D1134612

OXFORD EUROPEAN COMMUNITY LAW SERIES

General Editor: F. G. Jacobs
Advocate-General, The Court of Justice
of the European Communities

The European Internal Market and International Trade: A Legal Analysis

OXFORD EUROPEAN COMMUNITY LAW SERIES

The aim of this series is to publish important and original studies of the various branches of European Community Law. Each work will provide a clear, concise, and critical exposition of the law in its social, economic, and political context, at a level which will interest the advanced student, the practitioner, the academic, and government and Community officials.

The European Internal Market and International Trade

A Legal Analysis

PIET EECKHOUT

*Professor of EC Law, University of
Ghent (European Institute) and
Free University of Brussels; Assistant
to Advocate-General F. G. Jacobs,
Court of Justice of the European
Communities*

CLARENDON PRESS · OXFORD
1994

Oxford University Press, Walton Street, Oxford OX2 6DP

Oxford New York Toronto
Delhi Bombay Calcutta Madras Karachi
Kuala Lumpur Singapore Hong Kong Tokyo
Nairobi Dar es Salaam Cape Town
Melbourne Auckland Madrid
and associated companies in
Berlin Ibadan

Oxford is a trade mark of Oxford University Press

Published in the United States
by Oxford University Press Inc, New York

© Piet Eeckhaut 1994

British Library Cataloguing in Publication Data
Data available

Library of Congress Cataloging in Publication Data
Data available
ISBN 0–19–825903–4

1 3 5 7 9 10 8 6 4 2

Typeset by Create Text
Printed in Great Britain
on acid-free paper by
Bookcraft Ltd., Midsomer Norton, Avon

General Editor's Foreword

The internal market is familiar to all those acquainted with the laws and policies of the European Community. But both in scholarship and in practice, the law and policy of the Community's trade with the rest of the world has been remarkably neglected. Such neglect is all the more surprising given the economic and commercial significance of the Community's vast share of world trade and the frequent controversies surrounding its trading role.

The Community's trade policy—the 'common commercial policy'—is of special interest in a legal context, since it is one of the few areas where the Community has exclusive competence—a competence which precludes unilateral action by the Member States acting individually. That exclusive competence, which the Community has now exercised for more than 25 years, has given rise to debate, but the debate has concerned above all the precise scope of the common commerical policy. That question is of political and constitutional concern because it marks the boundary between Community competence and the competence of the Member States. But emphasis on that question seems to have preempted debate on the substance of the issues.

This book redresses the balance. It puts issues of substance, across the whole range of the subject, squarely in the foreground. Its coverage is exceptionally wide-ranging: not only does it tackle comprehensively many areas of general importance such as the Community's regime governing trade in services, its import regime for trade in goods and its export policy; at the same time it highlights areas of particular interest or sensitivity. These include financial services and the issue of reciprocity; transport services and the test case of civil aviation; audiovisual and telecommunication services; and the delicate issues raised by the Community's import regime for sensitive products such as textiles and Japanese cars. Throughout the discussion, the author places each topic in its economic and legal context.

Acute analysis of the novel issues raised in these and many other areas will be found in this book. Its perspective, also, is original. It takes as its starting-point the process of completion of the internal market, and examines from that basis the issues raised by international trade in goods and services. This approach provides a systematic framework within which the author addresses each issue in turn, combining law and policy on questions of great importance and topicality.

The book is exceptionally timely. 1993 saw the culmination of developments in many directions: the European Union, the European Economic Area, the North American Free Trade Area and the Uruguay round of the GATT negotiations, as well as the completion of the internal market. Even where the final details were not available at the time of writing, the author was able to discuss the issues relevant to his work. His book will provide a firm basis for understanding these developments and for evaluating the Community's policies.

Francis G. Jacobs

February 1994

Acknowledgements

This book is largely based upon my doctoral thesis on 'The External Dimension of the Completion of the European Community's Internal Market in Services and Goods: A Legal Analysis', presented at the Faculty of Law of the University of Ghent (Belgium). As such, it would not have been possible without the assistance and support of many individuals and institutions. Although it is not possible to list all of them here, some at least must be expressly mentioned.

In the first place, my thanks go to Professor Maresceau, my promotor, with whom I have been working now for about seven years, which have been most varied, instructive, and interesting. Moreover, the environment of the European Institute of the University of Ghent is excellent for pursuing research, both as regards colleagues and infrastructure. I have benefited a lot from discussions with the former, in particular Anne-Marie van den Bossche, Inge Govaere, and Philippe Vlaemminck.

I also wish to thank Messrs C. W. A. Timmermans and Hervé Jouanjean (both EC Commission), as well as Dr Jacques Pelkmans (CEPS). Francis Sarre corrected my abuse of the English language in an incredibly short amount of time, for which I am greatly indebted to him.

The General Editor of this series I thank for his support of my work and inspiring comments.

Indispensable financial assistance was granted by the Belgian FKFO (Joint Basic Research Fund), which funded a research project in the framework of which I was employed.

Last but not least, this study would not have been possible without the support of my wife, Hilde Coucke, to whom I dedicate this book.

Table of Contents

Table of Cases from the European Court of Justice and Court of First Instance

OPINIONS

European Community Treaties

Table of European Community Secondary Legislation

DIRECTIVES

REGULATIONS

DECISIONS

International Treaties and Agreements

Table of International Legislation

List of Abbreviations

ACP	African-Caribbean-Pacific
AETR	Accord européen relatif au travail des équipages des véhicules effectuant des transports internationaux par route (also ERTA)
ANSI	American National Standards Institute
BEUC	Bureau Européen des Consommateurs
BISD	*Basic Instruments and Selected Documents* (GATT)
Bull. EC	*Bulletin of the European Community*
CAP	Common Agricultural Policy
CCP	Common Commercial Policy
CCT	Common Customs Tariff
CDE	*Cahiers de droit européen*
CEN	Comité européen de normalisation
CENELEC	Comité européen de normalisation électrotechnique
CEPS	Centre for European Policy Studies (Brussels)
CES	Comité Économique et Social
CFSP	Common Foreign and Security Policy
CMIT	Committee on Capital Movements and Invisible Transactions
CMLR	Common Market Law Reports
CML Rev.	*Common Market Law Review*
COM	EC Commission document
CoCom	Co-ordinating Committee
CSIS	Centre for Strategic and International Studies (Washington, DC)
CU	customs union
Debates EP	*Debates of the European Parliament*
EAEC	European Atomic Energy Community
ECHR	European Convention on Human Rights
ECLR	*European Competition Law Review*
ECR	European Court Reports
ECSC	European Coal and Steel Community
ECU	European Currency Unit
EEA	European Economic Area
EFTA	European Free Trade Area
EJIL	*European Journal of International Law*

ELR	*European Law Review*
ERTA	European agreement concerning the work of crews of vehicles engaged in international road transport (also AETR)
ETSI	European Telecommunications Standards Institute
EuR	*Europarecht*
FDI	foreign direct investment
FTA	free trade area
GATS	General Agreement on Trade in Services
GATT	General Agreement on Tariffs and Trade
GDP	Gross Domestic Product
GSP	generalized system of preferences
ICAO	International Civil Aviation Organization
IEC	International Electrotechnical Commission
ILO	International Labour Organization
ISO	International Standards Organization
ITU	International Telecommunications Union
ISDN	integrated services digital network
JCMS	*Journal of Common Market Studies*
JWT	*Journal of World Trade*
JWTL	*Journal of World Trade Law*
Law Pol. Int. Bus.	*Law and Policy in International Business*
LIEI	*Legal Issues of European Integration*
MEP	Member of the European Parliament
MFA	Multi-Fibre Arrangement
MFN	most favoured nation
MITI	Ministry for Trade and Industry (Japan)
NAFTA	North American Free Trade Agreement
NATO	North Atlantic Treaty Organization
NJW	*Neue juristische Wochenschrift*
OECD	Organization for Economic Co-operation and Development
OEEC	Organization for European Economic Co-operation
OJ	Official Journal (of the European Communities)
ONP	open network provision
PSDS	packet-switched data services
PTT	Post, Telegraph, and Telephone companies
QR	quantitative restriction
RIIA	Royal Institute of International Affairs
RMC	*Revue du Marché Commun*
RMUE	*Revue du Marché unique européen*
RTDC	*Revue trimestrielle de droit commercial*

RTDE	*Revue trimestrielle de droit européen*
SEW	*Sociaal-economische Wetgeving*
STER	Stichting Etherreclame
TO	telecommunications organization
UACES	University Association for Contemporary European Studies
USITC	United States International Trade Commission
VER	voluntary export restraint
VRA	voluntary restraint agreement

Introduction

The Internal Market Programme

In the course of 1985 and 1986 the institutions of the European Communities (hereafter 'Community') devised and set in motion a programme to complete the Community's internal market by 31 December 1992. Much has been said about this programme, but its most important stages should nevertheless be very briefly reviewed.

The major starting-point was undoubtedly the Commission's White Paper on the completion of the internal market.[1] In this document the Commission presented a thorough study of the various barriers which stood in the way of having a genuinely single market,[2] as was (at least to some extent if not entirely) envisaged by the original EEC Treaty. The most ingenious aspect of the White Paper, however, was that the Commission managed to propose a list of about 300 measures which would enable the Community to complete its internal market, accompanied by a detailed timetable.

The Commission's approach was endorsed by the European Council, leading to the amendments of the EEC Treaty introduced by the Single European Act.[3] It would go beyond the scope of this introduction to analyse these amendments. Suffice it to say that according to Article 7a, EC Treaty, '[t]he internal market shall comprise an area without internal frontiers in which the free movement of goods, persons, services and capital is ensured in accordance with the provisions of this Treaty'. The same provision also constitutionalized the target date of 31 December 1992.

The internal market programme has been surprisingly successful. The large majority of the measures of which the programme was made up have been adopted in time. Admittedly, there are areas which lag behind (such as free movement of persons). Moreover, it has not always been possible to maintain the rigorous approach originally advocated by the Commission, and a lot remains to be done with regard to implementing the adopted measures at national level. Nevertheless, the essence of the internal market is in place, which finds perhaps its most spectacular expression in the complete abolition of controls at intra-Community borders on the movement of goods.

---

[1] *Completing the Internal Market: White Paper from the Commission to the European Council*, COM (85) 310 final, June 1985.

[2] The term 'single market' will only seldom be used in this book, because it is not often referred to in legal documents, which generally refer to the 'internal market'. Nevertheless, the concept of a single market expresses perhaps better what is at stake.

[3] The Act was signed on 28 Feb. 1986 and entered into force on 1 July 1987.

The Internal Market and International Trade: Is There an External Dimension to the Internal Market?

From an economic point of view, the question whether there is an external dimension to the internal market sounds almost ridiculous. How could, an economist would argue, a policy of economic integration that is as encompassing as the internal market programme and that applies to twelve developed countries which play an important role in international trade *not* affect trade and economic relations with the outside world? However, from the point of view of law- and policy-making the question could be raised in the early stages, as indeed it has been. One can safely say that until 1988 the attitude of the Community's institutions towards both the external effects of the internal market programme and the relationship between the programme and the Community's external policies was one of benign neglect. The Commission's White Paper contains only a few references to external policies.[4] There is also nothing in the definition of the internal market as laid down in Article 7a, EC Treaty, which provides a link with external relations, and the Single European Act did not amend the EEC Treaty provisions which do deal with this subject (the main ones being those on the Common Commercial Policy).[5] Even the famous Checcini report on the economic effects of 1992 did not take account of the external dimension.[6] The latter was only present in one very specific way: the internal market programme was (and is) clearly also aimed at improving the competitiveness of European industries in the face of Japanese and US competition. But this was only regarded as a strategic motive for the programme, unrelated to its contents, which would merely involve the elimination of barriers in the *internal* market.

The conclusion which a number of authors drew from all this was therefore at the time certainly defensible. It has for example been said that the concept of an internal market, as introduced in Community law by the Single European Act, does not have an external dimension, in contrast with the concept of a common market which includes a Common Customs Tariff and a Common Commercial Policy.[7]

[4] See *infra*, Ch. 5, p. 145.

[5] Art. 7a refers to a number of other provisions of the Treaty (7b, 7c, 28, 57 (2), 59, 70 (1), 84, 99, 100a, and 100b), none of them directly concerning external relations.

[6] See e.g. *Research on the 'Cost of Non-Europe': Basic Findings*, vol. i (Luxembourg: Office for Official Publications, for the Commission, 1988). See also Jacques Pelkmans, 'EC92 as a Challenge to Economic Analysis', in S. Borner and H. Grubel (eds.), *The European Community after 1992: Perspectives from the Outside* (Basingstoke: Macmillan Press, 1992), 17.

[7] See e.g. N. Forwood and M. Clough, 'The Single European Act and Free Movement: Legal Implications of the Provisions for the Completion of the Internal Market', 11 *ELR* (1986), 365; Jean De Ruyt, *L'acte unique européen* (Brussels: Éditions de l'ULB, 1987), 150; Pieter VerLoren van Themaat, 'The Contributions to the Establishment of the Internal Market by the Case-Law of the Court of Justice of the European Communities', in R. Bieber, R. Dehousse, J. Pinder and J. H. H. Weiler (eds.), *1992: One European Market?* (Baden-Baden: Nomos, 1988), 111.

However, subsequent developments have forced the Community to consider the external dimension of its internal market programme. At the beginning of 1988, the Commission issued a proposal for a Second Banking Directive which aimed at establishing the basic rules for the internal market in banking.[8] In this proposal provision was made for ensuring that Community banks would obtain access to other banking markets of the world, in return for the non-discriminatory access to the Community's market which non-Community banks were granted in the proposed directive. This reciprocity clause—which of itself was not revolutionary, since most of the Member States had a comparable clause relating to financial services on their statute book—provoked a storm of protests, and set in motion the debate on whether the establishment of the internal market would result in the construction of a protectionist Fortress Europe.

Although in October 1988 the Commission tried to demonstrate that nothing of the kind was being envisaged,[9] since 1988 the external dimension has figured high on the agenda of both political and academic discussions. A factor which certainly contributes thereto is the (at the time of writing) still ongoing Uruguay Round of multilateral trade negotiations, which covers a number of subjects which are also part of the 1992 programme. Numerous studies of the external dimension of the internal market programme have been published in the last few years. This book attempts to shed some additional light on the question by trying to provide a thorough analysis, from a legal point of view, of the relationship between the completion of the internal market and external trade in goods and services.

Approach and Structure of the Book

This book deals with what can be characterized as the key chapters of the internal market programme, to wit the Community's efforts aimed at integrating the various national markets in goods and services. These efforts lie at the heart of the programme because goods and services are basically what modern economies produce and market. Moreover, the internal market programme puts the regulation of transactions in goods and services much on the same footing, as will be demonstrated in the course of this study. The provision of services is no longer looked at as something merely ancillary to the production of goods, and the public service function of a number of important service sectors (such as telecommunications and transport), which in the past

---

[8] See Ch. 2.

[9] The Commission issued a statement, entitled 'Europe 1992: Europe World Partner', Press Release P-117 of 19 Oct. 1988, in which it emphasized that Europe 1992 would be of benefit to Community and non-Community countries alike, that 1992 would not mean protectionism, that the Community would meet its international obligations, and that 1992 should help to strengthen the multilateral system on a reciprocal basis.

served to shelter these sectors from genuine competition, is less and less emphasized. It is indisputable that in the framework of the internal market programme the production and marketing of goods and the provision of services are treated as two equivalent kinds of economic activity.

One could approach the subject of the external dimension of the internal market from a Cartesian, top-down perspective. That would imply drawing up a legal definition of the internal market concept and its various components in the fields of goods and services, in order to examine, on the basis of this definition, how the external dimension is being determined. Such an approach is not followed here, basically because it would be very difficult to draw up a 'universal' definition of the internal market concept. Notwithstanding the fact that it has been constitutionalized by the Single European Act, the internal market programme remains in the first place a political programme, which has been subject to evolution in the course of its implementation, and the boundaries of which are not always definite. This study therefore examines the concrete policies relating to goods and services which were developed in the course of the programme, in the first place of course those in which the external dimension plays an important role. However, it also aims at putting these concrete policies (which in many cases are still being shaped today) in perspective. For a subject such as the relationship between the internal market and international trade this perspective can only be twofold. On the one hand, it is the broader context of Community integration, in particular the development of the Community's external policies. On the other, it is the world trading system in which the Community is an active participant and which, from a legal viewpoint, consists of various sets of rules and disciplines laid down in multilateral and bilateral agreements, the most important being the General Agreement on Tariffs and Trade.

This book examines those chapters of the internal market programme which most directly affect trade in goods and services across the Community's external frontiers. That includes the regulation of imports and exports as such, but also issues such as establishment, technical regulations and standards, and public procurement. It does not deal with subjects such as competition policy, agricultural policy, fiscal policy, the internal energy market, and harmonization in the field of intellectual property, either because these policies are less directly related to the internal market programme, or because a comprehensive external policy is still lacking.

The book is not neatly divided into two parts, one dealing with goods and another with services. The reason is that there are two chapters covering subjects relating to both goods and services, namely one on public procurement and one on the extension of the internal market in the framework of the European Economic Area. These chapters are both situated at the end of the book.

An attempt has been made to put some logic in the order of the various chapters. Perhaps surprisingly, the services sector is examined first. This is justified on two accounts. It provides the opportunity to consider from the beginning two basic questions which the external dimension of the internal market programme raises. The first is the question of the scope and character of the Community's external competences, which are examined in Chapter 1, dealing with the relationship between international trade in services and Community law. The second issue concerns the Community's reciprocity policy, which lies at the heart of the external dimension of the internal market programme. This policy has first been proposed in the sector of financial services, which is the subject of Chapter 2.

As the approach towards completing the internal market in the field of services is of a sectoral nature, the analysis below is also sector-based. The three (or four) services sectors in which the Community is most active, and which are most important for the external dimension of the internal market, are examined: financial services (Chapter 2), transport services (Chapter 3), and audiovisual and telecommunications services (Chapter 4). The external regimes introduced in these sectors are addressed.

Then come three chapters on imports and exports of goods. First, the relationship between the completion of the internal market and the Community's import regime is dealt with from a general viewpoint (Chapter 5). The following chapter studies in somewhat more detail a number of more specific policies which have been devised in order to find solutions for the problems posed by imports of sensitive products, namely textiles and clothing, Japanese cars, and bananas (Chapter 6). Attention is also paid to the Community's export policy. Here the completion of the internal market raises one particular but significant question, namely to what extent should the Community become active in the field of strategic export controls (Chapter 7).

The two following chapters are comparable in that they deal with policies not concerning the regulation of imports and exports as such, but which nevertheless directly affect the Community's external trade. That is the case with Community action in the field of technical regulations and standards (Chapter 8), and with public procurement policies (Chapter 9). Chapter 10 examines the extension of the internal market to the EFTA countries, as envisaged by the Agreement on a European Economic Area (EEA). It is useful to look at this extension, because it raises a number of specific questions concerning the external dimension of the internal market. Chapter 11, lastly, attempts to draw a number of conclusions.

As mentioned above, this book was written before the conclusion of the Uruguay Round negotiations. It will be seen that many of the subjects dealt with are also on the agenda of these negotiations. If the latter are successful, the resulting multilateral policies and rules will add a dimension in a number of the areas analysed below. Nevertheless, the outcome of the negotiations has not been awaited, as this would have postponed the production of this book too much, a useful analysis of the results of the Uruguay Round requiring fresh study. That does not mean that the Uruguay Round is absent from the analysis. An attempt has been made to include references to the on-going negotiations, and in particular to the Draft Final Act submitted by GATT Director-General Dunkel in December 1991, as much as possible.

I should also add that, although the law is stated as of August 1993, references are to the (new) European Community (EC) Treaty, as amended by the Maastricht Treaty on European Union, because this book is put on the market after the entry into force of this Treaty. However, references to European Economic Community (EEC) Treaty provisions in quotations are not altered, which in some cases leads to discrepancies (e.g. Article 8*a*, EEC Treaty, is now Article 7*a*, EC Treaty). Moreover, when reference is expressly made to the original EEC Treaty, it is indicated as such. As a general rule, however, I assume that the amended EC Treaty is to be interpreted in the same sense as the original EEC Treaty, except in areas where there are substantial modifications.

1

International Trade in Services and Community Law

Introduction

This chapter serves as a general introduction to the three following ones, which deal with the external dimension of the completion of the internal market in three specific services sectors. It is necessary to include such an introduction, because otherwise a number of general issues would not stand out sufficiently.

As was mentioned in the introduction, the regulation of trade in goods and services is increasingly addressed on a comparable basis. The following section summarizes the main elements of this new approach towards international service transactions. It is followed by two sections on the basic rules guiding the Community's involvement in the field of services: the first deals with intra-Community movement of services, whereas the next, which is the most extensive one, examines the Community's powers to regulate service transactions in relations with third countries.

The Economic and Legal Context of Service Transactions from an International Perspective

Before going into the various legal questions that arise with respect to the external dimension of the single market in services, it is useful to consider the general economic and legal context in which international service transactions take place. Services are a relatively 'new' area in international economic relations. Both within and outside the Community their economic importance has only started to be commonly recognized in the course of the last decade. Before, services were more looked at as being ancillary to the production of, and trade in, goods.[1] As a result, there is not yet a settled general theory on international trade in services—even the concept itself has been debated.[2]

---

[1] Geza Feketekuty, *International Trade in Services: An Overview and Blueprint for Negotiations* (Cambridge, Mass.: Ballinger for the American Enterprise Institute, 1988), 60–2; Raymond J. Krommenacker, *World-Traded Services: The Challenge for the Eighties* (Dedham: Artech House, 1984), 3.

[2] Jagdish Bhagwati, 'Services', in J. M. Finger and A. Olechowski (eds.), *The Uruguay Round: A Handbook on the Multilateral Trade Negotiations* (Washington, DC: World Bank, 1987), 208; Geza Feketekuty, *supra* n. 1, pp. 67–70; Jacques Pelkmans, 'EC92 as a Challenge to Economic Analysis', in S. Borner and H. Grubel (eds.), *The European Community after 1992: Perspectives from the Outside* (Basingstoke: Macmillan Press, 1992), 13.

Moreover, service transactions are of themselves difficult to define and conceptualize. Quite naturally, these difficulties are reflected at the level of regulation. There is, to name only the most important example, as yet no established comprehensive framework governing international service transactions, as there is in the field of trade in goods through the GATT system. The Uruguay Round efforts are only a beginning in this respect.[3] Therefore, in order to allow a better overall understanding of the internal market enterprise in this area, and of some of the specific legal issues that are involved, clarification of the general economic and legal context of international service transactions is useful.

Below, the position of services in modern economies as well as economics will first be briefly addressed. Subsequently, the main characteristics of international service transactions are examined, keeping in mind the need to develop policies and rules governing such transactions. Lastly, one has to mention the various legal frameworks of services trade existing at the international level, be they general or sectoral. This analysis by no means claims to be original, but only serves as a general background and introduction.

Services in modern economies and economics

The importance of services for the world economy is steadily growing and has reached a high level. It has been calculated—although reliable data on services are scarce and not very sophisticated—that services account for 50 per cent of world output.[4] For developed countries, the share is even larger. In the Community, for example, service transactions produced 62.5 per cent of GDP in 1989.[5] They are, however, still more domestic in character than trade in goods. To take the Community example again, service transactions with third countries only reach about one third of the value of imports and exports of goods.[6]

---

[3] See *infra*, pp. 12–13.

[4] Henning Klodt, 'International Trade, Direct Investment, and Regulations in Services', 12 *World Competition* (1987), 2: 49.

[5] See Eurostat, *Basic Statistics of the Community*, 29th edn. (Luxembourg: Office for Official Publications of the EC, 1992), 43.

[6] See Eurostat, *International Trade in Services*, Theme 6D (Luxembourg: Office for Official Publications, 1991), 18. However, in these calculations foreign direct investment (FDI) in the services sector is not included. According to Klodt (*supra* n. 4, p. 57), the services sector accounts for a share of 30 to 50% of FDI in Japan, West Germany, and the USA. He concludes that: 'Evidently, the worldwide increase in foreign direct investment in services should probably not be attributed to a low tradeability, but to a rapidly increasing potential of international transactions in services. This has been realised in foreign direct investment, but is still latent in international trade' (p. 58). For the same view, see Carlo Secchi, 'Recent Trends in International Trade in Services', in G. Sacerdoti (ed.), *Liberalization of Services and Intellectual Property in the Uruguay Round of GATT* (Fribourg: University Press, 1990), 7.

This growing economic importance has been accompanied by what almost amounts to a discovery of services in economic theory. As was mentioned, services used to be perceived as purely ancillary to production and trade in goods by such 'classic' economists as Adam Smith, Ricardo, and Marx, and as adding no value to a country's economy.[7] Such was for a long time the prevailing opinion among economists, and theoretical interest in services trade was quite low. However, this changed radically in the course of the 1980s, and there is now a growing body of economic theory on the characteristics of services and, more important for our subject, on international transactions in services.

A number of economists have examined whether classic trade theory, built on the principle of comparative advantage, also applies to the services sector. Their conclusion is that, generally speaking, it does. Feketekuty has aptly summarized this conclusion:

The basic concepts of international trade theory can be articulated without any reference to what is produced and consumed and what is imported and exported. International trade theory is a logical construct that provides conclusions about market outcomes, no matter what is bought and sold in the marketplace. In other words the normative conclusions that can be drawn from international trade theory are as valid for shoes and oranges as for insurance and engineering.[8]

It follows from this conclusion that, at least from a theoretical point of view, there is a case for liberalizing international trade in services, because this would lead to overall economic gains.

Nevertheless, it is clear that there are major differences between service transactions and trade in goods. It is necessary to explore these differences, because they affect the question of how to regulate international trade in services.

The characteristics of trade in services

Services are extremely diverse. They range from so-called 'smokestack services'[9] such as banking and air transport to much more uncomplicated activities such as hairdressing and taxi driving. This diversity is also reflected in the way international trade in services takes place. Some examples may illustrate this. In tourism, it is the tourist who travels and consumes services abroad. In banking, it is possible to have financial transactions across the border, without the bank or the client moving towards one another. Or the foreign bank may wish to have some commercial presence in the client's country, in order to provide its services. Television allows the same

---

[7] See *supra* n. 2.   [8] *Supra* n. 1, pp. 123–4.
[9] The concept is used by Klodt, *supra* n. 4, p. 50.

programme to be broadcast at the same time in different countries, with sometimes up to billions of viewers watching it in their respective homes. In hairdressing, by contrast, there is very little international exchange.

As a result, it is difficult to define international trade in services. Nevertheless, it has been attempted to categorize international service transactions, and most of these attempts concentrate on the mobility of the 'actors' in the transaction, namely the producer and the consumer of services. Even then, however, there is no unanimity as to which categories should be distinguished.[10] In the author's view, one can perceive four main categories:[11]

1. The consumer moves towards the producer of the service, for example a Belgian tourist booking a room in an Austrian hotel.
2. The producer of the service moves to the consumer, as is the case when an orchestra performs abroad.
3. Consumer and producer of the service both move, the most important example being human transport.
4. Neither the producer nor the consumer moves, but it is the service itself which 'travels': television signals or a telephone call.

The fact that trade in services can involve the international movement of the producer and/or the consumer of services has important implications, which do not exist with respect to trade in goods. The latter does not require movement of people, except for the transporter (who performs a service!). The first implication is that one has to draw a line between international movement of people as such—in other words migration, which is a very sensitive issue— and service transactions involving people moving across borders. Often, it is not so easy to draw this line.[12] Secondly, international service transactions may require the mobility of companies. For a number of these transactions, in the financial sector for example, it is necessary that the service provider has some form of (more or less permanent) commercial presence in the consumer's

[10] Compare e.g. Deepak Nayyar, 'Some Reflections on the Uruguay Round and Trade in Services', 22 *JWT* (1988), 5: 37; Klodt, *supra* n. 4, p. 50; Raymond J. Krommenacker, 'Multilateral Services Negotiations: From Interest-Lateralism to Reasoned Multilateralism in the Context of the Servicization of the Economy', in Ernst-Ulrich Petersmann and Meinhard Hilf (ed.), *The New GATT Round of Multilateral Trade Negotiations: Legal and Economic Problems* (Deventer: Kluwer, 1988), 465; Phedon Nicolaides, *Liberalizing Service Trade: Strategies for Success* (London: Routledge for the RIIA, 1989), 7–17.

[11] Compare with the draft General Agreement on Trade in Services (see *infra*, pp. 12–13), which defines trade in services as 'the supply of a service: (a) from the territory of one Party into the territory of any other Party; (b) in the territory of one Party to the service consumer of any other Party; (c) through the presence of service providing entities of one Party in the territory of any other Party; (d) by natural persons of one Party in the territory of any other Party' (see Art. I (2)).

[12] Cf. the judgment of the European Court of Justice in *Rush Portuguesa*, discussed *infra* p. 17. See also Bhagwati, *supra* n. 2, p. 209; Feketekuty, *supra* n. 1, pp. 81–2; Krommenacker, *supra* n. 10, p. 467; Nayyar, *supra* n. 10, pp. 40–1.

country. In other words, one cannot fully address international trade in services without also addressing investment and establishment issues.[13]

Another important feature of most services is that they cannot be stored or circulate as is the case with goods. In other words, with most services production and consumption coincide. This means, among other things, that you cannot conceive of something like 'services that are in free circulation' within a customs union, by analogy with goods that are in free circulation.[14]

A last fundamental characteristic of service transactions is the fact that, all over the world, they are extensively regulated by governments. This regulation of service activities aims at furthering a wide range of policies, such as the protection of the consumer, development objectives, the protection of essential security interests and cultural policy, to name but a few. Most of this regulation of service activities is of a domestic nature, and is not aimed at regulating international service transactions in any specific way. This does not mean, however, that it does not affect such transactions. Although in most cases this regulation of service activities serves legitimate policy objectives, it often also acts as a barrier to trade. Quite rightly it has been observed that most barriers to trade in services are to be found at this regulatory level.[15] The reason for that is that most services do not physically cross borders, and that, as a result, it is very difficult to erect barriers to international trade in services at the border, by means of specific measures. This, in turn, means that it is impossible substantially to liberalize trade in services without addressing the regulation of service activities as such.[16] Community experience confirms this. The general prohibition of restrictions on the movement of services, laid down in Articles 59 and 60, EC Treaty, did not lead to substantial liberalization. The latter has only been accomplished within the framework of the single market programme, by addressing the various regulatory barriers to trade in services, through harmonization accompanied by the principle of mutual recognition.[17]

To conclude, it can be said that international service transactions display both significant similarities and critical differences with international trade in goods. Neither one of these elements should be overlooked when considering the regulation of international trade in services. There is, however, yet another factor which has to be referred to, and that is the existence of a large number of

[13] See e.g. Feketekuty, *supra* n. 1, pp. 87–8; Bhagwati, *supra* n. 2, pp. 208–9; Phedon Nicolaides, 'Economic Aspects of Services: Implications for a GATT Agreement', 23 *JWT* (1989), 1: 127–8. Klodt even argues that current growth of international transactions in services takes place mainly through foreign investment (see *supra* n. 4).

[14] Cf. *infra*, pp. 24–6.

[15] See e.g. Feketekuty, *supra* n. 1, p. 136; Jagdish Bhagwati, 'Economic Costs of Trade Restrictions', in *The Uruguay Round: A Handbook on the Multilateral Trade Negotiations*, *supra* n. 2, p. 29.

[16] For a candid analysis of the problems which this entails, see Martijn van Empel, 'The Visible Hand in Invisible Trade', *LIEI* (1990), 2: 23–43. Compare with Nicolaides, *supra* n. 10, pp. 40–8.

[17] See *infra*, p. 19.

international agreements governing international service transactions, next to the General Agreement on Trade in Services (GATS), which is being negotiated in the framework of the Uruguay Round.

Specific international agreements and the GATS

There is a host of international agreements governing specific aspects of international service transactions. Within the scope of this study it is clearly not possible to give a complete overview. Some examples may, however, illustrate the complexity of the network of international regulation which has been constructed over the years.

At a general level, the provision of services is sometimes dealt with in classic bilateral Treaties of Friendship and Commerce. It is also at this level that the OECD is to some extent active, which has led to the adoption of Codes on the Liberalization of Capital Movements and of Invisible Transactions, as well as of the so-called National Treatment Instrument. Basically, these instruments are aimed at liberalizing certain elements of international service transactions.[18]

Most international agreements are sectoral, however. In the field of transport, for example, there is a large number of bilateral agreements between countries concerning the exchange of traffic rights. Many of these agreements are based upon multilateral instruments, such as the Chicago Convention in the field of air transport.[19] With respect to telecommunications, there is the International Telecommunications Union (ITU) which forms the basis of international regulation. Nearly all these sectoral agreements emphasize the public service aspects inherent in the international provision of services, and involve strict regulation, leaving little room for genuine competition.

The approach of the negotiations on a General Agreement on Trade in Services is completely different. The essential aim of such a General Agreement is to set in train an overall liberalization of international trade in services, by providing basic rules and disciplines which are comparable to those of the traditional GATT system. These negotiations have led to a draft GATS which is included in the Draft Final Act proposed by the GATT's Director-General in December 1991.[20] It would lead too far to analyse this draft GATS here.[21] Suffice it to say that it introduces general principles such as most-favoured-nation treatment, transparency, free access to markets, and national treatment, and that it provides the framework for negotiating detailed concessions concerning specific services sectors or subsectors. In the following chapters,

[18] The Code on Capital Movements and the National Treatment Instrument are dealt with in Ch. 2, pp. 68–74.

[19] See Ch. 3, pp. 100–3.

[20] See MTN.TNC/W/FA, pp. 1–56 of the annex.

[21] See for such an analysis Bernard Hoekman, 'Market Access through Multilateral Agreement: From Goods to Services', 15 *World Economy* (1992), 6: 707–727.

this draft GATS will often be referred to, because if it enters into force it will play an important role in defining the external dimension of the internal market in services.

Community Regulation of Trade in Services between the Member States

Having touched upon the general economic and legal context of international trade in services, it is necessary to survey the Community's rules and policies towards trade in services between the Member States. After all, this is the substratum for the regulation of trade in services with third countries. This substratum consists of two main parts. On the one hand, there are the EC Treaty provisions on freedom to provide services and freedom of establishment. On the other hand, there are the Community's efforts aimed at harmonizing national legislation governing service transactions, with the objective of realizing a genuinely integrated market. These efforts have only really been developed with the single market programme.

The EC Treaty provisions on freedom to provide services and right of establishment

It is of course not possible to examine in depth here the content and implementation of the EC Treaty chapters on services and establishment. Only the basic rules and principles can be looked at. In addition, attention will be paid to part of the case-law of the Court of Justice which confirms the general features of services trade as described above. These references may serve as an illustration that, in essence, the problems inherent in regulating international service transactions are the same for both intra-Community trade and trade with third countries.

Freedom to provide services and non-discrimination

The prohibition of discrimination based on nationality or place of residence is a key principle embodied in the EC Treaty provisions on freedom to provide services and freedom of establishment. Let us first consider the services chapter. According to the Court of Justice in *Van Binsbergen*,

[t]he restrictions to be abolished pursuant to Articles 59 and 60 include all requirements imposed on the person providing the service by reason in particular of his nationality or the fact that he does not habitually reside in the State where the service is provided, which do not apply to persons established within the national territory or which may prevent or otherwise obstruct the activities of the person providing the service.[22]

[22] Case 33/74, *Van Binsbergen*, [1974] ECR 1299, at 1309.

To some extent, these restrictions need to be abolished through Community action, but the Court also decided in the same case that

the first paragraph of Article 59 and the third paragraph of Article 60 have direct effect and may therefore be relied on before national courts, at least in so far as they seek to abolish any discrimination against a person providing a service by reason of his nationality or of the fact that he resides in a Member State other than that in which the service is to be provided.[23]

In a substantial number of subsequent judgments the Court further clarified the scope of the directly effective principle of non-discrimination. The most important characteristic of this case-law is that it widens this scope to cases of so-called discrimination in substance, or factual discrimination.[24] This term serves to indicate the phenomenon that national legislation regulating services, although on its face applying equally to domestic and imported services, may in fact be more burdensome for services imported from other Member States. Some examples may illustrate this. In *Seco* the Court decided that, with respect to companies temporarily providing services in another Member State than the one in which they are established, and using their personnel in order to provide these services, such factual discrimination occurs when

the obligation to pay the employer's share of social security contributions imposed on persons providing services within the national territory is extended to employers established in another Member State who are already liable under the legislation of that State for similar contributions in respect of the same workers and the same periods of employment. In such a case the legislation of the State in which the service is provided proves in economic terms to be more onerous for employers established in another Member State, who in fact have to bear a heavier burden than those established within the national territory.[25]

In other words, although the obligation to pay social security contributions is equally applicable to domestic and foreign employers, it in fact amounts to discrimination because the foreign employers already pay such contributions in the Member State of establishment.

In *Van Wesemael*, the Court ruled on licensing requirements for employment agencies. It first emphasized that a Member State may legitimately impose such requirements for reasons of public policy. These requirements, however, may not be imposed on employment agencies established in other

---

[23] [1974] ECR at 1312.

[24] Discrimination in substance means, in general, to treat similar cases differently, or different cases identically, cf. Case 13/63, *Italy* v. *Commission*, [1963] ECR 165 at 177–8. See also Koen Lenaerts, 'L'égalité de traitement en droit communautaire', 27 *CDE* (1991), 1–2, 8–12.

[25] Joined Cases 62 and 63/81, *SECO* v. *EVI*, [1982] ECR 223, at 235.

Member States and operating on the domestic market, unless they are objectively justified. Such is not the case

when the service is provided by an employment agency which comes under the public administration of a Member State or when the person providing the service is established in another Member State and in that State holds a licence issued under conditions comparable to those required by the State in which the service is provided and his activities are subject in the first State to proper supervision covering all employment agency activity whatever may be the Member State in which the service is provided.[26]

This means that unnecessary duplication of licensing requirements may also amount to factual discrimination.

In recent cases, the Court has moved away from the concept of discrimination as regards the assessment of restrictions inherent in regulations applying equally to domestic and imported services. Instead it introduces concepts which are similar to those governing the free movement of goods. This case-law is aptly summarized in the *Stichting Collectieve Antennevoorziening Gouda* judgment. Because of the general language which the Court has used in this judgment, it is useful to quote extensively from it:

In this respect, the Court has consistently held ... that Article 59 of the Treaty entails, in the first place, the abolition of any discrimination against a person providing services on account of his nationality or the fact that he is established in a Member State other than the one in which the service is provided ...

In the absence of harmonization of the rules applicable to services, or even of a system of equivalence, restrictions on the freedom guaranteed by the Treaty in this field may arise in the second place as a result of the application of national rules which affect any person established in the national territory to persons providing services established in the territory of another Member State who already have to satisfy the requirements of that State's legislation.

As the Court has consistently held ... such restrictions come within the scope of Article 59 if the application of the national legislation to foreign persons providing services is not justified by overriding reasons relating to the public interest or if the requirements embodied in that legislation are already satisfied by the rules imposed on those persons in the Member State in which they are established.

In this respect, the overriding reasons relating to the public interest which the Court has already recognized include professional rules intended to protect recipients of the service ... ; protection of intellectual property ... ; the protection of workers ... ; consumer protection ... ; the conservation of the national historic and artistic heritage ... ; turning to account the archaeological, historical and artistic heritage of a country and the widest possible dissemination of knowledge of the artistic and cultural heritage of a country ...

Lastly, as the Court has consistently held, the application of national provisions to providers of services established in other Member States must be such as to guarantee the achievement of the intended aim and must not go beyond that which is necessary in

---

[26] Joined Cases 110 and 111/78, *van Wesemael*, [1979] ECR 35, at 53.

order to achieve that objective. In other words, it must not be possible to obtain the same result by less restrictive rules...[27]

The language which the Court employs here, as regards national regulations applying equally to domestic and imported services, is strikingly similar to the case-law on free movement of goods. There, too, national regulation may not in any way hinder imports, unless this is justified by certain mandatory requirements or by the exceptions of Article 36.[28] Whether this means that the concept of discrimination is no longer relevant at all for explaining the scope of the freedom to provide services, in so far as it affects equally applicable national legislation, is another matter. This question is addressed in the chapter on financial services, when analysing the concept of national treatment.[29]

The definition of services

Article 60, EC Treaty, defines services as follows:

Services shall be considered to be 'services' within the meaning of this Treaty where they are normally provided for remuneration, in so far as they are not governed by the provisions relating to freedom of movement for goods, capital and persons.

'Services' shall in particular include:

(a) activities of an industrial character;
(b) activities of a commercial character;
(c) activities of craftsmen;
(d) activities of the professions.

It is interesting to see that services are partly defined in a negative way. This could well reflect the fact that, as was described above, services were considered to be relatively unimportant when the original EEC Treaty was drafted. It also shows that the provision of services cannot be defined easily, something which has become clear in the Uruguay Round negotiations.[30]

The case-law of the Court of Justice also reveals some of the difficulties in defining the concept of services. There is, for example, the judgment in *Bond*

---

[27] Case C-288/89, *Stichting Collectieve Antennevoorziening Gouda* v. *Commissariaat voor de Media*, [1991] ECR I-4007, at I-4040–1. See also Case C-353/89, *Commission* v. *The Netherlands*, [1991] ECR I-4069, which is very similar.

[28] Mattera argues that the case-law on free movement of workers, freedom of establishment, and freedom to provide services is now the same, with respect to measures applying without discrimination, as the case-law in the field of free movement of goods. See his analysis in 'Les principes de "proportionnalité" et de la "reconnaissance mutuelle' dans la jurisprudence de la Cour en matière de libre circulation des personnes et des services: de l'arrêt "Thieffry" aux arrêts "Vlassopoulou", "Mediawet" et "Dennemeyer"', *RMUE* (1991), 4: 191–203. Compare with the analysis by Giuliano Marenco, 'The Notion of Restriction on the Freedom of Establishment and Provision of Services in the Case-law of the Court', in A. Barav and D. A. Wyatt (eds.), 11 *Yearbook of European Law* (1991) (Oxford: Clarendon Press, 1992), pp. 111–50, which is more extensive and at the same time less conclusive.

[29] Ch. 2, pp. 77–9.

[30] Cf. Hoekman, *supra* n. 21, pp. 717–18.

van Adverteerders, in which the Court ruled on a Dutch regulation prohibiting cable network operators to distribute television programmes from other Member States involving advertising intended especially for Dutch audiences.[31] In this case, it was not easy to identify the services which were actually performed. The Court distinguished two services:

The first is provided by the cable network operators established in one Member State to the broadcasters established in other Member States and consists of relaying to network subscribers the television programmes sent to them by broadcasters. The second is provided by the broadcasters established in certain Member States to advertisers established in particular in the Member State where the programmes are received, by broadcasting advertisements which the advertisers have prepared especially for the public in the Member State where the programmes are received.[32]

However, in the same case Advocate-General Mancini found, on the basis of several pages of analysis, that

for the purposes of Articles 59 and 60 of the Treaty, a programme broadcast in a Member State by the authorized television organization or organizations must be regarded as a single provision of services even if that programme is supplied to viewers in another Member State by satellite or is distributed by cable.[33]

Moreover, according to the advertisers there were three separate services involved; according to the Dutch government there was only one service affected by the Dutch regulation, namely that provided by the operator of the cable network to its subscribers; according to the German government and the Commission there were two services, but not the ones which the Court distinguished.[34]

The Court's case-law also displays the difficulties (which were mentioned above) in distinguishing between movement of persons (migration) and the provision of services, when labour-intensive services are performed across borders. In *Rush Portuguesa* the Court had to decide whether, when a Portuguese construction company moved its work-force to France to carry out construction works, such movement had to be characterized as movement of persons, or whether it was covered by the Treaty provisions on services. The Court found that the latter was the case, but it has to be noted that the Advocate-General again took a different view by saying that only the key personnel of the company had the right to move under the provisions on services.[35]

[31] Case 352/85, *Bond van Adverteerders* v. *The Netherlands*, [1988] ECR 2085.
[32] [1988] ECR 2131.
[33] [1988] ECR 2116.
[34] [1988] ECR 2093.
[35] Case C-113/89, *Rush Portuguesa*, [1990] ECR I-1417. The question was important because at that time there was not yet full free movement of persons between Spain and Portugal and the other Member States, by virtue of the Act of Accession.

It was also mentioned above that one cannot consider international trade in services without also looking at investment and establishment issues, especially in sectors such as financial services which often require the proximity of the service provider and his customer. But the EC Treaty distinguishes between free movement of services and the right of establishment. The question as to the dividing line between these two chapters has been submitted to the Court in the *German Insurance* case (which, by the way, confirms this importance of establishment in the financial sector).[36] The Court ruled that

an insurance undertaking of another Member State which maintains a permanent presence in the Member State in question comes within the scope of the provisions of the Treaty on the right of establishment, even if that presence does not take the form of a branch or agency, but consists merely of an office managed by the undertaking's own staff or by a person who is independent but authorized to act on a permanent basis for the undertaking, as would be the case with an agency.[37]

Clearly, this is a wide definition of establishment. It is therefore necessary to pay some attention to the Treaty provisions on establishment.

Right of establishment

According to Article 52 of the EC Treaty 'restrictions on the freedom of establishment of nationals of a Member State in the territory of another Member State shall be abolished'. This abolition also applies to 'restrictions on the setting up of agencies, branches or subsidiaries by nationals of any Member State established in the territory of any Member State'. Furthermore, Article 52 mentions the right to work as a self-employed person in another Member State, and the right to set up and manage undertakings, 'in particular companies or firms within the meaning of the second paragraph of Article 58'. This second paragraph defines these as 'companies or firms constituted under civil or commercial law ... '.

Most of the case-law on Article 52 relates to establishment requirements for the professions (lawyers, doctors, dentists, architects, etc.). Surprisingly perhaps, there are few judgments on freedom of establishment in the (for our subject) more important services sectors such as transport,[38] financial services, telecommunications, and broadcasting services, where establishment requirements for companies are at stake. There is little sense, therefore, in giving an overview here of the case-law on Article 52.

---

[36] See Case 205/84, *Commission* v. *Germany*, [1986] ECR 3755. See also, as to the Community context, Claus-Dieter Ehlermann and Gianluigi Campogrande, 'Rules on Services in the EEC: A Model for Negotiating World-Wide Rules?', in E.-U. Petersmann and M. Hilf (eds.), *The New GATT Round of Multilateral Trade Negotiations: Legal and Economic Problems* (Deventer: Kluwer, 1988), 484–5.

[37] [1986] ECR 3801.

[38] There are some exceptions here, see e.g. Case 167/73, *Commission* v. *French Republic*, [1974] ECR 359. This judgment is dealt with below, in Ch. 3, p. 91.

Harmonization of national legislation and the internal market programme

Experience within the Community has shown that the mere application of the
EC Treaty rules on the free movement of services is not sufficient to establish a
genuine internal market, but that complementary rule-making is necessary.
That, by the way, is a general characteristic of the completion of the internal
market. The originality of the 1992 programme lies in the fact that it encom-
passes an impressive agenda of legislative action. In the field of services, such
action consists mainly (although not exclusively) of harmonization of national
legislation, based on Articles 57 (2) or 100*a* of the Treaty, or on the relevant
provisions in the field of transport policy.

There are three main sectors which are the subject of Community action:
financial services, including banking, insurance, and transactions in securities,
transport services, and audiovisual and telecommunications services.[39] The
external dimension of the policies which are developed in these sectors is
examined in the following chapters.

The Community's Powers to Regulate Trade in Services with Third Countries

Before addressing the external dimension of the single market programme in
services it is also necessary to scan the Community's powers to regulate
international trade in services. The issue of the Community's powers and their
borders is a classic issue in European law; nevertheless, it needs to be considered here, because it is crucial for the formulation of substantive policies
regarding services. Moreover, with respect to international trade in services
the question is not yet settled.

There is only one provision in the EC Treaty dealing specifically with trade
in services with third countries, and it is of limited interest. According to
Article 59 (2),'[t]he Council may, acting by a qualified majority on a proposal
from the Commission, extend the provisions of the [services] Chapter to
nationals of a third country who provide services and who are established
within the Community'. To date, the Council has not used this power, and it is
obvious that it cannot be employed for regulating the more important aspects
of the Community's external trade in services. It is therefore necessary to
examine whether the EC Treaty supplies other powers which can be used to
that effect.

The first question which arises in this regard is whether and, if so, to what
extent the EC Treaty title on the Common Commercial Policy (CCP) applies

---

[39] Cf. the overview in Commission of the EC, *A Common Market for Services*, Current Status
1 Jan. 1993, based on the INFO 92 data base (Luxembourg: Office for Official Publications of the
EC, 1993), which also mentions action in the field of the professions. However, because the latter
is more related to free movement of persons it is not dealt with here.

to the services sector. Is there any room, legally speaking, for a CCP for services, and if the answer is positive, what is the scope of this CCP? The question is essential, first, because the CCP is of an exclusive nature: the Member States do not possess any autonomous powers with respect to commercial policy.[40] Secondly, if one assumes that the CCP extends to international trade in services, it follows that the Community has broad powers to regulate such trade, whereas if one does not accept this assumption, such Community powers may become more problematic. They then have to be based on the doctrine of so-called implied powers, the nature and scope of which are not very clear, as will be shown.

Below, both these possible 'power bases' are studied from the point of view of regulating service transactions with third countries. As the conclusion will be that both these bases provide a Community competence which, to some extent, may be overlapping, the question arises whether one of them has precedence over the other, or, conversely, whether they need to be used simultaneously. This question is dealt with in a third section.

The Common Commercial Policy and international trade in services

Does the CCP apply to services?

The question whether the CCP applies to the services sector is still not settled. There is no case-law specifically dealing with it, and there is no established Community practice.[41] This means that a commentator seems to be assigned a rather speculative task. Nevertheless, there are a number of significant indications that perhaps have not yet been completely explored and that make the task less speculative than it might look like at face value. Such an exploration should start with a summary of some of the basic principles which, according to the Court of Justice, command the scope of the CCP. Next, one needs to look at the literature which deals with the question. Finally, the indications from both these sources are examined more thoroughly.

One of the basic rules that flow from the Court's case-law on the CCP is that it is impossible to demarcate once and for all the field of commercial policy. This is clearly explained in the rulings concerning the relationship between

[40] This follows from Opinion 1/75 of the European Court of Justice, [1975] ECR at 1364. However, there are some authors who argue that this exclusivity of the Community's competence does not extend to the whole scope of the CCP. This thesis is examined *infra*, at pp. 32–4.

[41] See, however, Regulation 3155/90 on sanctions against Iraq in the area of financial services (OJ L 304/1 of 1 Nov. 1990) and Regulation 945/92 on sanctions against Libya in the field of air transport (OJ L 101/53 of 15 Apr. 1992). According to Pieter Jan Kuyper, the Council took the precaution of declaring that these regulations do not prejudice the general question of the applicability of Article 113 to trade in services, see 'European Economic Community', in K. M. Meessen (ed.), *International Law of Export Control* (London: Graham & Trotman, 1992), 76, n. 89 and 'Trade Sanctions, Security and Human Rights and Commercial Policy', in M. Maresceau (ed.), *The European Community's Commercial Policy after 1992: The Legal Dimension* (Dordrecht: Martinus Nijhoff, 1993), 395–6 and 398.

commercial policy and development policy, namely Opinion 1/78 and the *GSP* case.[42] The concept of commercial policy is open-ended, and one may in this respect recall the Court's formulation in Opinion 1/78:

It is therefore not possible to lay down, for Article 113 of the EEC Treaty, an interpretation the effect of which would be to restrict the common commercial policy to the use of instruments intended to have an effect only on the traditional aspects of external trade to the exclusion of more highly developed mechanisms such as appear in the agreement envisaged. A 'commercial policy' understood in that sense would be destined to become nugatory in the course of time.[43]

Essentially, there are two reasons for such an open-ended and evolutionary interpretation. The first is linked with the international context in which the Community develops its commercial policy. The Court recognizes that this context may require the extension of commercial policy to new fields of action; otherwise, the Community would not be able to play its role in these new areas (such as international commodity agreements in Opinion 1/78 or tariff preferences in the *GSP* case). The second reason, probably as important as the first, pertains to the Community's internal cohesion. In the words of Opinion 1/78,

[a] restrictive interpretation of the concept of common commercial policy would risk causing disturbances in intra-Community trade by reason of the disparities which would then exist in certain sectors of economic relations with third countries.[44]

Besides, Opinion 1/75 shows that the same risk of disparities prompts the exclusive character of the Community's commercial policy powers.[45]

It should also be recalled here that the Court has never taken sides in the dispute between the Commission and the Council whether an instrumental approach should be taken in deciding whether a measure falls within the scope of the CCP (the point of view of the Commission), or whether the objective of a measure is the decisive factor (the point of view of the Council).[46] Perhaps this reluctance again shows that, in the Court's view, it is not possible to lay down a comprehensive and definitive definition of commercial policy.[47] Accordingly, no attempt will be made here to devise such a universal definition.[48]

[42] Opinion 1/78, [1979] ECR 2871 and Case 45/86, *Commission* v. *Council*, [1987] ECR 1493.
[43] [1979] ECR 2913.
[44] Ibid.
[45] [1975] ECR 1364.
[46] See on these different approaches Jacques H. J. Bourgeois, 'The Common Commercial Policy: Scope and Nature of the Powers', in E. L. M. Völker (ed.), *Protectionism and the European Community*, 2nd edn. (Deventer: Kluwer, 1986), 4–5; Paul Demaret, 'La politique commerciale: perspectives d'évolution et faiblesses présentes', in J. Schwarze and H. G. Schermers (eds.), *Structure and Dimensions of European Community Policy* (Baden-Baden: Nomos, 1988), 71–2.
[47] Demaret, *supra* n. 46, pp. 72–3.
[48] For such an attempt, see Claus-Dieter Ehlermann, 'The Scope of Article 113 of the EEC Treaty', in *Mélanges offerts à Pierre-Henri Teitgen* (Paris: Pedone, 1984), 145–69; Bourgeois, *supra* n. 46, pp. 3–7. See however also Ch. 11, pp. 344 *et seq.*

In legal writing, one finds a whole range of opinions on the question whether trade in services falls within the scope of the CCP. Some argue that it does, because the chapter on commercial policy would cover external economic relations in general.[49] Others defend a more limited view, saying that only some aspects of international service transactions are related to commercial policy.[50] There are also commentators who believe that only services directly related to trade in goods can be addressed under the commercial policy heading.[51] Finally, there are those who contend that services have nothing to do with commercial policy.[52] Some of these different points of view, however, are indeed mere opinions, not backed up by thorough analysis. Moreover, a number of them were articulated more than a decade ago, when international trade in services was not yet on the agenda, so to speak. Their relevance may therefore be limited. That is not the case for a number of more recent contributions, in which the matter has been examined in more depth.

Perreau de Pinninck has pleaded against the extension of the CCP to trade in services.[53] His arguments may be summarized as follows. First, he refers to a literal interpretation of Article 113, EC Treaty, which, in his view, only mentions policy instruments relating to trade in goods. This argument is difficult to accept, however. Article 113 speaks of

changes in tariff rates, the conclusion of tariff and trade agreements, the achievement of uniformity in measures of liberalization, export policy and measures to protect trade such as those to be taken in case of dumping or subsidies.

Whereas tariffs are clearly linked to trade in goods,[54] the other instruments mentioned can certainly be used for regulating international service transactions. One can envisage trade agreements relating to services, an outstanding example being the Uruguay Round negotiations on a General Agreement on Trade in Services. Equally, measures of liberalization and of

---

[49] Albert Bleckmann, *Europarecht* (Cologne: Carl Heymanns, 1985), pp. 461–2; Pierre Pescatore, 'La politique commerciale', in *Les Novelles: droit des Communautés européennes* (Brussels: Larcier, 1969), 921–2.

[50] Christiaan W. A. Timmermans, 'Common Commercial Policy (Article 113 EEC) and International Trade in Services', in *Du droit international au droit de l'intégration: Liber Amicorum Pierre Pescatore* (Baden-Baden: Nomos, 1987), 675–89; Philippe Vigneron and Aubry Smith, 'Le fondement de la compétence communautaire en matière de commerce international de services', 28 *CDE* (1992), 5–6: 515–64.

[51] P. J. G. Kapteyn and P. VerLoren van Themaat, *Introduction to the Law of the European Communities*, 2nd edn., ed. Lawrence W. Gormley (Deventer: Kluwer, 1990), 790. See also Richard Lauwaars, 'Scope and Exclusiveness of the Common Commercial Policy: Limits of the Powers of the Member States', in J. Schwarze (ed.), *Discretionary Powers of the Member States in the Field of Economic Policies and their Limits under the EEC Treaty* (Baden-Baden: Nomos, 1988), 80–1.

[52] Michael d'Orville, *Die rechtlichen Grundlagen für die gemeinsame Zoll- und Handelspolitik der EWG* (Cologne: Carl Heymanns, 1973), 7–10.

[53] Fernando Perreau de Pinninck, 'Les compétences communautaires dans les négociations sur le commerce des services', 27 *CDE* (1991), 3/4: 390–422, especially at 401–8.

[54] Although it cannot be excluded that tariffication of trade in services would be introduced at one stage.

export policy could be used in the services sector as could measures to protect trade.[55] A literal interpretation of Article 113 is therefore not conclusive.[56]

Secondly, the author applies what he calls a systematic interpretation of the provisions on the CCP. Such an interpretation reveals the close link between the CCP and the customs union concept, which lies at the basis of the Community.[57] Without a uniform commercial policy, the essential aims of the customs union could be frustrated by the application of divergent commercial policies by the Member States, creating distortions of trade within the Community, because once goods are imported from third countries, they are in free circulation. As the customs union only relates to trade in goods, trade in services would not be covered by the CCP.[58] Moreover, services, once produced, cannot be traded further and therefore cannot be in free circulation. Although at first sight this argument appears cogent, it will be demonstrated below that its application to trade in services is not correct. The dangers for the internal market, inherent in divergent commercial policies, also apply to service transactions.[59]

Thirdly, the author concedes that a teleological interpretation of the provisions on the CCP may lead to extending them to trade in services, because otherwise the Community might not possess the necessary means to conclude agreements relating to services. For two reasons, however, he finds such an argument unconvincing. There are, in his view, other Community competences (implied powers) which may enable the Community to conclude such agreements. It would therefore not be necessary to rely on Article 113.[60] He maintains, furthermore, that the EC Treaty does not include an external regime governing services and establishment, because common rules in this area were of limited interest when the Treaty was drafted, and that would still be the case today. As to the first point, it is questionable whether the scope of implied powers is as wide as that of the CCP, when applied to services.[61] As to the second point, it is precisely the establishment of an internal market, also in the area of services, which renders common rules regarding service transactions with third countries much more necessary. This, too, is further explored below.

[55] See e.g. Council Regulation 4057/86 on unfair pricing practices in maritime transport, OJ L 378/14 of 31 Dec. 1986.

[56] Cf. Vigneron and Smith, *supra* n. 50, p. 535.

[57] This link is confirmed, the author argues, by a historical interpretation, based on the Spaak Report, see *supra* n. 53, p. 402.

[58] Similarly, the author argues that the Court's case-law on the scope of the CCP only relates to trade in goods, and cannot be extended to trade in services. For a refutation of this argument, see Paolo Mengozzi, 'Trade in Services and Commercial Policy', in M. Maresceau (ed.), *The European Community's Commercial Policy after 1992: The Legal Dimension* (Dordrecht: Martinus Nijhoff, 1993), 233–4.

[59] See pp. 25 *et seq.*

[60] Compare also with Paolo Mengozzi, *supra* n. 58, pp. 240–1, referring to the principle of the proper functioning of the Common Market, precisely as an argument *pro* the CCP.

[61] See pp. 35–41.

The contribution by Timmermans on the CCP and international trade in services provides a balanced, in-depth, and original study.[62] It deals both with the question whether international trade in services is covered by Article 113 of the EC Treaty (which receives an affirmative answer), and with the scope of the Community's competence to deal with services on the basis of Article 113. Only the first part is considered in this subsection, although it should be emphasized that the originality of the author's theses lies especially in the second part, where he argues that the scope of a CCP in services should reflect the division of competences between the Community and the Member States with respect to the regulation of trade in services within the Community. Although both these parts are of course intertwined, they are surveyed separately here, purely for analytical reasons.[63]

Basically, Timmermans perceives two reasons why Article 113 also covers international trade in services. First, there is the 'evolution of international practice'. The Court has ruled that the Community must be able to follow this evolution. Therefore,

if an international trade organisation like the GATT, decides to extend its activities to the services sector, the Community which has in fact replaced Member States as members of GATT, must, of course, be able to follow suit, without being hampered by an outdated interpretation of what is commercial policy.[64]

This, of course, is a reference to the Uruguay Round. Secondly, the author refers to the concepts of trade deflection[65] and distortion of competition. He rightly argues that the danger of deflections of trade is one of the most fundamental reasons why a uniform commercial policy is necessary within a customs union. Without such a uniform policy, such deflections are liable to occur because products can circulate freely within the customs union. But, as we have seen, most services cannot be traded on their own like goods. Accordingly, they cannot be put into free circulation. Therefore, deflections of trade 'are to be feared much less with regard to services than goods'.[66] However, there is another reason for a CCP in the services sector. It lies in the distortions of competition which could result from the absence of a uniform policy. The author gives the example of one Member State allowing

[62] See n. 50.

[63] The scope is dealt with *infra*, pp. 28–32.

[64] *Supra* n. 50, p. 684. A similar reasoning has been put forward by Demaret, *supra* n. 46, p. 77.

[65] Actually, Timmermans uses the term trade *diversion*. However, the phenomenon which he describes is generally described in customs union theory as *deflection* of trade. The latter indicates what takes place when a number of countries eliminate tariffs (or, for that matter, other import barriers) in trade with each other, and imports from third countries are directed to the country with the lowest external tariff (or other barrier). Trade diversion, on the other hand, is the fact that a customs union leads to a shift of trade with third countries to internal trade within the union. See on these terms, for example, Peter Robson, *The Economics of International Integration* (London: Allen and Unwin, 1980), 12–13 and 20. In the following résumé of Timmermans's arguments the term trade deflection is used instead of trade diversion.

[66] *Supra* n. 50, p. 684.

third-country insurance companies to operate within its market, whereas other Member States' markets are closed. Competition could then be distorted on two levels: insurance companies in the open Member State are subjected to more competition than those in other Member States, and, in the event that third-country companies have a competitive advantage over domestic companies, the insurance clients of the open Member State could acquire an artificial advantage over their competitors in other Member States.

Substantial differences in national regimes regarding international trade in services therefore create inequalities of economic chances which run counter to the basic philosophy of the Common Market.[67]

In conclusion, Timmermans refers to the Court's ruling in Opinion 1/75, where the danger of distortion of competition was invoked by the Court to warrant the exclusive nature of the Community's powers within the framework of the CCP.

One should further examine the different elements mentioned by Timmermans. Let us first take the problem of trade deflection. The assumption that there is little room for this concept in the area of international service transactions is built on the observation that most services, indeed, cannot be stored and traded on their own, since production and consumption often coincide. Yet here already, there are important exceptions, such as television signals and telecommunications networks. Clearly, in these services sectors something equivalent to trade deflection can occur. An example concerning television may illustrate this. Suppose a Canadian TV station would like to broadcast in all the EC Member States, but would not be allowed in a number of Member States to do so directly from Canada, by virtue of national legislation. This station could then, in order to circumvent this interdiction, establish itself in a Member State that does allow such transmissions, capture the Canadian programmes there, and broadcast them all over the Community, benefiting from the free movement of broadcasting services.[68] Would this not be a case of trade deflection, since the decision of where to set up the European 'antenna' would not be governed by purely economic considerations, but instead by the more or less liberal legislation of Member States?

Secondly, one has to put the question whether trade deflection can only occur with goods and services that can circulate and be traded on their own. Is it not also possible to envisage something comparable to trade deflection in a number of services sectors characterized by the fact that it is the consumer of services who travels? One can give an example here, combining air transport and tourism. Take transatlantic traffic in the direction USA–Europe. Part of this traffic is tourist-oriented. Now, the average American tourist does not visit 'France' or 'Germany' or 'Sweden', but he visits 'Europe'. Consequently,

[67] *Supra* n. 50, pp. 684–5. See also Vigneron and Smith, *supra* n. 50, pp. 537–8.
[68] Cf. Ch. 4, *infra*.

he probably does not care too much whether his transatlantic flight lands in, let us say, London, Paris, or Amsterdam. Accordingly, the US air carrier which transports him could also see these destinations as (to some extent) alternatives. However, suppose the Dutch aviation authorities offer much better opportunities and advantages to US air carriers in their bilateral dealings with US aviation authorities than the French or the British do.[69] Would this not mean that some of the transatlantic traffic is deflected, because US carriers would to a certain extent prefer to fly to Amsterdam? Could this not be qualified trade deflection? There is little doubt that the French and the British would characterize it as such. These examples show that trade deflection is not a phenomenon that only occurs with trade in goods; to some extent, it can take place in the services sector as well.

Let us now consider the danger of distortion of competition between undertakings of different Member States, in the absence of a uniform policy towards trade in services with third countries. The insurance example given by Timmermans makes sufficiently clear that this danger is real. There is an important additional observation to be made, however: with respect to those services that cannot circulate and be traded on their own, the danger of distortion of competition is *much greater* than with respect to trade in goods. Consider the following examples. If Member State *A* has a more liberal import regime for shoes than Member State *B*, shoe producers in both *A* and *B* will probably feel the pressure of imports, because the third-country shoes can be traded in the whole Community.[70] But in the event that Member State *A* has a more liberal regime than *B* concerning the provision of financial services in its territory by banks established in a third country, it will primarily be *A*'s domestic banks which will feel the pressure of competition, and it will only be the companies established in *A* which will benefit from any competitive advantages which the third-country banks might possess. There is much more distortion of competition in such a case. To some extent, therefore, the dangers of trade deflection and distortion of competition are alternative. Basically, they both reflect the same phenomenon: the absence of a uniform external policy leads to artificial economic results, disrupting the optimal allocation of resources. In this sense, there is probably as much a need for such a uniform policy in the area of service transactions as there is in the area of trade in goods.

It should also be remembered that the concept of trade deflection was coined in classic customs union theory, which is limited to the effects of tariffs on international trade. It is clear, however, that today the Community is much more in terms of integration than a mere customs union with a common

[69] As is actually the case, see the recently concluded 'Open Skies' agreement between the Netherlands and the USA, see ' "Open Skies" accord could set trend', *Financial Times*, 7 Sept. 1992, p. 4.
[70] The only exception to this is the application of Article 115, see Ch. 5, pp. 170–84.

external tariff. Looked at from this angle, the danger of trade deflection, which is linked to tariffs and other protective border measures, is only one of the dangers of not having a common external trade policy. The risk of distortion of competition is perhaps at least as important in economic terms. In any case, the Court of Justice has never limited the rationale of a CCP to deflection of trade, as is clear, for example, from Opinion 1/75.[71] In addition, the single market programme comes into play here. In the services sector, it is through this programme that a genuinely integrated European market is being realized.[72] It is clear that the more the EC market is integrated, the more acute the dangers of deflection of trade and distortion of competition become. With respect to services, the 'saut qualitatif' which the single market programme provides makes the adoption of a CCP for services all the more urgent.

Let us now consider the current international context. Timmermans rightly refers to the evolution of international practice, namely the inclusion of services in the Uruguay Round negotiations, and the need for the Community to be able 'to follow suit'. Again some additional observations can be made, taking a somewhat wider view. According to Article 110 of the EC Treaty the fundamental aims of the CCP are 'to contribute ... to the harmonious development of world trade, the progressive abolition of restrictions on international trade and the lowering of customs barriers'. In other words, trade liberalization is one of the fundamental aims of the CCP. One could therefore argue that, if there is a case for liberalizing international trade in services, there is also a case for a CCP for services. Now, it was mentioned above that economists tend to agree that indeed liberalization of international service transactions would in principle lead to economic gains. Admittedly, the opinions of economists alone are not forceful enough to determine the scope of the Community's CCP. In this case, however, these opinions do not stand alone. They have been officially endorsed by a large number of governments, *including* the Community, through the 1986 Ministerial Declaration opening the Uruguay Round multilateral trade negotiations. It is worth quoting this Declaration in this respect:

Negotiations in [the area of trade in services] shall aim to establish a multilateral framework of principles and rules for trade in services, including elaboration of possible disciplines for individual sectors, with a view to expansion of such trade under conditions of transparency and progressive liberalization and as a means of promoting economic growth of all trading partners and the development of developing countries.[73]

Clearly, these aims recognize the case for liberalization of trade in services and fall squarely within the aims of the Community's commercial policy as stated in Article 110. Therefore, since the Community has adopted the Ministerial

---

[71] See text at p. 21 *supra*.   [72] See *supra*, p. 19.   [73] *BISD*, 33 S., p. 28.

Declaration and since it has been taking part very actively in the negotiations on services,[74] one could conclude that a Community commercial policy for services is already being developed.

All these considerations warrant the view that, today, the Community's CCP also covers international trade in services. Implicitly, the different arguments set out above reflect the common-sense observation that trade in goods and trade in services are essentially similar, both being commercial transactions between people.[75] This observation alone already provides good argument in favour of a commercial policy for services, as well as for goods. The question that is really important, in my view, is how to determine the scope and borders of a CCP for services. For it is obvious that the range of commercial policy cannot extend to every inch of the regulation of international service transactions. Not every measure affecting international trade in services is necessarily a measure of commercial policy. It can as easily be a measure of consumer or public policy, for example. After all, the same is true for international trade in goods. How can one determine the scope of a CCP for services?

The scope of a Common Commercial Policy for services

According to Mengozzi, one should distinguish between the 'noyau central' of the CCP, being all aspects relating to the protection of the customs union as well as the conclusion of commercial agreements, and commercial policy measures falling within so-called 'domaines marginaux', because the commercial policy aspect is marginal, and linked to objectives such as consumer, environmental, and intellectual property protection.[76] As regards services, the author appears to imply that they fall within these 'domaines marginaux' of the CCP, because the regulation of service transactions involves the protection of a number of sensitive public interests. This distinction would be important for determining the extent to which the Community has the exclusive competence to act.[77]

---

[74] For example, on 18 June 1990 the Community tabled a draft General Agreement on Trade in Services (Commission Press Release IP/90/494 of 18 June 1990). Also see the 'Address by Mr Andriessen at the International Business Council—New York, 28 September 1990' (Commission Press Release Speech/90/74 of 28 Sept. 1990), in which the Commissioner stressed the importance of an agreement on services for the Community.

[75] Timmermans, *supra* n. 50, p. 679; C. S. Pisuisse, 'De bevoegdheid van de Europese Gemeenschap met betrekking tot de liberalisatie van de internationale dienstverlening', 35 *SEW* (1987), 3: 188; Peter Gilsdorf, 'Portée et délimitation des compétences communautaires en matière de politique commerciale', *RMC* (1989), 326: 205. Compare also with Ehlermann, who points to the increasingly similar interpretation of Arts. 59 *et seq.* and Arts. 30 *et seq.* as an argument in favour of extending the CCP to services, see 'Application of GATT Rules in the European Community', in M. Hilf, F. G. Jacobs, and E.-U. Petersmann (eds.), *The European Community and GATT*, 2nd edn. (Deventer: Kluwer, 1989), 130–1.

[76] Mengozzi, *supra* n. 58, pp. 248–50.

[77] This aspect is further examined *infra*, p. 32–34.

Although there is certainly some force in this distinction, it does not introduce any specific guide-lines for determining the scope of a CCP for services, leaving this to the Community's institutions. However, from an institutional point of view this is not an ideal solution, because the scope of the CCP determines the division of powers between the Community and the Member States. The various institutions have divergent interests in this regard.[78] Moreover, in Mengozzi's view the CCP has the potential to cover all aspects of the regulation of services, and that is difficult to justify.

Vigneron and Smith are of the view that considerations of democratic control should determine the scope of a CCP for services. As the European Parliament has no say in the development of the CCP, it would not be acceptable to use the commercial policy competence to adopt measures regarding services which involve the harmonization of substantive rules.[79] However, the lack of involvement of the European Parliament in the CCP is a general problem. Taken to its extreme, the above argument would result in a much-reduced CCP, all important external policies for which it is useful to have control by the Parliament being excluded from its scope. Moreover, who will determine when there has to be democratic control and when not?

More specific guide-lines are proposed by Timmermans. He maintains that one should define the notion of commercial policy—*in general*, and not just for services—in such a manner that it reflects the division of powers between the Community and the Member States with respect to intra-Community trade.[80] This is necessary, in his view, for basic reasons of coherence. If one did not limit the notion of commercial policy as indicated, the result would be that a specific measure which the Member States would still be allowed to take for intra-Community trade, could nevertheless be characterized as a commercial policy measure when applied to trade with third countries. But as the Member States have lost all autonomous competence to take commercial policy measures, this would mean that their freedom of action with respect to foreign trade would be more restricted than with respect to intra-Community trade. It is clear that such a result is difficult to defend and undesirable.

An example may illustrate this. Suppose a Member State wishes to restrict certain imports for genuine reasons of protection of public health. In intra-Community trade, it is allowed to do so by virtue of Article 36 of the EC Treaty (in the absence, of course, of any harmonization of national legislation). But if one were to consider such a measure, with respect to trade with third countries,

[78] Compare with René Barents, 'Milieu en interne markt', 41 *SEW* (1993), 1: 8–11, and 'The internal market unlimited: Some observations on the legal basis of Community legislation', 30 *CML Rev.* (1993), 1: 90–3.

[79] *Supra* n. 50, pp. 540–1.

[80] *Supra* n. 50, pp. 680–3. Also see, by the same author, 'La libre circulation des marchandises et la politique commerciale commune', in P. Demaret (ed.), *Relations extérieures de la Communauté européenne et marché intérieur: aspects juridiques et fonctionnels* (Bruges: Story for the College of Europe, 1988), 91–108.

as a commercial policy measure, this Member State would not be allowed to restrict direct imports from third countries for those same public health reasons, because it would not be competent to do so. Only the Community would be entitled to act.

Timmermans therefore proposes, as a kind of rule of reason, to let the interpretation of the notion of commercial policy be determined by the internal Community regimes governing trade in goods and trade in services respectively. For trade in services, this would mean that measures which in intra-Community trade are forbidden by virtue of Articles 59 and 60 of the EC Treaty, should be considered as being commercial policy measures if applied to trade in services with third countries. On the other hand, measures which amount to general, non-discriminatory regulation of certain service transactions, and which Member States consequently are allowed to take with respect to intra-Community trade in services, should not be characterized as commercial policy measures, if applied to service transactions with third countries. The result would be the following:

Measures discriminating directly or indirectly against international services are thus not forbidden but fall within the exclusive domain of the Community. Member States would be forbidden to take them, but the EC Council could do so, by virtue of Article 113 EEC. These discriminatory measures are in fact all those measures which regulate the 'status' of international services on the national market. These measures range from flat prohibitions on entering the market, and special regimes of stricter conditions, to granting national treatment whether or not on a basis of reciprocity.[81]

By the way, according to Timmermans such status measures also include discriminatory measures with respect to establishment by third-country nationals.[82] This is important in the light of the fact that, as we have seen, in a number of service sectors establishment is necessary, economically speaking, in order to trade services internationally.[83] In this respect the author's concepts run parallel with economic realities.

Timmermans's rule-of-reason approach to the concept of commercial policy is appealing. Its main force of attraction lies, of course, in the parallelism it establishes in the division of powers between the Community and the Member States as regards both intra-Community trade and trade with third countries. It is clear that a coherent functioning of economic regulation in the Community requires such a parallelism, at least to some degree.

The approach is also logical from the point of view of the basic rationale for a Common Commercial Policy. If it is accepted that the CCP's aim is to prevent trade deflection and distortion of competition within the single market caused by a non-uniform external trade policy, Timmermans's views are fully warranted: it is primarily the described 'status' measures, having a

---

[81] *Supra* n. 50, p. 687.   [82] Ibid. 688.
[83] *Supra*, pp. 10–11. Cf. Demaret, *supra* n. 46, p. 80.

discriminatory nature, which are liable to deflect trade or distort competition.[84] To limit ourselves to services, we can again refer to the above-mentioned insurance example. In this example, it is the fact that some Member States do not allow imports of insurance services from third countries, which distorts competition. If the various national regimes regulating insurance all applied indiscriminately to imported and domestic services, distortion of competition would only occur according to the strictness of these differing regimes. But such distortion is of an altogether different character. It is no longer attributable to a divergent external regime, but becomes a problem of intra-Community trade in services in general; a problem which can only be solved through harmonization based, for example, on Article 57 (2) of the EC Treaty. It is out of the question, in such a case, for the Community to have any exclusive competence by virtue of the provisions on the CCP.

Interestingly, Timmermans's approach also reflects, at Community level, proposals which were made concerning the liberalization of international trade in services at the multilateral level. It has indeed been argued that the latter exercise, in order to be workable, should concentrate on identifying discriminatory barriers to trade, and separate these functionally from domestic regulation for the purpose of negotiating their reduction.[85] To the extent that GATS indeed takes such an approach, the Community's competence to sign would also run parallel with this aspect of international trade in services.

The rule-of-reason approach probably needs some fine-tuning. First, it could create problems related to the fact that the EC Treaty entails far-reaching liberalization of intra-Community trade. Again limiting ourselves to services, the prohibition of restrictions on the movement of services, laid down in Articles 59 and 60 of the Treaty, is widely interpreted by the Court of Justice, extending to measures applying without distinction to domestic and imported services.[86] It is questionable whether the concept of commercial policy needs to be extended to those measures which do not infringe the rule of non-discrimination. This would deny the Member States a number of general regulatory powers that are not directly related to international trade in services.[87]

Secondly, the measures in question need not always be discriminatory towards imports from third countries. As was mentioned, trade liberalization is one of the basic aims of the CCP. Consequently, measures aimed at such liberalization, by for example aligning the import regime to the intra-Community regime would also have to be considered to be commercial policy.

[84] Timmermans also points this out, *supra* n. 50, p. 687.
[85] Geza Feketekuty, *supra* n. 1, p. 210–11. Also in other parts of the work there is a clear attempt to separate purely regulatory issues from trade policy issues.
[86] See *supra*, pp. 13–16.
[87] See for example the case-law, dealt with *supra* at pp. 14–15, concerning the duplication of licensing requirements. It can be argued that such duplication should not be considered as being a commercial policy measure, when applied towards trade with third countries.

Suppose that in the framework of the Uruguay Round the Community would agree to full national treatment of imported financial services, this would certainly be a commercial policy measure, not discriminatory, but conversely, liberalizing.

In conclusion, it is submitted that the rule-of-reason approach proposed by Timmermans offers a valuable tool for demarcating the field of commercial policy, also in the services sector. It should not, however, be interpreted as the final word on the question; it cannot amount to much more than a guide-line to be applied in specific cases. Below, when examining the external dimension of the different sectors of the internal market in services, the rule-of-reason approach will be employed in such a way.

Finally, one last general question concerning a CCP for services has to be dealt with. It relates to the exclusive character of the Community's competence in the sphere of commercial policy. There are commentators who have argued that in those areas which lie at the borders of commercial policy an a priori exclusive Community competence is not appropriate and should be abandoned. Services would be one of these areas. These suggestions may not be overlooked here, since they contain some forceful arguments.

Exclusivity reconsidered?

Gilsdorf has developed the argument that it is not realistic to claim an exclusive Community competence in areas such as services, which are not part of the classic core of commercial policy, and in which there are little or no Community instruments yet for exercising this competence.[88] Moreover, such an exclusive competence cannot be put in practice without difficulty, and it would not be improbable that the Council would just give a blank cheque to the Member States, which is of little value. From a more political point of view, he argues that one cannot have it all at once: a notion of commercial policy which largely surpasses traditional concepts and at the same time an unlimited exclusive Community competence. In support of his thesis, Gilsdorf points out that the Court of Justice has only twice affirmed the exclusive character of the CCP (in Opinion 1/75 and *Donckerwolcke*),[89] which hardly amounts to established case-law.[90]

For the services sector, there is the additional argument that free trade in services depends to a large extent on regulation, by contrast to free trade in goods, as the respective intra-Community regimes show. An exclusive

---

[88] Peter Gilsdorf, *supra* n. 75, pp. 197–8. Other authors also point to the fundamental contradiction between exclusive powers and a widening scope of the commercial policy concept, e.g. Demaret, *supra* n. 64, p. 83. See also Vigneron and Smith, *supra* n. 50, p. 541.

[89] Opinion 1/75, [1975] ECR 1355, at 1364 and Case 41/76, *Donckerwolcke*, [1976] ECR 1921, at 1937.

[90] *Supra* n. 75, p. 197.

Community competence, without the instruments to exercise it, would also not be appropriate from this point of view. Therefore, Gilsdorf proposes that the Member States retain their competence to regulate trade in services with third countries as long as the Community does not act.[91]

There are two important objections to this suggestion. From a legal point of view, it is difficult to reconcile Gilsdorf's views with the wordings of Opinion 1/75, which holds that

any unilateral action on the part of the Member States would lead to disparities in the conditions for the grant of export credits, calculated to distort competition between undertakings of the various Member States in external markets. Such distortion can be eliminated only by means of a strict uniformity of credit conditions granted to undertakings in the Community, whatever their nationality.[92]

Above, the disparities and distortion of competition which the Court mentions were considered to be the fundamental motive for a CCP for services. At the same time, they necessitate, according to the Court, an exclusive Community competence.

From a more political and institutional point of view, there is also an objection. Community experience indicates that, without an exclusive Community competence, there is little incentive for the Member States to allow the Community to play as important a role as may be necessary. The transport sector offers an obvious example in this respect. It may well be that to assume an exclusive Community competence is indispensable for ensuring that substantive and comprehensive EC policies are developed.

Admittedly, there is something artificial in claiming an exclusive Community competence in those areas where there are as yet no instruments to exercise this competence (as is the case, to some extent, in the services sector). But this is unavoidable, since the notion of commercial policy is subject to evolution, as the Court has emphasized. This means that it may extend to new areas of action. However, this evolutionary interpretation of the commercial policy concept should not encroach on the coherence of economic regulation, which would be the case if one abandons the exclusivity of the Community's competence. Moreover, the danger of inroads into this exclusivity, if the Community proves to be not yet able to act, should not be exaggerated. It is true that from a strictly legal point of view any autonomous Member State action in the field of commercial policy is illegal. However, such illegality would not necessarily lead to practical consequences of any dramatic nature, as past experience shows.[93]

These objections against abandoning the concept of exclusive Community powers in the case of international trade in services also apply to the reasoning

---

[91] *Supra* n. 75, pp. 204–5. [92] [1975] ECR at 1364.
[93] See in this connection Ch. 5.

developed by Mengozzi, regarding the distinction between 'noyau central' and 'domaines marginaux'.[94] Although it is not admitted by the author in so many words,[95] his thesis that the Member States may continue to regulate these 'domaines marginaux' (including services) as long as the Community does not act in effect boils down to a scheme of concurrent powers.

Two additional observations should be made. One is that these objections against abandoning exclusivity do not imply that in a number of cases the concept of exclusive Community powers in the area of commercial policy may not have become inappropriate. This is further explored in the chapter on export controls.[96] However, as regards commercial aspects of international service transactions, exclusivity is fully warranted because of the described link with the proper functioning of the internal market, especially the need to avoid deflections of trade and distortions of competition. Secondly, a case could perhaps be made for conferring on the Member States a more important role in implementing commercial policy, without surrendering the Community's exclusive competence. After all, Article 113 only states that the CCP should be accomplished through laying down uniform *principles*; it does not prescribe that each and every aspect of commercial policy must be in the hands of the Community's institutions. In the services sector, there might indeed be some scope for the Community deciding on the principles, and leaving part of their implementation to the Member States. As an example one could mention the air transport sector, with its host of bilateral agreements with third countries, which could perhaps further be negotiated by the Member States, but within the framework of a number of Community rules and guide-lines.[97]

Conclusion

It is submitted that international trade in services is covered by the EC Treaty provisions on the Common Commercial Policy. This does not mean that all kinds of regulation affecting international service transactions are to be characterized as commercial policy. In order to determine the scope of a CCP for services, the division of powers between the Community and the Member States concerning intra-Community trade in services can serve as a guide-line. Furthermore, although the Community's competence to devise a commercial policy is exclusive, the services sector is perhaps well suited to leave part of the implementation of the Community's commercial policy to the Member States.

---

[94] *Supra*, p. 28.
[96] Ch. 7, p. 258.

[95] He speaks of 'potential exclusivity', see *supra* n. 58, p. 249.
[97] See *infra*, Ch. 3, pp. 109–16.

Implied powers and international service transactions

According to the doctrine of implied powers, which is based on the Court's case-law in *AETR, Kramer,* Opinion 1/76, and Opinion 2/91,[98] the Community has the competence to act in external relations when specific Community objectives or internal Community regulation make such action necessary. Put as densely as this, the doctrine may appear rather simple. That, however, is deceptive. It is not an exaggeration to say that the subject of implied powers is one of the most difficult chapters of Community law, and there is little agreement among commentators on how exactly it should be interpreted and applied.[99] A comprehensive analysis would therefore go beyond the scope of the present study.[100] Below, only a summary of the debate is provided, followed by an attempt to define the extent to which implied powers could be used for regulating service transactions with third countries.

In the *AETR* case the Court of Justice answered the question whether it was the Community or rather the Member States which had the authority to conclude the European Agreement concerning the work of crews of vehicles engaged in international road transport.[101] The Court found that authority to enter into agreements does not only arise from express provisions of the EC Treaty (Articles 113, 114, and 238); it

> may equally flow from other provisions of the Treaty and from measures adopted, within the framework of those provisions, by the Community institutions … In particular, each time the Community, with a view to implementing a common policy envisaged by the Treaty, adopts provisions laying down common rules, whatever form these may take, the Member States no longer have the right, acting individually or even collectively, to undertake obligations with third countries which affect those rules.[102]

The Community alone may do so. Applying these principles to the *AETR* case, the Court subsequently examined Article 75, EC Treaty, finding that '[t]his

[98] Case 22/70, *Commission v. Council (AETR),* [1971] ECR 263; Joined cases 3, 4, and 6/76, *Kramer,* [1976] ECR 1279; Opinion 1/76, [1977] ECR 741; Opinion 2/91, 19 Mar. 1993, not yet published. It should also be mentioned that in Opinion 1/92, on the draft Agreement on a European Economic Area, the Court referred to the implied powers doctrine in order to establish the Community's competence to conclude international agreements in the field of competition policy, see paras. 38–42 of the Opinion, OJ C 136/11 of 26 May 1992. However, the Court's reasoning being very succinct this ruling is not further analysed here.

[99] Meinhard Hilf, 'The Single European Act and 1992: Legal Implications for Third Countries', 1 *EJIL* (1990), 1/2: 95.

[100] See for such a study, Christine Denys, *Impliciete bevoegdheden in de Europese Economische Gemeenschap* (Antwerp: MAKLU, 1990).

[101] The Commission had taken the view that Article 75, EC Treaty, regarding the common transport policy, applies 'to external relations just as much as to domestic measures'. The Council, by contrast, contended 'that since the Community only has such powers as have been conferred on it, authority to enter into agreements with third countries cannot be assumed in the absence of an express provision in the Treaty'. As Article 75 does not explicitly provide such authority, the Community would not be able to conclude agreements relating to transport ([1971] ECR 273–4).

[102] [1971] ECR 274. At 275 the Court reiterates that the Member States cannot assume obligations 'which might affect … or alter [the] scope' of Community rules.

provision is equally concerned with transport to and from third countries, as regards that part of the journey which takes place on Community territory',[103] assuming therefore 'that the powers of the Community extend to relationships arising from international law'.[104] Following this reference to Article 75, the Court referred to Regulation 543/69 on the harmonization of certain social legislation relating to road transport,[105] which 'necessarily vested in the Community power to enter into any agreements with third countries relating to the subject-matter governed by that regulation'.[106] As the AETR came within the scope of this regulation, the Community alone had the power to negotiate and conclude the agreement in question.[107]

In the *Kramer* case, concerning the North-East Atlantic Fisheries Convention, the Court reiterated that the Community's authority to enter into international commitments

arises not only from an express conferment by the Treaty, but may equally flow implicitly from other provisions of the Treaty, from the Act of Accession and from measures adopted, within the framework of those provisions, by the Community institutions.[108]

It then examined the provisions of the Treaty, the Act of Accession and two Council regulations relating to fisheries, concluding that

[i]t follows from these provisions taken as a whole that the Community has at its disposal, on the internal level, the power to take any measures for the conservation of the biological resources of the sea, measures which include the fixing of catch quotas and their allocation between the different Member States. It should be made clear that, although Article 5 of Regulation No 2141/70 is applicable only to a geographically limited fishing area, it none the less follows from Article 102 of the Act of Accession, from Article 1 of the said regulation and moreover from the very nature of things that the rule-making authority of the Community *ratione materiae* also extends—in so far as the Member States have similar authority under public international law—to fishing on the high seas. The only way to ensure conservation of the biological resources of the sea both effectively and equitably is through a system of rules binding on all the States concerned, including non-member countries. In these circumstances it follows from the very duties and powers which Community law has established and assigned to the institutions of the Community on the internal level that the Community has the authority to enter into international commitments for the conservation of the resources of the sea.[109]

However, since at the time the Community had not yet fully exercised its functions in the matter, the Member States were still entitled to conclude agreements. This (concurrent) power could, however, only be regarded as transitional, and would come to an end at the latest from the sixth year of the

---

[103] [1971] ECR 275.   [104] Ibid.
[105] OJ L 77/49 of 29 Mar. 1969, English Special edn. 1969 (I), p. 170.   [106] [1971] ECR 275.
[107] Ibid. and at 276.   [108] [1976] ECR 1308.   [109] [1976] ECR 1309.

(first) Accession, because Article 102 of the Act of Accession provides that the Council must by then have adopted measures for the conservation of the resources of the sea.[110]

Whereas in both *AETR* and *Kramer* the Community's authority to conclude international agreements was deduced from the provisions of the Treaty in conjunction with secondary Community law, Opinion 1/76 established such authority on the sole basis of the relevant provisions of the EC Treaty. In this case, the Commission had asked the Court whether the draft Agreement establishing a European laying-up fund for inland waterway vessels was compatible with the EC Treaty. This agreement, to be concluded by the Community, a number of Member States, and Switzerland, pursued the objective of rationalizing the economic situation of the inland waterway transport industry in the Rhine and Moselle basins, all the Netherlands inland waterways and the German inland waterways linked to the Rhine basin. The Court first examined the Community's competence to conclude such an agreement. It found that the objectives of the agreement came within the scope of the common transport policy, adding, however, that in this specific case the adoption of common rules by the Community would not be able to fully attain these objectives,

because of the traditional participation of vessels from a third State, Switzerland, in navigation by the principal waterways in question, which are subject to the system of freedom of navigation established by international agreements of long standing.[111]

Subsequently, the Court summarized its previous case-law on implied powers, stating that

whenever Community law has created for the institutions of the Community powers within its internal system for the purpose of attaining a specific objective, the Community has authority to enter into international commitments necessary for the attainment of that objective even in the absence of an express provision in that connection.[112]

The following paragraph is essential:

This is particularly so in all cases in which internal power has already been used in order to adopt measures which come within the attainment of common policies. It is, however, not limited to that eventuality. Although the internal Community measures are only adopted when the international agreement is concluded and made enforceable, as is envisaged in the present case by the proposal for a regulation to be submitted to the Council by the Commission, the power to bind the Community *vis-à-vis* third countries nevertheless flows by implication from the provisions of the Treaty creating the internal power and in so far as the participation of the Community in the international agreement is, as here, necessary for the attainment of one of the objectives of the Community.[113]

---

[110] [1976] ECR 1310.	[111] [1977] ECR 754–5.
[112] [1977] ECR 755.	[113] Ibid.

Lastly, in Opinion 2/91 the Court examined the question whether the Community was competent to conclude Convention No. 170 of the International Labour Organization, concerning safety in the use of chemicals at work.[114] Such competence was quickly established by the Court, because Article 118*a*, EC Treaty, provides for Community action in the field of health and safety of workers. However, the Commission argued that this competence was exclusive, in application of the rules laid down in *AETR*. That was only partly accepted by the Court, because both the ILO Convention and Article 118*a* (3) only provide for the adoption of minimum requirements. Hence, the Convention and Community directives adopted on the basis of Article 118*a* (3) could always be applied simultaneously, no matter which of them contains the strictest requirements. Nevertheless, the Court also found that a number of Community directives covering fields coming within the scope of the Convention contained rules which are more than minimum requirements. In so far as this is the case, the Community does have the exclusive competence to conclude the Convention. On the other hand, the Court also observed that to the extent that the Convention would apply to the overseas countries and territories of the Member States, the Community was not competent to conclude it, because its subject-matter lies outside the association scheme which the EC Treaty envisages for these countries and territories. In the end, it was established that '[t]he conclusion of ILO Convention No 170 is a matter which falls within the joint competence of the Member States and the Community'.

This case-law on implied powers is sometimes referred to as establishing the principle of parallelism of internal and external competences (*in foro interno, in foro externo*).[115] But that is too much of a simplification. The above-described judgments are more subtle than that.[116] First of all, it is necessary to distinguish between the power to conclude international agreements, on the one hand, and the power to regulate external relations from a substantive point of view, on the other. The main contribution of the implied powers case-law concerns the former power.[117] In the four decisions set out above, the Court emphasizes, without mincing words, the power of the Community to enter into international commitments, even in the absence of express

[114] See *supra* n. 98.
[115] e.g. Leslie Fielding, *Europe as a Global Partner*, UACES Occasional Papers 7 (London: 1991), 10; Vlad Constantinesco, 'Les compétences internationales de la Communauté et des États membres à travers l'Acte Unique européen', in *Relations extérieures de la Communauté européenne et marché intérieur: aspects juridiques et fonctionnels, supra* n. 80, p. 68.
[116] See Ami Barav, 'The Division of External Relations Power between the European Economic Community and the Member States in the Case-Law of the Court of Justice', in C. W. A. Timmermans and E. L. M. Völker (eds.), *Division of Powers between the European Communities and their Member States in the Field of External Relations* (Deventer: Kluwer, 1981), at 41.
[117] Cf. Denys, *supra* n. 100, ch. 7; also, be it implicitly, Jean-Victor Louis in J. Mégret *et al.* (eds.), *Le droit de la Communauté économique européenne*, xii: *relations extérieures* (Brussels: Éditions de l'ULB, 1980), 94–103.

provisions to that effect. However, when it comes down to determining whether the subject-matter of an agreement comes within the scope of the Community's competence, the Court's reasoning is far more elaborate, analysing the various elements of fact and law with great care. Thus, in *AETR* the Court did not broadly state that Article 75 of the EC Treaty, covers external relations in the transport sector. It looked for internal common rules, adopted in implementation of Article 75, covering the same subject area as the agreement in question. Only if such internal rules are affected, or if their scope risks being altered by the agreement does the Community have the exclusive competence to adopt it. Similarly, in *Kramer* the Court examined a whole set of rules stemming from the EC Treaty, the Act of Accession and two Council regulations in order to find that the Community has the power to adopt measures relating to fishing catch quotas on the high seas. It emphasized, moreover, the fact that the aim of conservation of fishing resources could not possibly be attained by the mere adoption of internal common rules, because of the 'very nature of things' (fish move rather freely). In Opinion 1/76, the Court in the absence of internal common rules only referred to Article 75, but again it did not state that this provision covers external relations as such. It highlighted the link with internal policies, pointing to the necessity to include Switzerland in the system for it to be effective. In Opinion 2/91, lastly, the Court took a close look at the scope of Article 118*a* and of Community directives in order to determine whether the Community had the exclusive competence to conclude the relevant ILO Convention. From a substantive point of view the latter does not deal with external relations, but aims at establishing minimum requirements to be observed by the domestic legislation of all signatories.

It is necessary, moreover, to distinguish between the *AETR* type of cases and the Opinion 1/76 type. According to *AETR*, the fact that the Community has adopted common rules creates its exclusive competence to negotiate and conclude international agreements covering the same subject area as these common rules. Put in other words, agreements which 'affect' or 'alter the scope' of these rules cannot be concluded by the Member States. It is not an easy thing to determine the exact range of this rule.[118] Most commentators appear to agree, however, that the words 'affect' and 'alter the scope' are to be interpreted in a legal sense, pertaining to the interplay of the rules as such, which is confirmed by Opinion

---

[118] For an analysis from a theoretical point of view, see John Temple Lang, 'The *ERTA* judgment and the Court's case-law on competence and conflict', F. G. Jacobs (ed.), 6 *Yearbook of European Law* (1986) (Oxford: Clarendon Press, 1987), 194–203; for an analysis based on practical examples, see Christiaan W. A. Timmermans, 'Division of External Powers between Community and Member States in the Field of Harmonization of National Law: A Case Study', in *Division of Powers between the European Communities and their Member States in the Field of External Relations, supra* n. 116, pp. 15–28.

2/91.[119] These words do not mean that external relations in the fields (internally) regulated by the Community come entirely within the scope of the Community's exclusive competence.[120] To give an example, the fact that the Community has adopted a comprehensive set of rules relating to air transport within the Community would not create, by virtue of *AETR*, an exclusive competence to deal with air transport relations with third countries.[121]

Under Opinion 1/76 it is the necessity of concluding an international agreement with a view to fully attaining a specific objective of the Community, which creates the Community's external competence. Both the concepts of 'necessity' and 'specific objective' limit the scope of this competence. It is therefore safe to say that this case-law does not create an external competence whenever the Community institutions find the exercise of such competence desirable or advisable.[122] Also, a mere reference to the general objectives of the EC Treaty (e.g. the unity of the internal market) would not be sufficient.

Applying these principles to the case of service transactions with third countries, it is doubtful whether the implied powers doctrine offers wide Community powers, especially when it comes down to regulating these transactions as such.[123] For example, does the fact that the Community has laid down common rules on the provision of financial services within the Community, harmonizing national legislation regarding the supervision of financial firms, create a competence regarding transactions in financial services with third countries? Do agreements relating to the latter necessarily affect or alter the scope of such common rules, as is required by *AETR* for the Community's competence to be present? Of course it is difficult to answer such questions purely in the abstract, in the absence of a detailed examination of the common rules in question and of what is meant by regulating service transactions with third countries. But this observation of itself already reveals that the implied powers doctrine is not well suited for developing a comprehensive regime regarding external service transactions or, to put it differently, for defining the external dimension of the internal market as regards services.

Let us also look at the Opinion 1/76 type of cases. Are there any provisions in the EC Treaty containing specific objectives, as regards services, which make it necessary for the Community to act in the field of external service transactions? The services chapter itself only mentions the provision of

---

[119] In this sense, R. Kovar, 'Les compétences implicites: jurisprudence de la Cour et pratique communautaire', in *Relations extérieures de la Communauté européenne et marché intérieur: aspects juridiques et fonctionnels, supra* n. 80, pp. 25–6; Louis, *supra* n. 117, pp. 110–11; more explicitly, Advocate-General Lenz in his Opinion in Case 165/87, *Commission* v. *Council* [1988] ECR 5545 at 5556.

[120] Louis, *supra* n. 117, p. 110: 'ce n'est pas tout le domaine réglé par le droit dérivé qui échappe comme tel à la sphère nationale'.

[121] Cf. Ch. 3, pp. 89–90.

[122] Barav, *supra* n. 116, p. 41.

[123] *Contra* Perreau de Pinninck, *supra* n. 53, pp. 408–14.

services within the Community. Harmonization of national legislation, on the basis of either Article 57 (2) or Article 100a, is only aimed at regulating the provision of services within the Community, for the purpose of creating an internal market. Of course one could argue that an internal market cannot be created without defining an external regime. But that argument is more of a political nature, involving an assessment from the point of view of desirability. It is basically the argument in favour of extending the CCP to trade in services, because otherwise deflections of trade or distortions of competition within the internal market may arise. From a purely legal point of view, however, it is perfectly possible to establish the internal market without regulating external relations. Article 7a of the Treaty, which defines the internal market, is in this regard indicative since it does not refer to external relations.

Perhaps in matters of transport policy, things are somewhat different. As was mentioned above, the Court held in *AETR* that Article 75, EC Treaty, also covers transport to and from third countries as regards that part of the journey which takes place on Community territory. This has been confirmed in Opinion 1/76. It may therefore be more easy to establish external Community competence in this area, also because both Articles 75 (1) and 84 (2) (relating to sea and air transport) define the Community's competence in broad terms. Again, however, attention must be drawn to the fact that both in *AETR* and Opinion 1/76 the Court was at great pains to emphasize the link between concluding an agreement and conducting an internal policy.

In the following chapters on services, especially the one on transport, the question of external competence based on implied powers will be further examined. Nevertheless, as a preliminary conclusion it is submitted that implied powers do not offer the appropriate tool for fully defining the external dimension of the internal market as regards services, although for some aspects of this definition implied powers can probably be used. However, it is not an easy matter—to say the least—to determine which these aspects are. The Community's implied powers have been the subject of debate ever since the Court has spoken about them. But it is probably in 'the very nature' of things implied that they are more intricate than what is expressly mentioned and described.

Concurrence of competence by virtue of the CCP and implied powers

The conclusion to be drawn from the two previous sections is that the Community's power to act in the field of external trade in services may stem both from the EC Treaty provisions on the CCP and from implied powers. It is certain that the scope of these two types of competence is not identical. Nevertheless, it cannot be ruled out that certain measures come under both these types. Do such measures have to be adopted on the basis of both these competences, or does one of them have precedence over the other? This is a question which has not yet been dealt with, although for a number of reasons it is quite important. First, it has procedural relevance. Under Article 113 of the EC Treaty, measures are adopted by the Council on a proposal from the Commission. The European Parliament, however, does not have to be consulted.[124] By contrast, under Article 57 (2) (to name but this provision) the co-decision procedure applies, systematically involving the European Parliament in decision-making. Secondly, the importance of the question lies in the concept of policy, which is essential in the implementation of the CCP but rather absent with regard to implied powers. The latter do provide a competence but they do not of themselves require the implementation of a comprehensive policy. For the subject-matter of this study, that is an important distinction. If implied powers were to precede the CCP, the definition and regulation of the external dimension of the internal market in services would be liable to suffer, because the Community institutions would appear to be less obliged, under the Treaty, to develop a comprehensive policy, 'based on uniform principles' (Article 113), and covering the whole field of external trade in services.

Most authors who have examined the question whether the regulation of trade in services with third countries comes under the commercial policy heading, seem to be of the (implicit!) view that, if the answer is affirmative, implied powers have no role to play when the Community acts in this field (to the extent that it remains within the scope of the CCP).[125] Only Perreau de Pinninck is of the view that since implied powers offer a sufficient basis for regulating external services transactions, recourse to Article 113 is not necessary. He argues that implied powers offer a specific and sufficient legal basis, making superfluous any reference to the general legal basis of Article 113.[126] One fails to see, however, in what sense the provisions on the CCP are of a more general nature than implied powers. Indeed, the opposite can as easily be maintained: the CCP is more specific in that it only deals with external relations, whereas implied powers are part of a broader internal competence.

The reason why so few commentators have dealt with the concurrence question is perhaps that the answer appears to be so evident: since the provisions of the EC Treaty on the CCP deal explicitly with external relations, the CCP must precede implied powers as a legal basis, because the latter are only implicit, deduced, as it were, from an internal competence.[127] As

---

[124] Although in practice it is often consulted in the framework of the so-called Luns-Westerterp procedure; see on this procedure Christian Tomuschat, in H. von der Groeben, J. Thiesing, and C.-D. Ehlermann (eds.), *Kommentar zum EWG-Vertrag*, 4th edn. (Baden-Baden: Nomos, 1991), pp. 5668–9.

[125] Thus, for example, Timmermans, *supra* n. 50, and Mengozzi, *supra* n. 58. The same view is present in COM (90) 17 final, on external aviation relations, analysed in Ch. 3.

[126] *Supra* n. 53, especially at pp. 414 and 421. Compare Lauwaars, *supra* n. 51, who appears to suggest something similar.

[127] Richard H. Lauwaars and Christiaan W. A. Timmermans, *Europees Gemeenschapsrecht in kort bestek* (Groningen: Wolters Noordhoff, 1989), 276.

Advocate-General Lenz has put it, 'the "implied powers" found in the [*AETR*] judgment by the Court of Justice must, however, take second place behind the express powers granted in the EEC Treaty'.[128] That conclusion indeed seems to be a matter of mere logic. It is supported, moreover, by the fundamental role which the CCP plays in preserving the unity of the internal market. The 'internal' motive for extending the CCP to trade in services, described above— which is precisely this unity—makes it difficult to perceive how it could be defended that the CCP competence does not take precedence over implied powers.

There is also case-law, however. The above-mentioned observation by Advocate-General Lenz is part of his Opinion in Case 165/87, *Commission* v. *Council*, concerning the legality of the Council's Decision regarding the conclusion of the International Convention on the Harmonized Commodity Description and Coding System.[129] The harmonized system which this Convention introduces is to be used by the contracting parties for their tariff and statistical nomenclature. The Council had based the said decision on Articles 28 (concerning autonomous alterations and suspensions of customs duties), 113 and 235, EC Treaty. The Commission argued that only Article 113 should have been relied upon. The Court, however, did not uphold either view. It decided that the Convention should have been concluded on the basis of Articles 28 and 113. The question therefore is: since Article 28 only mentions autonomous action, and not the conclusion of agreements, has the Court not decided that implied powers and the provisions on the CCP are to be used simultaneously as the legal basis for measures which come within the scope of both of these, especially since the Court ruled that 'where an institution's power is based on two provisions of the Treaty, it is bound to adopt the relevant measures on the basis of the two relevant provisions'?[130]

At first sight, this question may seem rhetorical. It is necessary, however, to examine the judgment more in depth. The Court distinguished between the tariff and statistical nomenclature aspects of the Convention.[131] It found that neither Article 28 nor Article 113 expressly give the Council power to establish a tariff nomenclature. However, as the establishment of a tariff nomenclature is indispensable to the application of customs duties, the power given to the Council to make changes in rates

necessarily implies, in the absence of express provision in the Treaty, power to establish and amend the nomenclature relating to the application of the Common Customs Tariff.

It follows from that observation that the Council has a general power in relation to tariff matters, which is based on Article 28 and on Article 113 of the Treaty, inasmuch

---

[128] See the Advocate-General's Opinion in Case 165/87, [1988] ECR 5556.
[129] [1988] ECR 5545. For the Decision, see OJ L 198/1 of 20 July 1987.
[130] [1988] ECR 5561.
[131] The statistical nomenclature is not further dealt with here.

as it has that power irrespective of whether Common Customs Tariff duties are amended autonomously (Article 28) or under tariff agreements or other measures of common commercial policy (Article 113).

The Commission's argument that the scope of Article 28 is covered by that of Article 113 of the Treaty must therefore be rejected.[132]

The last sentence is essential. What the Court actually says is that, as regards tariffs, the scope of Articles 28 and 113 is not identical, but complementary. In so far as autonomous alterations of duties are concerned, Article 28 is the relevant provision. In so far as conventional alterations are concerned, Article 113 applies.[133] This explains the Court's general statement, quoted above, regarding the adoption of measures on a dual legal basis. The case of tariff nomenclature is therefore different from the concurrence question raised above. This question relates to cases in which the scope of implied powers and the Community's competence by virtue of the CCP is identical, and not complementary. An example may illustrate the difference. Suppose it is accepted that under Article 84 (2), EC Treaty, the Community may conclude agreements with third countries relating to the exchange of traffic rights in civil aviation. Suppose it is equally accepted that the conclusion of such agreements is a matter for the CCP.[134] The scope of Articles 84 (2) and 113 would in this case be identical, which it is not in the case of the tariff nomenclature.

It is therefore submitted that the Court's judgment in Case 165/87 does not contradict the thesis that in the event of concurrence of implied powers and Community competence in the framework of the CCP, the latter takes precedence over the former.

There is another judgment, which suggests that the express external competence provided by the EC Treaty provisions on the CCP precedes implied powers. In *Greece* v. *Council* (the so-called *Chernobyl* judgment) the Court had to decide whether a regulation laying down maximum permitted levels of radioactive contamination for imports of agricultural products in the Community could be adopted on the basis of Article 113 of the Treaty.[135] The Greek government argued that, since the regulation aimed at protecting public health, it should have been based on the Treaty provisions on the protection of the environment (Articles 130*r* and 130*s*). The Court did not accept this argument, stating that these provisions 'leave intact the powers held by the Community under other provisions of the Treaty',[136] without examining whether the regulation should not have been adopted on the basis of both Articles 113 and 130*s*. This way of proceeding stands in contrast with the

[132] [1988] ECR 5560, italics added.
[133] By the way, the Court also says that as regards tariff nomenclature both Arts. 28 and 113 only provide, from the point of view of substance, an implied power. In addition, Art. 28 also implies the power to conclude agreements, whereas Art. 113 is an express provision in this regard
[134] See Ch. 3
[135] Case C-62/88, [1990] ECR I-1527. See also Ch. 7, pp. 254 *et seq.*
[136] [1990] ECR I-1550.

Court's judgment in the *Titanium Dioxide* case, which deals with the relation-ship between Articles 100*a* (on internal market harmonization) and 130*s*.[137] Here the Court found that a directive harmonizing national legislation on the reduction and elimination of titanium dioxide waste was at the same time aimed at protecting the environment and at establishing the internal market, and should in principle be based on both the above-mentioned provisions. For procedural reasons, however, this was not possible. The difference between the two judgments suggests that with respect to external trade, other Com-munity policies have to give way to the CCP, more than is the case in the internal sphere. In view of the important role which the CCP plays for ensuring the unity of the internal market, that is logical. The conclusion can only be that Article 113 of the EC Treaty precedes implied powers, and that once the Community's CCP competence is established in a given case, there is no need to check whether there are other provisions of the Treaty, supplying an implied power to regulate external relations.

Conclusions

This chapter offers two main conclusions. The first is that service transactions between countries are more and more looked at from a trade policy perspec-tive. That is the case both at the international level and within the Community. The Uruguay Round negotiations aim at establishing a General Agreement on Trade in Services, the system of which would to a large extent be com-parable to the General Agreement on Tariffs and Trade, which only covers goods. The case-law of the Court of Justice on the free movement of services clearly goes in the direction (to say the least) of treating cross-border service transactions in the same way as trade in goods. And the same can be said with respect to the treatment of services in the internal market programme, as the following chapters will bear out in a more detailed way. Basically, these chapters will look at the external dimension of the internal market in specific services sectors from this trade policy perspective.

This change of perception should be adequately reflected in the Com-munity's external competences. The Common Commercial Policy also covers international service transactions, in so far as commercial aspects of govern-ment regulation are involved. There is no reason, at least not in principle, to treat services transactions differently here from trade in goods. The basic question is not, it is submitted, whether services can be covered by the CCP, but to what extent that is the case. This question also applies to trade in goods (see the chapters on export controls, technical regulations and standards, and public procurement), and is becoming increasingly difficult as

---

[137] Case C-300/89, *Commission* v. *Council*, [1991] ECR I-2867. See also Ch. 5, pp. 147–8.

the effects on trade of domestic regulation aimed at protecting the consumer, the environment, or safeguarding cultural policies, are more and more scrutinized.[138]

Lastly, to the extent that the CCP covers trade in services, there is no need to look for implied powers in the EC Treaty which could provide a basis for external action by the Community.

[138] See also Ch. 11, pp. 348–9.

2

Financial Services and Reciprocity

Introduction

In the sector of financial services, the aim of the internal market programme is to create a framework allowing financial products to circulate freely within the Community.[1] The technique employed to achieve this is derived from the Community's experience with liberalizing trade in goods between the Member States. It is based on the well-known principle of mutual recognition, implying that a Member State has to recognize, at least to some extent, the way in which other Member States regulate the production and putting on the market of products, as being equivalent to its own system of regulation. This leaves only those parts of the regulatory system which are essential for safeguarding certain 'mandatory requirements', such as consumer, environmental, and public health protection, to be harmonized at Community level.[2] Such an approach is quite new with respect to services, and the financial sector clearly spearheads the efforts aimed at transposing this technique to services trade.

As much regulation of financial activities aims at supervising the actors involved (banks, insurance companies, securities firms), the principle of mutual recognition implies that the Member States respect each other's supervisory systems, without unnecessarily duplicating supervision in respect of financial institutions established in other Member States, offering their services abroad. This basic conclusion is called the principle of 'home country control': essentially, it is for the Member State in which a particular financial institution is established to supervise its functioning and operations. It flows from this principle that financial institutions need only a single licence, in their home country, to operate on a Community-wide scale.

The home country control principle has a considerable impact on the number and character of financial products that can be sold in any Member State. Indeed, it is sufficient for a financial institution to be allowed to market a product in its home Member State, for it to be able to sell this product throughout the Community by way of provision of services.[3] To take a

---

[1] Cf. the Commission's White Paper, COM (85) 310 final, para. 102.

[2] As is well known, this approach has been developed on the basis of the *Cassis de Dijon* judgment ([1979] ECR 649). Also see Ch. 8, p. 265.

[3] See for example Art. 18 of the second Council Directive of 15 Dec. 1989 on the co-ordination of laws, regulations, and administrative provisions relating to the taking up and the pursuit of the business of credit institutions and amending Directive 77/780/EEC, OJ L 386/1 of 30 Dec. 1989 (hereafter referred to as the Second Banking Directive).

concrete example: up until recently, Belgian legislation did not allow floating interest rates on mortgage loans. Under the internal market programme, Belgium is not obliged to abolish this restriction; but it cannot enforce it as regards mortgage loans emanating from banks established in other Member States, where flexible interest rates are allowed by virtue of national legislation.[4] The aim of this ground rule is to create some sort of competition between regulatory systems. There are of course noticeable differences in the way in which these fundamental principles are implemented in the three basic financial sectors, namely credit institutions (the Community term for banks), insurance companies, and securities firms. It would lead too far, however, to analyse these differences here.

Before examining the actual external dimension of the various instruments created for building a single market in financial services, it is useful to consider from a conceptual standpoint the various ways in which international trade in financial services can take place. In the writing on trade in services, the necessity of having some kind of presence abroad to be able to operate properly there is often emphasized.[5] Indeed, establishment is without doubt the most prominent factor in international trade in financial services, because the financial service provider often needs to have an establishment in the proximity of his clients. It is not, however, the only way in which such trade can be conducted. Cross-border provision of services, without establishment, is of course also possible.[6] The latter, moreover, is perhaps bound to become more important with the passage of time, because of the constant improvement and diversification in world-wide telecommunications networks, allowing transactions to take place without physical proximity of the actors.

Accordingly, barriers to international trade in financial services can be located at various levels. There can be restrictions on establishment, ranging from a flat prohibition for foreign companies to limitations on the scope of activities of such companies or on the degree of foreign control of financial institutions. On the other hand, there can be restrictions on the cross-border

---

[4] Cf. Bruno Mazzola, 'Some Thoughts on the Liberalization Process of European Banking and Financial Activity', in G. Sacerdoti (ed.), *Liberalization of Services and Intellectual Property in the Uruguay Round of GATT* (Fribourg: University Press, 1990), 208.

[5] On financial services, see for example Gary C. Hufbauer and Claudia Schmitz, 'The North American Argument about a "Fortress Europe"', in T. Oppermann and J. Molsberger (eds.), *A New GATT for the Nineties and Europe '92* (Baden-Baden: Nomos, 1991), 312. Also see Ch. 1, references in n. 13.

[6] It goes without saying that the concept of establishment itself may have different meanings, ranging from setting up a subsidiary or a branch to merely having a permanent representative abroad. The latter is sufficient, according to the Court of Justice, to speak of establishment in the sense of the EC Treaty (Case 205/84, *Commission* v. *Germany* [1986] ECR 3755, at 3801). It is obvious that if one considers establishment in such a broad sense, it becomes even more important for international trade in services.

provision of services without establishment, ranging from the requirement of having an establishment[7] to limitations on capital movements.

The preceding observations highlight the fact that the Community is far from having developed a comprehensive regulatory framework governing trade in financial services with third countries. Indeed, only the matter of establishment has really been dealt with, and even then Community rules have only been developed as regards subsidiaries, and not with respect to branches.[8] These rules centre around the concept of reciprocity, which was put forward for the first time in the banking sector, through the provisions of the so-called Second Banking Directive.[9] These provisions have since been copied in other financial legislation, and therefore also apply to the sectors of insurance and transactions in securities.[10]

Besides this legislation on establishment, there are of course the general provisions on free movement of capital, stating that the Member States shall endeavour to attain, in respect of movements of capital to and from third countries, the same degree of liberalization as in intra-Community transactions, where complete freedom exists.[11] However, the directive on liberalization of capital movements also provides that this rule

shall not prejudice the application to third countries of domestic rules or Community law, particularly any reciprocal conditions, concerning operations involving establishment, the provision of financial services and the admission of securities to capital markets.[12]

Furthermore, there are a number of less important provisions in proposed or adopted financial services legislation, concerning trade with third countries. None of them, however, relates to the basic questions concerning the external dimension of the single market in financial services.

As was mentioned, there are as yet no Community rules on the operations of branches in the Community of third-country financial services companies.

[7] This was the case in *Commission* v. *Germany* (n. 6 *supra*), dealing with the German *Versicherungsaufsichtsgesetz* which required that foreign insurers establish themselves in Germany before being allowed to operate on the German market.

[8] A branch is 'a place of business which forms a legally dependent part of a credit institution ...' (Article 1, Second Banking Directive, see n. 3), whereas a subsidiary is a 'place of business which forms a legally dependent part of a credit institution and which conducts directly all or some of the operations inherent in the business of credit institutions' (Art. 1, First Banking Directive, OJ L 322/30 of 17 Dec. 1977).

[9] *Supra* n. 3.

[10] (a) Life assurance: Arts. 8 and 9 of Council Directive 90/619/EEC, OJ L 330/50 of 29 Nov. 1990; (b) Non-life insurance: Art. 4 of Council Directive 90/618/EEC, OJ L 330/44 of 29 Nov. 1990; (c) Securities: see Art. 7 of Council Directive 93/22/EEC, OJ L 141/27 of 11 June 1993.

[11] Art. 7 of Council Directive 88/361/EEC of 24 June 1988 for the implementation of Art. 67 of the Treaty, OJ L 178/5 of 8 July 1988.

[12] Ibid. See also Arts. 73b and 73c of the EC Treaty, as amended by the Treaty on European Union, which 'constitutionalize' this rule.

Apparently, the Community's institutions are of the view that in this respect it is not necessary to provide for a uniform regime.[13]

This basically leaves only the reciprocity provisions to be studied. However, given the much-debated and contested character of these provisions, this is no small task. Accordingly, the concept of reciprocity is subjected to a detailed analysis under various angles, because it not only relates to financial services, but has been copied in some other areas.[14] Starting-point for the analysis is the legislative history of the reciprocity clause, linked as it is with the Second Banking Directive.[15] An attempt is then made at interpreting the clause. Furthermore, as some have voiced doubts concerning the conformity of the clause with the EC Treaty, as well as with a number of international obligations of the Member States, this aspect also has to be investigated. In the last point, the analysis is somewhat widened as the concept of national treatment (or non-discrimination), which lies at the heart of the reciprocity clause, will be further unravelled.

Reciprocity

Legislative history

At the beginning of 1988, the Commission presented to the Council its proposal concerning a Second Council Directive on the co-ordination of laws, regulations, and administrative provisions relating to the taking-up and pursuit of the business of credit institutions and amending Directive 77/780/EEC.[16] This (then proposed) directive is generally referred to as the Second Banking Directive. The proposal contained a provision on the setting-up or acquisition by third-country banks of a subsidiary in the Community (Article 7). According to this provision, the Member States would have had to inform the Commission of any request for authorization of such setting-up or acquisition. The Commission would then have examined, within a period of three months, 'whether all credit institutions of the Community enjoy reciprocal treatment, in particular regarding the establishment of subsidiaries or the acquisition of participations in credit institutions in the third country in question'. During this investigation, the Member States would have had to suspend their decision regarding these requests for authorization. Furthermore, the Commission would have had the authority, if it had found

---

[13] Cf. Paolo Clarotti, 'Harmonization for Banking and Securities Regulations in the European Communities: Its Implications for the Third Countries', in *Liberalization of Services and Intellectual Property in the Uruguay Round of GATT, supra* n. 4, p. 186.

[14] That is the case with airport slot allocation (see Ch. 3, p. 117), public procurement (Ch. 9, p. 319), and merger control (see Art. 24 of Regulation 4064/89, OJ L 395/1 of 30 Dec. 1989).

[15] *Supra* n. 3.

[16] COM (87) 715 final, OJ C 84/1 of 31 Mar. 1988.

that reciprocity was not ensured, to extend this suspension, and it would have had to 'present suitable proposals to the Council with a view to achieving reciprocity with the third country in question'.

As is well known, this proposal on reciprocity elicited quite a lot of comment and criticism, both from within the Community and from the Community's trading partners, especially the United States. Not only governments reacted,[17] but also the banking business community[18] as well as academic writing.[19] Without supplying a comprehensive study of the debate that took place on this subject, it is useful to describe the more important comments made on the Commission's proposal. These comments help to explain and interpret the clause on reciprocity as it was ultimately adopted.

First, it is clear that reciprocity is an extremely vague concept.[20] Linking this vague notion with the possibility of limiting establishment by foreign banks raised the fear that the Community could make demands concerning the treatment of Community banks abroad that would be virtually impossible to meet by any country. Indeed, what sort of reciprocity would the Community envisage? Would it go so far as to require mirror reciprocity, asking that third-country subsidiaries of Community banks be treated in exactly the same way as they are treated in the Community's single banking market? And if it were to do so, what exactly is this single market treatment, given the fact that the philosophy of the banking market integration is to allow the different regulatory systems of the Member States to continue to exist? Furthermore, the question could be raised as to the kinds of treatment that were envisaged: the range of activities banks are allowed to undertake, the geographical scope of their activities,[21] the organization of the banks' supervision, or even the general rules of company law?[22]

United States' authorities launched a frontal attack on the concept of reciprocity by contrasting it with the concept of national treatment. In their view,

---

[17] For a US government reaction, see the remarks by Thomas J. Berger, then Deputy Assistant Secretary for International Monetary Affairs, in 'Preparing for 1992: A Yankee View on Europe's Internal Market Program', *USA Text*, 15 Sept. 1988. Also see Youri Devuyst, 'The United States and Europe 1992', 13 *World Competition* (1989), 1: 30–1.

[18] On US banking business's reactions, see USITC, *The Effects of Greater Economic Integration within the European Community on the United States*, Publication 2204 (Washington, DC: 1989), 5/15–5/18. The Bankers' Association for Foreign Trade reacted with a paper on 'Reciprocity: A Step in the Wrong Direction' (Mar. 1989). On the position of the EC Banking Federation, on the other hand, see *Agence Europe*, No. 4986, 1 Apr. 1989, pp. 7–8.

[19] Hall S. Scott, 'La notion de réciprocité dans la proposition de deuxième directive de coordination bancaire', *RMC* (1989), 323: 45–56.

[20] That reciprocity is inherently a confusing concept is demonstrated by Geert Wils, 'The Concept of Reciprocity in EEC Law: An Exploration into these Realms', 28 *CML Rev.* (1991), 2: 245–74.

[21] See for example *infra*, p. 58, on the geographical fragmentation of the US banking market, by virtue of the McFadden Act.

[22] Cf. Scott, *supra* n. 19, pp. 50–5.

reciprocity that seeks to achieve identical commercial privileges in countries with different market structures and regulatory regimes will almost inevitably result in discrimination. In short, reciprocity that seeks identical treatment in different countries is a retreat to protectionism.[23]

On the other hand,

[t]he national treatment approach seeks to ensure that, in a given market, foreign firms are treated in the same way as domestic firms. By allowing domestic and foreign firms to compete on an equal footing in each market, national treatment accommodates national differences in regulatory regimes and supports the objectives of free access and non-discriminatory treatment.[24]

However, without pre-empting the analysis that follows below, it is worth pointing out already at this stage that reciprocity and national treatment are not by definition concepts with an opposite meaning. Indeed, the requirement of national treatment may well be interpreted as a form of reciprocity. Take the case of banking: if the Community asks that foreign subsidiaries of Community banks be given national treatment in their operations abroad, it in fact asks for the same treatment as it is giving third-country banks within the Community, because the latter also receive non-discriminatory treatment. Such a formal, non-substantive interpretation of reciprocity—which, by the way, may be the only one that is able to function well in an environment with substantially different regulatory systems—actually boils down to a national treatment requirement.[25]

Other comments focused on the rather cumbersome bureaucratic procedure that would result from the Commission's proposal.[26] Each time a foreign bank wanted to set up a subsidiary in the Community, its request would have to be suspended until the Commission had terminated its investigation of the situation in the bank's home country. This would have meant that the Commission would have had the opportunity to block any such request. Lastly, questions were raised as regards the status of already established Community subsidiaries of third-country banks. Would they also be affected by the reciprocity policy, or would they be protected by so-called grandfather rights?[27]

It is worth mentioning here that, in spite of the acrimonious debate sparked off by the Commission's proposal, the idea of requiring reciprocity with respect to establishment by foreign financial institutions was not new. On the contrary, all the Member States have some sort of reciprocity clause on their

---

[23] Berger, *supra* n. 17, p. 3.

[24] Ibid.

[25] Cf. Carter H. Golembe and David S. Holland, 'Banking and Securities', in G. C. Hufbauer (ed.), *Europe 1992: An American Perspective* (Washington, DC: The Brookings Institution, 1990), 70.

[26] See Philippe Vigneron and Aubry Smith, 'Le concept de réciprocité dans la législation communautaire: l'exemple de la deuxième directive bancaire', *RMC* (1990), 337: 353.

[27] Scott, *supra* n. 19, pp. 47–8.

statute book. Accordingly, the OECD Code of Liberalization of Capital Movements, more extensively dealt with below,[28] contains in its Annex E a Decision of the Council 'regarding measures and practices concerning reciprocity and/or involving discrimination among investors originating in various OECD member countries in the area of inward direct investment and establishment'.[29] This Decision recognizes and lists these reciprocity measures, and contains the principle that they shall be gradually abolished. The list mentions all the Member States, except Luxembourg, as having one or other reciprocity requirement, though not necessarily always in the banking sector.[30] Quite logically, therefore, the Commission has tried to justify its proposal on reciprocity by arguing that these national reciprocity requirements would become obsolete with the introduction of a single banking licence and that therefore a Community clause was necessary.[31]

Reacting to the waves of criticism of its reciprocity proposal, the Commission defended its views by issuing a general policy statement on the external dimension of the single market.[32] In this statement, it situates reciprocity in the overall aim of strengthening the multilateral trading system. More specifically, '[i]n sectors where there are no multilateral rules, the Community will endeavour to obtain greater liberalization of world trade through the negotiation of new international agreements' in the framework of the Uruguay Round. However,

[i]t would be premature ... to grant non-member countries automatic and unilateral access to the benefits of the internal liberalization process before such new agreements exist. ... In other words, the Commission reserves the right to make access to the benefits of 1992 for non-member countries' firms conditional upon a guarantee of similar opportunities—or at least non-discriminatory opportunities—in those firms' own countries.[33]

Furthermore, the statement seeks to elaborate the reciprocity concept, providing, however, merely a catalogue of what the 1992 version of reciprocity does *not* mean:

It does not mean that all partners must make the same concessions nor even that the Community will insist on concessions from all its partners. For example, it will not ask the developing countries to make concessions that are beyond their means. Nor does reciprocity mean that the Community will ask its partners to adopt legislation identical to its own. Nor does it mean that the Community is seeking sectoral reciprocity based

---

[28] pp. 68–74.
[29] This decision was adopted on 16 July 1986. See the OECD publication of the *Code of Liberalization of Capital Movements* (Paris: OECD, 1992).
[30] Reciprocity requirements regarding establishment of subsidiaries of foreign banks exist in France, Greece, Ireland, the Netherlands, Spain, and the UK. Apparently, the United States, too, have introduced some kind of reciprocity requirement, see Scott, *supra* n. 19, p. 53.
[31] Vigneron and Smith, *supra* n. 26, p. 352. On the single banking licence, see *supra*, p. 47.
[32] 'Europe 1992: Europe world partner', Commission Press Release P-117 of 19 Oct. 1988.
[33] Ibid. 2.

on comparative trade levels, this being a concept whose introduction into United States legislation has been fought by the Community.[34]

Equally worth mentioning is that, reportedly, the differences in views between the Community and the United States on reciprocity and national treatment in connection with (financial) services came to a head at the Uruguay Round mid-term review.[35] This resulted in a compromise formula, linking the concept of national treatment with that of effective market access:

To this end [of progressive liberalization of international trade in services] the adverse effects of all laws, regulations and administrative guidelines should be reduced as part of the process to provide effective market access, including national treatment.[36]

The Commission subsequently amended its proposal, also after hearing the views of the finance ministers in the Council.[37] The latter came to an agreement on the Second Banking Directive in June–July 1989,[38] and the directive was formally adopted in December 1989.[39] The final text on 'Relations with third countries' (Articles 8 and 9) no longer actually mentions the word 'reciprocity'. Nevertheless, it will be clear from the following description that a form of reciprocity is still what is intended.

Contents, interpretation, and implementation of the clause

Description

The recitals of the Second Banking Directive proclaim the rationale and aims of the reciprocity clause:

[W]hereas ... requests for the authorization of subsidiaries or of the acquisition of holdings made by undertakings governed by the laws of third countries are subject to a procedure intended to ensure that Community credit institutions receive reciprocal treatment in the third countries in question;

Whereas the authorizations granted to credit institutions by the competent national authorities pursuant to this Directive will have Community-wide, and no longer merely nationwide, application, and whereas existing reciprocity clauses will henceforth have no effect; whereas a flexible procedure is therefore needed to make it possible to assess reciprocity on a Community basis; whereas the aim of this procedure is not to close the Community's financial markets but rather, as the Community intends to keep its financial markets open to the rest of the world, to improve the liberalization of the

[34] Ibid.
[35] This review was held in December 1988 to April 1989, thus coinciding with the debate on the Commission's proposal for a Second Banking Directive. See Stephen Woolcock, *Market Access Issues in EC–U.S. Relations* (London: Pinter Publishers for the RIIA, 1991), 47.
[36] See GATT, MTN.TNC/11 of 21 Apr. 1989, p. 39.
[37] On these views, see 'EC deeply divided over banking reciprocity', *Financial Times*, 8 Nov. 1988. For Commissioner Brittan's views of the modifications, see *Agence Europe*, No. 4995, 14 Apr. 1989, p. 5.
[38] *Agence Europe*, No. 5048, 1 July 1989, pp. 5–6.
[39] *Supra* n. 3.

global financial markets in other third countries; whereas, to that end, this Directive provides for procedures for negotiating with third countries and, as a last resort, for the possibility of taking measures involving the suspension of new applications for authorization or the restriction of new authorizations.[40]

These recitals are almost more indicative of the reciprocity scheme than the actual provisions of the directive. Although the latter are quite elaborate, most of the text is concerned with procedural matters. Article 8 obliges the Member States to inform the Commission of any third-country undertakings setting up subsidiaries on their territory, either as a new establishment or through acquiring an existing credit institution.[41] Article 9 (1), on the other hand, also contains a duty to inform: 'The Member States shall inform the Commission of any general difficulties encountered by their credit institutions in establishing themselves or carrying on banking activities in a third country.' Similarly, Article 9 (2) requires that the Commission periodically draw up reports 'examining the treatment accorded to Community credit institutions in third countries, in the terms referred to in paragraphs 3 and 4, as regards establishment and the carrying-on of banking activities, and the acquisition of holdings in third-country credit institutions'. These reports must be submitted to the Council, accompanied by appropriate proposals.

Article 9 (3) and (4) contains the more substantive provisions. Paragraph 3 prescribes what can be done whenever it appears to the Commission 'that a third country is not granting Community credit institutions effective market access comparable to that granted by the Community to credit institutions from that third country ... '.

When such comparable treatment is not being offered, the Commission may propose to the Council that it negotiate with that third country. The aim of such negotiations is, obviously enough, to obtain 'comparable competitive opportunities for Community credit institutions'. Article 9 (3) only provides for negotiations, and no sanction in case these negotiations fail. The provision may therefore be considered as being declaratory, since under the Treaty the Commission probably has the power to propose to the Council to start such international negotiations in any event.[42]

Article 9 (4), on the other hand, deals with the situation in which 'Community credit institutions in a third country do not receive national treatment offering the same competitive opportunities as are available to domestic credit institutions and the conditions of effective market access are not fulfilled'. If this is the case, the Commission may also initiate negotiations, but, in addition, it may decide that undertakings from the third country concerned

---

[40] OJ L 386/2–3 of 30 Dec. 1989.

[41] A similar duty exists, as regards *requests* for authorization, when paragraphs 3 or 4 apply (see below).

[42] That is certainly the case if such negotiations are considered as part of the Community's commercial policy, cf. pp. 66–7 *infra*.

can no longer be authorized to set up or acquire banking subsidiaries in the Community.[43] Such a decision cannot operate longer than three months, but the Council may, before the end of this period, and in view of the results of the negotiations, decide whether the measures shall be continued.[44] However, these decisions are inapplicable to subsidiaries of third-country banks that are already established in the Community: their rights are protected by a grandfather clause.[45]

Also, Article 9 (6) confirms that '[m]easures taken pursuant to this Article shall comply with the Community's obligations under any international agreements, bilateral or multilateral, governing the taking-up and pursuit of the business of credit institutions'. Of course, this clause can only function as a reminder, because in any event, all the Community institutions have to observe, as regards any measures they may take, the international obligations that are binding on the Community.[46]

Article 9 therefore introduces a two-tier procedure. In what is perceived as the worst case—that in which Community banks do not receive national treatment in a third country and are not given effective market access—a real sanction is available. The Commission and the Council may block new establishments by banks from this country. On the other hand, if in a third country Community banks are not treated in a manner comparable to the way in which they are treated in the Community, only negotiations are possible. It is obvious that, by introducing this two-tier approach, the Commission and the Council have to some degree met the objections that were voiced in relation to the original Commission proposal. The same observation applies to the protection of grandfather rights and the fact that it will not be necessary for the Member States to pass on automatically all requests for authorization emanating from third-country banks to the Commission.

The basic question is of course how to interpret the provisions of Article 9 (3) and (4), asking for respectively comparable and national treatment of Community banks abroad. This basic question is further examined below.

[43] In has to do so in co-operation with a special committee, in which the Member States are represented, in accordance with the procedure laid down in Article 22 of the Directive.

[44] Acting, that is, on a proposal from the Commission. The decision is taken with a qualified majority.

[45] Article 9 (4), last sentence, provides that '[s]uch limitations or suspensions may not apply to the setting up of subsidiaries by credit institutions or their subsidiaries duly authorized in the Community, or to the acquisition of holdings in Community credit institutions by such institutions or subsidiaries'.

[46] The question can be raised whether this provision could have direct effect, so that in proceedings before a national court it could be invoked. If the answer is affirmative, this could be a way for circumventing the question of direct effect of the international obligations of the Community. A third-country bank subject to reciprocity measures could argue, in case it is of the view that the measures taken by the Community infringe certain international commitments, that the question of direct effect of these commitments does not arise, since the directive expressly refers to them.

Thereafter, it may also be useful to indicate some of the procedural questions that may arise in the application of the reciprocity provisions.

Effective market access comparable to that granted by the Community

At a glance, the reference to market access may give the impression that only *access* to the market, in other words all issues relating to establishment, is aimed at, and not the subsequent *treatment* that Community banks receive abroad, once they are established.[47] However, it would be difficult to reconcile such a restrictive interpretation with the overall scheme of Article 9. Clearly, paragraph 3 of Article 9 is more ambitious in addressing foreign trade barriers than paragraph 4. All commentators agree on this.[48] The general philosophy behind this provision may therefore be summarized as follows: through the internal market programme the Community is creating one of the most open financial markets in the world. After 1992, there will be few restrictions on the range of activities financial institutions will be able to carry on in the Community. It is logical for the Community to wish to see such a liberal regime also being applied in other major financial centres of the world. Otherwise, the world's major financial institutions, although in fact competing more and more in a global marketplace, will not be operating on a level playing field.[49]

Things become much more concrete, however, if one considers the relationship between the Community and the United States as regards the banking sector. EC Commissioners and officials have often complained that a number of internal US limitations on banking activities are out of date and are creating a too restricted market.[50] In this respect, the two most often mentioned limitations are the Glass Steagal and McFadden Acts.[51] Glass Steagal separates commercial and investment banking, not allowing one single financial

---

[47] Cf. Vigneron and Smith, *supra* n. 26, pp. 353–4. On market access versus subsequent treatment, see p. 59 *infra*. The concept of market access is interpreted here as relating only to establishment issues, and not to the cross-border provision of services. In itself, market access also implies the latter, but since in general the reciprocity policy only concerns establishment, such a wide interpretation does not seem appropriate. It could be argued, however, on the basis of the text that Article 9 (3) also allows negotiations on cross-border provision of services.

[48] Speech by Commissioner Andriessen, 'Implications of European Integration 1992 for U.S. and Japanese Financial Institutions', 27 Sept. 1989, p. 10; Vigneron and Smith, *supra* n. 26, p. 353; Christopher T. Toll, 'The European Community's Second Banking Directive: Can Antiquated United States Legislation Keep Pace?', 23 *Vanderbilt Journal of Transnational Law* (1990), 3: 627–8; Wils, *supra* n. 20, p. 268; USITC, *The Effects of Greater Economic Integration within the European Community on the United States: First Follow-up Report*, Publication 2268, Mar. 1990, p. 5/5.

[49] Cf. Clarotti, *supra* n. 13, p. 185.

[50] See especially the speech by Commissioner Brittan, 'Opening World Banking Markets', Washington, DC, 23 Mar. 1990, Commission Press Release IP/90/235.

[51] For a description of these Acts, see Golembe and Holland, *supra* n. 25, pp. 80–6 and 91–2; on Glass Steagal, also see Toll, *supra* n. 48, pp. 630–42, and Michael J. Levitin, 'The Treatment of United States Financial Services Firms in Post-1992 Europe', 31 *Harvard International Law Journal* (1990), 2: 517–18.

institution to operate in both markets and therefore to engage in 'universal banking'. However, such universal banking is exactly what is allowed throughout the Community after the coming into force of the Second Banking Directive. The McFadden Act, on the other hand, restricts interstate branching, which means that banks established in one US State are not allowed to open branches in other States. Such a territorial restriction will of course not be present in the Community's single banking market.[52]

It is obvious that these US restrictions are one of the immediate targets of Article 9 (3), and it may well be that in this respect the reciprocity policy already produced some results even before it came into force.[53] Nevertheless, it also is obvious that specific objectives of an institution such as the Commission, vested with the power to apply the reciprocity rules, cannot provide a definitive interpretation of these rules. On a more abstract level, therefore, the question as to what sort of 'comparable competitive opportunities for Community credit institutions' are envisaged, remains unanswered. Indeed, even if the aim were to draw a strict parallel with the internal market regime in financial services and the competitive opportunities that are available under this regime (so-called mirror reciprocity), one would still run into difficulties, because, as was mentioned earlier, this regime is not uniform in character, but instead allows a degree of competition between national regulatory systems.[54] The conclusion can therefore only be that Article 9 (3) gives the Commission and the Council a lot of discretion in deciding to open negotiations with third countries and on the subjects with which such negotiations would have to deal.

The Commission's first report on the implementation of the reciprocity policy confirms the above-described interpretation of Article 9 (3).[55] According to the Commission, the provision aims at addressing non-discriminatory restrictions on the provision of financial services, with the liberal character of the Community's financial services regime serving as a point of reference.

---

[52] It is not only the Community which would like to see these territorial restrictions disappear. In talks on the North American Free Trade Agreement, the Mexican and Canadian sides have also argued that national treatment is not enough because of these restrictions, see 'NAFTA free trade talks reaching most critical stage', *Financial Times*, 8 Oct. 1991, p. 8.

[53] Changes to the McFadden and Glass Steagal Acts are being discussed in the United States (see for example 'Moves to shatter Glass-Steagal', *Financial Times*, 3 Oct. 1990 and 'Reform of U.S. banking system proposed', *Financial Times*, 27 Sept. 1990). Commissioner Brittan has interpreted the US Administration's proposals for such changes as being influenced by the Community's banking legislation (*Agence Europe*, No. 5426, 7 Feb. 1991, p. 9). According to US banking experts Golembe and Holland, *supra* n. 25, 'those who argue that one of the most important consequences of Europe 1992 will be the restructuring of the U.S. financial system seem to us to be correct' (p. 97). See also Woolcock, *supra* n. 35, pp. 40–2.

[54] *Supra*, pp. 47–8. Also see Scott, *supra* n. 19, p. 50; Vigneron and Smith, *supra* n. 26, p. 354; Rudolf Dolzer, 'Reziprozität als Standard der EG-Drittlandsbeziehungen', in M. Hilf and C. Tomuschat (eds.), *EG und Drittstaatsbeziehungen nach 1992* (Baden-Baden: Nomos, 1991), 126–7.

[55] *Europe Documents*, No. 1800, 3 Oct. 1992, and No. 1801, 7 Oct. 1992.

National treatment offering the same competitive opportunities as are available to domestic credit institutions and effective market access

This is obviously the most important standard introduced by the reciprocity provisions, since the Community is willing to have it enforced through the sanction of not allowing banks of a third country not meeting the standard to establish themselves in the Community by way of subsidiaries. The first problem one is faced with when trying to interpret this standard is the conjunction of national treatment and market access. When looked at from the point of view of trade liberalization—which seems to be the proper perspective in view of the general aims of the reciprocity clause—this conjunction is somewhat peculiar as regards services. In relation to trade in goods, both concepts are easy to delineate. Market access is concerned with goods (physically) crossing a border, and with any barriers that may be associated with such crossing. National treatment, on the other hand, relates to the treatment that such goods are granted after having passed a border, when being put on the national market.[56] In the services sector, there is no such clear distinction, because services do not physically cross borders.[57] Accordingly, most barriers to trade in services are situated at the level of domestic regulation of the activities of service providers. It is arguable, therefore, that national treatment (or, in other words, non-discrimination) is a wider and more important standard for liberalizing international trade in services than free access to the market. In fact, such free access can be understood as merely being one of the components of national treatment. If, for example, a foreign service provider is not allowed to establish himself in a given country, it is clear that he is not receiving non-discriminatory treatment compared with domestic service providers.[58]

Implicitly, these observations are reflected in a number of the comments on the Second Banking Directive that have been published. Indeed, most commentators agree that the reference to effective market access in Article 9 (4) probably merely functions as some sort of correction to the concept of national treatment, which is considered as the principal standard. The correction would then be that not only purely formal or *de iure* national treatment is required, but also *de facto* or genuine national treatment. The emphasis on national treatment offering 'the same competitive opportunities as are available to domestic credit institutions' would point in the same direction.[59]

---

[56] Cf. Art. I and II of GATT, on the one hand, and Art. III, on the other.

[57] Cf. the comments by Jonathan Scheele, in *Liberalization of Services and Intellectual Property in the Uruguay Round of GATT, supra* n. 4, p. 228.

[58] Cf. Bernard Hoekman, 'Market Access through Multilateral Agreement: From Goods to Services', 15 *World Economy* (1992), 6: 720.

[59] Speech Commissioner Andriessen, *supra* n. 48, p. 11; Vigneron and Smith, *supra* n. 26, p. 354; Wils, *supra* n. 20, p. 268; Joseph Greenwald, 'Negotiating Strategy', in G. C. Hufbauer (ed.), *Europe 1992: An American Perspective* (Washington, DC: The Brookings Institution, 1990), 364–5; Woolcock, *supra* n. 35, p. 32; George S. Zavvos, 'Banking Integration and 1992: Legal

Another factor warranting this interpretation of Article 9 (4) is the Uruguay Round negotiations on services. As was mentioned, it is reported that at the mid-term review the differences of opinion between the Community and the United States on reciprocity versus national treatment came to a head, and that referring to effective market access was a compromise formula.[60] In the meantime, it seems that in the Uruguay Round negotiations a consensus has grown on the importance of achieving genuine, *de facto* national treatment as regards international trade in services.[61]

In its first report on the implementation of the reciprocity policy the Commission also interprets Article 9 (4) as referring to *de facto* national treatment, but it distinguishes more clearly the concepts of 'effective market access' and 'national treatment'.[62] The first concept, according to the Commission, refers to restrictions on establishment, whereas the second deals with the treatment of Community banks once they are already established in a third country.

Two considerations may help to explain the emphasis the Community is putting on *de facto* national treatment. The first one concerns relations with Japan. It has been reported that Community officials privately admit that Japan is the real 'target' of the reciprocity provision.[63] As is well known, there is a general feeling that obtaining access to the Japanese market is very difficult, not only because of some formal discriminations, but perhaps mainly because there are a number of administrative or other practices keeping the market closed.[64] It is not only the Community that has voiced this complaint; the United States have even developed a comprehensive programme, called the Structural Impediments Initiative, aimed at addressing these Japanese barriers to trade and investment.[65] Moreover, these complaints by the Community are not merely general in character. In the financial services sector also, a number of concerns on access to the Japanese market have been recorded.[66] A second factor may be the Community's internal experience in liberalizing

---

Issues and Policy Implications', 31 *Harvard International Law Journal* (1990), 2: 494, where the author gives some examples of absence of *de facto* national treatment.

[60] Scott, *supra* n. 19, p. 56. Both the terms 'effective market access' and 'national treatment' are mentioned in the Mid-Term Review Agreement as well as in Article 9 (4); see also Clarotti, *supra* n. 13, p. 187.

[61] See p. 76 *infra*.

[62] See n. 55.

[63] Gary Clyde Hufbauer, 'An Overview', in *Europe 1992: An American Perspective, supra* n. 25, p. 36; USITC, *The Effects of Greater Economic Integration within the European Community on the United States, supra* n. 48, p. 5/15.

[64] Cf. 'A Consistent and Global Approach: A Review of the Community's Relations with Japan', COM (92) 219 final of 21 May 1992.

[65] See e.g. Syed Tariq Anwar, 'The Impact of the Structural Impediments Initiative (SII) on U.S.–Japan Trade', 16 *World Competition* (1992), 2: 53–65.

[66] See COM (92) 219, *supra* n. 64, in particular p. 5; *Agence Europe*, No. 5670, 17 and 18 Feb. 1992, p. 9. See also Scheele, *supra* n. 57, p. 229; Dolzer, *supra* n. 54, pp. 130–1.

trade in services.[67] Articles 59 and 60 of the EC Treaty contain a prohibition of discrimination based on nationality or place of residence with respect to the provision of services. The case-law of the European Court of Justice on the scope of this prohibition has shown that, unless non-discrimination is understood in a factual rather than a formal way, it produces little effect in removing barriers to trade.[68]

However, this still leaves open the question of exactly how widely the standard of *de facto* national treatment may be construed. A definitive answer to this question is clearly not possible, but a number of experiences with the national treatment and non-discrimination concepts may supply valuable guide-lines and points of reference for interpretation and application. The two most important sources of such experiences are, it is submitted, the GATT national treatment provision and the non-discrimination clause of Articles 59 and 60 of the EC Treaty, since both of them deal with trade liberalization, which is also the aim of the reciprocity clause. An analysis of these experiences follows further below.[69] It has the purpose of sketching a background for employing the national treatment standard, not only for financial services, but for international trade in services in general.

Implementation of the reciprocity clause

In its first report on the implementation of the reciprocity provisions[70] the Commission has examined the treatment of Community financial services companies on a large number of third-country markets. The conclusion which the Commission draws from this examination is that it could take action with respect to a number of countries, on the basis of both paragraphs 3 and 4 of Article 9. However, in view of the fact that nearly all the countries examined participate in the negotiations on a General Agreement on Trade in Services, in the framework of the Uruguay Round, the Commission proposes to put the implementation of the reciprocity policy on hold and to try to obtain improved access and treatment in the context of these negotiations. However, the Commission also expresses its dissatisfaction with the concessions offered by its negotiating partners, which in the field of financial services would not go far enough. That is also the view of the Council of Ministers, which has sent a letter to thirteen countries, requesting them to improve their offers.[71]

Questions of procedure

The questions of a procedural nature which the implementation of the reciprocity provisions may raise are probably quite numerous. It is difficult,

[67] Cf. speech by Commissioner Andriessen, *supra* n. 48, p. 10.
[68] *Supra*, Ch. 1, pp. 13–16.   [69] pp. 76 *et seq.*
[70] *Supra* n. 55.   [71] *Agence Europe*, No. 5842, 22 Oct. 1992, p. 9.

however, to try to cover and analyse all these questions in any comprehensive way. Three possible problems that have been mentioned are the following:

1. If Article 9 (4) is applied, in the sense that credit institutions from a third country *X* are no longer allowed to establish themselves in the Community, will this refusal also apply to an already established Community subsidiary of a bank in third country *Y*, if this latter bank is itself acquired by a bank located in *X*? Or would this be covered by the grandfather clause?[72]

2. What if an already established Community subsidiary operating in, for example, the insurance sector, with a parent undertaking established in a third country not granting national treatment in the banking sector, asks for an authorization for banking activities? Would this be covered by the grandfather clause, or would it be considered to be a new establishment?[73]

3. There may be substantial difficulties in identifying the real parent undertaking of a request for authorization of a Community subsidiary.[74] In this respect, the Second Banking Directive refers to the definition of a subsidiary in the First Banking Directive.[75] But this may not solve the problem of a request for authorization emanating from a bank established in several third countries.

Reciprocity and the EC Treaty

There are two important questions as to the relationship between the provisions on reciprocity in the sector of financial services and the EC Treaty. First, it has been argued that some aspects of these provisions may be incompatible with Article 58 of the Treaty, which extends the freedom of establishment to companies. Secondly, it is generally assumed that the Community institutions have the power to regulate the creation and acquisition of subsidiaries by third-country undertakings, but little has been said about the nature of this power and its basis in the Treaty.

Compatibility or conflict with Article 58?

According to Article 58,

[c]ompanies or firms formed in accordance with the law of a Member State and having their registered office, central administration or principal place of business within the Community shall, for the purposes of this Chapter [on freedom of establishment], be treated in the same way as natural persons who are nationals of Member States.

This is a fairly liberal provision, in that it accords the freedom of establishment—and also the freedom to provide services[76]—to almost any company

[72] Vigneron and Smith, *supra* n. 26, p. 355.

[73] Ibid.; also Scott, *supra* n. 19, p. 48. Also see below on the scope of Art. 58, EC Treaty.

[74] Scott, *supra* n. 19, p. 49. See also Maria Dakolias, 'The Second Banking Directive: The Issue of Reciprocity', *LIEI* (1992), 1: 80–1.

[75] See *supra* n. 8.

[76] Art. 66 of the Treaty makes Art. 58 also applicable to free movement of services.

that has been set up under the law of one of the Member States. Through the 1962 General Programmes for the abolition of restrictions on the freedom of establishment and the freedom to provide services the Community has sought to introduce stricter requirements by adding that companies wishing to benefit from the provisions on freedom of establishment need to have an effective and continuous link with the economy of one of the Member States.[77] At first sight, this may seem like a condition without basis in the Treaty. However, a closer look at Article 52 does provide some foundation: freedom of establishment is guaranteed, in so far as the setting up of agencies, branches, or subsidiaries is concerned, to 'nationals of any Member State *established* in the territory of any Member State'.[78] The requirement of an effective and continuous link would aim at ensuring that companies benefiting from freedom of establishment already have a genuine first establishment in the Community, and have not simply been set up to benefit from free (secondary) establishment. But in practice there have probably not been many problems in this respect. At least, there is to my knowledge no case-law on the matter.

The relationship between Article 58 and the reciprocity provisions basically has two sides. First, one may wonder whether Article 58 has any bearing upon the subject of regulating first establishment, that is the setting-up or acquisition of a Community subsidiary by a third-country company or companies.[79] Secondly, and this is more complex, the question arises whether third-country companies are able to circumvent the reciprocity provisions by first setting up a subsidiary in Member State *A* and then relying on Articles 58 *juncto* 52 in order to set up or acquire a subsidiary in Member State *B*.

There is very little in the text of Article 58 justifying the interpretation that it in any way limits the powers of the Community institutions to regulate first establishment, as defined above. Such an interpretation would indeed be very wide. It would have to be built on the assumption that Article 58 introduces a general principle of freedom of establishment in relations with third countries; in other words, that it grants to all third-country nationals, be they private persons or companies, the right to set up companies within the Community. It will be clear that such a general principle is not present in Article 58, which deals with freedom of establishment within the Community, and simply defines what are to be regarded as the beneficiaries of this freedom in the case of companies. It may be that, in practice, there are few limits on first establishment, because the Member States' legislation is very liberal in this respect. However, this state of affairs is not a Community law principle endorsed by Article 58. This means that the Community institutions have considerable discretion over how to regulate first establishment—provided they have the

---

[77] Cf. Yvon Loussouarn, 'Le droit d'établissement des sociétés', 26 *RTDE* (1990), 2: 236–7.

[78] Italics added. See also Art. 59, speaking of 'nationals of Member States who are established in a State of the Community other than that of the person for whom the services are intended'.

[79] That is a company with no establishment in the sense of Art. 58 in the Community yet.

power, under the Treaty, to do so.[80] They could regulate first establishment in
a general way, by developing criteria for the setting up or acquisition, in the
Community, of companies by third-country nationals in general. Or they
could do so on a sectoral basis, as is the case with the reciprocity provisions in
the financial sector. There may, however, be one important limitation to this
discretionary power: if it is accepted that regulating first establishment comes
under the EC Treaty provisions on commercial policy, as is argued below, the
Community should not introduce restrictions which would run counter to the
principle of progressive liberalization of international trade, embodied in
Article 110 of the Treaty.

Secondly, there is the question of third-country companies already having a
subsidiary in the Community. An example may serve to clarify and illustrate
this question. Suppose the Community applies Article 9 (4) of the Second
Banking Directive to a specific third country, and suspends all requests for
authorization of a banking subsidiary emanating from banks having their
head office in this third country. Suppose bank X, being one of these banks,
already has a subsidiary in the Community, more specifically in Member State
A. If this subsidiary has the authorization, under the banking directives, to
operate as a credit institution, it is allowed to set up or acquire other subsidiaries in the Community by virtue of the grandfather clause. However, suppose
this subsidiary does not have a banking authorization, but is a mere company,
not engaged in banking. Would this subsidiary, being a company in the sense
of Article 58, established in Member State A, be able to rely on Articles 58
juncto 52 in order to set up or acquire, as a subsidiary, a *credit institution* in
Member State B?[81] In other words, would in such a case Articles 58 *juncto* 52
override the application of the reciprocity provisions? If these questions
receive an affirmative answer, it becomes very easy to circumvent the reciprocity policy.[82] Third-country banks would only have to set up a mere
company, not a bank, in one of the Member States, and this company could
then set up or acquire a banking subsidiary in any other Member State.

One argument to support such an interpretation would be the following:
Article 58 does not allow the Member States to introduce additional conditions to those enumerated in this provision, when granting free establishment to companies established in other Member States.[83] However, where the
reciprocity policy applies, this is exactly what would happen, since the
Member States would then have to look behind the company requesting
authorization to set up a bank: if this company is owned by a bank established

[80] See *infra*, pp. 65–8.
[81] The underlying assumption to this question is that such a case is not covered by the
grandfather clause of Art. 9 (4). See *supra*, p. 56.
[82] Cf. Jacques Steenbergen, 'Europe 1992 and the Uruguay Round', 8 *International Financial
Law Review* (1989), 4: 38.
[83] Ibid.

in a third country in respect of which the reciprocity policy applies, its request may not be granted.

The strength of this argument depends on how widely one interprets the EC Treaty provisions on establishment. If these provisions are basically limited to prohibiting all discrimination based on nationality, the argument cannot be upheld. Applied to the case of banking, it would mean that they do not grant all Community companies the right to set up a bank in another Member State without observing the various national regulations governing such setting-up. Member States may still apply these regulations which, in the case of banking, have been harmonized at the Community level, provided that in so doing they do not discriminate on the basis of nationality, *Member State* nationality, that is. The reciprocity test does not imply any such discrimination. It is not, in the example mentioned above, because the company requesting to set up a banking subsidiary in Member State *B* is established in Member State *A*, that its request cannot be granted. It is because this company is owned by a third-country bank, subject to the reciprocity policy. The absence of any discrimination based on nationality (again at Member State level) manifests itself particularly when one considers that the request also could not be granted if the company were established in Member State *B*, where the request for authorization is made.

However, the recent case-law of the Court of Justice tends to give a wider interpretation to the Treaty provisions on establishment and services.[84] If these provisions are to be construed as implying a concept of 'companies in free circulation', similar to the well-known concept of 'goods in free circulation', it is obvious that the above-mentioned argument would be quite forceful. The implementation of the reciprocity policy would in the above-described case lead to restrictions on the free movement of companies in the sense of the Treaty. However, the question would then have to be put whether these (non-discriminatory) restrictions, which are not based on independent action by the Member States, but on a Community policy, are unjustified. This policy on first establishment, which in my view (as argued below) is part of the Community's commercial policy, could well provide the necessary justification for these restrictions.

The Community's powers to regulate first establishment

The Second Banking Directive is based on Article 57 (2) of the EC Treaty, allowing for 'the coordination of the provisions laid down by law, regulation or administrative action in Member States concerning the taking up and pursuit of activities as self-employed persons'. Apparently, the Council is of the opinion that this provision is sufficiently wide in scope to cover relations with third countries, in so far as authorizing third-country banks to

---

[84] See Ch. 1, pp. 13–16 and *infra*, pp. 77–9.

establish themselves in the Community is concerned. Since Article 57 deals only with free establishment *within* the Community, it would have to be interpreted as granting an implied power to regulate first establishment in relations with third countries.

There may well be such an implied power, if one gives a broad interpretation to the Court's case-law on implied powers.[85] However, in Chapter 1 it was argued that, in cases in which the Community is competent both by virtue of the provisions on commercial policy and on the basis of implied powers, the commercial policy basis has to be preferred.[86] Hence, it is necessary to examine whether the reciprocity provisions in the sector of financial services have anything to do with commercial policy.

Bearing in mind the analysis in Chapter 1, the reciprocity policy indeed falls squarely within the Community's commercial policy. First, it will be clear that regulating access of foreign banks to the Community's internal market in financial services relates to international trade in services. The fact that the directives in question only apply to establishment, and not to the cross-border provision of services, does obviously not remove it from the ambit of services trade. There is general agreement on the conclusion that establishment abroad is one of the basic components of international trade in financial services.[87] Furthermore, if one takes the principle of parallelism between the EC Treaty provisions on freedom to provide services and the scope of the Common Commercial Policy, such parallelism is clearly present here: the Member States are certainly not allowed to operate a reciprocity policy in intra-Community trade. In this respect it is almost irresistible again to quote Timmermans, who in 1987 seems to have virtually predicted the reciprocity policy:

Measures discriminating directly or indirectly against international services are thus not forbidden but fall within the exclusive domain of the Community. Member States would be forbidden to take them, but the EC Council could do so, by virtue of Article 113 EC. These discriminatory measures are in fact all those measures which regulate the 'status' of international services on the national market. These measures range from flat prohibitions on entering the market, and special regimes of stricter conditions, *to granting national treatment whether or not on a basis of reciprocity.*[88]

Lastly, consider the basic rationale of the Common Commercial Policy, namely the prevention of distortion of competition and deflection of trade resulting from a disparate regime governing trade with third countries. If the Member States were to maintain their various rules on establishment by

---

[85] For this case-law, see Ch. 1, pp. 35–41.

[86] See pp. 41–5.

[87] *Supra*, p. 48.

[88] C. W. A. Timmermans, 'Common Commercial Policy (Article 113 EEC) and International Trade in Services', in *Du droit international au droit de l'intégration: liber amicorum Pierre Pescatore* (Baden-Baden: Nomos, 1987), 687, italics added.

third-country financial institutions, such distortion and deflection could easily occur. To some extent, foreign investment would be flowing to the Member State with the most liberal regime, not because of economic conditions, but because access is easier there. Consequently, there would be a lesser degree of competition in Member States with protected markets, where there would be less penetration by third-country companies. In this way, foreign investment—being an important mode of services trade in the financial sector— would be deflected and competition throughout the single market distorted. Moreover, the reciprocity provisions are framed in plain commercial policy language.[89] They mention the aim of trade liberalization and they refer to key GATT concepts such as market access and national treatment.

However, the practical relevance of the conclusion that the reciprocity provisions are to be considered as part of the CCP is limited. The financial services directives introducing these provisions are certainly not void because they only mention Article 57 (2); that would only be the case if the prerogatives of one of the institutions would be harmed by the incorrect choice of legal basis,[90] or if the choice could affect the content of the directives, because a different legislative procedure has to be followed (such as unanimity in the Council as opposed to qualified majority voting).[91] Neither one of these alternatives is present here.[92] Nevertheless, the fact that regulating first establishment in the financial services sector comes under the CCP does make it clear that the Community undoubtedly has a broad power to enact such regulation, something which could be disputed if one adheres to the implied powers theory.[93] Moreover, there are the limits imposed by Article 110, EC Treaty, setting 'the progressive abolition of restrictions on international trade' as one of the aims of the CCP. There can be little doubt that the actual reciprocity policy falls within these aims;[94] but more protectionist versions of reciprocity would probably be harder to justify under the rules of the Treaty.

The entry into force of the Treaty on European Union may have changed this picture. Indeed, according to the new Article 73*b* 'all restrictions on the movement of capital between Member States and between Member States and third countries shall be prohibited',[95] with the exception of a number of

[89] Piet Eeckhout, 'The External Dimension of the Internal Market and the Scope and Content of a Modern Commercial Policy', in M. Maresceau (ed.), *The European Community's Commercial Policy after 1992: The Legal Dimension* (Dordrecht: Martinus Nijhoff, 1993), 86.

[90] Cf. Case 138/79, *Roquette Frères* v. *Council*, [1980] ECR 3333 at 3360.

[91] See Case 45/86, *Commission* v. *Council (GSP)*, [1987] ECR 1493 at 1520.

[92] Both Art. 57 (2) and Art. 113 require qualified majority voting; the rights of the European Parliament have not been disregarded, quite the opposite, for under Art. 57 (2) the co-operation procedure applied, whereas under Art. 113 the Parliament does not even have to be consulted.

[93] Reference can again be made to the imprecision of the implied powers, cf. *supra*, Ch. 1, p. 41.

[94] Cf. Ch. 11, p. 365.

[95] This 'constitutionalizes' the provisions of the Capital Movements Directive, *supra* n. 11.

restrictions which were still in force on 31 December 1993 (Article 73c (1)). Moreover, Article 73c (2) provides that

the Council may, acting by a qualified majority on a proposal from the Commission, adopt measures on the movement of capital to and from third countries involving direct investment—including investment in real estate—establishment, the provision of financial services or the admission of securities to capital markets.

It is obvious that if the reciprocity policy had been adopted after the entry into force of the Maastricht Treaty, the described provision could have been used as its basis in the Treaty. However, whether this means that in the future the CCP will no longer be relevant for matters concerning investment and establishment, as defined in Article 73c, is in my view not certain. The latter provision addresses restrictions on first establishment from the perspective of capital movements. The perspective of the CCP is another one, and will continue to be valid. Accordingly, the scope of Articles 73c and 113 will have to be delineated.

Reciprocity and international obligations

In the course of the adoption of the Second Banking Directive, a number of questions were raised as to the compatibility of the provisions on reciprocity with existing international obligations of the Member States. More specifically, these questions concerned on the one hand the Code of Liberalization of Capital Movements, an OECD instrument, and on the other commitments relating to national treatment entered into by the Member States by virtue of bilateral Treaties of Friendship and Commerce. With respect to the latter, it was primarily United States' authorities who claimed that the reciprocity policy was liable to infringe rights the United States hold under such Treaties.[96] Secondly, some attention has to be paid to the relationship between the reciprocity provisions and the General Agreement on Trade in Services which is being negotiated in the Uruguay Round.

Reciprocity and OECD instruments

The Code of Liberalization of Capital Movements was adopted by the OECD Council in 1961.[97] All the EC Member States are parties to the Code, but the Community as such is not. This is due to the fact that the Community, although having a special relationship with the OECD, is not an actual member of the Organization. Such membership is necessary to be able to adhere to the Code.[98]

---

[96] USITC, *The Effects of Greater Economic Integration within the European Community on the United States*, *supra* n. 18, pp. 16/7–16/8; Berger, *supra* n. 17, p. 3.

[97] Cf. *supra* n. 29.

[98] Art. 21 defines a member of the Code as 'a Member of the Organization which adheres to this Code'.

Under the provisions of the Code, members commit themselves to liberalize, among other things, direct investment, including the 'creation or extension of a wholly-owned enterprise, subsidiary or branch, [and] acquisition of full ownership of an existing enterprise' by non-residents.[99] Article 9 of the Code confirms that the liberalization of these transactions must be implemented in a non-discriminatory manner: 'A Member shall not discriminate as between other Members in authorizing the conclusion and execution of transactions and transfers which are listed in Annex A and which are subject to any degree of liberalization.' In view of these provisions, the problem of the compatibility of the Community's reciprocity provisions with the Code is fairly obvious:[100] if the Community were to decide that banks from a country that is a party to the Code can no longer be authorized to set up or acquire a subsidiary in the Community, because Community banks do not receive national treatment in that country, the EC Member States would seem to be in breach of the liberalization commitments described above. Their refusal to grant requests for authorization emanating from such banks would be inconsistent with the provisions of Annex A to the Code.

However, one of the many difficulties that are linked with this problem appears already in the previous sentences. Indeed, it would be the *Member States* that would be in breach of their international obligations, and not the Community, which has never adhered to the Code. Other difficulties in assessing the alleged incompatibility result from other provisions of the Code, such as Article 10, dealing with exceptions to the principle of non-discrimination:

Members forming part of a special customs or monetary system may apply to one another, in addition to measures of liberalization taken in accordance with the provisions of Article 2 (a), other measures of liberalization without extending them to other Members ...

Can this exception, which applies to customs unions such as the Community, be invoked to justify the reciprocity policy? Furthermore, there is an Annex E to the Code, 'regarding measures and practices concerning reciprocity and/or involving discrimination among investors originating in various OECD member countries in the area of inward direct investment and establishment'. This Annex notes 'that some Member countries allow inward direct establishment under conditions of reciprocity'. It records these reciprocity measures and practices, and states that they shall be progressively abolished, without, however, specifying how soon this should happen.[101] Under the provisions of this Annex, some, but not all of the EC Member States have notified

---

[99] See Annex A, List A, I (A) (1).
[100] See also Dakolias, *supra* n. 74, pp. 88–90.
[101] This Annex is fairly recent: it dates from 16 July 1986.

reciprocity requirements in the banking sector.[102] How does this 'recognition' of reciprocity policies affect the compatibility of the Community's Second Banking Directive with the Code?[103]

These questions have also been examined within the OECD, namely by the Committee on Capital Movements and Invisible Transactions (CMIT), which monitors the implementation of the Code. This Committee has drawn up a report on the compatibility question, accompanied by some concrete proposals.[104] However, this report has not yet been adopted by the OECD Council.

Let us first consider the exception, in Article 10 of the Code, for customs unions. It allows that additional measures of liberalization, taken in the framework of such a union, are not extended to other parties to the Code. It has been argued that this provision may justify the Community's reciprocity policy.[105] The arguments in favour of this interpretation can be summarized as follows. Under Article 10, the Community has the liberty of reserving the single market liberalization in the banking sector for resident Community banks. However, it does not go as far as that. As a principle, non-Community banks will be able to enjoy the benefits of the single market under the same conditions as resident banks. There is only one exception, and that is if it were established that reciprocity is not guaranteed, in the sense that Community banks do not receive national treatment when operating abroad. In such a case, the benefits of the single market can be denied to foreign banks. However, as under Article 10 a *general* denial of these benefits is possible, surely a much more limited one is equally allowed by this provision. Moreover, the reciprocity policy could certainly not be considered as a deterioration in comparison with the previous situation, which was one of twelve separated markets. Due to the Second Banking Directive, the barriers between these markets have disappeared, also for foreign banks, under the condition of reciprocity. But overall the tendency is towards liberalization.

However, there is one basic component of the reciprocity policy which is overlooked in the development of this argument, and which undermines its justification under Article 10 of the Code. It is the fact that the sanction which the Community authorities can apply if national treatment is not granted, is not limited to denying foreign banks the benefits of the internal market.

---

[102] See *supra* n. 30. Reciprocity requirements also exist as regards insurance companies or financial services in general, as well as in other sectors, such as air transport.

[103] It has to be repeated that, whereas only the banking sector is discussed here, the same questions arise with respect to other financial services sectors, in which the reciprocity policy also applies.

[104] OECD, C (91) 5 of 22 Jan. 1991. Also see USITC, *The Effects of Greater Economic Integration within the European Community on the United States, supra* n. 18, pp. 16/6–16/7; ibid., *First Follow-up Report, supra* n. 48, pp. 17/7–17/9; ibid., *Second Follow-up Report*, Publication 2318 (Washington, DC: 1990), 14/3–14/4.

[105] CMIT Report (*supra*, n. 104), para. 29 and Vigneron and Smith, *supra* n. 26, pp. 358–9.

Establishment *as such* can be denied. Not only do foreign banks lose, in the case of Community sanctions, the opportunity to operate on a Community-wide scale—this being the 'additional liberalization' within the Community as a customs union, referred to in Article 10 of the Code—they also lose the opportunity of establishing themselves, through a subsidiary, in any of the Member States. That is precisely what Article 10 does not allow, because it infringes one of the liberalization commitments of the Code.[106] To be compatible with Article 10, the Community reciprocity sanction would have to be limited to denying foreign banks the right to offer their services throughout the Community, to denying them, in other words, the benefits of the Second Banking Directive. But to refuse them the right of establishment on Community territory is one step beyond the aperture of Article 10.

The problem with Annex E to the Code, concerning reciprocity measures, is that not all the EC Member States have notified such measures in the banking sector, as regards establishment through subsidiaries.[107] Only France, Greece, Ireland, the Netherlands, Spain, and the UK have done so. Therefore, the Community-wide reciprocity clause introduces new reciprocity requirements in the other Member States. Although Annex E does not explicitly prohibit new measures, these are clearly inconsistent with its thrust, being to eliminate existing measures. In the OECD Council's wording, 'a more extensive use of reciprocal and/or discriminatory approaches in matters pertaining to inward direct investment or the right of establishment ... could reduce the effective sphere of liberalization among Member countries'.[108] Consequently, the Council has also decided that existing measures and practices, as recorded in Annex E, should be progressively abolished.[109] It is obvious that it is difficult to reconcile the introduction of a new Community-wide reciprocity requirement with this aim of gradually abolishing existing restrictions.

As a first conclusion, it may therefore be said that it is difficult to justify the Community's reciprocity policy under either Article 10 of the Code, or Annex E. This brings us, however, to what is perhaps the essential problem in the relationship between the Community's policy and the Capital Code, namely the status of the Community within the OECD.[110] As was mentioned, the Community is not a party to the Capital Code, basically because the latter can only be adhered to by OECD members, which the Community as such is not. This does not mean, however, that the Community is totally absent from the OECD's activities. The EEC Treaty already provided that '[t]he Community shall establish close cooperation with the Organization for European

---

[106] Cf. CMIT Report, para. 27. [107] Ibid.
[108] Annex E, para. III. [109] Annex E, para. VII (2).
[110] See for an excellent study on this subject Christian Schricke, 'La CEE et l'OCDE à l'heure de l'Acte unique', 93 *Revue générale de droit international public* (1989), 4: 797–829; also see European Parliament, Report drawn up by Mr Saridakis, MEP, on relations between the European Community and the OECD, Document A 2–0313/88 of 14 Dec. 1988.

Economic Cooperation, the details to be determined by common accord'.[111] Accordingly, Protocol No. 1 of the OECD Convention provides that the Community's representation in the OECD is to be arranged according to the EEC and ECSC Treaties, and that the Commission participates in the OECD's activities. In practice, this almost amounts to full membership, with the exception, however, of the right to vote and to be a party to OECD Council Decisions.

The relationship between the Community and the Capital Code is therefore a rather mixed one. Although the Community is not a party to the Code, it is represented in the CMIT and it fully takes part in the activities of this Committee. Moreover, all the Member States have signed the Code. This suggests that the right step would be for the Community to adhere to the Capital Code, so as to become a full member. That such Community adherence is possible and could be acceptable for the other OECD members is illustrated by recent negotiations on the OECD National Treatment Instrument.[112] The revision of this Instrument resulted in a new OECD Council Decision, Article 7 of which specifies that it is open for accession by the Community. In this regard, this is the first Council Decision of its kind; but there is little doubt that it will act as a precedent case for future decisions dealing with matters coming under the Community's competence.

The CMIT did not go as far as suggesting that the Community adhere to the Code.[113] It did propose that Annex E be adapted so as to incorporate the reciprocity provisions of the Second Banking Directive, accompanied by more specific disciplines on the use which could be made of these provisions. As was said, the OECD Council has not yet acted on this proposal, some members of the Committee being of the view that the outcome of the Uruguay Round negotiations should be awaited.

In the meantime, however, the question arises whether the inconsistency between the Community's reciprocity policy and the Capital Code has any bearing on the lawfulness, under Community law, of the reciprocity provisions, or of any measures taken within their framework. There are three angles to this question.

---

[111] The OEEC was the OECD's predecessor.

[112] See for an account COM (91) 422 final, Proposal for a Council Decision on participation by the Community in the third revised OECD decision concerning national treatment. It is mentioned that 'consensus was quickly arrived at on the idea of the Community's becoming party to the decision, in view of the external implications of the single market and the existence of derogations from national treatment which could only be notified at Community level' (p. 2). It should be mentioned that the Commission has proposed that the Council adopt this decision on the basis of Arts. 57 and 113, EC Treaty. Most of the Member States are opposed to this, and the Council wishes to refer to Art. 235 of the Treaty. Belgium has asked the Court of Justice for an Opinion, on the basis of Art. 228, as to the correct legal basis (Opinion 2/92, see OJ C 255/4 of 2 Oct. 1992). The Court's Opinion will undoubtedly clarify the scope of Art. 113 in the field of investment and services.

[113] See n. 104.

First, it must not be overlooked that the Second Banking Directive as such does not limit establishment by banks from OECD countries, parties to the Capital Code. Restrictions on establishment that would be inconsistent with the Capital Code would only occur if the Community decided to use Article 9 (4) against an OECD country. It is not at all certain that the Community will ever do so.

Secondly, it would be difficult to argue that the Capital Code is legally binding on the Community, since it has not adhered to it. One would have to apply the reasoning which the Court of Justice developed in *International Fruit Company*, concerning the status of GATT in Community law.[114] In this judgment, the Court observed that the Community had effectively substituted the Member States in the GATT framework, and that this substitution had been recognized by the other GATT Contracting Parties. Until now, such a substitution has not taken place in the OECD framework, neither in general nor specifically relating to the Capital Code. Accordingly, the provisions of the Code are not binding for the Community and cannot have the effect of rendering the reciprocity policy illegal.

The third angle relates to Article 234 of the EC Treaty. The fact that the Capital Code is not binding for the Community does not mean that it has no status whatsoever in the Community's legal order. Article 234 (1) confirms that agreements concluded by the Member States before the entry into force of the EC Treaty are not affected by the Treaty. Although the Capital Code is of later date than the EC Treaty, to some extent this provision is applicable, because six Member States have joined the Community after they agreed to the Capital Code.[115] This does not only mean that the Capital Code is not affected by the EC Treaty, as Article 234 (1) provides. The Court of Justice has also decided that

[a]lthough the first paragraph of Article 234 makes mention only of the obligations of the Member States, it would not achieve its purpose if it did not imply a duty on the part of the institutions of the Community not to impede the performance of the obligations of the Member States which stem from a prior agreement. However, that duty of the Community institutions is directed only to permitting the Member State concerned to perform its obligations under the prior agreement and does not bind the Community as regards the non-member country in question.[116]

If it is accepted that there is a problem of compatibility of the reciprocity provisions with the Capital Code, the Community institutions might be acting in breach of the duty described by the Court, especially if they were to impose

---

[114] Cases 21–24/72, *International Fruit Company* v. *Produktschap voor groenten en fruit*, [1972] ECR 1219 at 1227. See also Ch. 3, p. 101.

[115] Cf. Case 812/79, *Attorney General* v. *Burgoa* [1980] ECR 2787, at 2802.

[116] Ibid., [1980] ECR 2803. See also Ch. 3, p. 100.

the sanction of Article 9 (4) as regards banks from an OECD country.[117] On the other hand, however, there is also paragraph 2 of Article 234, requiring that the Member States take all appropriate steps to eliminate incompatibilities between prior agreements and the EC Treaty. Combining Article 234 (1) and (2) in the case of the Second Banking Directive, the conclusion seems to be that the Member States and the Community as such (through the Commission representation) are under a duty to act, within the OECD framework, so as to eliminate the described incompatibility. As was mentioned above, accession of the Community to the Capital Code could be the most suitable approach in this respect.

One last observation has to be made concerning the compatibility of the Community's reciprocity policy with OECD commitments; perhaps it is the most fundamental one. The core of the problem, in my view, is the systemic conflict between a unilateral approach towards foreign trade barriers, and a multilateral one.[118] This conflict is more closely examined below.[119] It may be sufficient to indicate here that a unilateral approach, such as the reciprocity policy in the financial services sector, is bound to be incompatible with principles of non-discrimination that are a natural element, so to speak, of a multilateral approach, such as the Capital Code. The sanctions which can be imposed in the framework of a unilateral reciprocity approach contradict by their very character the principle of non-discrimination.

Reciprocity and Treaties of Friendship, Commerce, and Navigation

In the course of the adoption of the Second Banking Directive it was also maintained, especially by US authorities, that the reciprocity policy was inconsistent with existing bilateral Treaties of Friendship, Commerce, and Navigation, concluded between the Member States and, for example, the United States.[120] Most of these Treaties provide for national treatment, within the territory of each Party, as regards establishment and the carrying on of economic activities by nationals or companies of the other Party. As an example, the relevant passage of the US–German Treaty may be quoted:

Nationals and companies of either Party shall be accorded, within the territories of the other Party, national treatment with respect to engaging in all types of commercial, industrial, financial and other activity for gain, whether in a dependent or an independent capacity, and whether directly or by an agent or through the medium of any form of lawful juridical entity. Accordingly, such nationals and companies shall be permitted within such territories: (a) to establish and maintain branches, agencies, offices,

---

[117] Compare with Jacques H. J. Bourgeois, 'The Common Commercial Policy: Scope and Nature of the Powers', in E. L. M. Völker (ed.), *Protectionism and the European Community*, 2nd edn. (Deventer: Kluwer, 1986), 12 n. 29.

[118] Cf. the CMIT Report, *supra* n. 104, para. 28.

[119] See also Ch. 11, pp. 372–3.

[120] For a thorough examination of this question, see Levitin, *supra* n. 51, pp. 534–40.

factories and other establishments appropriate to the conduct of their business; (b) to organize companies under the general company laws of such other Party; and (c) to control and manage enterprises which they have established or acquired. Moreover, enterprises which they control, whether in the form of individual proprietorships, companies or otherwise, shall in all that relates to the conduct of activities thereof, be accorded treatment no less favourable than that accorded like enterprises controlled by nationals or companies of such other Party.[121]

It is clear that if the Community were to apply the sanction of Article 9 (4) of the Second Banking Directive against banks of a third country with which the Member States (or some of them) have contracted similar national treatment obligations, these Member States would have to disregard these obligations. However, since the Community's decision of not authorizing new establishment can only be taken if the third country concerned does not provide national treatment, this country would itself be infringing its national treatment obligations under the relevant Treaty.[122] It is therefore difficult to claim that the Community's reciprocity policy, in its current version with emphasis on national treatment, would be inconsistent with the existing Treaties of Friendship, Commerce, and Navigation.

But there is something more to be added. These Treaties are subject to regular examination by the EC Council, because some of their provisions are concerned with commercial policy. Until recently, this examination has always been rather formal, authorizing the maintenance in force of these Treaties, combined with emphasizing the duty of the Member States not to conduct a national commercial policy.[123] That has changed, however, as a result of a dispute between Germany and the Commission concerning the implementation of the so-called Utilities Directive, discussed in Chapter 9. For the legal aspects of this evolution the reader is referred to that discussion.[124]

Reciprocity and GATS

Within the scope of this chapter it is not possible fully to analyse the impact of a possible General Agreement on Trade in Services on trade in financial

---

[121] Quoted in USITC, *The Effects of Greater Economic Integration within the European Community on the United States supra* n. 18, p. 16/7. Some of these clauses contain an exception as regards banking activities (ibid.).

[122] Theoretically, this breach could occur with respect to banks from only some of the Member States. Other Member States would in such a case not be able to claim that the national treatment obligation in their bilateral agreement with the third country in question is breached, in the case of Community-wide sanctions. However, this hypothesis is probably not very realistic, since domestic legislation discriminating against foreign service providers is often of general scope.

[123] See e.g. the Council Decision of 25 Mar. 1991 authorizing the automatic renewal or maintenance in force of provisions governing matters covered by the common commercial policy contained in the friendship, trade, and navigation treaties and similar agreements concluded between Member States and third countries, OJ L 82/52 of 28 Mar. 1991.

[124] Ch. 9, pp. 317–18.

services between the Community and third countries.[125] Nevertheless, a number of observations have to be made. First, it is obvious that it is difficult to reconcile a bilateral approach based on reciprocity with a GATT-like multilateral agreement including the most-favoured-nation rule. The draft GATS included in the Dunkel package provides in Article II (1) that '[w]ith respect to any measure covered by this Agreement, each Party shall accord immediately and unconditionally to services and service providers of any other Party, treatment no less favourable than that it accords to like services and service providers of any other country'.[126] Hence, if this draft Agreement were to enter into force, covering financial services, it would no longer be possible for the Community to enforce reciprocity in relations with Parties to the Agreement. Secondly, the draft GATS confirms the emphasis on *de facto* national treatment. Article XVII, which deals with national treatment in the framework of specific commitments entered into by the various Parties, provides that 'each Party shall accord to services and service providers of any other Party, in respect of all measures affecting the supply of services, treatment no less favourable than that it accords to its own like services and service providers'.[127] It clarifies that such treatment may be formally identical or formally different, but requires that it does not modify the conditions of competition in favour of domestic services or service providers.[128] Thirdly, it is worth mentioning that the draft GATS includes an Annex on financial services which mainly deals with prudential measures, and which defines the various kinds of financial services.[129]

The concept of national treatment and trade liberalization

As was mentioned above, there are two important sources of experience in applying the concept of national treatment to barriers to trade. On the one hand, there are the EC Treaty provisions on free movement of services (and also on freedom of establishment), incorporating a prohibition of discrimination based on nationality. On these provisions there is a considerable body of case-law of the Court of Justice. It is of particular interest here because it is, to my knowledge, the only existing practice with respect to the application of a general principle of non-discrimination or national treatment to international trade in services. On the other hand, there is the national treatment clause of Article III of the GATT. Although not applicable to trade in services, it is useful to examine the GATT Panel Reports in which this clause has been

[125] On the negotiations in the field of financial services see Woolcock, *supra* n. 35, pp. 44–7.
[126] See the Draft Final Act of Dec. 1991, MTN.TNC/W/FA, p. 7 of the Annex.
[127] MTN.TNC/W/FA, p. 21 of the Annex.
[128] Ibid. See also *infra*, p. 80 on the interpretation of the national treatment clause of the GATT.
[129] See MTN.TNC/W/FA, pp. 35–8 of the Annex.

interpreted and further defined, because it is the only global, multilateral national treatment provision relating to trade liberalization. Also, it is clear that Article III of GATT has served as a point of reference for the negotiations on national treatment within the framework of a new General Agreement on Trade in Services; and, as was shown, these negotiations have exerted significant influence on the wording of the reciprocity provisions of the Second Banking Directive.[130]

Both these experiences reveal, as will be demonstrated, that the principle of national treatment or non-discrimination is capable of covering a wide range of regulations and practices, especially if emphasis is put on obtaining *de facto* national treatment, as is the case with the Community's reciprocity policy in the financial sector. Moreover, the succinct analysis below may be of some help, not only for interpreting the said reciprocity policy, but also for assessing more generally the function of a national treatment clause with respect to liberalization of trade in services. Again it has to be emphasized that most barriers to trade in services are situated at the level of general government regulation of the provision of services, and that the national treatment requirement plays a central role in addressing the way in which such regulation affects imported services.[131]

Non-discrimination and the EC Treaty

In Chapter 1, the scope of Article 59 of the EC Treaty has already been examined, by referring to a number of important cases dealt with by the Court of Justice.[132] It would not be very useful to repeat that analysis here. However, one important question has to be addressed. It is the question whether the concept of non-discrimination is still capable of fully explaining the Court's case-law on free movement of services, or whether, on the contrary, the Court has moved further, beyond this concept, in identifying barriers to intra-Community trade in services. The recent judgment in *Stichting Collectieve Antennevoorziening Gouda*, quoted in Chapter 1, seems to support the latter thesis.[133] It will be remembered that the Court made a distinction between, on the one hand, discrimination towards foreign service providers, and, on the other hand, the problem of national regulations applying equally to domestic and imported services, where discrimination is no longer mentioned.

Despite this distinction, it is submitted that at least some of the Court's rulings on equally applicable national regulations—or, in other words, general

---

[130] *Supra*, p. 60.   [131] See Ch. 11, p. 371.   [132] pp. 13–16.
[133] Case C-288/89, *Stichting Collectieve Antennevoorziening Gouda* v. *Commissariaat voor de Media*, [1991] ECR I-4007. See Ch. 1, pp. 15–16.

regulation of service transactions—could still be interpreted as referring to an element of discrimination, understood in a *factual* sense, that is.[134] The Court held in *Stichting Collectieve Antennevoorziening Gouda* that

> [i]n the absence of harmonization of the rules applicable to services, or even of a system of equivalence, restrictions on the freedom guaranteed by the Treaty in this field may arise in the second place as a result of the application of national rules which affect any person established in the national territory to persons providing services established in the territory of another Member State who already have to satisfy the requirements of that State's legislation.[135]

The discriminatory element to which the Court refers lies in the last part of this sentence: a difference exists in applying general national regulation of service activities to domestic as well as foreign service providers in so far as the latter already satisfy similar regulatory requirements in their home country.[136] If that is the case, equal treatment is not appropriate and amounts to factual discrimination, because the cases of domestic and foreign service providers are not similar. To take the example of the banking sector, it is obvious that there is a substantial difference between a request to carry on banking activities emanating from a domestic company which has never before operated as a bank, and a similar request from a well-established foreign bank, duly supervised in its activities by the authorities of the home country.

It has to be added that, when interpreting the concept of non-discrimination in such a broad manner, one probably reaches its boundaries in terms of handling barriers to trade in services. It is a far-reaching interpretation, because it requires that one looks not only at the situation on a given domestic market, but also at the way in which services are regulated abroad, in the country where the foreign service provider is established. Ultimately, it leads to a system of mutual recognition of national regulatory systems. It may well be that using such a wide discrimination test can only work in a system of strong economic integration, such as the Community's internal market. Moreover, to implement such a wide test requires intricate legal assessments, particularly when drawing the line between what is justified under certain 'imperative reasons of general interest', as identified by the Court in *Stichting Collectieve Antennevoorziening Gouda*, and what is an unnecessary duplication of other countries' systems of regulating service activities.

I should emphasize that I do not take the view that the Court would *limit* its interpretation of the prohibition of restrictions on services trade to cases of (formal or factual) discrimination. As the *Säger* case appears to suggest, the Court is probably also prepared to outlaw restrictions resulting from equally

---

[134] Cf. Ch. 1, p. 14.

[135] Case C-288/89, [1991] ECR I-4040.

[136] Cf. Christiaan W. A. Timmermans, 'Verboden discriminatie of (geboden) differentiatie', 30 *SEW* (1982), 6: 448–51.

applicable national regulation where no element of discrimination can be found whatsoever.[137]

National treatment and Article III of GATT

Article III of GATT deals with 'National Treatment on Internal Taxation and Regulation'. It is an elaborate provision, but nevertheless only indicates a number of broad rules, without specifying how exactly these rules have to be implemented. Its most important sections are paragraphs 1, 2, and 4. Paragraph 1 stipulates that the contracting parties recognize that

internal taxes and other internal charges, and laws, regulations and requirements affecting the internal sale, offering for sale, purchase, transportation, distribution or use of products, and internal quantitative regulations requiring the mixture, processing or use of products in specified amounts or proportions, should not be applied to imported or domestic products so as to afford protection to domestic production.

Paragraph 2 translates this principle, as regards taxes, into a commitment:

The products of the territory of any contracting party imported into the territory of any other contracting party shall not be subject, directly or indirectly, to internal taxes or other internal charges of any kind in excess of those applied, directly or indirectly, to like domestic products. Moreover, no contracting party shall otherwise apply internal taxes or other internal charges to imported or domestic products in a manner contrary to the principles set forth in paragraph 1.

Paragraph 4 does the same, as regards internal laws, regulations, and requirements:

The products of the territory of any contracting party imported into the territory of any other contracting party shall be accorded treatment no less favourable than that accorded to like products of national origin in respect of all laws, regulations and requirements affecting their internal sale, purchase, transportation, distribution or use ...

From GATT practice, especially the Panel reports in which the scope of Article III has been examined, it appears that the national treatment principle is able to cut quite deep into the way in which national regulatory systems affect the status of imported products. A few examples may illustrate this.

First, it is clear that Article III affects various domains of national regulation, such as taxes and subsidies, to name only the two most important ones.[138] It would, moreover, also apply to government procurement, if there was not a specific exception in this respect.[139] Already in an early case, a Panel

[137] Case C-76/90 *Säger* v. *Dennemeyer*, [1991] ECR I-4221; see in particular the Opinion by Advocate-General Jacobs. See also the annotation by Martijn van Empel, 41 *SEW* (1993), 9: 665–70.
[138] However, for subsidies there is the partial exemption of Art. III (8) (*b*).
[139] Art. III (8) (*a*).

ruled that Article III does not merely cover measures strictly governing trade. The Italian government had argued this, maintaining that special credit facilities offered to farmers buying domestically produced machinery were outside the scope of the General Agreement. The Panel observed that

the drafters of the Article intended to cover in paragraph 4 not only the laws and regulations which directly governed the conditions of sale or purchase but also any laws or regulations which might adversely modify the conditions of competition between the domestic and imported products on the internal market.[140]

Given the basic rationale of the national treatment clause, to which the Panel referred, this wide scope is logical. One Panel noted that

[t]he general prohibition of quantitative restrictions under Article XI ... and the national treatment obligation of Article III ... have essentially the same rationale, namely to protect expectations of the contracting parties as to the competitive relationship between their products and those of the other contracting parties.[141]

It need not be emphasized that in today's interdependent world large segments of domestic regulation may influence this competitive relationship between nationally produced and imported products.[142]

The fact that Article III aims to protect equivalent conditions of competition also produces other legal consequences. It need not be shown, in order for Article III to be applicable, that a measure has an actual negative effect on the volume of trade, for example. As one Panel put it, the aim of the national treatment provision is 'not only to protect current trade, but also to create the predictability needed to plan future trade'.[143] Similarly, to be inconsistent with Article III it is sufficient that a measure is capable of discriminating against imported products, without necessarily actually discriminating in each individual case. This was decided in a Panel Report on the Community's subsidy system in the sector of oilseeds and related animal-feed proteins. The Panel found that

[t]he Community Regulations are thus capable of giving rise to discrimination against imported products though they may not necessarily do so in the case of each individual purchase.

Having made this finding the Panel examined whether a purchase regulation which does not necessarily discriminate against imported products but is capable of doing so is consistent with Article III: 4. The Panel noted that the exposure of a particular imported product to a *risk* of discrimination constitutes, by itself, a form of discrimination. The Panel therefore concluded that purchase regulations creating such a risk

[140] Panel Report on Italian discrimination against imported agricultural machinery, *BISD*, 7 S., p. 64.
[141] Panel Report on US taxes on petroleum and certain imported substances, *BISD*, 34 S., p. 160.
[142] Cf. John H. Jackson, *World Trade and the Law of GATT* (Indianapolis: Bobbs-Merrill, 1969), 274 and *The World Trading System* (Cambridge: MIT Press, 1989), 189–90.
[143] Panel Report on US taxes, *supra* n. 141, p. 160. See also the Panel Report on the administration of the Canadian Foreign Investment Review Act, *BISD*, 30 S., p. 160.

must be considered to be according less favourable treatment within the meaning of Article III: 4.[144]

The wide scope of the national treatment clause also becomes manifest when analysing the sort of 'measures' which it covers. Paragraph 4 mentions 'all laws, regulations and requirements affecting' internal sale, etc. The word 'requirements' has especially been construed as including all sorts of governmental practices. For example, in a case concerning the Canadian foreign investment review system, Canada has argued that this word should be interpreted as referring to mandatory rules applying across the board. The Panel, however, could not agree to such an interpretation, because mandatory rules are already covered by the word regulations. It found that purchase undertakings, entered into by foreign investors in the framework of foreign investment review, were also to be considered 'requirements'. Also, in the Panel Report on the Community's anti-dumping laws regarding parts and components (the so-called screwdriver regulation) it is mentioned that

the comprehensive coverage of '*all* laws, regulations or requirements *affecting*' (emphasis added) the internal sale, etc. of imported products suggests that not only requirements which an enterprise is legally bound to carry out . . . , but also those which an enterprise voluntarily accepts in order to obtain an advantage from the government constitute 'requirements' within the meaning of [Article III: 4]. The Panel noted that the EEC made the grant of an advantage, namely the suspension of proceedings under the anti-circumvention provision, dependent on undertakings to accord treatment to imported products less favourable than that accorded to like products of national origin in respect of their internal use.[145]

An important question is whether Article III of GATT also covers cases of what, in Community law terminology, is called factual discrimination. There are, to my knowledge, no Panel Reports which would allow firm conclusions to be drawn in this respect. The Report concerning Community subsidies in the sector of oilseeds and animal-feed proteins might, however, be interpreted as going some way in this direction.[146] Moreover, one prominent GATT

[144] *BISD*, 37 S., p. 125.   [145] *BISD*, 37 S., p. 197.

[146] The Panel examined whether subsidies paid to processors buying domestic oilseeds merely served to offset the price differential between domestic and imported oilseeds, or whether, on the contrary, they served as an incentive for buying domestic products. It found 'that subsidy payments made to processors can be greater than the difference between the price processors actually pay to producers and the price that processors would have to pay for imported oilseeds. Whether such overcompensation creating an incentive to purchase domestic rather than imported products takes place depends on the circumstances of the individual purchase. The Community Regulations are thus capable of giving rise to discrimination against imported products though they may not necessarily do so in the case of each individual purchase.' It further noted 'that the exposure of a particular imported product to a *risk* of discrimination constitutes, by itself, a form of discrimination', and considered that the Community's Regulations were inconsistent with Article III (4) (*BISD*, 37 S., p. 125).

commentator clearly interprets the national treatment obligation in such a wider sense. On the question whether

a national regulation or tax which *on its face* appears to be nondiscriminatory, but which, because of various circumstances in the marketplace or elsewhere, has the effect of tilting the scales against the imported products

is consistent or not with Article III, it is said that

it can be strongly argued that even though a tax (or regulation) appears on its face to be nondiscriminatory, if it has an *effect* of affording protection, and if this effect is not essential to the valid regulatory purpose (as suggested by Article XX), then such tax or regulation is inconsistent with GATT obligations.[147]

Community lawyers will have little difficulty in recognizing that such an interpretation is comparable to the concept of factual discrimination in Community law.

The wide scope of national treatment

The analysis of Article III of GATT and of the provisions on services of the EC Treaty shows that one can distinguish three layers of national treatment. The first is only concerned with cases of formal discrimination against foreign products or economic actors. That is the lowest standard. It merely looks at whether laws or regulations openly discriminate. However, from the analysis above it follows that such purely formal national treatment is not what is aimed at in the financial services sector.

The second layer is concerned with cases of what in Community terminology is called factual discrimination. Undoubtedly, there are various definitions of this phenomenon. Broadly speaking, however, it is pretty clear what is meant by factual discrimination: it involves taking a closer look at the concrete effects of domestic laws, regulations, or administrative practices on imported goods or services, or on foreign economic actors. This implies looking at the market context in which competition between domestic and foreign products or actors takes place. If a given measure, taking into account this market context, operates in the direction of discriminating against foreign products or actors, it falls foul of the national treatment standard, interpreted in such a way. Obviously, this is the kind of national treatment test incorporated in the Community's financial services directives. However, it is also obvious that this version of national treatment, when implemented, requires difficult, intricate assessments of the various circumstances that affect the competitive relationship between foreign and domestic products or actors. Moreover, it entails drawing the line between legitimate government policy objectives and hidden discrimination, a line that may not always be so clearly

[147] Jackson, *The World Trading System, supra* n. 141, pp. 192–3. Art. XX is similar to Art. 36, EC Treaty.

visible. Therefore, to check in a correct and consistent manner whether this standard is applied probably requires judge-like impartiality.

Also, this version of national treatment is rather open-ended. How far does one go in examining the effects of a measure? There is no clear boundary in this respect, except in one sense, bringing us to the third layer of national treatment. In this third layer, one must not only look at the domestic market context, but also at the market context abroad, in the country of origin of the foreign products or actors. It is the sort of test of non-discrimination (if one can still characterize it as such) which the Court of Justice has developed, as was explained above.[148] If, for example, a foreign service provider already satisfies certain regulatory requirements in his home country, duplication of these requirements in the country where he wishes to establish himself amounts to discrimination, and is not allowed. The result is a rule of mutual recognition.

Again, it is conceded that such a wide test may be regarded as surpassing the principle of non-discrimination or national treatment; indicative in this respect is that the Court of Justice in its case-law on mutual recognition does not mention the concept of discrimination. But in any event such a broad interpretation of national treatment would be ill suited within the framework of the Community's reciprocity policy. To apply it would have little to do with reciprocity. It would be asking third countries much more than the Community itself is granting. For example, third countries would have to check, when a Community bank requests the authorization of establishing itself, whether their domestic regulations governing the setting-up of a bank do not duplicate the corresponding requirements laid down in Community or Member State-level regulation. If such duplication were present, those third countries would no longer be allowed to impose domestic requirements. They would have to recognize the regulatory system which exists in the Community, but this recognition would not be mutual because in Community law no corresponding recognition of the regulatory systems of third countries is present. Clearly, therefore, this third layer of national treatment is not appropriate for the implementation of the reciprocity provisions.

Conclusion

The Community's approach towards defining the external dimension in the field of financial services confirms that, in substance, the Community is increasingly looking at international service transactions from a trade policy perspective. In effect, a Common Commercial Policy for financial services is developed. The approach underlines, moreover, the importance of the national treatment standard for liberalizing trade in services, because re-

[148] p. 78.

strictions often result from general regulation, which at first sight does not particularly inhibit imported services. But in practice it may do so. The question is: how far does one go in looking at these practical effects on imports? The Community's internal experience with the non-discrimination rule may certainly serve as a useful point of reference here. Furthermore, the Community does not yet seem to have decided to what extent it attaches importance, not only to obtaining national treatment of its financial services companies on third-country markets, but also to achieving a 'level playing-field', meaning that its trading partners should create more open financial markets. This is linked to the tension which obviously exists between an autonomous external policy (which could pursue the latter aim more aggressively) and efforts aimed at arriving at multilateral liberalization (which will probably be limited to achieving a certain level of national treatment). All these elements are further examined in the concluding chapter.[149]

[149] See esp. pp. 365–6 and 372–3.

3

Transport Services: The Test Case of Civil Aviation

Introduction

From the perspective of international trade, the transport sector is in economic terms one of the most important services sectors. The regulation of transport activities in the Community is also an important segment of the internal market programme. The question of how the Community defines the external dimension of the internal transport market therefore arises almost automatically. One could examine this question for all the different transport modes, namely by sea, by air, by road, by train, and by inland waterways. However, that approach is not followed here. If it were, one would quickly discover that the Community has until now developed only a few external policies relating to transport.[1] That is not illogical in view of the fact that it took a lot of time, in spite of the fact that the EC Treaty envisages a Common Transport Policy, before the Community started to regulate even the intra-Community provision of transport services on a comprehensive scale.

This means that external relations in the transport sector—which is by tradition strictly regulated—are governed by bilateral agreements concluded between the Member States and third countries. In view of the completion of the internal market, which entails the free provision of transport services in the Community, this nationally oriented system cannot but pose problems. This has become most apparent in the field of civil aviation, in which the internal market programme has totally reversed the existing regulatory system within the Community. This sector of transport services is also characterized by a large measure of economic interdependence of external and internal traffic. It is the same air carriers, established in the Community, which offer their services for flights between and inside Member States and flights to and from third countries. Moreover, the latter kind of operations are in economic terms at least as important for these carriers as intra-Community air transport, if not more. It is not surprising, therefore, that the debate on how to define the external dimension of the Community's policies in the field of transport has mainly taken place in the area of civil aviation. That debate is examined below.

Nevertheless, a few words should be devoted to other transport sectors. The external dimension of the Community's policy is of course also very important

---

[1] Cf. the recent communication by the Commission, *The Future Development of the Common Transport Policy*, COM (92) 494 final of 2 Dec. 1992, pp. 91–2.

for shipping. However, there is less of a link here with the internal market for shipping (i.e. shipping between the Member States), which is of a modest size and the liberalization of which is not the subject of a comprehensive programme as is the case with civil aviation.[2] The Community's external shipping policy is surely worth discussing,[3] but it has less to do with the completion of the internal market. In the field of road transport the external dimension is made up of specific, almost geographical issues. There is the problem of transit through Switzerland, Austria, and the former Yugoslavia, which the Community is trying to solve by concluding transit agreements with the countries concerned.[4] Undoubtedly, this problem is important, but it raises few legal questions which are significant from the perspective of a general study of the external dimension of the internal market. The same observation applies to policies towards Central and East European countries, which are still in a stage of early development. In the sector of transport by inland waterways, the Community has recently started negotiations with a number of Central and East European countries.[5] Lastly, in the field of rail transport the Community is only starting to become active.

As regards civil aviation, policies aimed at completing the internal market have been developed in packages. There have been three of these, the third one, of July 1992, achieving the (almost) completely free movement of air transport services as well as freedom of establishment for air carriers.[6] These packages have been accompanied by a set of regulations concerning the implementation of competition policy in the area of civil aviation.[7] The Commission has also tried to have the packages accompanied by the development of a fully-fledged external policy, and has issued a number of proposals in this respect. These are, however, still under discussion. These proposals are analysed below, according to the following format: first the question of the Community's external competence is dealt with, followed by an examination of the compatibility with the Chicago Convention (the basis

[2] See Council Regulation 3577/92 of 7 Dec. 1992 applying the principle of freedom to provide services to maritime transport within Member States, OJ L 364/7 of 12 Dec. 1992.

[3] See e.g. Danielle Charles-Le Bihan and Joel Lebullenger, 'Common Maritime Transport Policy: Bilateral Agreements and the Freedom to Provide Services', A. Barav and D. A. Wyatt (eds.), 9 *Yearbook of European Law* (1989) (Oxford: Clarendon Press, 1990), 209–23.

[4] As regards the latter country, the problem is of course partly theoretical at the moment.

[5] See *Agence Europe*, No. 5875, 10 Dec. 1992, p. 10.

[6] The third package includes: Council Regulation 2407/92 on licensing of air carriers, OJ L 240/1 of 24 Aug. 1992, p. 1; Council Regulation 2408/92 on access for Community air carriers to intra-Community air routes, OJ L 240/8 of 24 Aug. 1992; Council Regulation 2409/92 on fares and rates for air services, OJ L 240/15 of 24 Aug. 1992.

[7] The two basic regulations are: Council Regulation 3975/87 laying down the procedure for the application of the rules on competition to undertakings in the air transport sector, OJ L 374/1 of 31 Dec. 1987, as last amended by Council Regulation 2410/92, OJ L 240/18 of 24 Aug. 1992; Council Regulation 3976/87 on the application of Article 85 (3) of the Treaty to certain categories of agreements and concerted practices in the air transport sector, OJ L 374/9 of 31 Dec. 1987, as last amended by Regulation 2411/92, OJ L 240/19 of 24 Aug. 1992. Since competition policy does not come within the scope of this study, these regulations are not analysed here.

for the world-wide regulation of civil aviation) of the Community's cabotage policies. Then the substance of the Commission's proposals, which relate to the future of the bilateral agreements concluded by the Member States and third countries, is discussed. Lastly, some other issues are touched upon.

External Competence: Common Commercial Policy or Common Transport Policy?

Importance of the question

In February 1990 the Commission presented a proposal to the Council for a Decision on a consultation and authorization procedure for agreements concerning commercial aviation relations between Member States and third countries.[8] In the communication which accompanies this proposal, the Commission defends the view that the commercial aspects of aviation relations with third countries come under the exclusive competence of the Community, by virtue of the provisions on the Common Commercial Policy (CCP).[9] The Commission's reasoning is quite uncomplicated. It is based on two assumptions. The first, the scope of the CCP extends to the regulation of trade in services with third countries. The second, aviation activities can without doubt be considered as the provision of services.

Nevertheless, this view has come under sharp criticism from the Council, the Member States, and the European Parliament,[10] as well as from legal writing.[11] The critics hold the view that the Community is only competent to deal with external relations in the air transport sector by virtue of the EC Treaty provisions on transport policy, in particular Article 84 (2). According to this thesis, the doctrine of implied powers is the only basis on which an

[8] COM (90) 17 final of 23 Feb. 1990.

[9] COM (90) 17 final, paras. 18–22. Ludwig Weber reports that the Commission defended this view already in 1960, see *Die Zivilluftfahrt im Europäischen Gemeinschaftsrecht* (Berlin: Springer-Verlag, 1981), 231.

[10] On the position of the Council and the Member States, see e.g. Ludwig Weber, 'External Aspects of EEC Air Transport Liberalization', 15 *Air Law* (1990), 5–6: 278; the various national reports in J. Schwarze, U. Becker, and C. Pollak (eds.), *The 1992 Challenge at National Level—Reports and Conference Proceedings 1991/1992* (Baden-Baden: Nomos, 1993); Thomas van Rijn, 'Transport Policy and Commercial Policy', in M. Maresceau (ed.), *The European Community's Commercial Policy after 1992: The Legal Dimension* (Dordrecht: Martinus Nijhoff, 1993), 255–6. For the position of the European Parliament, see Report on the legal basis of the Commission proposal for a Council decision on a consultation and authorization procedure for agreements concerning commercial aviation relations between Member States and third countries, DOC A 3–192/90 of 19 July 1990.

[11] Especially George Close, 'External Relations in the Air Transport Sector: Air Transport Policy or the Common Commercial Policy?', 27 *CML Rev.* (1990), 1: 107–27. See also, by the same author, 'External Competence for Air Policy in the Third Phase: Trade Policy or Transport Policy?', 15 *Air Law* (1990), 5/6: 295–305 and id. in P. D. Dagtoglou, J. M. Balfour, and J. Stuyck (eds.), *European Air Law Association*, iii: *Second Annual Conference* (Deventer: Kluwer, 1991), 31–44. See also R. Barents, 'Milieu en interne markt', 41 *SEW* (1993), 1: 10 and 14–16 and 'The Internal Market Unlimited: Some Observations on the Legal Basis of Community Legislation', 30 *CML Rev.* (1993), 1: 98.

external Community competence in the field of aviation can be built.[12] This thesis consequently dictates that such a competence only exists in so far as is necessary in the framework of the implementation of the internal Community transport policy.[13] The Commission, on the other hand, does not deny that there is an external competence based on Article 84 (2), but claims that commercial aspects are covered by the CCP. The implied powers doctrine would only apply to other aspects of aviation relations with third countries, such as social, environmental, technical, and security issues.[14]

In Chapter 1 the basic differences between the Community's competence in the context of the CCP and implied powers were examined.[15] The question of external competence in the sector of civil aviation is an outstanding example of these differences, and therefore offers a most interesting case study.

This question is not academic. If the Commission's reasoning is correct, then the effects on air transport relations with third countries are momentous. Member States would in principle lose all authority to conclude bilateral agreements with third countries dealing with commercial aspects of air transport[16] —which is precisely the core of all the existing agreements. That would probably not be the case if the Community's external competence only existed by virtue of an implied power offered by Article 84 (2) of the Treaty.

Moreover, if it is accepted that the Community's power is based upon the EC Treaty provisions relating to the CCP, there can be little doubt that the scope of this power is extensive and clear-cut, encompassing the essence of external relations in the field of civil aviation. It covers all commercial aspects of external aviation relations, including questions such as market access, pricing, and capacity determination.[17] Nevertheless, it has been objected that 'it would be extremely difficult to disentangle the purely commercial aspects of the common transport policy from its other aspects. There would be considerable demarcation disputes'.[18] As an example, the regulation of computer reservation systems is mentioned, which aims at protecting the consumer, preserving fair competition, and regulating market access.[19]

For some measures or agreements there may indeed be demarcation

---

[12] On implied powers, see *supra* Ch. 1, pp. 35–41.   [13] Cf. *infra.*

[14] COM (90) 17 final, paras. 18–27.   [15] See p. 45.

[16] But the Commission recognizes that it cannot, for the moment, replace the Member States in this respect. Hence, the Commission's proposal only aims at an authorization and consultation procedure, as a first phase. Nevertheless, it is clear that the final say will rest with the Community, and no longer with the Member States, see COM (90) 17 final. See also 'Air Transport Relations with Third Countries', Communication from the Commission to the Council, COM (92) 434 final of 21 Oct. 1992, containing modifications to the proposals of COM (90) 17 final. The substance of the policies proposed by the Commission in these two documents is discussed *infra*, pp. 109–16.

[17] COM (90) 17, para. 22.

[18] Close, 'External Relations in the Air Transport Sector ... ', *supra* n. 11, p. 121.

[19] Ibid. 120.

problems (as there are with the scope of any specific competence). But there are few similar problems for the main 'target' of a Community competence in aviation matters based on Article 113: the bilateral agreements which the Member States have concluded with third countries are first and foremost of a commercial nature. They specify traffic rights, they designate the carriers that are allowed to exercise these rights, and they contain provisions on capacity and pricing. That is the core of these agreements,[20] and it is commercial beyond any dispute. Furthermore, these agreements are themselves the core of external relations in the air transport field. This is due to the international framework which governs civil aviation, based on the Chicago Convention of 1944.[21] This framework is built on the principle that each State has sovereign power over its air space, and it therefore necessitates the conclusion of agreements in order to make air transport possible. For as long as this Chicago Convention system remains intact there will be a need for international agreements in which traffic rights are exchanged, and these will continue to be the pith of each country's external aviation relations. Therefore, it is not very difficult to ascertain what the essence is of a Common Commercial Policy in air transport. It is precisely this system of exchange of traffic rights with third countries.

By contrast, an external competence based on implied powers is much less clear-cut and may be a lot more narrow. In Chapter 1 it was explained that there are two types of implied powers.[22] According to the *AETR* type, the Community has the exclusive competence to conclude agreements which 'affect' internal rules. For civil aviation, the rules in question are those of the third package relating to the licensing of air carriers, access to intra-Community routes, and fares and capacity.[23] From a legal point of view, a bilateral agreement between a Member State and a third country on traffic between these countries does not affect the said rules, which only relate to intra-Community air transport. It is only if one defends a wider interpretation of the term 'affect' that an *AETR* type competence could be envisaged. But then the competence may become extremely wide, since there are a lot of external policies which may affect the operation of the internal rules on civil aviation. It would seem that such an external competence would almost be without borders.

On the other hand, the Opinion 1/76 type of implied powers exists whenever that is necessary for achieving a specific objective of the Community. Here, too, the scope of an external competence in the field of civil aviation cannot be easily determined. The assessment of what is necessary can in the final analysis

[20] See for example the Bermuda II type bilateral agreement, printed in Shawcross and Beaumont, *Air Law* (London: Butterworths, 1990), 4th edn., Vol. ii.
[21] For a concise description of the international regulatory system, see OECD, *Deregulation and Airline Competition* (Paris: OECD, 1988), 26–30.
[22] See p. 39.   [23] See *supra* n. 6.

only be the result of a political judgment. There are of course arguments for saying that the internal market necessitates a fully-fledged external policy. They are, by the way, basically the same as those in favour of a CCP for civil aviation, namely to prevent distortion of competition in the internal market. But these are only arguments, open to debate.

In consequence it can be said that an external competence of the Community in the field of civil aviation, based on implied powers, leaves a lot of discretion to the Council, the Community's main legislative body, which is composed of the Member States—which for the moment exercise external competences in this field.[24] By contrast, if the commercial policy qualification is correct, the Community is required to develop a genuine external policy of its own, since that is within its exclusive competence. There is a lot less political discretion in such a case.

The analysis below starts by charting the position of the provisions of the EC Treaty on air transport within the general system of this Treaty. Such an analysis reveals that, at first sight, there are good reasons for considering commercial aspects of external aviation relations as coming under the CCP. Nevertheless, serious arguments have been put forward against such a view. These arguments have to be closely examined.

Air transport in the EC Treaty

According to Article 3 (*f*) of the Treaty the activities of the Community include 'a common policy in the sphere of transport'. The provisions on this policy are situated in Title IV of the 'Community Policies', after the Titles on free movement of goods, agriculture, and free movement of persons, services, and capital. Article 74 lays down the basic principle that '[t]he objectives of this Treaty shall, in matters governed by this Title, be pursued by Member States within the framework of a common transport policy'. The provisions that follow incorporate specific rules and objectives for the development of this policy. However, these do not automatically apply to sea and air transport. Article 84 (2) states that 'The Council may, acting by a qualified majority, decide whether, to what extent and by what procedure appropriate provisions may be laid down for sea and air transport. The procedural provisions of Article 75 (1) and (3) shall apply.' Because of this second paragraph, it has in the past been argued that no other provisions of the Treaty (in general) apply to sea and air transport, unless the Council decides otherwise. In other words,

---

[24] That is confirmed by the position recently adopted by the Council, see *Agence Europe*, No. 5941, 17 Mar. 1993, p. 12. The Council maintains that Art. 84 (2) of the Treaty is the appropriate legal basis for external relations in the field of civil aviation and at the same time wishes to keep intact the system of national bilateral agreements, seeing room for Community agreements only in certain specific cases.

these sectors would in the absence of action by the Council remain outside the scope of the Treaty.[25]

However, in 1974 the European Court of Justice ruled otherwise in the so-called *French Seamen*'s case, in which it held that sea and air transport remain 'subject to the general rules of the Treaty'.[26] In order to reach this conclusion, the Court first examined the position of the provisions on transport in the system of the Treaty. It found that the Treaty aims at encompassing all economic activities. Therefore, the basic provisions on the establishment of the common market can only be rendered inapplicable 'as a result of express provision in the Treaty'.[27] Since Article 74 refers to the objectives of the Treaty, '[f]ar from involving a departure from these fundamental rules . . . , the object of the rules relating to the common transport policy is to implement and complement them by means of common action'.[28] This is confirmed by the existence of Article 61 (1) of the Treaty, which provides that '[f]reedom to provide services in the field of transport shall be governed by the provisions of the Title relating to transport'. Such a special exemption would not be necessary if the general rules of the Treaty did not apply to transport. Lastly, the Court determined the scope of Article 84 (2) which '[f]ar from excluding the application of the Treaty to [sea and air transport], provides only that the special provisions of the Title relating to transport shall not automatically apply to them'.[29]

The *French Seamen*'s case concerned the Treaty rules on freedom of establishment. One could perhaps have argued that the 'general rules' to which the Court referred only encompassed the basic freedoms (except freedom to provide services, see Article 61 (1)), and not the provisions on the policy of the Community (Part Three of the original EEC Treaty, including among other things the CCP).[30] In the *Lucas Asjes* case, also referred to as *Nouvelles Frontières*, the Court unequivocally rejected such a reasoning by deciding that the competition rules also apply to the transport sector.[31] In this ruling, it first summarized its views on the position of the Common Transport Policy in the system of the EC Treaty, then recalled Article 61 and added: 'However, no other provision in the Treaty makes its application to the transport sector subject to the realization of a common transport policy.'[32] The rest of the judgment deals with competition rules, but the passage quoted seems to leave little doubt that the whole EC Treaty as such applies to the transport sector.

[25] On this thesis, see Elisabeth Estienne-Henrotte, *L'application des règles générales du Traité de Rome au transport aérien* (Brussels: Éditions de l'ULB, 1988), 39–45, and Weber, *supra* n. 9, pp. 128–9.
[26] Case 167/73, *Commission v. France*, [1974] ECR 359, at 371.
[27] [1974] ECR 269.
[28] [1974] ECR 370.
[29] [1974] ECR 371.
[30] Estienne-Henrotte, *supra* n. 25, p. 52.
[31] Joined Cases 209 to 213/84, *Ministère public v. Lucas Asjes and others*, [1986] ECR 1425.
[32] [1986] ECR 1465.

This is confirmed by the Opinion delivered by Advocate-General Lenz in this case.[33]

Why then should the CCP not apply to the transport sector? In the light of the Court's case-law, the only valid objection which could be put forward against such application seems to be the view that trade in services *in general* cannot come under the provisions on the CCP. Above it was submitted that this view is not correct.[34] However, this is not the only objection which has been raised against the application of the CCP to civil aviation. Other counter-arguments are examined below. Most of them come down to characterizing the Common Transport Policy, in spite of the above-described case-law, as a sectoral policy encompassing in an exclusive manner all aspects of the regulation of transport activities.

The arguments against the application of the CCP

Case-law on transport

A first argument which has been put forward against the application of the CCP to air transport relates to the Court's case-law on external relations in the transport sector, especially Opinion 1/76.[35] In this case, the Court found that the Community could enter into an international agreement concerning inland waterway transport on the basis of Article 75 of the EC Treaty. Attention has been drawn to the fact that the subject of this Agreement, namely the creation of a European Laying-up Fund for Inland Waterway Vessels, concerned the question of market access, which is of course a highly commercial matter. From this fact it has been concluded that the Court considers Article 75 as 'the proper legal basis for the conclusion of commercial agreements by the Community with third countries in the inland transport sector'.[36] If this were true, there would be no reason not to apply this reasoning to air transport also, with Article 84 (2) then as the appropriate legal basis.

But closer analysis of Opinion 1/76 reveals that this argument is tenuous. It is true that the European Laying-up Fund was created for allowing withdrawal of temporary excess transport capacity, by providing for financial compensation for carriers that performed such withdrawal.[37] This relates to market access. But the object of the Agreement was not to regulate market access as such. It was the creation of a Fund as an international public institution with legal personality and with independent powers (even judicial

---

[33] [1986] ECR 1443, where the Advocate-General states: 'My view is that the Court's reference to "general rules" embraced all the provisions of the Treaty other than the "special provisions" of Title IV of Part Two relating to transport'.
[34] See Ch. 1, p. 34.
[35] [1977] ECR 741. For a description of this argument, see Close, 'External Relations in the Air Transport Sector...', *supra* n. 11, pp. 119–22.
[36] Ibid. 120.   [37] [1977] ECR 744.

and financial) to organize the laying-up procedures.[38] The delegation of powers to this new institution was precisely one of the main reasons for the Commission to ask the Court for its opinion. It is clear, therefore, that the Agreement went much further than simply regulating commercial matters. Arguably, the fact that an independent institution was created brought the Agreement outside the scope of commercial policy. Consequently, there was every reason to use Article 75 as a legal basis. It should also be mentioned that, even if one considers that commercial aspects of transport relations with third countries come under Article 113, there is good authority to allow the use of Article 75 in case commercial matters are involved, provided that these matters are ancillary to the main subject of an agreement.[39]

Commercial relations with third countries were also ancillary to the Agreement on a European Laying-up Fund in another sense. The Agreement concerned the Rhine and Moselle basins, including all the Netherlands inland waterways and the German inland waterways linked to the Rhine basin. The reason why an international agreement was necessary was that Switzerland had to be included. But it goes without saying that the Agreement would mainly regulate inland waterway transport activity *within* the Community. This was obviously one of the reasons why the Court considered that there was an implicit power to conclude an international agreement. Moreover, Opinion 1/76 was issued at a time when services transactions were not yet looked at from a trade perspective.[40] It would have been very peculiar for the Court to run ahead of the international developments which have taken place since then, the most important being the inclusion of services in the GATT Uruguay Round.

As a result, it is submitted that Opinion 1/76 is insufficient authority for concluding that the Court has made it clear that commercial relations with third countries in the transport sector do not come under Article 113 of the EC Treaty.

Case-law on the Common Agricultural Policy

A second argument is drawn from the Court's case-law on the Common Agricultural Policy (CAP), more specifically on the choice of legal basis of certain agricultural measures.[41] It is in this respect alleged that a comparison with the CAP, the other sectoral policy in the EC Treaty, can give indications on the scope of the Community's competences in the framework of the Common Transport Policy. There are two cases (both *UK* v. *Council*) in which it was maintained that Article 100, EC Treaty (on approximation of laws) should have been used as the legal basis for certain measures, next to Article 43

[38] [1977] ECR 745. [39] See Opinion 1/78, [1979] ECR 2917.
[40] See Ch. 1, p. 37. Cf. van Rijn, *supra* n. 10, p. 270.
[41] See again Close, 'External Relations in the Air Transport Sector...', *supra* n. 11, pp. 122–5.

(part of the agricultural chapter). These measures concerned trade in meat treated with hormonal substances (the famous hormones directive) and the protection of egg-laying hens kept in battery cages.[42] In both cases the Court ruled that Article 43 was the appropriate legal basis, and that there was no need to have recourse to Article 100. It is doubtful, however, whether the relationship between Article 43 and Article 100 is able to throw any light on the issue of external competence in transport matters. Admittedly, it is true that the Court considered 'the chapter on agriculture as a *lex specialis* which had precedence over the more general rules of the Treaty'.[43] But with respect to the relationship with Article 100, this is only natural. Article 100 concerns the establishment of the common market, and is a general provision in this respect. The chapter on agriculture also concerns the establishment of the common market—specifically in agricultural products. It is only logical, therefore, that measures relating to the establishment of the common market in those products be based on the provisions within this chapter, and not on the more general Article 100. Article 113, on the other hand, concerns the Community's external competences, a matter which is not explicitly covered by the chapters on agriculture and transport, and which is less directly related to the establishment of the common market.

A third case, *Commission* v. *Council*, is more important.[44] It concerned a directive aimed at facilitating trade in animal glands and organs, including blood, for pharmaceutical manufacturing purposes.[45] This directive relates both to importation from non-member countries and to intra-Community trade. It had been adopted on the basis of Articles 43, 100, and 113, a decision which was disputed by the Commission, arguing that only Article 43 should have been referred to. The Court first reiterated the above-mentioned principles on the relationship between Articles 43 and 100, finding that also in this case Article 43 was the only appropriate legal basis. Then it delivered its views on the use of Article 113. It held that:

Recourse to Article 113 as a legal basis for the contested directive was justified by the Council on the ground that the directive aims to facilitate importation of the products concerned into the Community.

In that connection, it must first be stated that the purpose of the contested directive is to provide uniform rules on the conditions under which the products concerned may be marketed, not only when they originate from non-member countries but also in intra-Community trade.

It must further be pointed out that the mere fact that the contested directive also concerns imports into the Community does not suffice to make Article 113 applicable. It is apparent from Article 40 (3) of the Treaty that measures taken in the context of the

---

[42] Case 68/86, [1988] ECR 855 and Case 131/86, [1988] ECR 905.
[43] Close, 'External Relations in the Air Transport Sector...', *supra* n. 11, p. 123.
[44] Case 131/87, [1989] ECR 3743.
[45] Council Directive 87/64, OJ L 34/52 of 5 Feb. 1987.

Common Agricultural Policy may also affect importation and exportation of the products concerned.

The contested directive accordingly falls within the field of application of Article 43 of the EC Treaty and in consequence the Council was not justified in adopting it on the basis of Articles 100 and 113 of the Treaty.[46]

From this passage, it has been concluded that the Court has decided 'that action taken within the context of the common agricultural policy is not to be based on Article 113 merely because it concerns imports and exports to the Community',[47] and that the chapter on agriculture, as a *lex specialis*, prevails over Article 113 in so far as external elements, also of a commercial nature, are concerned. Furthermore, it has been said that these conclusions are 'highly suggestive' in relation to the Common Transport Policy, the other sectoral policy in the Treaty.

Arguably, however, this inference goes beyond the Court's findings. Although the Court's reasoning is rather succinct, two arguments can be detected which led to the conclusion that the contested directive should have been based only on Article 43. The first one seems to be that the main object of the directive is not to regulate trade with third countries, but 'to provide uniform rules on the conditions under which the products concerned may be marketed'. The argument therefore goes more in the direction of considering the directive as *not* being a commercial policy measure, than in the direction of confirming that commercial policy measures in the agricultural sector come under the provisions on the CAP, and not under those of the CCP. This is confirmed by the next sentence, introducing the second argument:

'It must further be pointed out that the mere fact that the contested directive also concerns imports into the Community does not suffice to make Article 113 applicable'.

This sentence does not exclude, as a matter of principle, the use of Article 113 in the agricultural field at all; it only says that Article 113 is not applicable to every measure which '*also* concerns imports'. And the Court finds support for this statement in Article 40 (3) of the Treaty, which provides that a common organization of agricultural markets 'may include ... common machinery for stabilizing imports and exports'.

It is submitted that the *Commission* v. *Council* case actually deals with the borderline between the scope of the CAP and of the CCP, and does not in any way introduce the principle that genuine commercial policy measures relating to agricultural products do not come under Article 113. As a result, this ruling cannot provide indications on the Community's external competences in the transport sector and their legal basis.[48]

---

[46] [1989] ECR 3771.

[47] Close, 'External Relations in the Air Transport Sector...', *supra* n. 11, p. 124.

[48] Community practice shows that international agreements on trade in agricultural products are often concluded on the basis of Article 113, see C. S. Pisuisse, 'De bevoegdheid van de

The intentions of the authors of the EEC Treaty

A third argument against the application of the CCP with respect to air transport refers to the intentions of the authors of the EEC Treaty. It is maintained that these authors wished to keep transport, and especially sea and air transport, outside the general scope of the Treaty, until the Council decides otherwise. The reasons behind these intentions relate to the specificity of the transport sector.[49] This argument is untenable, and there is even no need to examine whether these intentions really existed or not. The Court of Justice does not consider reference to the intentions of the authors of the Treaty as an important method of interpreting EEC Treaty provisions. Instead, it relies much more on a teleological approach.[50] Moreover, as was explained above the Court has made it unequivocally clear in the *French Seamen*'s case that the Treaty is fully applicable to transport and that 'the object of the rules relating to the common transport policy is to implement and complement [the fundamental rules of the Treaty] by means of common action'.[51] Therefore, no legal value can be attached to the alleged intentions of the authors of the Treaty concerning transport.

The relationship with freedom to provide air transport services within the Community

The most delicate question when assessing whether commercial aspects of external aviation relations come under the provisions on the Common Commercial Policy lies in the relationship with the freedom to provide air transport services *within* the Community. Above it was argued that, if one accepts that trade in services forms part of the Community's commercial policy, there seem to be no reasons for not extending this also to transport services. But it was also argued (in Chapter 1) that there should be some parallelism in the scope of trade in services with third countries, coming under the CCP, and the scope of free movement of services within the Community.[52] In this respect, air transport poses a special problem, in that Article 61 (1) of the Treaty exempts transport from the provisions on free movement of services and thus makes the realization of such free movement dependent on measures taken in the

Europese Gemeenschap met betrekking tot de liberalisatie van de internationale dienstverlening', *SEW* (1987), 3: 187; Claus-Dieter Ehlermann, 'The Scope of Article 113 of the EEC Treaty', in *Mélanges offerts à Pierre-Henri Teitgen* (Paris: Pedone, 1984), 163; Jacques H. J. Bourgeois, in H. van der Groeben, J. Thiesing, and C.-D. Ehlermann (eds.), *Kommentar zum EWG-Vertrag*, 4th edn. (Baden-Baden: Nomos, 1991), 3176.

[49] Close, 'External Relations in the Air Transport Sector...', *supra* n. 11, p. 121.
[50] Cf. H. Kutscher, 'Methods of Interpretation as Seen by a Judge at the Court of Justice', in *Reports of the 1976 Judicial and Academic Conference* (Luxembourg: Court of Justice, 1976), p. I-21/22.
[51] [1974] ECR 370.   [52] See Ch. 1, pp. 29–32.

framework of the Common Transport Policy. If one maintains the doctrine of a degree of parallelism between the scope of the CCP and the scope of the Community's internal freedoms, one could conclude that transport does not come under the provisions on the CCP, since free movement of services is not automatically guaranteed by the Treaty. On a more political level the argument has been raised that the Commission is putting the cart before the horse by claiming an exclusive Community competence with respect to commercial aspects of external aviation relations while there is not yet a genuine internal market in civil aviation (which was the case when the Commission issued its proposals).[53]

However, it is not sufficient in this respect simply to refer to the existence of Article 61 (1). One should also examine to what degree the development of the Community's civil aviation policy has established a real internal market, including in the first place the freedom to provide services.[54] Clearly, with the adoption of the third package this freedom has been realized almost entirely.[55] Therefore, if the doctrine of parallelism referred to above is maintained, this loss of authority should at the level of external relations be translated into a widened scope of the CCP, encompassing commercial aspects of aviation relations.

It will perhaps be objected that this view makes the scope of the CCP dependent on whether the Community has taken certain actions or not, and not on a (more or less) definitive interpretation of the Treaty provisions on the CCP as such. This may be true, but it is in line with what the Court of Justice ruled in Opinion 1/78, in which it held that:

Article 113 empowers the Community to formulate a commercial 'policy', based on 'uniform principles' thus showing that the question of external trade must be governed from a wide point of view and not only having regard to the administration of precise systems such as customs and quantitative restrictions. The same conclusion may be deduced from the fact that the enumeration in Article 113 of the subjects covered by commercial policy (changes in tariff rates, the conclusion of tariff and trade agreements, the achievement of uniformity in measures of liberalization, export policy and measures to protect trade) is conceived as a non-exhaustive enumeration which must not, as such, close the door to the application in a Community context of any other process intended to regulate external trade. A restrictive interpretation of the concept of common commercial policy would risk causing disturbances in intra-Community trade by reason of the disparities which would then exist in certain sectors of economic relations with non-member countries.[56]

[53] See for example Weber, *supra* n. 9, p. 233.
[54] Moreover, one should also bear in mind that freedom of establishment is also an element which determines the freedom to provide transport services, and that the Treaty provisions on establishment are fully applicable to the air transport sector, cf. John M. Balfour, 'Freedom to Provide Air Transport Services in the EEC', 14 *ELR* (1989), 1: 30–46.
[55] Only for cabotage is there a transitional regime running until 1997, see Art. 3 of Regulation 2408/92, *supra* n. 6.
[56] [1979] ECR 2913. See also Ch. 1, p. 21.

A Common Commercial Policy for civil aviation

The arguments against developing a Common Commercial Policy in the field
of civil aviation do not carry enough weight. Things might have been different
if the internal market programme had not existed, if the Common Transport
Policy had developed in a different direction, continuing to emphasize the
specificity of the transport sector. However, the internal market programme is
about liberalizing service transactions (one is inclined to say services trade)
within the Community, *also* in the field of civil aviation. Instead of emphasizing the specificity of the transport sector, the programme aims at subjecting
this sector to the normal disciplines of free markets, not only as regards the
provision of services as such but also in the framework of competition policy.
Therefore, in terms of the completion and establishment of the internal market
the question of the external dimension is the same, whether applied to civil
aviation or to other services sectors.

In Chapter 1, the basic motives for developing a CCP in the field of services
trade were analysed.[57] It may suffice to recall here that these motives are very
much relevant for civil aviation. There is both the danger of deflection of
trade[58] and distortion of competition, the latter obviously being the most
notable one. The internal market programme has established a 'level playing
field' for competition between air carriers within the Community, with the
exception, however, of the external regime. Here, the Member States continue
to be able to distort the conditions of competition within the internal market if
they go on concluding bilateral agreements with third countries on the exchange of traffic rights. Field studies as well as press reports highlight that such
distortions are liable to occur, since the Member States are competing heavily
with a view to obtaining as favourable opportunities for external traffic as
possible for their national carriers, especially in bilateral negotiations with the
largest non-member countries, such as the United States.[59] In this connection
one should also bear in mind the economic importance of traffic to and from
third countries. For the air carriers, such traffic may even be more vital than
traffic within the Community.[60]

The fact that the commercial aspects of external relations in the field of civil
aviation come within the scope of the Community's exclusive competence by
virtue of the EC Treaty provisions on the CCP does not necessarily mean that
the bilateral agreements concluded by the Member States have suddenly
become illegal. The exercise of this competence can only be gradual. That is
recognized by the Commission in its proposals, the substance of which is

---

[57] See pp. 24–8.   [58] See Ch. 1, pp. 25–6.
[59] See Piet Eeckhout, in 'Belgium', in *The 1992 Challenge at National Level, supra* n. 10, p. 77;
' "Open skies" accord could set trend', *Financial Times*, 7 Sept. 1992, p. 4.
[60] See COM (92) 434 final, *supra* n. 16, p. 4.

examined below,[61] and it is in line with previous practice in the field of commercial policy. Indeed, as will be shown in Chapter 5, also in the field of trade in goods it takes quite some time before the CCP completely replaces all national policies. That is not to say that in the services sector the evolution has to be as slow. But a transitional regime is clearly desirable. What is important, however, is that the principle of full and exclusive Community competence is generally recognized.

Moreover, there may be room for a more extensive involvement of the Member States in implementing the CCP developed in the field of civil aviation than there is in the field of trade in goods. From a legal point of view this can be justified. Article 113 of the Treaty requires the development of a *uniform* commercial policy. With respect to trade in goods, achieving uniformity depends upon the details of the rules governing external trade. That may be less so in the field of services. For civil aviation, for example, what is important is that the conditions of competition concerning external traffic are equalized. That does not necessarily require that the Community regulates each and every aspect of external relations.

The European Community, Cabotage, and the Chicago Convention

As is well known, the principle of cabotage is one of the cornerstones of the regulation of transport activities throughout the world. According to this principle, the provision of transport services within the territory of a State is reserved for national carriers. With respect to air transport this principle is laid down in Article 7 of the Chicago Convention, which provides that:

Each contracting State shall have the right to refuse permission to the aircraft of other contracting States to take on in its territory passengers, mail and cargo carried for remuneration or hire and destined for another point within its territory. Each contracting State undertakes not to enter into any arrangements which specifically grant any such privilege on an exclusive basis to any other State or an airline of any other State, and not to obtain any such exclusive privilege from any other State.

For the future development of the Community's air transport policy this provision poses problems on two levels. First, the second sentence of Article 7 prohibits the granting of cabotage rights to other countries on an exclusive basis. But the Community only opens up cabotage, within the framework of the third package, for Community air carriers.[62] Secondly, the question arises whether it is possible under the Chicago Convention to consider the Community as a 'cabotage area', in which traffic would in principle be reserved for Community carriers. The problem is that Article 7 only speaks of 'States'.

---

[61] pp. 109–14.   [62] See Art. 3 of Regulation 2408/92, *supra* n. 6.

Does it (or any other provisions of the Chicago Convention) allow for cabotage areas that cover the territories of several States? This question is not hypothetical since the Commission proposed that such a policy be adopted.[63] Both these issues are examined below. But before doing so, the status of the Chicago Convention in Community law should first be defined.

The status of the Chicago Convention in Community law

The Chicago Convention was signed on 7 December 1944. All the Member States are parties to the Convention,[64] but the Community is not since the Convention is older than the EC Treaty. At first sight, therefore, one could conclude that the Community is not bound by the provisions of the Convention, and consequently cannot be restricted thereby when developing its air transport policy. However, closer analysis is necessary in order to check this far-reaching inference.[65]

The EC Treaty is not too eloquent on the status in Community law of agreements which the Member States have concluded with third countries before the entry into force of the Treaty. There is only Article 234, which contains two basic rules. First, rights and obligations arising from such agreements are not affected by the provisions of the EC Treaty. This is simply the expression of the *pacta sunt servanda* principle of international law, and does not deal with the status of these agreements in Community law.[66] Secondly,

[t]o the extent that such agreements are not compatible with this Treaty, the Member State or States concerned shall take all appropriate steps to eliminate the incompatibilities established. Member States shall, where necessary, assist each other to this end and shall, where appropriate, adopt a common attitude.

This, too, does not deal with the said status. Moreover, there is certainly no clear-cut incompatibility of the Chicago Convention with the EC Treaty, although it can be said that the aims of the common air transport policy tend to create some frictions with the rules of the Convention, based on national sovereignty. The issue of cabotage as dealt with below reveals this. Consequently, the possible application of Article 234 (2) will also have to be examined. However, this does not yet answer the question whether the Community is in any way bound by the Convention.

In the *Burgoa* case the Court of Justice held that Article 234 implies a duty on the part of the Community's institutions not to impede the performance of the obligations of a Member State stemming from a prior agreement.

---

[63] COM (90) 17 final.

[64] For a list of parties, see Shawcross and Beaumont, *supra* n. 20.

[65] See also for such an analysis Weber, *supra* n. 9, pp. 283–6.

[66] Ernst-Ulrich Petersmann, in *Kommentar zum EWG-Vertrag, supra* n. 48, p. 5730. Cf. A. T. S. Leenen, *Gemeenschapsrecht en volkenrecht* (Deventer: Kluwer, 1984), pp. 221–3.

However, that duty of the Community is directed only to permitting the Member State concerned to perform its obligations under the prior agreement and does not bind the Community as regards the non-member in question.[67]

But there is also case-law which does state that the Community is bound by a multilateral agreement concluded before the entry into force of the EC Treaty. In *International Fruit Company*[68] the Court of Justice had to rule on the status of the General Agreement on Tariffs and Trade in Community law. As is the case with the Chicago Convention, the GATT precedes the EC and was never signed by the latter, but only by the Member States. From this purely legal point of view, therefore, the GATT and the Chicago Convention are perfectly comparable. Nevertheless, the Court's judgment shows that there are also a lot of important differences.

The Court first sets out that the Member States wished to continue to observe the provisions of the General Agreement when the EC was established. This is clear from the EC Treaty: Article 110 embraces the same aims as the General Agreement and Article 234 (1) contains the *pacta sunt servanda* principle (see above). Also the fact that the Member States presented the EC Treaty to the CONTRACTING PARTIES in the framework of Article XXIV of GATT bears this out. Further, the Court observes that the Community conducts tariff and trade policy because this power was transferred to it by the Member States.[69]

Since the entry into force of the EEC Treaty and more particularly, since the setting up of the common external tariff, the transfer of powers which has occurred in the relations between Member States and the Community has been put into concrete form in different ways within the framework of the General Agreement and has been recognized by the other Contracting Parties.

In particular, since that time the Community, acting through its own institutions, has appeared as a partner in the tariff negotiations and as a party to the agreements of all types concluded within the framework of the General Agreement, in accordance with the provisions of Article 114 of the EEC Treaty which provides that the tariff and trade agreements 'shall be concluded ... on behalf of the Community'.

It therefore appears that, in so far as under the EEC Treaty the Community has assumed the powers previously exercised by Member States in the area governed by the General Agreement, the provisions of that Agreement have the effect of binding the Community.[70]

It is clear that the Community is much less involved in the operation of the Chicago Convention than in that of the GATT.[71] First of all, the Community

[67] Case 812/79, *Attorney General* v. *Burgoa*, [1980] ECR 2787, at 2803. See also Ch. 2, p. 73, and Ch. 9, pp. 317–18.
[68] Case 21–24/72, *International Fruit Company NV* v. *Produktschap voor groenten en fruit*, [1972] ECR 1219.
[69] [1972] ECR 1226–7.
[70] Paras. 16–18, [1972] ECR 1227.   [71] Petersmann, *supra* n. 66, pp. 5744–5.

has only very recently started to exercise its power to adopt a common air transport policy. By contrast, with respect to tariff and trade policies covered by the GATT it started to do so as soon as the Community was created. Moreover, there is no sign yet of the Community taking over the role of the Member States in the International Civil Aviation Organization (ICAO), created by the Chicago Convention.[72] Likewise, the other parties to this Convention do not consider the Community as the Member States' successor in this respect. All this makes it very difficult to infer from *International Fruit Company* that the Community is bound by the Chicago Convention. But perhaps there are other arguments for assuming such a binding effect.

Weber has introduced the concept of an indirect binding, based on the principle that, as a corollary to the fact that the Member States should respect the EC Treaty, the Community institutions should also take into account the Member States' interests and should not make it impossible for them to comply with their international commitments. In support of such a principle Article 6 of the original EEC Treaty is cited.[73] Perhaps there is more to be said for the line of reasoning proposed by Petersmann, who deduces from the *pacta sunt servanda* principle expressed in Article 234 (1) that the Community is under an obligation to observe as much as possible multilateral agreements dating from before the EC Treaty when implementing Community law.[74]

Moreover, there is a degree of difference between for example a simple bilateral agreement between a Member State and a third country and a multilateral agreement such as the Chicago Convention governing civil aviation world-wide. The Community cannot just ignore this multilateral framework when adopting and implementing its own air transport policy. Therefore, if there are no strict legal grounds for assuming that the Community is bound by the Chicago Convention, there are surely policy arguments that militate in favour of some degree of due respect for the provisions of the Convention. After all, air transport is very much a global industry, and as a result it is impossible to separate the Community's internal market and its regulation from the network of traffic with third countries.[75]

This does not necessarily mean that within the Community's legal order the provisions of the Convention could be invoked against internal air transport measures that conflict with them. It is submitted that the

---

[72] The Community only has observer status in ICAO, see Jürgen Erdmenger in *Kommentar zum EWG-Vertrag, supra* n. 48, p. 1199.

[73] Weber, *supra* n. 9, pp. 283 and 286. Article 6 (2) provided that '[t]he institutions of the Community shall take care not to prejudice the internal and external financial stability of the Member States'. Whether such language can be used in support of Weber's argument is debatable. Moreover, the provision has been deleted by the Treaty on European Union.

[74] Petersmann, *supra* n. 66, pp. 5736–7. Cf. also J. Megret *et al., Le droit de la Communauté économique européenne,* xii: *Relations extérieures* (Brussels: Éditions de l'ULB, 1980), 81.

[75] See COM (92) 434 final, *supra* n. 16, pp. 4–6.

Community is not bound by the Convention to the extent that this could invalidate Community law.[76]

Opening up cabotage within the Member States

As was mentioned, Article 7 of the Chicago Convention prohibits the granting of cabotage rights on an exclusive basis. Consequently, it poses problems to the opening up of cabotage traffic within the Community, which is limited to Community air carriers. The prohibition of Article 7 is somewhat paradoxical in that it introduces a most-favoured-nation principle in a field characterized by bilateralism and not by free trade.[77] Partly because of this paradox, the scope of Article 7 is not uncontested. According to the stricter doctrine, this provision leaves no room whatsoever for granting cabotage rights on an exclusive basis. But some also defend a more flexible interpretation, stating that there is room for doing so, provided that the grant does not 'specifically' mention the fact that it is exclusive.[78]

One would digress if one were to examine all the arguments which have been put forward in favour of one or other of these interpretations.[79] Moreover, this would be of little relevance since even the flexible interpretation does not accommodate the opening-up of cabotage traffic within the Community.[80] Indeed, this liberalization is couched in terms of exclusivity: it only applies to Community air carriers.[81] Actually, and this is perhaps overlooked by specialists in the field of air law, the language of Article 7 is totally unadapted to the Community's case. When cabotage traffic is liberalized it is not through a reciprocal 'grant' by the twelve Member States, parties to the Chicago Convention, but through a decision of the Council of the European Communities. The Council is not an intergovernmental organization. It is one of

[76] Compare with Case C-286/90, *Anklagemyndigheden* v. *Poulsen*, Judgment of 24 Nov. 1992, not yet published, where the Court held, in relation to a dispute concerning fishing, that the Community's competences must be exercised while respecting international law, and examined the provisions of a number of conventions relating to the law of the sea which were regarded as codifying customary international law in this field.

[77] According to Peter P. C. Haanappel it is not the Chicago Convention as such which promotes bilateralism, but rather State practice, see 'The External Aviation Relations of the European Economic Community and of EEC Member States into the Twenty-first Century', 14 *Air Law* (1989), 3: 141.

[78] See among others Jan Ernst C. de Groot, 'Cabotage Liberalization in the European Economic Community and Article 7 of the Chicago Convention', 14 *Annals of Air and Space Law* (1989), 157–61; Weber, *supra* n. 9, p. 280 and *supra* n. 10, pp. 277–87; Peter P. C. Haanappel, *supra* n. 77, p. 138; Joseph Z. Gertler, 'Towards a New, Rational and Fair Exchange of Opportunities for Airlines', in P. P. C. Haanappel *et al.* (eds.), *EEC Air Transport Policy and Regulation, and their Implications for North America* (Deventer: Kluwer, 1990), 200–2; Pablo Mendes de Leon, *Cabotage in Air Transport Regulation* (Dordrecht: Martinus Nijhoff, 1992), 37–52.

[79] See especially de Groot on this, *supra* n. 78, pp. 158–60.

[80] Cf. Haanappel, *supra* n. 77, p. 138.   [81] See n. 6.

the institutions of the Community, with supranational powers. Article 7 provides that '[e]ach contracting State undertakes not to enter into any arrangements which specifically grant any such privilege on an exclusive basis to any other State'. Such language does not cover a supranational Council decision.

The fundamental problem with the MFN rule of Article 7 is that there is no exception, as is often the case in international economic law, for customs unions such as the Community.[82] This is a problem which has to be addressed at the level of ICAO, the body created by the Chicago Convention.

How does one solve the issue? Haanappel has observed that in practice it would be very difficult to modify the text of the Convention, because of the two-thirds majority that is needed. Instead, he pleads for an intervention by the ICAO Council, defining the scope of Article 7 with respect to cases such as that of the EC.[83] This may be a workable solution and the Community could, through action by the Member States, try to obtain such an intervention. As was mentioned, it can be inferred from Article 234 (2) of the EC Treaty that the Member States are under an obligation to try to eliminate the inconsistencies between the Chicago Convention and the Community's air transport policy. To this end they should, in the words of Article 234 (2), 'assist each other ... and ... adopt a common attitude'. Perhaps such a common attitude could lead to a recognition by the other parties to the Convention that the Community has taken over much of the Member States' powers to regulate civil aviation, and to a role for the Community as such within ICAO. In any case, it can be argued that it would be wrong for the Community simply to ignore the language of Article 7 and the problems it poses to opening up cabotage in the Member States. As was said above, the Community should demonstrate some degree of due respect for the provisions of the Convention, in the sense that it should show its willingness to find a solution to these problems.

A European cabotage area

In its communication on Community relations with third countries in aviation matters the Commission proposes that the Community's air transport market be considered a cabotage area, defined as follows:

This means that all the traffic within and between Member States is considered to be equivalent to cabotage and is in principle reserved for Community carriers. This does not imply that, in the absence of equivalent market opportunities, existing fifth

---

[82] Weber, *supra* n. 9, pp. 281–2.
[83] Haanappel, *supra* n. 77, pp. 138–40. See also de Groot, *supra* n. 78, p. 170, where he draws an analogy with a GATT waiver.

freedom rights are withdrawn. In practice this would mean that Member States are no longer competent to grant new fifth freedom traffic rights to third countries but that they will have to refer requests for such fifth freedom rights to the Commission for consideration under Community procedures according to Article 113.[84]

The Commission discerns a number of reasons for adopting such a policy. First, the said fifth freedom traffic competes directly with intra-Community traffic taken care of by Community carriers, and 'therefore directly influences Community legislation and trade between Member States'.[85] Secondly, this fifth freedom traffic is not limited by Community legislation, in contrast with similar traffic operations by Community carriers. Thirdly, '[t]he Community should avoid to diminish the value of the traffic rights created by the Community legislation within the internal aviation market for Community air carriers'.[86] Fourth, 'the creation of the internal market has as a logical consequence for the outside world that the Community should be considered as one entity and therefore as a cabotage area'.[87] Lastly, the Commission is anxious to create a level playing field in negotiations with third countries, especially since 'individual Member States have faced the refusal of some very large partners in aviation to grant comparable traffic rights to European carriers'.[88] Of course here the Commission implicitly refers to the United States. There is indeed an imbalance in air transport relations between the United States and the European Community. This is due to the bilateral structure of civil aviation as a result of which each Member State has its own agreement with the United States on the exchange of traffic rights. The effect of this is that US carriers can serve a lot more destinations in Europe than any European carrier can serve in the USA.[89] Moreover, the USA also reserves cabotage traffic to US carriers, and European airlines are therefore not able to operate on the internal US market. By contrast, the United States possesses quite a lot of fifth freedom rights within Europe, and its carriers therefore have a share of the European internal market.[90]

It is clear that this imbalance is one of the most important reasons behind the Commission's intention to consider the Community's internal air transport market as a cabotage area.[91] In economic terms, the stakes are indeed high. The internal US market is the most important air transport market in the

---

[84] COM (90) 17 final, *supra* n. 8, para 42.   [85] Ibid. para. 38.
[86] COM (90) 17 final, para. 39.   [87] Ibid. para. 40.   [88] Ibid. para. 41.
[89] See COM (92) 434 final, *supra* n. 16, pp. 10–13 and 56–83, for an extensive analysis of civil aviation relations between the (Member States of the) Community and the USA. See also Paul V. Mifsud, 'New Proposals for New Directions: 1992 and the GATT Approach to Trade in Air Transport Services', 13 *Air Law* (1988), 4/5: 160–4.
[90] COM (92) 434 final, p. 11.
[91] See the statements by Professor Doganis and Mr Paice before the House of Lords Select Committee on the European Communities, *Civil Aviation: A Free Market by 1992?*, Session 1989–90, 16th Report (London: HMSO, 1990), 9 and 69; de Groot, *supra* n. 78, pp. 180–1.

world, and the transatlantic market is also very significant.[92] Moreover, it is only natural for an institution such as the Commission to perceive this imbalance as a matter of concern. In most other trade areas, the Community acts as a single negotiating party in international relations, and this is not least so in relations with the United States. Furthermore, as the internal market becomes fully established it is only logical that the Community speak with one voice to an ever greater extent. Not to do so in the field of air transport would indeed almost be an anachronism from this point of view. Nevertheless, the concept of a European cabotage area raises a number of legal and trade policy questions that need to be examined.

The concept of a cabotage area, consisting of the combined territory of a number of States, does not in fact exist in the Chicago Convention framework. The Commission argues that the Convention permits regional co-operation in its Article 77, which provides that:

Nothing in this Convention shall prevent two or more contracting States from consti-tuting joint air transport operating organisations or international operating agencies and from pooling their air services on any routes or in any regions.

From this provision, the Commission deduces that the Community has the right under the Convention to develop a regional air transport policy, and that to consider the Community as a cabotage area is only a logical consequence of such a regional policy. It is questionable, however, whether the scope of Article 77 is wide enough to cover the kind of integration that is inherent in the development of the Community's common transport policy.[93] Actually, there is little need to rely on this provision for the purpose of implementing a European cabotage area. It has rightly been observed that, in the current legal framework, such an area only implies limiting fifth freedom rights for third-country carriers.[94] Such rights are granted through agreements with the countries concerned. There is nothing in the Chicago Convention that could hold the Community back (whether acting as such or through the Member States) from not granting new fifth freedom rights. Existing rights are another matter, of course, but the Commission has explicitly stated that it does not intend to challenge those.[95] In fact, the concept of an international cabotage area is not new since there are already a number of precedents, such as the Arab countries, a number of South American countries, and Air Afrique.[96]

---

[92] There is, however, also quite some scepticism on whether European carriers would be able to compete in, for example, the intra-US market, see Haanappel, *supra* n. 77, p. 140, n. 106; de Groot, *supra* n. 78, pp. 184–5.

[93] Weber, *supra* n. 9, p. 278, n. 27.

[94] de Groot, *supra* n. 78, pp. 177–8. See also H. A. Wassenbergh, 'EEC-Cabotage after 1992', 13 *Air Law* (1988), 6: 283; Weber, 'External Aspects of EEC Air Transport Liberalization', *supra* n. 10, p. 286; various witnesses in House of Lords Select Committee on the EC, *Conduct of the Community's External Aviation Relations*, Session 1990–1, 9th Report (London: HMSO, 1991).

[95] Cf. *supra*, pp. 104–5.   [96] de Groot, *supra* n. 78, pp. 178–80.

Legally, therefore, there seem to be few obstacles to creating a European cabotage area. But the Commission's proposal also calls for some comments from a trade policy perspective.

It is not surprising that the proposal has fuelled fears in third countries for a Fortress Europe in civil aviation.[97] From the latter's point of view the creation of a European cabotage area and the prospect of having to negotiate with a large and very powerful bloc instead of twelve different States is not too encouraging. In this respect, one should not only concentrate on the United States. It is clear that currently there is some imbalance in aviation relations between the United States and the Community. It seems fairly logical that the Community, by negotiating as a bloc, wishes to restore this imbalance and obtain, for example, some access to US cabotage traffic in exchange for fifth freedom rights for US carriers in Europe. But the picture is totally different with respect to countries other than the United States, especially smaller ones. These are in a very weak position if they have to negotiate with the Community as such in a bilateral framework. If the Community were to try to obtain as much as possible from such negotiations, the ability of third-country airlines to compete with the European carriers could be severely damaged.[98]

In this connection it is important to bear in mind the economic context of a European cabotage area. The Community's air transport market is clearly one of the most developed in the world, and is something totally different from the market of an individual third country, except the United States and (perhaps) Canada and Japan. Therefore, it is in most cases much more important for a third-country carrier to have some access to the Community's internal market than vice versa. The following statement by Singapore Airlines illustrates this:

Foreign carriers operating to Europe face disadvantages without cabotage rights. Commonsense dictates that it is uneconomical to fly across vast sectors of Europe without passengers, or for foreign carriers to fly beyond the UK or Europe without the benefit of traffic rights. End to end operations are only possible if the necessary volume of traffic exists. Until such time multi-sector operations are essential. Singapore Airlines regrets that cabotage does not appear to be likely after 1993.[99]

These issues also point to the question of the future of the Chicago Convention framework in civil aviation, and whether it will be replaced by a more liberal system under a General Agreement on Trade in Services. This question is considered below. It may suffice here to say that such liberalization might change the bilateral structure of international air transport and thus also bear on the cabotage issue. In any event, it is clear that at the time of writing the

[97] See for example the comments by Singapore Airlines in a memorandum to the Select Committee on the European Communities of the House of Lords, *supra* n. 91, p. 151 and Gertler, *supra* n. 78, pp. 207–10.

[98] Cf. Gertler, *supra* n. 78, pp. 208–9.

[99] Select Committee on the European Communities, *supra* n. 91, p. 152. Cf. also Haanappel, *supra* n. 77, p. 140, where he pleads for an open European air space instead of beginning an aeropolitical war.

Community has not yet developed a coherent, well thought-out policy on relations with third countries in civil aviation, and therefore it is not surprising that there remains a lot of vagueness surrounding the concept of a European cabotage area.

Cabotage and sovereignty over the airspace

As a last point, it has to be mentioned that there is an altogether different legal approach to the cabotage issue, focusing on the concept of sovereignty. The Chicago Convention is based on the principle of *national* sovereignty, defined in Article 1: 'The contracting States recognise that every State has complete and exclusive sovereignty over the airspace above its territory'. This 'exclusive' link between sovereignty and the nation State was only natural in 1944, when the Convention was concluded. But, obviously, it is no longer as universal as it was then, with the advent of supranational organizations such as the Community, to which a number of States have transferred part of their sovereignty. In as far as this transfer of sovereignty concerns air transport, it is one of the basic reasons behind the legal difficulties affecting, from the viewpoint of the Chicago Convention, the concept of European cabotage. If this transfer were total with respect to civil aviation, it would only be logical that cabotage be addressed at the Community, and not the Member State level. Automatically the Community could be considered as a 'cabotage area', and Article 7 of the Chicago Convention would no longer apply to opening up cabotage traffic within the Member States.

However, it is clear that the Community has not yet acquired full sovereignty over civil aviation. There are a number of areas in which the Member States may still have powers.[100] The question then becomes one of degree: how much sovereignty needs to be transferred to the Community before it can be argued that the Community should be recognized as one single entity in the framework of the Chicago Convention? Recently, de Groot has tried to answer this question.[101] He argues that external relations are critical in this respect, in the sense that the Community would first have to obtain exclusive powers concerning external relations in the air transport sector. Above it was submitted that, to quite an extent, this is already the case. To date, however, this is still only a point of view, which has not yet been put into practice. As long as the latter is not the case, it will of course be very difficult to convince the other parties to the Chicago Convention that the Community has actually taken over Member States' sovereignty in the field of civil aviation.

Nevertheless, there is a case for proceeding along these lines. As argued above,[102] the Member States should adopt a common attitude within ICAO,

---

[100] Such as social, technical, and environmental issues relating to civil aviation.
[101] de Groot, *supra* n. 78, pp. 171–6.   [102] See p. 104.

and it would only be natural that, at a given time, they would concede their loss of sovereignty and argue within ICAO that the Community be considered a single entity, also with respect to cabotage. The GATT is a precedent in this respect. Such a step would presumably require negotiations with other members of ICAO, probably not the least over cabotage.

The Future of the Bilateral Agreements with Third Countries

Above it was submitted that the Community has the exclusive competence to deal with the commercial aspects of external relations in the field of civil aviation. It was said that this competence touches the essence of the networks of bilateral agreements which each Member State has developed. The question of how the Community can exercise its competence is therefore largely identical to the one concerning the future of these networks. Below, the Commission's proposals relating thereto are described and evaluated.

The Commission's proposals

In its first proposal, of February 1990, the Commission acknowledged that it could not immediately renegotiate all the bilateral agreements which the Member States have concluded, knowing that on average each Member State is bound by more than sixty such agreements. Such a drastic policy would create a serious risk 'that efficiency and speed would be impaired', also taking into account the delicate negotiating position of the Member States.[103] Instead the Commission proposed to take up its responsibilities gradually. To that end, transitional provisions would provide that the Council authorizes the Member States to continue, in certain cases, to conclude bilateral agreements. That would be the case 'when it appears that for compelling circumstances of an administrative or technical nature, Community negotiations prove to be not yet possible'.[104] Nevertheless, also in such cases there would be some form of supervision by the Community, to 'ensure that common elements are included in such agreements'.[105] One of these elements (undoubtedly the most important one) is a 'common nationality clause'. Indeed, because the international civil aviation system is based upon the notion of sovereignty, agreements between States typically reserve the exercise of traffic rights to national carriers.[106] That is also the case with the agreements

---

[103] COM (90) 17 final, *supra* n. 8, p. 9.   [104] Ibid. 10.   [105] Ibid.
[106] See e.g. Art. 3 (3) of the (standard) agreement annexed to COM (92) 434 final (*supra* n. 16): 'Each Contracting Party shall have the right to refuse to accept the designation of an airline or airlines from the other Contracting Party or to withhold or revoke the grant to such an airline or airlines of the rights specified in Article 2 of this Agreement or to impose such conditions as it may deem necessary on the exercise by the designated airline or airlines of those rights, in any case where it is not satisfied that the airline or airlines in question have their central administration and

concluded by the Member States. It is obvious that to continue this practice when there is an internal market in which Community air carriers can freely provide their services and freely establish themselves would be almost untenable. Already in September 1989 the Commission sent a letter to the Member States, arguing that these nationality clauses were incompatible with Community law and should be replaced by a Community clause.[107] This letter was largely ineffective—but this problem is further examined below.[108]

The Commission did not give many indications in this first proposal as to which negotiations would as a priority need to be conducted at Community level. It only mentioned the relations with EFTA and the granting of fifth freedom rights to third-country air carriers inside the Community.[109]

In order to give substance to the transitional regime the Commission proposed a Council Decision on a consultation and authorization procedure for agreements concerning commercial aviation relations between Member States and third countries.[110] It modelled this proposal (with some modifications) on Council Decision 69/494 on the progressive standardization of agreements concerning commercial relations between Member States and third countries and on the negotiation of Community agreements,[111] on the basis of which Member States are still from time to time authorized to prolong existing agreements.[112] The proposal has two sections. In title I the question of express or tacit extension of existing agreements is dealt with. According to Article 1, the Member States have to communicate to the Commission all the existing bilateral air services agreements within one year. However, for those agreements the extension of which is proposed, notification has to be made at the latest three months before the date of the extension. Article 2 provides that such extension may be subject to prior consultation, the purpose of which is

to establish whether the agreements or arrangements to be extended expressly or tacitly contain provisions relating to the common commercial aviation policy within the meaning of Article 113. If such is the case, it shall be established whether such provisions could constitute an obstacle to that policy.

If the Commission establishes that the latter is indeed the case, 'in particular by reason of divergencies between the policies of Member States', it submits

principal place of business in the territory of the other Contracting Party, that the majority of their shares are owned by nationals or by the Government of that other Contracting Party and are effectively controlled by such nationals or Government'.

[107] See Commission Press Release IP (89) 628 and COM (90) 17 final, *supra* n. 8, p. 4, according to which the Community clause should read (in rather imperfect English): 'The ownership of the air carriers designated to operate the services provided for in the Annex to this Agreement on behalf of the Party that is a member of the European Communities must have its central administration and principal place of business in the Community, the majority of whose shares are owned by nationals of Member States and/or Member States and which is effectively controlled by such persons or States'.

[108] pp. 114–15.   [109] COM (90) 17 final, *supra* n. 8, p. 9.   [110] Ibid. 15–21.
[111] OJ English Special edn. (1969), 603.   [112] See Ch. 9, p. 318.

according to Article 4 a detailed report to the Council and recommends, where appropriate, that the Commission open (Community) negotiations with the third countries in question. If, by contrast, the Commission establishes that the extension forms no obstacle to the CCP in the field of civil aviation, it may authorize such an extension.

The second section contains transitional provisions on new bilateral agreements. Article 5 provides:

1. Without prejudice to Article 113 of the Treaty and until 31 December 1992, the Council acting on a proposal from the Commission and after the required prior consultation may, by way of exception, authorize bilateral negotiations between Member States and certain third countries in cases where Community negotiations prove to be not yet possible as a result of compelling circumstances of an administrative or technical nature.

2. The provisions of this Article shall apply where, for any special reason, a Member State considers that, in order to avoid any interruption in commercial relations based on agreements, negotiations must be undertaken with some third country ...

The prior consultation referred to should cover

co-ordination as will ensure the proper functioning and the strengthening of the internal market, as will take account of the legitimate interests of the Member States ... and as will contribute towards the establishment of uniform principles of common commercial aviation policy in relation to the country in question.[113]

Consultations can be resumed during negotiations and their conclusions may serve as guide-lines. Further, the results of the negotiations must be communicated, allowing for objections to be raised by the Commission and the other Member States, in which case the agreement can only be concluded after authorization by the Council (Article 7).

As described above, this proposal has met with a lot of criticism, not only because of the competence claim. Both national authorities and the airline industry put questions concerning the proposed policies.[114] With which countries would the Community start negotiating and which policy would it pursue in such negotiations? Will centralized negotiations lead to better opportunities for Community air carriers? Is the Commission sufficiently staffed and has it the necessary expertise for replacing the Member States in bilateral negotiations? How will the traffic rights resulting from Community negotiations be allocated among Community air carriers?

The latter question was undoubtedly the most preoccupying. The Commission's proposal gave no answers in this respect—indeed it did not even mention the problem. That was certainly a lacuna in the proposal, since for the

---

[113] Art. 6.

[114] See the national reports in *The 1992 Challenge at National Level, supra* n. 10 and the evidence in Select Committee on the EC, *Conduct of the Community's External Aviation Relations, supra* n. 94.

air carriers much depends on how this question is answered. Suppose Community negotiations lead to more traffic rights on the Paris–New York route. Would all Community carriers be able to claim some of this traffic? Would these rights then be allocated on a proportional basis, would the 'first come, first served' rule apply, would carriers established in the Member State in question (here France) have first refusal, or would traffic rights be auctioned? It appears that no one could clearly conceive what the results of centralized negotiations would be. Given the economic importance of traffic to third countries for the airline industry, especially for the so-called national flag carriers, it is not surprising that the industry and national authorities reacted in a sceptical manner.

Apparently, the Commission was aware that its proposal was not yet 'complete', since in October 1992 it published a new communication on air transport relations with third countries,[115] in which it obviously tried to supply some answers to the above-mentioned questions. This communication contains more details on the system and economic importance of external traffic. On the basis of this description, the Commission tries to argue more forcefully that centralized negotiations with third countries are in the overall Community interest, in that additional opportunities can be obtained.[116] Not surprisingly, these arguments focus on air transport relations with the United States.

Furthermore, the communication tries to spell out the possible aims of a Community policy more clearly. In this respect, the Commission goes in the direction of also liberalizing trade in civil aviation with third countries, arguing that one of the aims of the establishment of the internal market is to make the Community's industry more competitive, and that once this is achieved restrictions on external traffic imposed by bilateral agreements are not in the interest of the efficient air carriers. The global context should not be lost sight of in this connection.[117]

More specifically, as regards nationality clauses the communication acknowledges that 'an immediate request for changing or deleting nationality clauses in existing [agreements] may not be readily granted in an individual negotiation'.[118] Therefore an acceptable transitional approach similar to Article 234 of the EC Treaty, will have to be worked out, boiling down to

[115] COM (92) 434 final, *supra* n. 16.
[116] Ibid. 10: 'It cannot be denied that the Community, as one of the most important trading blocks in the world, effectively creates additional opportunities to those created by a national approach'.
[117] The Commission gives an interesting example here: 'It is worth noting that the bilateral agreements between Member States and third countries are not the only factors which determine the competitive situation. Strong world-wide competition exists for example between EC and US air carriers. The fact that the bilateral agreement between e.g. the US and Japan is less restrictive than the agreements between Member States and Japan means that the US carriers can develop a much better position in Japan and thereby in the global competition' (ibid. 14).
[118] Ibid. 18.

temporarily tolerating existing agreements. For future agreements, however, the Commission puts a question mark against the usefulness of nationality policies (also at the overall Community level): '[i]n a worldwide competition it might not be sufficient to look only for direct market access possibilities but it could be more effective to invest in local expertise'.[119] Attention is drawn to the fact that in the framework of the Uruguay Round negotiations on a General Agreement on Trade in Services the Community has already proposed more flexibility in this area, but without a positive response from other parties.

Overall, one gets the impression that the Commission is forsaking the more or less doctrinal, legal approach, based on the above-discussed claim that the commercial aspects of external relations come under the heading of the CCP, to try and convince the Member States and the airline industry that a common external policy is useful, if not indispensable. Nevertheless, the Commission has not changed its views on the scope of Article 113 of the Treaty, as applied to civil aviation.

The new communication also includes more details on procedural aspects. As was mentioned, the problem of allocation of traffic rights occupies a central place in this connection. The Commission examines a number of alternative methods for carrying out this allocation.[120] The option of selling traffic rights is not to be preferred as this would raise the air carriers' costs and would increase barriers for new entrants. The establishment of a quota system, in which the quota would be divided according to the present market share of carriers, also has disadvantages. It would lead to a rigid system, making it virtually impossible for new entrants to develop. Instead, the Commission proposes a qualitative selection procedure.[121] This procedure would only be applied to the allocation of additional rights, not to existing ones. The air carriers interested in obtaining a share of these additional rights will have to submit a request, in which they supply detailed information in support of their claim. The selection among proposals should be based on a range of criteria, determining which of the requests offers most guarantees. The criteria which the Commission mentions are: service to the public, competition in the relevant market, use of scarce resources, and established Community policy. The Commission is aware that these criteria are rather general and difficult to apply. In specific cases, therefore, additional criteria can be added. Because the selection process is to some extent subjective, based on an assessment by the selecting authority, there will have to be guarantees of non-discrimination, transparency, and right of appeal. The selection would be performed by national authorities, in case the rights result from negotiations conducted by a Member State, and by the Commission (assisted by representatives from the Member States) in case they result from Community negotiations.

---

[119] Ibid.   [120] Ibid. 19–20.   [121] For the details of this procedure, see ibid. 26–7.

The original proposal for a decision concerning a consultation and authorization procedure is in some respects amended by the new communication. Concerning the extension of existing agreements, a provision has been added according to which the Commission may, until 31 December 1998, maintain in force the provisions governing matters covered by the common external aviation policy, contained in existing bilateral agreements.[122] Similarly, the Council may authorize the Member States, until the same date, to enter into bilateral negotiations 'where Community negotiations prove to be not yet possible', the reference to 'compelling circumstances of an administrative or technical nature' having been deleted.[123] The amended text also contains a reference to the problem of allocating traffic rights, without, however, laying down substantive criteria. That will have to be the subject of a separate Council decision.[124]

Comments

Not all the details of the Commission's proposals can be examined here. It remains to be seen, moreover, whether the Council will ever go along with the Commission's views.[125] From a legal point of view (and also, probably, from the policy viewpoint) the questions of ownership and control of air carriers, and of the allocation of traffic rights are fundamental. They are also interrelated.

The Commission argues that the nationality clauses in the existing bilateral agreements are incompatible with Community law. Although it is submitted that this is correct, the reasoning which the Commission puts forward in order to arrive at this conclusion may be supplemented by other arguments.[126] The Commission maintains that, as a result of the principle of freedom of establishment, a Community air carrier established in a Member State may well be owned or controlled by nationals of other Member States.[127] If such a carrier is excluded from traffic between this Member State of establishment and third countries, because of nationality clauses, it is being discriminated against on the basis of nationality, in breach of the Treaty provisions on establishment.[128]

However, the exclusion from external traffic rights is only indirectly related to the freedom of establishment. After all, establishment as such is not affected by it. The restrictions which a Member State would impose by applying a

[122] Art. 5 of the amended proposal.
[123] Art. 6 of the amended proposal. By way of derogation, the Commission may give such authorization, according to para. 3.
[124] Art. 11 of the amended proposal.
[125] See *supra* n. 24.
[126] See for this reasoning COM (92) 434 final, *supra* n. 16, p. 8.
[127] See Regulation 2407/92, *supra* n. 6.
[128] Compare with Case C-93/89, *Commission* v. *Ireland*, Judgment of 4 Oct. 1991, not yet published.

nationality clause are restrictions on the right to trade with third countries. As the Commission submits that the exchange of traffic rights is a commercial affair, and comes within the scope of the Community's competence for developing a Common Commercial Policy, Article 6 of the Treaty would appear to apply. As is well known this provision lays down that '[w]ithin the scope of application of this Treaty ... any discrimination on grounds of nationality shall be prohibited'. The scope of the prohibition of discrimination is then even wider than under the Commission's reasoning. The latter seems to imply that a Community air carrier first has to be established in the Member State which allocates the rights for traffic to and from third countries, before a non-discriminatory treatment can be enforced. That is not necessary if it is accepted that the prohibition of discrimination applies because trade in air transport services with third countries comes within the scope of application of the Treaty. Any Community air carrier, wherever it is established in the Community, can then claim access to external traffic from any Member State.

The Community has its own nationality clause. Regulation 2407/92 on licensing of air carriers provides that 'no undertaking shall be granted an operating licence by a Member State unless its principal place of business and, if any, its registered office are located in that Member State'.[129] Moreover,

[w]ithout prejudice to agreements and conventions to which the Community is a contracting party, the undertaking shall be owned and continue to be owned directly or through majority ownership by Member States and/or nationals of Member States. It shall at all times be effectively controlled by such States or nationals.[130]

The air carriers which have thus been licensed are Community air carriers, and it is only to them, by virtue of the provisions of the third package, that the freedom to provide transport services within the Community's internal market applies. As such, this definition of a Community air carrier, which is more narrow than the provisions of Article 58 of the Treaty,[131] comprises a restriction on first establishment in the Community. It is in this regard comparable to the reciprocity provisions applying in the financial services sector, which may also lead to such restrictions.[132]

The question of how to develop a common external policy in the field of aviation, and especially the issue of the allocation of traffic rights, demonstrate that it is difficult to reconcile, in terms of policy, a nationality clause (even if it is operated at the Community level) with an internal market in which free movement has been realized. Within the Community, air carriers decide freely

---

[129] Art. 4 (1) of the regulation (*supra* n. 6).   [130] Art. 4 (2).

[131] Art. 58 indicates that the freedom to provide services and the freedom of establishment applies to '[c]ompanies or firms formed in accordance with the law of a Member State and having their registered office, central administration or principal place of business within the Community'.

[132] See Ch. 2, pp. 63–4.

where and in which circumstances they provide their services. For traffic to and from third countries, however, that is not the case for as long as bilateral agreements restrict traffic rights. In such circumstances, the mechanism employed for allocating these rights among the interested carriers cannot but pose problems. Which criteria should one use, when internally free competition prevails? The qualitative criteria proposed by the Commission may be vague and subject to criticism, but are there others which are less artificial or distorting?

The foregoing demonstrates the difficulties inherent in combining internal free trade with a system of strictly regulated competition governing external trade. It is only logical, therefore, that in its latest communication the Commission suggests that also at the global level the Community should pursue a liberal policy with respect to ownership.[133] Quite indicative in this respect is that in mock negotiations between representatives of the Community and the United States, organized on the occasion of a seminar at the University of Leiden in 1991, the negotiators quickly discovered that a lot of the issues concerning how to open up civil aviation depends upon the fate of the nationality clauses.[134] If such clauses became obsolete, the whole system of government-determined exchanges of traffic rights would probably collapse.

Other Developments

To end, two other developments should be touched upon. One is the GATS negotiations. It is obvious that if GATT-like rules and disciplines were to be applied to civil aviation, the entire system of bilateral exchanges of traffic rights would fall apart, since it is patently inconsistent with the most-favoured-nation rule. That is of course also realized by the negotiators. The result is that in the draft GATS which is part of the 1991 Dunkel Package there is an Annex on air transport services, which provides that 'no provision of this Agreement shall apply to measures affecting ... traffic rights covered by the Chicago Convention, including the five freedoms of the air, and by bilateral air services agreements'.[135] Accordingly, the provisions of the draft GATS only cover a number of secondary services in the field of civil aviation, such as computer reservation services, aircraft repair and maintenance services, and the selling or marketing of air transport services. Apparently there is not yet sufficient support for subjecting civil aviation as such to free trade rules. It remains to be seen whether in the near future that will change. Much will depend in this respect on the policies developed by the Community.

[133] See *supra*, p. 113.
[134] See H. A. Wassenbergh (ed.), *External Aviation Relations of the European Community* (Deventer: Kluwer, 1992), 55–106.
[135] Para. 2 of the Annex, MTN.TNC/W/FA, p. 45.

A last development concerns slot allocation. Because of the high degree of airport congestion the Community considers it desirable to apply a number of common rules to airport slot allocation. These rules are the subject of a recent Council Regulation,[136] which contains a reciprocity clause comparable to the one applying in the field of financial services.[137] It provides that

[w]henever it appears that a third country, with respect to the allocation of slots at airports,

(a) does not grant Community air carriers treatment comparable to that granted by Member States to air carriers from that country, or

(b) does not grant Community air carriers *de facto* national treatment, or

(c) grants air carriers from other third countries more favourable treatment than Community air carriers, appropriate action may be taken to remedy the situation in respect of the airport or airports concerned, including the suspension wholly or partially of the obligations of this Regulation in respect of an air carrier of that third country, in accordance with Community law.[138]

It is not necessary to analyse fully the scope of this provision here, since its rationale and wording are basically the same as the financial services version of reciprocity. Nevertheless, a few observations have to be made.

First, one fails to see the difference between cases (*a*) and (*b*), since the kind of treatment which foreign air carriers receive in the Community with respect to slot allocation is national treatment. 'Comparable treatment' and 'national treatment' are therefore the same here. Secondly, the clause confirms the emphasis on *de facto* national treatment which this time is explicitly mentioned. Thirdly, there is an additional criterion, namely most-favoured-nation treatment. Again one may wonder what, in practice, the difference is with the two previously mentioned criteria. If in country *X* Community air carriers are discriminated against in comparison with other third-country air carriers, they will in all likelihood not be receiving national treatment either.

Conclusion

The case of the external dimension of the Community's policies in the field of civil aviation brings out the importance of the question whether the Community can regulate external trade in services in the framework of the Treaty provisions on the Common Commercial Policy. The legal dispute between the Commission on the one hand and the Council, the European Parliament, and the Member States on the other holds up all substantive progress. One could deplore that differences in opinion on the legal basis of Community action have the effect of blocking such action. However, the question has to be put

---

[136] Council Regulation 95/93 of 18 Jan. 1993 on common rules for the allocation of slots at Community airports, OJ L 14/1 of 22 Jan. 1993.

[137] See Ch. 2.

[138] Art. 12 (1) of the regulation.

whether the dispute does not serve as an alibi, in the case of the Member States, to maintain the existing system.[139] Given the importance of air transport to and from third countries, the internal market certainly requires Community action. This is one case of which it can be said that the internal market will not be genuinely completed before there is a common external regime. Accordingly, the absence of such a regime is a serious lacuna.

That is not to say that the establishment of such a regime is a simple matter. Essentially, the problem is that, as long as the Chicago Convention system of regulating world-wide civil aviation is more or less intact, the Community will need to link an internal system of free competition to limited external traffic rights. Cabotage is but one aspect of this problem, for which there probably are no instant solutions. In this respect, much depends on the rules on ownership and control of air carriers, which are the instrument for determining the subjects of traffic rights.[140] If one were to witness increased co-operation between, or even mergers of, air carriers of various countries (including across the Atlantic) it would become increasingly difficult to maintain rules of ownership and control, and, accordingly, limitations on traffic rights.

[139] Cf. *supra* n. 24.   [140] Cf. Ch. 11, pp. 353–4.

4

Audiovisual and Telecommunications Services

1. TELEVISION BROADCASTING

Introduction

Community action in the field of audiovisual services is almost exclusively directed towards television broadcasting. The latter is probably one of the most characteristic examples of the changes taking place in the nature of service transactions and, correspondingly, their perception, as referred to in Chapter 1. There it was said that services play an ever increasing role in modern economies, and are more and more looked at from an economic perspective.[1] That is certainly the case with television broadcasting in Europe, which until a few decades ago was exclusively government-organized, i.e. a public service, but which has evolved into a real industry. The picture emanating from this evolution is very mixed. There are, on the one hand, official broadcasting organizations, funded by governments and pursuing non-commercial objectives such as the provision of information, entertainment, and the diffusion of artistic performances. On the other, there are commercial broadcasters, funded mainly by private advertisers and operating with a view to making profits. Nevertheless, they also provide information, entertainment, and the like.[2]

Furthermore, through the advances of technology television is becoming more and more international in character. The use of satellites makes it possible to broadcast the same programme at the same time all over the world, and so-called direct satellite broadcasting allows a single television channel to reach a continental-scale audience. One should also mention the important role which television plays in modern societies as a medium for culture and information. Our age has been characterized as the age of television, because of the major influence it exerts on the ideas and behaviour of people.

It is not surprising, therefore, that television broadcasting did not remain outside the internal market programme. From a 'technical' point of view, the reason for television broadcasting's inclusion in the programme lies in the fact that the Member States maintained a number of regulatory barriers to

---

[1] See Ch. 1, p. 9.
[2] Cf. Vincent Porter, 'The Janus Character of Television Broadcasting', in G. Locksley (ed.), *The Single European Market and the Information and Communication Technologies* (London: Belhaven Press, 1990), 61–2.

cross-frontier television, mostly aimed at safeguarding national broadcasters.[3] However, the elimination of these barriers is not the only objective pursued by the Community's action in the field of television broadcasting. Especially under the impulse of the European Parliament, the aim is also to lay down common standards as regards such issues as advertising, sponsorship of programmes, the protection of minors, the preservation of cultural diversity, and the development of European audio-visual production.

All these subjects figure in the Council's Directive of 3 October 1989 on the co-ordination of certain provisions laid down by law, regulation or administrative action in Member States concerning the pursuit of television broadcasting activities.[4] The adoption of this directive, termed 'Television without Frontiers', has been extremely difficult because of the many conflicting interests involved, and in particular because of its external dimension. The European Parliament and some Member States strongly insisted on including provisions aimed at safeguarding and stimulating European audiovisual production in the face of competition from the United States, a large supplier of television programmes to European broadcasters.[5] These provisions, laying down some sort of minimum quota for European works, were the subject of intense debate, and have led to a protracted dispute between the Community and the United States regarding the relationship between free trade in television programmes and the preservation of cultural identity.

These quota provisions are the main subject of the following sections. But before analysing them and examining whether they are compatible with the GATT provisions regarding non-discrimination, it is useful to indicate briefly the place which television occupies in the system of the EC Treaty, to depict the debate leading to the adoption of the directive and to analyse the latter's external dimension in general.

The Television without Frontiers Directive: Marrying Cultural Policy and Free Movement of Services

The EC Treaty and television broadcasting

Problems concerning transfrontier television broadcasting have given rise to a number of rulings by the European Court of Justice, making it possible to

---

[3] See *Television without Frontiers: Green Paper on the Establishment of the Common Market for Broadcasting, especially by Satellite and Cable*, COM (84) 300 final of 14 June 1984, parts 5 and 6.
[4] Directive 89/552, OJ L 298/23 of 17 Oct. 1989.
[5] Exact figures are not available. For an overview of various studies, which estimate that between 20 and 40% of television programmes broadcast in Europe are US-made, see André Sapir, 'Le commerce international des services audiovisuels: une source de conflits entre la Communauté européenne et les États-Unis', in G. Vandersanden (ed.), *L'Espace audiovisuel européen* (Brussels: Éditions de l'ULB, 1991), 163–4.

locate the various aspects of such broadcasting in the system of the EC Treaty.[6] In the pioneering *Sacchi* judgment, the Court held that

[t]he transmission of television signals, including those in the nature of advertisements, comes, as such, within the rules of the Treaty relating to services.On the other hand, trade in material, sound recordings, films, apparatus and other products used for the diffusion of television signals is subject to the rules relating to freedom of movement for goods.[7]

The distinction is a clear one. Broadcasting as such is subject to Articles 59 and 60, EC Treaty, relating to the freedom to provide services, whereas trade in products, although it may be aimed at broadcasting programmes, comes within the rules on free movement of goods.

In subsequent judgments, the Court clarified the scope of the principle of free movement for services in relation to broadcasting. Most of the cases concerned restrictions on advertising.

The *Debauve* case concerned Belgian legislation prohibiting the broadcasting of commercial advertising.[8] This legislation was not only applied to Belgian broadcasters; it also covered the transmission of foreign programmes by cable distribution companies. The Court was asked whether the latter aspect of this legislation was consistent with the EC Treaty rules on freedom to provide services. It ruled that specific requirements imposed upon providers of services, founded upon the application of rules regulating certain types of activity and justified by the general interest, and applying to all persons and undertakings established within the territory of the Member State in question cannot be said to be incompatible with the Treaty to the extent to which a provider of services established in another Member State is not subject to similar regulations there. It found that restrictions on advertising were such rules justified by the general interest, and observed that in this respect there were widely divergent systems of law in the various Member States. The Court further decided that

[i]n the absence of any approximation of national laws ... the application of the laws in question cannot be regarded as a restriction upon freedom to provide services so long as those laws treat all such services identically whatever their origin or the nationality or place of establishment of the persons providing them.[9]

The Court concluded that since the Belgian legislation involved no discrimination, it was in keeping with these principles and therefore did not infringe the Treaty rules on freedom to provide services.

---

[6] See also the Commission's *Green Paper, supra* n. 3, part 5; Ivo E. Schwartz, 'Broadcasting and the EEC Treaty', 11 *ELR* (1986), 1: 7–60; Marianne Dony-Bartholme, 'L'audiovisuel et les règles relatives à la libre prestation des services', in *L'Espace audiovisuel européen, supra* n. 5, pp. 33–51.

[7] Case 155/73, [1974] ECR 409, at 427.

[8] Case 52/79, *Procureur du Roi* v. *Debauve and others*, [1980] ECR 833.

[9] [1980] ECR 856.

This judgment seemed to imply that the Member States remained rather free in regulating television broadcasting, as long as they did not discriminate against the cross-border provision of services. This appeared to be confirmed in the *Bond van Adverteerders* judgment,[10] dealing with a Dutch Ministerial Decree prohibiting the distribution by cable of programmes transmitted from other Member States and containing advertising intended especially for the public in the Netherlands or subtitled in Dutch. The aim of this Decree was to make sure that all revenue from television advertising directed at the Dutch public accrued to a public foundation (the 'STER') which funded the national broadcasting organizations (which are of a pluralistic, non-commercial nature, reflecting the main schools of thought in Dutch society). The Court ruled that the ban on advertising

involves a twofold restriction on freedom to provide services. In the first place, it prevents cable network operators established in a Member State from relaying television programmes supplied by broadcasters established in other Member States. Secondly, it prevents those broadcasters from scheduling for advertisers established in particular in the Member State where the programmes are received advertisements intended especially for the public in that State.[11]

The argument put forward by the Dutch government, that the Dutch broadcasting organizations were also not allowed to broadcast advertising, and that there was therefore no discrimination, was refuted by the Court, stating that one had to make a comparison with the situation of the Dutch television stations as a whole, since they benefited from the advertising by the STER. Thus, the Dutch Decree amounted to discrimination. Such discrimination could not be justified on the basis of Article 56, EC Treaty, which refers to public policy, public security and public health, because 'economic aims, such as that of securing for a national public foundation all the revenue from advertising intended especially for the public of the Member State in question, cannot constitute grounds of public policy'.[12]

However, the Court made clear in the *Stichting Collectieve Antennevoorziening Gouda* judgment that not only discriminatory restrictions on the freedom to provide services are inconsistent with Articles 59 and 60 of the Treaty.[13] The relevant passage was quoted in Chapter 1.[14] This case again concerned Dutch rules regarding advertising, which had replaced the above-mentioned Decree. This time the rules aimed at creating a non-discriminatory

---

[10] Case 352/85, *Bond van Adverteerders and others* v. *the Netherlands State*, [1988] ECR 2085.
[11] [1988] ECR 2132.   [12] [1988] ECR 2135.
[13] Case C-288/89, *Stichting Collectieve Antennevoorziening Gouda* v. *Commissariaat voor de Media*, [1991] ECR I-4007. See also Case C-353/89, *Commission* v. *The Netherlands*, [1991] ECR I-4069, which is very similar.
[14] See p. 15.

regime towards foreign television channels broadcasting advertising intended for the Dutch public, by subjecting them to the same limitations on advertising as those in force in the Netherlands. However, as these limitations only applied to advertising intended for the Dutch public, and not to all advertising by foreign broadcasters, the Court concluded that the regime was still aimed at safeguarding the revenue of the STER (an economic objective) and not at regulating the broadcasting of advertising as such. This aim could not justify restrictions on freedom to provide services.[15] The Court did acknowledge, however, that a national cultural policy aimed at safeguarding the freedom of expression for the various social, cultural, religious, or philosophical components of society could justify restrictions on freedom to provide services (in so far as these restrictions are non-discriminatory). In this regard it explicitly mentioned Article 10 of the European Convention on Human Rights, guaranteeing such freedom of expression, and stated that this was a fundamental right protected by the Community's legal order.[16]

In all, this case-law on the one hand appears to uphold the right for Member States to regulate television broadcasting within their territories, but on the other tolerates few restrictions on the cross-frontier provision of broadcasting services. This is confirmed by the *ERT-AE* judgment, on the Greek television broadcasting monopoly.[17] Here the Court ruled, in line with the *Sacchi* judgment,[18] that such a monopoly is in itself not incompatible with the freedom to provide services. However, if the single national broadcaster is also granted the exclusive right within the national territory to transmit programmes broadcast in other Member States, he is liable to favour his own programmes and to discriminate against foreign ones. In so far as this happens, Article 59 of the Treaty is being infringed.

The Court's case-law, especially the *Bond van Adverteerders* judgment,[19] also indicates that it is not an easy thing to exactly define the various services involved in television broadcasting. This aspect was examined in chapter 1 and it may suffice to refer to what has been said there.[20]

Furthermore, the Court has also examined the relevance of provisions such as Articles 90, 85, and 86, EC Treaty, for broadcasting.[21] But as this chapter only deals with television from the perspective of trade in services, these elements will not be addressed here.

---

[15] [1991] ECR I-4045.   [16] Ibid.

[17] Case C-260/89, *Elliniki Radiophonia Tileorassi AE* v. *Dimotiki Etaira Pliroforissis and Sotrios Kouvelas*, [1991] ECR I-2925.

[18] It was held there that '[n]othing in the Treaty prevents Member States, for considerations of public interest, of a non-economic nature, from removing radio and television transmissions, including cable transmissions, from the field of competition by conferring on one or more establishments an exclusive right to conduct them', see [1974] ECR 429.

[19] *Supra* n. 10.

[20] p. 17.

[21] See the *Sacchi* judgment, *supra* n. 18, and the *ERT-AE* judgment, *supra* n. 17.

The difficult birth of the directive; its contents

The above-mentioned case-law illustrates the tension which exists between the economic and non-economic (often broadly termed cultural) aspects of television broadcasting.[22] This tension was also very much present in the course of the adoption of the directive which was the subject of long and arduous debate.[23] Already at the beginning of the 1980s, the European Parliament suggested that the Community should regulate broadcasting. In 1984, the Commission published its Green Paper on 'Television without Frontiers', which served as a background document.[24] Then, in 1986 the Commission issued its proposal for a directive on television broadcasting.[25] This proposal was amended twice,[26] before it was finally adopted by the Council of Ministers in October 1989, more than three years after the proposal was presented.[27]

The most important stumbling block was probably the quota provisions which are the main subject of this chapter.[28] Some Member States, along with the European Parliament, strongly insisted on the insertion of binding provisions ensuring that European-made television programmes make up at least 60 per cent of overall broadcasting time. Other Member States, by contrast, were not in favour of such provisions. Neither were, of course, the United States, whose programme makers staged a piece of very aggressive lobbying in an attempt to influence the Community's decision-makers.[29]

Things were further complicated by the fact that not everyone recognized the Community's competence to regulate television broadcasting because, it was argued, cultural policy is a matter for the Member States.[30] This argument was buttressed by the fact that within the Council of Europe, which is competent for cultural matters, a Convention on Transfrontier Television was being negotiated.[31] At one time, it even looked as though the proposed

---

[22] According to Vincenzo Salvatore the Court's approach towards these non-economic aspects is superficial, see 'Quotas on TV Programmes and EEC Law', 29 *CML Rev.* (1992), 5: 968. See also, on the said tension, Denis Waelbroeck, 'La libre transmission des messages audiovisuels et la protection des intérêts culturels', in *L'Espace audiovisuel européen, supra* n. 5, pp. 138–54 and Porter, *supra* n. 2.

[23] It is summarized by Pascal Delwit and Corinne Gobin, 'Étude du cheminement de la directive "télévision sans frontières": synthèse des prises de position des institutions communautaires', in *L'Espace audiovisuel européen, supra* n. 5, pp. 55–74.

[24] *Supra* n. 3.

[25] Proposal for a Council Directive concerning broadcasting activities, COM (86) 146 final of 30 Apr. 1986, *Supp. Bull.* 5/86.

[26] See COM (88) 154 final of 21 Mar. 1988 and COM (89) 247 final of 31 May 1989.

[27] See *supra* n. 4.

[28] See Delwit and Gobin, *supra* n. 23; Rebecca Wallace and David Goldberg, 'The EEC Directive on Television Broadcasting', A. Barav and D. A. Wyatt (eds.), 9 *Yearbook of European Law* (1989) (Oxford: Clarendon Press, 1990), 177.

[29] See the remarks by Mr Collins, MEP, in *Debates of the European parliament*, No. 2–378/111 of 24 May 1989.

[30] That was the point of view of Denmark, see Wallace and Goldberg, *supra* n. 28, p. 177.

[31] See on this Convention Rusen Ergec, 'Le Conseil de l'Europe et l'espace audiovisuel européen', in *L'Espace audiovisuel européen, supra* n. 5, pp. 111–14.

directive would be abandoned in favour of the Council of Europe Convention.[32] In the end, however, a compromise was found within the Council of Ministers, one of the most important components of which was that the more loosely worded quota provisions of the Convention would be part of the directive.[33]

Before examining the external dimension of the directive in more detail, it is useful to give a broad overview of its overall content.[34] The aim of the directive is to ensure the free movement of broadcasts within the Community. This aim does not only find its origin in the EC Treaty. As the preamble indicates, it is a specific manifestation of the more general principle of freedom of expression, as contained in Article 10 of the ECHR. The technique used for achieving this aim is again, as in many other parts of the internal market programme,[35] that of mutual recognition. Each Member State must ensure that broadcasts transmitted by broadcasters under its jurisdiction comply with its laws regarding broadcasts intended for its own audiences.[36] That requirement is coupled with the following obligation:

Member States shall ensure freedom of reception and shall not restrict transmission on their territory of television broadcasts from other Member States for reasons which fall within the fields coordinated by this directive.[37]

Thus, one could almost apply the language of *Cassis de Dijon* to the free movement of broadcasting services, as defined in the directive: broadcasts lawfully produced and marketed in one Member State should not be subject to restrictions when transmitted to other Member States.

In addition to this general rule, the directive contains a few chapters on specific issues concerning the regulation of broadcasting. Chapter III deals with 'Promotion of distribution and production of television programmes'. Its main provisions concern the quota for European works (see below). There are also rules on the broadcasting of cinematographic works and on language policy.[38] Chapter IV concerns 'Television advertising and sponsorship', containing minimum rules on advertising and sponsoring of programmes. Chapter V deals with the protection of minors and chapter VI with the right of reply.

[32] The Convention was adopted on 15 Mar. 1989. For the text, see *European Treaty Series*, No. 132.

[33] This was much to the dissatisfaction of the European Parliament, see *Debates of the European Parliament*, No. 2–387/110–127 of 24 May 1989.

[34] See, for more details, Wallace and Goldberg, *supra* n. 28, pp. 179–91.

[35] See for example Ch. 2, p. 47.

[36] See Art. 2 (1) of the directive (*supra* n. 4). This also applies to 'broadcasters who, while not being under the jurisdiction of any Member State, make use of a frequency or satellite capacity granted by, or a satellite up-link situated in, that Member State', ibid.

[37] Art. 2 (2). However, Member States may provisionally suspend retransmissions of broadcasts in case of serious infringements against the rules of Art. 22, which prohibit 'programmes which might seriously impair the physical, mental or moral development of minors . . . '. For the conditions of such suspension, see also Art. 2 (2).

[38] See Arts. 7 and 8.

The Television without Frontiers Directive does not regulate broadcasting across the Community's external frontiers. In the words of the preamble, only 'broadcasts emanating from and intended for reception within the Community' are covered. This is reflected in Article 2 (1) which mentions 'broadcasts transmitted ... by broadcasters under [the] jurisdiction [of a Member State]'. Similarly, Article 2 (2) only mentions 'broadcasts from other Member States' as benefiting from the freedom of reception. This means that, according to the directive, the Member States remain free to regulate the transmission of broadcasts emanating from third countries. It would be useful to examine whether this lack of an external regime is liable to give rise to distortions of competition within the internal market.[39] If that is the case, such regulation needs to be looked at from the point of view of commercial policy, as argued in Chapter 1,[40] and the Community would have to develop a common policy in this respect.

However, there is of course an external dimension to the directive, because it prescribes that the Member States should ensure that broadcasters reserve a majority proportion of their transmission time to European works. In the next section, the relevant provisions are described and commented upon.

The quota for European works

Content

Article 4 (1) of the directive contains the basic rule:

Member States shall ensure where practicable and by appropriate means, that broadcasters reserve for European works, within the meaning of Article 6, a majority proportion of their transmission time, excluding the time appointed to news, sports events, games, advertising and teletext services.

It is added that this should be achieved progressively, on the basis of suitable criteria, having regard to the broadcaster's various responsibilities (informational, educational, etc.). What is striking is that this rule is carefully worded and appears to leave quite some discretion as regards implementation. The latter is confirmed in the second paragraph of Article 4: 'Where the proportion laid down in paragraph 1 cannot be attained, it must not be lower than the average for 1988 in the Member State concerned.'[41] To give such a large amount of freedom to the Member States for implementing and applying the rule has been necessary in order to find sufficient support in the Council of

---

[39] It may be that at the moment such distortions are unlikely, in view of the fact that few non-Community broadcasters transmit programmes in the Community and that competition between broadcasters is influenced by a lot of parameters, not all of them purely economic.

[40] pp. 26–7.

[41] For Greece and Portugal this reference year is 1990.

Ministers.[42] Furthermore, the formula is copied almost verbatim from the European Convention on Transfrontier Television.[43]

There is not only the majority rule of Article 4 (1). In order to stimulate not only European production of television programmes as such, but also production by producers who are independent of broadcasters, Article 5 provides that

Member States shall ensure, where practicable and by appropriate means, that broadcasters reserve at least 10% of their transmission time, excluding the time appointed to news, sports events, games, advertising and teletext services, or alternately, at the discretion of the Member State, at least 10% of their programming budget, for European works created by producers who are independent of broadcasters.[44]

It is of course one thing to lay down a quota for European television programmes, it is another to define which programmes are European and which not. There are no rules of origin for programmes and it is not a simple matter to devise such rules because a programme can be a very complex product, produced in various locations with the input of a lot of people and companies. Reflecting this complexity, the provisions of the directive defining the concept of European works are quite elaborate. According to Article 6 (1) there are three categories of European works:

(a) works originating from Member States;
(b) works originating from European third States that are a party to the European Convention on Transfrontier Television;
(c) works originating from other European third countries.

Works of categories (*a*) and (*b*) have to be 'mainly made with authors and workers residing in one or more States' referred to in these categories. In addition, they have to comply with one of the following conditions:

(a) they are made by one or more producers established in one or more of those States; or

(b) production of the works is supervised and actually controlled by one or more producers established in one or more of those States; or

(c) the contribution of co-producers of those States to the total production costs is preponderant and the co-production is not controlled by one or more producers established outside those States.[45]

Thus, the conditions relate both to the place of residence of authors and workers and the place of establishment of the producer(s).

---

[42] The question whether the quota rule is legally binding or not has been amply debated, see e.g. Salvatore, *supra* n. 22, pp. 978–80.

[43] See *supra*, p. 125.

[44] Again this should be 'achieved progressively, on the basis of suitable criteria'.

[45] Art. 6 (2).

On the other hand, the works of category (*c*) are

works made exclusively or in co-production with producers established in one or more
Member States by producers established in one or more European third countries with
which the Community will conclude agreements in accordance with the procedures of
the Treaty, if those works are mainly made with authors and workers residing in one or
more European States.

Until now, the Community has not yet concluded such agreements, so that this
provision remains theoretical.[46]

Lastly, those works which are not European in the sense of the above
definitions, shall nevertheless be considered to be European 'to an extent
corresponding to the proportion of the contribution of Community co-
producers to the total production costs', on condition that they are 'made
mainly with authors and workers residing in one or more Member
States'.[47]

Article 4 (3) and (4) contains provisions on reporting and review. The
Member States must provide the Commission every two years with a report on
the implementation of the above-mentioned rules.[48] The Commission must
then inform the other Member States and the European Parliament of the
reports, accompanied, where appropriate, by its opinion. The Commission
must also ensure the application of the rules, 'in accordance with the provisions of the Treaty'. The latter means that in the event of incorrect implementation the Commission can only institute proceedings against the
Member State in question on the basis of Article 169, EC Treaty. That the
quota rule is not particularly strict is again confirmed here, since it is stated
that

[t]he Commission may take account in its opinion, in particular, of progress achieved
in relation to previous years, the share of first broadcast works in the programming,
the particular circumstances of new television broadcasters and the specific situation of countries with a low audiovisual production capacity or restricted language
area.[49]

Next to these reporting requirements, it is provided in Article 4 (4) that the
Council shall review the implementation of the rules within a period of five
years. It shall do so on the basis of a report from the Commission which may
be accompanied by proposals for revision. This report shall 'take account ...
of developments in the Community market and of the international context'.

---

[46] See, however, also Ch. 10, p. 335.   [47] Art. 6 (4).

[48] This report should include a statistical statement on the achievement of the quota's proportion, the reasons for any failure to attain that proportion and the measures adopted and envisaged
to achieve it.

[49] Art. 4 (3), last sentence.

Comments

In the legal writing on the subject, the quota provisions of the directive have been extensively commented upon.[50] Not all that has been said there should be repeated here. Neither is this the place to repeat or add to the discussions concerning the merits of a quota for European works, looked at purely from a policy point of view. The observations below concentrate on issues which are important in the framework of this study, i.e. issues which are connected with regulating the external dimension of the internal market programme in the services sector. Whether the provisions are consistent with the GATT is examined in a separate section.

In Chapter 1, the question of the Community's competence in the field of international trade in services was examined. It was argued there that such a competence may be based on the EC Treaty chapter on the Common Commercial Policy (CCP), as well as on implied powers.[51] The television directive offers a concrete example of a measure for which this question of competence arises—and it shows how difficult the question may be. The directive has been adopted on the basis of Article 57 (2) of the EC Treaty. This Article provides that the Council shall 'issue directives for the coordination of the provisions laid down by law, regulation or administrative action in Member States concerning the taking up and pursuit of activities as self-employed persons'. Article 113 is not mentioned in the directive, neither is the concept of commercial policy. Obviously, this does not mean that the quota rules are not liable, at least potentially, to restrict exports of television programmes from non-European third countries to the Community. They may indeed have appreciable effects on trade[52] (leaving aside the question whether the sale of a television programme is trade in services or trade in goods).[53] If one were to apply to the quota rules the instrumental approach to the concept of commercial policy traditionally advocated by the Commission, they would have to be characterized as a measure of commercial policy.[54] That would also be the case if one follows the rule-of-reason approach defended by Timmermans.[55] The measure in question is of such a nature that the Member States are not

[50] See e.g. Wallace and Goldberg, *supra* n. 28, pp. 182–6; Porter, *supra* n. 2, pp. 69–70; Timothy M. Lupinacci, 'The Pursuit of Television Broadcasting Activities in the European Community: Cultural Preservation or Economic Protectionism?', 24 *Vanderbilt Journal of Transnational Law* (1991), 1: 113–54; Jean-Paul Hordies and François Jongen, 'La directive "télévision sans frontières": analyse juridique', in *L'Espace audiovisuel européen, supra* n. 5, pp. 78–80; Salvatore, *supra* n. 22.

[51] See p. 41.

[52] A lot depends on market developments, of course. According to François Danis demand for programmes will expand, leaving the United States a lot of room for augmenting their exports of programmes, see 'Le point de vue de la Commission des Communautés européennes', in *L'Espace audiovisuel européen, supra* n. 5, p. 117.

[53] This question is dealt with below, pp. 132–3.

[54] For this approach, see Ch. 1, p. 21.   [55] See Ch. 1, pp. 29–31.

allowed to adopt it in respect of intra-Community trade: if a Member State was to provide that all nationally established broadcasters have to transmit a majority of national programmes, this would surely be found to be inconsistent with the EC Treaty.[56] But if, on the other hand, one were to apply the Council's method of looking at the concept of commercial policy from the point of view of the objective pursued, it would certainly be argued that the aim of the quota rules is to preserve Europe's cultural identity by stimulating European audiovisual production, that this aim is one of cultural policy and that consequently the measure is not one of commercial policy.[57]

Abstracting from the question whether the latter approach is the proper one, the problem is that if one follows it the Community's competence to lay down the quota may become questionable. Indeed, at the time of issuing the directive the Community had no explicit competence to deal with cultural matters.[58] It then has to be argued that Article 57 (2), on which the directive is based, allows for the pursuit of cultural objectives, although it only speaks of 'the coordination of provisions ... concerning the taking up and pursuit of activities as self-employed persons' in the context of realizing the freedom of establishment and the free movement of services. Obviously, that is a very wide interpretation of Article 57 (2). Suppose, however, that the Community had adopted the quota rules on the basis of Article 113 of the EC Treaty. That would almost have amounted to openly admitting that the measure in question is of a 'crude' commercial nature, and has little to do with righteous cultural objectives.[59]

These observations illustrate the tension which exists between the commercial policy facet and other facets of regulating international trade in services. As was mentioned in Chapter 1, service transactions are the subject of much regulation, pursuing various policy objectives.[60] This complicates the exercise of determining the scope of commercial policy in the field of services.

Nevertheless, if one applies the guide-lines set out in Chapter 1, based on Timmermans's rule-of-reason approach, the quota rules have to be characterized as a measure of commercial policy. And indeed, if one looks at their substance, this is defensible. The directive itself acknowledges that the immediate aim of the quota rules is to stimulate European audiovisual

---

[56] Cf. Case C-17/92, *FEDICINE* v. *Spain*, Judgment of 4 May 1993, not yet published, in which the Court held that legislation aimed at promoting the distribution of Spanish films operated at the detriment of the distribution of films made in other Member States, and hence was inconsistent with Arts. 59 and 60 of the Treaty.

[57] On the Council's approach, see Ch. 1, p. 21.

[58] That has changed with the entry into force of the Treaty on European Union. However, according to Art. 128 (5) harmonization of laws is not possible in the framework of the Community's cultural policy.

[59] Leaving aside the question of whether this is not indeed its character, cf. the critique by Porter, *supra* n. 2, p. 70.

[60] See p. 11.

production.[61] Such an aim clearly has an economic character, and it is pursued through the adoption of a measure affecting trade with third countries. The conclusion that this measure comes within the scope of the CCP seems appropriate.[62] Of course there is also the objective of preserving Europe's cultural identity. But this objective lies beyond the immediate aim of stimulating European production, and it remains to be seen whether the quota rules will help to achieve it.[63]

The provisions determining the concept of European works demonstrate how difficult it is to lay down and apply detailed rules of origin for complex products.[64] Of course, these provisions are not ordinary rules of origin. The latter are only aimed at determining the nationality of products in a technical and perfectly neutral manner (at least in principle). The definition of European works in the directive is not neutral, in that it directly indicates the kind of audiovisual production the Community wishes to stimulate. Nevertheless, the complexity is there. Especially the requirement that the programmes have to be 'mainly made with authors and workers residing in one or more States referred to' may pose problems. Do all the people who contributed to the production of a programme have to be counted? And is a technician as important as an actor when determining whether the work is mainly made in one of the countries concerned?[65] Furthermore, with respect to the requirements concerning the place of establishment of producers, the question arises whether the provisions will not be easily circumvented. It is simple enough for US producers, for example, to set up subsidiaries within the Community in order to qualify as European producers for the purpose of the quota rules.[66] One wonders, in view of all this, whether the rules are really operational and whether a more or less uniform application throughout the Community is guaranteed.

It is interesting to compare the quota rules with another set of provisions adopted by the Community in the field of services, and aimed at (potentially) limiting access to the internal market, namely the reciprocity provisions applying to financial services.[67] Such a comparison reveals that the aims are completely opposite. In the case of financial services it is clear that the relevant

---

[61] According to the preamble 'it is ... necessary to promote markets of sufficient size for television productions in the Member States to recover necessary investments not only by establishing common rules opening up national markets but also by envisaging for European productions where practicable and by appropriate means a majority proportion in television programmes of all Member States'.

[62] *Contra* Salvatore, *supra* n. 22, pp. 976–7.

[63] Compare with the concept of external harmonization, put forward in Ch. 7 on export controls, pp. 252–8. Compare also with Case C-17/92, *supra* n. 56, in which the Court did not accept the argument that national legislation aimed at (quantitatively) furthering the distribution of domestic films served cultural and not economic objectives (see paras. 18–21).

[64] Compare with Ch. 6, p. 225, and Ch. 9, pp. 311–12.

[65] Cf. Wallace and Goldberg, *supra* n. 28, p. 183.

[66] Ibid. 184.   [67] See Ch. 2.

rules are not aimed at sheltering domestic production from competition from third countries. On the contrary, they are aimed at opening up third-country markets for Community companies. That, however, is not the goal of the quota rules. Their objective is to stimulate domestic production by guaranteeing and protecting a certain amount of output. The difference means that individual third countries cannot eliminate the quota rules by offering improved access to their markets in negotiations with the Community. Actually, the quota appears not to be negotiable.

The European Works Quota and the GATT

From the beginning the United States have strongly contested the legitimacy of the quota for European works, arguing that it is inconsistent with the provisions of the GATT. They have taken the matter before the GATT and they have threatened to take action on the basis of the famous (or infamous) Section 301 of the Trade Act.[68] In response, the Commission has explained the Community's point of view to the US authorities, which is that the GATT is not relevant for the quota provisions, since the latter only relate to trade in services (namely broadcasting) and that is not covered by the GATT.[69] Not surprisingly, the issue has also surfaced in the Uruguay Round negotiations on a General Agreement on Trade in Services (GATS). The Community has pushed for the insertion of a cultural exception which would safeguard its quota rules. The United States strongly object to such an exception.[70]

This debate is the subject of this section. First, the question has to be answered whether the quota rules have to be looked at from the angle of trade in services or trade in goods. Secondly, the (possibly) relevant GATT provisions are to be examined. Thirdly, the GATS negotiations are to be dealt with.

Goods or services?

Although the GATT does not provide in so many words that it only applies to trade in goods,[71] it is generally acknowledged that it was not intended to cover services.[72] The fact that services trade is the subject of a separate section of the Uruguay Round negotiations is the most visible token of this view. However,

---

[68] See '1992 National Trade Estimate Report on Foreign Trade Barriers', reported in *USA Text*, 30 Mar. 1992, p. 4. See also Lupinacci, *supra* n. 50, pp. 125–51. On Section 301 in general, see J. Bhagwati and H. T. Patrick (eds.), *Aggressive Unilateralism: America's 301 Trade Policy and the World Trading System* (New York: Harvester Wheatsheaf, 1990).

[69] See e.g. *Agence Europe*, No. 5147, 7 Dec. 1989, p. 9.

[70] Sapir, *supra* n. 5, p. 168.

[71] The General Agreement speaks of 'products', 'imports', and 'exports'.

[72] See John H. Jackson, *The World Trading System: Law and Policy of International Economic Relations* (Cambridge, Mass.: The MIT Press, 1989), 42.

the concept of 'good' or 'product' is not defined in the General Agreement, and there is little or no GATT practice which would assist in drawing up a definition of these concepts.[73] Thus, GATT experience does not provide accurate rules for determining whether television broadcasting comes within the scope of the Agreement or not.

The Community has consistently argued that broadcasting is the provision of services, and that, consequently, the quota rules are not to be scrutinized under the rules of the GATT. In view of the above-mentioned case-law of the European Court of Justice, which defines television broadcasting as a service, this argument appears logical. But things may not be as clear-cut. It is necessary to look at the effects of the quota rules in somewhat more detail.

The rules limit (at least potentially) the freedom of European broadcasters to transmit non-European works. There can be little doubt that this transmission itself is not a transaction involving goods. Neither television signals nor the images which they produce are tangible. However, the quota rules also affect (again at least potentially) imports of television programmes from non-European countries. The question therefore arises whether trade in programmes is to be regarded as trade in goods or trade in services. In this connection, it is useful to recall what the Court of Justice decided in the *Sacchi* case: 'trade in material, sound recordings, films, apparatus and other products used for the diffusion of television signals is subject to the rules relating to freedom of movement for goods'.[74] Similarly, in the *Warner Brothers* case the Court checked the consistency of restrictions on trade in video-cassettes with the provisions of Articles 30–6, EC Treaty.[75] On the other hand, in the *FEDICINE* case the Court decided that the distribution of cinema films is to be considered as the provision of services, and not movement of goods.[76]

Of course, the Community's internal rules and practices can only serve as a point of reference for determining whether trade in television programmes comes within the scope of the GATT or not. The question has also surfaced within the GATT itself, as the following examination of the relevant GATT provisions will show.

Relevant GATT provisions

The problem of cultural policies having an effect on trade already existed at the time when the General Agreement was drafted. There is, accordingly, one provision dealing with a specific aspect of this problem, then prevalent, and which is particularly relevant for the Community's quota rules. It is Article IV,

[73] Cf. John H. Jackson, *World Trade and the Law of GATT* (Indianapolis: Bobbs-Merrill, 1969), 259 *et seq.*
[74] See n. 18.
[75] Case 158/86, *Warner Brothers and Metronome Video* v. *Christiansen*, [1988] ECR 2605.
[76] Case C-17/92, *supra* n. 56. See also the Opinion of Advocate-General Van Gerven, paras. 7–11.

concerning 'Special Provisions relating to Cinematograph Films', which provides that '[i]f any contracting party establishes or maintains internal quantitative regulations relating to exposed cinematograph films, such regulations shall take the form of screen quotas'. These quotas had to conform to a number of subsequently enumerated requirements, and were to be the subject of 'negotiation for their limitation, liberalization or elimination'. The provision was aimed at addressing the then widely spread practice of countries protecting their national film production through the use of quotas, not by outlawing these quotas, but by subjecting them to a number of disciplines.[77] As such, Article IV is an exception to the rules of Article III, on national treatment of imported products.[78] It should be recalled that Article III (5) prohibits

any internal quantitative regulation relating to the mixture, processing or use of products in specified amounts or proportions which requires, directly or indirectly, that any specified amount or proportion of any product which is the subject of the regulation must be supplied from domestic sources.

It is obvious that if one were to characterize television programmes as products (and leaving aside Article IV), the Community's quota rules would have to be considered as infringing this provision.

At the beginning of the sixties, the United States made an effort to have trade in television programmes submitted to GATT disciplines.[79] They argued that the various restrictions on such trade infringed the GATT and were not covered by the exception of Article IV. At their request, a working party was established, but it was impossible to reach agreement on the issue. The question was not addressed any more after that, until the GATS negotiations.

The fact that the GATT contracting parties could reach no agreement on the applicability of the GATT to trade in television programmes is certainly an argument in favour of the Community's thesis that the quota rules are not covered by the GATT. And even if they are, one could maintain that the exception of Article IV should be applied by analogy.

The GATS negotiations

As was mentioned, the issue of television quotas also surfaced in the negotiations on a General Agreement on Trade in Services. These negotiations deal also with audiovisual services, and the United States has tried to obtain commitments for reducing existing quotas. The Community has defended the quota rules as a measure serving cultural objectives. Sapir reports that at the Ministerial Meeting of December 1990, which was aimed at concluding the

---

[77] See Sapir, *supra* n. 5, p. 166.   [78] See Ch. 2, pp. 79–82.
[79] See Jackson, *supra* n. 73, p. 294 and Sapir, *supra* n. 5, pp. 166–7.

Uruguay Round, the various participants defended three different approaches.[80] Some were in favour of a general exception for cultural matters, others were of the view that cultural objectives should be taken into account in a separate annex on audiovisual services. The United States and Japan, however, were against all exceptions for cultural reasons.

The issue has not yet been resolved in the course of subsequent negotiations. The General Agreement on Trade in Services, as taken up in the Draft Final Act of December 1991, does not contain any references to cultural objectives, nor is there a specific annex on audiovisual services.[81] Perhaps this will be dealt with in the framework of specific commitments on market access, based on Article XVI, which are still the subject of negotiations.[82]

Conclusion

The case of television quotas illustrates the tension between economic and cultural policy. Often the only instruments in the hands of governments for conducting a cultural policy are of an economic nature. That also applies to the quota policy. In order to achieve certain cultural objectives, restrictions on trade in television programmes are being enforced.

The said tension does not only manifest itself with respect to cultural policy, but also exists in other fields such as the protection of the environment. It is a delicate exercise to devise appropriate rules and concepts allowing to strike a balance between economic and non-economic policies. In this respect it must be said that the television quota is not very sophisticated. If multilateral rules were to be devised governing cultural exceptions in the field of services trade, one would hope that they would be somewhat more refined.

2. TELECOMMUNICATIONS SERVICES

Introduction

In the philosophy of the internal market programme, stimulating the development of the Community's telecommunications sector is one of the most

---

[80] *Supra* n. 5, p. 168.   [81] See MTN.TNC/W/FA, Annex.

[82] Art. XVI (1) provides: 'With respect to market access through the modes of supply identified in Article I, each Party shall accord services and service providers of other Parties treatment no less favourable than that provided for under the terms, limitations and conditions agreed and specified in its schedule.' In the second paragraph, the concept of market access is further defined by way of an enumeration of the kind of measures which are not allowed, unless otherwise specified in a country's schedule. Among these measures are 'limitations on the total number of service operations or on the total quantity of service output expressed in terms of designated numerical units in the form of quotas or the requirement of an economic needs test' (Art. XVI (2) (c)).

important objectives. Modern telecommunications are seen as a key component of a prospering post-industrial society. They are subject to rapid and fundamental technological change, and European industries are not always at the forefront compared with their US and Japanese counterparts, who operate in a much more deregulated environment. This lack of competitiveness is, if not entirely then in any case at least partly, caused by the fragmentation of the Community's market along national lines. Indeed, the protagonists in this sector are the national telecommunications organizations (TOs, or PTTs). In nearly all the Member States, they operate from a monopoly position, dominating both the markets of procurement of equipment and of telecommunications services. Their procurement policies have been nationally oriented, preventing the development of equipment manufacturers operating on a continental scale, and thereby precluding significant economies of scale.[83] And their monopolies with respect to the provision of services hinder the advancement of a range of new kinds of telecommunications services, based on high technology and responding to the fast growing need for the supply of information.

The Community's policies are aimed at reshaping this environment. From a legal point of view, they are multifaceted, based on various instruments of Community action.[84] Complementing the regulation of the provision of telecommunications services as such, which is discussed in this chapter, and which combines liberalization and harmonization, there are many other policies. Without attempting to be exhaustive, one can mention efforts in the field of technical regulations and standards, where the internal market programme has led to the creation of a European Telecommunications Standards Institute (ETSI);[85] directives in the field of public procurement, aimed at opening up the procurement practices of the TOs to intra-Community competition;[86] the establishment of a pan-European telecommunications infrastructure;[87] the application of competition law to the sector.[88] All of these policies

---

[83] See the Commission's *Green Paper on the development of the Common Market for Telecommunications Services and Equipment*, COM (87) 290 final of 30 June 1987, p. 72, where the Commission observed that none of the Member States represented more than 6% of the world market.

[84] See for recent overviews Richard Wainwright and Anders C. Jessen, 'Recent Developments in Community Law on Telecommunications', in A. Barav and D. A. Wyatt (eds.), 11 *Yearbook of European Law* (1991) (Oxford: Clarendon Press, 1992), 79–110 and A. Jaume, 'La libéralisation du secteur des télécommunications: aspects techniques et juridiques', *RMUE* (1992), 1: 117–42.

[85] See Ch. 8, p. 266.   [86] See Ch. 9.

[87] See Wainwright and Jessen, *supra* n. 84, pp. 88–90 and Jaume, *supra* n. 84, pp. 133–4.

[88] See in particular Colin Overbury and Piero Ravaioli, 'The Application of EEC Law to Telecommunications', in B. Hawk (ed.), *1992 and EEC/U.S. Competition and Trade Law: Annual Proceedings of the Fordham Corporate Law Institute 1989* (New York: Transnational Juris Publications, 1990), 286–312. Competition policy in the field of telecommunications will not be further discussed here, although it also has an external dimension, see ibid. 309–12 and Manuel Kohnstamm, 'Conflicts between International and European Network Regulation: An Analysis of Third Parties' Rights in European Community Law, *LIEI* (1990), 2: 45–99.

have to some extent an external dimension. However, as regards Community action in the field of the provision of telecommunications services as such, there are few initiatives dealing specifically with external relations, as the analysis below will demonstrate. This must not be interpreted as signifying that the Community's telecommunications policy is inward looking. One should bear in mind the components of this policy which are not studied in this chapter—a number of them being analysed in other chapters. Accordingly, the telecommunications dimension of this study is not confined to the following pages.

The analysis consists of two main sections. In the first, the policies undertaken by the Community in the course of the internal market programme which concern the provision of telecommunications services are described, and their external dimension is examined. The following section is prospective, looking at the direction in which future policies might go.

Community Policies Concerning Telecommunications Services

Overview

The Community's approach towards the provision of telecommunications services is based on two concepts: liberalization and harmonization.[89] The first concept indicates that the monopolies of the telecommunications organizations, in most cases laid down in national law, are gradually being abolished. The second refers to measures aimed at harmonizing the conditions for access to the basic telecommunications networks. This approach was for the first time described in the Commission's 1987 Green Paper on telecommunications.[90] The Commission then took the position that the national telecommunications administrations would continue to have exclusive or special rights over the provision and operation of the network infrastructure as well as over the provision of basic telecommunications services. The latter term was to be narrowly construed, but in any case encompassed voice telephony. All other services, however, including so-called value-added services,[91] were to be subject to free competition. Concerning access to the network, on the other hand, the adoption of a directive on what is termed 'Open Network Provision' was envisaged, meaning that the technical conditions under which service providers can obtain such access are harmonized. This was considered essential for the development of Community-wide competition in liberalized telecommunications services. On the basis of the Green Paper and the

[89] Overbury and Ravaioli, *supra* n. 88, pp. 287–8.
[90] *Supra* n. 83, especially at p. 18.
[91] See on this concept Herbert Ungerer with Nicholas P. Costello, *Telecommunications in Europe*, 2nd edn. (Luxembourg: Office for Official Publications of the EC, 1990), 53–62.

consultations and discussion to which it gave rise the Commission drew up a concrete action programme,[92] which was endorsed by the Council.[93]

The method which has been followed for liberalizing other than basic telecommunications services is much discussed. Instead of using the by now classical instrument of harmonization of national legislation on the basis of Article 100*a*, EC Treaty, the Commission has used its autonomous powers under Article 90 (3). As is well known, this provision allows the Commission to address directives or decisions to the Member States to ensure the application of the provisions of Article 90, which deals with public undertakings and undertakings to which Member States grant special or exclusive rights. With respect to such undertakings, the Member States 'shall neither enact nor maintain in force any measure contrary to the rules contained in this Treaty, in particular to those rules provided for in Article 7 and Articles 85 to 94'.[94]

This method was used for the first time in 1988, not in relation to telecommunications services but with a view to liberalizing the markets in telecommunications terminal equipment.[95] In essence, this directive provided that all special or exclusive rights granted by the Member States to public or private undertakings relating to the 'importation, marketing, connection, bringing into service of telecommunications terminal equipment and/or maintenance of such equipment' had to be withdrawn.[96] This way of proceeding has come under attack from a number of Member States, which brought a case before the Court of Justice against the directive. However, the Court basically upheld the Commission's approach, annulling only a few of the directive's provisions.[97]

In 1990 the Commission adopted its Directive on competition in the markets for telecommunications services.[98] In the preamble of this instrument the Commission refers to the policies proposed by the Green Paper and endorsed by the Council. It points to the fact that the technological advances

[92] Communication from the Commission, 'Towards a Competitive Community-wide Telecommunications Market in 1992—Implementing the Green Paper...', COM (88) 48 final of 9 Feb. 1988.

[93] Council Resolution of 30 June 1988 on the development of the common market for telecommunications services and equipment up to 1992, OJ C 257/1 of 4 Oct. 1988.

[94] Art. 90 (1). See, however, also para. 2, which provides that '[u]ndertakings entrusted with the operation of services of general economic interest or having the character of a revenue-producing monopoly shall be subject to the rules contained in this Treaty, in particular to the rules on competition, in so far as the application of such rules does not obstruct the performance, in law or in fact, of the particular tasks assigned to them...'.

[95] Commission Directive of 16 May 1988 on competition in the markets in telecommunications terminal equipment, OJ L 131/73 of 27 May 1988.

[96] See Arts. 1 and 2 of the Directive (*supra* n. 95).

[97] See Case C-202/88, *France* v. *Commission*, [1991] ECR I-1223. The Court found that the abolition of 'special rights' was not sufficiently motivated and that in a general directive on the basis of Art. 90 (3) of the Treaty the Commission could not lay down obligations directly addressed to undertakings.

[98] Directive of 28 June 1990, OJ L 192/10 of 24 July 1990.

of the last decades have given rise to an increasingly varied range of services and have made it technically and economically possible for competition to take place between various service providers.[99] It then refers to the monopoly positions occupied by the telecommunications organizations, which result from special or exclusive rights granted by the Member States. The granting of such rights inevitably causes restrictions in the sense of Article 59 of the EC Treaty.[100] These restrictions cannot be justified, either on the basis of Articles 55, 56, or 66 of the Treaty or on the basis of essential requirements recognized in the case-law of the Court of Justice.

The only essential requirements derogating from Article 59 which could justify restrictions on the use of the public network are the maintenance of the integrity of the network, security of network operations and in justified cases, interoperability and data protection.[101]

The Commission subsequently clarifies the sort of restrictions which Member States may still impose. It goes further by demonstrating that the granting of the said special or exclusive rights is inconsistent with Article 86 of the Treaty.[102] Moreover, the restrictions resulting from this grant can only partly be excused on the basis of Article 90 (2), which provides that the rules of the Treaty shall only apply to undertakings 'entrusted with the operation of services of general economic interest or having the character of a revenue-producing monopoly' to the extent that this 'does not obstruct the performance, in law or in fact, of the particular tasks assigned to them'. For telecommunications organizations, this task consists of providing and exploiting a universal network. Since the financial resources for the development of this network are derived mainly from the operation of the telephone service, the opening-up of voice telephony to competition could threaten the financial stability of these organizations.[103] The directive therefore does not apply to voice telephony. It also does not apply to telex services, as the Commission considers that an individual approach is necessary here.[104]

---

[99] Para. 1 of the preamble. Further on the Commission mentions a number of such services: services designed to improve telecommunications functions; information services providing access to data bases; remote data-processing services; message storing and forwarding services; transactions services such as teleshopping; teleaction services (see para. 6).

[100] The Commission mentions, as examples, the prohibition on connecting leased lines to the switched telephone network, the imposition of excess charges out of proportion to the service provided, the prohibition of routing signals by means of leased lines, the application of volume sensitive tariffs without justification and the refusal to give service providers access to the network (see para. 6).

[101] Para. 8. These concepts are defined in para. 9.

[102] Art. 86 prohibits abuse of a dominant position by undertakings.

[103] Para. 18. The Commission also acknowledges that the telecommunications organizations may require private operators not to offer a service consisting merely of the resale of leased lines (para. 19).

[104] Para. 21.

In accordance with these considerations the key provision of the directive requires that

Member States shall withdraw all special or exclusive rights for the supply of telecommunications services other than voice telephony and shall take the measures necessary to ensure that any operator is entitled to supply such telecommunications services.[105]

Other provisions deal with licensing or declaration procedures for the provision of packet- or circuit-switched data services (Article 3), with access to the network (Article 4), technical interfaces (Article 5), the abolishment of restrictions on processing of signals (Article 6), and with ensuring that regulatory functions are no longer carried out by the telecommunications organizations, but instead by an independent body (Article 7).

This directive has also been attacked before the Court of Justice, which again basically upheld the Commission's approach, annulling only the provisions on special rights in very much the same way as the above-mentioned judgment.[106]

It should be emphasized that, although the directive appears to be a great step towards liberalization, in economic terms it is not so since the major share of all revenue accruing from the provision of telecommunications services is still generated by voice telephony, which remains subject to the existing monopolies.[107]

Besides this directive, there are the efforts for achieving open network provision. The basic text governing these efforts is a Council Directive of 28 June 1990 on the establishment of the internal market for telecommunications services through the implementation of open network provision.[108] It lays down the principles governing ONP conditions, which must be based on objective criteria, transparent and published, 'they must guarantee equality of access and must be non-discriminatory'.[109] These conditions must not restrict access except for reasons based on the essential requirements, referred to above.[110] On the basis of this framework directive, a number of more specific instruments have been adopted or proposed concerning leased lines,[111]

[105] Art. 2.

[106] See Joined Cases C-271/90, C-281/90, and C-289/90, *Spain, Belgium and Italy* v. *Commission*, Judgment of 17 Nov. 1992, not yet published.

[107] See, however, *infra*, pp. 143–4. According to the Commission, '[v]oice telephony is the biggest and economically important service operated by telecommunications organizations', see proposal for a Council Directive on the application of open network provision (ONP) to voice telephony, COM (92) 247 final of 27 Aug. 1992.

[108] OJ L 192/1 of 24 July 1990. ONP is defined as 'the conditions, harmonized according to the provisions of this directive, which concern the open and efficient access to public telecommunications networks and, where applicable, public telecommunications services and the efficient use of those networks and services', see Art. 2 (10).

[109] Art. 3 (1).

[110] Art. 3 (2). For the essential requirements, see text at n. 101.

[111] See Commission proposal for a Council Directive on the application of open network provision to leased lines, OJ C 58/10 of 7 Mar. 1991.

integrated services digital network (ISDN),[112] packet-switched data services (PSDS),[113] and voice telephony.[114]

The external dimension

It goes without saying that telecommunications services are not only provided within the Community, but also to and from third countries. Nevertheless, the above-described regulatory instruments contain hardly any references to external trade in these services, and do not include a specific regime for such trade. That signifies, apparently, that the rules apply without distinction to the provision of services in and between Member States and to their provision to third countries. The directive on competition in the markets for telecommunications services,[115] for example, does not limit the withdrawal of exclusive rights, granted to telecommunications organizations, to services provided entirely within the Community. One may therefore assume that this abolition also applies to the provision of services to third countries. Similarly, the directive provides that the Member States must 'ensure that any operator is entitled to supply ... telecommunications services',[116] without limiting the concept of operator to service providers established in the Community and therefore also applying to foreign service providers.[117]

Comparable observations can be made with respect to ONP instruments. However, in this case there is one reference to external relations. The preamble of the framework directive provides that

the Community attaches very great importance ... to the increased participation of Community service providers in third country markets; whereas it will therefore be necessary, as specific directives are drawn up, to ensure that these directives are taken into account with a view to reaching a situation where the progressive realization of the internal market for telecommunications services will, where appropriate, be accompanied by reciprocal market opening in other countries;

Whereas this result should be achieved preferably through multilateral negotiations in the framework of GATT, it being understood that bilateral discussions between the Community and third countries may also contribute to this process.[118]

---

[112] Council Recommendation of 5 June 1992 on the provision of harmonized ISDN access arrangements and a minimum set of ISDN offerings in accordance with ONP principles, OJ L 200/10 of 18 July 1992.

[113] Council Recommendation of 5 June 1992 on the harmonized provision of a minimum set of packet-switched data services in accordance with ONP principles, OJ L 200/1 of 18 July 1992.

[114] COM (92) 247 final, *supra* n. 107.

[115] See *supra* n. 98.

[116] Art. 2.

[117] Although for technical reasons it will probably often be necessary to have an establishment in the Community.

[118] Directive on ONP, *supra* n. 108, OJ L 192/2 of 24 July 1990.

In spite of this declaration of intent, which is in line with the reciprocity policy applying in the financial services sector,[119] the other ONP instruments do not mention external relations.

There are, however, two possible developments which are likely to play a much more significant role in defining the external dimension of the internal market in telecommunications services. These are the Uruguay Round negotiations on a General Agreement on Trade in Services and the liberalization of voice telephony. They are examined below.

Prospects

GATS

The Uruguay Round negotiations of course also cover telecommunications services. Negotiations in this area have been difficult, for one thing because the United States have insisted on excluding telecommunications from the most-favoured-nation rule.[120] To understand this one should bear in mind that the United States have a system of open competition, in which access to the basic telecommunications networks is relatively unrestricted. It is reported that the US fear that the application of the MFN rule would expose US service providers to foreign competition, whilst they would not be able to compete on foreign markets because of monopolies that exist there. Indeed, the draft GATS included in the Draft Final Act submitted by GATT Director-General Dunkel does not prohibit monopolies or the granting of exclusive rights to service providers. It is mentioned in a footnote that '[n]othing in this Agreement condemns or condones the creation or maintenance of monopoly service providers'.[121] These monopolies are the subject of the negotiations on specific commitments, meaning that in case a Party includes in its schedule of concessions a specific kind of service it can no longer grant exclusive or monopoly rights in that regard. That follows from Article XVI on market access, which mentions as measures which a party shall not maintain or adopt in sectors or subsectors where market access commitments are undertaken: 'limitations on the number of service providers whether in the form of numerical quotas, *monopolies, exclusive service providers* or the requirements of an economic needs test'.[122] Consequently, the degree to which the Community opens up its market in telecommunications services to foreign competition in the framework of the GATS will depend on the specific commitments it will undertake.

---

[119] See Ch. 2.

[120] See e.g. 'U.S. blocks GATT telecoms deal at last minute', *Financial Times*, 19 Oct. 1990, p. 4 and 'U.S. stands firm on telecom deal', *Financial Times*, 11 Oct. 1991, p. 3.

[121] Note to Art. VIII, see MTN.TNC/W/FA, p. 14 of the annex. None the less, Art. VIII lays down a number of obligations with respect to monopolies and exclusive service providers.

[122] Art. XVI (2) (*a*), italics added.

It is reported by the Commission that the Community has made an offer regarding value-added services and basic data services, 'based on the current state of liberalisation within the Community'.[123]

The draft GATS also contains an Annex on Telecommunications, aimed at elaborating on the provisions of the Agreement concerning measures affecting access to and use of telecommunications networks and services.[124] Paragraph 5 of this Annex clarifies the obligations relating to such access and use. It provides, for example, that no conditions may be imposed other than those necessary to safeguard the public service responsibilities of suppliers of networks and services, to protect the technical integrity of networks or services and to ensure that service suppliers of other Parties do not supply other services than those included in a Party's schedule of concessions.[125] It would lead us too far, however, to study the contents of this Annex in any further detail.

Liberalizing voice telephony?

As was mentioned above voice telephony is in economic terms by far the most important sector of telecommunications services.[126] The Community's approach until recently has been not to challenge the exclusive or special rights granted in this field by the Member States to national telecommunications organizations. That has changed, however. In its 1992 review of the situation in the telecommunications sector the Commission observed that tariffs for voice telephony between Member States are still excessive, when compared with purely national calls. It put forward four possible options:

1. to maintain the status quo;
2. to introduce extensive Community regulation of tariffs and investments;
3. to liberalize all international and national voice telephony;
4. to liberalize only voice telephony between Member States, an option favoured at that time by the Commission.[127]

However, consultations based on this review have shown that there is general acceptance that in view of technological and market developments the option of phased full liberalization is to be preferred.[128] Accordingly, the Com-

---

[123] See the Communication to the Council and the European Parliament on the consultation on the review of the situation in the telecommunications services sector, COM (93) 159 final of 28 Apr. 1993, p. 29, n. 20.
[124] See MTN.TNC/W/FA, pp. 39–44 of the annex.
[125] See para. 5.6.
[126] See p. 139.
[127] See SEC (92) 1048 final of 21 Oct. 1992.
[128] See COM (93) 159 final (*supra* n. 123), p. 18.

mission has proposed a programme, running until 1998, for achieving such liberalization, and this approach was accepted by the Council.[129]

It goes without saying that the external policies of the Community accompanying this liberalization will substantially affect and determine the external dimension of the internal market in telecommunications services. The Commission is of the view that a balanced international environment should be achieved, and emphasizes the necessity to obtain equivalent opportunities in other markets. In other words, the concept of reciprocity is again referred to. The Commission refers to the GATS negotiations as the proper framework for pursuing multilateral liberalization (and reciprocity), and considers a purely bilateral approach as inappropriate.[130] In line with these views, the Council also stresses the goal of obtaining comparable and equivalent access to third country markets.[131]

Conclusion

In the case of telecommunications services the external dimension of the Community's policies is not yet the subject of a specific regime. The result is that these policies apply without discrimination to foreign service providers. However, the most important developments probably still lie ahead. If the Uruguay Round negotiations are successfully concluded, the GATS will provide the framework for the Community's external policy of multilateral liberalization. It remains to be seen how this policy will develop in the economically most important area of voice telephony. It would not be surprising if, in liberalizing voice telephony, the Community were to require reciprocity from its trading partners in much the same way as it did in the financial services sector (Chapter 2).

[129] See Council Resolution of 22 July 1993 on the review of the situation in the telecommunications sector and the need for further development in that market, OJ C 213/1 of 6 Aug. 1993.
[130] See COM (93) 159 final, *supra* n. 123, pp. 28–9.
[131] See the resolution, *supra* n. 129.

5

The Community Regime for Imports of Goods from Third Countries

Introduction

In the Commission's White Paper on the completion of the internal market there are few references to the external dimension of the programme. One of these—probably the most important one—concerns the application of Article 115, EC Treaty. The scope of this provision is well known. It allows that Member States restrict intra-Community trade in products, originating in third countries, for which there is not yet a uniform Community import regime. Hence, for a number of products Member States were still able to protect their national market, not only against direct imports from third countries, but also against indirect imports, against products which were in free circulation in the Community. However, to fend off indirect imports required controls at intra-Community borders. These controls are one of the main targets of the internal market programme. Their elimination is one of the most tangible elements of '1992' for the public at large. Consequently, some solution had to be found for the problem that Article 115 was still applied, giving rise to intra-Community border controls.

It is therefore not surprising to find the Commission's views on this problem in the White Paper chapter on the removal of physical barriers.[1] However, the problem at hand is a more fundamental one than simply eliminating one of a number of different controls on trade, taking place at intra-Community borders. The Commission acknowledged this in its White Paper, stating that '[i]t is worth noting that it is the absence of or failure to apply a common policy which give rise' to the application of Article 115. The common policy referred to is of course the Common Commercial Policy (CCP). Article 113 of the Treaty provides that this policy 'shall be based on uniform principles'. In *Donckerwolcke*, the Court of Justice clarified the relationship between Articles 113 and 115 and defined, with respect to importation of goods, how the requirement of 'uniform principles' has to be understood:

The assimilation to products originating within the Member States of goods in 'free circulation' may only take full effect if these goods are subject to *the same conditions of importation both with regard to customs and commercial considerations, irrespective of the State in which they were put into free circulation.*

[1] COM (310) final, paras. 35–6.

Under Article 113 of the Treaty this unification should have been achieved by the expiry of the transitional period and supplanted by the establishment of a common commercial policy based on uniform principles.[2]

Thus, it is the incomplete state of the CCP that gives rise to the application of Article 115. The fact that there are no uniform conditions of importation of third-country products—at least not with respect to all of them—is, in the Court's wording, 'one of a number of circumstances calculated to maintain in being between the Member States differences in commercial policy capable of bringing about deflections of trade or of causing economic difficulties in certain Member States'.[3]

From the point of view of completing the internal market, one could look at this incompleteness of the CCP rather indifferently. The main problem, in such an approach, would be to eliminate the controls at intra-Community borders resulting from the application of Article 115. If this aim can be reached by completing the CCP, so much the better. If, however, this proves to be impossible, perhaps alternative ways of protecting national markets can be found, which do not require controls at the borders between the Member States. To some extent, this seemed to be the sort of solution advocated by the Commission in its White Paper.[4] However, such an approach would fail to address the essence of the problem.[5] Trade with third countries is in economic terms very important for the Community.[6] This is characteristic of today's economic relations between countries, marked by increasing global interdependence.[7] Nevertheless, it is particularly the case for the Community.[8] It is also particularly the case for those product sectors in which there was not yet a

[2] Case 41/76, [1976] ECR 1936 (italics added).

[3] [1976] ECR 1937. It is not clear what the Court means when it refers to 'one of a number of circumstances'. Other circumstances than non-uniform conditions of importation, giving rise to differences in commercial policy are difficult to envisage.

[4] Para. 36 of the White Paper states: 'If Article 115 were no longer to be applicable, any import restrictions would have to be applied on a Community-wide basis. The enforcement of such quotas, which relies to a large extent on the administrations of Member States, would require intensive cooperation between national administrations and the Commission. Should it prove impossible to eliminate all individual quotas for Member States by 1992, internal frontier controls could no longer be the instrument of their application. Alternative ways of applying quotas would need to be found.'

[5] Cf. Henri Froment-Meurice, *L'Europe de 1992: espace et puissance* (Paris: La Documentation française, 1988), 28–9.

[6] In 1990, imports and exports accounted for 23.8 and 22.8% of GDP respectively, see Eurostat, *Basic Statistics of the Community*, 29th edn. (Luxembourg: Office for Official Publications of the EC, 1992), 271.

[7] On this interdependence, see for example John H. Jackson, *The World Trading System* (Cambridge, Mass.): MIT Press, 1989), 2–4; Arthur Dunkel, Director-General of GATT, in a speech reported in *News of the Uruguay Round*, No. 48, 17 May 1991, pp. 7–9.

[8] Compare the figures in n. 6 with those of the USA and Japan: in 1990, imports and exports of the USA accounted for 9.2 and 7.9% of GDP respectively; imports and exports of Japan were at 7.9 and 9.7% respectively (see Eurostat, *supra* n. 6). See also Jacques H. J. Bourgeois, 'The Common Commercial Policy: Scope and Nature of the Powers', in E. L. M. Völker (ed.), *Protectionism and the European Community*, 2nd edn. (Deventer: Kluwer, 1986), 2–3.

uniform CCP. These are sensitive sectors, in which some national industries, or even the Community industry as a whole, have difficulties in competing with imports from third countries, the latter occupying substantial market shares, or in any event having the potential of doing so in the absence of protection. Motor vehicles, textiles and clothing, and bananas are the most prominent examples. In such sectors the lack of a uniform import regime hindered the completion of the internal market in two ways. First, there is no genuine internal market for the products imported from third countries which are subject to diverging conditions of importation, leading to the application of Article 115. These products are not able to circulate freely within the Community. There was (and is) for example no internal or single market for Japanese cars.[9] Secondly, these disparities result in distortions of competition within the internal market: companies established in protected Member States do not operate under the same conditions of competition as those established in other Member States, fully exposed to competition from abroad. Suppose bicycles produced in third countries can freely enter Member State *A*, but are not allowed to enter Member State *B*. Producers of bicycles established in *A* will then be subject to the pressure of third-country imports into their national market, whereas that will not be the case for *B*'s bicycle makers. Both of them, however, are competitors—potentially at least—throughout the Community, by virtue of the internal market. The distortion of competition that is liable to result from the different national commercial policies is obvious. It should not be forgotten that avoiding such distortions of competition is one of the fundamental aims of the CCP.[10] Moreover, the Court has made it clear, when determining the scope of Article 100*a* of the Treaty in the *Titanium Dioxide* case, that eliminating distortions of competition is also one of the main components of the establishment of the internal market. The Court held that

[a]ccording to the second paragraph of Article 8a of the EEC Treaty, that market is to comprise 'an area without internal frontiers in which the free movement of goods, persons, services and capital is ensured'. By virtue of Articles 2 and 3 of the Treaty, a precondition for such a market is the existence of conditions of competition which are not distorted.

In order to give effect to the fundamental freedoms mentioned in Article 8a, harmonizing measures are necessary to deal with disparities between the laws of the

---

[9] See *infra* Ch. 6, part 2.

[10] Cf. Opinion 1/75, in which the Court ruled that unilateral action by the Member States in the field of commercial policy could lead to disparities 'calculated to distort competition between undertakings of the various Member States' ([1975] ECR 1364); Joined Cases 37 and 38/73, *Diamantarbeiders* v. *Indiamex* [1973] ECR 1609 at 1622–3, where the Court ruled that the aim of the common tariff is 'to avoid any deflection of trade in relation with those [third] countries and any distortion of free internal circulation *or of competitive conditions*' (italics added), and where it subsequently pointed to the similar function of the CCP. On the role of a uniform commercial policy in avoiding distortions of competition, also see Christiaan W. A. Timmermans, 'Community Commercial Policy in Textiles: A Legal Imbroglio', in *Protectionism and the European Community*, *supra* n. 8, pp. 165–6. See also Ch. 1, p. 26.

Member States in areas where such disparities are liable to create or maintain distorted conditions of competition.[11]

The completion of the internal market therefore requires, among other things, the completion of the CCP.[12] It requires uniform conditions for importing third country products in the Community. That is the basic problem onto which the application of Article 115 is grafted.

This chapter examines the progress which has been made, in the course of the implementation of the internal market programme, in developing a more uniform policy. The various kinds of measures conditioning importation which were not yet uniformly applied at the start of the programme are analysed, taking into account the Court's case-law and the efforts which have been made to achieve the completion of the CCP. Subsequently, the question of the further application of Article 115 is studied. Here, the central issue is of course whether and, if so, to what extent and under which conditions this provision can still be applied after 1 January 1993.

The analysis below is of a general nature. There are, however, three categories of sensitive products for which specific 'solutions' have been devised. They were already mentioned above: cars, textiles and clothing, and bananas. These solutions require special attention, because they raise a number of distinct legal and policy issues. They are dealt with in the following chapter.

The Completion of the Common Commercial Policy

Above reference was made to the *Donckerwolcke* judgment, in which the Court held that the assimilation of goods which are in free circulation to products originating in the Member States can only take full effect if these goods are subject to the same conditions of importation, irrespective of the State in which they are put in free circulation, and that such uniform conditions should have been brought about by the end of the transitional period (31 December 1969).[13] There is little doubt that the 'uniform conditions of importation' to which the Court refers only encompass regulatory measures affecting the importation of products in the Community, and do not extend to general economic conditions of importation, such as demand, price elasticity, and consumer preferences. Indeed, it would make no sense trying to make those conditions of importation uniform. Nevertheless, even when so limited, the concept of conditions of importation is fairly broad. There are a host of regulatory measures which have the potential of affecting the importation of goods. No attempt will be made here to list all these measures.[14] The analysis

---

[11] Case C-300/89, *Commission* v. *Council*, [1991] ECR I-2867, at I-2899.

[12] Leslie Fielding, *Europe as a Global Partner*, UACES Occasional Papers 7 (London, 1991), 4.

[13] *Supra* n. 2.

[14] That is the question of the scope of the CCP, on which there is a lot of literature. For an excellent overview, see Bourgeois, *supra* n. 8, pp. 1–16.

below concentrates on those measures the main purpose of which is to condition importation. These include tariffs, quantitative restrictions, safe-guard measures, voluntary export restraints, and measures aimed at combat-ing unfair trade (in the case of dumping or export subsidies). Only as regards the last category was full uniformity achieved before the internal market programme. Anti-dumping and countervailing duties were and are levied at the same level at all the Community's external borders, completely indepen-dent of the Member State of importation.[15] To a large extent, the same was of course true for tariffs: the Community has a uniform Common Customs Tariff.[16] However, a number of so-called tariff quotas, allowing certain quantities of goods to be imported free of or at a reduced rate of duty, were not administrated in a completely uniform fashion. Lastly, with respect to quanti-tative restrictions (QRs), safeguard measures and voluntary export restraints uniformity was still some way off.

The analysis below is subdivided, for each category of measures, in two sections. The first deals with the situation as it stood before the internal market programme, describing the then existing lack of uniformity and evaluating it in the light of the Court's case-law. The second section reports the progress which has been made towards bringing about uniformity in the course of the programme.

Quantitative restrictions

Starting-point and legal status

Most products enter the European Community free from quantitative re-strictions. That is in line with the rules of the GATT, which are binding on the Community.[17] There were, broadly speaking, two exceptions to this free access. On the one hand, for a number of products there still existed QRs at the level of one or more Member States. On the other, the Community has set a number of quotas for imports of textiles and clothing; these quotas were subdivided between the Member States.

(a) National QRs

In 1985–6, quite a number of products remained subject to national QRs, despite the fact that there had been a Common Commercial Policy for about

[15] See Regulation 2423/88 on protection against dumped or subsidized imports from countries not members of the EEC, OJ L 209/1 of 2 Aug. 1988. On the basis of Art. 10 of this regulation, the Commission may accept undertakings given by exporters, instead of imposing anti-dumping duties. It is reported that these undertakings sometimes consist of quantitative limits on exports to specific Member States, see Jean-François Bellis, 'The EEC Antidumping System', in J. H. Jackson and E. A. Vermulst (eds.), *Antidumping Law and Practice: A Comparative Study* (New York: Harvester Wheatsheaf, 1990), 52.

[16] See Regulation 2658/87 on the tariff and statistical nomenclature and on the Common Customs Tariff, OJ L 256/1 of 7 Sept. 1987.

[17] See Art. XI of GATT.

fifteen years. There were two categories, according to the country of origin of the products. The first category applied to the (now to some extent former) State-trading countries. For imports from these countries the products still subject to QRs were listed in Regulation 3420/83 on import arrangements for products originating in State-trading countries, not liberalized at Community level.[18] The implementation of this regulation required that each year the Council drew up a list of import quotas to be opened by the Member States.[19] The second category applied to imports from the rest of the world.[20] Regulation 288/82 determined, for these imports, which products were still subject to QRs in one or more Member States.[21]

The legal status of these national QRs was in many respects dubious. A number of them were probably inconsistent with the GATT.[22] More important, however, within the scope of this analysis is the question whether the enforcement of these QRs was consistent with the EC Treaty, and more specifically the exclusive Community competence as regards commercial policy.[23] In the *Donckerwolcke* case, the Court addressed this question. It held that

[a]s full responsibility in the matter of commercial policy was transferred to the Community by means of Article 113 (1) measures of commercial policy of a national character are only permissible after the end of the transitional period by virtue of specific authorization by the Community.[24]

Unfortunately, the concept of specific authorization has never been further defined by the Court. It has been argued that it implies that all relevant facts and circumstances of the case be considered, and that a blank authorization to the Member States is incompatible with the exclusive character of the Community's competence in the area of commercial policy, because it would result in a retransfer of powers to the Member States.[25] This is obviously a forceful

[18] OJ L 346/6 of 8 Dec. 1983, amended lastly by Regulation 2456/92, OJ L 252/1 of 31 Aug. 1992.

[19] See Art. 3. For the latest of these lists, see Regulation 2456/92, *supra* n. 18.

[20] With the exception of Cuba.

[21] Regulation 288/82 on common rules for imports, OJ L 31/1 of 9 Feb. 1982, as amended lastly by Regulation 2875, OJ L 287/1 of 2 Oct. 1992. The products subject to QRs are listed in Annex I of Regulation 288/82, completely published for the last time in Regulation 196/91, OJ L 21/1 of 26 Jan. 1991.

[22] Cf. Pieter Jan Kuyper, 'De invloed van het verdwijnen van de fysieke grenzen in de Gemeenschap op de handel in goederen met derde staten', 40 *SEW* (1992), 1: 19–22 and 'The Influence of the Elimination of Physical Frontiers in the Community on Trade in Goods with Third States', in M. Hilf and C. Tomuschat (eds.), *EG und Drittstaatsbeziehungen nach 1992* (Baden-Baden: Nomos, 1991), 53–5, where he also mentions some justifications, under GATT law, for some of the QRs. For an analysis of the legal status, from the point of view of GATT, of the QRs applied to imports from Japan, see Marco C. E. J. Bronckers, 'A Legal Analysis of Protectionist Measures Affecting Japanese Imports into the European Community—Revisited', in *Protectionism and the European Community*, *supra* n. 8, pp. 72–83.

[23] On this exclusivity, see Opinion 1/75, [1975] ECR 1364.

[24] [1976] ECR 1937.   [25] Timmermans, *supra* n. 10, p. 161.

argument. Nevertheless, the Court has allowed a fairly lax interpretation of the specificity requirement in its judgment in *Bulk Oil*.[26] The question at issue was whether the exception laid down in Article 10 of Regulation 2603/69 on common rules for exports,[27] excluding a number of products such as crude oil and petroleum oils from the principle of freedom of export, and therefore in effect allowing the Member States to impose restrictions on such exports, was consistent with the specificity requirement. Bulk had argued that this provision could not be construed as allowing the Member States to introduce new export restrictions after the adoption of the regulation, as had been the case in the United Kingdom: that would be incompatible with Article 113 of the Treaty. But the Court did not agree with this argument. It held that 'Article 10 of the regulation limits the scope of that principle [of free exportation] on a transitional basis with regard to certain products, until such time as the Council shall have established common rules applicable to them'.[28] The Court concluded that

Article 10 of Regulation No 2603/69 and the annex to that regulation constitute a specific authorization permitting the Member States to impose quantitative restrictions on exports of oil to non-member countries, and there is no need to distinguish in that regard between previously existing quantitative restrictions and those which are subsequently introduced.[29]

This judgment has been criticized for failing to buttress the exclusive character of the Community's competence in the area of commercial policy, by allowing too wide an interpretation of the concept of specific authorization. It has been said that the Court's interpretation would be better suited in a system of concurrent powers than in a system of exclusive Community powers, such as the CCP.[30] To some extent, this criticism is correct. It must, however, be somewhat qualified. The Court has also made it clear that excluding certain products from the scope of the CCP is only possible on a transitional, and not on a permanent basis. Refuting Bulk's argument based on Opinion 1/78, in which the Court has decided that the political importance of a product does not justify excluding this product from the domain of the CCP, the Court held that

[26] Case 174/84, [1986] ECR 559, at 587.
[27] OJ L 324/25 of 27 Dec. 1969. On this regulation, see also Ch. 7, p. 247.
[28] [1986] ECR 587.   [29] Ibid.
[30] E. L. M. Völker, in his annotation of *Bulk Oil*, 24 *CML Rev.* (1987), 1: 105–9. Cf. also Koen Lenaerts, 'Les répercussions des compétences de la Communauté européenne sur les compétences externes des États membres et la question de la "preemption"', in Paul Demaret (ed.), *Relations extérieures de la Communauté européenne et marché intérieur: aspects juridiques et fonctionnels* (Bruges: Story, 1988), 49–54; Timmermans, *supra* n. 10, p. 161; Paul Demaret, 'La Politique commerciale: perspectives d'évolution et faiblesses présentes', in J. Schwarze and H. G. Schermers (eds.), *Structure and Dimensions of European Community Policy* (Baden-Baden: Nomos, 1988), 97–8.

[i]t should be pointed out, however, that in that Opinion the Court was concerned only with the prohibition of a general exclusion, as a matter of principle, of certain products from the field of application of the common commercial policy and not with the Council's discretion to exclude, on a transitional basis, certain products from the common rules on exports.[31]

Moreover, the Court also mentioned two circumstances which are specific for oil, by referring to

the international commitments entered into by certain Member States and taking into account the particular characteristics of that product, which is of vital importance for the economy of a State and for the functioning of its institutions and public services.[32]

It might well be that the specificity requirement would need to be more narrowly interpreted in the case of other products which do not display the particular characteristics of oil.

Be that as it may, it is safe to assume that the national QRs listed in Regulations 288/82 and 3420/83 benefited from a specific Community authorization, as required by the Court.[33] Nevertheless, some doubts have been voiced over the procedures for modifying the import restrictions, which in some cases allowed the Member States to act autonomously.[34]

(b) Community quotas and regional subquotas in the textiles and clothing sector

The regulation of imports into the Community of textiles and clothing is extremely complex. The Community has concluded voluntary restraint agreements (VRAs) with the major supplying countries, partly within the framework of the Multi-Fibre Agreement. Broadly speaking these agreements contain, on the one hand, quantitative restrictions with regard to the most sensitive products, and, on the other hand, a system of indicative ceilings: if imports exceed the ceiling, the imposition of quotas becomes possible. Products falling within the scope of these agreements are subject to a double-checking system: the exporting countries have to set up a system of export licences, and the Community has its own system of import licences.

---

[31] [1979] ECR 587.

[32] [1979] ECR 588. Also see the opinion of Advocate-General Slynn, in the same case ([1979] ECR 571), in which reference is made to Case 72/83, *Campus Oil*, [1984] ECR 2727. In this judgment, the Court recognized that the public security exception of Article 36, EC Treaty, could be invoked with respect to oil. Cf. Demaret, *supra* n. 30, p. 98.

[33] Timmermans, *supra* n. 10, p. 163; E. L. M. Völker, 'The Major Instruments of the Common Commercial Policy of the EEC', in *Protectionism and the European Community*, *supra* n. 8, p. 35.

[34] Timmermans, *supra* n. 10, pp. 163–4. Under Regulation 288/82, Member States were allowed to enact proposed amendments to their quotas when, objections against these amendments having been lodged by other Member States or the Commission, the Commission does not submit a proposal to the Council within two weeks (see Article 20 (3) (*b*)). Of even more doubtful legality, in Timmermans's view, were the powers which the Member States still possessed under Art. 10 of Regulation 3420/83, namely to amend their national import arrangements autonomously in cases of extreme urgency.

A more detailed account of this system of protection is supplied in the next chapter.[35] Important to note here is that the import system was not uniform in character throughout the Community. The quotas set in the framework of the VRAs were allocated among the Member States (the Benelux being considered as one 'region', hence the term 'regional subquotas') according to a so-called burden-sharing key. It has to be emphasized that this subdivision of Community quotas into regional subquotas was not a purely administrative matter. It reflected the levels of protection which individual Member States wished to maintain as regards imports of textiles and clothing.[36]

The latter aspect was recognized by the Court of Justice—although it did not use the term protection—in the *Tezi Textiel* cases.[37] The Court considered that the system established by the basic import regulation concerning textiles[38] had not brought about complete uniformity as regards conditions of importation. It referred to the preamble to the regulation, which states that 'the extent of the disparities existing in the conditions for importation of these products into the Member States and the particularly sensitive position of the Community textiles industry mean that the said conditions can be standardized only gradually'.[39] Nevertheless, the Court considered that the basic regulation was 'undoubtedly a step towards the establishment of a common commercial policy based, in accordance with Article 113 (1) of the Treaty, on uniform principles'.[40] From the fact that uniform conditions of importation had not yet been achieved, the Court concluded that Article 115 of the Treaty could still be invoked for enforcing the national subquotas. This part of the judgment is discussed below.[41] Here it is important to note that the Court merely observed that uniformity had not yet been reached, and did not consider the system of subquotas to be incompatible with the Treaty chapter on commercial policy, at least not in legal terms. Given the *Donckerwolcke* and *Bulk Oil* judgments, this seems to be logical, since in these judgments even purely national commercial policy measures were declared not to be in breach of the Treaty, provided that there was a specific Community authorization.[42]

---

[35] See Ch. 6, pp. 187–8.

[36] Cf. Jacques Pelkmans, *Applying 1992 to Textiles and Clothing*, CEPS Working Document No. 67 (Brussels: CEPS, 1992), 4–7. This is also evidenced by the fact that Art. 115 has very often been invoked in order to enforce the subquotas, see *infra*, p. 177.

[37] Case 59/84, *Tezi Textiel BV* v. *Commission* [1986] ECR 887 and Case 242/84, *Tezi BV* v. *Minister for Economic Affairs* [1986] ECR 933. These judgments are largely identical; references below are to Case 59/84.

[38] At that time, Regulation 3589/82, OJ L 374/106 of 31 Dec. 1982. This regulation was similar to Regulation 4136/86 (OJ L 387/42 of 31 Dec. 1986), which was in force until 31 Dec. 1992.

[39] OJ L 374/107 of 31 Dec. 1982.

[40] [1986] ECR 924.   [41] pp. 173–5.

[42] Cf. *supra*, p. 150. One could also argue, though, that once a common policy is elaborated, it needs to be genuinely common, i.e. it may not maintain non-uniform conditions of importation.

Progress towards uniformity

(*a*) *National quantitative restrictions*

Theoretically, there were various solutions to the problem of the remaining national QRs, aimed at bringing about uniform conditions of importation. These QRs could be replaced by Community-wide restrictions. For example, instead of restrictions on imports of Japanese cars in Italy and Spain, a Community quota on such imports could be installed. On the other hand, the national QRs could simply be eliminated. Also, a number of inter-mediate solutions were possible. National restrictions could be replaced by a voluntary export restraint (VER), undertaken by the exporting country. This VER could apply to the entire Community, or could be limited to one or more national markets. In the latter case, clearly, the goal of uniformity would not be fully reached, but it would enable the Community to abandon the application of Article 115. Lastly, the quotas could be replaced by higher tariffs.

The analysis below will show that the last solution has only been used in the case of bananas.[43] That is not surprising in view of the fact that most of the Community's tariffs are bound in GATT, and that raising these tariffs would have been completely inconsistent with the ongoing Uruguay Round nego-tiations, which aim at tariff reductions.[44] The first solution (introducing Community-wide QRs) has in practice only been used for exports from State-trading countries. There are a number of reasons for this, also. From a legal point of view, it is difficult to justify this solution in so far as imports covered by GATT are concerned. To begin with, most of the existing national QRs are already of dubious character under GATT.[45] Introducing new re-strictions, which would be how one would have to characterize the introduc-tion of Community-wide quotas, would in nearly all cases clearly conflict with Article XI of GATT, prohibiting the use of QRs as a commercial policy instrument.[46] Moreover, it proved to be difficult to find a majority in the Council for the installation of such Community quotas. The more liberally-oriented Member States were not inclined to approve such a solution, from which they reap no benefit.[47]

---

[43] See especially Ch. 6, part 3.

[44] Cf. Jozef Kortleven, 'Enkele externe aspecten van de Europese interne markt', *Docu-mentatieblad Studie- en Documentatiedienst Ministerie van Financiën* (June 1991), pp. 148–50.

[45] Cf. *supra*, n. 22.

[46] Cf. Kuyper, 'De invloed van het verdwijnen van de fysieke grenzen . . . ', *supra* n. 22, pp. 20–1 and 'The Influence of the Elimination of Physical Frontiers . . . ', *supra* n. 22, pp. 54–5, where he looks at the question from the angle of Art. XXIV; Ariane Beseler, 'Intra-Community Protection with Regard to Goods Imported into the EC—Article 115 EC', *International Business Law Journal* (1991), 8: 1141. The question is also raised by Meinhard Hilf, 'The Single European Act and 1992: Legal Implications for Third Countries', 1 *EJIL* (1990), 1/2: 97.

[47] Beseler, *supra* n. 46, p. 1141.

The Community's approach towards achieving uniformity has not been guided by a concrete, transparent plan as has been the case in other sectors of the internal market programme. None the less, with the benefit of hindsight there may have been more strategy behind the policies initiated by the Commission than one would at first sight be inclined to think. It appears that the Commission first wanted to find solutions for the most sensitive products among those subject to QRs, such as Japanese cars, footwear, and bananas. It was only once these solutions were found or, at least, in the making, that the Commission put forward comprehensive proposals concerning the remaining QRs. These proposals were only issued in the course of 1992, at a very late stage, characterized by the pressure of time exerted by the 31 December 1992 target date. In addition, the Community has been forced (or perhaps aided), by a number of external developments, to abolish certain QRs. The latter aspect is examined first.

One of these external developments was the revolution in Central and Eastern Europe. As a result of this revolution, a large number of the QRs governed by Regulation 3420/83 regarding imports from State-trading countries were abolished.[48] The chronicle of this abolition is rather complicated, and will only be summarized here. The fact that the QRs in question had remained in force throughout the 1970s and 1980s was due to the fact that the Community was unable to conclude trade agreements with the then Communist countries (except Romania),[49] because of the political constellation.[50] These QRs were discriminatory in nature, as they only applied towards these countries, and therefore in all likelihood inconsistent with the GATT as regards those Communist countries that were GATT Contracting Parties.[51] In 1988, the Community started to negotiate trade and economic co-operation agreements with some of the Central and East European countries.[52] In the framework of these agreements it was agreed that the remaining QRs would be gradually abolished, according to a timetable running until 1995, and for some sensitive products until 1997. This, of course, did not solve the problem of what would happen with the quotas still in force on 1 January

---

[48] For the regulation, see n. 18.

[49] See the Agreement between the EEC and the Socialist Republic of Romania on trade in industrial products, OJ L 352/5 of 29 Dec. 1990.

[50] For an account, see John Maslen, 'European Community–CMEA: institutional relations', in M. Maresceau (ed.), *The Political and Legal Framework of Trade Relations between the European Community and Eastern Europe* (Dordrecht: Martinus Nijhoff, 1989), 85–92.

[51] Namely Hungary, Romania, Czechoslovakia, and Poland. See, specifically on the relationship between the Community and Hungary within the GATT, Anne-Marie Van den Bossche, 'GATT: The Indispensable Link Between the EEC and Hungary?', 23 *JWT* (1989), 3: 141–55.

[52] A first agreement was concluded with Hungary (OJ L 327/1 of 30 Nov. 1988), followed by the agreements with Poland (OJ L 339/1 of 22 Nov. 1989), the Soviet Union (OJ L 68/2 of 15 Mar. 1990), Bulgaria (OJ L 291/28 of 23 Oct. 1990), and Romania (OJ L 79/13 of 26 Mar. 1991).

1993.[53] The next step was PHARE, the Community's programme aimed at assisting the Central and East European countries in their conversion to market economies.[54] One of the objectives of this programme is to boost exports from these countries. Thus, it was decided, first with respect to Poland and Hungary, and subsequently with respect to Czechoslovakia, Bulgaria, and Romania, that the QRs under Regulation 3420/83 were to be immediately abolished.[55] More recently, similar decisions have been taken with regard to the (now former) Soviet Union and Albania.[56]

It is obvious that the elimination of QRs in trade relations between the Community and Central and Eastern Europe had nothing to do with the internal market programme. It has not been this programme that has provided the incentive for abolition. Rather, it was the revolutionary changes in the region which gave rise to a new kind of relationship with the Community.[57]

Quite a number of the remaining QRs were directed towards imports from Japan.[58] This was mainly a result of the circumstances which surrounded the accession of Japan to GATT.[59] The Community has never been able to develop a comprehensive commercial policy towards Japan through, for example, concluding a trade agreement.[60] Thus, the QRs remained in force. In

[53] Cf. Marc Maresceau, 'The Internal Market and its Impact on the Legal Framework of Trade Relations between the EEC and CMEA', in *Matters of Promoting CMEA–EC Economic Cooperation* (Moscow: CMEA, 1989), 179.

[54] This Programme was set up after the Commission had been attributed the task of co-ordinating economic assistance for Poland and Hungary, at the 'Sommet de l'Arche' of the G7, in July 1989.

[55] See Regulation 3381/89 of 6 Nov. 1989 liberalizing the specific quantitative restrictions with regard to Poland and Hungary and amending Regulation 3420/83 accordingly, OJ L 326/6 of 11 Nov. 1989; Regulation 3691/89 of 4 Dec. 1989 suspending non-specific quantitative restrictions in respect of Poland and Hungary and amending Regulation 3420/83 accordingly, OJ L 362/1 of 12 December 1989; Regulation 2727/90 of 25 Sept. 1990 liberalizing or suspending quantitative restrictions applying to certain countries of Central and Eastern Europe and amending Regulations 3420/83 and 288/82 accordingly, OJ L 262/11 of 26 Sept. 1990.

[56] See Regulation 2158/91 liberalizing quantitative restrictions applying to imports of certain products originating in the USSR and amending Regulation 3420/83 accordingly, OJ L 201/5 of 24 July 1991; Regulation 3859/91 of 23 Dec. 1991 amending Regulations 3420/83, 288/82, and 1765/82 in order to liberalize or suspend quantitative restrictions in respect of Albania, extending the suspension of certain quantitative restrictions in respect of countries of Central and Eastern Europe and laying down the import arrangements applicable to products originating in the Baltic States, OJ L 362/83 of 31 Dec. 1991.

[57] This has culminated in the signing of Association Agreements (the so-called Europe Agreements) with Hungary, Czechoslovakia, and Poland on 16 Dec. 1991, with Romania on 1 Feb. 1993, and with Bulgaria on 8 Mar. 1993. As a result of these Europe Agreements imports from the countries concerned are or will be governed by Regulation 288/82, see Regulation 517/92 of 27 Feb. 1992 amending the autonomous import arrangements for products originating in Hungary, Poland, and the Czech and Slovak Federal Republic (CSFR), OJ L 56/1 of 29 Feb. 1992.

[58] See Annex I of Regulation 288/82, *supra* n. 21.

[59] A number of GATT Contracting Parties, including some Member States, first opposed to Japan's accession, and subsequently invoked Art. XXXV of GATT, allowing them not to apply the General Agreement in their trade relations with Japan. See Bronckers, *supra* n. 22, pp. 58–64, and Kenjiro Ishikawa, *Japan and the Challenge of Europe 1992* (London: Pinter for the Royal Institute for International Affairs, 1990), 13–15.

[60] Bronckers, *supra* n. 22, pp. 67–8.

1988, on the occasion of political consultations between the Community and Japan, the latter raised this issue, maintaining that the QRs, being discriminatory, were inconsistent with GATT. Japan threatened to bring the matter before GATT if no acceptable solution was found.[61] Negotiations took place, resulting in the course of 1989 in what has been called a partial agreement.[62] The Community could not agree to the Japanese demand for a firm commitment to abolish all the discriminatory QRs by the end of 1992. However, it did offer to eliminate a number of the quotas gradually. Such eliminations took place in 1989 and 1990.[63] In return for satisfying progress in the abolition of the QRs, the Japanese side has agreed not to raise the matter in GATT.[64] It was reported that the attention of both sides shifted, in 1991, to the problem of restrictions on imports of Japanese cars.[65]

A number of the QRs have been abolished as a result of the Uruguay Round negotiations. Two categories can be distinguished. On the one hand, elimination has taken place in the framework of the rollback operation of the Uruguay Round, aimed at phasing out or bringing into conformity 'all trade restrictive or distorting measures inconsistent with the provisions of the General Agreement or Instruments negotiated within the framework of GATT or under its auspices'.[66] On the other hand, some QRs have been abolished in the framework of the Community's offer with respect to tropical products.[67]

With respect to the policies induced by the completion of the internal market itself and not by external developments, the Commission first addressed the most sensitive product categories. It negotiated with the Japanese government a voluntary restraint arrangement concerning imports of Japanese cars, concluded in the course of 1991, and it issued a proposal on a common organization of the market in bananas in the course of 1992. Both these initiatives are discussed in the following chapter. For footwear, a voluntary restraint arrangement was concluded with the major supplying countries

---

[61] Kuyper, 'De invloed van het verdwijnen van de fysieke grenzen...', *supra* n. 22, p. 21 and 'The Influence of the Elimination of Physical Frontiers...', *supra* n. 22, p. 55. On the consultations, see *Bulletin EC* 9–1988, p. 48 and 2–1989, p. 46; *Agence Europe*, No. 4950, 8 Feb. 1989, p. 8 and No. 4954, 13–14 Feb. 1989, p. 9.

[62] Cf. Agence Europe, No. 4979, 18 Mar. 1989, p. 9 and *Bulletin EC* 3–1989, pp. 51–2. See also Anna Murphy, *The European Community and the International Trading System*, ii: *The European Community and the Uruguay Round*, CEPS Paper No. 48 (Brussels: CEPS, 1990), 27.

[63] Regulation 2429/89, OJ L 230/6 of 8 Aug. 1989 and Regulation 3156/90, OJ L 304/5 of 1 Nov. 1990, both amending Regulation 288/82, *supra* n. 21.

[64] See n. 62.

[65] Kuyper, *supra* n. 22, pp. 21–2. None the less, in October 1991 and October 1992 two additional series of QRs applying to imports from Japan were abolished, see Regulation 2978/91, OJ L 284/1 of 12 Oct. 1991 and Regulation 2875/92, *supra* n. 21.

[66] Ministerial Declaration on the Uruguay Round, *BISD*, 33 S., p. 19, at 22. See Regulation 3365/89, OJ L 325/1 of 10 Nov. 1989, amending Regulation 288/82, *supra* n. 21.

[67] Regulation 2189/89, OJ L 209/7 of 21 July 1989, also amending Regulation 288/82, *supra* n. 21.

(South Korea and Taiwan) in 1990. This arrangement, since it was the result of a safeguard action initiated by the Community, is dealt with below, in the section on safeguard measures.[68] All these developments prepared the ground for the comprehensive proposals issued by the Commission in the second half of 1992. These proposals do not only relate to the fate of the remaining national QRs. They also concern the decision-making procedures governing anti-dumping, anti-subsidy, and safeguard measures. All of these proposals have been presented to the Council by the Commission as one overall package.[69]

With regard to the remaining QRs, the Commission proposes two kinds of measures: the abolition of quotas and their replacement with Community-wide restrictions. For imports subject to Regulation 288/82 (the general import regulation)[70] the first course of action is followed. The relevant proposal entails the complete abolition of all remaining national quantitative restrictions on imports. According to the proposed Article 1 (2) of this regulation, '[i]mportation into the Community of the products referred to in paragraph 1 shall be free, and therefore not subject to any quantitative restriction, without prejudice to measures which may be taken under Title V'.[71] The measures referred to are safeguard measures, which are dealt with in the next section. It is worth noting that this abolition of national quotas is justified, according to the Commission, because the 'completion of the common commercial policy as it pertains to rules for imports is ... a necessary complement to the completion of the internal market and is the only means to ensure that the rules applying to the Community's trade with third countries correctly reflect the integration of the markets'.[72] Moreover, mention is made of a number of sectoral back-up measures applying to cars, electronics, footwear, and bananas.[73]

For imports subject to the regulations on imports from State-trading countries the approach is different.[74] Although, according to the Commission, the rules should closely follow those of Regulation 288/82,

[s]traightforward abolition of [the national QRs] would, however, run the risk of aggravating the economic difficulties in certain sectors of the Community's industry,

---

[68] pp. 165–6.

[69] See, in chronological order, Proposal for a Council Regulation on the harmonization and streamlining of decision-making procedures for Community instruments of commercial defence and modification of the relevant Council Regulations, SEC (92) 1097 final, OJ C 181/9 of 17 July 1992; Proposal for a Council Regulation amending Regulation 288/82 on common rules for imports, COM (92) 374 final of 18 Sept. 1992; Proposal for a Council regulation on common rules for imports from certain third countries and repealing Regulations 1765/82, 1766/82, and 3420/83, COM (92) 455 final of 10 Nov. 1992; Proposal for a Council Regulation on common rules for imports of textile products from certain third countries initially covered by Regulations 288/82, 1765/82, 1766/82, and 3420/83, COM (92) 543 final of 15 Dec. 1992.

[70] See n. 21.   [71] COM (92) 374 final, *supra* n. 69.

[72] See the proposed preamble, COM (92) 374 final, *supra* n. 69.   [73] Ibid. 1 *bis*.

[74] See COM (92) 455 final, *supra* n. 69.

which are very sensitive and labour-intensive and have hitherto been protected ... Without every possible safeguard measure, these sectors would find it difficult to cope with competition from the imports from non-Community countries which are not subject to the constraints of a market economy and which (like, for example, China) are among the world's largest producers.[75]

The Commission therefore proposes to introduce, for some products, Community-wide QRs or surveillance measures.[76] These measures only apply to imports from China, North Korea, and Vietnam, although the proposed regulation itself also governs imports from the fifteen republics of the former Soviet Union, Albania, Bulgaria, Romania, and Mongolia. This difference in treatment reflects the different political course followed by these two groups of countries, the second one having set in motion the transition to a market economy, accompanied by democratization.[77]

In addition, there is a separate proposal for all textile and clothing products, imports of which will in the future no longer be covered by the two above-described regulations. This proposal is dealt with in the next chapter.[78]

As was mentioned, all these proposals were presented to the Council as one package. The Council only started to discuss them in December 1992, and was unable to reach agreement, not because of the almost complete abolition of the remaining national QRs which was proposed, but because a number of Member States do not wish to expand the Commission's competence to take anti-dumping, anti-subsidy, and safeguard measures.[79] As the Commission does not want to dissociate the two aspects of its proposals, these have remained blocked.

This absence of any decision has created serious difficulties with respect to imports governed by Regulation 3420/83. Under the terms of this regulation, the Council has to decide each year on the national import quotas that are actually opened. It was provided that, if no decision had been taken yet before 1 January of a given year, the quotas of the previous year were automatically extended on a provisional basis, until the Council took a new decision.[80] However, in July 1992 the Council amended this regulation, laying down, among other things, that this automatic extension would not apply for 1993, arguing that

from 1 January 1993, the continuation of import quotas to be opened solely at national level will be incompatible with the working of the single market to be put into operation

---

[75] Ibid. 1.

[76] See ibid., annexes 2 and 3. The remaining quotas apply to chloramphenicol, gloves, footwear, table- and kitchenware, glassware, radios, bicycles, and toys.

[77] This is also reflected in the agreements concluded by the Community with the second group. The appropriateness of this differentiation is not discussed here.

[78] COM (92) 543 final, *supra* n. 69. See Ch. 6, p. 196.

[79] See *Agence Europe*, No. 5888, 30 Dec. 1992, pp. 4–5.

[80] Art. 3 (2) of Regulation 3420/83, *supra* n. 18.

on that date; whereas consequently the present arrangements will have to be replaced by a Community mechanism covering any restrictions remaining on 31 December 1992.[81]

As there was no alternative regime on 1 January 1993 a genuine legal vacuum arose. Some Member States were of the view that, notwithstanding the above-mentioned amendment, the same quotas as in 1992 could be applied. Germany and the Netherlands even considered imports to be free.[82] Other Member States asked the Commission for its permission to open provisional quotas, and were granted such permission.[83] The views were even so conflicting that the Commission instituted proceedings, under Article 169 of the Treaty, against those Member States which allowed imports without having been authorized by it.[84]

(b) Regional subquotas for textiles and clothing

The regional subquotas in the textiles and clothing sector were gradually loosened by a system of so-called interregional transfers, started in 1987, which allowed the transfer of unused parts of one subquota to another subquota, which was already filled, up to a certain percentage of the subquota to which the transfer was made. These percentages were enlarged annually, to reach 40 per cent in 1992. The subquota system has been abolished as from 1 January 1993, leaving only the overall Community quotas intact. A more detailed description of this evolution is supplied in the next chapter.[85]

Safeguard measures and voluntary export restraints

Starting-point and legal status

Whereas quantitative restrictions provide more or less permanent protection in certain sectors, safeguard measures allow the Community to restrict imports of certain products from third countries in case these imports cause injury to Community producers. The general import regulations (288/82 and 1765 and 1766/82)[86] lay down the procedures to be followed for taking such

[81] Art. 5 and preamble of Regulation 2456/92 of 13 July 1992 fixing the import quotas to be opened by Member States in respect of State-trading countries in 1992 and amending Regulation 3420/83, OJ L 252/1 of 31 Aug. 1992.

[82] See *Agence Europe*, No. 5891, 6 Jan. 1993, p. 8; No. 5904, 23 Jan. 1993, pp. 7–8; No. 5911, 3 Feb. 1993, p. 10; No. 5913, 5 Feb. 1993, p. 8.

[83] See e.g. Commission communication pursuant to Art. 9 (9) of Regulation 3420/83, OJ C 38/2 of 12 Feb. 1993.

[84] *Agence Europe*, No. 5918, 12 Feb. 1993, p. 9 and No. 6014, 3 July 1993, p. 6; *Financial Times*, 'Brittan brings trade policy charges', 12 Feb. 1993, p. 6 and 'Brussels goes to Court over trade policy', 6 July 1993, p. 2.

[85] pp. 192–5.

[86] Regulation 288/82, *supra* n. 21; Regulation 1765/82 on common rules for imports from State-trading countries, OJ L 195/1 of 5 July 1982; Regulation 1766/82 on common rules for imports from the People's Republic of China, OJ L 195/21 of 5 July 1982.

measures.[87] Here too, however, full uniformity of import conditions was not yet achieved. In some cases, Member States themselves were still allowed to take safeguard measures. Moreover, Community safeguard measures were often regional in character, that is their scope was limited to one or more Member States.

(a) National safeguard measures

Under Regulation 288/82 Member States were still allowed to take interim protective measures, autonomously limiting imports of certain products into their territories. Until the end of 1984, these powers were still fairly wide, because they could be used whenever these imports caused substantial injury to national production. Thereafter they were limited to cases in which the national safeguard measure was justified by a protective clause in a bilateral agreement between a Member State and a third country.[88] The agreements referred to were trade agreements. As such, these agreements were incompatible with the Community's exclusive competence in the field of commercial policy; there was (and is), however, a Community procedure, subjecting these agreements to periodic review and regularly providing authorizations for their automatic renewal or maintenance in force.[89]

The protective measures in question were of an interim nature.[90] They only operated until the Commission took a decision, or, if the Member State referred the matter to the Council, until the Council took a decision, with a maximum of three months.

Questions could be raised as to the compatibility of these interim measures with the requirement of a specific Community authorization, discussed above.[91] Whenever a Member State took such a measure, there was no specific authorization. The only authorization then existing was the one concerning the bilateral trade agreement being invoked. But this was more like a blank cheque than an authorization to take a specific measure of commercial policy, because it could not be known beforehand at what moment and with regard to which product safeguard measures would be taken. Moreover, this competence of the Member States could not be justified on the basis that it was of a transitional nature, the CCP not yet being fully completed in the sense that there were no uniform conditions of importation. The national safeguard measures could be taken with respect to products already subject to such uniform conditions by virtue of the CCP. Consider a product that could be freely imported into the Community by virtue of Regulation 288/82, that is, in other words, a product not subject to any remaining national QRs. Without

---

[87] For a detailed analysis, see Völker, *supra* n. 33, pp. 39–44.

[88] See Art. 17.

[89] See e.g. Council Decision 92/53/EEC, authorizing extension or tacit renewal of certain trade agreements concluded between Member States and third countries, OJ L 22/55 of 31 Jan. 1992.

[90] For the details of the procedure, see Art. 17.

[91] See also Timmermans, *supra* n. 10, pp. 162–3.

previous Community authorization, Member States could nevertheless impose safeguard measures, restricting imports, hence acting autonomously in an area where there is a full common policy, and abrogating the common rule of free importation. Of course, the autonomous powers were limited, as has been observed, because they were of an interim nature, and embedded in a Community procedure.[92] This, however, does not take away the doubts cast on their lawfulness.

(b) Regional Community safeguard measures

The various import regulations all contain machinery allowing the Community to take safeguard measures. The conditions and procedure for such measures in Regulations 288/82 and 1765 and 1766/82 were quite similar. Safeguard measures could be taken

[w]here a product is imported into the Community in such greatly increased quantities and/or on such terms or conditions as to cause, or threaten to cause, substantial injury to Community producers of like or directly competing products, and where a critical situation, in which any delay would cause injury which it would be difficult to remedy, calls for intervention in order to safeguard the interests of the Community.[93]

Paradoxically, however, although according to the regulations there had to be injury to Community production as such,[94] it was also provided that the measures could be limited to imports intended for certain regions of the Community.[95] In the past, nearly all safeguard measures taken by the Community have been so limited, regional protection being the rule.[96] Such measures only applied to imports into one or more Member States, and injury was examined, not on a Community-wide basis, but merely as regards production in the Member States in question.[97]

From a legal point of view, this practice of regional protection was of questionable validity.[98] To begin with, regional Community safeguard measures are not the same as national measures, forming an exception to the rule of having a common policy, and benefiting from a specific authorization.

---

[92] Ibid. 162.

[93] Art. 15 (1) of Regulation 288/82, *supra* n. 21. Cf. Art. 11 of Regulations 1765 and 1766/82 (*supra* n. 86), which are similar.

[94] Timmermans argues that there should be 'an overall assessment of the situation of all Community producers and their need for protection', *supra* n. 10, p. 168.

[95] Art. 15 (3) (*a*) of Regulation 288/82, *supra* n. 21; Art. 11 (3) of Regulations 1765 and 1766/82, *supra* n. 86.

[96] Völker, *supra* n. 33, p. 42.

[97] See for example Regulation 1087/84 introducing protective measures in respect of certain electronic piezo-electric quartz watches with digital display, OJ L 106/31 of 19 Apr. 1984.

[98] Timmermans, *supra* n. 10, pp. 168–9 and 'La libre circulation des marchandises et la politique commerciale commune', in *Relations extérieures de la Communauté européenne et marché intérieur: aspects juridiques et fonctionnels*, *supra* n. 30, pp. 103–5; Völker, *supra* n. 33, p. 35.

The measures in question have an exclusive Community character. As such, however, they are not consistent with one of the basic requirements of the CCP, namely to lay down uniform conditions of importation. It is true that the Court has admitted that such uniform conditions need not be established at once. In *Tezi Textiel*, it acknowledged the validity of regional subquotas, because the Council had not yet managed to establish a full common policy.[99] But this state of affairs was considered to be something transitional, 'a step towards the establishment of a common commercial policy based ... on uniform principles'.[100] As was mentioned above, the Court characterized the subquotas as a continuation of former national commercial policies with respect to textiles, uniform conditions of importation not yet having been achieved.[101] The case of regional Community safeguards is totally different. These measures could (and can, as will be shown below) be applied to products previously imported under conditions of full uniformity. Therefore, they cannot be justified on the basis of being of a transitional nature, as a continuation of former national policies. That would only be possible if the specific measure in question were such a continuation. For example, an old national safeguard measure which was never abolished, but was converted into a Community measure. Otherwise, safeguard measures are by definition always 'new' measures, aimed at addressing an injurious surge in imports.

As Timmermans has emphasized, genuine Community safeguard measures should, as a rule, only be taken on the basis of an examination of the effects of the imports on the relevant Community industry as a whole, and should be directed to all imports into the Community of the products in question.[102]

(c) *Voluntary export restraints*

Voluntary export restraints (VERs) are a much less transparent trade policy instrument than quantitative restrictions or genuine safeguard measures because they are not always laid down in official texts, because their legal status is not always clear, and because the parties involved vary (from government–government over government–industry to industry–industry). This lack of transparency is almost by definition characteristic for VERs, since this instrument is in many cases used in order to 'circumvent' the standard rules and procedures governing action against injurious surges in imports

---

[99] Cf. *supra*, p. 153.   [100] [1986] ECR 924.

[101] Similarly, in the *Bulk Oil* case (*supra* n. 30), no common policy on exports of oil had ever been set up.

[102] Timmermans, *supra* n. 10, p. 168. He argues that to limit safeguard measures to one or more Member States would require a special justification, such as the fact that the relevant market is geographically limited. Moreover, because indirect imports remain possible, regional protection would only be successful in exceptional circumstances (highly perishable goods or goods with high transport costs). See also Kuyper, 'De invloed van het verdwijnen van de fysieke grenzen...', *supra* n. 22, p. 26 and 'The Influence of the Elimination of Physical Frontiers...', *supra* n. 6, pp. 60–1.

(i.e. safeguard measures), based on Article XIX of the GATT.[103] However, it makes it difficult to evaluate whether uniformity has already been achieved in this area.

In the context of the Community's commercial policy, the above-mentioned link (or tension) between VERs and safeguard measures is in one category of cases supplemented by a legal link. Indeed, when the Community activates the safeguards provisions of the basic import regulations[104] the procedure is often terminated with a VER offered by the exporting country or countries involved. Such a VER can be put on the same line as a safeguard measure.[105] Therefore, the above-made observations on regional safeguard measures also apply to this category of VERs, which have also often been regional in character.

However, these are not the only kind of VERs limiting exports to the Community. The latter has in some sectors also concluded voluntary restraint agreements with supplying countries outside the framework of standard safeguard procedures. That has been the case, for example, for textiles and clothing,[106] steel products and certain agricultural products.[107] Except for textiles and clothing, which are dealt with in the next chapter, these VERs were generally uniform in character, protecting the overall Community market and not individual Member States' markets.

In addition, the Member States and various branches of industry have also often concluded voluntary restraint arrangements with supplying countries or industries. Best known in this respect were the limitations on imports of certain Japanese cars in France and the United Kingdom.[108] It would be very difficult, if not impossible, to give a complete list of such VERs, which in many cases are not well known.[109] Nevertheless, it is obvious that nearly all (if not all) such VERs were non-uniform in character.

One could try to analyse the legal status, in terms of Community law, of all these different kinds of VERs. However, that is not the purpose of this study. Important here is the question whether non-uniform VERs, that is VERs which only protect some national markets or which entail differences in protection throughout the Community, are compatible with Community law. There is no case-law specifically dealing with this question. Nevertheless, some general observations can be made. When a Member State has concluded a voluntary restraint arrangement with a third country, one could argue that this arrangement must benefit from a specific authorization by the

---

[103] See also Ch. 6, pp. 209–10.   [104] See *supra* n. 93.

[105] See e.g. Regulation 1735/90, *infra* n. 116.

[106] See Ch. 6, p. 188.

[107] e.g. sheep- and goatmeat, a sector in which the Community has concluded voluntary restraint arrangements with the major supplying countries.

[108] See Ch. 6, p. 199.

[109] A fairly recent overview is provided in GATT, *Trade Policy Review: European Communities*, i (Geneva: GATT, 1991), 101–8.

Community, because it is only in the presence of such an authorization that the Member States are still allowed to take commercial policy measures. Moreover, as was argued, such an authorization can only apply to arrangements which already existed before the end of the transitional period, and not to new VERs.[110] In practice, the Community has to my knowledge never authorized a Member State to continue to apply a VER, except perhaps (implicitly) those taken in accordance with a trade agreement between a Member State and a third country which is still in force.[111]

Progress towards uniformity

(a) National safeguard measures

In conformity with the provisions of Regulations 288/82 and 1765/82 the competence of the Member States to take safeguard measures completely expired on 31 December 1987, with the exception, under Regulation 288/82, of measures 'justified by a protective clause contained in a bilateral agreement between the Member State and a third country'.[112] No applications of this provision have been reported, and the Commission's proposals concerning the reform of the basic import regulations no longer allow the Member States to take any safeguard measures.[113] This exception to the rule of uniformity of import conditions will therefore be eliminated.

(b) Regional safeguard measures

As was mentioned, before the internal market programme Community safeguard measures were nearly always regional in character, i.e. they applied only to imports in certain regions (or, in other words, Member States). That trend continued in the first few years of the programme. Thus, in 1988 the Commission adopted safeguard measures relating to imports into France and Italy of footwear originating in South Korea and Taiwan.[114] However, the Commission also made it known when taking these measures that

following requests from a number of Member States and in the light of the results of the investigation of the Italian and French markets and information forthcoming from the Community statistical surveillance of imports, the Commission intends in the near

---

[110] See p. 163.   [111] See p. 161.

[112] See Art. 17 (1) (*b*) and (5) of Regulation 288/82 (*supra* n. 21) and Art. 13 (5) of Regulation 1765/82 and Regulation 1766/82 (*supra* n. 86).

[113] For the proposals, see n. 69.

[114] Commission Regulation 561/88 of 29 Feb. 1988 instituting a system for the authorization of imports into Italy of footwear originating in South Korea and Taiwan, OJ L 54/59 of 1 March 1988; Commission Regulation 1857/88 of 30 June 1988 instituting a system for the authorization of imports into France of footwear originating in South Korea or Taiwan, OJ L 166/6 of 1 July 1988 (later confirmed by Council Regulation 3283/88, OJ L 291/74 of 25 Oct. 1988).

future to conduct an investigation of the overall situation of the industry Community-wide, taking account, with a view to the completion of the internal market, of the different import arrangements existing in the Member States.[115]

Such an investigation was indeed conducted, and in 1990 the safeguard measures applying to France and Italy were extended to the entire Community.[116] The Commission then reported that a number of Member States were 'opposed to the application of new regional measures'.[117] This created the impression that the practice of adopting regional Community safeguard measures would be eliminated with a view to the completion of the internal market.

That impression was however deceptive. Subsequent policies developed by the Community continue to insist on keeping open the option to adopt regional safeguard measures. Not only has this option twice been used again in the course of 1992,[118] the Community has also pleaded in favour of regional protection in the framework of the Uruguay Round negotiations on a safeguards agreement.[119] Apparently, this has been successful, since the text on safeguards in the Draft Final Act, submitted by GATT Director-General Dunkel in December 1991, contains the following footnote:

A customs union may apply a safeguard measure as a single unit or on behalf of a Member State. When a customs union applies a safeguard measure as a single unit, all the requirements for the determination of serious injury or threat thereof under this agreement shall be based on the conditions existing in the customs union as a whole. When a safeguard measure is applied on behalf of a Member State, all the requirements for the determination of serious injury or threat thereof shall be based on the conditions existing in that Member State and the measure shall be limited to that Member State. Nothing in this agreement prejudges the relationship between Article XIX and Article XXIV: 8 of the General Agreement.[120]

This text is self-evident, except for the last sentence. Article XXIV (8) provides that a customs union must apply 'substantially the same duties and other regulations of commerce' to external trade. The option of regional safeguards

[115] Regulation 1857/88 (*supra* n. 114), OJ L 166/8 of 1 July 1988.
[116] Commission Regulation 1735/90 of 21 June 1990 introducing prior Community surveillance of imports of certain types of footwear originating in South Korea and Taiwan, OJ L 161/12 of 27 June 1990. No restrictive measures were actually taken since the Korean authorities and the Taiwanese exporters undertook to voluntarily restrain exports. However, the result is of course the same as an actual safeguard measure. The regulation was confirmed by Council Regulation 3050/90, OJ L 292/17 of 24 Oct. 1990.
[117] Commission Regulation 1735/90.
[118] Commission Decision of 14 Aug. 1992 imposing protective measures in respect of certain steel pipes originating in the Czech and Slovak Federal Republic and imported into the Federal Republic of Germany, OJ L 238/24 of 21 Aug. 1992 and Commission Decision of 2 Dec. 1992 authorizing the French Republic to apply safeguard measures to the importation of bananas originating in the Republic of Cameroon and Côte d'Ivoire, OJ L 355/37 of 5 Dec. 1992.
[119] Kuyper, 'De invloed van het verdwijnen van de fysieke grenzen...', *supra* n. 22, p. 26 and 'The Influence of the Elimination of Physical Frontiers...', *supra* n. 22, p. 60.
[120] MTN.TNC/W/FA, p. M.1. See also, concerning textiles, p. O.11.

is clearly a derogation from this provision. It is therefore surprising that the draft safeguards agreement does not acknowledge it as such, but instead seems to leave the question of compatibility with Article XXIV unanswered.

The Commission's proposals on the reform of the basic import regulations also keep intact the possibility of taking regional safeguard measures.[121] The Commission argues that 'while the adoption of regional surveillance or protective measures will remain possible, it will be used only in exceptional circumstances, where no other alternative exists'.[122] However, what these exceptional circumstances and absence of any alternative could be is not clarified. The proposed preamble only adds that 'in the circumstances, surveillance and safeguard measures restricted to one or more regions of the Community may nevertheless prove more suitable than measures applying to the whole Community',[123] without specifying these 'circumstances'. The provisions itself of the proposed regulations are scarcely more articulate:

> Where ... it emerges that the conditions laid down for the adoption of [surveillance or protective] measures ... are met in one or more regions of the Community, the Commission, after having examined alternative solutions may exceptionally authorize the application of surveillance or protective measures limited to the region(s) concerned if it considers that such measures applied at that level are more appropriate than measures applied throughout the Community.[124]

The economic rationale for regional safeguard measures is not in any way explained in the Commission's proposals, and indeed it is difficult to discover such a rationale. One may be inclined to say: regional measures serve to protect, not the overall Community industry, but the industry of one or more Member States. However, there is the problem of indirect imports. As will be shown below, the Commission intends to abandon completely the use of Article 115, EC Treaty, no longer allowing that Member States shield off their markets against indirect imports (which, in any case, has become very difficult with the abolition of all intra-Community border controls on goods).[125] In the absence of such intra-Community protection, how will regional safeguard measures be made effective? Except for the (in practice) rare cases of products with truly high transportation costs or highly perishable goods a regional measure only applying to direct imports appears to be of quite limited economic use.[126]

---

[121] See *supra* n. 69.   [122] COM (92) 374 final, *supra* n. 69, p. 1 *bis*.

[123] Ibid. 2.

[124] Art. 17 of the amended Regulation 288/82, as proposed in COM (92) 374 final, *supra* n. 69. See also COM (92) 455 final and COM (92) 543 final, *supra* n. 69.

[125] See p. 178.

[126] Cf. Timmermans, *supra* n. 10, p. 169 and Kuyper, 'De invloed van het verdwijnen van de fysieke grenzen...', *supra* n. 22, p. 26 and 'The Influence of the Elimination of Physical Frontiers...', *supra* n. 22, pp. 60–1.

Moreover, as explained above regional safeguard measures are incompatible with the rule of uniformity of import conditions governing the CCP, which, in turn, is an essential component of the establishment of the internal market. This breach of the uniformity requirement cannot be justified on the basis that it is of a transitional nature, awaiting the establishment of a genuinely common policy. Regional safeguards will be applied with respect to imports which are already subject to a fully uniform policy. The conclusion must be that such measures infringe upon Article 113 of the Treaty.

The rationale for the maintenance of regional measures is perhaps more political than economic. It may be that it is aimed at softening the resistance against the general abolition of the remaining national QRs. However, that does not make this practice more acceptable.

(c) Voluntary export restraints

For VERs negotiated by the Community, the problem of non-uniformity did not actually exist. As to voluntary restraint arrangements concluded by the Member States, no efforts appear to have been undertaken to terminate these, although, arguably, they are not compatible with the Community's exclusive competence in the field of commercial policy. There is one important exception, namely the case of imports of Japanese cars, where the various restrictions have been replaced by a Community-wide arrangement, discussed in the next chapter.[127]

Tariff quotas

In the field of tariffs, the Council has in the past developed the practice to apportion tariff quotas, laid down in the framework of the Community's generalized system of preferences (GSP), among the various Member States. In *Commission* v. *Council*, the Court held that this practice was inconsistent with the EC Treaty, unless it was carried out according to a number of strict conditions.[128] It must be 'justified by administrative, technical or economic constraints which preclude the administration of the quota on a Community basis'.[129] The scheme for apportionment

must include machinery to ensure that, until the overall Community quota is exhausted, goods may be imported into a Member State which has exhausted its share without having to bear customs duties at the full rate or to be rerouted via another Member State whose share has not been exhausted. Such a result would be irreconcilable with the nature of the customs tariff and the commercial policy as a common tariff and a common policy.[130]

---

[127] Part 2.
[128] Case 51/87, *Commission* v. *Council* [1988] ECR 5459 at 5479.
[129] [1988] ECR 5479.   [130] Ibid.

Lastly, the free movement, within the Community, of the products covered by the quota must not be impaired by the apportionment and all the traders concerned, in every Member State, must have access to the share allocated to that State.[131] Clearly, the conditions laid down by the Court are aimed at guaranteeing uniform conditions of importation. In the Court's view, an apportionment into national shares must be something purely technical, in no way damaging the principle of uniform rules.

The Court found in *Commission* v. *Council* that the various GSP regulations were not consistent with the above-mentioned criteria. Special attention was paid to the regulations in the textiles sector. Here, the Commission admitted that there were certain economic and administrative constraints justifying an apportionment into national shares, 'particularly because of the close links with the arrangement regarding international trade in textiles'.[132] These links were not further elucidated,[133] and the Court did not deal with the alleged constraints. Instead, it found that the textiles regulations did not include the machinery referred to above, allowing importation at the reduced rate in every Member State until the overall Community quota is exhausted. On this basis, it declared the relevant regulation invalid.[134] This part of the judgment is difficult to interpret. Especially the concept of 'economic constraints', justifying an apportionment into national shares, is rather obscure. These constraints cannot be the need to shield off national markets, instead of the overall Community market. The other requirements laid down by the Court militate against such an interpretation. If imports at the reduced rate have to be possible in every Member State until the overall tariff quota is filled, different national needs for protection cannot be served through the GSP system. That is a fundamental difference with the system of Community QRs, subdivided into regional subquotas, in the framework of the MFA. The question therefore arises as to what precisely the economic constraints existing with regard to textiles and clothing are about.

Since the judgment, the Community institutions have brought their practice regarding tariff quotas into conformity with the requirements laid down by the Court. Hence, for most of the quotas there is no longer any apportionment into national shares.[135] It is interesting to note that, as far as the GSP system is concerned, the Council took the view that, among other reasons, such apportionment is not appropriate 'with the view to the achievement of the internal market foreseen by the "White Paper" for 1992'.[136] Instead of the

---

[131] Ibid.   [132] [1988] ECR 5466.

[133] The Commission probably refers to the fact that it is only MFA-bound suppliers that benefit from GSP. However, this does not make clear the constraints.

[134] [1988] ECR 5481.

[135] See for example Regulation 3380/89 opening and providing for the administration of Community tariff quotas bound in GATT for certain agricultural and industrial products, OJ L 326/2 of 11 Nov. 1989 and Regulation 3896/89 applying generalized preferences for 1990 in respect of certain industrial products originating in developing countries, OJ L 383/1 of 30 Dec. 1989.

[136] See the preamble to Regulation 3896/89 (*supra* n. 135), OJ L 383/3 of 30 Dec. 1989.

apportionment into national shares, there is now a system of close cooperation between the Commission and the Member States regarding the administration of tariff quotas.[137] When goods are imported in a Member State under the quota, it must draw a quantity, by means of notification to the Commission. The Commission keeps account of the quantities drawn and, once the quota is exhausted, brings this forthwith to the notice of the Member States.

Again, textiles and clothing are an exception, as could be expected after the Court's ruling.[138] In this area, there is still an apportionment into regional shares, according to a fixed scale. This apportionment is applied to a first tranche of 70 per cent of each of the Community quotas. The second tranche of the remaining 30 per cent constitutes a reserve, on which a Member State must draw when its share of the first tranche is exhausted. There are a number of provisions on how to use the reserve and on the returning of unused quantities to this reserve. Overall, the aim is to ensure that, until the Community quota is exhausted, imports are possible in every Member State, as required by the Court's ruling. In so far as this aim is reached, it remains unclear why in the textiles and clothing sector there still has to be an apportionment into national shares. It is difficult to imagine the sort of constraints giving rise to it. Be that as it may, the general conclusion must be that as a result of the Court's ruling in *Commission* v. *Council*, there are now genuinely uniform conditions of importation in the area of tariff quotas.

The Application of Article 115, EC Treaty

The effects of the incompleteness of the CCP on the Community's internal market was always most notable in those cases in which Article 115 of the Treaty has been applied. In such cases the disparate external regime gave rise to barriers to intra-Community trade which act as a fundamental derogation from the free movement of goods. Below, the application of Article 115 is examined from the perspective of the completion of the internal market. In a first part, it is necessary to deal with the law of Article 115, as it stands, through an analysis of the Court's case-law and the Commission's practice in authorizing the use of Article 115. Subsequently, the relationship between these authorizations and the various commercial policy instruments which are not yet uniformly applied, and which were listed above, has to be examined, as it is doubtful whether in these cases Article 115 may still be relied upon. Thereafter, three specific aspects of a potential post-1992 application of Article 115 are examined. First, an analysis is made of the modifications to this provision,

[137] See for example Arts. 3–5 of Regulation 3896/89.
[138] See for example Regulation 3897/89 applying generalized tariff preferences for 1990 in respect of textile products originating in developing countries, OJ L 383/45 of 30 Dec. 1989, in particular Arts. 3–5.

laid down in the Treaty on European Union. Secondly, the question is addressed whether, in legal terms, the date of 1 January 1993 affects the application of Article 115. Lastly, consideration is given to whether such application is possible without carrying out controls at intra-Community borders, in view of the abolition of these controls in the framework of the internal market programme.

The law and practice of Article 115

Article 115 deals with measures of commercial policy taken in accordance with the EC Treaty by the Member States. It mentions two potential dangers, relating to the execution of such measures. This execution could be obstructed by deflections of trade, or differences between these national measures could lead to economic difficulties in one or more Member States. If that is the case, the Commission must recommend the methods for the requisite co-operation between Member States or, failing this, authorize the Member States to take the necessary protective measures, determining, at the same time, the conditions and details of these measures.

Case-law

Already in the 1971 *Bock* judgment, the Court ruled that, because Article 115 is an exception to the provisions on free movement of goods, which are fundamental to the proper functioning of the common market, and constitutes an obstacle to the implementation of the CCP, it is to be strictly interpreted and applied.[139] The most important judgment, however, on the scope of Article 115 is undoubtedly the one handed down in the *Donckerwolcke* case.[140]

This case involved French measures applying to the importation into France of products, originating in third countries, but already in free circulation in the Community. On the one hand, the French authorities required a declaration of origin for these products. On the other, because the goods in question were textile products originating in a third country (the Lebanon), it was alleged that an import authorization should have been asked for. The question put to the Court by the national judge was whether these were measures equivalent to quantitative restrictions. It must be added that the Commission had not authorized the measures.

The Court started its analysis by referring to the fact that the Community is based upon a customs union, covering all trade in goods between Member States. This includes goods that are in free circulation, in accordance with Articles 9 (2) and 10 of the Treaty. Such goods are 'definitively and wholly assimilated to products originating in Member States'.[141] The Court then

[139] [1971] ECR 897, at 909.   [140] See n. 2.   [141] [1976] ECR 1935.

recalled the wide scope of the prohibition of measures of equivalent effect, which, on the basis of the preceding analysis, fully applies to goods in free circulation. It had no difficulty in finding that the French measures infringed this prohibition.

Subsequently, however, the Court found that the above-mentioned assimilation can only take full effect if uniform conditions of importation exist.[142] As long as that is not the case, differences in commercial policy between the Member States are liable to persist, with the resulting risks of deflection of trade or economic difficulties, mentioned in Article 115. This provision allows these risks to be avoided by giving the Commission the power to authorize Member States to take protective measures, derogating from the rule of free circulation. The Court subsequently repeated the principle of strict interpretation and application of Article 115, referred to above.[143] As regards the commercial policy measures lying at the basis of this application, the Court held that a specific authorization by the Community is necessary, because of the transfer of the competence to conduct commercial policy to the Community.[144]

Applying all these principles to the case at hand, the Court considered that requiring a declaration concerning the actual origin was only permissible if it did not amount to asking more than the importer may reasonably be expected to know, and if no disproportionate penalties were attached to non-compliance with such a purely administrative requirement.[145] To require an import licence was considered to be incompatible with the Treaty, unless the Member State in question had been duly authorized to do so by the Commission, on the basis of Article 115.

The *Donckerwolcke* judgment did not so much deal with the actual application of Article 115 but defined the setting in which the provision can be invoked: as a means of restricting the free movement of goods within the Community, the Article 115 mechanism constitutes a derogation from a fundamental rule, and needs to be strictly construed. Although this is rather obvious, it has to be borne in mind throughout any analysis of the scope and implementation of the provision.

There is, however, not only the derogation from the free circulation of goods, the Court also having mentioned that Article 115 is 'an obstacle to the implementation of the common commercial policy provided for by Article 113'.[146] This contradicts a point of view that has been put forward in legal writing, namely that the outlet provided by Article 115 allows progress in the

---

[142] Cf. *supra*, pp. 145–6.   [143] Cf. the *Bock* judgment.

[144] Cf. *supra*, n. 24.

[145] The Court justifies this on the basis of the relationship with the scope of the national commercial policy measures, but does not sufficiently indicate that origin may only be asked in the case of products which are still subject to national measures.

[146] [1976] ECR 1937.

development of the CCP because the Member States know that they can continue to protect national markets. Thus, they would be more prepared to support the common policy.[147] The Court is undoubtedly correct in its implicit criticism of such a reasoning. Indeed, the sort of common policy that a continued application of Article 115 is able to assist is not really a common one. Above it was shown that the requirement of uniformity governing the CCP is not a precept of the ideal world, but a basic component of the Community's commercial policy. And Article 115 is incompatible with full uniformity.

In subsequent cases, such as *Cayrol* v. *Rivoira, Ilford,* and *Levy* the *Donckerwolcke* ruling was confirmed.[148] However, the judgment in the *Tezi Textiel* cases has been criticized for failing to draw the appropriate practical conclusions from the strict criteria set out in the previous case-law.[149]

Tezi Textiel dealt with the application of Article 115 to intra-Community trade in textile products subject to the above-described system of Community import quotas, subdivided into regional subquotas.[150] The Tezi Textiel company argued that the Commission had unlawfully authorized the Benelux to exclude from Community treatment (or, in other words, to restrict intra-Community trade in) certain textile products originating in Macao. It contended that Article 115 could not be applied in order to protect regional subquotas and that, even if it could, the Commission's decision at issue did not comply with the requirements laid down in this provision. Both these arguments were examined by the Court.

First, the Court checked whether the Community's policy regarding textiles had brought about uniform conditions of importation. If that had been the case, it would have precluded any application of Article 115. However, the Court found that the basic import regulation did not fully establish such uniform conditions.[151] It was undoubtedly a step towards a genuine Common Commercial Policy, but the preamble stated that 'the extent of the disparities

---

[147] Pierre Vogelenzang, 'Two Aspects of Article 115 E.E.C. Treaty: Its Use to Buttress Community-Set Sub-Quotas, and the Commission's Monitoring System', 18 *CML Rev.* (1981), 2: 176–8.

[148] In *Cayrol* v. *Rivoira*, the Court confirmed the part of the *Donckerwolcke* ruling on declarations of origin and import authorizations (Case 52/77, [1977] ECR 2261, at 2280–1). In *Ilford*, the strict relationship between the application of Art. 115 and the underlying national commercial policy measures was emphasized by the President of the Court (Case 1/84 R, [1984] ECR 423). In *Levy*, the Court clarified which kind of penalties could be attached to non-compliance with the obligation to state the origin of goods which are indirectly imported and with the prohibition of importation, duly authorized by the Commission on the basis of Art. 115 (Case 212/88, [1989] ECR 3511; see also *infra*, n. 199).

[149] For *Tezi Textiel*, see *supra* n. 37. The criticism has been voiced by Timmermans, in 'Community Commercial Policy on Textiles: A Legal Imbroglio', *supra* n. 10, pp. 172–6; *supra* n. 98, pp. 101–6; in 'Noot onder Tezi', *SEW* (1986), 11: 762–7; also by R. J. P. M. van Dartel, 'The EEC's Commercial Policy concerning Textiles', in *Protectionism and the European Community*, *supra* n. 8, p. 154.

[150] Cf. *supra*, p. 153.   [151] Cf. *supra*, n. 40.

existing in the conditions for importation of these products into the Member States and the particularly sensitive position of the Community textiles industry mean that the said conditions can be standardized only gradually'.[152] From this passage, the Court concluded that the disparities in question could not be attributed solely to the regulation in question, but were the result of measures taken by the Member States, on their own initiative, but in accordance with the requirements of Community law. The import regulation merely maintained existing disparities, whilst proclaiming their elimination as the end goal.[153] Therefore, the Court characterized the regional subquotas as a continuation of pre-existing national commercial policies, and not as something essentially brought about by the common policy itself. Accordingly, the conclusion was that Article 115 could be invoked in order to protect the subquotas.

As to the actual application of Article 115, and more precisely the presence of economic difficulties justifying protective measures, the Court referred to the rule of strict interpretation, laid down in *Donckerwolcke*. In addition, it said that since the textiles regulation constituted a step towards a Common Commercial Policy based on uniform principles, 'the Commission must show great prudence and moderation in exercising the powers which it still has under Article 115'.[154] This means that it may only authorize protective measures for serious reasons and for a limited period, after a full examination and having regard to the general interests of the Community. The Court then applied these criteria to the case at hand, and found that they had been observed.[155]

The acceptance by the Court of the application of Article 115 in order to protect regional subquotas in the textiles sector has been convincingly criticized.[156] The crucial part of the judgment is indeed not very articulate. What are the 'measures taken by the Member States, on their own initiative', resulting in disparities in the conditions of importation? As Timmermans has argued, they are not the subquotas laid down by the import regulation; neither are they autonomous national trade policy measures, benefiting from a Council authorization. Also, it is contested that the subquotas are a continuation of pre-existing national commercial policies. The explanation that the Court 'has shrunk away from the indeed considerable, political impact' of outlawing the use of Article 115 in the textiles sector seems plausible.[157] Be that as it may, the Court has perhaps taken the view that, overall, in the textiles and clothing sector, a genuine common policy had not yet been reached, which is correct.

---

[152] See [1986] ECR 924.   [153] [1986] ECR 924–5.   [154] [1986] ECR 928.

[155] The Court referred to the level of indirect imports, the growth of overall imports from non-member countries, and the level of prices of imports ([1986] ECR 929). It must be said that this part of the judgment is not very convincing. Little or no evidence is given of the sort of economic difficulties caused by the indirect imports in question.

[156] See n. 149.   [157] Timmermans, *supra* n. 10, p. 173.

Trade in textiles has for decades been governed by a restrictive regime, in which first the Member States took part individually, later being replaced in the MFA framework by the Community.[158] *Tezi Textiel* therefore highlights that Article 115 does not only protect 'national measures', but also Community measures that do not bring about uniform conditions of importation. However, such extended protection can only be justified if the Community measures are a step towards a genuinely common policy. Arguably, the Court has tried to make clear that this can only be transitional, and that a 'renationalization' of the CCP would not be allowed, and could not lead to applying Article 115. It interpreted the textiles regulation as an element of such a transition, and stated that the fact that it was a step towards a Common Commercial Policy should induce an even stricter interpretation of the requirements laid down in Article 115.[159] The Court has therefore *not* given a blank cheque to the further application of Article 115; instead, it has allowed itself some room for finding, in due course, that the common policy has become sufficiently uniform in character to rule out the use of Article 115.

Overall, the Court's case-law on the scope of Article 115 emphasizes the link with the transitional character of the non-completion of the CCP. The provision may still be invoked in order to limit trade in those products for which uniform conditions of importation have not yet been laid down in the framework of the CCP. This was the case with the remaining national QRs and the regional subquotas in the textiles and clothing sector. However, as uniformity is being achieved in this respect, Article 115 will no longer have a role to play with respect to such QRs. As regards a number of other non-uniform commercial policy measures, there may be more doubts over whether Article 115 may be legitimately applied. That is especially the case with regional safeguard measures.[160] In so far as these measures concern products already subject to uniform conditions of importation, such as products that can be freely imported into the Community by virtue of the basic import regulations, safeguard measures should also be uniform in character, as was argued above. If they are not, which is not acceptable, it is certainly not acceptable that Article 115 be applied so as to fend off indirect imports. If it were, that would come down to characterizing Article 115 as a permanent mechanism for derogating from the free movement of goods. The Court's language does not

---

[158] See Niels Blokker, *International Regulation of World Trade in Textiles* (Dordrecht: Martinus Nijhoff, 1989). The MFA was preceded by the Cotton Textile Arrangements, to which all Member States were parties (p. 112), and to which the Community acceded in September 1970 (p. 114). The MFA was negotiated by the Community itself (p. 148). These various arrangements are similar in scheme, but differ as to their scope—both in terms of products and countries—which has widened in the course of time.

[159] [1986] ECR 928.

[160] Cf. *supra*, p. 118.

allow such a qualification, which is incompatible with the rules and principles of the customs union on which the Community is based.[161]

The Commission's policy

There is a large body of cases in which protective measures have been authorized by the Commission on the basis of Article 115. It would not be very useful to provide a comprehensive examination here of the Commission's past policies in granting such authorizations, since the aim of the internal market programme is precisely to do away with them.[162] Only the general lines are analysed, as well as the run-up to the pivotal date of 1 January 1993.

After *Donckerwolcke* it became clear that there was a need for precise criteria governing the application of Article 115. In 1980 the Commission drew up a general decision, laying down such criteria.[163] This decision was replaced by a stricter one in 1987, in view of the completion of the internal market and the consequences this was to have for the application of Article 115.[164] Nevertheless, here again, as in its White Paper, the Commission proceeded rather cautiously. The preamble mentions the objective of an area without internal frontiers, as introduced by the Single European Act, and adds that

this implies, on the one hand, that the disparities still existing among commercial policies applied by the Member States shall be progressively eliminated or reduced and, on the other, that the Commission must be fully aware of these objectives when assessing the need to authorize measures pursuant to Article 115 of the Treaty.[165]

Full elimination of the use of Article 115 by 1 January 1993 is not mentioned as the prime objective. Also in 1987, the Commission seemed to wish to maintain some latitude when addressing the problems posed by Article 115.

Decision 87/433 is primarily of a procedural nature. It provides for two kinds of measures. First, Member States may ask for the authorization to subject certain indirect imports to intra-Community surveillance, allowing them to monitor these imports. This can only be granted if there is a danger

---

[161] The Commission has indeed authorized Art. 115 measures in cases of regional safeguard measures (see van Dartel, *supra* n. 149, p. 154 and Timmermans, *supra* n. 10, pp. 169, 176–7, both criticizing this practice).

[162] For such examinations, see Beseler, *supra* n. 46, pp. 1124–37; Colette Nemé, '1992 et la clause de l'article 115: à quand une politique commerciale commune?', *RMC* (1988), 322: 578–81; Francis Sarre, 'Article 115 EEC Treaty and Trade with Eastern Europe', 23 *Intereconomics* (1988), 5: 233–40.

[163] Decision 80/47/EEC, OJ L 16/14 of 22 Jan. 1980.

[164] Decision 87/433/EEC, OJ L 238/26 of 21 Aug. 1987.

[165] OJ L 238/26.

that the imports in question lead to economic difficulties.[166] Secondly, authorization to take protective measures may be granted if the imports indeed give rise to such difficulties. The Member States must in this respect supply detailed information, substantiating the case for protection.[167] Moreover, it is the Commission which determines the conditions and details of the protective measures.

Decision 87/433 does not specify the kind of protective measures that may be taken. In practice, protection has nearly always amounted to quantitatively limiting indirect imports of the product concerned. This is accomplished through the import licensing system provided for in the Decision.[168]

Although Article 115 is, as the Court has stressed, of an exceptional nature, the use of it has not been something exceptional. Throughout the late 1970s and the 1980s, the number of applications for protection lodged by the Member States with the Commission annually has ranged from 110 to 356, of which on average the Commission granted an authorization in 70 per cent of the cases.[169] Throughout this period, more than 50 per cent of these authorizations pertained to the sector of textiles and clothing.[170] There are, to my knowledge, no comprehensive studies on the economic effects of these applications of Article 115, in terms of impact on intra-Community trade and conditions of competition.[171] Nevertheless, it is safe to assume that this impact was more than merely marginal. That is certainly the case if one looks at the specific sectors involved. Motor vehicles and textiles are the most important in this respect. As regards the former, Article 115 has induced very low levels of penetration of Japanese cars in a number of Member States, compared to the corresponding level in non-protected States. The same is true regarding MFA-type textiles and clothing.

The Commission's policy regarding the problems which the continued application of Article 115 has posed to the completion of the internal market has been pragmatic and not very transparent.[172] There have been efforts

---

[166] Moreover, according to Art. 2 (2) the Commission will not give the authorization unless: '(a) there have been significant imports of the product in question from other Member States in the calendar year preceding the year in which the application is made; (b) import opportunities for the product in question opened by the Community *vis-à-vis* the third country of origin exceed 1% of the total import opportunities opened by the Community *vis-à-vis* all third countries subject to similar rules.'

[167] Art. 3 (3) (*e*) provides that the alleged economic difficulties must be shown by such factors as: 'production, utilization of capacity, consumption, sales, market shares held by the third country concerned, all third countries and national production respectively, prices (that is to say, depressed prices or prevention of normal price rises), profits or losses, employment'.

[168] See Art. 2 (5).

[169] See Beseler, *supra* n. 46, pp. 1134–5.

[170] Ibid. 1136.

[171] For a sectoral study see L. Alan Winters, 'Integration, Trade Policy and European Footwear Trade', in L. A. Winters (ed.), *Trade Flows and Trade Policy after '1992'* (Cambridge: University Press, 1992), 175–209.

[172] Decisions authorizing protective measures are not even fully published in the Official Journal, but only notified to the public in the C section.

aimed at eliminating the disparities in commercial policy measures giving rise to the use of the provision. These were described above. On the other hand, the Commission has gradually tightened the conditions under which it has been prepared to authorize protective measures, especially as regards the requirement of imports causing economic difficulties.[173] Moreover, mention has often been made of certain 'flanking' measures, of an industrial policy character, aimed at cushioning the shocks produced by free(r) imports.[174] It is not clear, however, what these measures precisely entail.[175]

As a result of this tightening of the conditions for recourse to Article 115, the number of authorizations has fallen drastically in the last few years.[176] Apparently, the Member States themselves implicitly accept that the article will become obsolete, at least to some degree, since the number of applications has diminished, almost to the same extent as the authorizations. Hence, in the course of 1992 no more than a couple of authorizations have been in force, relating to cars, motor cycles, shoes, and bananas.[177] For cars, an alternative regime was put in place by 1 January 1993, so that recourse to Article 115 could be dropped.[178] However, the common organization of the market for bananas was only decided upon in the course of February 1993, and entered into force on 1 July 1993. In order to cover this delay, Article 115 was still being applied, which is discussed in the next chapter.[179] Regarding motor cycles and shoes the authorizations have not been extended beyond 1992.

At first sight, the Commission's success in eliminating the application of Article 115 by the end of 1992 (with the single exception of bananas), combined with the fact that there will no longer be national quantitative restrictions in case the Commission's proposals to that effect are adopted, may seem to render superfluous any additional comments on the prospects regarding this provision. That is not necessarily correct, however. The elimination of the remaining QRs has not yet been officially decided. Moreover, Article 115 itself has not been abolished; it has even been modified by the Treaty on European Union. It is not to be ruled out, therefore, that the article is at some stage 'resurrected'. This possibility leads to the question of how to define the legal status of Article 115 after 1 January 1993. In more precise terms, this question comes down to measuring the impact of Article 7a of the Treaty (formerly Article 8a, EEC)—providing for the completion of the internal

---

[173] See for example the *Twenty-fifth General Report of the EC* (1991), 38.

[174] Ibid.

[175] With the exception, that is, of the RETEX programme, involving regional aid in the textiles sector.

[176] According to the Commission, authorizations for protective measures have fallen from 112 in 1990 to 48 in 1991 (also *Twenty-fifth General Report of the EC*, 38). Beseler, however, produces different figures, although allegedly based on information given by the Commission, see *supra* n. 46, pp. 1134–5.

[177] *Twenty-sixth General Report of the EC* (1992), 46–7.

[178] See *infra*, Ch. 6, part 2.					[179] pp. 243–5.

market by the said date—on the application of Article 115. Since it can be argued that one aspect of this impact is to bar the instrument of intra-Community border controls, attention must also be paid to alternative methods of implementing the article.

The Treaty on European Union

The new version of Article 115, as amended by the Treaty on European Union, is rather curious. On the one hand, it grants greater discretion to the Commission for deciding whether protective measures may be taken or not. This results from the amendment of the first paragraph: instead of 'the Commission *shall* authorize', it is provided that 'the Commission *may* authorize'.[180] On the other hand, however, the new second paragraph seems to return some powers to the Member States: in cases of urgency, they may take the necessary measures themselves, under the condition of requesting authorization from the Commission. This text is almost a copy of the previous version of the second paragraph, but the latter only applied to the transitional period, which ended on 1 January 1970. At first sight, therefore, this would appear to be a serious setback in terms of eliminating the use of Article 115 as a derogation from the free movement of goods within the internal market.

Essential is the question whether the modified second paragraph grants the Member States any new powers with respect to taking protective measures. It is difficult to give a conclusive answer to this question, because the new text is utterly ambiguous and almost incomprehensible, taking into account the existing practice in the application of Article 115.

First, the second paragraph applies 'in the event of urgency'. But the state of urgency is almost inherent to the application of Article 115. As was mentioned, the Commission has only authorized protective measures in the case of serious economic difficulties—and more and more so in the last few years. In those circumstances there is always some degree of urgency. As a result, it is not clear in which cases the second paragraph would apply. It would certainly be difficult to argue that the second paragraph covers all applications of Article 115, since the first paragraph has not been eliminated.

Secondly, what is meant by the Member States may 'take the necessary measures themselves'? This was exactly the existing practice. It was never the Commission which took protective measures; it was the Member States which could do so, after having obtained the Commission's authorization. Perhaps it will be argued that the difference with the first paragraph lies in the power of the Commission to determine the conditions and details of such measures. This power is not mentioned in the second paragraph. However, it *is* stated that the Commission must give its authorization by way of a decision, and that it may at any time decide that 'the Member States concerned shall amend or

---

[180] Italics added.

abolish the measures in question'. Does this not imply that the Commission may, already in its decision pursuant to a Member State's request under the second paragraph, determine the conditions and details of the measures that can be taken? Arguably, if the Commission may at any time amend or abolish the national measures, it may also at any time determine their conditions and details.

Reference should also be made to the rule of strict application and interpretation of Article 115, pronounced by the Court in *Donckerwolcke*.[181] The Court also emphasized that in this respect a proper authorization by the Commission is essential.[182] Interpreting the modified second paragraph in line with these principles can only lead to the conclusion that it confers no autonomous powers upon the Member States. Actually, the only real innovation would seem to be that, in case of urgency, the Commission must take a decision 'as soon as possible'.[183]

To conclude, a rational interpretation of the new second paragraph, taking into account the system of the Treaty and the existing practice in the application of Article 115, reveals that it changes almost nothing to the system as it operated in the past.[184]

The modification of the first paragraph of Article 115 is probably more significant. The degree of discretion which the Commission has at its disposal in authorizing protective measures has, to my knowledge, never really been analysed, and no Member State has ever brought the Commission before the Court for not granting such an authorization. In practice, therefore, the Commission has always exercised considerable discretion.[185] However, with the modified version there can no longer be any doubt that this discretion is considerable indeed. The Commission would therefore in the future be entitled to employ an altogether different interpretation of the concept of 'economic difficulties', justifying recourse to protective measures. This concept has always been interpreted on a sectoral basis, but it could be argued that, in view of the exceptional character of Article 115 as a derogation from the free movement of goods within a genuinely single, internal market that *is* in place, it refers to real crisis situations affecting the economy of a Member State as such, and not just one sector. Such an interpretation would close the door on using Article 115 as an instrument of standard protection of national markets, which it has been in the past, but which is incompatible with a

---

[181] [1976] ECR 1937.   [182] [1976] ECR 1938, paras. 39–40.

[183] In practice, however, this has also been the case. Art. 3 (7) of Decision 87/433/EEC provides that the Commission must decide on a request for protection 'within five working days of its receipt'.

[184] It is perhaps not to be excluded that at the basis of this modification lay the fear of some Member States that the Commission would refuse granting authorizations for protective measures after 31 Dec. 1992.

[185] The Court's case-law, especially *Tezi Textiel*, *supra* n. 37, may also be read in the sense of acknowledging such discretion.

genuine internal market. Did not the Court in *Tezi Textiel* rule that, when authorizing protective measures, the Commission must keep in mind 'the general interests of the Community'?[186] And is the unity of the internal market not an overriding interest of the Community, in comparison with claims for sectoral protection at Member State level?

The impact of Article 7*a*

Article 7*a*, EC Treaty, provides that '[t]he Community shall adopt measures with the aim of progressively establishing the internal market over a period expiring on 31 December 1992'. Moreover, the internal market comprises 'an area without internal frontiers in which the free movement of goods, persons, services and capital is ensured in accordance with the provisions of this Treaty'. Article 115, on the other hand, is a derogation from the free movement of goods, and it has been applied by means of controls at the internal frontiers that were to be eliminated. So the question arises whether Article 7*a* has any bearing, legally speaking, on Article 115. Does Article 7*a* imply, for example, that from 1 January 1993 Article 115 may no longer be applied?

There are various angles to this question. There is, to begin with, the Declaration on Article 7*a* annexed to the Final Act of the Single European Act, which introduced the article into the EC Treaty. This Declaration provides, among other things, that '[s]etting the date of 31 December 1992 does not create an automatic legal effect'. That has been interpreted by most commentators as expressing the intention of the drafters to avoid what happened at the end of the first transitional period, laid down in Article 7 of the Treaty, and related to the common market. As is well known, the Court found that a number of provisions of the Treaty acquired direct effect at the end of this period, even in the absence of implementing measures that should have been taken.[187] Leaving aside for one moment the issue of what kind of provisions would be apt for becoming directly effective on 1 January 1993, the first question is whether the Declaration itself creates any legal effect. Toth has dealt with this question in great detail, mainly from the point of view of international law.[188] It is submitted, however, that that is not the proper perspective. In so far as the problem is the legal effect of the Declaration on the EC Treaty and its implementation, it is a question of Community law, and not of international law.[189] Nevertheless, the author has pointed to some elements that are able to supply an appropriate answer.[190] Article 236 of the EEC

---

[186] [1986] ECR 928–9.

[187] See e.g. the in-depth study by Marc Maresceau, *De directe werking van het Europese Gemeenschapsrecht* (Antwerp: Kluwer, 1978), ch. 2.

[188] A. G. Toth, 'The Legal Status of the Declarations Annexed to the Single European Act', 23 *CML Rev.* (1986), 4: 803–12.

[189] *Contra*, implicitly, H. G. Schermers, 'The Effect of the Date 31 December 1992', 28 *CML Rev.* (1991), 2: 275–6.

[190] Toth, *supra* n. 188, pp. 808–11.

Treaty (now Article N of the Union Treaty) stipulates that amendments to the Treaty shall enter into force after being ratified by all the Member States. In the case of the Single European Act it was only the Act itself, in accordance with its Article 33, that was subject to ratification, and not the Final Act of the Conference, containing the various Declarations. Moreover, one can draw a comparison with the Declarations that were attached to the EEC Treaty itself and to the three Acts of Accession. In these four treaties, it was provided that the Annexes and Protocols 'form an integral part thereof', not mentioning the Declarations, which, *a contrario*, do not form part of these treaties.[191] There is no reason, as Toth rightly states, why the same should not be true with respect to the Declarations annexed to the Single European Act. Lastly, there is Article 31 of the Act, providing that the Court has no jurisdiction over the provisions of the Act except those of Title II (the modifications to the EEC Treaty) and Article 32. Thus, the Court has no jurisdiction over the Declaration on Article 7a, but only over the article itself. As a result, Toth's conclusion that this Declaration 'cannot in any way restrict, exclude, qualify or amend the clear provisions' of Article 7a has to be considered to be correct.[192] Therefore, in examining the impact of Article 7a on the application of Article 115, the wording of the Declaration has no role to play.

On the other hand, it cannot be maintained that the effect of Article 7a is to preclude any further application of Article 115 from 1 January 1993. Neither the Single European Act nor the Treaty on European Union has abolished Article 115. Moreover, Article 7a provides that the internal market shall be established 'without prejudice to the other provisions of this Treaty', including Article 115, which therefore remains intact. To argue differently would come down to advancing the thesis that on 1 January 1993 all the Treaty provisions allowing derogations from the free movement of goods, persons, services, and capital have become obsolete. That would include, among others, Articles 36, 48 (3), and 56. There is no basis whatsoever for such a thesis which, by the way, if it were correct would render completely pointless large segments of the internal market programme, aimed at suppressing recourse to these articles, through harmonizing national legislation.

Does this mean that Article 7a has no impact at all on Article 115? That is not the correct conclusion. The fact that, as a matter of principle, recourse to Article 115 remains available after 1 January 1993 does not preclude imposing

[191] Toth also refers to Cases 7 and 9/54, *Groupement des Industries Sidérurgiques Luxembourgeoises* v. *High Authority* [1956] ECR 175 at 194, where the Court held that the Annexes and Protocols attached to the ECSC Treaty were 'equally binding' only by virtue of the fact that they were expressly incorporated in the ECSC Treaty through Article 84.
[192] *Supra* n. 188, p. 812. See also, Meinhard Hilf, 'The Single European Act and 1992: Legal Implications for Third Countries', 1 *European Journal of International Law* (1990), 1/2: 92, n. 10. Schermers (*supra* n. 189, p. 276) argues that there may be consequences under international law. This may be true, but then it is a matter between the Member States, and cannot have any bearing within Community law, since the Declaration is not an international agreement to which the Community is a party.

a number of constraints on the way in which the article is put into effect. One of these would be that, since the internal market should have been established by the said date, applying Article 115 has to become much more exceptional, in line perhaps with the views on the concept of 'economic difficulties' defended above.[193]

Another constraint relates to the way in which Article 115 functions. Until now, this has always been the case through controls at intra-Community borders. However, the internal market is 'an area without internal frontiers' and eliminating the various controls that took place at intra-Community borders has been one of the major aims of the internal market programme.[194] Undoubtedly, therefore, the Community's institutions as well as the Member States are under a duty to eliminate such border controls, a view which is also defended by the Commission.[195] As regards Article 115, one can indeed envisage other ways of applying the provision, no longer necessitating border controls.[196] Consequently, it is submitted that the Commission may no longer, by virtue of Article 7a, authorize protective measures that operate through a licensing system which requires controls at the Community's 'internal frontiers'. If Article 115 is further applied, other methods should be sought.

Applying Article 115 in the absence of border controls

Taking protective measures in intra-Community trade without using the instrument of border controls is to some extent an untested area. It is not the aim of this section to explore, at technical level, the various ways in which this could be achieved. What has to be mentioned, however, are the constraints which, from a legal point of view, impose themselves on such measures. These constraints flow from the fact that Article 115 allows derogations from the rule of free movement, and as such needs to be strictly interpreted and applied.[197]

---

[193] pp. 180–1.

[194] It is one out of the three chapters of the Commission's White Paper (COM (85) 310 final), and has become the Commission's major preoccupation as regards the completion of the internal market, during 1992.

[195] See the 'Prise de position de la Commission relative à l'interprétation de l'article 8A du Traité CEE', reproduced in *Europe Documents*, No. 1773, 12 May 1992. The Commission argues that the abolition of frontier controls 'est une obligation de résultat qui ne laisse aucune marge d'appréciation: dans la Communauté doivent être abrogés tous les contrôles frontaliers qui sont instaurés en vertu d'une législation communautaire et tous les autres contrôles que les États membres effectuent aux frontières intérieures, quelle que soit leur forme et quelle que soit leur justification'.

[196] Cf. Kuyper, 'De invloed van het verdwijnen van de fysieke grenzen ... ', *supra* n. 22, pp. 28–9 and 'The Influence of the Elimination of Physical Frontiers', *supra* n. 22, p. 63; Alfonso Mattera, 'L'achèvement du marché intérieur et ses implications sur les relations extérieures', in *Relations extérieures de la Communauté européenne et marché intérieur: aspects juridiques et fonctionnels*, *supra* n. 30, p. 213. *Contra* Beseler, *supra* n. 46, pp. 1138–9, where she argues that none of the alternative solutions envisaged is a realistic option.

[197] Cf. *supra*, p. 172.

In this respect, the Court's case-law concerning Article 36 of the Treaty may provide a useful point of reference.[198] The principle of proportionality, basic to the application of Article 36, should especially be respected when recourse is had to Article 115. The measures that are taken must be proportional to the objective that is pursued, which is to ensure that differences in commercial policy measures do not lead to economic difficulties. It is difficult, of course, to compile a catalogue of which measures would be proportional and which would not. Nevertheless it is arguable that, as an example, setting up a heavy administrative system burdening all companies trading in certain sensitive products (textiles and clothing, for instance), merely with a view to being able to intervene in case economic difficulties occur, would not withstand the proportionality test. Similarly, any (penal or other) sanctions for non-compliance with new systems of protective measures may not be disproportionately severe.[199]

Conclusion

The Community has come part of the way towards establishing uniform conditions of importation, as a genuine internal market requires. If the Council accepts the Commission's most recent proposals,[200] there will no longer be national quantitative restrictions. To some extent this will be a success, keeping in mind that the Community did not manage to achieve this in the past, although uniformity should have been reached by the end of 1969. This is one case in which the internal market programme has obviously nothing to do with the creation of a Fortress Europe, quite the opposite.[201] The abolition of national quotas, it is submitted, produces the effect that Article 115 can no longer be applied. Indeed, this provision could only be used on a transitional basis, as long as uniform import conditions were not yet established.

The result of all this is that the Community's desire to retain the option of taking regional safeguard measures can be strongly criticized, both from an economic and legal point of view. What is the use of regional safeguard

[198] On this case-law, see e.g. Alfonso Mattera, *Le marché unique européen: ses règles, son fonctionnement*, 2nd edn. (Paris: Jupiter, 1990), 585–600 and Laurence W. Gormley, *Prohibiting Restrictions on Trade within the EEC* (Amsterdam: North-Holland, 1985), ch. 6.

[199] On the question of sanctions, see also the *Levy* judgment, *supra* n. 148. In this case, the Court distinguished between the kinds of sanctions that could be imposed according to whether the Commission has authorized protective measures or not. In the absence of such an authorization, false declarations as to the origin of imported goods cannot 'attract the criminal penalties provided for in the case of false declarations made with a view to effecting prohibited imports' ([1989] ECR 3530). If, however, a 115 authorization is present, 'Member States may declare that imports effected without an advance licence are subject to the criminal penalties attaching to the undeclared importation of prohibited goods' ([1989] ECR 3531).

[200] See n. 69.   [201] Cf. Ch. 11, p. 357.

measures if Article 115 is no longer available to fend off indirect imports? And how can regional measures be squared with the rule of uniformity? The suggestion must be that the Community should no longer have recourse to such regional measures, which are incompatible with an internal market, and that the basic import regulations have to be amended in this respect.

However, at the time of writing the Commission's proposals have not yet been adopted because of what appears to have become a fundamental debate on the direction of the Community's commercial policy, in particular the operation of instruments of commercial defence (anti-dumping, anti-subsidy, and safeguard measures). This illustrates that the Community continues to have difficulties in conducting a genuinely *common* commercial policy.

But this chapter does not yet offer a complete picture. Specific Community action with respect to the most sensitive products is examined hereafter.

6

The Community Import Regimes for Sensitive Products: Textiles and Clothing, Japanese Cars, and Bananas

1. TEXTILES AND CLOTHING

Introduction

The Community's policy concerning imports of textiles and clothing has to some extent already been dealt with in the preceding chapter.[1] Nevertheless, it is necessary to analyse it in some more detail here, because not all the important developments that are taking place in the framework of this policy could be examined in the general overview which that chapter offers. Moreover, textiles and clothing are, from an economic point of view, a very sensitive sector, in which the Community's industry experiences a lot of difficulties in competing with third-country suppliers. This was in the past reflected in the frequent application of Article 115, EC Treaty, with a view to shielding national markets from indirect imports of textile products originating in third countries.[2] In turn, this frequency was already an important indicator of the lack of uniformity in the Community's regulation of textile imports. Seen from this angle, this sector certainly also deserves some special attention in this study.

However, the analysis provided below does not attempt to explain all the details of the Community's import regime governing textiles and clothing. That would require another study. The emphasis lies on the lack of uniformity which this regime displayed, and on how this is being remedied. Furthermore, like in other sectors the fundamental changes were only set in motion in the second half of 1992. As a result, not all the relevant proposals have yet been adopted. The analysis is therefore by no means definitive. First, the

---

[1] pp. 152–3 and 160. The terms 'textiles and clothing' and 'textiles' will be used as synonyms hereafter.

[2] At the end of the 1970s and in the beginning of the 1980s often more than two thirds of the authorizations granted by the Commission related to textiles, see R.J.P.M. van Dartel, 'The EEC's Commercial Policy Concerning Textiles', in E. L. M. Völker (ed.), *Protectionism and the European Community*, 2nd edn. (Deventer: Kluwer, 1986), 152–3 and C. W. A. Timmermans, 'Community Commercial Policy on Textiles: A Legal Imbroglio', ibid. 171.

import regime is described as it stood in the past, with its lack of uniformity, lying mainly in the system of regional subquotas. Secondly, the most important segments of the reform of this regime are described and commented upon.

Overview of the Import Regime

General framework

A major part of world trade in textiles and clothing is governed by the Multi-Fibre Arrangement (MFA), negotiated in the context of GATT between the major importing and exporting countries.[3] This Arrangement basically aims at bringing this trade outside the scope of normal GATT rules, by allowing that bilateral agreements are concluded between importing and exporting countries, in which the exporting party undertakes to restrain its exports. These restraints must comply with a number of conditions set out in the MFA, the most important being that trade should be gradually liberalized by expanding the quotas. In return for the VERs which the exporting countries apply, they are guaranteed that no safeguard action will be taken against their exports.

The Community is a Party to the MFA.[4] In the framework of its participation, it has concluded a series of bilateral agreements with textiles-supplying countries, regulating imports from these countries.[5] These agreements essentially contain the following provisions:[6]

- The Parties confirm that their mutual trade in textiles is governed by the MFA.[7]
- The Community undertakes not to introduce quantitative restrictions under Article XIX of the GATT (on safeguard measures) or Article 3 of the MFA (on market disruption).[8]

[3] For the text of this Arrangement, see *BISD*, 21 S., p. 3. The Arrangement was extended for the third time ('MFA IV') by the Protocol of 31 July 1986 (*BISD*, 33 S., pp. 7–14), for a period running until 31 July 1991. In view of the fact that the Uruguay Round negotiations are not terminated yet, MFA IV has now been extended until 31 Dec. 1993 (see the Community's Council Decision of 9 Feb. 1993 on the conclusion of the Protocol maintaining in force the Arrangement regarding international trade in textiles (MFA), OJ L 38/33 of 16 Feb. 1993). For a description of the history and the contents of the MFA, see Niels Blokker, *International Regulation of World Trade in Textiles* (Dordrecht: Martinus Nijhoff, 1989).

[4] See Council Decision 74/214, OJ L 118/1 of 30 Apr. 1974. On the Community's participation, see van Dartel, *supra* n. 2, pp. 134–40.

[5] These include Argentina, Bangladesh, Brazil, Hong Kong, India, Indonesia, Macao, Malaysia, Pakistan, Peru, the Philippines, Singapore, South Korea, Sri Lanka, and Thailand.

[6] See e.g. the Agreement between the EEC and Hong Kong on trade in textile products of 2 Oct. 1986, OJ L 97/2 of 14 Apr. 1988.

[7] Art. 1 (1) of the Agreement with Hong Kong.

[8] Art. 1 (2).

- The third country concerned agrees to restrain its exports in conformity with quotas set out in the agreement. Such exports are subject to a double-checking system, requiring both export licences granted by the third country to its exporters and import licences granted by the Community's Member States.[9]
- For exports not subject to quotas, limitations are possible if certain indicative ceilings are exceeded. These limitations are the subject of negotiations, but if no agreement is reached the Community may itself set the limitations in accordance with a number of abstract criteria relating to past imports.[10]

In addition, the Community has concluded similar voluntary restraint agreements with other textiles-exporting countries, which are not a party to the MFA, such as the countries of Central and Eastern Europe and China. The import system set up by these agreements is essentially the same as the one laid down in the MFA-type agreements.[11] Furthermore, imports from Taiwan are governed by an autonomous regime, again, however, similar to the MFA-type agreements.[12] And with respect to a number of Mediterranean countries (essentially Egypt, Malta, and Turkey) a system of monitoring applies.[13]

Next to these systems of protection,[14] the basic import Regulations 288/82 and 3420/83 also contain (national) quantitative restrictions relating to textiles and clothing products.[15] However, most of these restrictions are not actually enforced as the quotas set in the framework of the above-mentioned agreements prevail.

Imports of textiles are of course also subject to the Common Customs Tariff, and in so far as they originate from developing countries (among which, paradoxically enough, are also the major suppliers whose exports are subject to quotas) benefit from the Generalized System of Preferences. The previous lack of uniformity of the GSP system was discussed in the preceding chapter and will not be further dealt with here.[16]

---

[9] Art. 3 and Protocol A.   [10] Art. 7.

[11] It should be noted that in the framework of the Europe Agreements (see Ch. 5, n. 57) the newly associated countries will obtain better access than MFA-type suppliers, once the Uruguay Round negotiations are terminated.

[12] Regulation 4134/86 on the arrangements for imports of certain textile products originating in Taiwan, OJ L 386/1 of 31 Dec. 1986, now replaced by Regulation 395/92, OJ L 405/6 of 31 Dec. 1992.

[13] See Regulation 2819/79 making imports of certain textile products from certain third countries subject to Commission surveillance, OJ L 320/9 of 15 Dec. 1979, as lastly extended by Regulation 3788/91, OJ L 356/67 of 24 Dec. 1991.

[14] See, for the implementation of the voluntary restraint agreements within the Community, Regulation 4136/86 on common rules for imports of certain textile products originating in third countries, OJ L 387/42 of 31 Dec. 1986, as lastly amended by Regulation 1539/92, OJ L 163/9 of 17 June 1992.

[15] For these regulations, see Ch. 5, nn. 18 and 21.

[16] See Ch. 5, pp. 168–70.

Regional subquotas

The non-uniform character of the described import regimes was due to the fact that the quotas agreed upon (or set autonomously by the Community) were subdivided into so-called regional subquotas.[17] Not only was the overall Community quota indicated for each product, but the share of the quota for each Member State (the Benelux counting as one 'region') was also specified.[18] Products subject to restrictions could only be imported in a Member State if its subquota had not yet been filled. According to the preamble of Regulation 4136/86 (the basic regulation for imports of textiles) this subdivision was based on the following considerations:

Whereas, in order to ensure the best possible utilization of the Community quantitative limits, they should be allocated in accordance with the requirements of the Member States and with the quantitative objectives established by the Council; whereas, however, the extent of the disparities existing in the conditions for importation of these products into the Member States and the particularly sensitive position of the Community textiles industry mean that the said conditions can be standardized only gradually; whereas, for these reasons, allocation of supplies cannot immediately be effected on the basis of requirements alone.[19]

The subdivision was carried out according to a so-called 'burden-sharing' key (referring to the consideration that the burden of imports should be shared),[20] but, as the analysis by Pelkmans has shown, past imports were so important in the annual adjustment of the quotas that actual burden-sharing would only have been achieved by 2038.[21] In other words, this subdivision reflected the level of protection which individual Member States wanted to maintain more than a genuine sharing of the burden of imports.

Uniformity was also absent in the above-mentioned ceiling system. Here, too, the burden-sharing key applied, meaning that not only did the imposition of quotas become possible once the overall ceiling was reached, but also if one Member State's share of this ceiling was attained. Import quotas could then be laid down for this Member State alone.[22]

As described in the preceding chapter, in the *Tezi* cases the Court of Justice

[17] See also Ch. 5, pp. 152–3.

[18] For some products, there were even no overall Community quotas, but only quotas for one or more specific regions.

[19] OJ L 387/42 of 31 Dec. 1987.

[20] The key is described in Art. 11 (3) of Regulation 4136/86, *supra* n. 14.

[21] Jacques Pelkmans, *Applying '1992' to Textiles and Clothing*, CEPS Working Document No. 67 (Brussels: CEPS, 1992), 5–6.

[22] See Art. 11 (3) of Regulation 4136/86, *supra* n. 14: 'Should the imports referred to in paragraph 2 into a given region of the Community exceed, in relation to the total quantities calculated for the whole Community according to the percentage specified in paragraph 2, the percentage set for the region in the table below, such imports may be made subject to quantitative limits in the region in question: Germany 25.5%; Benelux 9.5%; France 16.5%; Italy 13.5%; Denmark 2.7%; Ireland 0.8%; United Kingdom 21.0%; Greece 1.5%; Spain 7.5%; Portugal 1.5%.

did not object against this subquota system.[23] Moreover, it allowed that Article 115 of the Treaty be applied in order to shield the subquotas from indirect imports. However, in 1988 the Court delivered its judgment in the *Commission* v. *Council* case concerning the apportionment among the Member States of tariff quotas allotted by the Community to imports from developing countries, in the framework of the Generalized System of Preferences (GSP).[24] The Court then held that such an apportionment, in order to be compatible with Articles 9 and 113 of the Treaty, can only be carried through in accordance with a number of strict conditions, one of which is that until the overall quota is exhausted imports must be possible in each Member State. That condition was clearly not fulfilled in the case of regional subquotas for textiles. The question therefore arose whether this ruling, applying to tariff quotas, had any consequences on the lawfulness of the subquotas set in the framework of the Community's policy regarding imports of textiles and clothing.[25]

However, it is submitted that the ruling on tariff quotas did not apply to the textiles subquotas.[26] There was a significant difference between the Community's policy regarding tariffs compared with the one concerning QRs. The Common Customs Tariff (CCT) has been effective since the end of the transitional period. Since then, uniform conditions of importation have been realized in respect of tariffs. In this area, no national measures have survived the transitional period.[27] Moreover, the GSP system was introduced after the adoption of the CCT; from the beginning, it has been a common policy. Therefore, a national apportionment of tariff quotas could not be justified on the basis that in this field a common policy had not yet been achieved. Such apportionment, if damaging the uniform conditions of importation into the Community, was in effect a step backwards from the common regime, and went in the direction of a renationalization of the common policy. It is a well-established principle of Community law that common policies cannot be renationalized.[28] The case of QRs on imports of textiles and clothing was different. In *Tezi Textiel*, the Court considered the national subquotas as a

---

[23] Case 59/84, *Tezi Textiel BV* v. *Commission*, [1986] ECR 887 and Case 242/84, *Tezi BV* v. *Minister for Economic Affairs*, [1986] ECR 933; see Ch. 5, p. 153.

[24] Case 51/87, [1988] ECR 5459, see Ch. 5, p. 168.

[25] Cf. Pieter Jan Kuyper, 'De invloed van het verdwijnen van de fysieke grenzen in de Gemeenschap op de handel met derde staten', 40 *SEW* (1992), 1: 24 and 'The Influence of the Elimination of Physical Frontiers in the Community on Trade in Goods with Third States', in M. Hilf and C. Tomuschat (eds.), *EG und Drittstaatsbeziehungen nach 1992* (Baden-Baden: Nomos, 1991), 58.

[26] The question is also raised, though not answered, by Kuyper, *supra* n. 25, p. 24.

[27] At least not in so far as tariffs as such are concerned. On charges having equivalent effect, see Joined Cases 37 and 38/73, *Diamantarbeiders* v. *Indiamex*, [1973] ECR 1609.

[28] Cf. Case 7/71, *Commission* v. *France* [1971] ECR 1003, at 1018, where the Court held, concerning Euratom, that '[t]he Member States agreed to establish a Community of unlimited duration, having permanent institutions vested with real powers, stemming from a limitation of authority or a transfer of powers from the States to that Community. Powers thus conferred could

continuation of existing national commercial policy measures.[29] Although this assessment is not uncontested,[30] it was clearly a decisive factor in the Court's reasoning. In this field, uniformity had not yet been achieved. Therefore, until such uniformity was brought about, national subquotas were allowed as a transitional measure.

From 1987 onwards the subquota system was made more flexible by a system of so-called interregional transfers. The mechanism was laid down in Article 7 (3) of Regulation 4136/86.[31] It provided that supplier countries could, each year after 1 June, transfer the unused quantities of the shares allocated to Member States of a Community quantitative limit to the shares of the quantitative limit allocated to other Member States. Thus, if country *X* had a quota of 100 tonnes in Member State *A*, which had been used up, and a quota of 500 tonnes in Member State *B*, not yet filled, it could transfer quantities of its *B* quota to *A*, and import more products in *A*. There were, however, strict limits to this interregional transfer. In the example, the *B* quota had to have been used for less than 80 per cent. More importantly, the transfer was limited to a certain percentage of the *A* quota. It is this percentage which has been increased on an annual basis, from merely 2 per cent in 1987 to 16 per cent in 1991, and jumping to 40 per cent in 1992.[32] In the above example, country *X* could then transfer a maximum of 40 tonnes from its *B* share to its *A* share in 1992. As can be seen from the example, the flexibility offered by this transfer system was entirely dependent on the size of the quota to which the transfer was made. If this was very small (in other words if national protection was strict), then the system could not effect substantial change.[33]

The Reform of the Import Regime

As was mentioned, the reform of the Community's regime for imports of textiles and clothing was only set in motion in the course of 1992. In May of

not, therefore, be withdrawn from the Community, nor could the objectives with which such powers are concerned be restored to the field of authority of the Member States alone, except by virtue of an express provision of the Treaty.' Similarly, Case 32/79, *Commission* v. *United Kingdom* [1980] ECR 2403, at 2434 and Case 804/79, *Commission* v. *United Kingdom* [1981] ECR 1045, at 1073. See also Timmermans, *supra* n. 2, pp. 164–5.

[29] Case 59/84, *supra* n. 23, para 38.

[30] Timmermans, *supra* n. 2, p. 173 and 'La libre circulation des marchandises et la politique commerciale commune', in P. Demaret (ed.), *Relations extérieures de la Communauté européenne et marché intérieur: aspects juridiques et fonctionnels* (Bruges: Story-Scientia for the College of Europe, 1988), 103 and 'Noot onder *Tezi*', 36 *SEW* (1986), 11: 763–4.

[31] See *supra* n. 14.

[32] For the percentages over the period 1987–91, see the original version of Regulation 4136/86, *supra* n. 14. In this period, there were smaller percentages for the major suppliers. For the percentage in 1992, see Regulation 369/92, OJ L 45/1 of 20 Feb. 1992.

[33] Cf. Pelkmans, *supra* n. 21, p.38, where he gives 'the example of Portugal's 1990 quota of cotton fabrics (category 002) from India, which is 123 tons. The UK quota from India is 26214 tons. A transfer of 213% would still represent only 1% of the UK quota and hardly reduce the restrictiveness of the Portuguese quota'.

that year the Commission issued a communication to the Council on the implications of the completion of the internal market for this regime.[34] It described which measures needed to be taken in order to arrive at a uniform import regime consistent with the internal market. Two sets of measures can be discerned. On the one hand the abolition of the subdivision of Community quotas into regional subquotas (and the abolition of regional-specific quotas), on the other the abolition of the national quotas laid down in the general import regulations (288/82 and 3420/83) or, in some cases, their replacement by Community quotas. The Council agreed to these orientations in June 1992.[35] Before discussing them, however, a few words should be said about the negotiations in the framework of the Uruguay Round aimed at bringing textiles back into the GATT fold.

The Uruguay Round negotiations

As regards textiles and clothing, the objective of these negotiations is to reach an agreement providing for a transitional period after which trade in these products will be fully integrated into the GATT. Accordingly, the Draft Final Act of the Round submitted in December 1991 contains an 'Agreement on textiles and clothing', providing that this integration will have to be achieved by 2003 (a ten-year period of transition)[36] and determining in detail the various stages of this integration. During this transition period, a specific safeguard mechanism applies, allowing action against injurious surges in imports.[37] It should be recalled that here, too, as with the general safeguards agreement of the Draft Final Act, a footnote allows customs unions to apply safeguard measures, either as a single unit or on behalf of a Member State.[38]

It is obvious that in the Uruguay Round the substance of the Community's system of protection against imports of textiles and clothing is at stake. One should keep this in mind when judging the Community's efforts to achieve uniformity of import conditions. Compared to the consequences of an Uruguay Round agreement, the effects of abolishing the subquota system on the level of protection are probably only minimal.

The abolition of the subquota system and the anti-concentration clause

Since 1 January 1993 there are no longer regional subquotas pertaining to products subject to quantitative restrictions in the framework of bilateral

---

[34] 'Implications of the internal market for commercial policy in the textile and clothing sectors', SEC (92) 896 of 27 May 1992.

[35] Resolution of 17 June 1992 on the textile and clothing industries, OJ C 178/3 of 15 July 1992.

[36] See Art. 2 (8), MTN.TNC/W/FA, p. O.4.

[37] Art. 6, ibid. O.11–15.   [38] Ibid. O.11. Cf. Ch. 5, p. 166.

agreements concluded by the Community with supplying countries. In order to achieve this the following modifications were introduced.[39] First, Article 11 (1) of the Hong Kong Agreement (which can serve as an example) now provides that '[t]he quantitative limits established under this Agreement on imports into the Community of textile products of Hong Kong origin will not be broken down by the Community into regional shares'. Accordingly, the annex to the Agreement containing the quotas which Hong Kong undertakes to apply is modified and contains only global Community QRs. Similarly, in Article 7, dealing with the imposition of quotas where the indicative ceilings are reached, all references to regional measures have been deleted. However, provisions have been inserted which are aimed at ensuring that the abolition of the subquotas does not lead to a disruption of traditional trade flows. This is what in textiles circles is called the anti-concentration clause. Article 11 (2) and (3) of the Hong Kong Agreement now provide:

2. The Parties shall cooperate in order to prevent sudden and prejudicial changes in traditional trade flows resulting in regional concentration of direct imports into the Community.
3. Hong Kong shall monitor its exports of products under restraint into the Community. Should a sudden and prejudicial change in traditional trade flows arise, the Community will be entitled to request consultations in order to find a satisfactory solution to those problems ...

These provisions raise a number of questions. Is it the aim to replace the previous subquota system with informal restraints imposed by the exporting countries? Does this mean that the import regime is still not uniform in character? What is the use of further having regional restraints applying to direct imports when there is completely free circulation within the Community? How will the anti-concentration clause be applied, and how will the Hong Kong authorities be able to know the direction of trade flows and how can they influence them?

To pick up the last question first, the amended Agreement contains a number of additional provisions which allow the anti-concentration clause to be applied in practice, in the framework of the double-checking system governing imports (i.e. export and import licences). Article 5 of protocol A now provides:

The export licence ... shall be valid for export throughout the customs territory to which the Treaty establishing the EEC is applied. However, where the Community has made recourse to the provisions of Article 7 in accordance with the provisions of Agreed Minute No. 1, or to the Agreed Minute No. 2, the textile products covered by

---

[39] See the Agreements annexed to Council Decision 92/625 of 21 December 1992 on the provisional application of agreements between the European Economic Community and certain third countries on international trade in textiles, OJ L 410/1 of 31 Dec. 1992.

the corresponding export licences can only be put into free circulation in the region(s) of the Community indicated in those licences ... [40]

The Agreed Minutes referred to relate, precisely, to the anti-concentration clause. According to Agreed Minute No. 2,

[n]otwithstanding Article 11 paragraph 1 of the Agreement [on the abolition of regional subquotas], for imperative technical or administrative reasons or to find a solution to economic problems resulting from regional concentration of imports, or in order to combat circumvention and fraud of the provisions of the Agreement, the Community will establish for a limited period of time a specific management system in conformity with the principles of the internal market.

However, if the Parties are unable to reach a satisfactory solution during the consultations provided for in Article 11 paragraph 3, Hong Kong undertakes, if so requested by the Community, to respect temporary export limits for one or more regions of the Community ... [41]

Attached is a 'note verbale' saying that the Community has decided to apply the specific management system referred to in Agreed Minute No. 2 as from 1 January 1993, and that, consequently, the corresponding provisions of Protocol A shall also be applied.

Combining all these provisions, the picture becomes clearer. Although from 1 January 1993 there are no longer regional subquotas, the old system of import/export administration continues to be applied for some time.[42] That means that the authorities of the exporting country will still have to indicate, when issuing export licences, the Member State of destination; that an import licence can only be obtained in the Member State indicated in the export licence; and that the products can only be imported in the Member State which has granted the import licence. However, the Hong Kong authorities remain free in deciding which Member State is indicated in the export licence, provided that there is no regional concentration of exports. It is only when the Community decides that such regional concentration occurs that it can ask Hong Kong actually to limit its exports to the region concerned.

It may be expected that this system is of a transitional nature, aiming at a smooth passage from the regional subquota system to a completely uniform

[40] See also Art. 10 (1) of Protocol A which contains similar language with respect to the corresponding import licences.

[41] See also Agreed Minute No. 1, with provides that 'Article 7 of the Agreement [on the imposition of quotas once the indicative ceilings are reached] does not preclude the Community, if the conditions are fulfilled, from applying the safeguard measures referred to in Article 7 for one or more of its regions in conformity with the principles of the internal market'.

[42] According to a 'Notice to importers' published in OJ C 347/2 of 31 Dec. 1992, it is expected that this will continue throughout 1993. In a second phase, expected to commence on 1 Jan. 1994, the exporting country will continue to indicate a Member State on the export licence, but with such a licence an import licence can be requested in any Member State. Imports will only be possible in the Member State indicated in the import licence. In the third and final phase, expected to commence on 1 Jan. 1995, the export licence can be presented to any Member State and the import licence will be valid throughout the Community.

import regime. None the less, the economic rationale of the anti-concentration clause is not obvious.[43] It is clearly the Community's aim that once textile products are imported they can circulate freely within the Community, and that Article 115 of the Treaty will no longer be applied. Given this principle of free movement, the Member State of direct importation may not necessarily be the Member State of consumption. Large importers which serve the overall Community market will be interested in having their imports concentrated in one or only a few places, independently of the Member State of final consumption. Correspondingly, there may result a serious regional concentration of direct imports in, for example, Belgium and the Netherlands, which have large seaports. That concentration would not necessarily hurt the textiles industries of these countries, as the goods may be destined for other Member States. Regional concentration of direct imports is therefore by no means a correct indicator of regional concentration of consumption.

As with the question of regional safeguards, one gets the impression that the rationale of the anti-concentration clause is more political than economic.[44] It remains to be seen, of course, whether and to what extent the clause will actually be applied. From a legal point of view, it can probably be justified provided that it is genuinely provisional, guaranteeing a smooth transition to a completely uniform regime. It has to be noted, moreover, that even if the clause is applied this will only entail administrative costs for exporters and importers, who may have to change the destination of exports. However, once imported into the Community the rules on free movement apply.[45]

It should also be mentioned that the Commission is setting up a system of central management for the quota system. As there are no regional subquotas any more, such a central system is necessary in order to check whether the quotas are not being exceeded. This system is described in a regulation recently adopted by the Council.[46] Because it is mainly technical in character, it is not analysed here. Suffice it to say that the Member States continue to grant import licences, under the authority of the Commission which checks whether there is still room within a quota, and which authorizes the Member States to issue licences on a 'first come—first served' basis.

Abolition of national quantitative restrictions and replacement with Community restrictions

As was mentioned, the basic import Regulations 288/82 and 3420/83 also lay down national quantitative restrictions in the field of textiles and clothing. In

[43] Compare with the question of regional safeguards, discussed in Ch. 5, p. 167.
[44] Ibid.
[45] See also *infra*, pp. 196–7, on Art. 115, EC Treaty.
[46] Council Regulation 958/93 of 5 Apr. 1993 establishing a Community procedure for administering quantitative import restrictions and monitoring of textile and clothing products originating in certain third countries, OJ L 103/1 of 28 Apr. 1993.

the preceding chapter, the Commission's proposals regarding the reform of these basic regulations were discussed.[47] This reform also applies to the QRs regarding textiles, albeit the subject of a separate proposal which aims at bringing together all the rules applying to imports of the products concerned (in so far, of course, as such imports are not covered by bilateral agreements).[48] This proposal is essentially similar to the ones discussed in the previous chapters. For imports from (former) State-trading countries not all the QRs are abolished; some are replaced by Community restrictions.[49] The safeguard procedures are reformed, but they still allow the adoption of regional safeguard measures under the same conditions as described in the preceding chapter.[50] There are also provisions on the management of Community QRs. One basic difference between the textiles proposal and the general ones has to be noted. The national QRs laid down in Regulation 288/82 are not abolished; they are merely suspended 'until the Agreement on trade in textile and clothing products resulting from the Uruguay Round GATT Trade negotiations is concluded and entered into force'.[51] Their elimination will only take effect on that date. The reasons for this suspension are not indicated, and thus the subject of conjecture. Perhaps the Community wishes to maintain the possibility of reintroducing these QRs if no agreement is reached in the Uruguay Round. It is questionable, however, whether that is legally possible. As was mentioned, the QRs on textiles and clothing of Regulation 288/82 are at the moment not applied, since these imports are covered by the system of bilateral agreements. That system is clearly a common policy developed by the Community. To enforce the national quotas again would come down to 'renationalizing' a common policy which is the exclusive competence of the Community. Moreover, the uniformity of import conditions which now exists, and which is prescribed by Article 113 of the EC Treaty, would be eliminated again. That is clearly incompatible with the Treaty.[52]

The application of Article 115

Lastly, a few words on the application of Article 115 of the Treaty to imports of textiles and clothing. The analysis in the preceding chapter has shown that Article 115 is of a transitional character, and can therefore only be applied

[47] See Ch. 5, pp. 158–60.

[48] Proposal for a Council Regulation on common rules for imports of textile products from certain third countries initially covered by Council Regulations 288/82, 1765/82, 1766/82, and 3420/83, COM (92) 543 final of 15 Dec. 1992.

[49] Ibid. see Annex IV. The exporting countries concerned are: China, Vietnam, Mongolia, North Korea, the republics of the former Soviet Union (with the exception of the Baltic States) and the republics of the former Yugoslavia.

[50] p. 167.   [51] Art. 2 (2) of the Proposal, *supra* n. 48.

[52] Timmermans, *supra* n. 2, pp. 164–5.

with respect to products not yet subject to a uniform import regime.[53] For textiles, such uniformity was absent as long as the system of regional subquotas existed. However, now that this system has been abandoned, and uniformity achieved, Article 115 has no role to play any longer. It should be recalled that in the *Tezi* case the Court characterized the subquota system as being 'undoubtedly a step towards the establishment of a common commercial policy based, in accordance with Article 113 (1) of the Treaty, on uniform principles'.[54] The final step has now clearly been taken, meaning that Article 115 can no longer be invoked.

2. JAPANESE CARS

Introduction

The (in economic terms) single most important product which has been the subject of intra-Community restrictions based on Article 115, EC Treaty, is the motor vehicle (or car).[55] These restrictions have served to insulate some Member States' domestic markets from imports of Japanese cars, governed by national QRs. The problem which this has posed for the completion of the internal market has been (and will perhaps continue to be) perplexing, for a number of reasons. The Community is the world's biggest car producer. This production is undoubtedly a vital element of the European economy, especially in terms of employment.[56] At the same time, the Community's car industry has quite some difficulty in competing with its Japanese counterpart, considered to be more efficient.[57] If Japanese cars were imported into the Community free of all restrictions (both tariffs and quotas), they would in all likelihood capture a far greater share of the European market, with corresponding reductions in European output.[58] These imports are therefore perceived as a threat to the prospering of the Community's car industry and, by

---

[53] p. 175.

[54] Case 59/84, *Tezi Textiel BV* v. *Commission*, [1986] ECR 887 at 924.

[55] The latter term, being more common, will be used throughout this chapter.

[56] In a recent communication to the Council on the car industry, the Commission mentions that the Community produces almost 40% of all cars and estimates that about 10% of all employment in the Community depends directly or indirectly on car production, see *Europe Documents*, No. 1781/82, 12 June 1992, pp. 2–3. The communication is summarized in Commission Press Release P-24 of 29 Apr. 1992.

[57] See the communication mentioned in the previous note and Alasdair Smith and Anthony J. Venables, 'Automobiles', in G. C. Hufbauer (ed.), *Europe 1992: An American Perspective* (Washington, DC: Brookings Institution, 1990), 157–8.

[58] Compare the Japanese share of the overall Community car market, 9%, with the Japanese share of the car market in a number of less-protected countries such as Finland, Ireland, and Norway, averaging 40%, see *A Single Market for Cars*, 22nd Report by the Select Committee on the European Communities of the House of Lords (1990), 19.

some, as a threat to the European economy as such.[59] An element that has to be added, moreover, is the large trade deficit on the Community's side in trade with Japan and the probably corresponding allegations that the Japanese market still remains rather closed to imports.[60] Because of this background, the option of simply abolishing the existing national QRs (and other protectionist devices, analysed below) for the benefit of completing the internal market has never been seriously considered. That would have created the impression that the internal market was 'given away' to Japan, or even stronger, that it was created for the benefit of foreign competition and to the detriment of local production. On the other hand, however, the internal market would hardly be credible where the market for cars continued to be fragmented along national lines. As Sir Leon Brittan has said, '[a] car, after all, is one of the biggest purchases which most people ever make'.[61] The question therefore has been how to combine eliminating the existing fragmentation with not giving up all protection against Japanese imports. Complicating matters further has been the traditional antagonism within the Council between the more liberally oriented Member States and those who regard some degree of protection as vital to their interests.[62] As regards Japanese cars, the former were not inclined to agree to significant restrictions on imports at Community-wide level.[63]

It is well known that the Community has tried to solve the problem by concluding a voluntary restraint arrangement with Japan.[64] In this arrangement, Japan agrees to monitor its exports to the Community as a whole, as well as to the formerly protected markets, until the end of the century. This part of this chapter is aimed at analysing this arrangement from a legal point of view. That is quite obviously not the only kind of study on the subject that is of interest. The economic merits of the export restraints agreed upon are questionable,[65] necessitating an analysis from the viewpoint of (commercial) policy as such. That, however, would go beyond the scope of this review. It will nevertheless be clear that, in the end, a legal examination also leads to considering policy issues.

---

[59] See e.g. Bernard Cassen, 'Une question de survie pour l'automobile européenne', 37 *Le Monde diplomatique* (Mar. 1990); 'Peugeot's chief attacks Britain on Japan plants', *Financial Times*, 3 Oct. 1990.

[60] See e.g. *A Consistent and Global Approach: A Review of the Community's Relations with Japan*, COM (92) 219 final of 21 May 1992.

[61] Speech on 'The Single Market for Cars', Commission Press Release SPEECH/91/13 of 5 Dec. 1991.

[62] On this antagonism, see Anna Murphy, *The European Community and the International Trading System*, ii (Brussels: CEPS Paper No. 48, 1990), 124–5.

[63] See e.g. the statements by Christopher Roberts, UK Deputy Secretary for State and Industry, reported in *A Single Market for Cars*, supra n. 58, at p. 4 of the evidence.

[64] See *infra*, p. 201.

[65] Specifically as regards cars, see Alasdair Smith and Anthony J. Venables, 'Counting the Cost of Voluntary Export Restraints in the European Car Market', in E. Helpman and A. Razin (eds.), *International Trade and Trade Policy* (Cambridge, Mass.: MIT Press, 1991), 187–213.

Even a 'mere' legal analysis of the EC–Japan arrangement may cover a range of questions. This chapter focuses on three main issues, considered to be central in the framework of studying the relationship between the completion of the internal market and regulating imports from third countries. These are the status of the arrangement under the rules of the GATT, the relationship between the extended protection of some national markets and (mainly) EC competition law, and the problem of so-called Japanese transplant production, i.e. Japanese cars made in Europe. First, however, follows a description of the EC–Japan arrangement and its antecedents.

The EC–Japan Arrangement

Antecedents

The previously existing national restrictions on Japanese car imports were various in origin and type. As regards Italy, Spain, and Portugal, these were official quantitative restrictions.[66] France had since the 1970s limited Japanese imports to 3 per cent of domestic sales. Apparently, she enforced this by means of delaying type-approval procedures once the maximum amount of imports was reached.[67] Lastly, the British car industry had concluded an informal arrangement with the Japanese Automobile Manufacturers' Association, aimed at limiting the Japanese share of the British car market to 10–11 per cent.[68]

The lawfulness of some of these measures, either under Community law or under the rules of the GATT, has always been doubtful.[69] However, since as a result of the EC–Japan arrangement all these restrictions have been abolished, no further comments on this issue are added here.[70]

[66] They were listed in the annex to Regulation 288/82 (see Ch. 5, p. 150).
[67] See Marco C. E. J. Bronckers, 'A Legal Analysis of Protectionist Measures Affecting Japanese Imports into the European Community—Revisited', in E. L. M. Völker (ed.), *Protectionism and the European Community*, 2nd edn. (Deventer: Kluwer, 1986), 78–9. See also Court of First Instance, Case T-28/90, *SA Asia Motor France et al.* v. *Commission*, Judgment of 18 Sept. 1992, not yet published, and Case T-7/92, *SA Asia Motor France et al.* v. *Commission*, Judgment of 29 June 1993, not yet published. The latter judgment contains a detailed description of how the French policy operated..
[68] Bronckers, *supra* n. 67, p. 79.
[69] Ibid. 75–83. Also see Case T-28/90, *supra* n. 67, as well as the case brought by the Bureau Européen des Consommateurs and The National Consumer Council against the Commission for not acting against the arrangement pertaining to the British market, see OJ C 160/14 of 26 June 1992 and *infra*, p. 222.
[70] It must be mentioned, though, that in an action brought against the Commission before the Court of Justice (see *supra* n. 69), the Bureau Européen des Consommateurs (BEUC) and The National Consumer Council contend that the arrangement pertaining to the British market has not been terminated and will be used for implementing the EC–Japan arrangement which, indeed, does not explicitly mention the abolition of the said arrangement.

The negotiations leading to the arrangement were protracted and strenuous. It is reported that in November 1988 the Commission decided that the existing national restrictions had to be abolished by the end of 1992 and that Japan ought to stabilize its exports until then, and possibly for a limited period afterwards.[71] In the same period the question surfaced whether Nissan cars produced in the UK were to be regarded as European or not; France and Italy were in disagreement with the Commission and the UK, the former wanting to curb exports of these cars to their respective national markets, the latter arguing that that would be illegal under Community law and that the Nissan cars were to be regarded as European.[72]

Apparently, the most difficult part of the negotiations lay inside the Community. It took more than two years for the Commission and the Member States to come to some kind of agreement as to what would be asked of the Japanese side.[73] Among the main points of disagreement were:[74]

- the length of the transitional period during which Japan would limit its exports;
- the scope of these limitations, namely whether to include Japanese cars produced outside Japan, especially the European transplant production;
- how to prevent leakage from free to protected markets within the Community;
- the extent to which the limitations should be adapted to take account of fluctuations in demand in the EC market.

The negotiations seemed to gather pace in the course of 1991. At the same time, the Commission and Japan were preparing a Joint Declaration on EC–Japan relations, following up the example of the EC–US Joint Declaration of 1989.[75] Gradually, this preparation was linked up to the car negotiations, among other things because no agreement could be reached on how to phrase the objective of reciprocal market access in the Declaration.[76] In the course of July, the Joint Declaration was finally signed[77] and by the end of that month it was made public that the Community and Japan had reached agreement on the car issue.

[71] See *Agence Europe*, No. 4891, 11 Nov. 1988, pp. 7–8 and the *Financial Times*, 10 Nov. 1988, p. 10.
[72] See *infra*, p. 224.
[73] On 1 May 1991, *Agence Europe* reported that the Commission had defined the Community's negotiating position, see No. 5483, p. 6.
[74] Cf. the evidence in *A Single Market for Cars*, supra n. 58; 'EC move to limit Japanese car imports under threat', *Financial Times*, 25 Sept. 1990, p. 1; 'EC carmakers want 10-year protection from Japanese', *Financial Times*, 3 Oct. 1990; 'Keeping Japanese cars at bay', *Financial Times*, 15 Oct. 1990, p. 6; *Agence Europe*, No. 5439, p. 25 and 26 Feb. 1991, p. 6.
[75] *Bull. EC* 12–1989, point 2.2.16.
[76] *Agence Europe*, No. 5531, 10 July 1991, pp. 9–10 and No. 5536, 17 July 1991, p. 8.
[77] See *Bull. EC* 7/8–1991, points 1.3.33 and 1.4.8.

Contents of the arrangement

The EC–Japan arrangement is not an official agreement between the Community and Japan. The text is called 'Elements of Consensus', and has not been published. What has been published in the specialized press are official declarations issued by Commissioner Andriessen and Mr Nakao, Japan's Minister of International Trade and Industry.[78] The elements contained in these declarations are the following:

- The Community undertakes to cease authorizing the application of Article 115, EC Treaty, as regards Japanese cars, to abolish the existing quantitative restrictions and to achieve full Community acceptance of type approval, all by the end of 1992.
- Japan will monitor its exports to the Community until the end of 1999. This monitoring will be applied to the Community as a whole, as well as to the individual markets of France, Italy, Spain, Portugal, and the UK. It will be based on forecast levels of exports in 1999.[79]
- As to procedure, both sides will meet twice a year to hold consultations on the implementation of the arrangement. They will also make a notification to the GATT.
- The Community will take the necessary measures 'to ensure that the operation of competition law does not constitute an obstacle to the operation of the cooperative measures on the Japanese side', and it will not ask Japan to co-operate beyond the end of 1999.

The text of the arrangement itself, parts of which have been described in press reports,[80] contains some additional elements. (1) The objectives of the arrangement are phrased in terms of achieving progressive and full liberalization of the EC market, avoiding market disruption by Japanese exports and contributing to the necessary adjustments of the EC manufacturers towards adequate levels of international competitiveness. (2) It is stated that there will be no restrictions on Japanese investment or on the free circulation of its products in the Community. (3) The biannual consultations will be held in autumn and in spring. The autumn discussion will cover the export trend for the current year, the forecast of exports for the following year and a preliminary outlook on the year after that. The spring discussions will include the actual results of exports for the previous year, the forecast level for the current year and any adjustments to be made, as well as a preliminary outlook for the following year. (4) As the monitoring commitment operates on the basis of

[78] See *Agence Europe*, No. 5547, 2 Aug. 1991, pp. 6–7.
[79] These levels are: for the Community as a whole 1.23 million cars, with demand estimated at 15.1 million cars; for the restricted markets: France 150,000 cars exported, demand 2.85 million; Italy 138,000, demand 2.6 million; Spain 79,000, demand 1.4 million; Portugal 23,000, demand 0.275 million; UK 190,000, demand 2.7 million.
[80] See 'EC vehicle sales accord with Japan to include light trucks', *Financial Times*, 5 Aug. 1991, p. 4.

202 *Import Regimes for Sensitive Products*

forecast levels of demand in 1999, there are two clauses on what should be done in case this forecast proves incorrect. The levels will be adjusted in an equitable manner if the actual trend of demand and of forecast demand for 1999 deviates from the original assumption. Moreover, 'Japan bears in mind the EC's concern that the necessary adjustments of the EC manufacturers towards adequate levels of international competitiveness would be adversely affected if the EC manufacturers cannot enjoy the adequate benefit of market growth or they face improper decrease in the production level in a contracting market.' (5) As to notification to the GATT, it is stated that the Community and Japan will jointly defend the monitoring system as being consistent with the GATT and as a significant measure related to liberalization. (6) Lastly, the Commission insists that there should not be an excessive concentration of sales of Japanese cars produced in Europe, causing market disruption on specific national markets. The Japanese side undertakes to convey this concern to the Japanese manufacturers.

Questions of law and interpretation

The arrangement raises a host of questions of law and interpretation (which are often intermingled). Without claiming to be exhaustive, the following overview may be useful, before addressing the main questions in more detail.

First comes the question as to the precise legal status of the EC–Japan arrangement, both under Community and international law. The arrangement is certainly not an official agreement between the Community and Japan in the sense of Articles 113 and 228, EC Treaty. According to these provisions, agreements shall be concluded by the Council, and there are no indications of such a conclusion, which requires the Council to sign the agreement and to take a decision pertaining to its conclusion.[81] It is doubtful therefore whether under Community law the arrangement is binding upon the Community and its Member States. Similarly, under international law signing an agreement is a minimum requirement in order for it to be binding.[82] The conclusion must be that in all likelihood the commitments entered into by both parties are not legally binding. However, that does not mean that the arrangement is beyond the law. It does call for a number of comments from a legal point of view, as the analysis below will reveal. It must also be added that the form of the arrangement was a point of discussion during the negotiations, it having been reported that the Member States wanted the arrangement to be informal 'because such trade restraints are questionable under GATT rules'.[83]

[81] Cf. Christian Tomuschat, on Article 228 in H. von der Groeben, J. Thiesing, C.-D. Ehlermann (eds.), *Kommentar zum EWG-Vertrag*, 4th edn. (Baden-Baden: Nomos, 1991), 5671.
[82] Cf. Tomuschat, *supra* n. 81, p. 5671.
[83] 'EC reaches accord on plan for sales of Japanese cars', *Financial Times*, 20 June 1990, p. 1. Allegedly, Commissioner Sir Leon Brittan wanted restrictions on intra-Community trade in Japanese cars to be formally enshrined in Community legislation, see 'EC move to limit Japanese car imports under threat', *Financial Times*, 25 Sept. 1990, p. 1.

The scope of the arrangement is unclear. It has not been clarified whether only exports from Japan are covered, or whether Japanese-labelled cars produced outside Japan are also included.[84] Given the large output of the latter kind, especially in the USA, the question is obviously significant,[85] and it could well become an issue in the course of the implementation of the arrangement.[86] Even more ambiguous and contested is the status of European-made Japanese cars. As was mentioned, the arrangement provides that there will be no restrictions on Japanese investment within the Community, or on the free circulation of its products. Nevertheless, there are two 'déclarations conclusives' attached to the arrangement (which are anything but conclusive),[87] one by Commissioner Andriessen, stating that

the Commission has based itself on various working assumptions concerning the automobile market developments in the future, including an estimate of 1.2 million vehicles, by the end of the transitional period, for the annual output, to be sold in the Community, of Japanese owned factories located in the EC.

Whereas this seems to imply that the evolutions in the European output of Japanese car manufacturers may play some role in the implementation of the arrangement, the second declaration, by Mr Nakao, radically denies this. It says:

Let me call your attention to your commitment in the 'Elements of consensus' that Japanese investment or sales of its products in the Community shall not be restricted.

Press reports have already highlighted the scope for controversy inherent in these conflicting points of view.[88]

Furthermore, the impact of fluctuations in demand on the level of exports from Japan is not specified beyond the terms indicated above. Various hypotheses have been voiced,[89] but the arrangement itself is rather silent on this

---

[84] i.e. cars produced by a producer of Japanese origin. Press reports are inconclusive as to the intentions of the parties in this regard. Compare 'Japan, EC agree on car imports', *Financial Times*, 1 Aug. 1991, p. 6, stating that '[t]he deal ... does not affect imports into the EC of Japanese brand cars made in the USA or any other third country', with 'EC vehicle sales accord with Japan to include light trucks', *Financial Times*, 5 Aug. 1991, p. 4, where it is mentioned that 'Japanese exports to the EC from all sources except "transplants" ' are included. Commissioner Bangemann has declared that exports of Japanese cars made in the U.S. are not subject to the arrangement, see Written Question No. 1277/92 by Mr Christian de la Malène, MEP, OJ C 51/12 of 22 Feb. 1993.

[85] It is also relevant for the GATT context because if US-made cars were included, the arrangement would affect US exports without the USA being a party to it. See *infra*, p. 213.

[86] For the moment, few Japanese-labelled cars are shipped from outside Japan to the Community. However, this could change in view of the increasing pressure by the United States on Japan relating to trade in cars, cf. e.g. 'Japan freezes car export quota for U.S.', *Financial Times*, 9–10 Jan. 1993, p. 3. It is not to be excluded that this pressure would at some stage be focused on the level of exports to the Community of Japanese-labelled cars produced in the USA.

[87] Also see 'Car sales accord light on consensus', *Financial Times*, 23 Sept. 1991, p. 4.

[88] Ibid. and 'Japan and Europe set to clash on car trade', *Financial Times*, 12 Sept. 1991, p. 1.

[89] Cf. again 'Car sales accord light on consensus', *supra* n. 87.

issue. Undoubtedly, this will be one of the main subjects of the biannual consultations that are to be held, since fluctuations in demand are of course liable to occur.[90]

Monitoring and the Rules of the GATT

Under the arrangement, Japan undertakes to 'monitor' its exports to the Community as a whole, as well as to some Member States' national markets individually. How the term monitoring is to be understood is not indicated in the arrangement, and it would therefore be difficult to give a precise definition of the commitment Japan entered into. Neither is it possible to specify with any certainty the methods which the Japanese side will use for implementing its commitment. But in view of the circumstances surrounding the negotiation and the conclusion of the arrangement, it is beyond doubt that Japan has agreed to restrain its exports of cars to the Community. Japan's commitment must therefore be characterized as a voluntary export restraint (VER). As such, the arrangement is nothing new. It is, on the contrary, almost the archetype of the so-called grey area measures that are proliferating in international trade, and which are aimed at protecting a country's market against imports of sensitive products *without* reverting to the established rules and disciplines of the world trading system, as laid down in the GATT.[91] These grey area measures are clearly at odds with the GATT system, although it is not always easy to firmly establish their incompatibility with the General Agreement in legal terms.[92] Since there is a great variety in these measures, a

[90] The first rounds of consultations confirm this. As car sales have fallen in Europe, the Community argues that the burden of this decline should be shared by the Japanese exporters. That was accepted by the Japanese side, see e.g. 'Further cuts in Japanese car exports to Europe agreed', *Financial Times*, 6 Sept. 1993, p. 1.

[91] The literature on this subject is abundant. See e.g. David Roberts, *GATT Rules for Emergency Protection*, Thames Essay No. 57 (London: Harvester Wheatsheaf for the Trade Policy Research Centre, 1992), in particular ch. 4; Marc Beise, 'Out of the Grey? Grey Area Measures and the Future of Multilateralism', in T. Oppermann and J. Molsberger (eds.), *A New GATT for the Nineties and Europe '92* (Baden-Baden: Nomos, 1991), 89–96; Phedon Nicolaides, *The Hydra of Safeguards: An Intractable Problem for the Uruguay Round?*, RIIA Discussion Paper No. 21 (London: RIIA, 1989); John H. Jackson, *The World Trading System* (Cambridge, Mass.: The MIT Press, 1989), 177–83 and 'Consistency of Export-restraint Arrangements with the GATT', 11 *World Economy* (1988), 4: 485–500; Niels M. Blokker, 'GATT en vrijwillige exportbeperkingen; het panelrapport over Japanse halfgeleiders', 37 *SEW* (1989); 2: 90–104; Mitsuo Matsushita, 'Coordinating International Trade with Competition Policies', in E.-U. Petersmann and M. Hilf (eds.), *The New GATT Round of Multilateral Trade Negotiations* (Deventer: Kluwer, 1988), 395–435; E.-U. Petersmann, 'Grey Area Trade Policy and the Rule of Law', 22 *JWT* (1988), 2: 23–44; Michel Kostecki, 'Export-Restraint Arrangements and Trade Liberalization', 10 *World Economy* (1987), 4: 425–53; Brian Hindley, 'Voluntary Export Restraints and the GATT's Main Escape Clause', 3 *World Economy* (1980), 3: 313–41.

[92] Cf. Jackson, 'Consistency of Export-restraint Arrangements with the GATT', *supra* n. 91.

lot depends on their individual characteristics.[93] Also, to some extent a finding of incompatibility depends on how one interprets some of the GATT's provisions, which were drafted without any knowledge of the phenomenon of grey area measures, non-existent at that time.

Both the Community and Japan are bound by the GATT, which governs their trade relations.[94] The question therefore arises whether the arrangement regarding exports of Japanese cars is consistent with the provisions of the General Agreement. The format of the attempt below to answer that question is as follows. First to be explored is whether the Japanese export restraints violate Article XI, GATT, which as a rule prohibits quantitative restrictions. As the conclusion will be that this might indeed be the case, it is examined whether the restraints can be justified on the basis of Article XIX, relating to safeguard measures. Some attention is also paid to the issue of whether the Community and Japan are entitled to conclude a so-called *inter se* agreement, through which they put their respective GATT rights and obligations on the sideline. Lastly, the problem of how to enforce Article XI of the GATT is considered.

Export restraints and Article XI

Article XI (1), GATT, provides that

[n]o prohibitions or restrictions other than duties, taxes or other charges, whether made effective through quotas, import or export licences or other measures, shall be instituted or maintained by any contracting party on the importation of any product of the territory of any other contracting party or on the exportation or sale for export of any product destined for the territory of any other contracting party.[95]

This is radical language, not allowing, on the face of it, any government-inspired restrictions on exports. The problem is, however, that there are no indications of any formal restrictions in the case of the EC–Japan arrangement. It could be that the Japanese government merely informs the Japanese car manufacturers about the desired level of exports, and that these manufacturers behave 'wisely', having due regard to the advice of the government and to the dangers inherent in overstrained trade relations between the Community and Japan. Would this violate Article XI? How wide is the scope of this provision, and more specifically of the term 'other measures' than quotas and import and export licences, making effective restrictions on exports?

[93] One class of VERs has even been officially admitted into the GATT system, namely the restrictions on trade in textile products which exist in the framework of the Multi-Fibre Arrangement (cf. *supra*, p. 187).

[94] It will be remembered that in *International Fruit Company* the Court of Justice held that the provisions of the GATT have the effect of binding the Community, see Joined Cases 21 to 24/72, [1972] ECR 1219, at 1227. Japan joined the GATT in 1955, see *BISD*, 4 S., pp. 7–10. .

[95] Art. XI (2) contains some exceptions to this rule which are, however, irrelevant for trade in cars.

These questions have to some extent been answered in the GATT Panel Report following the Community's complaint against the bilateral arrangement between the governments of Japan and the United States on trade in semi-conductor products.[96] This arrangement was the result of US anti-dumping proceedings against semi-conductor exports from Japan. It contained a section on the prevention of dumping, in which Japan undertook to monitor (!) costs and prices of semi-conductors exported, not only to the United States, but also to third markets. This was one of the elements of the arrangement to which the Community objected, arguing that it contravened the provisions of Article VI (on dumping) and Article XI.[97] The Panel Report is very instructive as regards the way in which the Japanese government implements export restraints. In the case of semi-conductors, no legally binding measures had been adopted, but the government had set up a system of 'administrative guidance', allowing it to exert decisive influence on the level of prices of exported products.[98] The Panel examined this practice in the light of Article XI (1).[99] It noted that the wording of this provision was comprehensive and that it did not, unlike other provisions of the General Agreement, refer to laws or regulations, but more broadly to measures. It concluded from this wording that the legal status of the measures restricting exports was irrelevant, and found support for that finding in an earlier Panel Report.[100] The Panel then recognized that not all non-mandatory requests made by governments could be regarded as measures within the meaning of Article XI (1). It distinguished two essential criteria for this to be the case: there had to be reasonable grounds to believe that sufficient incentives or disincentives existed for non-mandatory measures to take effect; the operation of the measures had to be essentially dependent upon government action or intervention. If these criteria were met,

the measures would be operating in a manner equivalent to mandatory requirements such that the difference between the measures and mandatory requirements was only

[96] See *BISD*, 35 S., pp. 116–63. For comments, see Blokker, *supra* n. 91.

[97] The Community also objected to Japan's commitments as regards access to the Japanese markets, maintaining that these discriminated in favour of US-made semi-conductors.

[98] For a description of the system, see *BISD*, 35 S., pp. 120–2. Japan requested its producers and exporters not to resort to dumping. The export approval system applying to semi-conductors in the framework of CoCom enforcement was used in order to monitor prices. Producers and exporters had to report data on export prices and costs, with the possibility of intervention by the Ministry for Trade and Industry (MITI) in case it considered prices to be too low. Lastly, MITI published Semi-Conductor Supply-Demand Forecasts on a quarterly basis. Also instructive as regards administrative guidance is the Panel Report on Japanese restrictions on imports of certain agricultural products, *BISD*, 35 S., pp. 136–245, at pp. 188 and 242, as well as Kenjiro Ishikawa, *Japan and the Challenge of Europe 1992* (London: Pinter Publishers for the RIIA, 1990), 35–6 and Michael William Lochmann, 'The Japanese Voluntary Restraint on Automobile Exports: An Abandonment of the Free Trade Principles of the GATT and the Free Market Principles of United States Antitrust Laws', 27 *Harvard International Law Journal* (1986), 1: 105 and 145–9.

[99] See *BISD*, 35 S., pp. 152–9.

[100] On Japanese restrictions on imports of certain agricultural products, *supra* n. 98.

one of form and not of substance, and that there could be therefore no doubt that they fell within the range of measures covered by Article XI (1).[101]

Examining the system of administrative guidance set up in the case of semi-conductors, the Panel found that it indeed met these criteria and was inconsistent with Article XI (1).

The Panel Report in the semi-conductors case clearly indicates under what circumstances measures taken by the Japanese government in order to restrict exports of cars to the Community would violate Article XI (1) of the General Agreement. Since at the time of writing no information is available on how the Japanese side implements the car arrangement, it is not possible to reach a definitive conclusion in the matter. It must be said, however, that the above-analysed Panel Report has delivered a wide interpretation of the prohibition of Article XI (1), which would cover any action by Japan that would effectively restrict exports of cars.[102] However, the EC–Japan arrangement itself keeps out of the range of the GATT prohibition of quantitative restrictions. Article XI (1) only addresses unilateral measures by governments, although these may result from an international agreement. The agreement as such does not really violate the GATT, it is its implementation by one of the parties which does. Implicitly though it may be, the Panel Report in the semi-conductors case confirms this. The conclusion of the Panel was that the Japanese measures violated the GATT, not the agreement, although the GATT Council had defined the Panel's terms of reference as the task of examining 'trade by Japan in semi-conductors, in the context of the arrangement between Japan and the United States'.[103] On the basis of the wording of Article XI (1), this was probably the only conclusion the Panel could reach.[104]

This aspect highlights that the GATT provisions were not designed for addressing the problem of VERs. It is a major loophole, because in many cases the exporting country has little choice, politically speaking, than to conclude a voluntary restraint arrangement, because of the pressure and threats (implicit or explicit) on the part of the importing country. VERs would be much easier

---

[101] *Supra* n. 99, p. 155.

[102] As regards the wide interpretation of Art. XI (1), see also Blokker, *supra* n. 91, p. 97.

[103] See the Report, *supra* n. 99, p. 116.

[104] Nevertheless, an argument could be constructed along the following lines. In the Panel Report on Japanese measures on imports of leather (*BISD*, 31 S., pp. 94–114) the Japanese argument that the official import quotas had not been filled and that there was therefore no effect on trade was rebutted on the ground that 'the existence of a quantitative restriction should be presumed to cause nullification or impairment not only because of any effect it had had on the volume of trade but also for other reasons e.g. it would lead to increased transaction costs and would create uncertainties which could affect investment plans' (p. 113; cf. *infra*, n. 111). This means that the formal existence of a restriction is sufficient in order to find a breach of Art. XI (1). Hence, it could be argued that in case an international agreement between GATT contracting parties contains a formal commitment to restrict exports, this commitment in itself runs foul of Art. XI (1). That would come fairly close to considering the agreement as such to be incompatible with the said provision, a result which would surely be consistent with the spirit of the GATT.

to police under the GATT if the General Agreement contained a provision prohibiting agreements between governments, the object or effect of which is to restrain trade.[105]

There is one fundamental difference between the semi-conductors case and the EC–Japan arrangement regarding cars which has not yet been mentioned, namely the fact that the agreement between the USA and Japan contained provisions on monitoring exports to *third-country* markets, including the Community, without any involvement of these countries in the agreement, nor even any consultations with them. Only this side of the monitoring was attacked by the Community, arguing that

[i]t could not be the intention of the General Agreement to condone unilateral measures which, applied to the advantage of one or two contracting parties, led to the manipulation of supply of a key component of modern technology, to the detriment of other contracting parties. Nor could it be condoned that such action was taken bilaterally, in the absence of any form of meaningful consultation and without transparency.[106]

Taken further, this argument might imply that export restraints, if applied only between two contracting parties at the request of the importing country, do not violate Article XI (1). Indeed, it has been maintained that the prohibition of quantitative restrictions on exports is aimed at ensuring unrestrained supplies to an importing country. In case this country does not want to be supplied, Article XI (1) would not be violated.[107] The Panel Report on semi-conductors does not, however, support such an argument. The Panel did not at any stage of its reasoning take into account the fact that the Community had not asked Japan to monitor its exports of semi-conductors. As emphasized above, it found the restraints on exports *as such* to be incompatible with the General Agreement. With respect to the actual harm that these restraints might have caused to the Community, the Panel said nothing. It only concluded, as is customary in Panel proceedings, that a violation of a GATT provision constitutes a case of prima facie nullification or impairment of benefits accruing to the Community under the General Agreement.[108] Indeed, Article XI (1) is not merely aimed at ensuring continued supplies to importing countries.[109] The prohibition of quantitative restrictions is one of the most fundamental provisions of the General Agreement, in that the latter prefers

---

[105] Such a provision could be analogous to Art. 85 (1), EC Treaty, replacing the concepts of 'undertakings' and 'distortion of competition' with 'governments' and 'trade restriction'. Compare with the (provisional) results of the Uruguay Round negotiations on a safeguards agreement, see below, p. 212.

[106] See the Report, *supra* n. 99, p. 138.

[107] Cf. Horst G. Krenzler, 'Exportselbstbeschränkungen: ein aktuelles Problem der Handelspolitik der Europäischen Gemeinschaft', 12 *EuR* (1977), 2: 178.

[108] This means that the burden of proof is reversed, in that the defendant contracting party then has to demonstrate that there has not been any 'nullification or impairment'. In practice, the latter has proved to be very difficult. Cf. Jackson, *The World Trading System, supra* n. 91, pp. 94–6.

[109] Cf. Petersmann, *supra* n. 91, p. 32.

the use of tariffs as a trade policy instrument as these are less harmful than non-tariff barriers.[110] This fundamental character of the prohibition is confirmed in a Panel Report in which it was found that both Article XI and Article III (on national treatment)

have essentially the same rationale, namely to protect expectations of the contracting parties as to the competitive relationship between their products and those of the other contracting parties. Both articles are not only to protect current trade but also to create the predictability needed to plan future trade.[111]

The fact that the prohibition of quantitative restrictions is about undistorted competitive relationships between products imported and exported by the contracting parties precludes that export restraints be justified on the basis of the importing country having requested them. Accordingly, the fact that the Community has asked Japan to restrict its exports of cars to the Community does not affect the conclusion reached above.

Justification on the basis of Article XIX?

If Japan actually restricts exports of cars in a manner inconsistent with Article XI (1), the question arises whether this cannot be justified on the basis of Article XIX. This provision allows GATT contracting parties to take safeguard measures against imports which cause or threaten to cause serious injury to domestic producers of like or directly competitive products. Such measures consist of suspending a GATT obligation or withdrawing or modifying a GATT concession. It is accepted GATT practice that Article XI (1) is one of the 'obligations' that can be suspended when a contracting party has recourse to Article XIX.[112] Thus, when applying this provision a contracting party may install an import quota which would otherwise violate Article XI (1).

The above-mentioned question must be studied against the background of the tense relationship between VERs and Article XIX. For some decades now, VERs have been proliferating and recourse to Article XIX has been declining.[113] Often, these tendencies are regarded as being intertwined: contracting

---

[110] Tariffs are more transparent, they do not eliminate the price mechanism, there are no 'quota rents' accruing to the exporters but instead there is additional revenue in the importing country, and they are mostly laid down in legislative acts which cannot be amended by a mere administrative decision, cf. Petersmann, *supra* n. 91, p. 30 and Jackson, *The World Trading System*, *supra* n. 91, p. 116.

[111] Panel Report on United States taxes on petroleum and certain imported substances, *BISD*, 34 S., p. 160. Cf. Ch. 2, p. 141. The reference to 'expectations of the contracting parties' must not be understood as implying that if an importing country does not 'expect' imports, the corresponding exports may be restrained. The reference must be read in its context, the Panel having referred to the above-mentioned Panel Report on Japanese measures on imports of leather (see the quotation in n. 104).

[112] Jackson, 'Consistency of Export-restraint Arrangements with the GATT', *supra* n. 91, p. 494.

[113] See e.g. Nicolaides, *supra* n. 91.

parties would prefer the leeway offered by VERs, avoiding the shackles of the substantive and procedural requirements of the General Agreement's safeguard clause. That is considered to be one of the major deficiencies of the world trading system. VERs are not often transparent, they tend to discriminate against the most efficient suppliers, they are not subject to any procedural constraints (at least not at international level), it is difficult to have them reviewed in the GATT, and they tend to promote power-oriented rather than rule-oriented diplomacy.[114] Since the Tokyo Round of multilateral trade negotiations, reform of Article XIX has been attempted with a view to deflecting the road to VERs (politically often more passable than recourse to Article XIX) in the direction of GATT orthodoxy. So far, these attempts have not been successful.[115]

A first obstacle to justifying the EC–Japan arrangement under Article XIX lies in the fact that this provision allows an *importing* country to take safeguard measures, whereas in the framework of the arrangement it is the *exporting* country which restricts exports in a manner which may violate Article XI (1).[116] Of course, it could be asked whether Article XIX would not authorize such restrictions in case the importing country has requested them on the basis of alleged injury to its domestic industry. Indeed, one prominent GATT commentator sees some scope for such an interpretation in the following terms:

If, in certain cases, a safeguard measure under Article XIX of the GATT would have been possible, but the countries involved prefer an export-restraint arrangement, such a measure should be allowed if it would not affect third parties.[117]

However, even if one were to accept this interpretation, it is questionable whether it is able to 'acquit' the EC–Japan arrangement. There are two hurdles to overcome. First, Article XIX requires that safeguard measures be taken in a non-discriminatory manner, i.e. against all imports of the product concerned, whichever the exporting country. It has been questioned whether such a requirement is inherent in this provision, but it is now generally accepted that it is (although there are voices in favour of abandoning it in the framework of a redrafting of Article XIX).[118] Obviously, the EC–Japan arrangement does not

[114] This list of vices is surely not a complete one. Compare with the literature referred to in n. 91.
[115] See, however, *infra*, p. 212.
[116] Cf. Jackson, 'Consistency of Export-restraint Arrangements with the GATT', *supra* n. 91, p. 494.
[117] Ibid.
[118] Marco C. E. J. Bronckers has tried to make a case for an interpretation of Art. XIX allowing so-called selective, i.e. discriminatory safeguard measures, see *Selective Safeguard Measures in Multilateral Trade Relations* (Deventer: Kluwer, 1985), chs. 1 and 2. However, there is a GATT Panel Report in which it has been stated that if quantitative restrictions are chosen as a safeguard measure under Article XIX, these have to be administered in accordance with Article XIII, i.e. in a non-discriminatory manner (Panel Report on Norwegian restrictions on imports of certain

satisfy this requirement of non-discrimination, since the Community only takes action against imports of Japanese cars. The above-mentioned interpretation must certainly not allow the contracting parties to circumvent the non-discrimination principle. Secondly, it is doubtful whether the EC–Japan arrangement leaves third countries unaffected. The car market is very much a global one.[119] Restrictions on exports of Japanese cars to the Community may very well induce Japanese car manufacturers to export more to other markets.[120] Of course it might then be argued that the same would be likely to happen if the Community were to take genuine safeguard measures under Article XIX. The latter, however, offer some procedural guarantees of transparency and the possibility of review within the GATT, which are absent from the EC–Japan arrangement.[121] The fact that in today's interdependent world restrictions on imports or exports are likely not just to affect trade between the countries involved is an additional argument in favour of interpreting Article XIX rather strictly as regards the room it may provide for concluding voluntary restraint arrangements.[122]

This brings us to the procedural side of the matter. The Community has its own procedure for the adoption of safeguard measures.[123] It includes an official investigation into the effects of imports on the domestic industry, it allows all interested parties to be heard, and subjects the decision-making to a number of legal constraints. All of this is lacking in the EC–Japan arrangement. Whether imports of Japanese cars cause or threaten to cause serious injury has not been publicly examined, there have been no official hearings and since the arrangement is not published and its legal status is uncertain, it would be very hard to subject it to judicial review within the Community. All this precludes justifying the arrangement on the basis of Article XIX, since the Community has not observed its own rules applying to safeguard action. If the Community had followed these rules, as it has done in a number of other cases

textile products, *BISD*, 27 S., pp. 119–26, at p. 125). This Report provides the authority for a non-discriminatory interpretation of Article XIX (also accepted by Bronckers, *supra*, pp. 80–1). The Community is in favour of creating some scope for selective safeguard measures, which is one of the elements of its negotiating position in the Uruguay Round (see *News of the Uruguay Round*, No. 34, 23 Feb. 1990, pp. 2–4 and No. 41, 9 Oct. 1990, pp. 5–6).

[119] Cf. 'L'industrie automobile européenne: situation, enjeux et propositions d'action', *supra* n. 56 and Smith and Venables, *supra* n. 57, pp. 119–27.

[120] Smith and Venables, *supra* n. 57, p. 152.

[121] When a contracting party wishes to take action under Article XIX, notice must be given in advance to the GATT as well as to the contracting parties exporting the product concerned, followed by consultations. Admittedly, the Community and Japan have indicated that they would notify the GATT.

[122] Cf. Petersmann, *supra* n. 91, p. 32. VERs are probably not completely incompatible with Art. XIX, since para. 3 (*a*) of this provision mentions the reaching of an agreement among the interested contracting parties as a possible outcome of safeguard action. Such an agreement could contain a VER.

[123] Art. 15 of Regulation 288/82 (see Ch. 5, p. 164) for imports from market economy countries.

which have resulted in VERs,[124] it might have been possible to invoke Article XIX. On balance, that now seems to be excluded.

However, the preceding considerations could become irrelevant if the Uruguay Round is concluded. The safeguards issue is one of the items on the agenda of these negotiations.[125] This has resulted in a draft Agreement on Safeguards which is part of the Draft Final Act presented by the GATT's Director-General in December 1991.[126] This text contains much more detailed provisions on the conditions under which safeguard measures can be taken than Article XIX. In addition, it includes a section on 'Prohibition and elimination of certain measures', providing, among other things, that

a contracting party shall not seek, take or maintain any voluntary export restraints, orderly marketing arrangements or any other similar measures on the export or the import side. These include actions taken by a single contracting party as well as actions under agreements, arrangements and understandings entered into by two or more contracting parties. Any such measure in effect at the time of entry into force of this agreement shall be brought into conformity with this provision or phased out...[127]

The latter should be done within a period of four years. However, each contracting party is entitled to maintain one such measure for a longer period, namely until 31 December 1999. The draft Agreement contains one example of such a measure: the EC–Japan car arrangement.[128] It is obvious that in case this Agreement enters into force, it would have to be considered as providing a sufficient justification for the arrangement in terms of compatibility with the General Agreement.

Inter se agreements

In the literature on VERs, the question has been put whether GATT contracting parties can conclude a so-called *inter se* agreement, through which they put aside their respective GATT rights and obligations.[129] Even accepting that this would be possible,[130] it could certainly not apply to the EC–Japan

[124] See e.g. Regulation 1735/90 introducing prior Community surveillance of imports of certain types of footwear originating in South Korea and Taiwan, OJ L 161/12 of 27 June 1990.
[125] See for more details, Robertson, *supra* n. 91, ch. 7.
[126] MTN.TNC/W/FA, pp. M.1-M.11.   [127] See Art. 22 (*b*).
[128] See the Annex to the draft Agreement.
[129] See Blokker, *supra* n. 91, p. 100. Compare with Jackson, 'Consistency of Export-Restraint Arrangements with the GATT', *supra* n. 91, p. 492 and Petersmann, *supra* n. 91, pp. 31–2, both of whom do not use the term *inter se* agreement, but do discuss the question.
[130] Which is not obvious, cf. the literature in n. 129. Art. 41 (1) of the Vienna Convention on the Law of Treaties provides:

Two or more parties to a multilateral treaty may conclude an agreement to modify the treaty as between themselves alone if:...
(b) the modification in question is not prohibited by the treaty and:
    (i) does not affect the enjoyment by the other parties of their rights under the treaty or the performance of their obligations;
    (ii) does not relate to a provision, derogation from which is incompatible with the effective execution of the object and purpose of the treaty as a whole.

As regards VERs, the conditions of (i) and (ii) do not seem to be fulfilled.

arrangement for two very simple reasons: the arrangement is not a proper agreement under international law[131] and the parties to it did not have the intention to 'amend' the General Agreement as between them, since they expressly provided that the GATT would be notified and that they would 'jointly defend the monitoring system in that forum as a GATT consistent measure'.[132]

The problem of enforcement

Assuming that Japanese restrictions on exports of cars implemented in the framework of the EC–Japan arrangement violate the rules of the GATT (and in the absence of a Uruguay Round agreement 'legalizing' this violation), the question of enforcement arises. How can one restore GATT orthodoxy? Obviously, neither the Community nor Japan are likely to complain. Private citizens or companies considering themselves to be damaged by the restrictions would be faced with the fact that the GATT has no direct effect and therefore cannot be relied upon before the courts.[133] This only leaves third countries with an effective possibility of having the arrangement reviewed. The GATT would of course be the proper forum for such a review. The question then is broached whether a formal complaint by a third country would have any chance of succeeding.[134] After all, it is not certain whether third countries are directly affected by the EC–Japan arrangement.[135]

Article XXIII of the General Agreement requires a contracting party, when bringing a complaint, to show 'that any benefit accruing to it ... is being nullified or impaired or that the attainment of any objective of the Agreement is being impeded'. However, it is established GATT practice that a breach of a GATT obligation amounts to a case of prima-facie nullification or impairment. This shifts the burden of proof to the defendant country, which must demonstrate that there is no nullification or impairment.[136] In the case of the EC–Japan arrangement, that would probably be rather complicated in view of

[131] See *supra*, p. 202. [132] See p. 202.

[133] Joined Cases 21 to 24/72, *International Fruit Company et al.* v. *Produktschap voor Groenten en Fruit*, [1972] ECR 1219, at 1227–8. Only in direct proceedings before the Court of Justice has the doctrine of direct effect no role to play, as has become evident in Case C-69/89, *Nakajima all Precision Co.* v. *Council* [1991] ECR I-2069. However, direct access for private citizens is only possible in a limited number of cases of which in the case of the arrangement only the action for compensation of damages seems to have any chances of being admitted. On the principles governing Japanese law as to direct effect of GATT, see John H. Jackson, Jean-Victor Louis, and Mitsuo Matsushita, *Implementing the Tokyo Round* (Ann Arbor, Mich.: The University of Michigan Press, 1984), 83–9.

[134] Cf. Jackson, 'Consistency of Export-Restraint Arrangements with the GATT', *supra* n. 91, pp. 492–3; Blokker, *supra* n. 91, pp. 100–1.

[135] This depends among other things on the scope of the arrangement, namely whether exports originating outside Japan are included or not, cf. *supra*, p. 203.

[136] See n. 108.

the global character of the car market. Hence, third countries would seem to have a good chance of succeeding if a complaint were to be brought within the GATT, provided they are able to show the inconsistency of the Japanese restrictions on exports of cars with the General Agreement. Whether there is any political willingness on the part of third countries to complain, however, is an altogether different matter.[137]

Protecting National Markets and Community Law

This section examines the relationship between the export restrictions laid down by the arrangement and Community law in a narrow sense, i.e. without having regard to international agreements which are binding on the Community. The first question which in this respect needs to be addressed is whether the Community is entitled, under the Treaty, to conclude voluntary restraint arrangements with third countries, in which these countries undertake to limit their exports to the Community *as a whole*.[138] In so far as these arrangements are laid down in a genuine international agreement, the Community would indeed seem to have the authority to conclude them, by virtue of its competence to conduct commercial policy. There is the constraint of Article 110, EC Treaty, which sets 'the progressive abolition of restrictions on international trade' as one of the aims of the Common Commercial Policy. However, there can be little doubt that the Community's institutions have considerable discretionary powers when taking commercial policy measures, probably allowing them to conclude the said agreements.[139] The problem with the EC – Japan arrangement is that it is *not* a genuine international agreement. To the extent that the parties have chosen this course of action in order to

---

[137] It is one of the recommendations of the famous 'Leutwiler Report', drawn up by seven 'wise men' on the request of the GATT's Director-General, that '[t]hird parties should use their rights to complain when bilateral agreements break the rules', see *Trade Policies for a Better Future: The 'Leutwiler Report', the GATT and the Uruguay Round* (Dordrecht: Martinus Nijhoff, 1987), 15 and 54–5.

[138] Quite a lot of such arrangements exist. One need only refer to the various bilateral agreements between the Community and textiles-exporting countries, see *supra* p. 187.

[139] In Opinion 1/78, the Court decided that '[a]lthough it may be thought that at the time when the Treaty was drafted liberalization of trade was the dominant idea, the Treaty nevertheless does not form a barrier to the possibility of the Community's developing a commercial policy aiming at a regulation of the world market for certain products rather than at a mere liberalization of trade', see [1979] ECR 2913. This language probably covers the case of VERs. It must be added that most of the existing VERs protecting the overall Community market are permitted under the relevant international rules: the textiles agreements are in conformity with the MFA, whereas the VERs resulting from safeguard action are probably allowed under Art. XIX, GATT. One could also regard as VERs the undertakings which are often offered by exporters whose exports are the object of an anti-dumping investigation (see Art. 10 of Regulation 2423/88, OJ L 209/11 of 2 Aug. 1988). These undertakings are foreseen by Art. 7 of the GATT Anti-Dumping Code (*BISD*, 26 S., p. 171).

avoid inconsistency with the GATT,[140] we are back to the question of compatibility with the GATT.[141] Furthermore, there is little than can be added without ending up in some sort of circular argument. It could indeed be argued that the Community is not entitled to conclude a voluntary restraint arrangement without observing the rules of the Treaty on concluding international agreements and that the arrangement, as a result, is unlawful. However, as has already been mentioned the arrangement is not legally binding, so that a verdict of illegality would produce little effect.[142]

However, the arrangement does not merely contain a restriction on exports to the Community as a whole. It also contains restrictions on exports to five national markets within the Community. The latter appear more questionable under Community law (in the above-indicated sense), since they lead to a partitioning of the market, which sharply contrasts with the rules and principles guiding the completion of the internal market. Below, this aspect of the arrangement is looked at from two angles, the first being the requirement of a uniform commercial policy whereas the second relates to competition law and policy.

The subquotas and the requirement of a uniform commercial policy

In the preceding chapter, emphasis was laid on the requirement of uniformity inherent in the development of the Common Commercial Policy. Departures from this requirement, it was maintained, are only permissible on the condition that they are of a transitional nature, full uniformity not yet having been reached. To some extent, this rule of transitional exceptions may perhaps justify the restrictions on exports of Japanese cars to national markets within the Community. That could be the case with respect to Italy, Portugal, and Spain, because these Member States have restricted imports of Japanese cars before the Common Commercial Policy became effective for them.[143] Thus, it could be argued that the Japanese VER is only a transitional prolongation of these import restrictions, offering, admittedly, more scope for access of Japanese cars than previously[144] as well as the perspective of unrestricted trade by

[140] See *supra*, n. 83.

[141] Compare with Petersmann, *supra* n. 91, p. 34, where he characterizes the respect of rules such as those of the GATT as being a basic constitutional requirement of most developed nations. Much more extensive in this respect, by the same author, is *Constitutional Functions and Constitutional Problems of International Economic Law* (Fribourg: University Press, 1991).

[142] Perhaps an action for compensation of damages, based on Arts. 178 and 215, EC Treaty, would be possible.

[143] The Italian quotas existed before the CCP came into effect on 1 Jan. 1970; the Portuguese and Spanish quotas predate these countries' accession to the Community (see Bronckers, *supra* n. 67, pp. 77–8).

[144] The export estimates mentioned in the arrangement (see *supra* n. 79) amount to larger Japanese market shares than existed under the previous restrictions, except for the UK, access to which is limited to 7% whereas the arrangement between the British and Japanese car manufacturers provided for a limit of 10–11% (see p. 199).

the end of the century. Even then, it is questionable whether the length of the transitional period is still reasonable, especially in the case of the Italian market, access to which normally should have been the subject of a uniform commercial policy since 1 January 1970.

The above justification, however, does not exist as regards restrictions on exports to France and the UK. These restrictions do not replace official quotas, but rather, in the case of the UK, an industry-to-industry arrangement and, in the case of France, administrative barriers to entry.[145] Both these devices were of dubious standing under Community law.[146] Moreover, they did not precede the establishment of the Common Commercial Policy, so that it cannot be maintained that there has never been a uniform policy concerning imports of cars in France and the UK. The rule of transitional exceptions can therefore not be invoked. As a result, it can be seriously questioned whether the Community was entitled to conclude a voluntary restraint arrangement with Japan relating to exports to France and the UK, in view of the requirement of uniformity inherent in the Common Commercial Policy.

Again, however, there is the problem of enforcement. Since the arrangement is not a legally binding act emanating from one of the Community's institutions, a verdict of illegality is not likely to produce much effect. The only prospect for judicial review would be to start proceedings before the Court of Justice against one or more of the institutions (which ones?), invoking the Community's non-contractual liability. That could perhaps be done by an importer of Japanese cars considering himself to be harmed by the restrictions resulting from the arrangement. However, it would undoubtedly be very difficult to prove that the Community has committed a wrongful act by concluding the arrangement and that this has caused demonstrable damage.[147]

The subquotas and EC competition law and policy

As was mentioned, the arrangement itself establishes a link with the Community's competition policy, by providing that the Commission will 'ensure that the operation of competition law does not constitute an obstacle to the operation of the arrangement', without, however, further clarifying this

[145] See *supra*, p. 199.

[146] Bronckers, *supra* n. 67, pp. 78–82. Attempts have been made to have these restrictions reviewed by the Court of Justice and the Court of First Instance, see *supra* n. 69. In its judgment in Case T-7/92 the latter Court held that the Commission unduly rejected the complaints addressed to it by the applicants in the framework of the Community's competition policy. These complaints alleged that the division between a number of Japanese manufacturers of the import quotas set by the French government was an anti-competitive agreement liable to fall foul of Art. 85, EC Treaty.

[147] On the Court's case-law on non-contractual liability, see e.g. Henry G. Schermers and Denis Waelbroeck, *Judicial Protection in the European Communities*, 5th edn. (Deventer: Kluwer, 1992), 328–64.

link.[148] One possible explanation is that Japanese car manufacturers wish to be certain that any agreements which they may reach regarding the sharing of the exports subject to voluntary restraint will not be declared incompatible with the EC Treaty provisions on competition.[149] But there is also a second explanation, relating to the subquotas. It immediately springs to mind if one considers the problem of how to implement the restrictions on exports to national markets within the Community. There are no official import quotas, and there is no longer any corresponding application of Article 115. How can one then make sure that Japanese cars, once imported into the Community, are not sold on one of the protected markets in larger numbers than agreed? That can only be achieved through restrictions on competition: the Japanese manufacturers have to organize the distribution of their products in such a way as to allow them to control the final destination, thus limiting the scope for competition at the distribution level. The question then becomes whether they can do so under EC competition law, and whether the above-mentioned provision of the arrangement plays any role in that.

The main element of EC competition law which governs this question is Commission Regulation 123/85 on the application of Article 85 (3) of the EEC Treaty to certain categories of motor vehicle distribution and servicing agreements.[150] This regulation exempts the distribution networks set up in accordance with its provisions of the prohibition laid down in Article 85 (1) regarding agreements that distort competition. Below, it is examined to what degree the regulation allows restrictions on distribution of cars along national lines. Appended is an analysis of the more general question whether the Community's institutions are entitled to subordinate competition policy to a goal such as the implementation of the EC–Japan arrangement.

Regulation 123/85 and the role of intermediaries

The regulation allows that car manufacturers set up a distribution network on a territorial basis. Each dealer is then assigned a contract territory and may be prohibited, outside this territory, from maintaining branches or depots, from seeking customers, and from entrusting third parties with the distribution of the cars in question.[151] This means that the dealer is not entitled to develop an active sales policy outside his area. These territorial restrictions are justified, in the Commission's view, because they 'lead to more intensive distribution and servicing efforts in an easily supervised contract territory, to knowledge of

---

[148] See *supra*, p. 201.
[149] Cf. Commission Decision of 29 Nov. 1974 relating to proceedings under Art. 85 of the Treaty (IV/27.095—*Franco-Japanese ball-bearings agreement*), OJ L 343/19 of 21 Dec. 1974, also dealing with voluntary restraints on exports from Japan. See also n. 146.
[150] OJ L 15/16 of 18 Jan. 1985.
[151] Art. 3 (8) and (9).

the market based on closer contact with consumers, and to more demand-orientated supply'.[152] However, they must not provide absolute territorial protection. In the words of the Notice accompanying the regulation, 'the European consumer's basic rights include above all the right to buy a motor vehicle and to have it maintained or repaired wherever prices and quality are most advantageous to him'.[153] All persons residing and companies established within the Community must therefore be able to buy a car with whichever dealer they wish to. Accordingly, dealers must also satisfy demand from outside their territory. However, that only applies to orders placed by private persons, as the dealers may be prohibited from selling to a reseller, unless the latter is part of the distribution network.[154]

Although probably the aim, this scope for parallel imports has not worked as a corrective for too widely differing prices of car models in the various national markets.[155] Consumers have not made use of this opportunity on a large scale, even though the Commission has concluded from a recent study that the said prices indeed differ considerably throughout the Community.[156] One possible explanation is that consumers have no knowledge of this facility, or find it too cumbersome to shop for a car in another Member State. To the extent that this explanation is correct, the described shortcoming in the operation of Regulation 123/85 could be offset by the activities of specialized companies acting as intermediaries between car buyers in one Member State and dealers in another. The regulation allows such activities, provided that they do not amount to reselling.[157]

There is a palpable fear among the Commission and the Member States that a substantial growth in the activities of these intermediaries may endanger the implementation of the EC–Japan arrangement. The Commission has implicitly acknowledged this in a communication to the Council on the car

---

[152] Recital 9.   [153] OJ C 17/3 of 18 Jan. 1985.   [154] Art. 10.

[155] This aim is implicitly present in the provisions of Regulation 123/85, as well as in the Notice accompanying it (*supra* n. 153). Cf. also F. L. Lukoff, 'European Competition Law and Distribution in the Motor Vehicle Sector: Commission Regulation 123/85 of 12 December 1984', 23 *CML Rev.* (1986), 4: 854–5 and 863–5.

[156] See 'Intra-Community Car Price Differentials Report', Commission Press Release IP/92/355 of 6 May 1992; also see 'Car prices vary by 40 per cent in parts of the EC', *Financial Times*, 27 Apr. 1992, p. 14 and *Agence Europe*, No. 5718, 27 and 28 Apr. 1992, pp. 11–2. See also *Agence Europe*, No. 5880, 16 Dec. 1992, pp. 11–2, referring to a study by the BEUC. In December 1992, the Commission and the European car manufacturers reached an agreement on regular publications of the various prices of cars across the Community, see *Agence Europe*, No. 5879, 14/15 Dec. 1992, p. 9 and 'Carmakers agree to publish comparative prices across EC', *Financial Times*, 11 Dec. 1992, p. 20.

[157] Art. 3 (11). The Commission has made it known that the study on car price differentials does not demonstrate that Regulation 123/85 is the chief cause of these differentials. Nevertheless, '[t]he persistence of price differentials over time supports the conclusion that the selective distribution system, as it currently operates, may be a factor in sustaining such differentials insofar as it limits trade between Member States in the Single Market, and thereby reduces effective pressure on manufacturers to align prices more closely' (see the Press Release referred to in n. 156).

industry,[158] whereas some Member States have made their consent to Community-wide type approval of cars conditional on the Commission clarifying its position on the role of intermediaries.[159] These fears are understandable since the Japanese car manufacturers have no direct influence on intermediaries.[160] In so far as the latter are allowed under Regulation 123/85 to develop their activities, a parallel market could indeed emerge, making it impossible for the manufacturers to abide by the subquotas set in the framework of the arrangement without infringing EC competition law.

With regard to this problem, the *Eco System/Peugeot* case has served as a catalyst. It is named after a French company, specialized in acting as an intermediary between French consumers and Peugeot car dealers (among others) established in Belgium, allowing the former to take advantage of lower Belgian prices. At one stage, the Peugeot company sent a circular to its Belgian dealers, instructing them not to supply any more cars to Eco System. The latter then lodged a complaint with the Commission, which after a full investigation concluded that the activities of Eco System came within the scope of the intermediary concept in Regulation 123/85 and ordered Peugeot to recommence supply.[161] Simultaneously, the Commission issued a notice in which it clarified the activities of car intermediaries.[162] This notice distinguishes two principles, namely

that the intermediary referred to in the Regulation is a provider of services acting for the account of a purchaser and final user; he cannot assume risks normally associated

[158] See *L'industrie automobile européenne*, *supra* n. 56. In the words of the accompanying Press Release, 'if the selective distribution system were employed to allow major price differences between the various national markets it would create the risk of a sizeable parallel market emerging. This would make it considerably more difficult to implement the EC–Japan arrangement ... However, the Commission does not condemn the selective distribution system: on the contrary, it considers that the implementation of the EC–Japan arrangement on motor vehicles ... calls for a "satisfactory and efficient system of selective distribution over the transitional period to ensure that the objectives of the arrangement are not endangered by large-scale indirect importation". The Commission believes that a selective distribution system operated in a satisfactory and efficient way would be useful for the management of the transitional period of the EC–Japan arrangement on motor vehicles', P-24 of 29 Apr. 1992, p. 5. Also see the speech by Commissioner Sir Leon Brittan, then responsible for competition policy, 'The Single Market for Cars', Commission Press Release Speech/91/13 of 5 Dec. 1991.

[159] Community-wide type approval of cars will make it impossible for individual Member States to hinder or block imports through the type approval procedure. Obviously, a number of Member States did not wish to hand over this weapon without being reassured on the scope for intermediary activities under Regulation 123/85, see *Agence Europe*, No. 5605, 8 Nov. 1991, pp. 7–8; 'Spain could clear way for progress in EC car dispute', *Financial Times*, 8 Nov. 1991, p. 6, and the speech by Sir Leon Brittan, *supra* n. 158. Also see *A Single Market for Cars*, *supra* n. 58, pp. 12 and 29–30 of the evidence.

[160] See, however, Jacques Pelkmans, '1992: Economic Effects on Third Countries', in M. Hilf and C. Tomuschat (eds.), *EG und Drittstaatsbeziehungen nach 1992* (Baden-Baden: Nomos, 1991), 174–5, who plays down these fears.

[161] Commission Decision of 4 Dec. 1991 (Case IV/33.157—*Eco System/Peugeot*), OJ L 66/1 of 11 Mar. 1992.

[162] OJ C 329/20 of 18 Dec. 1991. This Notice is a supplement to the general Notice on Regulation 123/85, *supra* n. 153.

with ownership, and is given prior written authority by an identified principal, whose name and address are given, to exercise such activity. The second is the principle of the transparency of the authorization, and in particular the requirement that, under national law, the intermediary pass on to the purchaser all the benefits obtained in the negotiations carried out on his behalf.[163]

On the basis of these principles, the Commission has worked out a number of practical criteria regarding the organization of the intermediary's activities. Rather surprisingly, some of these criteria are phrased in terms of obligations for the intermediary, although he is not part of the distribution network and does not (normally) engage in any competition-distorting activities. In fact the contrary.[164] The relationship with Regulation 123/85 is, however, clearly stated:

Activities which do not conform to these guidelines and criteria will justify the presumption, in the absence of evidence to the contrary, that an intermediary is acting beyond the limits set by Article 3 (11) of Regulation (EEC) No 123/85, or creating a confusion in the mind of the public on this point by giving the impression that he is a reseller.[165]

Therefore, the intermediary is not obliged to do anything, but if he does not respect the criteria laid down by the Commission, he runs the risk of not being supplied by dealers, without being able to lodge a justified complaint.

The most important criteria set out in the notice seem to be those relating to the relationship between the intermediary and the car dealers. The Commission judges that this relationship should not become a privileged one, that the intermediary should obtain supplies on normal market conditions, that he must not make agreements by which he undertakes obligations to buy, and that he should not receive discounts different from those which are customary.[166] Then follows the last sentence of the notice, which is probably the most critical one in the framework of this study:

In this context, sales of more than 10% of his annual sales by any one authorized dealer through any one intermediary would create the presumption of a privileged relationship contrary to the Articles cited above.[167]

---

[163] Ibid.

[164] These obligations relate to the organization of the structure of the intermediary's activities, to the use of supermarket buildings as an outlet, to the risks which the intermediary may assume, to the services offered to the clients and to advertising.

[165] Ibid. One question which arises in this respect is whether the individual dealers need to check whether an intermediary acts in accordance with the described criteria, if so, whether they need to do so with regard to each individual transaction through an intermediary, or whether, on the contrary, the dealer may get instructions from the part of the manufacturer as to which intermediaries respect the criteria. This question, which is obviously important for the smooth operation of the system, is not dealt with in the Notice.

[166] OJ C 329/21.

[167] Ibid. The Articles are those of Regulation 123/85, namely 3 (8) (*a*) and (*b*), 3 (9) and (4) (1) (3) (*sic*).

How the Commission has arrived at this 10 per cent figure is not clarified.

It is impossible to define beyond mere conjecture the role played by the existence of the EC–Japan arrangement in drawing up the above-described clarification.[168] One would assume, however, that the arrangement—and especially its provision which states that competition law will not obstruct the operation of the arrangement—has militated in favour of limiting the scope for large-scale intermediary activities,[169] whereas pure competition policy considerations would normally have tended to work in favour of strengthening parallel imports in order to combat unwarranted price differences between national markets. In the light of these observations, the 10 per cent limit appears to be rather restrictive. Applied to the EC–Japan arrangement, there would have to be quite a lot of intermediary companies in the markets protected by subquotas (which encompass the largest EC markets, with the sole exception of Germany) for parallel imports to undermine the implementation of the arrangement. If we take the Eco System example, this company would only be able to supply Japanese cars to its customers with an absolute maximum of 10 per cent of all Japanese cars sold in Belgium.[170] That would probably not be a threat to the subquotas, unless there were many companies similar to Eco System.

Subordination of competition policy?

The broad question which all this raises is whether the Commission is entitled to let the EC–Japan arrangement play a role in (first) devising and (secondly) implementing its competition policy relating to the distribution of cars.

As to the devising part, the question may not be a very practical one. After all, Regulation 123/85, including its leeway for setting up a distribution system along national lines and its limited scope for parallel imports, was adopted long before the EC–Japan arrangement. How can one demonstrate, furthermore, that the clarification of the activities of intermediaries was not induced by considerations of a purely competition policy nature? How will one be able to demonstrate, if the regulation is extended in 1995, when it needs to be revised,[171] that the EC–Japan arrangement affects the terms of such an extension?

However, the implementing part is much trickier. Suppose in the next few years intermediary activities do develop to the extent of threatening the

---

[168] For an analysis of the intermediary concept in the context of the basic principles of competition policy guiding exclusive distribution, see Wernhard Möschel, 'La distribution sélective d'automobiles en droit européen de la concurrence', 44 *RTDC* (1991), 1: 1–26.

[169] The Commission has itself formally acknowledged the link, see *supra* n. 158.

[170] That is if it continues to import only from Belgium. It could of course also go to Holland and Germany, for example.

[171] According to Art. 14, the regulation remains in force until 30 June 1985.

implementation of the arrangement as regards subquotas, and that Japanese car manufacturers instruct their dealers not to supply them any more, as Peugeot did in the *Eco System/Peugeot* case. Would the Commission be entitled *not* to act against such instructions, even if it was to receive a number of complaints?[172] Suppose, secondly, that the various distributors of Japanese cars supply cars to one another (within their respective distribution networks), as they are allowed to under Regulation 123/85,[173] and that the manufacturers intervene so as to make sure that the subquotas are respected. Again, would the Commission be entitled *not* to act, even if the dealers were to complain, given the fact that in the comparable *Ford* case it was established that manufacturers were obliged to continue to supply dealers?[174] In this connection, it must be recalled that complaints lodged with the Commission in the framework of EC competition law cannot simply be dismissed on a purely discretionary basis. Complainants with a legitimate interest have the right to have their case properly examined, and they can subject the Commission's decision to judicial review by the Court of Justice.[175]

Could the Commission argue, if such a case were to be brought up, that the EC–Japan arrangement precludes it from taking action? As such, that would be difficult since, as was mentioned, the arrangement is not a proper international agreement and thus is not binding on the Community. Could the Commission then, in a broader argument, maintain that the Community's commercial policy towards imports of Japanese cars takes precedence over competition law, and that it is therefore not in the Community's interest to act against restrictions on competition which are necessary in order to implement the car arrangement?[176]

It is submitted that also this argument would be unfounded, at least in so far

[172] In this respect, it has to be noted that in reaction to the car price differentials study (*supra* n. 156), Commission Vice-President Sir Leon Brittan sent a letter to the European car manufacturers in which he requested, among other things, that they write a standard letter to their dealers indicating the scope, under Regulation 123/85, for supplies to other dealers and intermediaries (Press Release IP/92/355 of 6 May 1992). At the same time, the Commission indicated that it 'is also planning to launch proceedings against dealers/manufacturers where it receives evidence that parallel imports between national markets or dealer-to-dealer sales across national frontiers are being deliberately obstructed' (see the Press Release referred to in n. 156).

[173] Art. 3 (10) (*a*). In the *Eco System/Peugeot* case it appeared that Peugeot dealers did not build up supplies among themselves, see para. 14 of the Decision, OJ L 66/3 of 11 Mar. 1992.

[174] This case concerned the refusal by Ford to continue the supply to its German dealers of right-hand-drive cars, see Decision IV/30.696 (*Ford Werke AG*), OJ L 327/31 of 24 Nov. 1983 and Joined Cases 25 and 26/84, *Ford-Werke AG and Ford of Europe Inc* v. *Commission* [1985] ECR 2725.

[175] See Court of First Instance, Case T-24/90, *Automec* v. *Commission*, Judgment of 18 Sept. 1992, not yet published, paras. 71–81. For an application relating to Japanese cars, see Case T-7/92, *supra* n. 146.

[176] Compare with the action brought by the BEUC and The National Consumer Council against the Commission for not acting against the voluntary restraint arrangements between the British and Japanese car manufacturers (*supra* n. 69). The Commission apparently rejected the relevant complaint arguing that the 'arrangements were permitted by the United Kingdom authorities for commercial policy reasons'.

as the subquotas are concerned. It is not a legitimate aim of commercial policy to maintain barriers to *intra-Community* trade, as the Common Commercial Policy should be uniform in character. Admittedly, there is some scope for non-uniform measures on a transitional basis, as the analysis in the previous chapter has shown. It would be too far-reaching, however, to allow these measures to transgress competition law.[177] Moreover, the arrangement is not a genuine measure taken pursuant to the Common Commercial Policy since it has not been concluded in accordance with the rules of Article 113, EC Treaty. It has therefore not been possible to exercise standard democratic control on its adoption.[178] In such circumstances, it should not be tolerated that alleged commercial policy objectives are invoked for not taking action against restrictions on competition within the Community, restrictions that are incompatible with the concept of an internal market.[179]

The Status of Japanese Transplant Production

The ambiguities surrounding the status of Japanese transplant production under the arrangement (i.e. Japanese-labelled cars produced within the Community) have already been referred to above.[180] Some additional observations should, however, be made, concentrating mainly on the famous *Nissan* case and the rules determining which cars are to be considered as European and which are not.

---

[177] Compare with the words of the Court of Justice in Case 6/72, *Europemballage and Continental Can* v. *Commission* [1973] ECR 244: 'But if Article 3 (f) [of the EEC Treaty] provides for the institution of a system ensuring that competition in the Common Market is not distorted, then it requires *a fortiori* that competition must not be eliminated. This requirement is so essential that without it numerous provisions of the Treaty would be pointless. Moreover, it corresponds to the precept of Article 2 of the Treaty according to which one of the tasks of the Community is "to promote throughout the Community a harmonious development of economic activities". *Thus the restraints on competition which the Treaty allows under certain conditions because of the need to harmonize the various objectives of the Treaty, are limited by the requirements of Articles 2 and 3. Going beyond this limit involves the risk that the weakening of competition would conflict with the aims of the Common Market*' (italics added).

[178] The elements allowing such control are: an official and published proposal by the Commission, the so-called Luns-Westerterp procedure through which the European Parliament is consulted (see for a description Tomuschat, *supra* n. 81, pp. 5668–9) and the formal adoption of the measure by the Council, followed by publication, thus allowing for judicial review.

[179] Compare with the following dialogue between Lord Carr of Hadley and Mr Christopher Roberts, Deputy Secretary, UK Department of Trade and Industry, part of the evidence reproduced in *A Single Market for Cars*, *supra* n. 58, p. 6: Lord Carr of Hadley: 'If, say, Nissan could only sell its cars to its concessionaires in Germany provided those companies undertook in turn not to send them on to other countries in Europe, would either the German government or the Commission have any objection to that?' Mr Roberts: 'This would be Nissan (Japan)?' Lord Carr of Hadley: 'Yes.' Mr Roberts: 'I think it would go on quite quietly. It is not a matter to which anybody would wish to draw attention.' Lord Carr of Hadley: 'A funny sort of Single Market . . .' Mr Roberts: 'It is a definite weakness in the Single Market situation.'

[180] p. 203.

In the course of 1988, the question arose whether cars produced by Nissan in the United Kingdom were to be regarded as European or not.[181] It was an important question in the framework of the then existing restrictions. Should these Nissan cars be treated as Japanese when imported into Italy and hence be counted against Italy's quota, or should they have free access like other European cars? Both the French and the Italian governments argued that the Nissans were merely assembled in Britain and that all the main components were of Japanese origin. They pleaded for the enforcement of a local content rule, determining the amount of content of Community origin required for a car to be characterized as European, and threatened not to allow the Nissan cars to be imported in excess of the existing quotas. Figures as high as 80 per cent local content were mentioned.

The Commission reacted by stating that under the Community's rules of origin the Nissans were to be regarded as European products,[182] and that they hence could not be subjected to restrictions in intra-Community trade. Furthermore, the Commission ruled out that it would draw up special local content rules for the automobile sector.[183] After quite some debate, the French and Italian governments accepted the Commission's view.

The matter of transplant production came up again in the negotiations on the EC–Japan arrangement, as was to be expected considering the build-up of car production capacity in the Community by three of the leading Japanese manufacturers.[184] As described above, there appears as yet to be no agreement between the Community and Japan on whether this transplant production is to be included in the monitoring exercise or not.[185]

From a legal point of view, however, the current state of affairs does not give rise to much comment. As the EC–Japan arrangement does not result in official restrictions on imports of Japanese cars, the Community's rules of

---

[181] See Kenjiro Ishikawa, *supra* n. 98, pp. 76–81; Richard Eccles, 'When is a British car not a British car? Issues raised by Nissan', 10 *ECLR* (1989), 1: 1–3; 'Nissan row touches a raw nerve', *Financial Times*, 30 Sept. 1988; 'La Commission de la CEE veut exercer un contrôle sur les investissements japonais', *Le Monde*, 5 Oct. 1988; 'Car makers dispute local content', *Financial Times*, 27 Feb. 1989; 'Confused EC drives into impasse on Nissan', *Financial Times*, 10 Mar. 1989; 'UK and Italy settle dispute over import of Nissan cars', *Financial Times*, 2 May 1989.

[182] Then Regulation 802/68 on the common definition of the concept of the origin of goods, OJ English Special edn. 1968 (I), 165, now replaced by the Community Customs Code, Regulation 2913/92 of 12 Oct. 1992, OJ L 302/1 of 19 Oct. 1992 (which contains the same rules). According to Art. 5 of Regulation 802/68 (now Art. 24 of the Customs Code), goods originate in the country in which the last substantial transformation has taken place. Also see Edwin Vermulst and Paul Waer, 'European Community Rules of Origin as Commercial Policy Instruments?', 24 *JWT* (1990), 3: 55–99.

[183] Cf. the Commission's communication *Un grand marché intérieur de l'automobile*, *Europe Documents*, No. 1593, 8 Feb. 1990, p. 7.

[184] See e.g. 'Honda chooses UK for first European car assembly plant', *Financial Times*, 14 July 1989, p. 1 and 'Clash likely over Japan's EC car quotas', *Financial Times*, 5 Aug. 1991, p. 1. For a recent overview of Japanese carmakers' manufacturing activities in Europe, see 'Trickle swells to a flood', *Financial Times*, 3 Sept. 1992, p. 12.

[185] See p. 203.

origin have no role to play in determining which cars are subject to the VER and which not.[186] That will simply be a point of negotiation in the implementation of the arrangement. Perhaps this is an advantage, since cars are an outstanding example of the ever increasing artificiality inherent in laying down rules determining the nationality of products. It is not possible to analyse this problem in any detail within the scope of this study. Suffice it to say that, as regards cars, the difficulties are illustrated by the negotiations on a North American Free Trade Agreement.[187] The above-mentioned Community rules of origin are far too unsophisticated for delivering a satisfactory answer to the question of the origin of cars, as becomes apparent when reading the judgment of the Court of Justice in *Brother International* v. *Hauptzollamt Giessen*,[188] in which the Court of Justice had every difficulty in applying the rules with respect to something as simple (in comparison with cars) as electronic typewriters.

3. BANANAS

Introduction

Defining a regime governing as from 1 January 1993 the importation of Japanese cars into the Community may have been laborious and politically sensitive, but it was not nearly as complex as resolving the problems posed by the different national systems regarding the importation of bananas. This is a field mined with a set of conflicting and long-vested interests of various producers, traders, and governments. For the outsider, this may come as a surprise since there is not much banana production in the Community. But there is some, and in the relevant Member States it has always been shielded from external competition (mainly originating from the so-called dollar zone in Latin America), because it would be unable to compete under normal market conditions, due to a number of structural disadvantages. Moreover, some Member States import bananas from their ex-colonies, where production is subject to similar disadvantages. Within the framework of the Lomé Conventions (linking the Community to the ACP countries), these traditional trade flows have always been protected. The other Member States, with no production of their own and not importing from ex-colonies, buy their bananas where they are cheapest, namely in the dollar zone. In one Member State, Germany, there is even such a strong interest in importing at low cost from Latin America that already in 1957, when the Community was created, a

---

[186] Cf. Commissioner Andriessen in a speech on 'Latest EC thinking concerning external aspects of automotive trade and investment', Press Release Speech/90/12, 23 Feb. 1990, p. 3.

[187] Cf. US International Trade Commission, *Rules of Origin Issues Related to NAFTA and the North American Automotive Industry*, USITC Publication 2460, Nov. 1991.

[188] Case C-26/88, [1989] ECR 4253.

226

Import Regimes for Sensitive Products

protocol was added to the EEC Treaty, providing for duty-free entry of bananas in this country up to certain annual quotas. Of course, these greatly diverging national regimes could only coexist by derogating from the free movement of goods within the Community. On the basis of Article 115, EC Treaty, the Member States producing bananas and those importing them from ACP countries have always been authorized to limit indirect importation of dollar zone bananas. As described in Chapter 5, such compartmentalization had to be eliminated with a view to completing both the Common Commercial Policy and the internal market.

The political difficulties associated with agreeing upon a common regime in the field of bananas can be easily illustrated. The issue has been so controversial and sensitive that Latin American leaders have said that proposed Community decisions would have grave effects on the consolidation of democracy in their countries[189] and have called for the offices of the Director-General of the GATT;[190] that a German minister has threatened that his country would not ratify the Maastricht Treaty on European Union;[191] and that Prime Ministers from Caribbean countries have publicly stated that the fate of these countries' entire economies depends upon the kind of regime which the Community introduces.[192]

As with other segments of the completion of the Common Commercial Policy, the Community has only really become active in the course of 1992. It was as late as August 1992 when the Commission issued a proposal for a Council regulation which would subject the production and marketing of bananas to a common market organization, a traditional recipe in the field of agricultural products. This proposal, which contained the necessary uniform rules on importation of bananas from third countries, could not be agreed upon by the Council in time for the fatidical date of 1 January 1993. It took until February 1993 to reach final agreement, and the regulation only entered into force on 1 July 1993.

The format of the analysis below is as follows. First, the various pre-existing national regimes governing importation of bananas are described. Subsequently, the common market organization which has been adopted is analysed, especially, of course, the rules on external trade. In particular, the compatibility of these rules with, on the one hand, the Community's international obligations and, on the other, general principles of Community law is examined. The former because of the above-mentioned provisions of the Lomé Convention and the GATT context. The latter because there are provisions on the distribution of import licences which differentiate between

---

[189] *Agence Europe*, No. 5892, 7 Jan. 1993, p. 13.
[190] *GATT Focus* (Oct. 1992), 94: 3–4.
[191] *Agence Europe*, No. 5830, 7 Oct. 1992, p. 10.
[192] See e.g. J. F. Michell, Prime Minister of St Vincent and the Grenadines, 'The Caribbean's need for Europe', *Courier* (1992), 132: 59.

different groups of importers. Lastly, as there were no common rules on 1 January 1993, the application of Article 115 was continued beyond that date in the case of bananas, and this calls for some specific comments.

The Starting-Point: The Various National Import Regimes

Before the common market organization was adopted the only element of common policy governing imports of bananas was the Common Customs Tariff, providing for the levying of a 20 per cent *ad valorem* tariff on bananas.[193] And even this element was only to some extent really common. By virtue of Article 168 (1) of the Lomé Convention bananas originating in the ACP countries entered the Community free of customs duties.[194] Moreover, as was mentioned there is the Protocol on the tariff quota for imports of bananas, annexed to the EEC Treaty, and providing for annual quotas which can be imported duty-free by the German Federal Republic.[195]

Community production of bananas is mainly situated in four areas: the Canary Islands (Spain), Madeira (Portugal), Martinique and Guadeloupe (French overseas departments), and Crete (Greece). In the words of the Commission, this is 'politically, economically and socially sensitive ... production situated in regions on the very outer edges of the Community and the maintenance of which requires adequate protection'.[196] This protection was afforded by quantitative restrictions on third-country imports. As regards Spain and Portugal, these were allowed by the Act of Accession[197] and listed in Regulation 288/82 (the general import regulation).[198] The latter is also the case for France and Greece, whose import regimes have been the subject of cases brought before the Court of Justice. In *Commission* v. *Greece* the Court condemned the Greek practice of requiring an import licence for the

---

[193] See Council Regulation 2658/87 of 23 July 1987, OJ L 256/1 of 7 July 1987, as last amended by Regulation 2913/92, OJ L 301/1 of 19 Oct. 1992.

[194] Lomé IV is published in OJ L 229/3 of 17 Aug. 1991.

[195] These quotas are determined on the basis of imports of bananas for 1956, taking into account the subsequent evolution of consumption. According to the last sentence of para. 4, '[a]ny decision to abolish or amend this quota shall be taken by the Council, acting by a qualified majority on a proposal from the Commission'.

[196] Explanatory memorandum attached to the Commission's proposal for a Council Regulation on the common organization of the market in bananas, COM (92) 359 final, 7 Aug. 1992, p. 5.

[197] Protocol No. 2 of the Act of Accession, concerning the Canary Islands and Ceuta and Melilla, provides in Art. 4 (2) that bananas originating in the Canary Islands can be imported free of customs duties in Spain (the Protocol states that the customs territory of the Community does not include the Canary Islands), but may not be deemed to be in free circulation in the Community, when thus imported. Moreover, Spain was allowed to maintain quantitative restrictions on imports of bananas through other Member States, until the setting up of a common organization of the market.

[198] OJ L 31/1 of 9 Feb. 1982 (see *supra* Ch. 5, n. 21).

importation of bananas originating in other Member States or in free circulation there, and of systematically refusing to issue such licences.[199] As regards France, Belgian and French traders have complained that they could not obtain import licences from the French authorities with a view to importing bananas. However, the importers were unable to have the substance of their complaints reviewed by the Court because their applications were considered to be inadmissible.[200]

Imports from ACP countries mainly take place in the United Kingdom, France, and Italy. The United Kingdom is traditionally supplied by Caribbean countries,[201] France by Cameroon and Côte d'Ivoire, and Italy by Somalia. These trade flows have always benefited from a privileged status under the provisions of the Lomé Conventions, by way of a specific Protocol on bananas. Article 1 of Protocol 5 of Lomé IV, which is currently in force, provides that '[i]n respect of its banana exports to the Community markets, no ACP State shall be placed, as regards access to its traditional markets and its advantages on those markets, in a less favourable situation than in the past or at present'.[202] It should be added that at the time of negotiating Lomé IV, the problems which the various import regimes regarding bananas would pose for the completion of the internal market were already envisaged. This is reflected in a Joint Declaration relating to Protocol 5, and stating that this Protocol does not prevent the Community from establishing common rules 'as long as no ACP State, traditional supplier to the Community, is placed as regards access to, and advantages in, the Community, in a less favourable situation than in the past or at present'.[203] Moreover, the Community undertook to consult with these traditional suppliers in case, following the completion of the

---

[199]   Joined Cases 194 and 241/85, [1988] ECR 1037.

[200]   In Case 247/87, *Star Fruit* v. *Commission*, [1989] ECR 291, the applicant claimed that all import licences were systematically allocated to the French 'groupement d'intérêt économique bananier', and asked the Commission to intervene on the basis of Art. 169, EC Treaty, which the Commission refused. The subsequent application to the Court against this decision was, logically, held to be inadmissible. In Case 206/87, *Lefebvre Frère et Sœur* v. *Commission*, [1989] ECR 275, the applicant contested the lawfulness of authorizations granted by the Commission on the basis of Article 115, EC Treaty. This application, too, was quite logically considered inadmissible. See furthermore on the French import regime Written Question No. 1328/87 by Mr Ernst Mühlen, MEP, OJ C 121/19 of 9 May 1988 and Written Question No. 2199/91 by Mr Jacques Vernier, OJ C 269/5 of 19 Oct. 1992.

[201]   Mainly the Windward Islands (Saint Vincent and the Grenadines, Saint Lucia, Dominica, and Grenada) and Jamaica. On the importance of banana exports for these countries' economies, see e.g. Michael Davenport, with Sheila Page, *Europe: 1992 and the Developing World* (London: Overseas Development Institute, 1991), 94–5.

[202]   The Protocol also provides that all the means of the Convention (financial, technical, agricultural, industrial, and regional co-operation) shall be used with a view to improving the production and marketing of ACP bananas, that the two parties shall confer in a permanent joint group and that, should the banana-producing ACP States set up a joint organization, the Community will lend its support to this organization.

[203]   Annex LXXIV of the Final Act of the Convention.

single market, substantial modifications took place in the Community.[204] The ACP countries have always attached great importance to these guarantees, as is evidenced by various statements made by the ACP–EEC Council of Ministers and by resolutions regularly adopted by the ACP–EEC Joint Assembly.[205] France, the United Kingdom, and Italy have protected these traditional trade flows by operating quantitative restrictions against importation of dollar zone bananas, in conformity with Regulation 288/82.[206] In the case of Italy, the application of Article 115, EC Treaty, which was linked to these restrictions has also been challenged before the Court of Justice, again, however, unsuccessfully because the application was judged to be inadmissible.[207] It must be added here that applying Article 115 in order to protect ACP market shares is a peculiar exercise. Normally, the Commission only grants Article 115 authorizations if indirect imports are liable to cause harm to national production.[208] ACP bananas are the only non-Community products which have benefited from the protection afforded by this article.[209]

The other Member States, which do not produce bananas and do not have traditional trade links with ACP suppliers, mainly import bananas originating in the dollar zone, i.e. a number of Latin American countries.[210] Production in these countries is characterized by advantageous conditions of climate, soil, and terrain, and takes place in large plantations some of which are in the hands of multinational companies.[211] This production is, consequently, cost-efficient and of good quality.

[204] Ibid.

[205] See, in recent years, the Annual Report of the ACP–EEC Council of Ministers (1989), 22; Annual Report (1990), 24; Annual Report (1991), 29. For the resolutions adopted by the ACP–EEC Joint Assembly, see the Resolution on ACP bananas adopted at Bridgetown, OJ C 186/46 of 24 July 1989; Resolution on the effects of the '1992' EEC Single Market on the ACP States adopted in Versailles, OJ C 45/30 of 26 Feb. 1990; Resolution on ACP bananas adopted in Kampala, OJ C 216/69 of 19 Aug. 1991; Resolution on bananas adopted in Amsterdam, OJ C 31/63 of 7 Feb. 1992; Resolution on the implementation of the Lomé Convention in the Caribbean ACP States with reference to the specific problems and concerns of the region, adopted in Santo Domingo, OJ C 211/38 of 17 Aug. 1992; Resolution on bananas and GATT, adopted in Santo Domingo, OJ C 211/55 of 17 Aug. 1992 and Resolution on bananas, adopted in Santo Domingo, OJ C 211/60 of 17 Aug. 1992.

[206] See Ch. 5, note 21.

[207] Case 191/88, *Co-Frutta* v. *Commission*, [1989] ECR 794. Again the Court decided that a private operator could not request, in direct proceedings before the Court, the annulment of an authorization granted by the Commission on the basis of Art. 115.

[208] See Ch. 5, p. 177.

[209] See further *infra*, pp. 243–5.

[210] The banana-exporting Latin American countries are Bolivia, Colombia, Costa Rica, Cuba, Ecuador, El Salvador, Guatemala, Honduras, Mexico, Nicaragua, Panama, and Venezuela.

[211] Often, the debate on competition in the banana sector is conducted in terms of small, independent ACP farmers against these multinationals operating in Latin America, see e.g. the Information Report drawn up by the Section for Agriculture and Fisheries of the Economic and Social Committee, on the Community's banana market in the run-up to 1993, CES (91) 1012, pp. 5–7.

The Common Organization of the Market in Bananas

Elaboration

In the course of 1990 and 1991, an 'interservices group' established within the Commission studied the problems posed by the above-described national regimes governing importation of bananas, with a view to suggesting solutions. However, the first indication of the direction of future policy did not come from this group. On 15 December 1989 Lomé IV was signed, keeping intact the Protocol on bananas at a time when it was obvious that the completion of the internal market would require the adoption of common rules in the banana sector. The above-mentioned Joint Declaration bears witness thereof.[212] Clearly, therefore, the Community then already chose to continue to protect the traditional ACP banana exports, regardless of the completion of the internal market.[213]

On the basis of the report of the interservices group, which indicated a number of alternative policies, the Commission drew up its proposal in the course of the first half of 1992, while consulting a number of parties concerned. The proposal, finally adopted on 7 August 1992,[214] was classical in that it recommended the introduction of a common market organization, on the basis of Articles 42 and 43, EC Treaty. It was obvious, however, that the function of this common market organization was as much (if not more) to determine the rules governing importation of bananas from third countries, as it was to regulate internal production. Although one could argue that rules on importation have to be laid down in the framework of the Common Commercial Policy, the fact that common market organizations include rules on external trade has been accepted by the Court of Justice.[215]

In the explanatory memorandum attached to the proposal, the Commission set out the aims of the common market organization. First, prices must be supported 'through measures affecting imports of bananas from the dollar zone, while ensuring reasonable prices for the consumer'.[216] Secondly, there

[212] See n. 203.

[213] It must be said that the Community did not always interpret the provisions of the banana Protocol in such a sense. In the Report of the ACP–EEC Council of Ministers (1976–80) it is said that the Community maintained that, if it were to establish a common market organization for bananas, the ACP countries would not be granted a more favourable status than that laid down in the general provisions of the Convention on imports of products subject to a common market organization. For these provisions, see *infra*, p. 236.

[214] See n. 196 and OJ C 232/3 of 10 Sept. 1992.

[215] In Case 52/81, *Faust* v. *Commission*, [1982] ECR 3745, the Court refuted the applicant's claim (at 3760) that '[u]nder Article 40 (3) of the Treaty, a common organization of the market is to be "limited to pursuit of the objectives set out in Article 39", which do not include objectives of external commercial policy'. Indeed, as Advocate-General Slynn put it in his Opinion in this case, '[i]n the nature of things, I doubt whether the operation of a common organization of the market can be divorced from the Community's trade policy towards third countries and its international obligations' ([1982] ECR at 3770).

[216] COM (92) 359 final, p. 2.

should be a fair division of the advantages and costs of marketing bananas, 'in particular by encouraging importers in the "dollar banana" sector to participate in the marketing of preferential bananas'.[217] Thirdly, effective competition must be ensured.[218] More specifically, as regards the proposed trading system, the Commission considered that five important factors needed to be taken into account:

- the existence of politically, economically, and socially sensitive Community production, requiring adequate protection;
- ensuring reasonable prices for the consumers;
- honouring the commitments of the Lomé Convention;
- taking account of the interests of the dollar zone countries;
- the GATT context.[219]

Reconciling these factors comes down to setting 'the priority objective of maintaining various sources of supply'.[220] To achieve this, the Commission proposed the introduction of a quota system, operating by means of import certificates (in other words, licences). Because Community production and imports from traditional ACP suppliers were not likely to increase, 'controlled management of quantities proves necessary only in relation to non-traditional ACP bananas and those originating in other non-member countries'.[221] This controlled management was to take place by means of a quantitative restriction. The Commission suggested that there would be a consolidated quota of 2 million tonnes, representing (according to the Commission) the present level of imports, and a yearly additional quota if the forecast supply balance would show an increase in consumption. The tariff on these imports would remain at the existing level, namely 20 per cent, except for ACP bananas, which would enter free of duty.[222]

Of course, once a quota is established the question arises how import licences are to be allocated. As was mentioned, the Commission wanted to 'encourage' dollar zone banana importers to import ACP and Community bananas, fearing that without doing so the latter would not be sufficiently marketed. To that effect it proposed what it called an importers' partnership system. The above-mentioned quotas would be divided into two tranches. Import licences for the first tranche, amounting to 70 per cent of the quotas, would be allocated to traditional importers of dollar zone bananas. For the remaining 30 per cent licences would be distributed among all importers, but they would only be available on the basis of a commitment to import

---

[217] Ibid.

[218] Ibid. Other objectives were the involvement of all interested parties in the operation of the scheme and a system of specific aid for Community producers. The internal elements of the common market organization are not further dealt with here.

[219] Ibid. 5.   [220] Ibid.   [221] Ibid. 6.

[222] Ibid. 6. But Germany would of course have to give up its duty-free quota.

traditional ACP and Community bananas. These licences would be granted on the basis of a 'banana coefficient', determining how many dollar zone and non-traditional ACP bananas could be imported in relation to the amount of Community and traditional ACP bananas the importer would undertake to market. This undertaking would have to be backed up by lodging a guarantee, to make sure that the protected category of bananas would be actually imported.[223]

The Commission acknowledged that this proposed quota system conflicted with the provisions of the GATT, which in principle prohibits all quantitative restrictions.[224] Accordingly, it suggested that the Community should obtain a waiver under Article XXV (5) of the GATT.[225]

Furthermore, the proposal envisaged support for Community and traditional ACP production, as well as the creation of a diversification and development fund for the benefit of Latin American countries supplying bananas.[226]

The Commission's proposal met with diverse reactions. The ACP countries welcomed it at the ACP–EC Council of Ministers held in May 1992.[227] By contrast, Latin American banana-exporting countries were very hostile to it and made clear that they would oppose it by all means available.[228] Although there was no definitive decision, they brought the issue before the GATT Council, invoking a specific procedure in favour of developing countries and requesting the mediation of the Director-General of the GATT.[229] Serious criticism was also voiced by two World Bank officials who made a study of the likely economic consequences of the proposed quota system and came to the conclusion that it was grossly inefficient.[230]

Within the Community, the European Parliament and the Economic and Social Committee approved of the proposed policies,[231] although in the

[223] Ibid., and Arts. 17–22 of the proposal.

[224] Art. XI, see *supra*, pp. 205–9.

[225] This provision states that '[i]n exceptional circumstances not elsewhere provided for in this Agreement, the CONTRACTING PARTIES may waive an obligation imposed upon a contracting party by this Agreement; *Provided* that any such decision shall be approved by a two-thirds majority of the votes cast and that such majority shall comprise more than half of the contracting parties...'.

[226] COM (92) 359 final, pp. 10 and 12. See also the Commision's proposal for a Council Regulation establishing a special system of assistance to traditional ACP suppliers of bananas, COM (92) 465 final of 11 Nov. 1992, OJ C 344/9 of 29 Dec. 1992.

[227] See 'The 17th ACP–EC Council of Ministers', *Courier* (1992), 134: 8–9.

[228] *Financial Times*, 'Latin American banana producers attack EC quota plan', 20 Aug. 1992, p. 22 and 'Talks fail to resolve EC banana quotas row', 10 Sept. 1992, p. 7; *Agence Europe*, No. 5801, 27 Aug. 1992, p. 8 and No. 5807, 4 Sept. 1992, p. 11.

[229] See n. 190. See also *GATT Focus* (July 1992), 91: 4.

[230] Brent Borrell and Maw-Cheng Yang, *EC Bananarama 1992: The Sequel*, World Bank Working Paper (Washington, DC, 1992).

[231] See European Parliament, Document A3–0410/92 and Economic and Social Committee, Opinion on the proposal for a Council Regulation on the common organization of the market in bananas (93/c 19/26), OJ C 19/99 of 25 Jan. 1993.

Committee a strongly dissenting opinion was heard. According to a minority of Committee members, the proposed scheme was inconsistent with the new approach to agricultural policy, with efforts at liberalizing world trade in the framework of the Uruguay Round and with Community law.[232]

Within the Council of Ministers, reactions were also mixed. On the whole, the Member States which operated restrictions on third-country imports of bananas were reported to by satisfied, whereas those which allowed free access to their markets were opposed. A compromise solution was found, as part of a larger package deal and in spite of rejection by Germany and Denmark, in the last Agriculture Council of 1992, although only pertaining to the essential elements of the external trade regime.[233] On the basis of this compromise, a definitive text was drawn up and decided on in February 1993.[234]

The external trade regime of the common market organization

Content

The broad lines of the Commission's proposal were retained in the regulation adopted by the Council.[235] However, instead of introducing quantitative restrictions, the text adopted lays down a tariff quota of 2 million tonnes for the importation of non-traditional ACP and other third-country (i.e. dollar zone) bananas. Imports within this quota can be effected at a customs duty rate of 100 ECUs/tonne, which is more or less equivalent to the previous 20 per cent *ad valorem* tariff.[236] Each year, the volume of this quota can be revised on the basis of the forecast supply balance. If the quota is exceeded, imports can still be effected, but with customs duties at a prohibitively high level, namely 750 ECUs/tonne for non-traditional ACP bananas and 850 ECUs/tonne for dollar zone bananas.[237] The latter is in the range of a 170 per cent *ad valorem*

---

[232] OJ C 19/102 of 25 Jan. 1993. The reference to infringements of Community law is rather succinct and vague: 'The partnership arrangements which are to apply to 30 per cent of the overall quota conflict not only with the provisions of the EEC Treaty—in particular Articles 39 to 43 and the Articles on competition—but also with general law: prohibition of tying agreements. The European Court of Justice has rejected such a procedure in tying cases (requirement to add skimmed milk powder to feedingstuffs)' (para. 2.10). See also *infra*, pp. 239–43.

[233] See e.g. 'EC sets banana quota and tariffs', *Financial Times*, 18 Nov. 1992, p. 26 and *Agence Europe*, No. 5882, 18 Dec. 1992, pp. 7–8.

[234] Council Regulation 404/93 of 13 Feb. 1993 on the common organization of the market in bananas, OJ L 47/1 of 25 Feb. 1993.

[235] See Arts. 15–20.

[236] Cf. the preamble to the regulation: 'a tariff of ECU 100 per tonne, which corresponds to the current rate under the Common Customs tariff' (OJ L 47/2 of 25 Feb. 1993).

[237] The preamble provides that 'imports not falling within the tariff quota must be subject to sufficiently high rates of duty to ensure that Community production and traditional ACP quantities are disposed of in acceptable conditions' (ibid.).

tariff.[238] On the other hand, traditional ACP banana imports will enter the Community free of duties.[239]

Licences allowing for importation within the tariff quota are allocated on the following basis:

- (*a*) 66.5 per cent for operators who in the past have marketed certain minimal quantities of non-traditional ACP and other third-country bananas;
- (*b*) 30 per cent for operators who have marketed Community and/or traditional ACP bananas;
- (*c*) 3.5 per cent for newcomers.

The quantities which each importer under (*a*) and (*b*) can import is determined on the basis of past trade performance, namely the average annual quantity of bananas which he has sold in the three most recent years for which statistics are available. Provision has been made for ensuring that licences distributed to original category (*a*) operators do not diminish each year by virtue of the fact that category (*b*) operators will also be allowed to market non-traditional ACP and third-country bananas. It is said that 'the initial allocation of licences between the two categories of operators [will remain] identical',[240] which probably signifies that the three categories of operators are fixed, in that operators cannot move from one category to another.[241]

Although the formulas adopted by the Council differ from the Commission's proposal, the results will probably be rather similar. The tariff quota theoretically allows additional imports above the quota, but the duties which are then imposed are so high that such additional imports will in any event be very limited. As to the distribution of import certificates, the effects will also be similar to the partnership system proposed by the Commission. Importers of dollar zone bananas who wish to maintain or expand their market share will have to import Community and traditional ACP bananas, because their share of the 2 million tonnes tariff quota is limited to 66.5 per cent.

It must be added that the system is very technical and that it will only be possible to evaluate its concrete effects properly once it is in operation and implementing measures have been taken.[242] Nevertheless, already at this stage a number of questions can be put.

[238] See 'EC sets banana quota and tariffs' n. 233 above.

[239] The quantities qualifying as traditional ACP imports are indicated in the Annex to the regulation.

[240] Art. 19 (2).

[241] This provision was probably inserted because dollar zone importers feared that they would obtain fewer licences from year to year, because they would have to share them more and more with importers of Community and traditional ACP bananas, see *Agence Europe*, No. 5897, 14 Jan. 1993, p. 8.

[242] One of the most important implementing measures is the definition of the term 'operator' and the determination which banana traders are operators and to which category they belong. For the procedure governing implementing measures, see Art. 27.

For example, within the 2 million tonnes tariff quota third-country as well as non-traditional ACP bananas can be imported. However, the latter are bananas imported from the ACP countries in excess of the traditional quantities. How will operators and customs authorities be able to determine when these traditional quantities have all been imported, and further imports come within the quota? This will require very close monitoring of all banana imports, not just those of the third-country category.[243] Moreover, will this system not be detrimental to ACP banana imports? Operators who are allocated licences for imports within the tariff quota have the choice between importing third-country bananas (of which there is certainly sufficient supply) and non-traditional ACP bananas. Will they not choose to import third-country bananas, as there is no guarantee that in a given year the level of traditional ACP supplies will ever be reached, which is a condition for non-traditional ACP imports to be possible?[244]

Another question relates to the distribution of licences for imports within the quota. For category (*a*) operators (i.e. traditional importers of dollar zone bananas) this distribution will be based on the average quantities of bananas sold in the three most recent years. However, not all sales are taken into account; only 'sales of third country and/or non-traditional ACP bananas' serve as a basis. Does this not mean that for this category of operators the distribution will remain fixed (provided that all of them continue to use their licences), as the amounts of future sales of such bananas are entirely determined by the licences which they will now obtain?

Next to these technical questions on the operation of the import scheme, more fundamental legal issues have to be addressed. The first is how the external trade regime of the common market organization is to be assessed in the light of the Community's international obligations. The second is whether the import allocation system, containing restrictions on the freedom to import, is compatible with Community law, and especially such principles as equality of treatment and proportionality.[245]

---

[243] That is indeed provided for by Commission Regulation 1442/93 laying down detailed rules for the application of the arrangements for importing bananas into the Community, OJ L 142/6 of 12 June 1993.

[244] With the exception of imports from ACP countries which are not mentioned in the list of traditional suppliers, such as the Dominican Republic.

[245] These questions will have to be answered by the European Court of Justice, as both the German government and a number of importers have lodged actions with the Court against the external regime of the common market organization. The latters' actions for annulment have already been declared inadmissible because the importers were considered not to be directly and individually concerned (see Art. 173 of the Treaty). Some of them, however, have also asked for compensation for damages, and these cases are still pending (see the orders of the Court reported in OJ C 215/10–14 of 10 Aug. 1993). The German government also asked for the annulment of the relevant provisions. Its claim for interim measures has been dismissed, because the alleged damage to German importers and consumers was not considered to be sufficiently probable by the Court, see Case C-280/93 R, *Germany* v. *Council*, Order of 29 June 1993.

Compatibility with the Community's international obligations?

First, let us consider the Lomé IV Protocol on bananas.[246] It is obvious that the Community has made every effort to ensure that no traditional ACP supplier is placed 'in a less favourable position than in the past or at present'.[247] Imports from competing non-traditional ACP and dollar zone suppliers will be more or less limited to their previous market shares (if not substantially less)[248] . Thus, if the Commission's presumption that Community production will remain stable is correct,[249] traditional ACP suppliers will have a guaranteed market share, which will only diminish in case there is a fall in demand. The latter, however, does not appear to be a circumstance covered by the Protocol, which only provides for guarantees against deliberate action by the Community.[250] Moreover, there is the proposed Council Regulation on assistance to the traditional ACP suppliers which, when adopted, will provide additional support.[251]

However, doubts can be raised as to the compatibility of the tariffication of non-traditional ACP supplies of bananas with the Lomé Convention.[252] According to Article 168 (2) (*a*) of this Convention there are two alternative regimes governing importation into the Community of products originating in the ACP countries and subject to a common market organization:[253]

(i) those products shall be imported free of customs duties for which Community provisions in force at the time of import do not provide, apart from customs duties, for the application of any measure relating to their import;
(ii) for products other than those referred to under (i), the Community shall take the necessary measures to ensure more favourable treatment than that granted to third countries benefiting from the most-favoured-nation clause for the same products.

It would appear that the first indent is applicable to the case of bananas. In the Commission's proposal, that was not so since there were quantitative restrictions in addition to customs duties. That would have made the second indent applicable. But as the Council regulation only retains customs duties—be they extremely high for imports above the tariff quota—as import measures, all ACP bananas should be imported free of duties in accordance

---

[246] See *supra* p. 228.   [247] Art. 1 of the Protocol.
[248] It is reported that current annual consumption of dollar zone bananas in the Community is well above 2 million tonnes, at about 2.5 million tonnes, see 'Ecuador in a bind over EC banana quotas', *Financial Times*, 20 Jan. 1993, p. 24.
[249] See *supra* p. 231.
[250] The Protocol provides that no ACP State 'shall be placed' in a less favourable situation.
[251] See n. 226.
[252] i.e. the 100 ECUs/tonne duties for imports within the tariff quota and the 750 ECUs/tonne duties for additional imports.
[253] Art. 168 (2) (*d*) makes these provisions also applicable to newly set up common market organizations.

with the first indent. Only if one characterizes the high duty of 850 ECU/tonne for imports above the quota as a measure having an equivalent effect to a quantitative restriction can the status of non-traditional ACP banana imports be considered as being in conformity with the Lomé Convention. But such an interpretation runs counter to the Community's position in the framework of GATT (see below), namely that the external regime of the common market organization merely involves tariffication.

Let us now consider the GATT context. It is reported that the Commission first contended that the external regime, as agreed upon, does not require a GATT waiver (in contrast with its proposal) since it only involves a modification of the tariff binding for imports of bananas.[254] However, a recent GATT Panel Report undermines this appreciation. As mentioned above a number of Latin American countries, producing dollar zone bananas, complained in the GATT that the new regime is inconsistent with the Community's GATT commitments. But they also directed their complaints against the restrictions which the Member States operated before the entering into force of the new regime. The latter complaints have already led to a Panel Report which has severe consequences, not only for the new banana regime but also, even more importantly, for the entire network of preferential agreements with developing countries which the Community has concluded. The Panel held that the non-reciprocal tariff preferences which the Community grants in the framework of the Lomé Convention are contrary to the most-favoured-nation rule of Article I of the GATT, and are not covered by the exceptions of Article XXIV (on customs unions and free-trade-areas) and of Part IV (on trade and development).[255] This means that all these preferences, including of course those granted to ACP countries in the framework of the new banana import regime, would be illegal under GATT rules. The Report has not yet been adopted by the GATT Council, which is a condition for it to be binding, because the Community strongly opposes its conclusions. In the meantime a new Panel has been established, with the task of examining the new common market organization. It remains to be seen what will be the outcome of negotiations within the GATT on this subject. If the above-mentioned Panel Report gets adopted, the Community will have to obtain a waiver for its non-reciprocal preferential policies.

Moreover, the restrictions introduced by the new common market organization for bananas are not in line with the approach taken in the Uruguay Round negotiations towards reducing support of the production of, and restrictions on trade in, agricultural products, as well as restrictions on trade in

---

[254] See *Agence Europe*, No. 5920, 15 and 16 Feb. 1993, p. 9. Modifications of tariff schedules are governed by Art. XXVIII of the General Agreement, which does not require a two-thirds majority as in the case of a waiver, but only requires negotiations on compensation with the major suppliers.

[255] For a summary of the Panel Report, see *GATT Focus*, No. 100, (July 1993), 2–4.

tropical products. With respect to tropical products the aim of the Uruguay Round is to achieve the fullest liberalization of trade.[256] For unprocessed products (such as fresh bananas) the Mid-Term Review Agreement has even set the aim of a total elimination of customs duties.[257] The Community, which has made a generous offer in this field already in 1990,[258] has had to exclude bananas from this offer.[259] With respect to agricultural products in general the Draft Final Act of the negotiations provides for the conversion of all border measures in customs duties ('tariffication').[260] It has been suggested that this circumstance induced the Council of Ministers to abandon the concept of quantitative restrictions, proposed by the Commission.[261] However, tariffication alone is not sufficient. The Draft Final Act also lays down that these customs duties must on average be reduced by 36 per cent in a period from 1993 to 1999, with a minimum reduction per tariff line of 15 per cent.[262] It is obvious that the new banana regime cannot easily be reconciled with these requirements. Therefore, in the event of the Uruguay Round negotiations being successfully concluded, the Community may have to negotiate an exception for bananas. That is a delicate and politically sensitive affair in view of the widespread criticism of the Community's agricultural policies and of the fact that there are other requests for exceptions from new disciplines on agricultural policies, the main one concerning the ban on rice imports in Japan and South Korea.[263] Too many requests for exceptions risk leading to an unravelling of the entire package.

One can also put the question whether the new regime is not inconsistent with the agreements on standstill and rollback included in the Punta del Este ministerial meeting which launched the Uruguay Round. The contracting parties then committed themselves 'not to take any trade restrictive or distorting measure inconsistent with the provisions of the General Agreement or the Instruments negotiated within the framework of GATT or under its auspices', and to phase out or bring into conformity with the General Agreement all such measures.[264]

---

[256] See the Ministerial Declaration of the Uruguay Round, *BISD*, 33 S., p. 23.

[257] Ibid.

[258] See 'Tropical Products: Revised Offer by the European Community', Commission Press Release IP/90/981 of 4 Dec. 1990.

[259] Anna Murphy, *The European Community and the International Trading System*, i: *Completing the Uruguay Round of the GATT*, CEPS Paper No. 43 (Brussels: CEPS, 1990), 127; Michael Davenport with Sheila Page, *supra* n. 201, p. 54.

[260] Para. 4 of Part B ('Agreement on modalities for the establishment of specific binding commitments under the reform programme') of the text on agriculture, MTN.TNC/W/FA, p. L.19.

[261] 'EC qualifies quota proposals in move to break banana trade reform deadlock', *Financial Times*, 11 Dec. 1992, p. 30.

[262] Para. 5 of Part B of the text on agriculture (*supra* n. 260).

[263] See e.g. 'Dunkel is reminded of Far Eastern farm lobby', *Financial Times*, 27 Nov. 1992, p. 3.

[264] See Ministerial Declaration on the Uruguay Round, *BISD*, 33 S., p. 22.

The foregoing shows that there is more at stake than a simple, isolated modification of tariff schedules. Furthermore, the observation needs to be formulated that in the case of bananas the Community gives preference to commitments towards a specific group of third countries (the traditional ACP exporters) to the detriment of abiding by the rules governing the world trading system laid down in the General Agreement, and by the general direction of multilateral trade policies.

Compatibility with general principles of Community law?

The above description of the system governing the distribution of certificates for imports will have made clear that the conditions of competition between the various importers of bananas established in the Community are (at least) liable to be affected by the common market organization, and that competition is to some extent restricted. That is in any case the judgment of some of the importers themselves.[265] This raises the question whether the regulation is consistent with the Community's competition policy. In this regard it must be emphasized that the EC Treaty itself provides for quite some manoeuvring room in the case of common market organizations. According to Article 42 '[t]he provisions of the Chapter relating to rules on competition shall apply to production and trade in agricultural products only to the extent determined by the Council' when setting up a common market organization. However, there is also Article 40 (3) of the Treaty, stating that the common organization of agricultural markets 'shall exclude any discrimination between producers or consumers within the Community'. This provision on equal treatment has given rise to quite some case-law of the Court of Justice, against which the import certificate scheme of the common market organization for bananas needs to be tested.[266]

Article 40 (3) only mentions producers and consumers, and not importers. However, the Court has consistently held that the provision is merely the enunciation of the general principle of equal treatment which is part of the Community's legal order.[267] This principle therefore also applies to importers.

The Court has handed down two judgments on equal treatment of importers which are relevant for the import system for bananas. In *Faust v. Commission* quotas on imports of preserved mushrooms from third countries were

---

[265] *Agence Europe*, No. 5898, 15 Jan. 1993, p. 14.

[266] On this case-law, see e.g. Giancarlo Olmi, *Commentaire Mégret*, ii: *Politique agricole commune*, 2nd edn. (Brussels: Études européennes, 1991), 302–6; Heinz-Wolfgang Kummer in H. von der Groeben, J. Thiesing, and C.-D. Ehlermann (eds.), *Kommentar zum EWG-Vertrag*, 4th edn. (Baden-Baden: Nomos, 1991), 643–4; John A. Usher, *Legal Aspects of Agriculture in the European Community* (Oxford: Clarendon Press, 1988), 41–4; Francis G. Snyder, *Law of the Common Agricultural Policy* (London: Sweet & Maxwell, 1985), 57–60.

[267] See e.g. Joined Cases 117/76 and 16/77, *Ruckdeschel v. HZA Hamburg-St. Annen*, [1977] ECR 1753 at 1769. See also the literature referred to in n. 266.

the subject of the case.[268] The applicant, an importer of mushrooms from Taiwan, argued that the Commission had arbitrarily fixed the import quota granted to each non-member country, and had privileged imports from China because the Community had concluded a trade agreement with that country. The Court did not accept that argument:

Although Taiwan certainly appears to have been treated by the Commission less favourably than certain non-member countries, it should be remembered that there exists in the Treaty no general principle obliging the Community, in its external relations, to accord to non-member countries equal treatment in all respects. It is thus not necessary to examine on what basis Faust might seek to rely upon the prohibition of discrimination between producers or consumers within the Community contained in Article 40 of the Treaty. It need merely be observed that, if different treatment of non-member countries is compatible with Community law, different treatment accorded to traders within the Community must also be regarded as compatible with Community law, where that different treatment is merely an automatic consequence of the different treatment accorded to non-member countries with which such traders have entered into commercial relations.[269]

Applied to the case of bananas, this means that any different treatment of importers which is merely an automatic consequence of the difference in treatment of the third countries from which they import bananas does not infringe the principle of equal treatment.[270] Thus, the fact that dollar zone and non-traditional ACP bananas are treated less favourably than Community and ACP bananas cannot be challenged by relying on the principle of equal treatment as applied to importers. However, the import certificate system introduced by the regulation establishing the common market organization clearly goes further than the mere automatic consequences of the difference in treatment of third-country exporters. There is a second judgment which is relevant in this respect.

In *Krohn* v. *Bundesanstalt für landwirtschaftliche Marktordnung* the Court reviewed certain elements of the regime governing imports of manioc from non-member countries.[271] Such imports, although free from quantitative restrictions, were subject to a licensing system. In order to obtain the licences, importers had to lodge a security aimed at ensuring that the licences would actually be used.[272] In the course of 1982, the Council concluded agreements with some third countries fixing import quotas for manioc. As a result, imports within the quotas could further be effected at the normal import levy of 6 per cent, whereas additional imports were subject to a 50 per cent import

---

[268] See *supra* n. 215.   [269] [1982] ECR 3762.

[270] In so far, of course, as the difference in treatment of the exporting countries is compatible with Community law, especially international obligations, see *supra*, pp. 236–9, and the principle of proportionality, see *infra*, p. 242.

[271] Case 165/84, [1985] ECR 3997.

[272] Such a system is common practice in the agricultural sector, see e.g. Olmi, *supra* n. 266, p. 94 n. 100.

levy. However, the effects of this quota system on importers differed according to whether manioc was imported from Thailand or whether it was imported from other third countries subject to the system. In the latter case, provision had been made for importers to cancel the import licences which they had obtained before the quota system came into effect, and to have the corresponding security released. But in the case of licences for importation from Thailand this was not possible. The Court noted that this placed importers of manioc from Thailand 'in an unfavourable competitive position *vis-à-vis* importers of manioc from other non-member countries',[273] which it described as follows:

From 28 July 1982, holders of previously issued licences for the import of manioc from Thailand found themselves faced with the choice of either carrying out the importations covered by the licences and paying the very high rate of levy or losing their security. The consequence for them was additional charges which importers of manioc from other non-member countries could avoid . . .[274]

The Court concluded that '[s]uch a situation is contrary to the principle in Community law of equal treatment of traders in comparable situations'.[275]

The difference in treatment of importers was rather clear-cut in the *Krohn* case. It is less so in the framework of the import certificate scheme applying to the tariff quota for bananas. It is true that traders who have traditionally imported bananas from the dollar zone are faced with serious restrictions; there is not only the tariff quota of 2 million tonnes, but in addition they will only be granted licences up to 66.5 per cent of this quota. Their opportunities to trade in these bananas are therefore diminished by at least one-third, which is not the case for importers of Community and traditional ACP bananas.[276] However, dollar zone importers are of course allowed to start importing these Community and traditional ACP bananas. That is precisely what the regulation aims at. None the less, it is not to be ruled out that quite some practical difficulties may be associated with such a change in sources of supply. There may for example be long-term contracts between traditional ACP suppliers and importers established in the Community. To what extent such practical difficulties exist cannot be measured here. But it goes without saying that, the greater they are, the more discrimination there is against traditional importers of dollar zone bananas.[277]

[273] [1985] ECR at 4021.
[274] [1985] ECR at 4022. This was aggravated by the fact that for imports from Thailand the quota system entered into force two months earlier than for imports from other sources.
[275] Ibid.
[276] On the contrary, these importers get access to imports of dollar zone bananas within the 30% share of the tariff quota, in addition to their traditional access to imports of Community and traditional ACP bananas.
[277] Compare with Case C-280/93 R (*supra* n. 245) in which the Court held that it was unclear for which reasons the German importers of dollar zone bananas would not be able to import Community and traditional ACP bananas.

In this respect, a second important principle of Community law comes into play, namely the principle of proportionality.[278] Restrictions imposed upon the above-mentioned group of importers must be proportional to the aims which the common market organization seeks to achieve. In other words, they may not go further than what is necessary for guaranteeing the marketing of Community and traditional ACP production. The Community must therefore be able to demonstrate that without the licence distribution system set up by the regulation this marketing would not be ensured. On the face of it, doubts can be entertained whether that is feasible.

In addition, the principle of proportionality is also clearly relevant for assessing the external discrimination of the banana regime, i.e. the fact that third-country and non-traditional ACP supplies are treated much less favourably than traditional ACP supplies (and Community production). Here, too, the question arises whether the rules are proportional, whether a less strict regime would not have been sufficient. In this respect, a group of three recent judgments of the Court of Justice may provide some indications. In the *Faust* and *Wünsche* cases,[279] the Court decided that a levy imposed on imports of mushrooms from China was incompatible with the principle of proportionality because it was too high. The levy was aimed at preventing excessive disturbance of the Community market, and was set at a level corresponding to the full cost of production of top-quality mushrooms in France, without taking into account that mushrooms of lower quality were imported. Moreover, the levy came on top of the normal customs duties of 23 per cent, and therefore went much further than equalizing the prices of imported and Community products. It was declared invalid by the Court.

It remains to be seen whether the aims of the common market organization in bananas warrant the prohibitively high tariffs on imports of third-country or non-traditional ACP bananas above the tariff quota. However, one should also add that the Court of Justice has decided that with respect to agricultural policies the Community legislature has a broad discretion, implying that

where [he] is obliged, in connection with the adoption of rules, to assess their future effects, which cannot be accurately foreseen, its assessment is open to criticism only if it

---

[278] This principle has been defined by the Court in Case 265/87, *Schräder*, [1989] ECR 2237 at 2269–70, where it also held that 'in matters concerning the common agricultural policy, the Community legislator has a discretionary power which corresponds to the political responsibilities imposed by Arts. 40 and 43. Consequently, the legality of a measure adopted in that sphere can be affected only if the measure is manifestly inappropriate having regard to the objective which the competent institution intends to pursue.'

[279] Case C-24/90, *Hauptzollamt Hamburg-Jonas* v. *Faust* and Cases C-25/90 and C-26/90, *Hauptzollamt Hamburg-Jonas* v. *Wünsche*, Judgments of 16 Oct. 1991, not yet published. These judgments are discussed by Francis G. Jacobs, 'Review by the Court of Justice of Commercial Policy Measures: Recent Trends and Future Prospects', in M. Maresceau (ed.), *The European Community's Commercial Policy after 1992: The Legal Dimension* (Dordrecht: Martinus Nijhoff, 1993), 75–6.

appears manifestly incorrect in the light of the information available at the time of adoption of the rules in question.[280]

The Interim Application of Article 115, EC Treaty

As was mentioned above, Article 115 has in the past always been applied in the banana sector, not only to protect the national production of some Member States, but also to protect traditional imports from ACP countries. The latter kind of Article 115 authorizations were a special case in that ACP bananas were the only third-country products benefiting from such protection. The text of Article 115 appears to allow this, as it envisages two alternative situations: national commercial policy measures being obstructed by deflection of trade *or* differences in such measures leading to economic difficulties in one or more of the Member States. It is obvious that in the absence of applying the Article for the purpose of protecting traditional ACP bananas having guaranteed access to some of the Member States (which therefore limit other banana imports), deflection of trade would indeed occur, although one cannot speak of economic difficulties in those Member States. None the less, this interpretation of the scope of Article 115 has become more and more exceptional, since the Commission has in the course of time tightened the conditions under which it was prepared to grant authorizations, by requiring that in the absence of protection serious economic difficulties had to be liable to occur. In practice, therefore, the two situations envisaged in Article 115 have been interpreted as being cumulative and not alternative.[281] That is indeed more in line with the place of Article 115 in the system of the EC Treaty: as a derogation from the free movement of goods and an inhibiting factor in establishing the Common Commercial Policy the article should be strictly interpreted.[282]

Be that as it may, the case of bananas became even more exceptional in the first half of 1993. Indeed, as no agreement could be reached on the common market organization in time for it to enter into force on 1 January 1993, bananas were the only product for which Article 115 was still being applied. In December 1992, the Commission authorized France and the United Kingdom to exclude from Community treatment bananas originating in the dollar zone

---

[280] Joined Cases C-267/88 to C-285/88, *Gustave Wuidart and Others* v. *Laiterie coopérative eupenoise*, [1990] ECR I-435 at 481.

[281] See Ch. 5, p. 177.

[282] See Ch. 5, p. 175. One commentator has therefore implicitly criticized the fact that in the case of ACP bananas Art. 115 is applied, see Francis Sarre, 'Article 115 EEC Treaty and Trade with Eastern Europe', *Intereconomics* (1988), 197: 233. The Commission has also consistently referred to the Community's commitments under the Lomé Convention. From a legal point of view, however, this argument adds nothing: if Art. 115 had to be interpreted as not allowing the protection of third-country exports, that could under Community law not be changed by an agreement concluded by the Community, which has to be consistent with the Treaty.

and imported in other Member States, until 30 June 1993.[283] This, of course, calls for some comments.

In Chapter 5, it was argued that the date of 1 January 1993 does not have the effect of precluding the application of Article 115; that, however, such application should become even more exceptional than it has been in recent years; that using the instrument of border controls is no longer permissible; and that all measures related to the application of this Article must be proportionate to the objectives that are pursued.[284] It must be acknowledged that the continued application of Article 115 in the banana sector was of an exceptional nature. It was due to the fact that the common market organization could not be agreed upon in time. Obviously, if Article 115 had no longer been employed this would have endangered the objectives which are aimed at by the common market organization. The application was therefore clearly temporary.

As to controls at intra-Community borders, it is common knowledge that these disappeared on 1 January 1993, at least in so far as movement of goods is concerned. In line with this disappearance, the authorizations granted by the Commission to France and the United Kingdom did not allow these Member States to continue to enforce the ban on indirect imports by performing border controls. The following recitals of the decision addressed to the United Kingdom indicate how the Commission looked at this situation:

Whereas the request from the British government to apply measures under Article 115 of the Treaty raises delicate problems as a result of the realisation of the internal market and Article 8a of the Treaty prohibits any check of goods at borders between Member States after 31 December 1992;

Whereas it is advisable that the United Kingdom government gives the Commission preliminary notification of the entering into force of the measures which it considers appropriate in order to maintain the advantages of the ACP States which traditionally supply the United Kingdom market, in conformity with Lomé Convention commitments;

Whereas the Commission will scrutinize such measures in the light of Article 8a of the Treaty and communicate, if considered necessary, the terms and conditions which are to be respected to the United Kingdom authorities.[285]

---

[283] Commission Decision C (92) 3382 final of 28 Dec. 1992, 'autorisant la République française à appliquer des mesures de protection au titre de l'article 115 du Traité à l'égard des bananes fraîches originaires de certains pays tiers' (existing only in French) and Commission Decision C (92) 3381 of 28 Dec. 1992 authorizing the United Kingdom to apply protective measures on the basis of Art. 115 of the Treaty concerning imports of fresh bananas originating in certain third countries, both not published. A request to apply Art. 115, made by Italy, has been rejected because there are at this stage virtually no traditional ACP imports (which in the case of Italy come from Somalia) to be protected, see *Agence Europe*, No. 5897, 14 Jan. 1993, pp. 9–10. In the case of Spain and Portugal, the relevant provisions of the Act of Accession simply continued to be applied, see *supra* n. 197.

[284] Ch. 5, pp. 170–84.

[285] See *supra* n. 283. The Decision regarding France contained similar wording. See also Art. 1 (2) and (3) of the Decision addressed to the United Kingdom:

The decision thus prohibited controls at intra-Community borders, but did not determine which other measures were possible. In the press it was reported that in the United Kingdom a licence continued to be required for importing dollar zone bananas, and that unauthorized importation was a criminal offence.[286] One may assume that a similar system was being applied in France. In the *Levy* judgment, such a practice was found to be acceptable. If an Article 115 authorization is present, 'Member States may declare that imports effected without an advance licence are subject to the criminal penalties attaching to the undeclared importation of prohibited goods.'[287] However, in the present case there may have been problems of transparency and legal security. The major traditional banana traders were undoubtedly aware that the 'old' system of restrictions on indirect imports continued to be applied in France and the United Kingdom. But smaller, non-traditional traders may not have been aware that restrictions on intra-Community trade were still allowed. In the past, this posed no problems since there were controls at the borders and unauthorized imports could simply not get through. But there were no such controls any more after 31 December 1992, which might have induced smaller traders even more to think that there were no longer any restrictions. Moreover, it was certainly not the Commission's decisions which would have attracted their attention: these decisions were not published, but only notified in the C section of the Official Journal. That was consistent with the existing practice, which was deplorable, looked at from the point of view of transparency and legal security. It is submitted that the Commission should have published its decision, and should also have made public exactly which measures the United Kingdom and French authorities were allowed to take.

4. CONCLUSIONS

The cases of textiles, Japanese cars, and bananas present a varied picture. As regards textiles, the Community is well on the way towards achieving a fully uniform commercial policy. In view of past experience in this sector (one must keep in mind that this was the main field of application of Article 115), this is no small achievement. However, as with the proposals concerning the reform of the general import regulations, dealt with in Chapter 5,[288] the Community keeps open the option of taking measures aimed at 'regional' protection,

---

2. To this end, the United Kingdom authorities shall notify the Commission, prior to entering into force, the measures which are considered appropriate in order to maintain the advantages of the ACP States which traditionally supply the United Kingdom market in conformity with Lomé Convention commitments. These measures shall not lead to checks at borders between Member States;

3. The Commission shall scrutinize such measures in the light of the provisions of Article 8a of the EEC Treaty and inform when considered necessary, the United Kingdom authorities of the particular terms and conditions to be respected.

[286] *Financial Times*, 'EC sets banana quota and tariffs', 18 Dec. 1992, p. 26.
[287] Case 212/88, [1989] ECR 3511 at 3531.   [288] See pp. 158–60.

primarily through the anti-concentration clause. For the same reasons as explained above, this should be strongly criticized.[289] Moreover, it would not be surprising that if this option is ever used, it will be in the textiles sector, precisely because of this past experience. It is, however, encouraging that until the time of writing (summer 1993), the anti-concentration clause has remained dormant, and that the uniform import regime appears to work. It goes without saying that the longer this situation continues, the more difficult it will become to justify departures from the rule of uniformity.

By contrast, in the case of Japanese cars it remains to be seen whether full uniformity will be attained by the end of the century, as provided in the EC–Japan arrangement. It has always been more easy to take a trade sector outside the scope of normal GATT rules, than to restore free trade disciplines. Trade in cars is increasingly 'managed', not only by the Community but also by the United States. However, the conclusion of a Uruguay Round Agreement on safeguard measures will perhaps be able to avert this trend.

Moreover, the Community appears to subordinate its competition policy to the aim of (differentiated) external protection. That can only be deplored and should not be repeated in other trade sectors. The conduct of the Community's commercial policy cannot justify derogations from the basic rules on competition, certainly not those concerned with the removal of barriers to trade between the Member States. This is one clear case in which external policies related to the completion of the internal market operate to the detriment, paradoxically, of the unity of this same internal market.[290]

In the case of bananas, finally, the saga of the Community's external regime is certainly not yet finished. It is one thing to restrict imports from certain third countries, but the import licensing system employed to enforce these restrictions appears to be stricter than necessary, and can be regarded as discriminating against importers of so-called third-country bananas. It remains to be seen what the final outcome will be of the new 'banana cases' pending before the Court of Justice and of the GATT negotiations in this area.

[289] Ibid. See also Ch. 11, p. 355.   [290] Cf. the conclusions in Ch. 11, p. 355.

7

The Community's Export Policy and the Case of Strategic Export Controls

Introduction

In the previous chapters the incomplete state of the Community's commercial policy with respect to the regulation of imports was discussed. However, it is not only with respect to imports that, at the time when the internal market programme was devised, full uniformity had not yet been achieved. The Community's rules on exports—basically proclaiming the principle of free exportation—did not yet apply to all products.[1] The exceptions could be classified in two categories. The first were the products expressly mentioned in the basic regulation as not benefiting from the rule of free exportation.[2] These included, on the one hand, a variety of products for which for one or other reason export restrictions were still in force, and, on the other, petroleum products. The latter were kept outside the scope of the regulation because of their importance for the various Member States in terms of securing the supply of energy, and because of the fact that trade in these products is to some extent regulated by the International Energy Agency.[3] The former category has been almost completely eliminated, whereas a provisional solution was found for the latter.[4] These restrictions will not be further discussed here, for one thing because they were not that important from the perspective of completing the internal market (unless one looks at the creation of an internal market for energy products, a subject which is not addressed in this study).

The second category of exceptions does not strictly relate to a well-defined set of products. The basic export regulation provides, in a similar manner to the various basic import regulations,[5] that the Member States remain competent to restrict exports on grounds of 'public morality, public policy or public security; the protection of health and life of humans, animals or plants; the protection of national treasures possessing artistic, historic or archaeological value, or the protection of industrial and commercial property'.[6] Whereas

[1] See Council Regulation 2603/69 establishing common rules for exports, OJ L 324/25 of 27 Dec. 1969.

[2] See Art. 10.

[3] See Pieter Jan Kuyper, 'De invloed van het verdwijnen van de fysieke grenzen in de Gemeenschap op de handel in goederen met derde staten', 40 *SEW* (1992), 1: 29–30.

[4] Regulation 3918/91, OJ L 372/31 of 31 Dec. 1991.

[5] See Ch. 5, p. 150.

[6] Art. 11 of Regulation 2603/69 (*supra* n. 1).

most of these grounds are probably not very relevant for exports, by contrast the aim of protecting public security has served to enforce ever since World War II a set of so-called strategic export controls, restricting exportation of a variety of products (and even technologies) which were deemed vital for safeguarding the security of the Western world. Most of these controls are co-ordinated within the framework of CoCom, which is a rather secretive inter-national 'committee' based in Paris, whose membership consists mainly of the NATO countries.[7] Although the decisions taken within CoCom are not legally binding on its members, the lists of goods subject to export controls which are laid down in the national legislation of the various members reflect the above-mentioned decisions. Nevertheless, the EC Member States (which are all members of CoCom, with the exception of Ireland)[8] do not only enforce these strategic controls on exports to third countries, but also on all exporta-tion as such. These controls are therefore also a barrier to intra-Community trade in the products concerned, a barrier whose elimination has been on the agenda of the internal market programme.[9]

Both from the perspective of the external dimension of the internal market and from that of Community law, these strategic export controls are a fascinating subject. On the one hand, they clearly relate to trade, regulation of which comes within the Community's competence, but on the other, the objective of safeguarding national security is (as clearly) one which is within the national province. This poses important questions of competence, which are further complicated by the fact that the Treaty on European Union provides for new competences in the field of security. Moreover, looked at from another angle these controls are almost a prototype of the barriers to trade which the internal market programme seeks to remove. Increasingly, these are barriers which do not result from policies aimed at regulating the exchange of products as such, but often serving entirely different purposes. This raises difficult questions as to how to strike a balance between the objective of removing these barriers and the equally valid objective of keeping intact the policies concerned.

The analysis below is as follows. First the status of strategic export controls under the rules of the EC Treaty is examined. On the basis of this examination, it is possible to deal more thoroughly with the question whether the

---

[7] Minus Iceland, that is, but with Japan and Australia. CoCom is not a genuine international organization, see e.g. Richard T. Cupitt, 'The Future of CoCom', in G. K. Bertsch and S. Elliott-Gower (eds.), *Export Controls in Transition* (Durham, NC: Duke University Press, 1992), 234–6; Stuart Macdonald, *Technology and the Tyranny of Export Controls: Whisper Who Dares* (Basingstoke: Macmillan, 1990), 11–8. For a recent comprehensive analysis of the law of export controls, see Karl M. Meessen (ed.), *International Law of Export Control* (London: Graham & Trotman, 1992).

[8] But this country is reported to operate a similar system.

[9] Although it is not mentioned in the Commission's White Paper on the completion of the internal market (COM (85) 310 final). However, it is touched upon in the Report on the progress required by Art. 8b of the Treaty, COM (88) 650 final of 17 Nov. 1988, para. 47.

Community has any competence in this field. Lastly, the action which the Community envisages to undertake, and which is still at the stage of a Commission proposal, is (briefly) commented upon.

Strategic Export Controls and the EC Treaty

In a fairly recent case, the European Court of Justice has had to answer the question whether CoCom controls were compatible with the EC Treaty.[10] It is useful to take this judgment, which has been discussed more extensively elsewhere,[11] as a starting point for analysing the status of strategic controls under the rules of the Treaty.

The *Aimé Richardt* case concerned measures taken by Luxembourg aimed at preventing the exportation to the Soviet Union of high-technology goods, sold by a French company to a Soviet state trading company, and at one stage in transit on Luxembourg territory. No licence had been requested from the Luxembourg authorities for the exportation of these goods, which apparently were on the CoCom list of so-called dual use goods subject to control,[12] and which were therefore confiscated. In the subsequent criminal proceedings which were instituted against the exporter, the question was raised whether the requiring of an export licence by Luxembourg was consistent with the rules of the EC Treaty.[13]

The Court merely examined this question with reference to the rules on intra-Community movement of goods, without taking into account the Community's rules on exportation, which arguably was not the proper perspective.[14] Be that as it may, the Court analysed the scope of Article 36 of the Treaty, which mentions public security as a ground for derogating from the free movement of goods, and decided that this concept includes the external security of a Member State. Although it reiterated the general principles

[10] Case C-367/89, *Aimé Richardt, Société en nom collectif 'Les Accessoires Scientifiques'*, Judgment of 4 Oct. 1991, not yet published.

[11] Inge Govaere and Piet Eeckhout, 'On Dual Use Goods and Dualist Case Law: The *Aimé Richardt* Judgment on Export Controls', 29 *CML Rev.* (1992), 5: 941–65.

[12] There are three CoCom lists of products subject to controls, one concerning arms, one concerning nuclear material, and one concerning dual use goods. The latter are products that can be used for civil and military purposes. See Stuart Macdonald, *supra* n. 7, pp. 12–13.

[13] The question was technically raised in terms of the Community regulation on transit, but was obviously broader in scope.

[14] The goods had been confiscated when they were to be put on a plane leaving from Luxembourg to Moscow. They were leaving from Luxembourg because the Air France flight from Paris to Moscow which should have carried the goods was cancelled. By the time the goods were confiscated, the intra-Community transit procedures had run their course, and what the Luxembourg authorities actually prevented was the exportation to the Soviet Union. The Court uses the fiction that the goods were not actually imported into Luxembourg, in order to be able to characterize the contested measures as restrictions on transit. This reasoning can be criticized, see Govaere and Eeckhout, *supra* n. 11, pp. 947–9 and 953.

governing the scope of Article 36 (such as the principles of strict interpretation and of proportionality), the Court held without further ado that the importation, exportation, or transit of goods which can be used for strategic purposes may indeed affect the public security of a Member State, and that the Member States are therefore entitled to subject the transit of such goods to a licensing system. It did add, however, that the sanctions imposed when such a licence is not requested may not be disproportionate.[15]

The judgment can be criticized for failing to carry out any substantive review of the national measures in question and for simply accepting the alleged threat to public security as put forward, an attitude which contrasts with other judgments on the scope of Article 36.[16] But it remains a fact, of course, that the Court does not have the capacity of assessing and checking the risks for public security inherent in the exportation to a variety of third countries of a variety of complex high-technology products. The result is that the Member States have considerable discretion with respect to strategic export controls, even when enforced in the context of intra-Community trade, and that the barrier-to-trade element of these controls remains intact.

As was mentioned, the Court did not look at the facts of the *Aimé Richardt* case from the angle of the Community's export policy. That was done by Advocate-General Jacobs in his Opinion in the case.[17] He examined whether the CoCom controls were compatible with the rules of the basic export regulation, and in this respect referred to Article 11, quoted above.[18] Similarly as the Court did with regard to Article 36, he thought that 'the concept of public security is in principle broad enough to embrace restrictions on the transfer of goods or technology of strategic importance to countries which are thought to pose a military threat'.[19] Although discussing the provisions of the basic export regulation, the Advocate-General did not expressly deal with the status of CoCom controls under the EC Treaty rules on the Common Commercial Policy (CCP), on which the regulation is based. Since these rules grant to the Community the exclusive power to regulate trade matters, the question pertaining to the relationship between the said controls (which, of course, also regulate trade) and the Community's power to conduct commercial policy must be asked. The next section is an attempt to answer this question.

The EC Treaty contains two other provisions that are often mentioned in connection with strategic export controls. Article 223 (1) (*b*) provides that

---

[15] The Court is of the view that confiscation of the goods is disproportionate to the extent that the products could have been sent back to the Member State of origin, but then leaves it to the national judge to appreciate whether the principle of proportionality has been observed, see paras. 24 and 25 of the judgment.

[16] Govaere and Eeckhout, *supra* n. 11, pp. 949–52.

[17] Opinion delivered on 8 May 1991, not yet published.

[18] See p. 247.   [19] Para. 28.

[a]ny Member State may take such measures as it considers necessary for the protection of the essential interests of its security which are connected with the production of or trade in arms, munitions and war material; such measures shall not adversely affect the conditions of competition in the common market regarding products which are not intended for military purposes.

In the second paragraph it is added that the Council shall draw up a list of the products concerned, during the first year after the entry into force of the Treaty. This was indeed done in the course of 1958, but the list has never been officially published, nor amended.[20] Although the English text of Article 223 (2) is not unequivocal in this respect, the other language versions of the Treaty make clear that this list is to be exhaustive, i.e. that products not mentioned on the list are not covered by Article 223.[21] As a result, this provision does not apply to a lot of the strategic export controls currently enforced. If one takes the CoCom case, there are three lists of products subject to controls: arms, nuclear material, and dual use goods. By definition the latter are not to be characterized as arms or war material (which is implicitly confirmed by the fact that in *Aimé Richardt* the Court did not mention Article 223), and it is reported that not all arms mentioned in the first CoCom list are taken up in the Article 223 list,[22] which is not surprising in view of the age of the latter. Furthermore, for those products which are covered by Article 223 it is not entirely clear what kind of national measures are permissible. One would, however, assume that export controls are among them.[23]

Besides Article 223, there is Article 224, which provides that

Member States shall consult each other with a view to taking together the steps needed to prevent the functioning of the common market being affected by measures which a Member State may be called upon to take in the event of serious internal disturbances affecting the maintenance of law and order, in the event of war, serious international tension constituting a threat of war, or in order to carry out obligations it has accepted for the purpose of maintaining peace and international security.

This provision also has only a limited role to play with respect to export controls. If one again takes the case of CoCom controls, it is difficult to argue that they are enforced in a context of (threat of) war; neither are they the kind

[20] See Pieter Jan Kuyper, 'European Economic Community', in *International Law of Export Control, supra* n. 7, p. 70.

[21] The Dutch version mentions 'de lijst van *de* produkten'; the French version 'la liste *des* produits'; the German version 'die Liste *der* Waren' (italics added). See also Peter Gilsdorf in H. von der Groeben, J. Thiesing, and C.-D. Ehlermann (eds.), *Kommentar zum EWG-Vertrag*, 4th edn. (Baden-Baden: Nomos, 1991), 5592–3.

[22] Gilsdorf, *supra* n. 21, p. 5593.

[23] Cf. Gilsdorf, *supra* n. 21, pp. 5591–2. In this respect, reference must also be made to Art. 225, EC Treaty, which provides that '[i]f measures taken in the circumstances referred to in Articles 223 and 224 have the effect of distorting the conditions of competition in the common market, the Commission shall, together with the State concerned, examine how these measures can be adjusted to the rules laid down in this Treaty'.

of obligations mentioned in the article, since CoCom is not an official international organization.[24] This, too, is confirmed by the fact that the Court did not mention Article 224 in the *Aimé Richardt* case.

Lastly, with regard to both Articles 223 and 224 it has to be said that the Court has ruled in the *Johnston* v. *Chief Constable of the Royal Ulster Constabulary* case that these provisions are to be put on the same level as others allowing for exceptions to the fundamental rules of the Treaty, such as Articles 36, 48, and 56.[25] This means that they have to be strictly interpreted, and that they do not amount to giving an exclusive competence to the Member States.[26] For all these reasons, the relevance of Articles 223 and 224 for action in the field of strategic export controls is probably rather limited.

The Community's Competence: Commercial Policy and External Harmonization

The Commission has in the course of 1992 issued a proposal for a regulation aimed at eliminating the (intra-Community) barrier-to-trade aspect of export controls on dual use goods.[27] It maintains that Article 113 of the EC Treaty, is the appropriate legal basis for such a regulation. This competence claim needs to be examined, because it has far-reaching implications. Has not the Court of Justice consistently ruled that the conduct of commercial policy is an exclusive Community competence? Does the reference to Article 113 then mean that the Member States have no competence at all for enforcing strategic export controls, although they have always done so without any intervention by the Community?

Before addressing these questions, one may wonder whether there are no other provisions in the Treaty which furnish the power to eliminate the barriers to intra-Community trade resulting from export controls. In this regard, Article 100*a* immediately springs to mind. It applies 'for the achievement of the objectives set out in Article 7*a*', namely the establishment of the internal market, and provides that the Council shall 'adopt the measures for the approximation of the provisions laid down by law, regulation or administrative action in Member States which have as their object the establishment and functioning of the internal market'. One might take the view that the Commission's proposal, in so far as it is connected with the completion of the

---

[24] See the Commission's views as recorded in the Report for the Hearing in *Aimé Richardt* (n. 10), para. 25; Gilsdorf, *supra* n. 21, p. 5605; Kuyper, *supra* n. 20, pp. 72–3.

[25] Case 222/84, [1986] ECR 1651, at 1684.

[26] Pieter Jan Kuyper, 'Trade Sanctions, Security and Human Rights and Commercial Policy', in M. Maresceau (ed.), *The European Community's Commercial Policy after 1992: The Legal Dimension* (Dordrecht: Martinus Nijhoff, 1993), 414.

[27] Proposal for a Council Regulation on the control of exports of certain dual use goods and technologies and of certain nuclear products and technologies, COM (92) 317 final of 31 Aug. 1992.

internal market, could be based on Article 100*a*. However, it is not possible to simply dissociate the internal barrier-to-trade aspect from the substance of export controls, which is the regulation of exports to third countries. If one aims at establishing a genuine internal market for dual use goods, where products can circulate freely as long as they are on Community territory, some degree of harmonization must be carried out both as regards restricted products and as regards restricted destinations, in order to prevent deflections of trade.[28] But that comes down to regulating exportation, a matter for which Article 100*a* does not appear to be suitable and which is explicitly mentioned in Article 113. Therefore, one should first explore whether Article 113 is applicable to export controls.[29]

Rule of reason and the *Chernobyl* judgment

In previous chapters, the rule of reason proposed by Timmermans for the interpretation of the concept of commercial policy, as laid down in Article 113 of the Treaty, has been used as a guide-line.[30] If one applies it to the case of export controls, however, the conclusion must be that such controls do not come within the scope of the CCP. Indeed, as the Court has ruled that national measures taken within the framework of export control systems and restricting intra-Community trade are justifiable under the public security concept in Article 36, and as the rule-of-reason approach relies on such a qualification for determining that the measures in question, if applied to trade with third countries, are not to be regarded as commercial policy measures, this conclusion seems unavoidable. That is confirmed if one looks at the substance of export controls, as applied by the Member States. These controls have nothing to do with commercial policy (or at least they should not have).[31] Their purpose is to prevent that products exported from a State would be used

[28] Otherwise, goods risk being exported from the Member State with the most liberal regime regarding export controls, the stricter regimes thus being circumvented.

[29] The Court's case-law on the relationship between Arts. 43 and 100 of the Treaty is relevant in this respect. In two judgments, the Court decided that recourse to Art. 100 was not appropriate for measures regulating production and marketing of agricultural products, because the chapter on agriculture is to be considered as a *lex specialis* which has precedence over the more general rules of the Treaty (see Case 68/86, *UK* v. *Council*, [1988] ECR 855 and Case 131/86, *UK* v. *Council*, [1988] ECR 905; these cases are also discussed in Ch. 3, pp. 93–4). Assuming that Art. 100*a* allowed for the adoption of measures relating to exportation to third countries, because of the link with the completion of the internal market, it would seem that as regards such regulation of exports the chapter on the CCP is a *lex specialis* which has precedence over Art. 100*a*.

[30] See Ch. 1, pp. 29–31.

[31] It is not excluded, of course, that measures taken in the framework of export controls are in reality aimed at reaching certain more commercially oriented objectives. The discussions within CoCom on whether certain high-technology products can receive an export authorization are often described by insiders as hidden commercial battles between the CoCom members, cf. Paul Freedenberg, 'The Commercial Perspective', in *Export Controls in Transition*, *supra* n. 7, pp. 39–40.

for jeopardizing the external security of that State. Only if one advocates the instrumental approach to the concept of commercial policy, which used to be put forward by the Commission,[32] is it possible to defend the qualification of export controls as commercial policy measures, because the instruments which are used to enforce these controls are instruments of trade regulation (export licences and restrictions). But such a view is difficult to accept and has undesired effects. One of these is that the Community would have the exclusive competence to set up and enforce a system of export controls, which completely contradicts the existing practice. The latter would only be justified under the rules of the Treaty if the Member States were to benefit from a specific authorization by the Community, in line with *Donckerwolcke*.[33] There is no such authorization, unless one so characterizes Article 11 of the basic export regulation.[34] But that provision is not specific at all: it does not specify for which products the public security exception can be invoked, nor does it indicate which destinations are subject to controls. To characterize Article 11 as a specific authorization boils down to emptying this concept of all meaning. That would amount to going down a road which is very dangerous for the 'hard core' of the CCP, which with such an interpretation could in effect be easily renationalized. Of course, one could in this field also drop the concept of exclusivity, as has been suggested by Gilsdorf.[35] But that, too, seems undesirable and difficult to rationalize.[36] How can one determine which sections of the CCP are within the Community's exclusive powers, and which not? And what would be the division of competences between the Community and the Member States in the field of export controls? Are these competences simply concurrent, meaning that the Community can regulate the whole field of export controls and thus determine how the external security of the Member States is to be safeguarded?

In this respect, one should also mention the Treaty on European Union, which puts policies aimed at preserving external security firmly outside the EC Treaty, and within the Common Foreign and Security Policy.[37] This also indicates that one cannot simply characterize strategic export controls as commercial policy measures.

Does this mean that the CCP has nothing to do with such controls? The Court of Justice has handed down a judgment which suggests that such a conclusion would not be correct. In *Greece* v. *Council*[38] the Court was asked

---

[32] It is not clear whether the Commission still adheres to this approach in all its consequences. It did so in its conclusions in Case C-62/88, *Greece* v. *Council*, [1990] ECR I-1527 at I-1534 (this judgment is extensively discussed *infra*, p. 255). However, the Commission's proposal regarding export controls (*supra* n. 27) appears to depart from the purely instrumental approach, see p. 262.

[33] See Ch. 5, p. 150.   [34] See *supra* p. 247.

[35] *Supra* n. 21, pp. 5589, 5596–7 and 'Portée et délimitation des compétences communautaires en matière de politique commerciale', *RMC* (1989), 326: 197–8.

[36] See Ch. 1, pp. 32–4.

[37] With the exception, that is, of Article 228a, discussed *infra*, p. 259.

[38] See n. 32.

whether the Council had correctly adopted a regulation on the conditions governing imports of agricultural products originating in third countries following the accident at the Chernobyl nuclear power station,[39] on the basis of Article 113, EC Treaty. This regulation laid down certain maximum permitted radioactive levels, compliance with which was a condition for releasing a number of agricultural products, imported from third countries, for free circulation within the Community. Member States should verify this, and, in the event of non-compliance, take the requisite measures, which may include a prohibition of importation. The Greek government argued that this regulation aimed at protecting public health within the Community—which of course it did—and that consequently it should have been adopted on the basis of Article 31 of the EAEC Treaty, or of Articles 130r and 130s of the EC Treaty.[40]

The analogy with the case of export controls is the following. Public health is also one of the grounds mentioned in Article 36, alongside public security. Therefore, if one applies Timmermans's rule-of-reason approach, measures applying to trade with third countries but which are aimed at safeguarding public health would remain outside the scope of the CCP, even if instruments for regulating trade are used. This means that the Court, if it endorses the rule of reason, should have upheld Greece's action for annulment. It did not, however.

The Court's reasoning with respect to the legal basis of the Chernobyl regulation, although succinct, is worth citing *in extenso*:

The Court held in its judgment in Case 45/86, *Commission* v. *Council*, [1987] ECR 1493 (paragraph 11), that in the context of the organization of the powers of the Community the choice of the legal basis for a measure must be based on objective factors which are amenable to judicial review.

As far as the objective pursued is concerned, the preamble to Regulation No. 3955/87 indicates that 'the Community must continue to ensure that agricultural products and processed agricultural products intended for human consumption and likely to be contaminated are introduced into the Community only according to common arrangements' and that those 'common arrangements should safeguard the health of consumers, maintain, without having unduly adverse effects on trade between the Community and third countries, the unified nature of the market and prevent deflections of trade'.

Regulation No. 3955/87 establishes uniform rules regarding the conditions under which agricultural products likely to be contaminated may be imported into the Community from non-member countries.

It follows that, according to its objective and its content, as they appear from the very terms of the regulation, the regulation is intended to regulate trade between the

---

[39] Regulation 3955/87, OJ L 371/14 of 30 Dec. 1987.

[40] According to Art. 30, EAEC Treaty, '[b]asic standards shall be laid down within the Community for the protection of the health of workers and the general public against the dangers arising from ionizing radiations', whereas Art. 31 lays down the procedures to be followed. Arts. 130r and 130s deal with environmental policies.

Community and non-member countries; accordingly it comes within the common commercial policy within the meaning of Article 113 of the EEC Treaty.[41]

What are the implications of this ruling? Has the Court decided that the scope of the CCP is wider than the rule-of-reason approach suggests? Is it saying that the Commission's instrumental approach is correct, that all measures which make use of instruments regulating trade with third countries come within the Community's exclusive competence by virtue of the provisions on the CCP, notwithstanding any non-commercial objectives that might be pursued? Does this mean that strategic export controls are entirely a matter for the CCP, and that the Member States have no competence in this area? It is submitted that the last two questions should receive a negative answer, and that the Court's decision can be fully and more appropriately explained by introducing the concept of 'external harmonization'.

Chernobyl and the concept of 'external harmonization'

Let it first be emphasized that the Court's reasoning does not seem to confirm the instrumental approach proposed by the Commission.[42] The Court hardly mentions the instruments used by the Chernobyl regulation. Instead, it analyses both the objective and the content of the regulation. The reference to the objectives pursued is almost blasphemous in the instrumental approach. Yet the Court takes these objectives fully into account when determining that the regulation comes within the scope of the CCP.

It is precisely this reference to the objectives of the regulation which is crucial. Indeed, as the preamble makes clear, the regulation is not only intended to safeguard the health of consumers within the Community. It is also aimed at maintaining the unified nature of the market and preventing deflections of trade. To this effect, it lays down uniform rules regarding the conditions under which certain products can be imported into the Community. Of course such uniformity was not guaranteed as long as the Member States acted independently in order to prevent the importation of contaminated products, as was the case before the relevant regulations were adopted.[43] That makes the regulation essentially different from corresponding measures taken by the Member States. It is aimed not only at preserving public health, but also at laying down uniform conditions of importation in order to prevent deflections of trade or distortions of competition within the internal market. This aspect is absent from independent Member State action providing for

---

[41] [1990] ECR I-1549.   [42] See *supra* n. 32.
[43] The accident at Chernobyl took place in Apr. 1986, and was immediately followed by action by the Member States. On 30 May 1986 the Council adopted Regulation 1707/86, OJ L 146/88 1986, which was substantially identical to the regulation under discussion here.

maximum levels of contamination. It will be recalled from previous chapters that it is also one of the essential objectives of the CCP. As Advocate-General Darmon put it in his Opinion in the *Chernobyl* case:

> In order to avoid any change in patterns of trade and any distortion of competition in dealings with non-member countries, the Community must be able, under the common commercial policy, to adopt uniform rules regarding the conditions under which products from non-member countries may be imported into its territory. Those conditions may include in particular compliance with maximum permitted levels of radioactivity without the measure in question thereby being of a different nature or not capable of adoption under Article 113. The contested regulation thus seems to me by its very nature to come within the scope of the common commercial policy.[44]

Things may become clearer if one looks at them from the perspective of the rule of reason, and the parallelism which it proposes between the rules on free movement within the Community and the concept of commercial policy. Under the Treaty provisions on free movement of goods, the Member States are not entitled to take measures which are capable of hindering intra-Community trade, unless such measures are justified on the basis of Article 36 or on the basis of the so-called mandatory requirements.[45] Nevertheless, the Community has an instrument at its disposal for removing these legitimate barriers to trade: Article 100*a* allows for the harmonization of national legislation, which in effect removes the barriers.[46] Let us now look at the CCP. Interpreting the concept of commercial policy according to the rule of reason, there are also measures (relating to trade with third countries this time) which the Member States are not entitled to take, because they infringe on the Community's exclusive competence. But there are also measures pursuing non-commercial objectives, such as the protection of public health or of public security, which do *not* come within the scope of the CCP. However, as regards the latter category there may be as much a need for harmonization by the Community as there is with respect to national measures applied to intra-Community trade. One can call this kind of harmonization, which is necessary in order to prevent deflections of trade and distortions of competition—in short, to preserve the unity of the market—*external* harmonization. Article 100*a* does not appear to be the appropriate legal basis for it, since external trade is at stake. By contrast, Article 113 has always been interpreted as essentially aiming at laying down a uniform regime for trade with third countries. It therefore provides the proper basis for carrying out such external harmonization. In this respect, Article 113 is the 'outside' of Article 100*a*.[47]

[44] [1990] ECR I-1542.

[45] On mandatory requirements, see Ch. 8, p. 265.

[46] The term harmonization is used here in its general meaning. Technically, one can distinguish between unification, harmonization, and approximation of national legislation.

[47] Art. 100*a* also aims at eliminating distortions of competition within the internal market, cf. Case C-300/89, *Commission* v. *Council (Titanium Dioxide)*, [1991] ECR I-2867, at 2899, quoted in Ch. 5, p. 147.

The fact that measures taken by the Community with a view to such external harmonization are essentially different from corresponding measures taken by the Member States also radically affects the rule of exclusive Community powers in the field of commercial policy: it is irrelevant in the areas subject to external harmonization. The competence of the Community concerns the bringing about of uniformity; the competence of the Member States relates to the protection of public health, public security, and the like. As long as the Community has not acted, the Member States remain competent to enact the measures which they deem to be necessary—as long as these measures are genuinely aimed at safeguarding these essential policies. But once the Community has harmonized the conditions of importation or exportation, the Member States are of course obliged to respect the rules laid down in Community instruments.

Implicitly, this approach may be confirmed by the practice of the Community in the field of economic sanctions. This practice has now settled in the following way:[48] the fundamental decision as to which economic sanctions should be enforced in a given situation is taken within the framework of European Political Co-operation. This reflects the fact that, essentially, the competence to take such sanctions remains with the Member States. The decision is subsequently 'implemented' by way of Community measures based on Article 113 of the Treaty. That is possible because this way uniform conditions of importation or exportation remain intact. It should also be mentioned that in 1989 the Council adopted a regulation concerning the export of certain chemical products which are likely to be used for the production of chemical weapons.[49] The regulation subjects such exports to the requirement of a prior export authorization conferred by the competent authorities of the Member States. It includes a common list of products, and was adopted on the basis of Article 113. This regulation can also be characterized as providing for external harmonization.[50]

In conclusion, it is submitted that there exists a Community competence to act in the field of strategic export controls, with a view to eliminating or preventing deflections of trade or distortions of competition within the internal market caused by a non-uniform external regime, and that this competence is based on Article 113 of the Treaty. There are no reasons for not extending this competence to products covered by Article 223, because this provision does not amount to a reservation of competence in favour of the Member States.[51]

[48] See Kuyper, *supra* n. 26, p. 404; Gilsdorf, *supra* n. 21, pp. 5603–4.

[49] Regulation 428/89, OJ L 50/1 of 22 Feb. 1989.

[50] Another example, which does not relate to export controls but which does concern security questions, is Regulation 900/92 amending Regulation 3677/90 laying down measures to be taken to discourage the diversion of certain substances to the illicit manufacture of narcotic drugs and psychotropic substances, OJ L 96/1 of 10 Apr. 1992, which is also based on Art. 113.

[51] See *supra*, p. 252.

The Treaty on European Union

As the Treaty on European Union lays down new provisions on a Common Foreign and Security Policy (CFSP), the question arises whether the Community's competence to deal with export controls changed when the Treaty entered into force.[52] It is in any event clear that strategic export controls come within the scope of the CFSP, since Article J.1 (2) provides that one of the objectives of this policy is 'to strengthen the security of the Union and its Member States in all ways'. Does this mean that the CCP is no longer relevant for export controls? Such a view runs counter to Article M of the European Union Treaty, providing that 'nothing in this Treaty shall affect the Treaties establishing the European Communities ... '. In so far as the EC Treaty applies to export controls, that is not changed by the Maastricht Treaty. This means that in this field the relationship between the CFSP and the CCP will need to be sorted out. However, it would not be surprising if the existing practice regarding economic sanctions were also to take hold of common policies regarding export controls: fundamental decisions taken within the framework of the CFSP and implemented by way of a regulation based on Article 113.[53]

But that is not all. Within the EC Treaty, the European Union Treaty introduces a new provision which may be relevant. Article 228a states that

[w]here it is provided, in a common position or in a joint action adopted according to the provisions of the Treaty on European Union relating to the common foreign and security policy, for an action by the Community to interrupt or to reduce, in part or completely, economic relations with one or more third countries, the Council shall take the necessary urgent measures. The Council shall act by a qualified majority.

Kuyper has argued that this provision, which in any case relates to imposing economic sanctions, also applies to the case of strategic export controls. However, the fact that the article refers to 'urgent' measures may cast some doubt on this qualification. Export controls, albeit reducing economic relations with the non-member countries involved, are not necessarily urgent measures, although with the end of the Cold War and the resulting world-wide instability, they may increasingly become so.[54]

---

[52] See also Govaere and Eeckhout, *supra* n. 11, pp. 962–4.

[53] In this respect, the second paragraph of Art. C of the Union Treaty should also be referred to: 'The Union shall in particular ensure the consistency of its external activities as a whole in the context of its external relations, security, economic and development policies. The Council and the Commission shall be responsible for ensuring such consistency. They shall ensure the implementation of these policies, each in accordance with its respective powers.'

[54] With the end of the Cold War, strategic export controls are acquiring a different dimension, see SEC (92) 85, p. 3; Kuyper, *supra* n. 26, p. 414.

The Commission's Proposal

In August 1992, the Commission issued a proposal for a Council Regulation on the control of exports of certain dual use goods and technologies and of certain nuclear products and technologies,[55] which is aimed at removing the barriers to intra-Community trade resulting from these controls. This proposal has been carefully prepared, the Commission having extensively examined the question in co-operation with the Member States.[56] There are therefore some chances that it will be adopted in the course of the next few months, without many radical modifications. Nevertheless, as the regulation is not yet on the Community's statute-book, it would be premature to analyse it in great detail here. What is presented below is a description of the main facets of the proposed regulation, as well as some comments.

Description

According to the explanatory memorandum, the aim of the proposed regulation is to dismantle the controls on intra-Community trade applied by the Member States in the field of export controls on dual use goods and technologies. In other words, the result should be that 'such goods and technologies should move as freely between Member States as they do within each of them'.[57] To that end, there must be effective controls in all the Member States, based on common standards and applying to all kinds of export controls.[58] More concretely, discussions with the Member States have revealed that there are five prerequisites for achieving these aims. There must be:

- a common list of dual use goods and technologies;
- a common list of destinations;
- common criteria for the issuing of licences;
- a co-ordinating forum or mechanism;
- explicit procedures for administrative co-operation between customs and licensing offices throughout the Community.[59]

The Commission is of the view that a regulation is indispensable for ensuring that all the Member States apply effective controls, which in turn is necessary to generate a sufficient degree of mutual confidence in the controls applied by the various Member States. The Commission points out that that regulation does not amount to full harmonization of export controls policies. It is 'limited

---

[55] See n. 27.   [56] Cf. SEC (92) 85 final.   [57] COM (92) 317 final, p. 2.

[58] Mentioned are: CoCom, the Nuclear Non-Proliferation Treaty, the Australia Group, and the Missile Technology Control Regime, as well as foreign policy controls applied by the Member States, see ibid.

[59] Ibid. 2–3.

to the essential requirements necessary for the completion of the internal market'.[60] Hence it is 'based on the fact that decisions concerning list of goods and of destinations, are essentially strategic in nature and therefore part of national competence'.[61] Furthermore, the Commission will also propose the establishment of a co-ordinating group, composed of representatives of the Member States and chaired by a representative of the Commission.[62]

The system of the proposed regulation is as follows. It applies to the exportation or re-exportation of certain dual use goods and technologies (Article 1), which are defined as goods and technologies 'which can be used for both civil and military purposes' (Article 2 (*a*)). This clearly is a wide definition, but the regulation does not apply to all such goods and technologies. The Council will have to enact a complementary regulation containing a list of the goods and technologies that are actually covered by the regulation.[63] According to Article 3, an authorization shall be required for exporting the goods concerned. In addition, such an authorization will also be required for the exportation of dual use goods which are not mentioned in the complementary regulation, provided that

the exporter is aware, or has been informed by his government, that the goods in question are, in their entirety or in part, intended for use in connection with the development, production, maintenance, detection, identification or dissemination of conventional, chemical, biological or nuclear weapons and the development, production, maintenance or storage of missiles capable of delivering such weapons. (Article 4)

Moreover, the regulation does not prevent the Member States from enforcing still other export prohibitions, provided that they inform the Commission and the other Member States (Article 5).

As regards the competence to grant an export authorization, it is stated that this shall be done 'by the competent authorities in the Member State in which the exporter is established' (Article 6 (1)). In principle, such an authorization is required for each export transaction, but simplified formalities may be applied, and in particular there may be a system of general authorizations for exports to non-sensitive countries, which will also be listed in the complementary regulation (Article 7). The export authorization shall be valid throughout the Community. It must be presented to the customs office handling the export declaration, at the time of completing the customs formalities for export (Article 10). The competent authorities of the Member States may decide that only a limited number of customs offices, within their jurisdiction, have the competence to complete the export formalities for dual use goods subject to the regulation.

Of course, it is one thing to provide that a number of goods are subject to

---

[60] Ibid. 3.   [61] Ibid. 4.   [62] Ibid.
[63] Work on this list is not yet completed.

export control, but it is another to lay down the criteria on the basis of which export authorizations are actually granted. The proposed regulation merely enacts these criteria in a general way:

> In deciding whether to grant an export authorization the competent authorities shall have regard to the following criteria:
> (a) respect for the international commitments of the Member States of the Community...;
> (b) respect of human rights in the country of final destination;
> (c) the internal situation in the country of final destination...;
> (d) the preservation of regional peace, security and stability;
> (e) the national security of the Member States... as well as that of friendly and allied countries;
> (f) the behaviour of the buyer country with regard to the international community, as regards in particular its attitude to terrorism, the nature of its alliances, and respect for international law;
> (g) the existence of a risk that the equipment will be diverted within the buyer country or re-exported under undesirable conditions.[64]

Lastly, there are also provisions on administrative co-operation, on control measures, on penalties, and on implementing measures.

Comments

The proposed regulation is obviously very much characterized by the desire of the Commission not to make any competence claims which the Member States would not accept. The scope of the regulation is limited to removing the barriers to trade within the internal market, and to preventing deflections of trade and distortions of competition. There is no attempt to make export controls subject to a fully-fledged common policy, replacing national policies. This approach is not only justifiable for pragmatic reasons. It reflects the division of competences as set out above. At this stage, the Community does not have the competence to deal with pure security issues. What it does have is the power to harmonize export control policies, in order to reach a uniform external regime.

At the same time, this respect for the division of powers between the Community and its Member States may give rise to a number of difficulties. Because the proposed harmonization is of limited scope, genuine co-operation between the Community's institutions and the Member States is required. If such co-operation is not present, the proposed system will probably not be able to achieve its aims, namely to eliminate barriers to intra-Community

[64] Art. 8. These criteria are the ones which were adopted by the European Council in its June 1991 'Declaration on Non-Proliferation and Arms Exports', see the explanatory memorandum, p. 5.

trade. The question moreover arises whether the proposed harmonization is not too limited to be workable.[65]

The combination of Community and national competences must surely be assessed in the light of the Treaty on European Union. The Commission's reasoning regarding prior agreement between the Member States on lists of dual use goods and destinations may only be really workable with the development of a Common Foreign and Security Policy. As such, the regulation of export controls on dual use goods may become a test case for the co-ordination of the CFSP and the CCP (and, especially, its legal dimension), which undoubtedly is one of the more important problems concerning the application of the Treaty on European Union. It has for example been observed that the practice of first reaching political consensus makes of the following Article 113 decision a measure of mere implementation and risks to deprive the qualified majority voting rule provided for in this article of its relevance.[66] It would not be surprising if this procedural problem were to become paramount.

Conclusion

The case of export controls illustrates the gradual widening of the Community's external competences. From a political perspective, the end of the Cold War enables the Community to become more active in the field of general foreign and security policy. The Maastricht Treaty provides for a number of instruments devised to achieve this. If this trend is confirmed, the problem of co-ordinating economic and non-economic external policies will undoubtedly become crucial. Such co-ordination will only be effective if the CCP is not relegated to merely regulating classic trade policy instruments. With a view to avoiding this, the concept of external harmonization might be useful. Without this concept, there is the obvious risk of a gap in the Community's external powers related to the internal market, not only with respect to export controls, but also in relation to other policy fields, such as external environmental measures.[67]

[65] Cf. Kuyper, *supra* n. 26, p. 418.

[66] Gilsdorf, *supra* n. 21, pp. 5603–4.

[67] See Ch. 11, pp. 348–9, where the concept of external harmonization is discussed as part of a general analysis of the scope of the CCP in relation to the internal market.

8

Technical Regulations and Standards

Introduction

Policies relating to technical regulations and standards are of key importance to the internal market programme.[1] Not only do the measures adopted in this field represent a majority of the overall number of 1992 measures.[2] Leaving aside quantitative restrictions, technical regulations and standards have long been considered to be the non-tariff trade barrier *par excellence*, which is perhaps best evidenced by the large body of case-law of the Court of Justice on Article 30 of the EC Treaty. As the internal market programme is essentially about doing away with trade barriers, distortions caused by the different national regulatory regimes governing the characteristics of products, their packaging, marking, labelling, or testing,[3] have been made a clear target. Moreover, action in the field of technical regulations and standards is undoubtedly also critical for one of the underlying aims of the 1992 programme, which is to strengthen the technological base of the European industries, in order for them to become more competitive on world markets.[4] Standards can embody leading-edge technologies and, as such, are able to play a major role in global competition.[5] An outstanding illustration is the battle between the Community and Japan over the elaboration of standards for high-definition

---

[1] For a definition of the concepts 'technical regulation' and 'standard', see *infra* n. 22.

[2] Jacques Pelkmans and Michelle Egan, 'Tackling Technical Barriers', paper presented at the CEPS/CSIS conference on 'Reconciling Regulation and Free Trade', Dec. 1992, p. 5.

[3] Cf. the GATT definition of a 'technical specification', laid down in the Agreement on Technical Barriers to Trade, *BISD*, 26 S., p. 29.

[4] In the words of the Commission's White Paper on the completion of the internal market (COM (85) 310 final), '[f]ailure to achieve a genuine industrial common market becomes increasingly serious since the research, development and commercialisation costs of the new technologies, in order to have a realistic prospect of being internationally competitive, require the background of a home market of continental proportions' (para. 60). Reference can also be made to the Commission's policy statement on *Industrial Policy in an Open and Competitive Environment* (COM (90) 556 final, 16 Nov. 1990), which mentions that 'European standards are not only required for the purpose of removing technical barriers to trade, but increasingly they are also becoming a key item for the promotion of industrial competitiveness' (p. 12). See also Henri Froment-Meurice, *L'Europe de 1992: espace et puissance* (Paris: La Documentation française, 1988), 40–1.

[5] See e.g. Jacques Pelkmans, 'The New Approach to Technical Harmonization and Standardization', 25 *JCMS* (1987), 3: 260–1.

television, a product considered, rightly or wrongly, to be of vital importance for the future of Europe's electronics industry.[6]

From the above observations, the scope for tensions with the Community's trading partners already becomes apparent, as does the (from an external point of view) ambivalent character of the Community's actions in this area.[7] On the one hand, the removal of barriers in trade between the Member States cannot but also benefit foreign suppliers wishing to sell their products throughout the Community.[8] On the other, however, in so far as new, Europe-wide technical regulations and standards are developed, this may well happen with the objective of handicapping foreign competition at the back of the regulators' minds.

Characteristic for the internal market programme is the 'new approach' towards technical regulations and standards.[9] It has its roots in two developments. The first is the Community's experience with previous attempts at harmonizing the various national technical regulations. The aim was for such harmonization to be all encompassing, so that all elements of national law would be replaced by common rules. This proved to be virtually unworkable. For some products, it took more than a decade to lay down harmonized rules, which were sometimes outdated by the time they entered into force. Moreover, the problem of divergent industrial standards, which are of a private and voluntary nature, but are none the less able to act as a barrier to trade, was left largely unaddressed. The second development was the case-law of the Court of Justice. It appeared, especially after the famous *Cassis de Dijon* judgment,[10] that all-encompassing harmonization was not indispensable for eliminating the barrier-to-trade aspect of national technical regulations. As is well known, the Court decided in *Cassis de Dijon* that a Member State must, by virtue of Article 30, EC Treaty, allow the marketing on its territory of goods produced and/or marketed in another Member State in accordance with domestic law. Only the protection of a number of so-called mandatory requirements or of one of the public goods mentioned in Article 36 could justify derogations from

---

[6] See e.g. *Financial Times*, 'The battle to enter your living room', 5 Apr. 1989, and 'Battlelines drawn on the small screen', 21 May 1990, p. 15.

[7] Cf. Thomas Bruha, 'Normen und Standards im Wahrenverkehr mit Drittstaaten', in M. Hilf and C. Tomuschat (eds.), *EG und Drittstaatbeziehungen nach 1992* (Baden-Baden: Nomos, 1991), 85–6.

[8] See *infra*, p. 270 *et seq*.

[9] The new approach was officially set in motion by a Council Resolution of 7 May 1985, OJ C 136/1 of 4 June 1985. It is also described in the White Paper (n. 4), paras. 61–73. For more details, see Denis Waelbroeck, 'L'harmonisation des règles et normes techniques de la CEE', 24 *CDE* (1988), 3: 243–75; Jacques Pelkmans, *supra* n. 5, pp. 249–69; Richard H. Lauwaars, 'The "Model Directive" on Technical Harmonization', in R. Bieber, R. Dehousse, J. Pinder, and J. H. H. Weiler (eds.), *1992: One European Market?* (Baden-Baden: Nomos, 1988), 151–73; Sebastian Farr, *Harmonisation of Technical Standards in the EC* (London: Chancery Law Publishing, 1992), ch. 3.

[10] Case 120/78, *Rewe* v. *Bundesmonopolverwaltung für Branntwein*, [1979] ECR 649.

this basic principle.[11] The latter was then baptized as 'mutual recognition', meaning that the Member States must, as a rule, mutually recognize national regulations governing the production and marketing of products.

This principle of mutual recognition is one of the cornerstones of the new approach towards technical regulations and standards. Accordingly, harmonization is no longer aimed at completeness. Instead, only the essential requirements to which products have to conform become the object of common rules. As a result, there is now for example one very general directive on the safety of machines, governing approximately 55,000 types of machines.[12] A manufacturer who is able to demonstrate that his products correspond to the safety requirements set out in the directive can market them throughout the Community.

But mutual recognition and harmonization of essential requirements alone are not sufficient for the elimination of barriers to trade. In the above-mentioned example of machines, there is quite some scope for divergent interpretations and applications of the general requirements of the directive by the various national authorities responsible for checking safety. This problem is partly obviated by the elaboration of Europe-wide standards, translating the general requirements of the directives into detailed technical specifications. These standards are drawn up by European standards bodies, the main ones being CEN, CENELEC, and ETSI.[13] Although such standards are of a private nature and compliance with them is not mandatory, they are linked to the harmonization process. The Commission, pursuant to the adoption of a 'new approach' directive, gives a mandate to the said bodies to produce standards for the products concerned. A manufacturer who is able to demonstrate that his products conform to these standards benefits from a presumption of conformity with the essential requirements of the directive in question.[14] Thus, the scope for divergent interpretations is to some extent eliminated, and the manufacturer is given the choice to produce either in

---

[11] Mandatory requirements include the effectiveness of fiscal supervision, the protection of public health, the fairness of commercial transactions, the protection of the consumer, the protection of the environment, standardization of products, anti-inflation policy, public spending curbing and protection of cultural works and values, see Alfonso Mattera, *Le marché unique européen*, 2nd edn. (Paris: Jupiter, 1990), 272–3.

[12] Council Directive 89/392/EEC on the approximation of the laws of the Member States relating to machinery, OJ L 183/9 of 29 June 1989, amended by Directive 91/368, L 198/16 of 22 July 1991. The figure is mentioned by Jacques Pelkmans and Michelle Egan, *Fixing European Standards: Moving beyond the Green Paper*, CEPS Working Document No. 65, May 1992, p. 24.

[13] CEN stands for 'Comité européen de normalisation', CENELEC for 'Comité européen de normalisation électrotechnique', and ETSI for European Telecommunications Standards Institute. These bodies are (mainly) composed of the EC and EFTA countries. For a description of their work in its relationship with the new approach, see the *Commission Green Paper on the Development of European Standardization*, COM (90) 456 final, 8 Oct. 1990, pp. 12–17 and Farr, *supra* n. 9, ch. 4. Also, on CEN and CENELEC, Florence Nicolas and Jacques Repussard, *Common Standards for Enterprises* (Luxembourg: Commission, 1988).

[14] See e.g. Article 5 (2) of Directive 89/392/EEC (n. 12).

accordance with the relevant standards or to demonstrate 'directly' that his products comply with the essential requirements of the relevant directive. In practice, therefore, the new approach rests on a combination of legislative harmonization and very active Europe-wide standard-setting of a semi-private nature, bearing the stamp of official recognition.[15]

The new approach does not govern all actions undertaken by the Community in the field of technical regulations and standards. For a number of product categories, the old approach of full, detailed harmonization is still more or less applied. This is the case with motor vehicles, tractors and agricultural machinery, and chemicals, mainly because old-type harmonization was already at an advanced stage when the new approach was devised. It is also the case with foodstuffs and pharmaceutical products, for which voluntary standards are considered inappropriate because of the dangers for public health and the environment which these products pose.[16]

The new approach has been applied to products such as toys, machines, simple pressure vessels, medical devices, and weighing instruments.[17] Although the list of directives is limited, their scope is fairly wide, as the machine example makes clear. Therefore, and as the new approach is typical for the single market programme, the emphasis in this chapter lies on its impact on trade with third countries.

As was mentioned above, technical regulations and standards are typical non-tariff trade barriers. As such, this is of course not a problem which is confined to intra-Community trade. Accordingly, there have been some efforts within the GATT system aimed at drawing up multilateral rules designed to combat the trade-distorting effects of these regulations.

At the time when the General Agreement itself was drafted, however, the problem was not nearly as manifest as it is today. Consequently, there are few provisions addressing it.[18] One can mention Article III, on national treatment, providing in paragraph 4 the rule of non-discrimination in respect of all domestic 'laws, regulations and requirements affecting [the] internal sale, offering for sale, purchase, transportation, distribution or use' of products. This rule, important though it may be, is not further elaborated, which softens its impact on the barrier-to-trade aspect. As regards technical regulations and standards, prescribing non-discrimination is more like stating the overall

---

[15] The Commission has calculated that the completion of the internal market requires the adoption of at least 1600 European standards, see the *Commission Green paper* (n. 13), p. 3. For a critical review of the European policy regarding standard-setting, see Pelkmans and Egan, *supra* n. 2; also Ad van de Gevel (rapporteur), *The European Community without Technical Barriers*, CEPS Working Party Report No. 5 (Brussels: CEPS, 1992), 52–8.

[16] See Denis Waelbroeck, *supra* n. 9, pp. 256–7.

[17] See *A New Community Standards Policy*, Vol. iv of the Commission's 'current status' reports on completing the internal market (Luxembourg: Commission), based on the INFO 92 data base.

[18] See Jacques H. J. Bourgeois, 'The Tokyo Round Agreements on Technical Barriers and on Government Procurement in International and EEC Perspective', 19 *CML Rev.* (1982), 1: 6–7.

aim than setting out the ways of achieving it, since it is often difficult to demonstrate actual discrimination in specific cases.[19] Furthermore, Article XI (2) (*b*) allows '[i]mport and export prohibitions or restrictions necessary to the application of standards or regulations for the classification, grading or marketing of commodities in international trade,' as an exception to the general prohibition of quantitative restrictions. Also, Article XX provides under the heading of 'General Exceptions' that 'nothing in [the] Agreement shall be construed to prevent the adoption or enforcement by any contracting party of measures: ... (*b*) necessary to protect human, animal or plant life or health', provided that 'such measures are not applied in a manner which would constitute a means of arbitrary or unjustifiable discrimination between countries where the same conditions prevail, or a disguised restriction on international trade'. Thus, the legitimacy of drawing up regulations applying, for example, to the safety of products is fully recognized in the General Agreement.[20]

Since the trade problems caused by technical regulations and standards really became apparent in the course of the seventies, the subject was put on the agenda of the Tokyo Round of multilateral trade negotiations. These resulted in the adoption, among other things, of an Agreement on Technical Barriers to Trade, shortly called the Standards Code.[21] The Code contains provisions both of a procedural and a substantive nature. According to Article 2, technical regulations and standards should not be prepared, adopted, or applied *with a view* to creating obstacles to international trade, and neither must they have the *effect* of creating unnecessary obstacles. Also, national treatment of imported products must be guaranteed.[22] Parties must also in principle make use of existing international standards (Article 2.2). In cases in which this is not done, there is a duty to give notice to other Parties, and to take

---

[19] Perhaps this is one of the reasons why the European Court of Justice has quickly abandoned references to the concept of discrimination, when interpreting the scope of Art. 30, EC Treaty, cf. the broad definition in Case 8/74, *Dassonville*, [1974] ECR 837 at 852.

[20] Compare with Bourgeois, *supra* n. 18, pp. 7–8.

[21] See n. 3. For analyses, see Robert E. Sweeney, 'Technical Analysis of the Technical Barriers to Trade Agreement', 12 *Law Pol. Int. Bus.* (1980), 1: 179–217; R. W. Middleton, 'The GATT Standards Code', 14 *JWTL* (1980), 3: 201–19; Jacques Nusbaumer, 'The GATT Standards Code in Operation', 18 *JWTL* (1984), 6: 542–52; Jacques Pelkmans and Nial Bohan, 'Towards an Ideal GATT TBT Code', paper presented at the conference 'Reconciling Regulation and Free Trade' (see n. 2), pp. 14–17. From an EC perspective, see Bourgeois, *supra* n. 18, and Jacques Steenbergen, 'Trade Regulation since the Tokyo Round', in E. L. M. Völker (ed.), *Protectionism and the European Community*, 2nd edn. (Deventer: Kluwer, 1986), 187–91.

[22] Art. 2.1. The degree of obligation differs according to whether technical regulations and standards are drawn up by central government bodies, local government bodies, private standard bodies and regional standard bodies, see Arts. 2.9, 2.10, 3, and 4. A technical regulation is defined as '[a] technical specification, including the applicable administrative provisions, with which compliance is mandatory'. Standards, on the other hand, are 'technical specification[s] approved by a recognized standardizing body for repeated or continuous application, with which compliance is not mandatory' (see Annex 1 to the Code).

comments into account.[23] The second part of the Code deals with the problem of controlling conformity with technical regulations and standards and with certification systems. Here, too, there is a general obligation of national treatment, with some specifications as regards testing conformity.[24] The above-mentioned obstacles-to-trade language is repeated for certification systems, as is the duty of notification.[25] A third part deals with information and assistance. Parties should install enquiry points which have the duty to answer questions concerning, among other things, technical regulations, standards, and certification systems (Article 10). Also, Parties should advise and assist each other, especially the developing countries among them (Article 11). The latter benefit moreover from special and differential treatment (Article 12).[26] The last part deals with institutional questions. A Committee on Technical Barriers to Trade has been established with the purpose of supervising the implementation of the Agreement (Article 13). There is also a procedure for consultation and dispute settlement, in which there is room for both the constitution of a panel and the establishment of a technical expert group.[27]

The Community is a Party to the Standards Code, oddly enough, however, together with the individual Member States.[28] This has been a compromise solution in response to the conflicting views over where the competence lay to conclude the Tokyo Round Agreements: only with the Community or partly also with the Member States. It is an odd solution, because the Community's approval is based on Article 113, EC Treaty, according to which the Community has the exclusive competence to conduct commercial policy.[29] This means that it has been acknowledged within the Community that the Agreement is essentially situated within the commercial policy domain. One wonders therefore (and it has not been indicated)

---

[23] See *infra*, pp. 279–80.   [24] Arts. 5.1 and 7.2.

[25] Art. 7. Again, the degree of obligation differs depending on whether central government bodies are involved, as opposed to local, non-governmental, and regional bodies (Arts. 8 and 9).

[26] According to Art. 12.3, for example, Parties 'shall take account of the special development, financial and trade needs of developing countries, with a view to ensuring that ... technical regulations, standards, test methods and certification systems and the determination of conformity with technical regulations and standards do not create unnecessary obstacles to exports from developing countries'.

[27] Art. 14. The expert groups should examine questions of a technical nature, whereas panels should deal with the commercial policy questions in a dispute between Parties.

[28] For the adoption by the Council, see Decision 80/271/EEC, OJ L 71/1 of 17 Mar. 1980. On the difficulties related to the acting together by the Community and the Member States, see Jacques H. J. Bourgeois, *supra* n. 18, pp. 21–2; Jacques Steenbergen, *supra* n. 21, pp. 187–90 and Meinhard Hilf, 'The Application of GATT within the Member States of the European Community, with Special Reference to the Federal Republic of Germany', in M. Hilf, F.-G. Jacobs, and E.-U. Petersmann (eds.), *The European Community and GATT*, 2nd edn. (Deventer: Kluwer, 1989), 164–5 and 169.

[29] See *supra*, Ch. 1, p. 21.

which elements of the Agreement could fall outside the Community's competence.[30]

A full review of the impact of the 1992-related policies concerning technical regulations and standards on trade with third countries would require a drawn-out analysis, which cannot be undertaken within the scope of this study.[31] Instead, this chapter is aimed at portraying the major issues which have arisen in the course of the implementation of the internal market programme, concentrating mainly on the above-described new approach. Such a limitation is warranted because, in all, the general questions of law are limited in scope. In the absence of global harmonization, doing away with barriers to trade resulting from divergent technical regulations and standards ultimately depends on adopting and implementing the relevant domestic policies in good faith.[32]

This chapter contains two sections. The first deals with technical regulations and standards as such, the second relates to checking conformity, which in Community terminology is called certification and testing. Each section begins with an introductory part, indicating the basic principles governing trade relations with third countries. More specific issues are subsequently reviewed.

Technical Regulations and Standards

The basic principle: non-discrimination

Non-discrimination is the basic principle governing the impact of Community policies relating to technical regulations and standards on imports from third countries.[33] The provisions of directives harmonizing national technical

[30] On the question of competence, see also *infra*, p. 292. The Agreement has been revised in the Uruguay Round negotiations. The text taken up in the Draft Final Act (MTN.TNC/W/FA, pp. G.1–27) contains a number of important improvements. It makes a clearer distinction between technical regulations and standards. It introduces the rule of proportionality with respect to the trade-restrictive effects of technical regulations pursuing legitimate policy objectives (Art. 2.2). This is in effect very similar to the way in which Arts. 30–6, EC Treaty, are interpreted by the Court of Justice. It urges Parties mutually to recognize equivalent technical regulations (Art. 2.7). As regards standardization, it includes a Code of Good Practice for standardizing bodies. The rules on conformity assessment are also strengthened.

[31] See e.g. the various reports by the US International Trade Commission, *The Effects of Greater Economic Integration within the European Community on the United States*, Investigation No. 332–267, USITC Publication 2204, July 1989; USITC Publication 2268, Mar. 1990 (*First Follow-up Report*); USITC Publication 2318, Sept. 1990 (*Second Follow-up Report*); USITC Publication 2368, Mar. 1991 (*Third Follow-up Report*); US Deparment of Commerce, *EC 1992: A Commerce Department Analysis of European Community Directives* (May 1991).

[32] Jacques Nusbaumer, *supra* n. 21, p. 545. See also Bruha, *supra* n. 7, p. 106.

[33] See the Commission's policy statement on *Europe 1992: Europe World Partner*, Press Release P-117 of 19 Oct. 1988 and Art. 1 of the Council's Decision of 15 Jan. 1980, OJ L 14/36 of 19 Jan. 1980. Also John Farnell, 'The Global Approach to Conformity Assessment', speech presented at the CEN/CENELEC Conference on '1992: European Standardization in the International Context', Feb. 1990, p. 6. See, however, also Lauwaars, *supra* n. 9, pp. 168–9, and Paul

regulations, whether old-approach or new-approach style, apply to all products put on the Community market, whether produced inside the Community or imported from third countries. The directive on the safety of machines, for example, provides that 'Member States shall not prohibit, restrict or impede the placing on the market and putting into service in their territory of machinery which complies with the provisions of this Directive',[34] without referring to the place of production of machinery. Generally, the directives contain no provisions specifically dealing with imports, except, in a number of cases, on certification and testing.[35]

This is in line with the rules of the EC Treaty applying to goods which have been imported into the Community. By virtue of the fact that the Community is a customs union, the rules relating to the free movement of goods within the Community 'shall apply to products originating in Member States and to products coming from third countries which are in free circulation in Member States' (Article 9 (2), EC Treaty). According to Article 10 (1),

[p]roducts coming from a third country shall be considered to be in free circulation in a Member State if the import formalities have been complied with and any customs duties or charges having equivalent effect which are payable have been levied in that Member State, and if they have not benefited from a total or partial drawback of such duties or charges.[36]

Interpreting this rule, the Court of Justice has made it unequivocally clear that 'as regards free circulation of goods within the Community, products entitled to "free circulation" are definitively and wholly assimilated to products originating in Member States'.[37] In this respect, the concept of free movement of goods is not even limited to the Treaty provisions under Title 1, named 'Free

Demaret, 'La politique commerciale: perspectives d'évolution et faiblesses présentes', in J. Schwarze and H. G. Schermers (eds.), *Structure and Dimensions of European Community Policy* (Baden-Baden: Nomos, 1988), 89, regarding the resistance which in the past has been put up by some Member States against this non-discriminatory application.

[34] Art. 4 (1), OJ L 183/11 of 29 June 1989.

[35] This leaves aside Community measures in the area of veterinary and phytosanitary controls which generally do contain specific provisions on imports. These measures will not be discussed here. For certification and testing, see *infra*, pp. 286–95.

[36] On the scope of the import formalities, see Nikolaus Vaulont, in H. von der Groeben, J. Thiesing, and C.-D. Ehlermann (eds.), *Kommentar zum EWG-Vertrag*, 4th edn. (Baden-Baden: Nomos, 1991), 256–8.

[37] Case 41/76, *Donckerwolcke*, [1976] ECR 1935. This has been confirmed in Case 119/78, *S. A. des Grandes Distilleries Peureux* v. *Directeur des Services Fiscaux de la Haute-Saône et du Territoire de Belfort*, [1979] ECR 975, at 986: 'It follows that the prohibition of measures having an equivalent effect to quantitative restrictions in intra-Community trade has *the same scope* as regards products imported from another Member State after being in free circulation there as for those originating in the same Member State' (italics added); Case 288/83, *Commission* v. *Ireland*, [1985] ECR 1775; Case 193/85, *Cooperative Co-Frutta* v. *Amministrazione delle finanze dello Stato*, [1987] ECR 2112; Case 212/88, *Levy*, [1989] ECR 3529; Case C-83/89, *Openbaar Ministerie en Minister van Financiën* v. *Vincent Houben*, [1990] ECR I-1161.

movement of goods', but also applies to a provision such as Article 95, on non-discrimination in the area of taxation, although it is located in the 'Competition, Taxation and Approximation of Laws' Title of the Treaty and only mentions 'products of other Member States'.[38]

All this means that imported goods do not only benefit, on equal terms with domestically produced goods, from the provisions of directives harmonizing technical regulations, but also from the Treaty provisions limiting the Member States' right to draw up technical regulations that may hinder intra-Community trade.[39] One important result is that the operation of the principle of mutual recognition does not depend upon the origin of the products. In the *Cassis de Dijon* example, if the liquor imported into Germany had been American, but previously imported and marketed in France in accordance with French regulations, it would also have benefited from the mutual recognition rule. It is true that the *Cassis de Dijon* judgment speaks of products 'lawfully *produced and* marketed in one of the Member States',[40] at first sight excluding products imported from third countries. But in view of the above-mentioned fundamental and unequivocal language on the assimilation—with respect to free movement—of imports to domestic goods, there seem to be no reasons for not also extending the rule of mutual recognition.[41] Submitting the opposite would produce insurmountable difficulties. Where would one draw the line between the rules on free movement which would apply to goods in free circulation and those which would not? In *Donckerwolcke*, the Court held that

the provisions of Article 30 concerning the elimination of quantitative restrictions and all measures having equivalent effect are applicable without distinction to products originating in the Community and to those which were put into free circulation in any one of the Member States, irrespective of the actual origin of these products.[42]

---

[38] See *Co-Frutta* (*supra*, n. 37).
[39] That is, in particular, Art. 30.
[40] [1979] ECR 664, italics added.
[41] The same view is held by the Commission in *A Global Approach to Certification and Testing*, COM (89) 209 final, OJ C 276/26 of 19 Oct. 1989; E. L. M. Völker, *Barriers to External and Internal Community Trade* (Deventer: Kluwer, 1993), 92–4; Paul Demaret, 'Environmental Policy and Commercial Policy: The Emergence of Trade-Related Environmental Measures', in M. Maresceau (ed.), *The European Community's Commercial Policy after 1992: The Legal Dimension* (Dordrecht: Martinus Nijhoff, 1993), 366; Thomas Bruha, *supra* n. 7, pp. 104–6; Peter-Christian Müller-Graf, in *Kommentar zum EWG-Vertrag* (*supra* n. 36), 467; Alfonso Mattera, *supra* n. 11, pp. 30–1 and 'L'achèvement du marché intérieur et ses implications sur les relations extérieures', in P. Demaret (ed.), *Relations extérieures de la Communauté européenne et marché intérieur: aspects juridiques et fonctionnels* (Bruges: Story-Scientia for the College of Europe, 1988), 214; André Sapir, 'Does 1992 Come before or after 1990? On Regional Versus Multilateral Integration', in R. W. Jones and A. O. Krueger (eds.), *The Political Economy of International Trade* (Cambridge, Mass.: Basil Blackwell, 1990), 109; Meinhard Hilf, 'The Single European Act and 1992: Legal Implications for Third Countries', 1 *EJIL* (1990), 1/2: 99; Klaus Winkel, 'Die Grundsätze des freien Warenverkehrs im Verhältnis zu Drittländern', 44 *NJW* (1977), 1994.
[42] [1976] ECR 1935; confirmed in Case 212/88, *Levy*, [1989] ECR 3529.

As the rule of mutual recognition is an essential component of the interpretation and application of Article 30,[43] it would be both impossible and blatantly contrary to the Court's rulings to refuse its application to products which are in free circulation.

The above basically answers the argument which White has developed against the extension of the Court's *Cassis de Dijon* case-law to goods in free circulation.[44] He derives from the passage in *Donckerwolcke* where the Court held that the assimilation of imports to domestic goods can only take full effect 'if these goods [in free circulation] are subject to the same conditions both with regard to customs and commercial considerations, irrespective of the State in which they were put into free circulation',[45] that this assimilation does not apply to national measures of equivalent effect of the type invalidated by *Cassis de Dijon*. Indeed, the argument goes, these national measures are not uniform throughout the Community, which means that in this respect imports from third countries are not subject to the 'same conditions' mentioned above. However, the problem with such an interpretation is that it comes down to saying that the Court, after stating the rule of assimilation, immediately revoked it. National measures of equivalent effect are by definition not uniform: otherwise they would not restrict intra-Community trade. If the assimilation does not apply to such measures, why then has the Court said in the same judgment that the prohibition of quantitative restrictions and measures having equivalent effect is 'applicable without distinction' to goods produced in the Community and those which are in free circulation? Again it must be said that one cannot conceive of a way to determine which rules regarding the free movement of good would apply to goods in free circulation, and which not. The above quotation from *Donckerwolcke* referring to the uniformity of conditions of importation must be read in the light of what followed, namely an analysis of the scope of Article 115 of the Treaty, a provision which does allow restrictions on intra-Community trade in imported products in the framework of national commercial policy measures.[46]

The assimilation rule is also not invalidated, contrary to the suggestion by Oliver,[47] by the *EMI* judgment, in which the Court decided that

[s]ince [Arts. 10 (1) and 9 (2)] only refer to the effects of compliance with customs formalities and paying customs duties and charges having equivalent effect, they cannot be interpreted as meaning that it would be sufficient for products bearing a mark applied in a third country and imported into the Community to comply with the

[43] See for a candid analysis of the relationship between the rule of mutual recognition and Art. 30, Mattera, *supra* n. 11, pp. 247–80.
[44] Eric L. White, 'In Search of the Limits to Article 30 of the EEC Treaty', 26 *CML Rev.* (1989), 2: 259–63.
[45] [1976] ECR 1936. See also Ch. 5, p. 150.
[46] See Ch. 5, pp. 171–3.
[47] Peter Oliver, *Free Movement of Goods in the E.E.C.*, 2nd edn. (London: European Law Centre, 1988), 16–17.

customs formalities in the first Member State where they were imported in order to be able then to be marketed in the common market as a whole in contravention of the rules relating to the protection of the mark.[48]

These sentences must not be interpreted in the sense of denying the application of Article 30 to products in free circulation. The reason why Article 30 had no bearing on the case was that the products were imported under the trade mark of a third country, namely the United States. Thus, the issue was not one of the exercise of various national trade marks *within* the Community having an effect on intra-Community trade.[49]

The extension of the mutual recognition rule calls for some comments, first relating to its implementation. How does mutual recognition work in practice for goods which are in free circulation?[50] To my knowledge, there have been no cases which could provide some authority on this question. One can therefore only rely on general principles of Community law.

As mentioned above, *Cassis de Dijon* speaks of goods 'lawfully produced and marketed in one of the Member States'. The production requirement must of course be dropped in the case of imported products.[51] That leaves us with the condition that goods be 'lawfully marketed' in one of the Member States. What this condition means in practice will depend on both the type of product and the regulations governing its marketing in the Member State in question. As such, this is not uncommon to the operation of the mutual recognition rule, which, in general, depends on these specifications. For some products, there will have to be an authorization preceding marketing.[52] For others, there will only be a general rule as to the conditions for marketing, combined with *ex post facto* controls for checking whether these conditions are adhered to, and possibly penal sanctions in case of infringement.[53] The concept of having been lawfully marketed depends on these elements.[54]

---

[48] Case 51/75, *EMI Records* v. *CBS UK*, [1976] ECR 811, at 846.

[49] Cf. Inge Govaere, 'Intellectual Property Protection and Commercial Policy', in M. Maresceau (ed.), *The European Community's Commercial Policy after 1992: The Legal Dimension* (Dordrecht: Martinus Nijhoff, 1993), 212.

[50] Compare with the theoretical analysis of the various possibilities by L. A. Winters, 'Partner Interests in Customs Union Formation: An Economic View', in P. Demaret, J. Bourgeois, and I. Van Bael (eds.), *Trade Laws of the European Community and the United States in a Comparative Perspective* (Brussels: Story-Scientia for the College of Europe, 1992), 289.

[51] As Völker points out (*supra* n. 41, p. 94) the Court no longer refers to the production requirement in the judgments which followed *Cassis de Dijon*.

[52] That is the case with cars, for example. (However, type-approval of cars is subject to Community rules, see Council Directive 92/53/EEC, OJ L 225/1 of 10 Aug. 1992).

[53] See e.g. the German legislation on beer, as recorded in Case 178/84, *Commission* v. *Germany* [1987] ECR 1229.

[54] The test of whether a product can be marketed in a Member State is not necessarily performed when the customs formalities are fulfilled, so that a good brought into free circulation is not necessarily a good that can be lawfully marketed. However, in November 1992 the Commission issued a proposal for a Council Regulation on checks for conformity with the rules on product safety in the case of products imported from third countries (COM (92) 466 final of 11 Nov. 1992). The aim of this proposal is to ensure that customs

However, it would seem that there first has to be some degree of marketing in one Member State, before the benefit of mutual recognition in another Member State can be invoked. To give an example, if a German importer of a beer brewed in the United States, which does not conform to the *Reinheitsgebot*, but which does conform to the relevant Belgian regulations, wishes to sell that beer in Germany, he can only invoke the mutual recognition rule in case it has first been marketed in Belgium.[55] In the absence thereof, he would not have the right to claim access to the German market, even if he can show that the beer complies with the Belgian regulations. That follows from the scope of the mutual recognition rule, which does not apply to direct imports from third countries, but only to goods in free circulation.[56] This state of affairs is somewhat artificial, and could give rise to deflections of trade.[57] To the extent that such deflections materialize, there is a case for laying down common rules on the marketing of the products concerned.[58]

For the scope of the marketing requirement, the Court's case-law on the so-called U-turn construction could also be relevant. In the *Leclerc* case, the Court held that Article 30 does not apply where the goods in question were exported for the sole purpose of reimportation in order to circumvent domestic price legislation.[59] Similarly, it could be maintained that the extension of the mutual recognition rule to goods in free circulation does not apply where the goods have been imported in a Member State for the sole purpose of re-exporting them to another Member State.[60]

A second question relates to mutual recognition in direct trade with third countries. As mentioned above, it is obvious that the Treaty does not require that a Member State, say Germany, recognizes the technical regulations of a

authorities competent for releasing imports for free circulation, exercise control on the safety of the products concerned, as well as on their conforming with Community and national rules. The proposal was recently adopted, see Council Regulation 339/93 of 8 Feb. 1993, OJ L 40/1 of 17 Feb. 1993.

[55] Cf. Demaret, *supra* n. 11.

[56] That clearly follows from the *EMI* judgment, *supra* n. 41, at 845. There is a difference, though, between *EMI* and the beer example. In the latter case, no mutual recognition of US and German regulations would be asked for; the German importer would invoke intra-Community mutual recognition for direct importation from a third country. See also the next paragraph.

[57] In the beer example, shipping the beer through Antwerp instead of through Hamburg. The size of such deflections depends, among other things, on the scope of the marketing requirement. Does it suffice to market one can of the US beer in Belgium, in order to rely on mutual recognition in Germany? Or do all the cans which are to be sold in Germany first have to be marketed in Belgium? In view of the rationale of the marketing requirement, which is to make sure that the products concerned conform to the relevant regulations of a Member State, the first, most liberal hypothesis would seem to be justified. In its judgments on mutual recognition, the Court has never formulated the marketing requirement as referring to each individual product.

[58] Cf. Bruha, *supra* n. 7, p.106. Compare with the concept of external harmonization, put forward in the chapter on export controls (see Ch. 7, pp.252–9).

[59] Case 229/83, *Leclerc* v. *Au Blé Vert*, [1985] ECR 1, at 35.

[60] In the beer example, that could be the case if only a couple of cans are marketed in Belgium.

third country, say the United States, as being equivalent to its own.[61] However, there is the GATT Standards Code, containing a most-favoured-nation (MFN) rule which prohibits discrimination between the Parties in the area of technical regulations and standards. Since not only the Community as such, but also the Member States are Parties to the Code, it could be argued that the MFN rule compels those Member States to extend mutual recognition to third countries. Taking the provisions of the Code at face value, the commitment that 'products imported from the territory of any party shall be accorded treatment *no less favourable* than that accorded to like products ... originating in any other country in relation to ... technical regulations and standards'[62] seems to demand such an extension.[63] But it is clear that it was not the Community's intention—nor that of the Member States, for that matter—to extend with one stroke of the pen the mutual recognition system to trade with other Parties to the Code. Neither, apparently, have the other Parties claimed that the Community should operate such an extension. The problem has therefore remained rather theoretical.[64] It would not arise if the Standards Code were to contain an exception to MFN treatment for customs unions (CUs) and free trade areas (FTAs), similar to Article XXIV of the GATT. This provision allows contracting parties to engage in further trade liberalization among each other, without extending this to other trading partners. The mutual recognition rule is covered by this exception. Moreover, countries invoking Article XXIV must ensure that 'duties and other restrictive regulations of commerce ... are eliminated with respect to substantially all the trade between the constituent territories'.[65] It could therefore be argued that Article XXIV *requires* that the Community develop a system of mutual recognition of technical regulations, because the trade-distorting effects of the latter can be regarded as 'other restrictive regulations of commerce' which need to be eliminated.[66]

---

[61] See n. 41. Compare with E. L. M. Völker, 'Technical Regulations and Standards and Commercial Policy', in M. Maresceau (ed.), *The European Community's Commercial Policy after 1992: The Legal Dimension* (Dordrecht: Martinus Nijhoff, 1993), 299–300.

[62] Art. 2.1 (italics added). The national treatment rule also applies to determination of conformity (Art. 5.1.1) and certification systems (Art. 7.2).

[63] Steenbergen, *supra* n. 21, pp. 187–8. Compare with Jacques H. J. Bourgeois, 'Some Comments on the Practice', in C. W. A. Timmermans and E. L. M. Völker (eds.), *Division of Powers between the European Communities and their Member States in the Field of External Relations* (Deventer: Kluwer, 1981), 107.

[64] It is not completely theoretical, though: see *infra*, pp. 278–82, on the question of access to the European standardization bodies. See also Pieter Jan Kuyper, 'De invloed van het verdwijnen van de fysieke grenzen in de Gemeenschap op de handel in goederen met derde staten', 40 *SEW* (1992), 1: 18.

[65] Art. XXIV (8).

[66] However, the Community is probably the only CU or FTA which goes as far as mutual recognition when eliminating restrictive regulations of commerce. Compare with Kuyper, *supra* n. 57, p. 19.

Not only is there no Article XXIV-like provision in the Standards Code,[67] neither has the relationship between Article XXIV, GATT, and the MFN rule of the Standards Code been clarified. (This, by the way, is only one element of the broader problem that the relationship between the General Agreement and the Tokyo Round agreements lacks definition.)[68] This silence can be interpreted either as a rejection of the GATT exception for CUs and FTAs in the field of technical regulations and standards, or merely as avoiding the issue. In the latter case, it could probably be argued that the Community can continue to invoke Article XXIV as a shelter for its internal mutual recognition rule. After all, the fact that the Community as such has signed the Code, be it together with the Member States, furnishes an indication that also with regard to the field covered by the Code, the Community, being a customs union, must be regarded as one entity.

Three additional observations are worth making. The first is that it is difficult to envisage how an extension of the mutual recognition rule to non-Community Parties to the Standards Code would be implemented. These Parties would not have to reciprocate, which would strongly tip the balance of concessions to the disadvantage of the Community. Moreover, it must not be forgotten that mutual recognition stems from the case-law of the Court of Justice and would probably not work in the absence of regular judicial decisions.[69]

Secondly, and most importantly, the problem is but one expression of the lack of satisfactory guide-lines within the GATT system for the scope and limits of regional integration. The ambivalent approach towards such integration has been present from the system's conception.[70] Time has only aggravated it because of the inexorable increase of non-tariff trade barriers— such as technical regulations and standards—which have been more successfully combatted within systems of regional integration (and especially within the Community), than at the multilateral level. The question of the external dimension of the internal market reveals, more than anything, the many edges to this problem, which is further analysed in the concluding part of this study.[71]

Lastly, the question of the extension of internal market integration to other Parties, by virtue of the MFN principle of the Standards Code, does not only

---

[67] That is also the case with the revised version of the Code, see n. 2.

[68] As to the relationship between the MFN requirement and the Tokyo Round agreements (but not specifically as regards the Standards Code), see G. C. Hufbauer, J. Shelton Erb, and H. P. Starr, 'The GATT Codes and the Unconditional Most-Favored-Nation Principle', 12 *Law Pol. Int. Bus.* (1980), 1: 59–93 and John H. Jackson, *The World Trading System* (Cambridge, Mass.: MIT Press, 1989), 137–8.

[69] See also *infra*, p. 284.

[70] See e.g. the recent overview by Youri Devuyst, 'GATT Customs Union Provisions and the Uruguay Round: The European Community Experience', 26 *JWT* (1992), 1: 15–34. See also Chapter 11, p. 359.

[71] Ch. 11, pp. 358–62.

arise with respect to the mutual recognition rule. Comparable is the issue of access to the work of the European standards bodies, such as CEN, CENELEC, and ETSI, dealt with in the next section.

Access to standard-setting

It is understandable that third countries exporting to the Community's market have tried (and continue to try) to influence the process of adopting new technical regulations and setting new standards. In practice, these efforts have been primarily directed at the latter process. For a number of reasons, that is also understandable. New, Community-wide technical regulations are adopted by way of directives, harmonizing the existing national laws and regulations. This is an official, legislative exercise, interference with which is limited to some equally official avenues. One of these is the Standards Code, through its provisions on notification, consultation, and dispute settlement.[72] In the course of the implementation of the internal market programme, this avenue may have been used by third countries, but there were no cases that reached the stage of official dispute settlement.[73] One explanation for this may be that the new approach in the area of technical regulations and standards produces very general directives, with provisions limited to the essential requirements with which products have to comply, requirements which are probably indisputable in most cases. The practical effect on imports into the Community is much more dependent upon the standards developed as the result of these directives (and on the process of certification and testing).[74] In this connection, it should not be forgotten that, although compliance with standards is by definition not obligatory, in the case of the new approach it provides an important advantage because of the presumption that it equals compliance with the essential requirements of the directives.

As described above, standard-setting is mainly done by the European standards bodies, CEN, CENELEC, and ETSI.[75] These organizations are composed of the national standardization bodies of the EC and EFTA member countries.[76] Thus, the Community's major trading partner (EFTA) already has full access to the 1992-related standard-setting operations.[77] That is not the case with the United States, and it is in this country that a very thorough review has been undertaken of the impact of the Community's standard-setting process on its industries, both by government and industry

---

[72] Arts. 13 and 14.
[73] The hormones dispute between the Community and the United States is not dealt with here.
[74] For certification and testing, see *infra*, pp. 286–95.
[75] See n. 13.
[76] ETSI also has Cyprus, Malta, and Turkey as members, see Farr, *supra* n. 9, p. 39.
[77] Such full access is logical in view of the agreement on a European Economic Area (for the text, see 63 *CMLR* (1992), Part 859, p. 921 *et seq.*), which covers technical regulations.

branches.[78] This review has set in motion a dialogue on third-country access to European standardization, portrayed below.[79]

There are various forms and levels of access to standardization. The lowest level is that of information. It is in the interest of third-country exporters that they be adequately and timely informed on the development of standards, if only in order to be able to adapt their products (if necessary) by the time the new standards enter into force. Timely information is also important for the next step towards better access, namely the right to submit comments in the course of the process of drafting new standards. Such a right can be granted on an *ad hoc* basis, but it can also be institutionalized by admitting third-country standardization bodies as permanent observers to the development of standards. And the final level of access is of course full membership of the standardization bodies.

The Standards Code contains a number of obligations relating to these different levels of access, although with respect to the European standards bodies, which are 'regional standardizing bodies' in the terms of the Code, these obligations are only a best-endeavours commitment.[80] The point of departure is that existing international standards should be relied upon as much as possible.[81] If that is not possible or appropriate, other Parties should be informed and should be allowed to submit comments.[82] Thus, Parties shall publish a notice that they propose to introduce a particular standard; provide upon request and without discrimination to interested companies established in other Parties particulars or copies of the proposed standard; allow reasonable time for such interested parties to make comments, discuss

[78] Cf. e.g. the reports by the US International Trade Commission (n. 31); the Report, to the Secretary of Commerce, of the Federal Advisory Committee on the EC Common Approach to Standards, Certification, and Testing in 1992, May 1991; US Department of Commerce, *supra* n. 31. See also René Schwok, *U.S.–EC Relations in the Post-Cold War Era* (Boulder, Colo.: Westview Press, 1991), 63–72.

[79] Cf. 'Talks between U.S. and EC Commission Officials on Standardization and Certification', Commission Press Release IP/89/746 of 6 Oct. 1989; 'Factsheet on U.S. and EC communiqué on standards, testing and certification', US Department of Commerce, 21 June 1991.

[80] See Art. 2.9, saying that 'Parties shall take such reasonable measures as may be available to them to ensure that regional standardizing bodies of which they are members comply with the provisions of Article 2, paragraphs 1 to 8', the latter setting out the obligations relating to technical regulations and standards. The USA has urged more stringent provisions regarding regional standardizing bodies in the framework of the Uruguay Round, see *The Effects of Greater Economic Integration within the European Community on the United States: First Follow-up Report, supra* n. 31, p. 6/36. This aim was only partly achieved. The revised Code (n. 30) contains a Code of Good Practice for standardization bodies, with a stricter and more elaborated preference for international standardization. According to Art. 4.1 of the revised Code, 'Parties shall ensure that their central government standardizing bodies accept and comply with the code of good practice'; however, as regards local government, non-governmental, and regional standardizing bodies, they shall only 'take such reasonable measures as may be available to them to ensure' that these bodies accept and comply with the Code of Good Practice.

[81] Art. 2.2. On international standards, see the following section.

[82] Art. 2.5. As regards information, see also the enquiry points which all Parties have to install according to Art. 10.

these comments with them and take the comments and the results of the discussions into account.[83] Moreover, 'Parties shall ensure that all ... standards which have been adopted are published promptly in such a manner as to enable interested parties to become acquainted with them.'[84] It will be noticed that these obligations concern the first two levels of access described above, namely information and a right of comment. On observer status and full membership of regional standardizing bodies, the Code is silent.

It is also in these areas of information and the right of comment that the United States has clearly succeeded in influencing the process of developing new, internal-market-related standards. Responding to criticisms, CEN and CENELEC have started to issue monthly reports providing details of ongoing standardization activities. They have stated that they would allow comments by third-country bodies, as well as presentations from third-country experts, and they have concluded a number of private co-operative agreements with the American National Standards Institute (ANSI).[85] However, the United States has at one stage also claimed 'a seat at the table' of the European standards bodies, wishing to participate fully in the development of European standards.[86] That claim was not received with much enthusiasm, and has only been successful in the case of ETSI, the telecommunications standards body, which has granted observer status to US organizations concerned with telecommunications.[87] The Community's position as regards such participation in the work of the European standards bodies is set out in a Commission Green Paper on standardization.[88] A distinction is made there between European and non-European countries. With respect to the latter, the Commission is of the view that 'it is primarily up to the European standardization bodies to decide whether it is in their interest to offer a limited degree of input into their work to the standardization bodies of these countries'.[89] The advantages may be improved transparency and state-of-the-art input. However, the Commission also points to some of the potential costs of such an approach,

[83] According to Art. 2.6, however, 'where urgent problems of safety, health, environmental protection or national security arise or threaten to arise for a Party, that Party may omit such of the steps enumerated in Article 2, paragraph 5 as it finds necessary', provided that it takes a number of other steps which are enumerated.

[84] Art. 2.7.

[85] See *The Effects of Greater Economic Integration within the European Community on the United States: First Follow-up Report* (n. 31), pp. 6/32–5; van de Gevel, *supra* n. 15, p. 65; Michael Calingaert, *The 1992 Challenge from Europe*, 5th edn. (Washington, DC: National Planning Association, 1990), p. xxiii.

[86] *First Follow-up Report*, p. 6/32; Schwok, *supra* n. 78, p. 63; Youri Devuyst, 'The United States and Europe 1992', 13 *World Comp.* (1989), 1: 35; van de Gevel, *supra* n. 15, p. 65.

[87] *The Effects of Greater Economic Integration within the European Community on the United States: First Follow-up Report* (n. 31), p. 6/32 n. 120; Peter F. Cowhey, 'Telecommunications', in G. C. Hufbauer (ed.), *Europe 1992: An American Perspective* (Washington, DC: The Brookings Institution, 1990), 205. ETSI differs from CEN and CENELEC in that it also has private companies as members (including third-country companies), see Farr, *supra* n. 9, p. 39 and GATT, *Trade Policy Review: European Communities*, i (Geneva, 1991), 122.

[88] See n. 13.   [89] Para. 54.

such as the risk of delays and the concern that discussions which ought to take place within international standardization bodies might take place at the European level. Moreover, the Commission is of the opinion that, where limited participation is granted, reciprocity must be ensured.[90]

For European countries which are not yet members, such as the Central and East European countries, the approach is different. For these, full membership is a desirable option for the longer term. In the short term, however, membership would slow down the development of European standards at a time when acceleration is needed.[91] Nevertheless, these countries 'should be closely associated with the work of European standardization bodies', because '[t]he widespread adoption and use of European standards outside the member countries of the EEC and EFTA is in Western Europe's economic interest'.[92] The Commission has therefore proposed 'associate member' status for those European countries, implying 'a right to participate in the work of European standardization without the right to vote'.[93] This suggestion has been taken up by CEN and CENELEC, which have granted 'affiliate' status to a number of Central European countries.[94]

This different approach towards European and non-European countries again highlights the tension between the multilateral non-discrimination rule and regional integration. In the area of regional standardization bodies, however, the Standards Code appears to tolerate the exception to the MFN rule. The latter, according to Article 2.1, only concerns the treatment of imports, and not the setting of standards.[95] Moreover, express mention is made in the Code of the existence of regional standardizing bodies, whose legitimacy is therefore recognized.[96] It is obvious that if these regional bodies had to open up to all interested countries, they would merely become a duplicate of the existing international (in the sense of global) standardizing bodies, and thus lose their *raison d'être*.[97]

---

[90] Ibid.

[91] On this acceleration, see the introduction to the Green Paper, *supra* n. 13, where the Commission states that, at that time (Oct. 1990), the completion of the internal market still required the adoption of 800 standards, or about one standard a day.

[92] Para. 53.   [93] Ibid.

[94] *Agence Europe*, No. 5601, 1 Nov. 1991, p. 16; *Standardization in the European Economy*, COM (91) 521 final, 16 Dec. 1991, p. 28.

[95] However, one could regard the emphasis on international standards as an alternative to MFN. See also the next section.

[96] Art. 2.9.

[97] In this sense, there may be a difference between access to the European bodies and access to US bodies. US authorities claim that their standardization bodies are completely open and offer full national treatment to foreign companies as regards standard-setting (*The Effects of Greater Economic Integration within the European Community on the United States: First Follow-up Report* (n. 31), p. 6/36). However, the European bodies are essentially composed of national standardization bodies. They would of course lose their regional character if they were to grant full participation to non-European bodies. For a positive appreciation of regional integration in the area of technical regulations and standards from a trade policy perspective, see Pelkmans and Bohan, *supra* n. 21, pp. 20–1.

    This tolerance of regional standardization does not, however, eliminate the tension with the MFN principle. It surfaces again when one considers one of the most important obligations of the Code regarding standard-setting, namely that '[w]here technical regulations or standards are required and relevant international standards exist or their completion is imminent, Parties shall use them'.[98] Clearly, if regional standardization bodies should merely implement existing international standards, what is their use beside the national bodies of their member countries?

Reliance on international standards

As mentioned, the Standards Code urges its Parties to rely on international standards. However, this does not apply in cases

> where, as duly explained upon request, such international standards or relevant parts are inappropriate for the Parties concerned, for *inter alia* such reasons as national security requirements; the prevention of deceptive practices; protection for human health or safety, animal or plant life or health, or the environment; fundamental climatic or geographical factors; fundamental technological problems.[99]

These exceptions have been characterized as a loophole, although there is a duty to notify and explain departures from international standards to other Parties.[100]

    Again, it has been the United States which has complained that the European standardization bodies, when drawing up new 1992-related standards, did not sufficiently rely on international standards.[101] In response to these complaints, the Community institutions have on a number of occasions confirmed their fundamental commitment to international standardization.[102] Similarly, the European standardization bodies have declared that they would base their work on existing international standards and that, if such standards do not yet exist, they would refer planned standards work to the international standardization bodies,[103] and would adopt the resulting standards, provided they can be developed within the timeframe imposed by

---

[98] Art. 2.2.   [99] Ibid.

[100] Bourgeois, *supra* n. 18, p. 10.

[101] See the various reports on *The Effects of Greater Economic Integration within the European Community on the United States* (n. 31), throughout the chapters on standards; Schwok, *supra* n. 78, p. 65.

[102] See the statements by Commissioner Bangemann, reported in *Agence Europe*, No. 5026, 1 June 1989, p. 5; 'European and International Standardization Should Go Hand in Hand', Commission Press Release IP/91/488 of 31 May 1991; Resolution of the European Parliament on European standardization, certification, and testing, OJ C 240/208, at 211, of 16 Sept. 1991.

[103] i.e. the International Standards Organization (ISO) and the International Electrotechnical Commission (IEC).

the EC Commission. They have also strengthened co-operation with the international standardization bodies.[104]

Furthermore, in its 1990 Green Paper, the Commission outlined the measures which had already been taken in order to improve co-ordination between the European and the international standardization bodies, and presented some proposals for improving this.[105] However, the Commission also issued a warning to the effect that

[t]he Community expects that its leading economic partners, and particularly the United States and Japan, will be prepared to commit more resources to international standardization in the coming years, and, equally important, to implement international standards at the national level.[106]

That the Commission does not want unconditionally to support international standardization also became clear when it published a follow-up communication to the Green Paper. Therein it on the one hand reported that the overwhelming majority of those who had responded to the Green Paper were of the view that the development of international standards should remain the main objective of standardization work, and declared that it shared this view.[107] On the other hand, however, the Commission attached a number of conditions to referring new standardization work, necessary in the framework of Community legislation, to the international standardization bodies. These should be able to deliver the standards within the timescale imposed by such legislation, the essential requirements of which should be fully taken into account, and the European standardization bodies should retain final contractual responsibility for delivery of the standards.[108] At the same time, the Commission thought that '[t]he international standards bodies may find it difficult to meet these conditions'.[109] Nevertheless, it invited them to take up

---

[104] *The Effects of Greater Economic Integration within the European Community on the United States: First Follow-up Report* (n. 31), p. 6/34; Pelkmans and Egan, *supra* n. 2, p. 12; Stephen Cooney, 'Similarities in the Reform Debate: A Comparison with Special Attention to the U.S. and EC Standards and Conformity Assessment Systems', paper presented at the conference 'Reconciling Regulation and Free Trade' (see n. 2), p. 7.

[105] See n. 13, at paras. 59 and 60.

[106] Para. 60. The lack of US commitment to international standardization has also been admitted and criticized within the United States, see *The Effects of Greater Economic Integration within the European Community on the United States: Second Follow-up Report, supra* n. 31, p. 4/16 and the Report to the Secretary of Commerce (n. 2), 6–14. Also see Pelkmans and Egan, *supra* n. 2, pp. 12–13; Stephen Woolcock, *Market Access Issues in EC-US Relations* (London: Pinter Publishers for the RIIA, 1991), 93 and 102–3.

[107] Paras. 10 and 45. Also see Pelkmans and Egan, *supra* n. 2, pp. 16–17.

[108] Para. 46. Also see the statement to the IEC General Assembly by Commission Vice-President Andriessen, Rotterdam, 30 Sept. 1992, pp. 7–8.

[109] The Commission noted that the average time taken to deliver an ISO standard is usually double that accorded to CEN, CENELEC, and ETSI and that '[o]ther parties in international standardization may not wish to aim at the high level of performance required by the standards needed for Community product legislation, or may not be interested in the development of some standards because their national authorities directly regulate the sector in question', see para. 47.

the challenge and signalled that the main European and US standards organizations had agreed jointly to promote faster international standardization and to identify priority areas.[110] . In the mean time, it is reported that the European standardization bodies do indeed base their work to a considerable extent on international standardization.[111]

International harmonization and mutual recognition

That the Community does not wish to jeopardize the timely implementation of its internal market programme by giving unconditional priority to the development of international standards is understandable. In this connection, it should be mentioned that some argue that international standardization may not always be the best solution, in economic terms, for solving the barrier-to-trade problems posed by divergent technical regulations and standards, because of the difficulties inherent in reaching compromise at international level and the consequent watering-down of the technologically innovative character of new standards.[112]

Basically, this raises the question as to the appropriate policy mixture of pursuing global harmonization of technical regulations and standards (of which international standards are an essential component) and setting up systems of mutual recognition. Although this question cannot be fully addressed here, the few observations made below from a Community perspective may perhaps stimulate the debate.[113]

The Community's internal experience shows that there are actually two types of mutual recognition, which can be called judicial and administrative. The judicial type is the one resulting from the Court's case-law on the prohibition of measures having equivalent effect to quantitative restrictions (Articles 30–6, EC Treaty). Uniform interpretations by the judiciary are vital for making this type of mutual recognition work, because it depends on applying a very broad rule. Even then, it has its disadvantages for international trade, because rulings inevitably come *post factum* and depend on the arising of disputes.[114] Therefore, at the current stage of international

---

[110] Ibid.

[111] Pelkmans and Egan, *supra* n. 2, p. 17; Andriessen speech (n. 108), 6; Pelkmans and Bohan, *supra* n. 21, p. 13; Farr, *supra* n. 9, p. 42; GATT, *supra* n. 87, p. 123.

[112] Jacques Nusbaumer, *supra* n. 21, pp. 546 and 550. Also see Pelkmans and Egan, *supra* n. 2, pp. 17–18; Pelkmans and Bohan, *supra* n. 21, p. 10. At the conference on 'Reconciling Regulation and Free Trade' (n. 2), various experts emphasized that for a variety of reasons international harmonization is not beneficial in all cases.

[113] Compare with Pelkmans and Bohan, *supra* n. 21.

[114] Cf. Denis Waelbroeck, *supra* n. 9, p. 244. It should be mentioned that in the Community's new approach to technical regulations and standards the principle of mutual recognition is not seen by everyone as providing a definitive solution, but rather as an intermediate instrument in the absence of total harmonization, see Waelbroeck, pp. 254–5.

economic integration it would not seem advisable to develop the judicial type of mutual recognition at the global level. The GATT dispute settlement procedures do not (yet) have the strength to guarantee uniform interpretations of a basic rule aimed at removing the trade-distorting effects of divergent technical regulations and standards.[115]

The administrative type is more clear-cut. It implies that the various competent authorities sit together and draw up lists of those technical regulations and standards which they consider to be equivalent and therefore to become subject to mutual recognition. Within the Community, there is no actual experience yet with such an approach, though there is the (to date unused) Article 100*b*, EC Treaty, which provides that

[d]uring 1992, the Commission shall, together with each Member State, draw up an inventory of national laws, regulations and administrative provisions which fall under Article 100a and which have not been harmonized pursuant to that Article.

The Council, acting in accordance with the provisions of Article 100a, may decide that the provisions in force in a Member State must be recognized as being equivalent to those applied by another Member State.

A similar procedure could be installed at the multilateral level, within the framework of the Standards Code, although some modifications would have to be introduced. For one thing, there is not within the GATT system a central policy-making institution having powers similar to the EC Council.[116] Therefore, the decisions on mutual recognition would have to result from detailed negotiations between the various trading partners. These are already possible today, under the existing rules,[117] but there is not a real institutional setting in which they can take place. To create such a setting, one suggestion could be to introduce a rule requiring all Parties to the Standards Code who adopt new technical regulations or standards which are not based on existing international standards, to conduct negotiations with other Parties showing an interest in having their own technical regulations and standards recognized as being equivalent. Such a rule could create a permanent exchange of concessions regarding mutual recognition.

Perhaps such a system of administrative (or negotiated) mutual recognition would produce more results than efforts in the direction of global

---

[115] This is confirmed by the fact that the General Agreement has actually always contained such a broad rule, namely Art. III, if properly construed, without this yielding substantial case-law regarding the trade-distorting effects of technical regulations and standards. It remains to be seen whether the strengthening of the GATT dispute settlement procedures, negotiated in the Uruguay Round (see MTN.TNC/W/FA, pp. S.1–23), will make these procedures more judicial and less diplomatic.

[116] On the limits on the powers of the CONTRACTING PARTIES and the GATT Council, see John H. Jackson, *The World Trading System* (Cambridge, Mass.: MIT Press, 1989), 48–9.

[117] Art. 5.2 of the Standards Code. For an EC example of the possibility of concluding mutual recognition agreements, see Art. 9 of Directive 70/156/EEC on type-approval of cars, as amended by Directive 92/53/EEC (n. 52).

harmonization.[118] This is not to say that international standardization is to be abandoned, far from it. But there are a number of limits inherent in it, such as the fact that it is of a private nature and therefore cannot replace government policies aimed at protecting essential interests, the sheer magnitude of the task of developing international standards for all traded products, as well as the difficult and time-consuming process of consensus-seeking. Next to international standardization, there is of course also the method of negotiating international agreements containing mandatory product specifications. This method may be preferable in areas such as the protection of the environment, where mutual recognition might be less workable.[119]

In any case, the Community, with its solid experience in doing away with trade barriers resulting from divergent technical regulations and standards, should play a leading role in the process of devising appropriate rules and procedures at the multilateral level, especially when the internal market programme in this area has been completed. It will then no longer be able to invoke the pressure of this programme's timetable to concentrate mainly on internal developments.

It must be added that the question of harmonization versus mutual recognition of technical regulations and standards cannot be dissociated from the question of how conformity with such regulations and standards is tested, in other words the issue of certification and testing. Although logically speaking this comes second, in practice the trade-distorting effects which can result from certification and testing procedures have been considered to be as important, if not more, as differences in the contents of technical regulations and standards.[120] Furthermore, it is in this area, analysed in the next section, that agreements on mutual recognition have already been envisaged in concrete terms.

Certification and Testing

Outline of the 'global approach'

The systematic review of the trade-distorting effects of national policies relating to technical regulations and standards, undertaken within the framework of the internal market programme, as well as the implementation of the new approach, described above, quickly revealed that Community action was

---

[118] Cf. Steenbergen, *supra* n. 21, pp. 218–19.

[119] Because the emphasis lies on the strictness of standards, and not so much on their content. A country with higher standards will not easily accept recognition of less stringent standards.

[120] See for example the US reactions (*The Effects of Greater Economic Integration within the European Community on the United States: First Follow-up Report* (n. 31), pp. 6/23–4) and Jacques Nusbaumer, *supra* n. 21, p. 547.

not only needed at the level of harmonizing technical regulations and developing European-wide standards, but also at the level of assessing the conformity of products with those regulations and standards.[121] The difficulties associated with conformity assessment are probably as diverse as those related to the content of technical regulations and standards. This led the Commission to propose, by way of a memorandum, what it called 'A global approach to certification and testing'.[122] In this document, the various problems concerning conformity assessment are analysed and the direction of future policy is described. The latter part contains two main sections, one on confidence-building measures and another on new legislative techniques for conformity assessment. The second is the most important one with a view to evaluating how certification and testing is going to take place within the Community's internal market.

The basic principle governing these new legislative techniques is that there are, as a rule, various procedures at Community level for assessing conformity of a given product. Accordingly, manufacturers have a choice of how to demonstrate conformity. These procedures are called modules.[123] The factor distinguishing these modules from each other is the role played by the manufacturer, on the one hand, and the so-called notified bodies, on the other. The latter is a general term for those institutions (mainly test laboratories) which the Member States, when implementing a directive harmonizing technical regulations, assign with the task of assessing the conformity of products.

Some examples may serve to illustrate this interplay between manufacturers and notified bodies. Under module A it is the manufacturer who declares that his product conforms to the essential requirements set out in the relevant directive, and there is no intervention by a notified body, except, in some cases, as regards tests on specific aspects of the product or product checks at random intervals. This is obviously a very simple procedure, minimizing the burden on manufacturers. Much less simple is the combination of modules B and F. Module B, called type examination, concerns the design phase of a product, and implies that the manufacturer submits both technical documentation and a specimen to a notified body, which ascertains conformity with the essential requirements of the relevant directive, carries out tests, if necessary, and then issues an EC type-examination certificate. In some cases it is combined with module F, called product verification and relating to the production phase. In

[121] See the examples mentioned in the Commission's memorandum (n. 122 *infra*).

[122] COM (89) 209 final of 15 June 1989, OJ C 267/3 of 19 Oct. 1989.

[123] For a description, see the Commission's memorandum (n. 122 *supra*) as well as the Council's Decision of 13 Dec. 1990 concerning the modules for the various phases of the conformity assessment procedures which are intended to be used in the technical harmonization directives, OJ L 380/13 of 31 Dec. 1990. See also J. McMillan, 'La "certification", la reconnaissance mutuelle et le marché unique', *RMUE* (1991), 2: 181–211. Farr, *supra* n. 9, ch. 5.

module F, the manufacturer declares that a product conforms to the type described in the type-examination certificate and the notified body either tests every product or tests the products on a statistical basis (by means of random samples). These modules imply a high degree of involvement by the notified bodies. Still another possibility is the combination of type examination in the design phase (module B) with the manufacturer operating an approved 'quality system' for inspection and testing in the production phase (modules D and E). This implies that the notified body does not test the products themselves, but carries out surveillance of the said quality system.

The global approach also provides for the setting-up of a new European Organization for Certification and Testing (EOTC), which will furnish 'information, experience and a framework within which appropriate structures and agreements for the different industrial sectors can be negotiated'.[124] It will also provide 'the common technical basis that is indispensable for the negotiation of mutual recognition agreements with non-Community partners'.[125]

This brings us to the external dimension of the global approach to certification and testing. The final chapter of the Commission's memorandum deals with external aspects. It first points to the principles guiding these aspects. In accordance with the commitments undertaken within the GATT framework, and especially the Standards Code, '[t]he Community will continue to grant non-discriminatory access to its conformity assessment procedures to products originating in third countries'.[126] Such non-discriminatory treatment is indeed a requirement of the Standards Code,[127] and the global approach appears to respect it. In any case, there is no formal discrimination against non-EC manufacturers. The various modules apply without distinction to domestically produced and imported products. The only specific requirement relating to imports is that a non-EC manufacturer must have an authorized representative within the Community for the purpose of conducting the dialogue with the notified bodies.[128] Given the complexity of the conformity assessment procedures, this requirement is probably justified for administrative reasons.

However, the fact that there is no formal discrimination does not mean that the various modules do not represent obstacles to trade, especially for non-EC producers. The size of these obstacles depends, of course, on which module applies. If only self-certification is required (module A), there is little or no hindrance. If, on the other hand, modules B and F apply, non-EC producers have to submit to a notified body within the Community a specimen for type examination, as well as all imported products for testing conformity with the

---

[124] Commission's memorandum, OJ C 267/25 of 19 Oct. 1989.
[125] Ibid. See also J. McMillan, *supra* n. 123, pp. 181–211.
[126] OJ C 267/26 of 19 Oct. 1989.   [127] Art. 5.
[128] See the various modules as set out in the Council's Decision (n. 123).

type certificate. That may entail costs which are higher than those borne by manufacturers based in the Community.[129] It may also entail a duplication of tests which have already been carried out in the producer's home country. Understandably, therefore, third countries will try to minimize these obstacles. Again, it was primarily the United States which sought to obtain less cumbersome procedures for its exporters.[130] The USA has asked that Member States be allowed to appoint notified bodies located in the USA, that EC notified bodies be able to subcontract some of the tests to US laboratories, and that greater scope for self-certification be given. These issues are examined in the next section.

Closely related, yet analytically distinct is the question of mutual recognition agreements. The Commission has proposed that the Community conclude agreements with third countries for mutual recognition of declarations and marks of conformity, tests, certificates, and the like. Such agreements are possible under the Standards Code.[131] The Council has agreed to this proposal, which is examined in the final section.

Notified bodies and imports

Notified bodies play a crucial role in the implementation of the global approach. It is understandable, therefore, that third countries try to obtain the highest possible degree of access to these bodies for their exporters. The above-mentioned claims made by the United States correspond to this desire. If Member States were allowed to notify test labs located in the USA (in addition to the labs located in the Community) as bodies responsible for testing and certifying conformity with Community directives, that would of course simplify matters for US exporters. If that is not possible, an alternative might be to allow Community-based notified bodies to subcontract a substantial part of their testing and certification activities, as applied to foreign exporters, to foreign test laboratories.[132]

Undoubtedly, these claims have partly been induced by the fact that the relationship between notified bodies and imported products has not been regulated by the Community when the first set of new approach directives was issued. The requirements regarding notified bodies, laid down in these directives, are only of a qualitative nature, and do not mention the questions of relationship with a Member State, location or subcontracting.[133] Neither are

---

[129] Such as transport and transaction costs.
[130] See e.g. *The Effects of Greater Economic Integration within the European Community on the United States: First Follow-up Report* (n. 31), p. 6/23–8.
[131] Art. 5.2.   [132] See n. 31.
[133] See e.g. Council Directive 90/385/EEC on the approximation of the laws of the Member States relating to active implantable medical devices, OJ L 189/17 of 20 July 1990, particularly Annex 8 regarding minimum conditions to be met when designating inspection bodies to be notified.

there any indications on how notified bodies should proceed towards manufacturers not established in the Community with regard to an item such as
surveillance of quality systems operated by manufacturers, which, in the case
of foreign manufacturers, implies that controls are carried out outside the
territory of the Community.

The Community has not reacted very enthusiastically to the demands made
by the United States. It is reported that the Commission has made it clear that,
in its view, the Member States are not allowed to notify, for the purpose of
certification and testing, inspection bodies located outside the Community.
There would, according to the Commission, be some scope for subcontracting
part of the activities related to testing to foreign laboratories, but this would
have to be limited to ancillary activities, because the final responsibility
regarding type approval, certification of conformity and surveillance would
always remain with an EC-based notified body. The only way in which third
countries could get around these limitations would be by concluding agreements on mutual recognition with the Community. In the absence of such
agreements there could be no question of foreign inspection bodies performing controls that could be recognized inside the Community.[134]

The Commission's stance may well be worth defending from a policy point
of view, because in the absence of agreements on mutual recognition there are
no guarantees that Community exporters are not put in a less advantageous
position than their foreign counterparts. If, for example, US manufacturers
can have the conformity of their products with Community directives certified
in the United States, it would clearly be desirable that, conversely, Community
exporters can have the conformity of their products with US technical regulations certified inside the Community. However, from a legal point of view
the Commission's position is not indisputable. In the absence of provisions in
the relevant harmonization directives regarding the location of notified bodies
or the question of subcontracting, it would seem that the Member States have
some latitude in notifying the bodies of their choice and in organizing the
system. After all, a directive, according to Article 189, EC Treaty, 'shall leave
to the national authorities the choice of form and methods'. It would therefore
be difficult to argue that a Member State does not have the right to notify a
body located in a third country, provided the Member State is able to
guarantee that it can effectively supervise such a body.[135]

In the most recent directives, however, an express limitation has been

---

[134] *The Effects of Greater Economic Integration within the European Community on the United
States: Second Follow-up Report* (n. 31), pp. 4/21–2; speech by Farnell (n. 33), p. 7; Cooney, *supra*
n. 104, pp. 7–8.

[135] Such a guarantee could be the subject of an agreement between the Member State and the
third country in question. In so far as such an agreement would be strictly limited to the
designation of notified bodies, the Member States would seem to be competent to conclude it,
because this is a matter of implementing a directive. By contrast, agreements relating to mutual
recognition of testing itself fall within the competence of the Community, see *infra*, p. 292.

introduced in this respect. The directive on type-approval of motor vehicles, for example, provides that 'third country services may only be notified as an appointed technical service' for performing the necessary tests 'in the framework of a bilateral or multilateral agreement between the Community and the third country'.[136] If such a limitation is to be the general policy, it would be preferable to have it inserted into all the relevant directives, including those which have already been adopted. Moreover, there is certainly scope for some additional Community legislation on how notified bodies should operate with respect to non-Community manufacturers. Such legislation could serve to mitigate some of the fears of foreign governments and exporters.

The United States has also proposed in the framework of the Uruguay Round negotiations that, as an amendment to the Standards Code, the rule of national treatment be applied with respect to the appointment of notified bodies, implying that foreign test laboratories be granted notified body status on equal terms with domestic laboratories.[137] Such a rule, if adopted, would make superfluous detailed bilateral agreements on mutual recognition (discussed in the next section). That could be in the interest of smaller countries wishing to acquire better access to EC certification and testing, because in the absence of multilateral rules the Community will primarily be interested in negotiating with its largest trading partners, since access to these countries' markets is most important for EC industries. It is not certain, however, whether such a general national treatment rule is able to generate an adequate balance of concessions, because of the different mixtures in various countries between governmental and non-governmental, and central and local certification and testing.[138] In any case, the rule is not included in the revised version of the Standards Code, as taken up in the Draft Final Act.[139]

Agreements providing for mutual recognition

In its memorandum on the global approach to certification and testing the Commission has indicated that the Community is prepared 'to conclude agreements for mutual recognition of tests, reports, certificates and marks'

[136] Art. 1 of Directive 92/53/EEC, modifying Art. 14 of Directive 70/156/EEC (n. 45).

[137] *The Effects of Greater Economic Integration within the European Community on the United States: First Follow-up Report* (n. 31), p. 6/26. Such a national treatment rule does not yet form part of the Standards Code, which only provides for non-discrimination towards foreign *products*, and not towards foreign *test laboratories*, cf. Arts. 5.1 and 5.2.

[138] The US system, for example, is entirely different from that of the Community, see Saunders, *infra* n. 158.

[139] See n. 30. According to Art. 6.1, 'Parties shall ensure, whenever possible, that results of conformity assessment procedures in other Parties are accepted, even when those procedures differ from their own, provided they are satisfied that those procedures offer an assurance of conformity with applicable technical regulations or standards equivalent to their own procedures.' However, '[i]t is recognized that prior consultations may be necessary in order to arrive at a mutually satisfactory understanding...' (see also *infra*, n. 156).

with third countries.[140] This suggestion was confirmed by the Council in its resolution on the global approach, in which the Council asked the Commission to submit as soon as possible recommendations for detailed negotiating directives.[141] In September 1992, the Council gave the Commission a formal mandate to start negotiations. Countries which are mentioned as candidates are the USA, Canada, Australia, and New Zealand.[142] Talks with the USA started in October 1992. Three aspects of such agreements need to be commented upon. First the Community's competence, secondly their relationship with existing agreements regarding mutual recognition concluded by the Member States with a number of third countries, and finally their possible content.

As regards the Community's competence, the Commission is of the view that

[i]nternational agreements between governments on mutual recognition of test reports or certificates, although they seek to ensure that the public policy objectives of technical legislation are achieved, are primarily intended to promote international trade, and therefore are a matter of common commercial policy under Article 113 of the Treaty.[143]

The Council has subscribed to this view,[144] which therefore seems to be generally accepted. Indeed, there can be little doubt that a present-day interpretation of the concept of commercial policy (which, as the Court of Justice has emphasized, is the only valid interpretation)[145] includes the kind of mutual recognition agreements envisaged by the Community.[146] Undoubtedly, the principal aim of such agreements is to facilitate international trade by eliminating an important non-tariff barrier to trade.

The commercial policy qualification may become somewhat less certain if the said agreements were also to provide for mutual recognition of technical regulations and standards as such, and not merely of certification and testing. The ingredients of non-commercial policies (protection of public health, of the environment, of the consumer, etc.) would then be more prominent. Nevertheless, mutual recognition is, as the Community's experience reveals, essentially a trade-promoting technique. All agreements involving mutual recognition in the area of technical regulations and standards may therefore be regarded as pertaining to commercial policy.

[140] OJ C 267/26 of 19 Oct. 1989. See also Farr, *supra* n. 9, ch. 8.
[141] Council Resolution on a global approach to conformity assessment, OJ C 10/1–2 of 16 Jan. 1990.
[142] See EC Council, 'Communication à la Presse 8634/92 (Presse 160)' and the speech by Vice-President Andriessen (n. 108), p. 5.
[143] OJ C 267/27 of 19 Oct. 1989.
[144] See n. 141.   [145] See Ch. 1, p. 21.
[146] E. L. M. Völker, 'Technical Regulations and Standards and Commercial Policy', *supra* n. 61, p. 307.

Even if one were to dismiss the commercial policy qualification, the Community would still retain the exclusive competence to conclude agreements for mutual recognition of certification and testing, in so far as these agreements relate to harmonized technical regulations. That follows from the implied powers doctrine, inaugurated by the *AETR* judgment.[147] Whatever the difficulties associated with the interpretation of the implied powers rule, it is beyond doubt that agreements with third countries relating to certification and testing of products subject to common rules would 'affect' these rules, and therefore would have to be concluded by the Community.

A question closely related to competence concerns the impact of the Community's competence and of future agreements negotiated by the Community, on existing agreements providing for mutual recognition of certification and testing, concluded by individual Member States with third countries.[148] Analysis of this question reveals one angle of the Community's competence claim which has not yet been mentioned. The Community has the exclusive competence to conduct commercial policy, meaning that the Member States cannot lawfully enter into agreements relating to commercial policy with third countries. Applied to the field of certification and testing, this raises no problems for those products which are regulated at Community level. It is logical that the Member States cannot, for example, conclude agreements providing for mutual recognition of conformity assessment with respect to the safety of machines, because there is a directive on this matter.[149] If there are to be agreements with third countries in this area, such agreements should bind the Community as a whole, because the rules are common. If one or more Member States have concluded a mutual recognition agreement pertaining to machines before the common rules were adopted, the provisions of Article 234, paragraph 2 of the EC Treaty, apply: the Member States concerned should eliminate the incompatibilities with the new common rules.[150] In practice, this may mean that the existing agreements would have to be terminated.[151] However, what about products that are not regulated at Community level? Clearly, this means that the Member States continue to be entitled to adopt or modify a technical regulation of their own. Yet if one looks at relations with third countries, by virtue of the Community's exclusive competence to conduct commercial policy the Member States would not be allowed to conclude agreements on mutual recognition of testing conformity with such a regulation. That is not a very satisfactory result. Why, if a Member State is

---

[147] See Ch. 1, p. 35–6.
[148] A number of such agreements exist with the USA, see *The Effects of Greater Economic Integration within the European Community on the United States: First Follow-up Report* (n. 31), p. 17/9–10.
[149] See n. 12.   [150] See Ch. 3, p. 100.
[151] That would be the case if the harmonization by the Community is total, meaning that it leaves no room for divergent national technical regulations.

entitled to adopt a technical regulation, would it not be entitled to conclude an international agreement relating to this regulation?

This result can be avoided, though, without giving up the view that agreements on mutual recognition come under the commercial policy heading. The exclusive character of the Community's commercial policy competence does not mean that all national measures in this area are invalid. The Court has acknowledged that such measures remain possible, provided that there is a specific Community authorization.[152] Thus, the Council could authorize a Member State to uphold an existing agreement on mutual recognition, or to enter into a new one. It must be added that supervision by the Community of such agreements would not be unwelcome.[153] One thing which the Council would have to check would be the relationship between the mutual recognition system of the agreement and the application of the technical regulation to intra-Community trade. Thus, questions which would need to be clarified are:

- Can a third-country producer benefiting from the agreement with respect to his exports to the Member State in question also invoke this benefit in intra-Community trade, combining it with the mutual recognition rule of Article 30 of the EC Treaty?
- Does the third country in question not receive a more favourable treatment than other Member States?[154]
- Is some form of Community action relating to the products concerned (harmonization, conclusion of an agreement with third countries, etc.) necessary or not?

The existence of a fully-fledged single market certainly warrants such Community supervision, because mutual recognition agreements, even if concluded by just one Member State, determine the access of third-country products to this market.

The exact content of mutual recognition agreements regarding certification and testing, concluded by the Community, will depend on the outcome of negotiations. Nevertheless, the Community's institutions have already made known some of their views on the matter. In its memorandum on the global approach, the Commission has indicated that three conditions would need to be met.[155] First, the technical competence of the non-Community partner would have to be adequate, meaning that 'tests or inspections carried out by a non-Community body will [have to] offer the same guarantees as those located in the Community'. Secondly, the mutual benefits flowing from the agreement would have to be equivalent and guaranteed in an identical manner, so that the

---

[152] Ch. 5, p. 150.

[153] Compare with Decision 69/494, OJ English Special edn. (1969), 603, on the supervision of 'traditional' commercial agreements between Member States and third countries.

[154] Such more favourable treatment would probably be inconsistent with Community law, see Bourgeois, *supra* n. 18, p. 30.

[155] C 267/26 of 19 Oct. 1989.

practical effects in terms of ease of market access are the same for both sides. Thirdly, the agreement would have to be limited to the activities of specifically designated bodies, excluding automatic extension to third parties by further agreements on mutual recognition. These conditions have been endorsed by the Council.[156]

Although these conditions (especially the second one, concerning reciprocity) appear to be legitimate, there are already indications that they may pose problems. It has been reported that the US authorities are of the view that EC testing laboratories are already granted national treatment in the United States, and that, consequently, US labs should also receive such treatment in the Community, without any further concessions.[157] Next to this fundamental objection, there also appear to be practical problems, not least because there is no single unified institutional mechanism in the United States which assesses the competence of laboratories, and because there are differences between the Community and the USA in which products are regulated and whether products are regulated at the level of central or local government.[158]

Such difficulties can only be compounded if the Community were to negotiate with various third countries. The result could be a network of different agreements which would be difficult to manage and which would not be transparent for companies. In such circumstances, multilateral rules would be preferable.

Conclusions

This chapter shows the complexity, in legal terms, of efforts aimed at eliminating the barrier-to-trade aspects of technical regulations and standards. There are in this field no magic formulas. The road towards a global system ensuring that all barriers are eliminated, or at least minimized, is a long one.

[156] See the resolution mentioned in n. 141. In *The Effects of Greater Economic Integration within the European Community on the United States: First Follow-up Report* (n. 31), at p. 6/28, it is suggested that the Council's resolution reflects a more liberal approach than the Commission's memorandum. It is difficult to detect such nuances in the various wordings, though. Compare also with Art. 6.1 of the revised Standards Code (n. 30), recognizing that mutual recognition agreements regarding conformity assessment may require 'a mutually satisfactory understanding regarding, in particular: (a) adequate and enduring technical competence of the relevant conformity assessment bodies in the exporting Party, so that confidence in the continued reliability of their conformity assessment results can exist; in this regard, verified compliance, for instance through accreditation, with relevant guides or recommendations issued by international standardizing bodies shall be taken into account as an indication of adequate technical competence; (b) limitation of the acceptance of conformity assessment results to those produced by designated bodies in the exporting Party.'

[157] *The Effects of Greater Economic Integration within the European Community on the United States: First Follow-up Report* (n. 31), p. 6/27.

[158] Ibid.; Mary Saunders, 'Can the U.S. Move to a Centralised Standards and Conformity Assessment System?', paper presented at the conference 'Reconciling Regulation and Free Trade' (see n. 2), p. 4.

The chapter also shows, perhaps more than any other, the fundamental approach of non-discrimination towards the definition of the external dimension of the internal market programme. Indeed, in spite of certain frictions which in this field are almost unavoidable, the Community has made every effort to ensure that its policies do not discriminate against imports from third countries, and it is at the forefront of multilateral policy-making. Its internal experience is of great value in this respect, especially the operation of the mutual recognition rule within the Community, and its relation to harmonization of technical regulations. One could qualify this experience, which in the case of the new approach is certainly still subject to evolution, as a possible test-bed for multilateral efforts directed at liberalization. This test-bed function of the completion of the internal market can also be found in other policy areas.[159]

[159] Cf. Ch. 11, pp. 368–72.

9

Public Procurement

Introduction

Governments are, in all their branches, important buyers of goods and services. It has been calculated that within the Community public procurement amounts to 15 per cent of GDP.[1] At the same time, there are strong indications that governments continue, in this field, to use their purchasing power in order to favour domestic undertakings, often creating so-called national champions, and thus to discriminate against imports. In spite of the existence of a common market within the Community since the end of the transitional period (1970), entailing free movement of goods and services, this observation is equally valid for the procurement policies of the Member States.[2] One need not be an accomplished economist to realize that such discriminatory policies generate a significant 'cost of non-Europe'. The fact that domestic undertakings are being preferred as government suppliers, to the detriment of lower-cost imports, increases government spending. It leads, moreover, to a partitioning of the markets, most prevalent in those sectors in which public procurement is dominant.[3] Conversely, the economic benefits induced by opening up public procurement markets have been indexed as follows:[4]

- A static effect, resulting from buying from the cheapest source, and consisting of public savings.

---

[1] 'Public Procurement in the Excluded Sectors', *Bull. EC*, Supplement 6/88, p. 6. For a detailed study of the volume of public-sector procurement, see 'The "Cost of Non-Europe" in Public-Sector Procurement', in *Research on the 'Cost of Non-Europe'*, Basic Findings, Vol. v, Part A (Luxembourg: Office for Official Publications of the EC, for the Commission, 1988), 183–251.

[2] Cf. the Commission's White Paper on completing the internal market, COM (85) 310 final, paras. 81–7. The size of these discriminations becomes apparent if one compares the general level of imports in a Member State with import penetration in the field of public procurement. In Belgium, for example, the overall percentage of imports compared with internal demand was 43 in 1985, whereas imports in public purchasing accounted merely for 2.6%. Data for other Member States show comparable ratios, see 'Public Procurement in the Excluded Sectors', *supra* n. 1, pp. 7 and 12.

[3] Such as telecommunications, to mention only the most important example. For a more sophisticated analysis of the costs resulting from discriminatory procurement policies, see D. L. McLachlan, 'Discriminatory Public Procurement, Economic Integration and the Role of Bureaucracy', 23 *JCMS* (1985), 4: 359–61.

[4] 'Public Procurement in the Excluded Sectors', *supra* n. 1, p. 7, and 'The "Cost of Non-Europe" in Public-Sector Procurement', *supra* n. 1, p. 9.

- A competitive effect, namely downward pressure on prices because of stronger competition.
- A restructuring effect, caused by increased competition, and leading to economies of scale.

Estimates of the total economies that could result from such opening up are in the range of 0.6 per cent of Community GDP.[5] It is not surprising, therefore, that the Community's institutions have often stated that action in this field is vital for achieving a genuine single market.[6]

The non-existence in 1985, when the internal market programme was devised, of a single market in public procurement was not due to a lack of legal instruments. All discriminatory procurement practices operated by the Member States are clearly caught by the basic rules of the EC Treaty on free movement, i.e. Article 30 regarding goods, Article 52 regarding establishment, Article 59 regarding services.[7] Moreover, in order to clarify the application of these provisions to public contracts the Council had in the course of the 1970s adopted a number of directives, laying down common rules aimed at eliminating discrimination.[8] However, it appeared that these various instruments were largely ineffective with regard to opening up procurement practices. Quite a number of reasons for this ineffectiveness have been put forward.[9] The directives were inadequate because they were not strict and precise enough with respect to such issues as information and award procedures and the use of standards, and also because a number of important sectors were excluded (namely water, energy, transport, and telecommunications). Moreover, national authorities did not adequately implement and enforce these directives, and enterprises largely abstained from trying to win contracts outside their domestic market because they considered it to be too difficult, in the absence, among other things, of effective national procedures for obtaining

[5] 'Public Procurement in the Excluded Sectors', *supra* n. 1, p. 9. Compare with 'The "Cost of Non-Europe" in Public-Sector Procurement', *supra* n. 1, p. 54, estimating total savings around half a per cent of GDP.

[6] T. L. Margue, 'L'Ouverture des marchés publics dans la Communauté', *RMUE* (1991), 2: 144–5.

[7] For an application of Art. 30 to public procurement, see Case 45/87, *Commission* v. *Ireland*, [1988] ECR 4929. As regards Article 59, see Case 76/81, *Transporoute* v. *Minister for Public Works*, [1982] ECR 417 and Case C-113/89, *Rush Portuguesa*, [1990] ECR I-1417. Cf. e.g. T. L. Margue, *supra* n. 6, pp. 149–52; Friedl Weiss, 'The Law of Public Procurement in EFTA and the EEC: The Legal Framework and its Implementation' F. G. Jacobs (ed.), 7 *Yearbook of European Law* (1987) (Oxford: Clarendon Press, 1988), 85–7 and 'Public Procurement in the EEC: Public Supply Contracts', 13 *ELR* (1988), 4: 319–20..

[8] Directive 70/32, OJ L 13/1 of 19 Jan. 1970; Directive 71/304 concerning the abolition of restrictions on freedom to provide services in respect of public work contracts and on the award of public works contracts to contractors acting through agencies or branches, OJ L 185/1 of 16 Aug. 1971; Directive 71/305 concerning the co-ordination of procedures for the award of public works contracts, OJ L 185/5 of 16 Aug. 1971; Directive 77/62 co-ordinating procedures for the award of public supply contracts, OJ L 13/1 of 15 Jan. 1977.

[9] See especially T. L. Margue, *supra* n. 6, pp. 158–61.

redress in cases of discrimination. Lastly, the Commission did not have at its disposal sufficient means for controlling the implementation of the directives by public purchasers.

The internal market programme is aimed at addressing these problems.[10] It involves legislative action in four different fields. First, the two existing directives on public works and public supplies were redrafted, with a view to improving transparency and tightening the rules.[11] Secondly, a directive was adopted regarding the application of review procedures to the award of public contracts,[12] the objective being to make it easier for companies to obtain redress in cases of infringement. Thirdly, there are now specific common rules for the previously excluded sectors, laid down in the so-called Utilities Directive.[13] And lastly, provisions were adopted regarding the extension of procurement disciplines to services (other than public works).[14]

A thorough examination of this set of new directives would go beyond the scope of the present study, and has been carried out elsewhere.[15] This chapter analyses the external dimension of the Community's policy in the field of public procurement, that is the impact of the newly adopted rules on imports from third countries, as well as on tenders submitted by firms located outside the Community. However, in order to understand this impact it is useful first to explore how the 'old' directives on public works and public supplies related

[10] See the White Paper, *supra* n. 2, paras. 84–7.

[11] See Directive 88/295 amending Directive 77/62 relating to the co-ordination of procedures on the award of public supply contracts, OJ L 127/1 of 20 May 1989, and Directive 89/440 amending Directive 71/305 concerning co-ordination of procedures for the award of public works contracts, OJ L 210/1 of 21 July 1989. A new, codified version of both directives has recently been issued, see Directive 93/36 co-ordinating procedures for the award of public supply contracts, OJ L 199/1 of 9 Aug. 1993; Directive 93/37 concerning the co-ordination of procedures for the award of public works contracts, OJ L 199/54 of 9 Aug. 1993.

[12] Directive 89/665 on the co-ordination of the laws, regulations, and administrative provisions relating to the application of review procedures to the award of public supply and public works contracts, OJ L 395/33 of 30 Dec. 1989.

[13] Directive 90/351 on the procurement procedures of entities operating in the water, energy, transport, and telecommunications sectors, OJ L 297/1 of 29 Oct. 1990, now replaced by a new, codified version (including services), see Directive 93/38 co-ordinating the procurement procedures of entities operating in the water, energy, transport, and telecommunications sectors, OJ L 199/84 of 9 Aug. 1993.

[14] Directive 92/50 relating to the co-ordination of procedures for the award of public service contracts, OJ L 209/1 of 24 July 1992 and Directive 93/38, *supra* n. 13.

[15] See e.g. T. L. Margue, 'L'Ouverture des marchés publics dans la Communauté', *RMUE* (1991), 2: 143–79, 3: 177–221, 4: 111–73; Jean-Pierre Gohon, *Les marchés publics européens*, Que sais-je No. 2625 (Paris: Presses universitaires de France, 1991); Michael Erhart, 'Öffentliches Auftragswesen', in M. Röttinger and C. Weyringer (eds.), *Handbuch der europäischen Integration* (Vienna: Manzsche Verlags- und Universitätsbuchhandlung, 1991), 735–57; N. F. Spencer Chapman and C. Grandjean, *The Construction Industry and the European Community* (Oxford: BSP Professional Books, 1991), 70–114; Alfonso Mattera, *Le marché unique européen*, 2nd edn. (Paris: Jupiter, 1990), 362–95; Friedl Weiss, 'Public Procurement in the EEC: Public Supply Contracts', *supra* n. 7, pp. 318–34 and 'The Law of Public Procurement in EFTA and the EEC: The Legal Framework and its Implementation', *supra* n. 7, pp. 83–107; the various articles in 'Les Marchés publics et la Communauté européenne', *RMC* (1989), 332: 592–664 and Maurice-André Flamme and Philippe Flamme, 'Vers l'Europe des marchés publics?', *RMC* (1988), 320: 455–79.

to trade with third countries, what action has been taken at multilateral level (in the GATT), and in what way these directives have been amended in the course of the internal market programme. That is the subject of the next section. Subsequently the 'external' provisions of the Utilities Directive are examined. The following section does the same as regards services contracts. The final section takes a (horizontal) look at the provisions on technical specifications and standards in the various directives.

The External Dimension of the Directives on Public Supplies and Public Works

The original public works and public supplies directives[16]

When reading the provisions of the original public works and public supplies directives, one might at first glance conclude that there was no external dimension. These instruments aimed at fully attaining the free intra-Community movement of goods and services in the field of public procurement.[17] Although this was not expressly stated, it was obvious that they only applied to tenders submitted by companies established in the Community.[18] Neither was any mention made of goods and services originating outside the Community, with the small but important exception of one recital of the public supplies directive, stating that 'access to public supply contracts for products originating in countries other than the Member States is the subject of the Council resolution of 21 December 1976 and of the Commission statement of 21 December 1976'.[19] This made it clear that the directive did not apply to imports from third countries. At the same time, however, the said resolution and statement contained the views of the Council and the Commission on the relationship between opening up public procurement within the Community and trade with third countries. In the resolution it was acknowledged that the Community should determine the conditions under which public supply contracts can be awarded to tenders consisting of goods originating in third countries. These conditions should be in the nature of safeguarding the interests of Community producers, by ensuring reciprocity. However, until such an external regime was adopted, the Member States remained free to take measures of commercial policy in the field of public supply contracts, with

---

[16] Directives 71/305 and 77/62, *supra* n. 11.

[17] See the respective preambles.

[18] See for example Art. 21 of the original version of Directive 77/62, stating that '[a]ny supplier wishing to take part in a public supply contract may be requested to prove his enrolment in the professional or trade register under the conditions laid down by the laws of the Community country in which he is established'. See also Friedl Weiss, 'The Law of Public Procurement in EFTA and the EEC: The Legal Framework and its Implementation', *supra* n. 7, p. 91.

[19] See OJ L 13/1 of 15 Jan. 1977; Council Resolution concerning access to Community public supply contracts for products originating in non-Member countries, OJ C 11/1 of 15 Jan. 1977; Commission Statement concerning Art. 115, EEC Treaty, OJ C 11/2 of 15 Jan. 1977.

regard to products or categories of products originating in third countries. In addition, the Council took note of the fact that Article 115 of the EC Treaty, allowed the adoption of protective measures in case the execution of those national measures would be obstructed by deflection of trade.[20] This point is elaborated in the Commission's statement. It is said there that the execution of national commercial policy measures might run into difficulties in the case of tenders consisting of goods originating in third countries but put into free circulation in the Community. The Commission made known that it intended to allow the Member States, on the basis of Article 115, to exclude such tenders in all cases where equivalent tenders, but consisting of products directly imported from third countries, were the subject of exclusion measures enforced by the Member States. The Commission clarified, furthermore, that its authorization would only produce its effects at the moment when tenders were examined, and not at the moment of importation, and that it therefore would not require any controls or limitations at intra-Community borders, and would not affect the import regimes regarding third-country products.

These views and policy statements call for some comments. It is noteworthy, first of all, that already in 1976 the Council and the Commission recognized in unison that to determine the conditions under which public procurement is opened up for third-country products is a matter of commercial policy. It follows, although not explicitly confirmed, that by virtue of Article 113, EC Treaty, the Community has the exclusive competence to set these conditions. This probably explains the first point of the Council's resolution, i.e. the recognition, in the absence of a Community policy, of the Member States' power to take commercial policy measures in the field of public supply contracts. As the Court decided in *Donckerwolcke*,[21] national commercial policy measures are only permissible if there is a specific authorization by the Council.

This recognition of the commercial policy character of the external dimension of policies regarding public supply contracts is to be supported. It is in line with the rule-of-reason approach to the concept of commercial policy developed by Timmermans, as set out and defended above.[22] To determine specific conditions for foreign access to public contracts is clearly a measure of commercial policy.[23] Perhaps more questionable is whether the Council's resolution could be regarded as a sufficiently specific authorization of the

---

[20] On Art. 115, see *supra* Ch. 5, p. 170–84.

[21] Case 41/76, [1976] ECR 1921, at 1937.

[22] Ch. 1, pp. 29–31.

[23] It is a measure which, if applied to intra-Community trade, comes squarely within the scope of the interdiction of Art. 30 of the EC Treaty, because it discriminates against imports. Under the rule-of-reason approach, such a measure, if applied to trade with third countries, comes within the Community's exclusive competence regarding the pursuit of commercial policy, cf. Christiaan W. A. Timmermans, 'La libre circulation des marchandises et la politique commerciale commune', in P. Demaret (ed.), *Relations extérieures de la Communauté européenne et marché intérieur: aspects juridiques et fonctionnels* (Brugge: Story-Scientia, 1988), 94–9.

Member States' powers to take measures themselves, in line with the *Donckerwolcke* doctrine. One would at least have expected that some mechanism would have been created for reviewing national policies. However, in view of the latitude furnished by the *Bulk Oil* judgment, it is difficult to answer this question definitely.[24] In any case this does not take away the fact that the Community was and is required, under the EC Treaty, to adopt a comprehensive policy of its own. To what extent the Community has lived up to this requirement is examined below.

Secondly, there is the reference to Article 115. Again this is in line with *Donckerwolcke*, where the Court decided that, as regards free movement, goods imported from third countries and put into free circulation are 'definitively and wholly assimilated to products originating in Member States'.[25] Since the Community's policy in the field of public supply contracts is aimed at ensuring precisely such free movement, it is simply a matter of mere logic that this policy also applies to third-country products which are in free circulation.[26] However, if Article 115 had not been available, this rule of assimilation would have provided an irreparable loophole in the national powers which the Council's resolution recognized. In order to circumvent national measures excluding tenders consisting of third-country products, it would have been sufficient first to import these products in another Member State, in which case they benefit from the free movement of goods. To put it in more practical terms, third-country firms would only have needed to set up one or two subsidiaries in the Community, importing goods produced abroad, and subsequently invoking the free movement of goods in order to submit public supply tenders in the various Member States.[27]

The GATT Agreement on Government Procurement

The above-mentioned resolution alluded to ongoing negotiations within the GATT and OECD frameworks as an avenue to determining at Community level the conditions for third-country access to public contracts. Indeed, during the Tokyo Round of GATT multilateral trade negotiations public (or rather, in that context, government) procurement figured high on the agenda, resulting in the adoption of an Agreement on Government Procurement

---

[24] Case 174/84, [1986] ECR 559, at 587, see Ch. 5, p. 151. In this judgment, the Court accepted that the Council could, in 1969, exclude petroleum products from the scope of the common rules on exports without ever reviewing this policy afterwards, at least not until the time of the judgment.

[25] [1976] ECR 1935. This is extensively dealt with in Ch. 8, p. 271 *et seq.*

[26] This also appears from Directive 70/32, *supra* n. 8.

[27] That in practice Art. 115 does not seem to have been applied in this regard, and that no such problems were signalled may be due to the fact that the discussed directives did not lead to a real opening-up of public procurement.

(commonly called Government Procurement Code).[28] The Community took part in these negotiations, and signed and concluded the Code, on the basis of Article 113, EC Treaty.[29]

The provisions of the Code apply to all procurement of products, above a certain contract threshold, by a number of specifically designated entities in the territories of the various Parties (Article I).[30] The main obligations concern national treatment and non-discrimination (Article II). Parties shall provide to the products and suppliers of other Parties offering products originating within the customs territories of the Parties, treatment no less favourable than that accorded to domestic products and suppliers (national treatment), and than that accorded to products and suppliers of any other Party (most-favoured-nation treatment). Parties shall ensure that their entities do not treat a locally established supplier less favourably than another locally established supplier on the basis of degree of foreign affiliation or ownership. They shall also ensure that their entities do not discriminate against locally established suppliers on the basis of the country of production of the good being supplied. Furthermore, the Code contains provisions on special and differential treatment for developing countries (Article III), on technical specifications (Article IV), on tendering procedures (Article V), on information and review (Article VI), on enforcement of obligations (Article VII), and on exceptions (Article VIII).

At the time of adoption, the Code was at the same time more restrictive as well as more liberal than the Community's internal rules.[31] More restrictive because the list of entities to which it applies in the Community is shorter than the various national authorities that are subject to the public supplies directive. More liberal on the other hand, because the Code's threshold was lower than that of the directive and the provisions on non-discrimination were more strict.[32] However, as the Code was concluded by the Community as such, its provisions did not apply to 'internal' public procurement, that is tenders submitted in a Member State by companies established in the Community and consisting of products originating in the Community—public procurement between the Member States, to put it shortly. In so far as the Code's provisions were more liberal than those of the directive, this would have led to the

---

[28] *BISD*, 26 S., pp. 33–55, amended in 1987–8, see *BISD*, 35 S., p. 365.

[29] See Council Decision 80/272, OJ L 71/44 of 17 Mar. 1980.

[30] Procurement of products includes purchase, lease, rental, or hire-purchase, with or without an option to buy, as well as services incidental to the supply of products. The threshold is SDR 130,000. The entities covered are listed in Annex I of the Agreement.

[31] i.e. Directive 77/62 regarding public supply contracts, *supra* n. 11. Public works are not covered by the Code.

[32] See Jacques H. J. Bourgeois, 'The Tokyo Round Agreements on Technical Barriers and on Government Procurement in International and EEC Perspective', 19 *CML Rev.* (1982), 1: 30; Thiébaut Flory, 'Les marchés de fournitures et les accords GATT', *RMC* (1989), 332: 655–6; Friedl Weiss, 'Public Procurement in the EEC: Public Supply Contracts', *supra* n. 7, p. 325.

paradoxical result that non-Community Parties to the Code would have been entitled to more favourable treatment, in some respects, than other Member States. This result was avoided by supplementing the public supplies directive with some new provisions, aimed at ensuring that intra-Community public procurement was subject to as favourable treatment as procurement in the relations with the other Parties to the Code.[33]

To implement the Code as such, however, the Community took no specific measures other than its conclusion. From a purely legal point of view, admittedly, this was sufficient. Agreements concluded by the Community are part of the Community's legal order, and are binding upon the Community institutions as well as the Member States.[34] It was therefore left to the Member States to ensure such implementation 'on the field'.[35] There are some drawbacks to this approach, however. One of these is that there are two different sets of rules, the first (the directive) applying to 'internal' and the second (the Code) to 'external' public procurement. That does probably not enhance consistency and may make it more difficult to supervise procurement practices. Another drawback may be that it is not certain whether the provisions of the Code have direct effect, in other words whether they can be enforced by the national judiciaries.[36] If the Community had implemented the Code by way of a directive, it would probably have been easier to establish such direct effect, which would enable private companies to enforce their rights. Moreover, as the conclusion of the Code was a measure of commercial policy, coming within the scope of the Community's exclusive competence, the question can be put whether the Community ought not to have taken the necessary implementing measures itself.

The Code determines the conditions for third-country access to public contracts in the Community, as envisaged in the 1976 Council resolution. However, it does so only to a limited extent: it applies only to trade with the Parties to the Code, to the government entities specifically designated, to public purchases and not public works, and to contracts above a certain threshold. The conclusion of the Code by the Community does therefore not amount to a comprehensive external policy. This was recognized in a second Council resolution, dating back from 22 July 1980.[37] Again the Council acknowledged that the Member States could continue to take commercial policy measures with regard to public supply contracts, in so far as such measures did not come within the scope of the Code. Again reference was made to Article 115. And again it was decided that these national measures should be gradually co-ordinated and unified.

---

[33] See Directive 80/767, OJ L 215/1 of 18 Aug. 1980.

[34] Cf. Bourgeois, *supra* n. 32, p. 29.

[35] Perhaps this was a first token of subsidiarity.

[36] As is well known, the Court of Justice has decided that the GATT itself has no direct effect, see Joined Cases 21–24/72, *International Fruit Company*, [1972] ECR 1219.

[37] OJ C 211/2 of 19 Aug. 1980.

The amendments to the public supplies and public works directives

In view of what precedes, one would have expected that the Community would have used the opportunity of the internal market programme, which led to a major revision of the public works and public supplies directives, to elaborate a comprehensive external policy also. That has unfortunately not been the case. The amended directives contain as little on external policies as the original ones.[38] These policies are therefore still left to the individual Member States, and they are not subject to any review mechanism at Community level. Moreover, to my knowledge there have been no authorizations for applying Article 115 in the field of public supplies, at least not in recent years. Whether this means that no tenders consisting of goods that are in free circulation have been excluded by the Member States, or simply that the national authorities do not bother to ask for such authorization, is unknown. Clearly, there is an utter lack of transparency in this field.

However, the fact that no external regime has been worked out for public works and public supply contracts does not mean that there is no external dimension at all to the internal market programme in the area of public procurement. Such a dimension is apparent in other directives adopted by the Council, in the first place the Utilities Directive.

The Utilities Directive and its Community Preference Clause

The directive relates to procurement procedures of entities operating in the water, energy, transport, and telecommunications sectors, which were excluded from the scope of the public works and public supplies directives, as well as from the scope of the Government Procurement Code.[39] As was the case with previous directives, it is aimed at ensuring full free movement of goods and services[40] by providing for detailed disciplines for the procurement practices of the said entities. From an economic point of view, procurement in these sectors is important.[41] That is perhaps especially the case for telecommunications, large segments of which have traditionally been closed off from competition. For opening up these segments, the directive is crucial.[42]

The main reason why the entities operating in these sectors were not covered by the previous directives was that in some cases they were governed by private

---

[38] See Directive 88/295, amending Directive 77/62, *supra* n. 11, and Directive 89/440, amending Directive 71/305, *supra* n. 11.

[39] Directive 90/351, now replaced by Directive 93/38, *supra* n. 13. References below are to Directive 90/531.

[40] As regards services, however, only works contracts were covered by the directive, cf. Arts. 1 (3) and 4 (1). Other services than works are the subject of Directive 93/38, *supra* n. 13.

[41] T. L. Margue, *supra* n. 6, 3: 193–4. For an overview of procurement in these sectors, see 'Public Procurement in the Excluded Sectors', *supra* n. 1, pp. 22–53.

[42] Cf. Reinhard Schulte-Braucks, 'L'ouverture des marchés publics des télécommunications', *RMC* (1989), 332: 649–50.

and not by public law. Accordingly, it is one of the principal features of the Utilities Directive that it covers not only public authorities, but also undertakings controlled by these authorities (public undertakings), as well as entities operating on the basis of special or exclusive rights.[43]

There is undoubtedly an element of industrial policy present in the directive. It is feared that without the creation of a market of a continental scale, European industries will continue to lag behind those of the United States and Japan, in particular in so far as high-technology products are concerned. Again telecommunications is perhaps the outstanding example. Hence, one of the aims of opening up procurement practices is to create a much larger market with a view to improving the competitive position of Community industries.[44] This brings us to the directive's external dimension. At the centre is the provision on Community preference, i.e. Article 29 of the directive,[45] discussed below.

Background

In contrast with some of its other internal-market related proposals, the Commission made great efforts, when publishing its proposals on public procurement in the excluded sectors, carefully and extensively to formulate its views on which external policy ought to be pursued.[46] These views therefore deserve to be set out at some length.

The Commission first observes that the Community 'has a considerable measure of choice as to how far it extends the direct benefits of open procurement to third-country partners'.[47] It could, on the one hand, adopt a 'fortress Europe' policy, offering the advantage that industrial restructuring could take place without the threat of increased third-country competition. However, such a policy would also have serious disadvantages. There would be some loss of efficiency in the absence of foreign competition. In a number of product areas, it would amount to cutting off traditional suppliers, resulting in

[43] See Arts. 1 (1) and (2) and 2 (1).

[44] One of the effects of opening up public procurement, revealed by the research on the cost of non-Europe, is an external one: 'the more effective use of R&D and marketing effort may have a profound effect, not just on innovation and growth, but on the survival of some sectors of European industry. In key high technology sectors such as computers, telecommunications, aerospace, transport equipment and defence goods the historical fragmentation of European industry into national preserves has made it increasingly uncompetitive, both at home and in world markets. Even though imports from outside the EC are likely to increase in the short term, major restructuring and increased competition can bring costs down and enable European industry to remain viable, compete and possibly gain new export markets in the long term', see 'The "Cost of Non-Europe" in Public-Sector Procurement', *supra* n. 1, p. 46.

[45] Now Art. 36 of Directive 93/38, *supra* n. 13.

[46] See 'Public Procurement in the Excluded Sectors', *supra* n. 1, pp. 11–12, 59–60, and 70–1. This compares favourably with, for example, the proposal for a Second Banking Directive, COM (87) 715 final (see Ch. 2, p. 50) and with the new approach to technical regulations and standards (Ch. 8).

[47] 'Public Procurement in the Excluded Sectors', *supra* n. 1, p. 11.

economic and technological losses. Lastly, such a fortress Europe policy would not be likely to facilitate access to extra-Community markets for Community companies. On the other hand, not taking any measures to defend Community interests would create substantial opportunities for third-country suppliers, who already benefit from the Community's very liberal policy on establishment.

[T]hird-country suppliers with subsidiaries established in the Community ... would be well placed to exploit the single market, without the Community acquiring corresponding access to foreign markets. Such a policy ... could weaken the position of Community producers relative to their third-country competitors at world level.[48]

The logical conclusion was that the Community should steer a middle course. The Commission suggested that

[i]f the Community were to opt for a balanced and progressive opening up of public procurement in the excluded sectors to third countries, in the sense of securing concessions from third countries on a basis of mutual access and phasing the opening of its markets, it could hope to be in a position to achieve some of the benefits of internal reorganization before facing the challenge of a more open relationship with third countries.

   At the same time, the existence of possible means of protection of the Community market would constitute a strong position from which to negotiate with the Community's trading partners for mutual access to markets.[49]

Put in other terms, the Community ought to pursue two general objectives.

First, provisions are needed to defend the Community's commercial interests and preserve its negotiating position by making no unilateral concessions but on the contrary creating a positive incentive for third countries to give guarantees of equal access to similar markets. Second, Community producers should, where necessary, be given the necessary time for the industrial adaptation required to meet the objectives of 1992 and the day when reciprocal access is finally agreed.[50]

The first objective can only be fully understood in connection with the ongoing Uruguay Round negotiations which are aimed at extending the scope of and reviewing the Government Procurement Code, among other things. It is obvious that the Commission wished to safeguard the Community's negotiating position, which would have been extremely difficult if the Community had unilaterally extended the benefits of opening up procurement in the excluded sectors to third countries.[51]

   How were these objectives to be translated into a specific legislative proposal? The Commission addressed only the problem of offers made by firms established within the Community, because, it argued, '[s]ituations in which

---

[48] Ibid. 12.   [49] Ibid.   [50] Ibid. 70.   [51] Ibid. 71.

offers are made by firms established entirely outside the Community are in practice relatively rare and, in any case, the directives will simply not apply to them'.[52] Therefore, the proposed regime did not concentrate on the place of establishment of tenderers, but rather on the concept of 'origin of offers'. A number of offers, although submitted by tenderers established in the Community, were to be considered as having their origin outside the Community. That would be the case 'when more than half of the price offered represents the value of products manufactured or services performed outside the Community or a combination thereof'.[53]

The Commission proposed that two rules be applied to such offers. First, the various procurement entities would be entitled to reject such offers (Article 24 (1)). Secondly, in cases of equivalence between a 'non-Community' and a 'Community' offer, the latter would have to be preferred, unless there were technical reasons for not doing so.[54] However, both these rules would only be applied in so far as they do not conflict with the international obligations of the Community or its Member States.[55] Moreover, in the event of a revision of the Government Procurement Code, the Council would decide by a qualified majority that the Article did not apply to offers covered by the Code.[56] Lastly, it is worth mentioning that the Commission, in line with the existing practice, proposed that the directive be adopted on the basis of Article 113 of the EC Treaty (next to Article 100a), making clear that the described preference clause is a measure of commercial policy.

The Commission's proposal on preference was somewhat amended in the course of the legislative process, but its main features remained intact.[57] The most important change relates to the scope of the concept of 'offers having their origin outside the Community'. To determine this services included in the offer will not be taken into account, but only products, by contrast to the Commission's proposal. This amendment, stemming from the Council, was considered acceptable by the European Parliament

[52] Ibid. It has to be recalled here that the establishment of companies inside the Community is easy, which enables third-country companies to set up subsidiaries without much trouble, see Ch. 2, p. 62.

[53] Art. 24 (1). Para. 4 contained further rules on how to determine origin: '(a) the value of products manufactured outside the Community shall include the value of all finished or semi-finished products imported, directly or indirectly, from third countries; (b) the value of services performed outside the Community shall include the value of all activities performed on the territory of third countries that contribute to the rendering of the services of the contract.'

[54] In the sense that acceptance of the 'Community' offer 'would oblige the contracting entity to acquire material having different technical characteristics from existing material which would result in incompatibility or disproportionate technical difficulties in operation and maintenance' (Art. 24 (3)).

[55] Art. 24 (1). This reference may be explained by the fact that a few of the entities covered by the directive also come within the scope of the GATT Government Procurement Code.

[56] Art. 24 (5). The language is more general, but the reference to the Code is obvious.

[57] See Art. 29 of the directive for the definitive text (Art. 36 of Directive 93/38, *supra* n. 13). On the debate within the Council, see Stephen Woolcock, *Market Access Issues in EC–US Relations* (London: Pinter Publishers for the RIIA, 1991), 78–9.

because a very high proportion of the services provided under works contracts are necessarily performed in the Member State where the contracting entity is based, which guarantees that a considerable proportion of the value of the products covered by these contracts is of Community origin.[58]

Furthermore, one amendment clarifies the methods to be employed for determining the origin of products, and another requires that the Commission submits annual reports on the state of international negotiations in the field covered by the directive.

Analysis and comments

The first paragraph of the provision defines its scope:

This Article shall apply to tenders comprising products originating in third countries with which the Community has not concluded, multilaterally or bilaterally, an agreement ensuring comparable and effective access for Community undertakings to the markets of those third countries. It shall be without prejudice to the obligations of the Community or its Member States in respect of third countries.

Two elements are noteworthy. One is that, as proposed by the Commission, the directive does not apply to tenders submitted by companies which are not established in the Community. It may be that, as the Commission has indicated, such tenders do not often occur.[59] Nevertheless, they are not impossible. In view of the fact that to determine the conditions for third-country access to public procurement is a matter of commercial policy, and therefore comes within the Community's exclusive competence, it is difficult to accept that there are no Community rules for such tenders. From a purely legal point of view, it can even be argued that this amounts to full-scale liberalization, because in the absence of a specific authorization by the Council the Member States are no longer entitled to take commercial policy measures themselves.[60] This can be interpreted as meaning that the Member States cannot determine specific conditions for or exclude altogether tenders submitted by third-country companies. Obviously, that is not the desired result.

Secondly, the first paragraph sets out what the Community aims at in international negotiations on liberalization. Community undertakings should acquire 'comparable and effective access' to third-country markets. The terms comparable and effective seem rather tautological here. Can it not be assumed that, where Community undertakings acquire access to other markets,

[58] See the report drawn up by Mr Herman, MEP, Document A 3–129/90 of 23 May 1990, p. 17.
[59] Cf. *supra*, p. 308.
[60] Unless it can be argued that the Council's resolution of 1980, authorizing the Member States to take commercial policy measures with regard to public procurement contracts not covered by the GATT Code, is still applicable.

comparable to the access to the Community's market which third-country undertakings would in the event acquire, there will also be effective market access? Or would the Community itself offer less than effective access?

Perhaps the origin and meaning of the concept of effective market access is the same as that contained in the Second Banking Directive.[61] If that is the case, it points to the Community's desire for not only obtaining formal but also *de facto* access.[62] The reference is of less practical importance than the one in the Second Banking Directive, however, because it is only an objective for negotiations. In effect, it merely states that it can be expected that the Community will only conclude an agreement that guarantees effective access.

The second paragraph contains the rule on rejection of tenders having their origin outside the Community:

Any tender made for the award of a supply contract may be rejected where the proportion of the products originating in third countries, as determined in accordance with Council Regulation (EEC) No 802/68 of 27 June 1968 on the common definition of the concept of the origin of goods ... exceeds 50% of the total value of the products constituting the tender. For the purposes of this Article, software used in the equipment of telecommunications networks shall be considered as products.[63]

The fifth paragraph qualifies this provision in so far as third countries are concerned with which the Community has concluded an agreement within the meaning of the first paragraph (i.e. providing for comparable and effective market access). For the purpose of determining the proportion of non-Community products, those originating in the said third countries shall not be taken into account. An example may illustrate this qualification. Suppose a tender is submitted, consisting of 40 per cent products (by value) of Community origin, 20 per cent originating in third country *X* and 40 per cent in third country *Y*, with which the Community has concluded an agreement within the meaning of the fifth paragraph: such a tender will not be subject to the rejection rule, because the 40 per cent of *Y* will not be taken into account for determining the proportion of products originating in third countries.

A first observation which has to be made in connection with the rejection rule is that it employs the concept of origin of goods, and makes no distinction between products directly imported from third countries and products which are in free circulation within the Community. It is doubtful whether this approach is compatible with the principle of free movement of goods.

[61] See *supra*, Ch. 2, pp. 56–61.

[62] Again Japan may be the prime target. For an overview of Japanese procurement practices, see J. Léonard, 'L'ouverture des marchés publics japonais', *RMC* (1989), 332: 658–60.

[63] Regulation 602/68 has in the meantime been replaced by the Community Customs Code, see OJ L 302/1 of 19 Oct. 1992.

Because of its importance, this question is examined in a separate section below.

Secondly, it is difficult to believe that the rejection rule amounts to a genuinely common external policy. The fate of tenders having their origin outside the Community is decided by the Member States,[64] responsible as they are for implementing the directive. Given the non-committal language of the directive ('[a]ny tender ... *may* be rejected'), this could give rise to divergent interpretations as well as divergent policies regarding such tenders. The question therefore has to be put whether the rejection rule, being, as is generally accepted, a measure of commercial policy, is in keeping with the basic requirement of Article 113, EC Treaty, i.e. that 'the common commercial policy shall be based on uniform principles'. Such uniformity does not appear to be guaranteed in the case of the rejection rule.

It is interesting to consider the consequences of a non-uniform interpretation and application of the rejection rule. The rationale of the uniformity requirement is well known.[65] Without a uniform commercial policy, complementing the common external tariff, deflections of trade are liable to arise. In the case of tenders consisting of third-country products this would mean that such products are first imported in another Member State than the one in which the tender is submitted, with a view to benefiting from the free movement of goods. However, the rejection rule seems also to apply to goods which are in free circulation. Again this brings us to the problem dealt with in the next section, dealing with the compatibility of the rejection rule with the free movement of goods.

Thirdly, it must be said that the exclusion rule appears to be rather cumbersome, based as it is on the origin of products. At face value, there is the neat reference to the basic Council regulation on rules of origin. However, applying these rules is not an easy matter at all, and procurement entities have no experience with them. The relevant regulation contains only a few very broad provisions, the most important of which is Article 24, stating in effect that a product originates in the country where its last substantial transformation has taken place.[66] The difficulties associated with applying this rule to the whole spectrum of existing products, a lot of them highly sophisticated and containing many components produced in various countries, have been analysed

[64] With the exception, that is, of the preference rule in case of equivalent offers, examined hereafter.

[65] See Ch. 5, p. 147.

[66] It provides that '[a] product in the production of which two or more countries were concerned shall be regarded as originating in the country in which the last substantial process or operation that is economically justified was performed, having been carried out in an undertaking equipped for the purpose, and resulting in the manufacture of a new product or representing an important stage of manufacture'. For a number of products more detailed regulations exist, implementing and applying the general rule of Art. 24 (see e.g. Regulation 2071/89 on photocopiers, OJ L 196/34 of 12 July 1989). One can argue that the reference in the Utilities Directive to Regulation 802/68 is at the same time to be interpreted as a reference to these specific regulations.

elsewhere.[67] These difficulties may be illustrated with the example of software, mentioned in the last sentence of the rejection rule. It is said there that for the purpose of determining origin 'software used in the equipment of telecommunication networks shall be considered as products'. One must assume, therefore, that the substantial transformation rule applies when procurement entities have to determine the origin of software.[68] But where does the last substantial transformation of software take place? Is it the country in which the company that has developed the software is established? Is it the country where the decisive intellectual work took place? Or is it, in the case of standardized software, the country where it was copied to diskettes?

Moreover, the exclusion rule does not determine how the term 'product' is to be interpreted. For example, suppose Belgacom, the Belgian telecommunications undertaking, wishes to award a contract for the supply of telephone switching equipment. Is such equipment to be regarded as one product for the purpose of determining origin, or should one also look at the origin of the many individual components (most of them probably also being individual products) of which such an exchange is made up? If the former is correct, Belgacom will be confronted with the difficult question of the origin of an assembled product.[69] If the latter solution is to be preferred, then tenderers will have to supply long lists of components and their origin. That in turn highlights that the application of the exclusion rule is liable to impose a considerable burden on companies tendering for supply contracts in the excluded sectors.

It could be argued, of course, that procurement entities are not obliged to apply the exclusion rule, and that therefore the cumbersome process of determining origin can be avoided. However, that would be overlooking the provisions of the third and fourth paragraphs of Article 29 of the Utilities Directive.

These paragraphs contain a preference rule. It is provided that

where two or more tenders are equivalent in the light of the award criteria defined in Article 27, preference shall be given to the tenders which may not be rejected pursuant

---

[67] See on the Community's practice Edwin Vermulst and Paul Waer, 'European Community Rules of Origin as Commercial Policy Instruments?' *JWT* (1990), 3: 55–99. Rules of origin are now regarded as a possible barrier to trade in themselves, hence their inclusion in the Uruguay Round, cf. the Draft Final Act embodying the results of the Uruguay Round of Multilateral Trade Negotiations, MTN.TNC/W/FA, pp. D.1–14.

[68] There are in Community law no specific rules for determining the origin of software. The explicit inclusion of the latter in the rejection and preference rules of the Utilities Directive may be explained by its importance in the telecommunications sector. It is reported that 70–80% of the total development cost of modern switching equipment relates to software, see 'Public Procurement in the Excluded Sectors', *supra* n. 1, p. 51. Also see Peter F. Cowhey, 'Telecommunications', in G. C. Hufbauer (ed.), *Europe 1992: An American Perspective* (Washington, DC: Brookings Institution, 1990), 199.

[69] On this question, see Case C-26/88, *Brother International* v. *Hauptzollamt Giessen*, [1989] ECR 4253, in which the Court experienced great difficulty in determining the origin of mere electronic typewriters, assembled in Taiwan with components imported from Japan.

to paragraph 2. The prices shall be considered equivalent for the purposes of this Article, if the price difference does not exceed 3%.

Therefore, when a 'Community' and a 'non-Community' tender are equivalent, the 'Community' tender must be preferred. There is, however, an exception to this rule. The 'Community' tender shall not be preferred 'where its acceptance would oblige the contracting entity to acquire material having technical characteristics different from those of existing material, resulting in incompatibility or technical difficulties in operation and maintenance or disproportionate costs'. As a result of this preference rule, procurement entities are obliged to examine the origin of tenders, at least when there are two or more equivalent ones. The concept of equivalence has only been defined in terms of price difference. The price of tenders is not, however, the only criterion on the basis of which contracts can be awarded. Article 27 of the directive, to which Article 29 (3) refers, provides for two criteria between which procurement entities can choose when they award a contract: the most economically advantageous tender and the lowest price.[70] The interpretation of the concept of equivalence in cases in which the former method is chosen is apparently left to the procurement entities. Given the wide range of criteria that can be applied for determining the economically most advantageous offer[71] it is perhaps doubtful whether there will often be two or more equivalent tenders in terms of this criterion.

Furthermore, the difficulties associated with determining the origin of products, described above, apply equally to the preference rule, as does the problem of the relationship with the free movement of goods within the Community.

Lastly, the exception of paragraph 4 is almost self-evident. It ensures that the preference rule does not operate to the disadvantage of the procurement entities by creating unnecessary costs resulting from technical incompatibilities. One would expect that this exception will not often apply, because the procurement entities will normally take care to specify the technical requirements of products subject to tendering when they issue a call for competition.[72]

The last paragraph of Article 29 provides that the Commission shall submit annual reports to the Council on progress in and results of international negotiations in the fields covered by the directive. Finally, '[t]he Council, acting by a qualified majority on a proposal from the Commission, may amend the provisions of this Article in the light of such developments'. As the

---

[70] The most economically advantageous tender involves the application of 'various criteria depending on the contract in question, such as: delivery or completion date, running costs, cost-effectiveness, quality, aesthetic and functional characteristics, technical merit, after-sales service and technical assistance, commitments with regard to spare parts, security of supplies', see Art. 27 (1) (*a*).

[71] See n. 70.

[72] On technical specifications, see *infra*, pp. 322–4.

Uruguay Round is the main negotiating forum for public procurement, no results have yet been achieved.[73]

Incompatibility of the rejection and preference rules with the free movement of goods within the Community?

Article 30 of the EC Treaty prohibits all quantitative restrictions on imports and all measures having equivalent effect between Member States. As is well known, this provision has been widely interpreted by the Court of Justice, as encompassing all trading rules enacted by the Member States liable to hinder, directly or indirectly, actually or potentially, intra-Community trade.[74] On several occasions the Court has indicated that the prohibition covers public procurement practices.[75] Indeed, the full realization of the free movement of goods is one of the main objectives of the Community's action in the field of public procurement, as the preambles of the various directives make clear.[76]

As analysed in previous chapters, the free movement of goods extends to all products that are in free circulation, i.e. all products which have been imported into the Community and for which all customs formalities have been fulfilled.[77] Such products are 'definitively and wholly assimilated to products originating in Member States'.[78] Applied to the field of public procurement this means that not only should a Member State not discriminate against tenders consisting of products manufactured in another Member State, but also that it may not discriminate against tenders consisting of products that are in free circulation. This has been recognized by the Council and the Commission: it is the subject of the above-mentioned resolutions and statement on national commercial policy measures in the area of public supply contracts.[79] The only way for the Member States legitimately to exclude tenders consisting of products which are in free circulation is to have recourse to Article 115 of the EC Treaty.

The rejection and preference rules run counter to these principles. They differentiate between products originating in and outside the Community; they do not differentiate, as regards the latter, between products which are in free circulation and those which are directly imported from third countries. So interpreted, the rejection and preference rules allow Member States to exclude tenders consisting of products which are in free circulation.

---

[73] See also *infra*, p. 317.

[74] See Case 8/74, *Procureur du Roi* v. *Dassonville*, [1974] ECR 837, at 852.

[75] Case 45/87, *Commission* v. *Ireland, supra* n. 7 and Case C-21/88, *Du Pont de Nemours Italiana* v. *Unità sanitaria locale n° 2 di Carrara*, [1990] ECR I-889.

[76] See Directives 77/62 and 90/531, *supra* nn. 11 and 13.

[77] See Arts. 9 and 10 of the EC Treaty, and Ch. 8, pp. 271–8.

[78] Case 41/76, *Donckerwolcke*, [1976] ECR 1935.

[79] *Supra*, nn. 19 and 37.

Such an application of these provisions is clearly capable of hindering intra-Community trade in a manner inconsistent with the free movement of goods. An example may illustrate this. Suppose a contract for the supply of switching equipment is awarded by Belgacom, the Belgian telecommunications company. Two companies are competing for the contract, *X* from Belgium and *Y* from Germany. Suppose *Y* mainly uses components of US origin in the manufacture of the products to be supplied to Belgacom, in contrast to *X* which uses components originating in the Community. The offer of *Y*, although the lowest in terms of price, is rejected on the basis of the rejection rule. Obviously, this affects intra-Community trade.[80]

However, there is an important difference with classical Article 30 cases. The latter are concerned with measures taken by the Member States independently, and not with legislative action by the Community. In legal writing on the subject, doubts have been raised about whether the EC Treaty rules on the free movement of goods are as such binding upon the Community institutions.[81] However, there cannot be a shadow of a doubt that the institutions are obliged to observe the principles underlying these rules. In *Ramel* v. *Receveur des douanes* the Court decided that

the extensive powers ... granted to the Community institutions ... must, in any event as from the end of the transitional period, be exercised from the perspective of the unity of the market to the exclusion of any measure compromising the abolition between Member States of customs duties and quantitative restrictions or charges or measures having equivalent effect.[82]

Admittedly, there is some case-law, primarily in agricultural matters, which gives the Community institutions some room for manoeuvre in observing and applying these principles.[83] Analysis of these cases shows, however, that derogations are only allowed in exceptional circumstances, such as the monetary situation in the context of monetary compensatory amounts or the still incomplete state of the common market organization in sheepmeat and goatmeat.[84] The commercial policy objective of providing some degree of external protection, which explains the rejection and preference rules, would appear not to be able to justify a derogation from the free movement of goods.

[80] Perhaps it is even possible, under the rules of the directive, that contracting authorities discriminate against undertakings established in other Member States by using the rejection rule. Suppose the tenders of both *X* and *Y* mainly consist of products originating outside the Community, but that Belgacom rejects the tender of *Y* and accepts that of *X*. This would seem to be possible, since there is nothing in the directive requiring a coherent policy of rejection; the rejection rule can be applied on a case-by-case basis.

[81] Peter Oliver, *Free Movement of Goods in the EEC*, 2nd edn. (London: European Law Centre Ltd, 1988), 51.

[82] Joined Cases 80 and 81/77, [1978] ECR 927, at 946–7.

[83] See Oliver, *supra* n. 81, pp. 46–50.

[84] On monetary compensatory amounts, see e.g. Case 5/73, *Balkan-Import-Export* v. *Hauptzollamt Berlin-Packhof*, [1973] ECR 1091; on sheep- and goatmeat, see Case 106/81, *Kind*, [1982] ECR 2885 and Case 61/86, *UK* v. *Commission*, [1988] ECR 431.

The fact that the Community is a customs union requires that this protection effectively be external, that it only be enforced against direct imports from third countries. There is only one exception, namely Article 115 of the EC Treaty, and this exception is of a transitional nature, applying to national commercial policy measures which have not yet been replaced by a common regime.[85] Taking the opposite view comes down to giving the Community institutions the power to set aside the fundamental principles concerning the free movement of goods whenever they deem external protection to be more in the Community's interest. This cannot be readily accepted. It is incompatible with the very concept of completing the internal market, implying as was shown that even the application of Article 115, the only Treaty provision allowing the implementation of external protection to take precedence over the free movement of goods, is put an end to.[86]

The conclusion should therefore be that the rejection and preference rules cannot be relied upon for rejecting tenders consisting of products which are in free circulation, because this conflicts with the fundamental principles governing the free movement of goods in the Community. That, however, completely undermines the external policy of the directive, which of itself is not invaluable, especially in view of the international context.[87] As was emphasized by the Commission when it proposed the directive, the Community operates a liberal policy regarding establishment of companies. Accordingly, it is relatively simple for third-country companies interested in competing for government contracts within the Community to set up a subsidiary which merely functions as a tenderer and as an importer of products manufactured abroad. To some extent, the Community is 'trapped', in this field, by the fact that it is a customs union, with the corresponding concept of goods in free circulation. If the Community were a single country, the objections raised above would not exist, as the US example of the so-called Buy American Act demonstrates. This Act, too, contains preference rules for products of domestic origin.[88]

But there may be a way out of the trap. Instead of concentrating on the origin of products, Community rules could be directed at the 'nationality' of tendering companies. One requirement could be that such companies not only be established in the Community, but also show an effective link with the Community's economy.[89] That would eliminate the submission of tenders by mere mailbox subsidiaries.

[85] See Ch. 5, pp. 175–6.
[86] Compare with Ch. 2, pp. 62–5, concerning the reciprocity policy in the field of financial services and the scope of Art. 58 of the Treaty. In the latter case there does seem some scope for justifying restrictions on establishment on the basis of the Community's commercial policy.
[87] In particular the safeguarding of the Community's negotiating position at the multilateral level is clearly a worthwhile policy.
[88] On this Act, see Woolcock, *supra* n. 57.
[89] Compare with the Commission's proposal regarding public service contracts, dealt with in the next section.

The international context

The Utilities Directive has come under fierce criticism from the United States government, which threatened retaliation under the notorious Section 301 of the US Trade Act, because of the possible discrimination against US products. This led to strenuous and protracted negotiations between the Community and the USA, resulting in a partial agreement reached in the course of April 1993.[90] This agreement in the form of a memorandum of understanding provides for the mutual opening-up of certain categories of procurement contracts, including electrical utilities covered by the Utilities Directive. The Community, consequently, waived to some extent the application of the exclusion and preference rules of this directive with respect to tenders comprising products of US origin.[91] Moreover, the Community and the US shall jointly sponsor a study of the procurement opportunities that would arise from their respective offers and requests in the negotiations on the GATT Government Procurement Code. The agreement is thus situated in this negotiation process which is to continue. However, the USA was not completely satisfied with this agreement, which does not cover telecommunications, and imposed limited sanctions, against which the Community retaliated by doing the same.[92]

Against this background of tense US–EC relations the German government saw fit to dissociate itself from the Community's policy by making it known to US authorities that it interpreted the national treatment clause of its Treaty of Friendship, Commerce, and Navigation with the USA, dating from 1954, as precluding it from applying the exclusion and preference rules of the Utilities Directive, as well as the sanctions adopted by the Council.[93] This led to a major dispute between Germany, on the one hand, and the Community's institutions, in particular the Commission, as well as the other Member States on the other. The legal questions which this dispute raises are most interesting.

Germany appears to argue that Article 234 of the EC Treaty allows it to continue to honour its commitments towards the United States. This provision, as will be recalled,[94] concerns agreements concluded before the entry

[90] See the Council Decision of 10 May 1993 concerning the conclusion of an Agreement in the form of a Memorandum of Understanding between the European Economic Community and the United States of America on government procurement, OJ L 125/1 of 20 May 1993.
[91] See the Council Decision of 10 May 1993 concerning the extension of the benefit of the provisions of Directive 90/531 in respect of the United States of America, OJ L 125/54 of 20 May 1993, which is based on Art. 29 (5) of the directive (see *supra* p. 310).
[92] See Council Regulation 1461/93 concerning access to public contracts for tenderers from the United States of America, OJ L 146/1 of 17 June 1993.
[93] See e.g. *Financial Times*, 'German fury at minister's telecoms line', 15 June 1993, p. 7; 'Crossed lines over telecoms trade-off', 16 June 1993, p. 5; 'Paris tries to avert split on telecoms', 18 June 1993, p. 5; *Agence Europe*, No. 5999, 12 June 1993, p. 8, and No. 6000, 14 and 15 June 1993, p. 7. For the text of this national treatment clause, see Ch. 2, pp. 74–5.
[94] Compare with Ch. 2, pp. 73–4, and Ch. 3, pp. 100–1.

Public Procurement

into force of the Treaty between one or more Member States and one or more third countries. According to paragraph 1 rights and obligations arising from such agreements shall not be affected. Paragraph 2 provides that the Member States should eliminate any incompatibilities between such agreements and Community law. However, the latter is irrelevant, according to the German government, since Article 29 (1) of the Utilities Directive provides that the exclusion and preference rules apply 'without prejudice to the obligations of the Community *or its Member States* in respect of third countries'.[95] This reference to existing agreements concluded by the Member States would have been included on the request of the German government, although there appears to be no trace of such a request and the action of the German government came as a complete surprise to the other Member States and the Commission. Be that as it may, from a strict legal point of view this German argument appears well founded.

However, that is not all. Treaties of Friendship, Commerce, and Navigation concluded between Member States and third countries are clearly liable to affect the Community's commercial policy and to disregard the Community's exclusive competence to conduct such a policy. Their renewal or maintenance in force is therefore subject to supervision under the terms of a Council decision of 1969.[96] In the framework of such supervision the German-US Treaty was always allowed to be maintained, under the condition, however, that its provisions 'are not contrary to existing common policies'.[97] In so far as the national treatment clause of the German-US Treaty is interpreted as precluding the application of the exclusion and preference rules of the Utilities Directive towards tenders consisting of US products, it indeed appears to be contrary to, if not the letter, then surely the substance of the common external policy in this field.

The Commission now tries to solve the matter by no longer proposing the renewal or maintenance in force of the German-U.S. Treaty, as well as similar ones to which other Member States are parties, because that 'could create problems of compatibility with existing common policies'.[98] It remains to be seen whether the Council and the German government will go along with this approach.

[95] Italics added.
[96] Council Decision 69/494 on the progressive standardization of agreements concerning commercial relations between Member States and third countries and on the negotiation of Community agreements, OJ L 326/39 of 29 Dec. 1969. See also Ch. 2, p. 75.
[97] See lastly Council Decision 92/234 authorizing the automatic renewal or maintenance in force of provisions governing matters covered by the common commercial policy contained in the friendship, trade, and navigation treaties and similar agreements concluded between Member States and third countries, OJ L 120/37 of 5 May 1992, in particular Art. 1.
[98] See proposal for a Council Decision authorizing the automatic renewal or maintenance in force of provisions governing matters covered by the common commercial policy contained in the friendship, trade, and navigation treaties and similar agreements concluded between Member States and third countries, COM (93) 326 final of 9 July 1993, p. 2.

Public Service Contracts

The internal market programme also involves the extension of public procurement disciplines to the award of public service contracts, other than public works covered by Directive 71/305.[99] Accordingly, the Council has adopted a general directive, relating to the co-ordination of procedures for the award of public service contracts.[100] There is, in addition, a specific regime governing public service contracts in the excluded sectors.[101] Both these instruments need to be discussed here because the approach towards their external dimension differs (again) from the directives examined above.

Directive 92/50 on the award of public service contracts

When the Commission drew up its proposal regarding public service contracts,[102] largely inspired by the existing rules on public works and public supply contracts, it inserted a provision on relations with third countries. This provision (Article 40 of the proposal) was similar to the rules on reciprocity issued in the financial services sector, and discussed in Chapter 2. As such, this approach had the merit of aiming at the definition of a coherent policy with respect to external relations in the services sector.

The proposed Article 40 contained five paragraphs. In the first, the Member States were asked to inform the Commission 'of any general difficulties encountered, in law or in fact, by their undertakings in securing the award of public service contracts or public service concessions in third countries'. Under the second paragraph, the Commission was to inform the Council periodically of the opening-up of public service contracts in third countries and on the state of international negotiations on this subject. The third and fourth paragraphs were the most important ones, because they would have allowed the Community to take action against certain undesired forms of treatment of Community undertakings, by third countries, in the field of public service contracts. Paragraph 3 defined such treatment in the following terms: (*a*) a third country 'does not grant Community undertakings *effective access comparable* to that granted by the Community to undertakings from that country';[103] (*b*) a third country 'does not grant Community undertakings *national treatment or the same competitive opportunities* as available to

---

[99] See n. 11.

[100] Directive 92/50 relating to the co-ordination of procedures for the award of public service contracts, OJ L 209/1 of 24 July 1992.

[101] See Directive 93/38, *supra* n. 13.

[102] COM (90) 372 final, OJ C 23/1 of 31 Jan. 1991.

[103] Italics added. Compare with Art. 9 (3) of the Second Banking Directive (Ch. 2, pp. 55–6), mentioning the case in which 'a third country is not granting Community credit institutions effective market access comparable to that granted by the Community to credit institutions from that third country'.

national undertakings';[104] (c) a third country 'grants undertakings from other third countries *more favourable treatment* than Community undertakings'.[105] In all three cases, the Commission could 'initiate negotiations in order to remedy the situation'. In addition, however, in cases (b) and (c) the Commission could decide according to paragraph 4 that

the award of public service contracts or concessions to:
    (a) undertakings governed by the law of the country in question;
    (b) undertakings affiliated to the undertakings specified in (a) and having their registered office in the Community but having no effective and continuous link with the economy of a Member State;
    (c) tenders which have as their object services originating in the country in question;
may be suspended or restricted during a period to be determined in the decision.

Such a decision could be overruled by the Council, within a period of four weeks after its adoption, acting by qualified majority upon request of any Member State. Lastly, in the fifth paragraph it was said that '[t]his Article is without prejudice to the obligations of the Community in relation to non-Member countries'.

Comparing this provision with the reciprocity rules in the financial services sector, it is obvious that the concepts are similar. There is one important addition: the Community can take action, not only where Community undertakings do not receive national treatment, but also where they do not get most-favoured-nation treatment. Because the latter will almost invariably amount to the former, this addition is somewhat awkward.[106] Indeed, if country A grants preferential treatment to country B in the field of public procurement, not extending this to the Community, it is difficult to imagine that this treatment would be more beneficial than the one received by A's own undertakings. In such a case, no MFN treatment is granted to the Community, but national treatment is lacking at the same time. There could be instances, however, in which B is receiving less than national treatment, but nevertheless more preferential treatment than the Community. But whether this is a realistic hypothesis is another matter. It implies rather sophisticated external policies on the part of country A.[107]

It is also striking that the Commission proposed that it could take action independently, without the Council's consent. There would only have been an obligation for the Commission previously to consult an advisory committee,

[104] Italics added. Compare with Art. 9 (4) of the Second Banking Directive, dealing with the situation in which 'Community credit institutions in a third country do not receive national treatment offering the same competitive opportunities as are available to domestic credit institutions and the conditions of effective market access are not fulfilled'.

[105] Italics added.

[106] See also Ch. 3, p. 117.

[107] Unless, perhaps, it is in the framework of a customs union or free trade area that preferential treatment is granted. An interesting question is whether the Community would object to such preferential treatment.

composed of Member States' representatives, and to 'take the utmost account' of this committee's opinion.[108] Apparently, this aspect of the proposal was unacceptable for the Council. Although the European Parliament strongly backed the adoption of the reciprocity provision,[109] it did not survive the legislative process, reportedly because the Commission and the Council could not reach agreement on the advisory committee procedure. Since the latter was rejected unanimously by the Council, the Commission considered that the reciprocity clause had lost its usefulness, the argument apparently being that the Council can always take commercial policy measures on the basis of Article 113, EC Treaty, and that no special provision needs to be inserted to that effect.[110] This indicates that the Commission considered it to be essential that it be allowed to take action itself. Such a desire may have its roots in two broader policy goals of the Commission. One is its general preoccupation with the 'comitologie', i.e. the various procedures in Community law instruments assigning executive powers to the Commission, on advice of committees in which the Member States are represented. The Commission wants stronger powers in relation to these committees.[111] Secondly, the Commission has recently asked to be given more powers for adopting commercial policy measures in the fields of anti-dumping, anti-subsidies, and safeguards.[112]

Be that as it may, the deletion of the reciprocity provision is regrettable, not necessarily because of its merits on policy grounds (which may be debatable), but because it appears to reduce the scope of the directive, limiting it to intra-Community trade in services and forsaking the elaboration of a common external policy. Indeed, as it now stands the directive only seems to address tenders emanating from service providers established in the Community, since some of its provisions mention possible tenderers only in connection with the Member States.[113] The above language is conditional, however, because there

---

[108] Art. 40 of the proposal, referring to Art. 39.

[109] See the amendments in the second reading, OJ C 150/98–9 of 15 June 1992 and the corresponding debate, *Debates EP* (1992), No. 3-418/36–7.

[110] See the statements by Commission Vice-President Sir Leon Brittan in *Debates EP* (1992), No. 3-418/37.

[111] See for example the first progress report on the completion of the internal market, as required by Article 7*b*, EC Treaty, COM (88) final, p. 9.

[112] See its proposal for a Council Regulation on the harmonization and streamlining of decision-making procedures for Community instruments of commercial defence and modification of the relevant Council regulations, SEC (92) 1097 final, OJ C 181/9 of 17 July 1992.

[113] Art. 26 (2) speaks of '[c]andidates or tenderers who, *under the law of the Member State in which they are established*, are entitled...' (italics added); Art. 27 (4), says that, concerning restricted negotiated procedures, '[e]ach Member State shall ensure that contracting authorities issue invitations without discrimination to those *nationals of other Member States* who satisfy the necessary requirements...'; Art. 30 (2) and (3) provide that candidates or tenderers may be requested to prove their enrolment in a professional or trade register, and lists only the registers existing in the various Member States. The Commission's proposal, on the other hand, clearly intended also to cover tenders submitted by service providers not established in the Community, see Erhart, *supra* n. 15, p. 757.

is one article which also refers to third countries. Under Article 39, Member States are obliged to forward every other year a statistical report on the service contracts awarded by contracting authorities. This report should, according to the second paragraph, list 'the number and value of the contracts awarded to each Member State and to third countries'. Whether this means that the directive also applies to tenders submitted by service providers established in third countries, and not in the Community, is unclear. However, it would appear to be doubtful given the fact that this is the only provision in which third countries are mentioned, that the preamble no longer mentions Article 113, EC Treaty, as did the Commission's proposal, and that the above-mentioned articles connect tenderers with the Member States.[114]

As a result the Member States are probably entitled to develop their own policies regarding trade in services with third countries in the field of public procurement. In this respect, the public services directive is in line, unfortunately, with the public works and public supplies directives. Even the beginning of a common external policy is completely lacking.

Public service contracts in the excluded sectors

The Directive extending the scope of the Utilities Directive to services does include the above-described reciprocity clause.[115] There is one difference with the above description, namely that instead of the Commission being able to decide on suspensions or restrictions of the award of services contracts to third-country undertakings, it is the Council which would decide. The above observations on the contents of the clause apply *mutatis mutandis*.

Public Procurement and Technical Specifications

All of the public procurement directives contain largely similar rules on technical specifications which are part of public contracts.[116] It is obvious that such specifications could easily be drawn up by contracting authorities so as to afford protection to domestic undertakings. That could be done, for example, by obliging tenderers to use products which comply with existing national standards. However, in *Commission* v. *Ireland* the Court of Justice made clear that such specifications come within the scope of Article 30, EC Treaty, and that, consequently, the general rules regarding mutual recognition of technical regulations and standards are equally applicable in the field of public

---

[114] Compare with Directives 71/305 and 77/62, *supra* n. 11, dealt with *supra* pp. 300–2, which have the same character in this regard, and of which the Council and the Commission have made clear that they do not apply to tenders submitted by third-country undertakings.

[115] See Art. 37 of Directive 93/38, *supra* n. 13.

[116] See Art. 10, Directive 93/37; Art. 8, Directive 93/36; Arts. 18 and 19, Directive 93/38; Art. 14, Directive 92/50.

procurement.[117] It does not matter, in this respect, whether the public contract in question involves the supply of products, the execution of works, or the provision of services. To the extent that the contract includes the supply or use of products, Article 30 is applicable.

The rules in the directives are clearly aimed at translating the general rule of Article 30 into more detailed obligations. The basic provision states that

[w]ithout prejudice to the legally binding national technical rules and insofar as these are compatible with Community law, such technical specifications shall be defined by contracting authorities by reference to national standards implementing European standards or by reference to European technical approvals or by reference to common technical specifications.[118]

For a number of specified reasons, however, contracting authorities may depart from this rule. That is the case:

- if there are no means yet to establish the conformity of a product with these standards, approvals or specifications;
- if application of the rule were to prejudice certain other Community efforts regarding standardization and mutual recognition;
- if application of the rule were to lead to the use of products or materials incompatible with already existing equipment or entail disproportionate costs or technical difficulties, provided there was a strategy for the transition to European standards, technical approvals, or common technical specifications;
- if the project is of a genuinely innovative nature.

Moreover, where there are no European standards, European technical approvals, or common technical specifications, the directives allow contracting authorities to refer to other documents, but they also establish an order of preference, consisting of:

1. national standards implementing international standards;
2. other national standards;
3. any other standard.[119]

Finally, Member States are to prohibit technical specifications mentioning goods of a specific make or source or of a particular process and having the effect of favouring or eliminating certain undertakings or products.

---

[117] Case 45/87, *supra* n. 7.

[118] Art. 14 (2), Directive 92/50. The comparable provisions in the other directives differ only slightly.

[119] Directives 71/305 and 92/50 provide that, before recourse is had to this order of preference, technical specifications 'shall be defined by reference to the national technical specifications recognized as complying with the basic requirements listed in the Community directives on technical harmonization' (Arts. 10 (5) and 14 (5) respectively). It is not clear why a similar provision was not inserted in the other directives.

It is not possible to provide an in-depth analysis of these provisions here. What needs to be examined, however, is their impact on trade with third countries. At first sight, the preference given to the use of European standards and the fact that reference to international standards is only impossible if no European standards exist, may seem to work to the disadvantage of third-country products (in so far, of course, as such products are not excluded from the scope of the various directives). That need not be the case, however. In this respect, reference should be made to what has been said in the previous chapter regarding the relationship between European and international standardization.[120] To the extent that European standardization duly respects the work done within the international standardization bodies, and that international standards are relied upon as much as possible, the negative effects on the competitive position of third-country products will be limited. Therefore, the impact of the preference given to European standardization in the public procurement directives depends entirely upon the direction which European standardization policies take.

Moreover, given the absence of a common external policy in most of the public procurement directives, the emphasis on European standardization is quite logical. Since the directives only apply to tenders submitted by undertakings established within the Community, a preference for international standardization would be rather surprising, in that it would almost amount to an official declaration of lack of confidence in the work done by the European standardization bodies.

Conclusion

One must conclude that the Community's external policies in the field of public procurement are not very coherent nor comprehensive. It cannot be said that the external dimension of the relevant directives is fully defined yet. For a number of products and services, there is simply no common external regime. For others, in particular those covered by the Utilities Directive, the common rules leave quite some scope for divergent interpretation and application by national authorities. Such a state of affairs is clearly liable to distort competition within the internal market, which points to the necessity to work out a fully-fledged external policy. The Uruguay Round may offer the forum for agreeing to such a policy.

Moreover, in the case of the Utilities Directive the Community forsakes the basic rules governing the customs union on which it is based in order to provide for external protection, which is certainly deplorable. This is comparable to the case of imports of Japanese cars, where the Community appears to subordinate its internal competition policy to the goal of differentiated protection within the Community.[121]

[120] Ch. 8, pp. 282–4.   [121] See Ch. 5, part 2. See also Ch. 11, p. 355.

10

The Extension of the Internal Market in the Framework of the European Economic Area

Introduction

In the previous chapters the external dimension of the internal market programme was analysed, taking as a basis the (internal) legal instruments
adopted or applied by the Community. The aim was to study this external
dimension as it applies to trade and economic relations between the Community and third countries in general. Of course, there have been references to
relations with certain specific third countries, such as the United States and
Japan, but these references were mainly part of sketching the setting of
Community measures. In general, the content of the latter does not discriminate between the various trade partners of the Community.[1] That, by the way,
compares favourably with the often-voiced criticism that the Community
operates a network of preferential and discriminatory trading arrangements,
and by so doing undermines the principle of non-discrimination which lies at
the heart of the world trading system.[2] There is, however, one major and
radical exception to this non-discriminatory character of the external dimension of the internal market programme, and that is the Agreement on the
European Economic Area (EEA).[3] This Agreement is aimed at extending the
acquis communautaire concerning the internal market to the EFTA countries.
From the point of view of the external dimension of the internal market
programme, the Agreement is rather ambivalent. On the one hand, there is
little 'external' to it, since the EFTA countries have committed themselves to
taking over the relevant *acquis communautaire* almost completely, and as the
same rules will apply as within the Community, there is no question of

[1] There are of course some exceptions, the most important one being the common market
organization for bananas, see Ch. 6, part 3.
[2] See e.g. GATT, *Trade Policy Review: European Communities*, Vol. i, the Report by the GATT
Secretariat (Geneva, 1991), 7–8, 12–14, and 61–75; Josef Molsberger and Angelos Kotios, 'The
Single European Market of 1992 within the GATT of the Nineties', in T. Oppermann and J.
Molsberger (eds.), *A New GATT for the Nineties and Europe '92* (Baden-Baden: Nomos, 1991),
359. See also Ch. 11, p. 360.
[3] This Agreement was signed by the Community, its Member States and the EFTA States on 2
May 1992 in Oporto. It was due to come into force on 1 Jan. 1993, but because of the
non-ratification by Switzerland, this date has been delayed. References in this chapter to the text
of the Agreement are based on the edition by the EC Council and Commission (Luxembourg:
Office for Official Publications of the EC, 1992).

applying a specific regime governing external relations. On the other hand, however, the EFTA countries remain of course non-member States and the Agreement, although from a substantive point of view simply transposing the internal Community rules, is part of the Community's external policies.

One can look at this ambivalence from various angles. From the point of view of policy the question can be put whether it is appropriate that the Community treats a given set of third countries in such a preferential way as to extend the internal market to them. In terms of the world trading system, this question raises the problem of regionalism versus multilateralism, which is, however, not limited to the EEA but is relevant for the internal market programme itself as well. This problem has been touched upon in previous chapters and will, as it is not specific for the EEA, be further explored in the concluding chapter below.[4]

However, there is another angle which provides a perspective on the EEA, interesting for the purpose of this study. In the previous chapters, the relationship between the internal market programme and the Community's commercial policy (both as a concept and an actual policy) has often been indicated and analysed. In this respect, the EEA offers an entirely different picture. The EEA is not a customs union, which means that the Community and the various EFTA countries do not employ a common customs tariff, nor a common commercial policy. Therefore, although the EEA is an extension of the internal market to the EFTA countries, the external dimension of the internal market is (generally speaking) *not* extended. Obviously this raises a number of important questions.

In the next section, the aims, system, and scope of the EEA are briefly set out in order to allow a better understanding of the basic questions involved. Subsequently, the external dimension of the EEA is analysed (in so far as it exists), by looking at the various subjects dealt with in the previous chapters. That is followed by a number of questions and comments on this (lack of an) external dimension of the EEA. As the Agreement on the EEA is of recent date and has not yet been implemented, and as there is virtually no literature on the issues which are considered here, this chapter is of limited scope.

Aims, System, and Scope of the EEA

According to Article 1 of the Agreement, its aim is 'to promote a continuous and balanced strengthening of trade and economic relations between the Contracting Parties with equal conditions of competition, and the respect of the same rules, with a view to creating a homogeneous European Economic

---

[4] Ch. 11, p. 358–62.

Area'.[5] In order to achieve this, the Agreement contains provisions on the free movement of goods, persons, services, and capital, on competition law, and on closer co-operation in a number of other fields.[6] These provisions (except the latter category) are modelled on, and in some cases even copied from, the EC Treaty.[7] Moreover, in its 22 annexes the agreement lists an enormous amount of Community secondary acts which, each with some modifications so as to allow them to be applied in the EEA instead of in the Community, are an integral part of the Agreement.[8] The great majority of these acts are related to the establishment of the internal market.[9] All this demonstrates that the aim of the Agreement is to extend the internal market to the EFTA countries. That is further confirmed by Article 6, stating that the provisions of the Agreement and the acts referred to 'shall, in their implementation and application, be interpreted in conformity with the relevant rulings of the Court of Justice of the European Communities given prior to the date of signature of this Agreement'.

The fact that the Contracting Parties wished to incorporate, as much as possible, the internal market rules in the EEA has also created great difficulties in the negotiations. It was one thing for the EFTA countries to agree to adapt their legal systems to the existing *acquis communautaire*, but this *acquis* is of course subject to almost continuous change, renewal, and expansion. It would

[5] The term Contracting Parties, it has to be noted, has a variable content. According to Art. 2 (*c*), 'the term "Contracting Parties" means, concerning the Community and the EC Member States, the Community and the EC Member States, or the Community, or the EC Member States. The meaning to be attributed to this expression in each case is to be deduced from the relevant provisions of this Agreement and from the respective competences of the Community and the EC Member States as they follow from the Treaty establishing the European Economic Community and the Treaty establishing the European Coal and Steel Community.' This provision is necessary because the EEA is a mixed Agreement, concluded by the Community and its individual Member States, because it is thought that some areas do not come within the scope of the Community's competences.

[6] There are 'Horizontal provisions relevant to the four freedoms', pertaining to social policy, consumer protection, the environment, statistics, and company law. 'Cooperation outside the four freedoms' is also envisaged; it relates to research and technological development, information services, the environment, education, training and youth, social policy, consumer protection, small and medium-sized enterprises, tourism, the audiovisual sector, and civil protection.

[7] Provisions of the EC Treaty which were virtually copied are: Arts. 30, 34, 36 (free movement of goods), 48 (free movement for workers), 52 (freedom of establishment), 59–60 (free movement of services), and Arts. 85 and 86 (competition policy).

[8] Cf. Art. 7: 'Acts referred to or contained in the Annexes to this Agreement or in decisions of the EEA Joint Committee shall be binding upon the Contracting Parties and be, or be made, part of their internal legal order as follows: (a) an act corresponding to an EEC regulation shall as such be made part of the internal legal order of the Contracting Parties; (b) an act corresponding to an EEC directive shall leave to the authorities of the Contracting Parties the choice of form and method of implementation.'

[9] The annexes concern: veterinary and phytosanitary matters; technical regulations, standards, testing, and certification; product liability; energy; free movement of workers; social security; mutual recognition of professional qualifications; right of establishment; financial services; audiovisual services; telecommunications services; free movement of capital; transport; competition; state aid; procurement; intellectual property; health and safety at work, labour law, and equal treatment for men and women; consumer protection; environment; statistics; company law.

have been completely useless only to refer to the *acquis* existing on the date of signature of the Agreement, without including a system allowing for the adaptation of the rules of the Agreement in parallel with the future development of the *acquis*. It has, however, been very difficult to devise such a system, because the Community could not allow the EFTA countries to take part in Community decision-making, whereas the latter naturally did not want to take over newly developed rules without being able to influence the adoption and content of such rules. The solution found for this problem distinguishes, in a subtle way, between the 'decision-shaping' and 'decision-making' aspects of drawing up new Community rules. The EFTA countries will be able to take part in the former, but not in the latter.[10]

Closely related to these difficulties was the issue of the judicial system set up by the Agreement. As much as the EFTA countries did not want to sign a blank cheque regarding the future development of the *acquis communautaire*, they also did not want to commit themselves to observing the future case-law of the Court of Justice.[11] Therefore, the Agreement first contained provisions on the establishment of an EEA Court which would have been allotted the task of interpreting the EEA rules. The Commission asked for the opinion of the Court of Justice on the compatibility of this judicial system with the EC Treaty,[12] and the Court concluded that the system was liable to endanger the uniform interpretation of Community law and therefore conflicted with 'Article 164 of the EEC Treaty and, more generally, with the very foundations of the Community'.[13] It is interesting to note that the Court, in order to arrive at this conclusion, analysed the difference in objectives between the Agreement and the EC Treaty. It was of the view that the Agreement was (merely) 'concerned with the application of rules on free trade and competition in economic and commercial relations between the Contracting Parties',[14] whereas these rules, in the context of the EC Treaty, are part of the legal order of the Community, the objectives of which are economic integration leading to a single market and an economic and monetary union, and, ultimately, to contribute to making concrete progress towards European unity.[15] The Contracting Parties subsequently modified the draft Agreement with a view to eliminating the incompatibility with the EC Treaty. The concept of an EEA Court was abandoned and replaced by the creation of an EFTA Court, leaving

[10] See Arts. 97 to 104.

[11] See Art. 6, quoted *supra* p. 327, which only refers to judgments handed down before the signing of the Agreement.

[12] Cf. Art. 228, EC Treaty, providing that '[t]he Council, the Commission or a Member State may obtain beforehand the opinion of the Court of Justice as to whether an agreement envisaged is compatible with the provisions of this Treaty. Where the opinion of the Court of Justice is adverse, the agreement may enter into force only in accordance with Article N of the Treaty on European Union' (regarding amendments to the Treaty).

[13] See Opinion 1/91, [1991] ECR I-6079, para. 46.

[14] Ibid. para. 15.   [15] Ibid. paras. 16–17.

it to the Contracting Parties (through the EEA Joint Committee) to ensure the uniform interpretation of the relevant rules where there are divergent decisions by the Court of Justice and the EFTA Court.[16] This solution was considered acceptable by the Court in its second opinion on the draft Agreement.[17]

As was mentioned, the EEA is not a customs union, which means that there is no common external tariff and no common commercial policy. Although at the beginning of the negotiations the Community suggested that it would be useful also to coordinate the external policies relevant to the EEA,[18] some EFTA countries have been very reluctant to give up anything of their independence in the field of external relations, which may be explained by the tradition of neutrality which a number of them nurture.[19] Moreover, as the analysis by Wijkman shows, a customs union requires more common decision-making than a mere extension of the internal rules governing the single market.[20] Nevertheless, the Agreement on the EEA contains a few provisions on external policies; moreover, the fact that the EEA is not a customs union entails a number of consequences that needed to be taken care of. Both aspects are surveyed and commented on in the next section.

The External Dimension of the EEA

Overview

Trade in goods

Because the EEA does not include a common customs tariff and a common commercial policy, the prohibition of customs duties, quantitative restrictions, and measures of equivalent effect only applies to products originating in

---

[16] See Arts. 105–7.

[17] Opinion 1/92, OJ L 136/1 of 26 May 1992. For comments on the two Opinions, see the annotations by H. G. Schermers, 29 *CML Rev.* (1992), 5: 991–1009; Jacques Steenbergen, 40 *SEW* (1992), 5: 402–31; Marc-André Gaudissart, *RMUE* (1992), 2: 121–36.

[18] Commission President Delors observed in his 1989 speech to the European Parliament in which he made the proposal to strengthen the ties with EFTA, that '[t]he single market is first and foremost a customs union. Are our partners prepared to abide by the common commercial policy that any customs union must apply to outsiders?', see *Debates EP*, No. 2-373/76. See also Jacques Steenbergen, 'EG/EFTA en de Europese economische ruimte', 39 *SEW* (1991), 1: 27; *Financial Times*, 'Problems of the single market', 21 Mar. 1989, p. 23 and 'Brussels sets targets for talks on future of EFTA', 9 May 1990, p. 2.

[19] Cf. Philippe Nell, *Les pays de l'AELE face au marché intérieur de la CE: défi, enjeu et stratégie*, EFTA Occasional Paper No. 24 (Geneva, 1988), 30; Detlev C. Dicke, 'Switzerland as an EFTA-Country and the "Fortress Europe"', in *A New GATT for the Nineties and Europe '92*, *supra* n. 2, p. 341.

[20] Per Magnus Wijkman, 'Economic Interdependence', in H. Wallace (ed.), *The Wider Western Europe: Reshaping the EC/EFTA Relationship* (London: Pinter for the RIIA, 1991), 60–8. See also Meinhard Hilf, 'The Single European Act and 1992: Legal Implications for Third Countries', 1 *EJIL* (1990), 1/2: 112.

the EEA. Seen from this angle, the EEA is a 'mere' free trade area, in which goods imported from third countries do not circulate freely. It is not fundamentally different, in this respect, from the existing free trade agreements linking the Community to the individual EFTA States.[21] Such a free trade area requires, in order to prevent deflections of trade, a set of rules of origin, determining which products benefit from free circulation and which not.[22] The application of these rules prevents the varying commercial policies of the Contracting Parties being circumvented by the importation of products in the country with the most liberal external regime. At the same time, it implies that controls at the borders between the Contracting Parties (i.e. the borders between the various EFTA States, and between these States and the Community) have to be performed. As a result the EEA is not an 'area without internal frontiers' in the sense of Article 7a of the EC Treaty. However, although it is beyond doubt that the system and content of the rules of origin laid down in the Agreement are important and merit to be thoroughly studied, they are not directly relevant for the subject of this study and will not be further dealt with here.[23]

The foregoing applies mainly to the relationship between the EEA and the classic chapters of the Community's common commercial policy, i.e. the rules specifically governing imports from third countries.[24] But as we have seen, there are of course also other instruments of Community law affecting the marketing of imported products. One category of these concerns technical regulations and standards.[25] In this field, the Agreement on the EEA takes over the bulk of the _acquis communautaire_.[26] That raises the question of the effect of this take-over on third-country imports.

As regards the directives harmonizing national rules governing the production and marketing of products this effect would appear to depend on the scope of these directives. As a rule the latter are equally applicable to domestic (in the sense of Community) and imported products. Since the aim of the EEA is to extend the provisions of these directives to the EFTA countries with as little modification as possible, the same rule should apply within the EEA. Take the example of the directive on the safety of machines, providing that

---

[21] These agreements were concluded in 1972, see OJ L 300 and 301 of 31 Dec. 1972, English Special edn. (1972) II, pp. 3 _et seq._

[22] See Protocol 4.

[23] Analyses are to be found in Frank Emmert, 'Die Entwicklung der Ursprungsregeln bis zum EWR-Abkommen' and Anton Egger, 'Ursprungsregeln aus schweizerischer Sicht (Art. 9 EWR-A)', both in O. Jacot-Guillarmod (ed.), _EEA Agreement: Comments and Reflexions_ (Zürich: Schulthess Polygraphischer Verlag, 1992), 115–32 and 133–48; Jacques H. J. Bourgeois, 'L'Espace économique européen', _RMUE_ (1992), 2: 14. In this connection it should also be mentioned that according to Protocol 13 measures can be taken by the Contracting Parties aimed at preventing circumvention of anti-dumping and countervailing duties and measures against illicit commercial practices (i.e. the fair trade side of import rules). The Agreement eliminates the possibility of taking such measures against one of the Contracting Parties, see Art. 26.

[24] See Chs. 5 and 6.   [25] See Ch. 8.   [26] See Annex II.

Member States shall allow the placing on the market and putting into service of machinery which complies with the directive.[27] This rule applies, *mutatis mutandis*, in the EEA. In the absence of clear indications that the origin of machinery is in any way relevant for determining the scope of this rule, the conclusion must be that all machines are covered, also those imported from third countries.[28]

Things are different for the basic rules governing the free movement of goods within the EEA. As was said, the prohibition of quantitative restrictions and measures of equivalent effect only applies to products originating in the Contracting Parties.[29] This means, among other things, that the principle of mutual recognition does not apply to non-originating products, by contrast to the state of affairs within the Community.[30] There is clearly something of a paradox in this discrepancy between the scope of the EEA equivalent of the directives and the scope of the basic rules, in that the directives are precisely aimed at fully ensuring the free movement provided for in these basic rules.

There is one more element to be added regarding technical regulations and standards. As described in Chapter 8, the Community intends to conclude agreements with third countries on mutual recognition of certification and testing. By virtue of such agreements it would become possible for third-country manufacturers to have the compliance of their products with Community technical regulations and standards certified within their own countries. But as the same regulations and standards apply within the EEA, will these agreements also be valid throughout the EEA? That question was considered in the negotiations. Protocol 12 specifically deals with it; it provides that

[m]utual recognition agreements with third countries concerning conformity assessment for products where the use of a mark is provided for in EC legislation will be negotiated on the initiative of the Community. The Community will negotiate on the basis that the third countries concerned will conclude with the EFTA States parallel mutual recognition agreements equivalent to those to be concluded with the Community. The Contracting Parties shall cooperate in accordance with the general information and consultation procedures set out in the EEA Agreement. Should a difference arise in relations with third countries, it will be dealt with in accordance with the relevant provisions of the EEA Agreement.

[27] Art. 4 (1) of Directive 89/392/EEC, OJ L 183/9 of 29 June 1989 (see Ch. 8, n. 12). For the reference in the EEA Agreement, see Annex II, Section XXIV, p. 450 of the edition referred to *supra* n. 3.

[28] *A contrario* this can also be deduced from Article 8 (2), determining the provisions on free movement of goods which are only applicable to products originating in the EEA, and which does not mention Art. 23, which in turn refers to the Annex on technical regulations and standards. Therefore, one can argue that the rules referred to in this Annex are *not* only applicable to products originating in the EEA.

[29] Art. 8 (2) *juncto* Arts. 11 and 12.

[30] See Ch. 8, pp. 291–5.

Two elements can be noted here. First, it is confirmed that the Community will take the initiative to negotiate and conclude these agreements—as indeed it has already done.[31] That is only logical, in view of the fact that it is the Community which has drawn up (and will continue to draw up) the directives to which the agreements will relate. Secondly, the Community will not formally negotiate in the place of the EFTA States, but the practical results may be similar, since it is provided that these States will conclude parallel agreements. These agreements will by definition be very similar to the ones concluded by the Community, as the substantive rules within the EEA are the same. Accordingly, this is at least one area in which, in the words of one commentator, 'EC and EFTA edge towards a common external regime'.[32]

The Agreement on the EEA also incorporates the *acquis communautaire* in the field of public procurement.[33] As was shown in chapter 10, the relevant directives contain very few references to trade relations with third countries. The most important of these are the rejection and preference rules of the Utilities Directive.[34] Those rules are also taken over in the Agreement, be it with some modifications, which, however, do not relate to their substance.[35] Accordingly, the external policy of possibly rejecting tenders of third-country origin and preferring equivalent domestic (in the sense of Community, and in this context of EEA) tenders will also have to be implemented by the EFTA countries. The modifications relate mainly to the conclusion of agreements ensuring 'comparable and effective' access to third-country markets, which remains within the competence of the Community and of each EFTA State.[36] Nevertheless, the aim again is to have maximum convergence, and to that effect it is provided that 'the Contracting Parties consult closely in their negotiations with third countries'.[37] The fact that the negotiations referred to primarily take place within the framework of the Uruguay Round, in which the EFTA countries also participate, facilitates the achieving of such convergence.

Trade in services

It was mentioned in Chapter 1 that the EC Treaty contains only minor explicit references to external relations in the area of service transactions.[38] It is not surprising, therefore, that the general provisions on services of the EEA

[31] Ch. 8, p. 292.

[32] Nikolaus G. van der Pas, 'The European Economic Area Aspects Concerning Free Movement of Goods', in *EEA Agreement: Comments and Reflexions*, *supra* n. 23, p. 109.

[33] But not yet the public services directive (see Ch. 9, p. 319).

[34] These rules are explained and commented on in Ch. 9, p. 309 *et seq.*

[35] See Annex XVI, pp. 611–12 of the edition mentioned *supra* n. 3.

[36] See the modifications of Art. 29 (1) of the Utilities Directive, as laid down in Annex XVI, p. 611.

[37] Ibid. 612.   [38] See p. 19.

Agreement do not mention these relations, especially since the EFTA countries did not wish to take over the Community's external policies, which in the services sector are in any event still in an embryonic stage. This absence of common external policies does not have the same effects as with trade in goods, where free movement has to be limited to products originating in the Contracting Parties. Since as a rule services do not circulate and, once produced, cannot be further traded,[39] there is no need to have rules of origin in order to limit the scope of the rules on free movement. Nevertheless, as with goods there are some specific provisions in the Agreement on relations with third countries. It is useful, therefore, to examine the status of external relations in the three services sectors which have been dealt with in previous chapters.

As regards civil aviation the Agreement still refers to the so-called second package of Community acts, which since the signing of the Agreement was replaced by the third package.[40] This illustrates the pace at which the *acquis* laid down in the Agreement is subject to change. The Contracting Parties will probably take the necessary decisions to adapt the Agreement in this respect, because it is inconceivable that the EFTA countries apply the second package, whereas the EC Member States apply the third.[41] As the second package contains no provisions on external relations (and neither does the third), there is nothing on external policies in the Agreement. However, suppose the Member States decide to go along with the Commission's views on developing a comprehensive external policy in the field of civil aviation, gradually replacing the existing bilateral agreements with third countries by agreements concluded by the Community. This would undoubtedly affect the operation of the civil aviation chapter of the EEA Agreement. Given the economic importance of air transport to and from third countries, it is extremely difficult to conceive a smooth combination of a common external policy which is only valid for the Community with an internal market that is extended to the EFTA countries. Some form of co-ordination would be unavoidable.

In the field of financial services, there is of course the Community's reciprocity policy.[42] This policy is not incorporated in the EEA Agreement, and thus not extended to the EFTA countries. Nevertheless, it is confirmed that the EEA rules corresponding to the financial services directives also apply to the setting-up of subsidiaries by third-country financial companies and that, as a result, authorizations granted to such subsidiaries are valid throughout the EEA.[43] But this immediately raises the question as to what happens when the

[39] See, however, also *supra* Ch. 1, p. 25.
[40] See Annex XIII, Section VI of the Agreement (pp. 588–9 of the edition mentioned *supra* n. 3). For the third package, see Ch. 3, p. 86.
[41] These packages contain different rules on the same subjects and thus cannot be combined.
[42] See Ch. 2.
[43] See Annex IX, the sections on insurance (pp. 551 and 554–5 of the edition mentioned *supra* n. 3) and banks and other credit institutions (pp. 557–8 of the same edition).

Community, within the framework of this policy, decides that (for instance) banks of a certain third country are no longer allowed to establish themselves in the Community.[44] Can such a prohibition be circumvented by setting up a subsidiary in an EFTA country? The Annex of the Agreement on financial services contains rules aimed at avoiding this. It is therefore provided that if the Community takes the above-mentioned decision, 'authorizations granted by a competent authority of an EFTA State to such credit institutions shall have validity only in its jurisdiction, except where another Contracting Party decides otherwise for its own jurisdiction'.[45] This excludes the possibility of circumvention. Moreover, provision has also been made for the situation in which EFTA financial companies are discriminated against in third countries. Again taking the case of banks, it is said that

when a third country imposes quantitative restrictions on the establishment of credit institutions of an EFTA State, or imposes restrictions on such credit institutions that it does not impose on Community credit institutions, authorizations granted by competent authorities within the Community to credit institutions being direct or indirect subsidiaries of parent undertakings governed by the laws of that third country shall have validity only in the Community, except where an EFTA State decides otherwise for its own jurisdiction.[46]

This means that the EFTA States are allowed to operate a reciprocity policy of their own which cannot be circumvented by establishment in the Community. It should lastly be noted that the Community commits itself, when negotiating with third countries in order to obtain national treatment and effective market access, to 'endeavour to obtain equal treatment for the credit institutions of the EFTA States'.[47]

The results of this approach are to some extent comparable to the free-trade-area concept. In the case of financial companies which are not allowed to establish themselves in one of the Contracting Parties, but which can set up a subsidiary in the other Contracting Parties, the services which these companies provide cannot 'circulate' freely within the EEA, in similar vein as non-originating goods.

In the field of audiovisual services the rules of the directive on television broadcasting are also extended to the EEA, including the quota for European works.[48] One must assume that this means that the concept of European works is broadened so as to include the EFTA States.[49] Moreover, it will be

---

[44] See Ch. 2, pp. 55–6.

[45] See at p. 558 of the edition mentioned *supra* n. 3; for insurance, see n. 43.

[46] *Supra* n. 3, p. 558.   [47] Ibid.

[48] Council Directive 89/552/EEC, OJ L 298/23 of 17 Oct. 1989, discussed in Ch. 4, part 1. In the EEA Agreement, see Annex X on audiovisual services.

[49] See Art. 6 (1) (*a*) of the directive. This broadening is not entirely certain, though, because no reference to that effect can be found in the EEA Agreement, neither in the relevant Annex nor in Protocol 1 on horizontal adaptations. However, it is difficult to construe the Agreement in any other way, because otherwise the EFTA States have to broadcast a majority of programmes made in the Community.

remembered that the quota rules also provide for the possibility of concluding agreements with 'other European third countries' in order to let their television programmes be counted as European works. In the EEA Agreement, the rules of the directive are adapted so that the EFTA States are also allowed to conclude such agreements. Consultations concerning the contents of such agreements are possible.[50]

In the field of telecommunications services, the relevant Annex mentions all the Community instruments dealt with in Chapter 4,[51] without any specific modifications. Accordingly, the external dimension of these instruments also applies to the EEA.

Comments

In previous chapters the function of having a common commercial policy for achieving a genuinely single market has been amply treated. Not only is a common commercial policy necessary to prevent deflections of trade. Without it, the conditions of competition throughout the market are likely to be distorted. An abstract example clarifies this.[52] Suppose Member State *A* allows bicycles to be freely imported from third countries; it applies no tariffs and no quantitative restrictions. Member State *B*, by contrast, makes such importation much more difficult by applying a 20 per cent tariff and rather strict quantitative restrictions, because otherwise imports would be too harmful for domestic producers. In a free trade area, the foreign bicycles imported in *A* and re-exported to *B* are subject to the same above-mentioned restrictions, because free trade only applies to products originating in the area. However, suppose there are bicycle producers in both *A* and *B*. All these producers are able to distribute their products in the whole of the free trade area. They are therefore direct competitors. But the conditions of competition under which these producers operate are fundamentally different according to whether they are established in *A* or *B*, because those of *B* are sheltered against third-country competition and those of *A* are not. Moreover, in the event that foreign bicycles occupy a large share of A's market (e.g. 40 per cent), there is not much of a real internal market in bicycles in the free trade area.[53]

In the EEA, the problem of avoiding deflection of trade is taken care of. But the problem of avoiding distortions of competition caused by divergent commercial policies is not. From this point of view, the EEA is not really an internal market. Indeed, one commentator at least is of the view that the fact that the EEA is not a customs union prevents it from being a genuine internal

[50] See Annex X, p. 562 of the edition mentioned *supra* n. 3.
[51] See Annex XI, p. 563.
[52] Cf. Ch. 5, p. 147.
[53] Cf. Ch. 6, part 2, on the regime regarding Japanese cars. This practical example is also illustrative for the EEA, since at least a number of EFTA countries do not restrict importation of Japanese cars, the latter occupying substantial market shares, see Ch. 6, n. 58.

market.[54] Nevertheless, the aim of the Contracting Parties is clearly to extend as much as possible the Community's internal market to the EFTA countries. The absence of the customs union dimension could cripple the EEA in this respect.[55] Looked at from the angle of equalizing the conditions of competition, which according to the preamble of the Agreement is one of the EEA's fundamental objectives,[56] it is as though one of three legs is missing. The Agreement harmonizes internal rules governing economic transactions with a view to equalizing those conditions, it sets up common rules on competition policy so that private enterprises are not able to distort competition, but it does not equalize the conditions of external competition.

The foregoing is of course theoretical. It may be that in practice the Community's and the EFTA States' commercial policies do not always diverge very much. After all, they are all members of the GATT, which determines the basic rules governing their external trade relations. If the Uruguay Round is concluded these rules will become broader in scope and more detailed, leaving even less independence in commercial policy-making. Perhaps the divergences are greater in a number of specific sectors such as cars and textiles.

Moreover, as we have seen in some areas provision has been made in the Agreement for co-ordinating (at least to some extent) external policies. That is the case with mutual recognition agreements regarding conformity assessment, agreements concerning the opening-up of public procurement in the excluded sectors and the objective of obtaining reciprocity in the financial services sector. It is therefore certainly not entirely true that commercial policies are completely left out of the EEA Agreement. To the extent that such co-ordination actually takes place, it goes without saying that the danger of distortions of competition diminishes.

It may well be, however, that in some fields much more co-ordination will be needed. The most striking example is civil aviation. As was said, from the moment the Community actually develops a common external policy in this area, it is difficult to conceive how this policy, if it is not extended to the EFTA

[54] Van der Pas, *supra* n. 32, pp. 112–13. It should be noted that in standard theories on economic integration the customs union always comes in between a free trade area and a common market, see e.g. Jacques Pelkmans, 'EC92 as a Challenge to Economic Analysis', in S. Borner and H. Grubel (eds.), *The European Community after 1992: Perspectives from the Outside* (Basingstoke: Macmillan, 1992), 17; Peter Robson, *The Economics of International Integration* (London: Allen and Unwin, 1980), ch. 5. Cf. also Nell, *supra* n. 19, p. 2, where he puts the question: 'Existe-t-il un statut "intermédiaire" entre une zone de libre-échange et une union économique et monétaire en devenir, sans passer par une union douanière?' See, lastly, also Bourgeois, *supra* n. 23, p. 13, stating: 'L'EEE n'est donc pas une "union douanière" entre la Communauté et les États de l'AELE, encore moins un "marché commun"'. That seems to be overstating, in view of the fact that a common market has always been defined as entailing the free movement of factors of production, which is precisely the objective of the EEA.

[55] *Contra* Wijkman, *supra* n. 20.

[56] 'Considering the objective of establishing a dynamic and homogeneous European Economic Area, *based on common rules and equal conditions of competition* ... ' (italics added).

countries, can be combined with the EEA internal market in civil aviation. Indeed, the rules of the third civil aviation package allow completely free establishment which will (probably) apply to the whole EEA.[57] But if the Community concludes agreements on traffic rights with third countries, all Community air carriers will be able to exercise these rights. All kinds of problems would emerge if the EFTA States continued to operate their own networks of bilateral agreements, limiting traffic rights to national carriers, as is now the case. That would surely be liable seriously to distort the conditions of competition within the EEA. At the same time there is perhaps a danger that the fact that in areas such as civil aviation co-ordination of external policies will be unavoidable, may make the development of the Community's external policy even more cumbersome and time-consuming than it already is today.

In conclusion, it is obvious that only the implementation of the EEA Agreement will show whether the absence of common external policies actually distorts the conditions of competition within the EEA, thereby damaging the internal-market character of the EEA. However, again one gets the impression that the Community does not take the external dimension of its internal market too seriously, since it has agreed to extending all the substantive rules governing the internal market to the EFTA countries without looking upon the absence of common external policies as something which stands in the way of this extension.

[57] This is not completely certain yet because the Contracting Parties have not yet decided to apply the third package to the EEA.

11

Conclusions

The above analysis shows that the external dimension of completing the internal market in the field of trade in goods and services is a subject with many facets, even if looked at 'merely' from a legal perspective. Moreover, it is a subject which is in constant evolution, making the target of this study a moving one. Within the next couple of years, it may perhaps be said that this target has been completely missed. Be that as it may, an attempt has been made to expose the more general questions which the external dimension of the internal market programme raises. 'Questions' is indeed the right word, since this is a field in which few definitive answers have as yet been given. This study can therefore amount to no more than a *status quaestionis*.

This concluding chapter is aimed at bringing together the basic questions and by so doing putting them in a more general perspective. It seems appropriate, in this respect, to look at the subject from two angles. The first is the internal angle, i.e. Community integration. After all, defining the external dimension of the internal market is in the first place one element of the Community's policies concerning the completion of this market. It cannot be dissociated from these policies as it is bound to affect them substantially, bearing in mind the ever increasing economic interdependence to which the Community is subject. However, it is equally obvious that defining the external dimension does not take place in an international vacuum. The Community is an active participant in what one distinguished commentator calls the world trading system.[1] The external policies which it develops are thus bound to play an important role in the development of this system, as the Uruguay Round negotiations illustrate. The world trading system is therefore the second angle from which the external dimension of the internal market is to be looked at (see below).

If the preceding chapters have not already done so, this chapter certainly goes beyond purely legal issues to address matters of policy. The latter, however, are not insulated from their legal setting. The law is, in one sense, an instrument for developing certain policies. It is this instrumental function which the overview below tries to explore.

---

[1] John H. Jackson, *The World Trading System: Law and Policy of International Economic Relations* (Cambridge, Mass.: MIT Press, 1989).

The External Dimension and Community Integration

The non-completion of the external dimension

The first, most obvious observation that has to be made is that the external dimension of the internal market has been insufficiently defined. Whereas the programme for the completion of the internal market has in general been successful, in that the deadline of 1 January 1993 has more or less been met, that is not the case for the external dimension. This aspect of the programme has certainly not yet been completed. Two elements of this non-completion are worth emphasizing.

First, the Community's institutions did not pay much attention (to say the least) to the external dimension of the internal market programme when it was devised.[2] In the White Paper, there were hardly any references to external relations and the Single European Act merely introduced new provisions concerning general foreign policy (the title on European Political Co-operation) and did not mention external relations in internal market-related areas.[3] It was only in the course of 1988, when the proposal for a Second Banking Directive was published, that as a result of the Fortress Europe incrimination the Community was forced to pay more attention to the external dimension. It should be borne in mind that the programme was at that time, if not in substance then at least as regards timing, almost half-way.

There are varying views on the causes of this omission. Pelkmans argues that the external dimension was really overlooked by most,[4] whereas Tsoukalis is of the opinion that the omission was 'a deliberate attempt to sidestep a potentially controversial issue at a delicate stage of the intra-EC negotiations'.[5] Perhaps the truth lies somewhere in between. Undoubtedly, the Community's institutions, and in particular the Commission, responsible for setting up the programme, concentrated their efforts in the beginning exclusively on the internal side, as the most important objective then was to convince the various political and industrial circles inside the Community that the programme was worthwhile and that it could be realized. In this marketing effort, the external dimension had no role to play, since it would only have raised the vexed questions of whether a Fortress Europe was under construction or whether, conversely, the internal market would primarily benefit third-country competitors. The fact that the external dimension was so

[2] See Introduction, p. 2.

[3] Only Art. 130*n*, on research and technological development, and Art. 130*r* (5), concerning environmental protection, deal with external relations.

[4] Jacques Pelkmans, 'Europe 1992: A Handmaiden to GATT', in F. Laursen (ed.), *Europe 1992: World Partner? The Internal Market and the World Political Economy* (Maastricht: European Institute of Public Administration, 1991), 148–9 and 'EC92 as a Challenge to Economic Analysis', in S. Borner and H. Grubel (eds.), *The European Community after 1992: Perspectives from the Outside* (Basingstoke: Macmillan, 1992), 7.

[5] Loukas Tsoukalis, *The New European Economy: The Politics and Economics of Integration* (Oxford: Oxford University Press, 1991), 268.

consistently neglected leads one to suspect that the real policy-makers indeed deliberately omitted it. However, this does not explain why in 1988, three years after the White Paper, the Community was still caught off guard when the Fortress Europe campaign was launched. It looks as though by that time a certain degree of complacency had set in with respect to leaving aside the external dimension. In this sense, Pelkmans is probably right in characterizing it as being overlooked.

The observation made by Hilf is striking in this connection. He indicates that the almost exclusive preoccupation with internal policies also character-ized the conception itself of the Community, since the three founding Treaties are poorly drafted as regards external relations.[6] Perhaps this reflects the eminently political aim underlying Community integration: to build, in the words of the EC Treaty, 'an ever closer union among the peoples of Europe', which is much more inward-looking than less ambitious forms of integration such as 'mere' free trade areas and customs unions.

The second observation is that the Community has not been able to make up the arrears. At the time of writing, i.e. the summer of 1993, the external dimension of the internal market is far from being fully defined. In some fields, common policies have been set in train but have not yet been completed. That is the case with the regime governing imports of goods from third countries:[7] the effort to replace national commercial policies with a genuinely uniform common policy is on course, but not yet finished.[8] This is also the case with the problem of strategic export controls.[9] In the field of civil aviation, a common policy was proposed by the Commission already in 1990 but appears to be totally blocked by the Council of Ministers.[10] In other areas, there are common rules governing external policies, but upon closer examination there is little common in these policies. That is primarily the case with the rejection and preference rules in the field of public procurement in the excluded sectors.[11] As was mentioned, these rules leave a lot of discretion to the Member States as to which kind of external policies are pursued. Lastly, in some areas, mainly related to services, there is nothing as yet with respect to the external dimension. There are, for example, no common rules regarding Community branches of third-country financial services companies[12] nor regarding the provision of transfrontier services (in the absence of establish-ment) in the fields of financial, audiovisual, and telecommunications services.[13]

---

[6] Meinhard Hilf, 'Europa '92: Festung oder Partner?', in M. Hilf and C. Tomuschat (eds.), *EG und Drittstaatsbeziehungen nach 1992* (Baden-Baden: Nomos, 1991), 9.
[7] See Chs. 5 and 6.
[8] See the example of Japanese cars, Ch. 6, part 2.
[9] See Ch. 7.   [10] See Ch. 3.
[11] See Ch. 9, pp. 305 *et seq.*   [12] Ch. 2, pp. 49–50.   [13] Chs. 2 and 4.

There are various reasons for these arrears. One is, of course, that the Community was late in even starting to develop external policies related to the completion of the internal market. But this late start is not sufficient to explain why the Commission issued important proposals such as those pertaining to the abolition of national quotas, textiles and clothing, bananas, and strategic export controls only in the course of 1992, the last year of the programme, with the knowledge that it would be very difficult to have them adopted in time for the magical date of 1 January 1993. There are other factors which have contributed to delaying or not dealing with the external dimension. First, some of the issues on the agenda of the external dimension are politically difficult because, for example, the protection of sensitive sectors is at stake, third country exporters are the first to benefit from liberalization, and the various Member States have conflicting interests.[14] In these cases, agreement was only likely to be reached when the Member States started to feel 1993 breathing down their neck. In a second category of areas there is a power struggle between the Commission and the Council (or, in other words, the Member States) regarding the competences of the Community. That applies, in general, to the entire services sector, and especially civil aviation, where the Member States are unwilling to go along with the views of the Commission concerning the scope of the Common Commercial Policy. This power struggle has held up much of the substantive debate. Thirdly, there are the Uruguay Round negotiations. The relationship between these negotiations and the internal market is investigated in the second section, below.[15] Suffice it to say here that a lot of the topics which are on the agenda of these negotiations are related to the external dimension of the internal market.[16] The Community's institutions clearly have in mind to have part of the external dimension of the internal market determined by the outcome of these negotiations. Unfortunately, the latter are at the time of writing still not concluded, and this circumstance has cast its shadow on the formulation of the Community's external policies. Although the dragging on of the negotiations can be partly attributed to the Community's own behaviour, it is not particularly the internal-market issues which have blocked the Round. Fourthly, in some cases the Community's institutions are apparently of the opinion that there are no compelling reasons for laying down common rules.[17]

[14] See especially Ch. 6.

[15] pp. 366–8.

[16] See Christopher Milner and David Allen, 'The External Implications of 1992', in D. Swann (ed.), *The Single European Market and Beyond: A Study of the Wider Implications of the Single European Act* (London: Routledge, 1992), 175, who report that of the fifteen Uruguay Round negotiating groups nine dealt with issues figuring on the 1992 agenda.

[17] That applies, for example, to the various regimes governing branches of third-country financial services companies, see Ch. 2, pp. 49–50.

The basic policy question: Community preference[18]

The basic policy question underlying the external dimension of the internal market can be called the question of Community, or internal preference.[19] In its essence it is a simple one. Should the Community, when developing its policies concerning the completion of the internal market, extend without much ado the benefits which this internal liberalization entails to trade with third countries? Should it attach certain conditions to such an extension? Or should it reserve these benefits for internal trade? To put it in more technical language: when the Community lays down new regulation aimed at completing the internal market, should it simply 'ignore' the external dimension, thus ensuring that the law applies to both internal and external trade alike, or to both domestic and foreign economic actors? Or should it install a special regime governing external relations? Phrased in these terms the question looks beguilingly simple. However, for a complex of reasons it is extremely difficult for the Community to give one basic answer to this question.

Economists would come out with one simple answer. Liberalization of trade improves economic efficiency and enhances welfare. The Community should therefore automatically extend its internal liberalization policies to external trade.[20] But how can this be achieved in practice, given the fact that the completion of the internal market is situated at such a complex level of economic integration and involves such a variety of policies, which are often only indirectly related to external trade? What does it mean, for example, to extend the benefits of intra-Community liberalization in the field of technical regulations and standards to trade with third countries? Should the Community simply take over international standards, even when these are not considered appropriate or sufficient? Should it apply mutual, or even unilateral recognition of technical regulations and standards in direct trade with third countries, without looking at the content of these regulations and standards? Should it, to give another example, allow third-country financial services companies to provide their services within the Community, without itself performing any prudential supervision of these companies' operations, leaving this to their home country authorities? It is obvious that in all cases in which policies other than pure trade policies are at stake, such as the

---

[18] For the analysis in this section and in the following one, see also Piet Eeckhout, 'The External Dimension of the Internal Market and the Scope and Content of a Modern Commercial Policy', in M. Maresceau (ed.), *The European Community's Commercial Policy after 1992: The Legal Dimension* (Dordrecht: Martinus Nijhoff, 1993), 79–101.

[19] This concept is often used in the context of the Common Agricultural Policy. However, it is not the author's intention when employing this term here to drag in all the connotations linked to the external effects of the Community's agricultural policies.

[20] Cf. L. Alan Winters, 'Partner Interests in Customs Union Formation: An Economic View', in P. Demaret, J. Bourgeois, and I. Van Bael (eds.), *Trade Laws of the European Community and the United States in a Comparative Perspective* (Brussels: Story-Scientia for the College of Europe, 1992), 287–90.

protection of public health, of the environment and of the consumer (and these cases are, by the way, the bulk of the programme) the Community cannot simply extend the benefits of internal integration in the absence of guarantees that these non-commercial objectives continue to be achieved. A specific, substantive regime governing external relations is therefore required.

Moreover, an automatic, unilateral extension to external trade of the benefits which internal liberalization entails is in political terms perceived as unilateral disarmament.[21] Why give away the benefits of the internal market without being ensured that Community companies are given equivalent access to third-country markets? Is that not contrary to the Community's interests? Why open up unilaterally in those areas in which there are no international rules, binding on the Community, which require the same? After all, the only general provision of international law governing the effects of economic integration on third countries is Article XXIV of the GATT, and it only deals with customs unions and free trade areas, merely requiring (as regards the former) that

the duties and other regulations of commerce imposed at the institution of any such union . . . in respect of trade with contracting parties not parties to such union . . . shall not on the whole be higher or more restrictive than the general incidence of the duties and regulations of commerce applicable in the constituent territories prior to the formation of such union . . . .[22]

This provision does not require that economic integration aimed at establishing a real internal market be automatically extended to external trade. Why, moreover, open up unilaterally while such opening-up is on the agenda of the Uruguay Round negotiations?

The key word may be uttered now: reciprocity. For what reasons should the Community extend the benefits of the internal market to trade with third countries if reciprocity is not ensured? Again, many economists will argue that this is an outdated, mercantilist concept and that reciprocity is not required for free trade to be beneficial. That opens up a very fundamental debate on the right course towards trade liberalization, a debate which is dealt with further below.[23] Suffice it to say here that reciprocity continues to be the 'ruling paradigm'[24] of the world trading system, as exemplified by the Uruguay Round negotiations.

Have we thus not arrived at the basic answer to the preference question? Is

[21] Cf. Edmund Dell, 'Of Free Trade and Reciprocity', 9 *World Economy* (1986), 2: 138. Cf. also the famous expression used by Commission President Delors: 'la Communauté sera ouverte, mais elle ne sera pas offerte'.

[22] Art. XXIV (5) (a).

[23] See pp. 362–6.

[24] The term is used by Jan Tumlir, though not in exactly the same context, in 'GATT Rules and Community Law: A Comparison of Economic and Legal Functions', in M. Hilf, F. G. Jacobs, and E.-U. Petersmann (eds.), *The European Community and GATT*, 2nd edn. (Deventer: Kluwer, 1989), 19.

reciprocity not the fundamental answer to this question? Yes and no. Yes because it does touch upon the essence of the Community's approach towards defining the external dimension of the internal market. And no because reciprocity is only a superficial, formal answer and does not apply to all segments of the programme.

It is a superficial and formal answer since there are many kinds of reciprocity. The term of itself does not indicate what exactly the Community wishes to obtain in return for extending the benefits of the internal market. Does the Community seek reciprocal national treatment? Does it wish to impose its own approach towards the regulation of certain economic activities? Does it wish sectoral or overall reciprocity? Does it wish a reciprocal balance of trade flows? Since all these questions cannot be dissociated from the Uruguay Round negotiations and the broader context of the world trading system, they are examined in the next section.[25]

Moreover, reciprocity clearly does not apply to all segments of the internal market programme. The concept is not relevant, for example, for the completion of the Common Commercial Policy in the area of imports of goods and the elimination of restrictions on intra-Community trade in third-country goods. Neither is it relevant for the problem of strategic export controls.

As a preliminary conclusion, it can be said that the Community's institutions have not given one single substantive answer to the basic preference question which the external dimension of the internal market programme raises. Neither have they devised a comprehensive strategy.[26] They have only given a formal answer: reciprocity. Given the complexity of the programme, more than that was probably either impossible or inappropriate.[27]

The scope of the Common Commercial Policy

The preference question brings us to the problem of the Community's powers to regulate external relations. As was mentioned, this is an important problem since divergences of opinion between the institutions on the scope of the Community's external powers often block or inhibit the elaboration of a common external policy. In a number of the preceding chapters, a lot of attention was devoted to the function and scope of the Common Commercial Policy (CCP).[28] Indeed, it is clear that, in the system of the EC Treaty, the CCP is the external side of the establishment of the internal market. If the latter were a building, the CCP would be its façade. It is useful to bring together here the various observations which were made in this connection in

[25] pp. 362–6.
[26] This is welcomed by Pelkmans, 'Europe 1992: A Handmaiden to GATT', *supra* n. 4, p. 149, because in his view it has lead to more liberal external policies.
[27] Cf. Henri Froment-Meurice, *L'Europe de 1992: espace et puissance* (Paris: La Documentation française, 1988), 14–15.
[28] See particularly Chs. 1, 3, and 7.

previous chapters, and to try to demonstrate that, when we are looking at the CCP, we are indeed standing before the façade of the internal market.

Various commentators have referred to the need to extend the scope of the CCP so that it covers the external side of the internal market. Already in 1984, *in tempore non suspecto*, Ehlermann stated in his famous paper on the scope of the CCP: 'The Tokyo Round Codes on subsidies, government procurement and standards are excellent illustrations of the need to extend modern trade policy to measures which apply to imports, exports *and* the internal market.'[29] Perhaps even more indicative than this and similar statements by distinguished Community lawyers, who are often under suspicion of preferring pro-integrationist solutions, is the fact that some economists, who are much less burdened by the legal consequences which their views entail, have put forward the same reasoning. In the words of André Sapir,

The completion of the European internal market will require an extension of the Community's jurisdiction on external trade in areas covered by the 1992 program. In other words, common attitudes will have to be adopted by the 12 EC Member States toward third countries in such areas as safeguard clauses, technical barriers, government procurement, and services.[30]

The preference question confirms these views. Indeed, it is obvious that this basic question underlying the external dimension of the internal market—namely whether and under what conditions the benefits of intra-Community liberalization are extended to trade with third countries—is eminently a question of commercial policy. It is a question which pulls a whole range of domestic policies into the commercial policy stream. When the Community decides that third-country banks may establish themselves in the internal market and thus benefit from the increased opportunities which the internal financial services market offers, on the condition, however, that Community banks are not discriminated against on third-country markets, that is clearly a measure of commercial policy. The same goes for the preparedness to accept that the conformity of foreign products with Community technical regulations is checked in third countries, but on the condition that this takes place in the framework of a mutual recognition agreement offering comparable

---

[29] C. D. Ehlermann, 'The Scope of Article 113 of the EEC Treaty', in *Mélanges offerts à Pierre-Henri Teitgen* (Paris: Pedone, 1984), 154. See also Jacques H. J. Bourgeois, 'The Common Commercial Policy: Scope and Nature of the Powers', in E. L. M. Völker (ed.), *Protectionism and the European Community*, 2nd edn. (Deventer: Kluwer, 1986), 6; Ulrich Everling, 'The Law of the External Economic Relations of the European Community', in *The European Community and GATT*, supra, n. 24, p. 103.

[30] André Sapir, 'Comments', in J. J. Schott (ed.), *Free Trade Areas and U.S. Trade Policy* (Washington, DC: Institute for International Economics, 1989), 314. See also, by the same author, 'Does 1992 Come before or after 1990? On Regional versus Multilateral Integration', in R. W. Jones and A. O. Krueger (eds.), *The Political Economy of International Trade* (Cambridge, Mass.: Basil Blackwell, 1990), 205. Cf. L. Alan Winters, supra n. 20, p. 288 and 'European Trade and Welfare after "1992"', in L. A. Winters (ed.), *Trade Flows and Trade Policy after '1992'* (Cambridge: University Press, 1992), 27.

opportunities to Community exporters. And a lot of other examples could be mentioned. Consequently, all specific measures adopted by the Community and relating to the internal market, be they autonomous or conventional, which in one way or another provide some kind of answer to this preference question, should be characterized as being measures of commercial policy.

Such an interpretation of the commercial policy concept is consistent with the system of the EC Treaty. To understand this, one should place the CCP in its historical perspective. It is uncontested that the CCP complements the customs union upon which, in the words of Article 9 of the EC Treaty, the Community is based. Such a union entails a common external tariff, and without a common commercial policy accompanying this common tariff the aim of having a uniform regime governing external trade would be frustrated. The fact that the CCP was seen as a complement to the customs union[31] has its origin in the GATT setting. The General Agreement, which in Article XXIV provides the legal basis for the establishment of customs unions and free trade areas, prefers the use of tariffs over other trade policy instruments. The aim of the Agreement was to have all non-tariff border measures inhibiting international trade eliminated as quickly as possible, by in principle outlawing them,[32] and then to reduce tariffs in multilateral negotiations.[33] The CCP should be seen in this perspective. In the ideal world, it would almost have been self-destroying. The Community, in parallel with its GATT partners, would have abolished all quantitative restrictions as well as other border barriers, while participating in negotiations on tariff reductions. But the ideal world never materializes. Instead of being eliminated, non-tariff barriers gradually became a major problem of international trade. Not only did it prove difficult to do away with classical obstacles such as quantitative restrictions, governments also displayed great creativity in developing an entire arsenal of other protectionist measures and did not shy away from using internal, domestic policies to that effect. The Uruguay Round can be characterized as one big attempt at dismantling this arsenal.

This development took place not only in international trade but also within the Community. There, too, it was something which was clearly not foreseen when the founding Treaties were drafted. Article 30, EC Treaty, merely prohibits quantitative restrictions and 'measures having equivalent effect'. For Community lawyers, the latter phrase sounds all-encompassing, but that is entirely due to the case-law of the Court of Justice which has, correctly, given a very wide interpretation to this provision. Taken literally, however, the phrase is of rather limited scope.

---

[31] See also Art. 3 (*b*), original EEC Treaty, describing as one of the activities of the Community: 'the establishment of a common customs tariff and of a common commercial policy towards third countries'.

[32] See especially Art. XI.   [33] Cf. Jackson, *supra* n. 1, p. 115.

The Court's case-law on the prohibition of non-tariff barriers in intra-Community trade has been very effective, but a jurisprudential approach has its intrinsic limits. It is precisely the aim of the internal market programme to push the elimination of these barriers much further than that.

The conclusions for the scope of the CCP are evident. As much as the provisions of the Treaty prohibiting the use of non-tariff barriers in intra-Community trade needed to be widely interpreted, in view of the developments which took place since the founding of the Community, the provisions on the CCP also have to be given an extensive interpretation, in parallel with the internal market concept.

The approach defended here is in line with the Court's case-law on the scope of the CCP. This case-law refers both to the external context (the world trading system) in which the CCP has to play its part and to the internal function of having a common trade policy. The latter facet is not often emphasized, yet it is crucial for the establishment of the internal market. The Court, as analysed above,[34] has indicated that the requirement of uniformity inherent in the CCP is aimed at avoiding deflections of trade and distortions of competition within the Community which would result from a non-uniform external regime. Especially the criterion of distortion of competition is important, in view of the internal market programme, as is evidenced by the *Titanium dioxide* judgment.[35] Indeed, the more integrated this market becomes, acquiring the characteristics of a genuinely single market, the less tolerable are distortions of competition caused by divergent government policies, be they internal or external. It is for example not tolerable that the establishment of the internal market in civil aviation, entailing the general freedom to provide transport services within the Community, is not accompanied by a uniform external regime, but that, instead, the Member States continue to be able to distort the conditions of competition prevailing on this market by determining external traffic rights through bilateral agreements with third countries.

Exactly how wide is the scope of the CCP, as regards external policies related to the establishment and functioning of the internal market? To which kind of measures does it apply? Above it was submitted that the rule-of-reason approach proposed by Timmermans offers a valuable tool for demarcating the field of commercial policy.[36] According to this approach, one should look at the scope of the free movement of goods and the freedom to provide services within the Community in order to determine whether a given measure, when applied to external trade, comes within the range of the CCP. For example, a measure aimed at protecting public health may, by virtue of Article 36 of the Treaty, restrict intra-Community trade. Similarly, one cannot uphold the view

[34] Ch. 1, pp. 24 *et seq.*
[35] Case C-300/89, *Commission* v. *Council*, [1991] ECR I-2867, see Ch. 5, p. 147. See especially the Opinion of Advocate-General Tesauro, [1991] ECR I-2887–2889.
[36] See Ch. 1, pp. 29–31.

that the same measure, when applied to external trade, would come within the Community's exclusive competence by virtue of the Treaty provisions on the CCP.

This rule-of-reason approach is of course only a tool, and not a strict rule. It must be refined to take into account the differences between internal integration and external policies. For example, the Court has given a wide interpretation to the prohibitions of Articles 30, 59, and 60 of the Treaty, which encompass measures which apply without distinction to domestic and imported goods and services. It is doubtful whether the scope of the CCP is as extended as that. It would be better to limit this scope to measures which discriminate, be it openly or covertly, against foreign products.

The rule-of-reason approach is also fully in line with the preference question underlying the external dimension of the internal market. When measures are aimed at protecting public health, the environment, or the consumer, they do not provide an answer to the preference question; they do not, in other words, aim at determining the conditions of competition between goods and services originating in the Community and those imported from third countries. Accordingly, they are not commercial policy measures.

The internal market implies the free movement of goods, the freedom to provide services, freedom of establishment, free movement of workers, and free movement of capital. It is obvious that the CCP does not cover all external policies which are related to these freedoms. The CCP applies to trade relations, and though this is a continuously widening concept, it cannot be used for issues such as migration and purely monetary capital movements. Trade refers to exchanges of goods and services. However, there are measures relating to investment, establishment, and movement of workers which are surely relevant for these exchanges. It is widely acknowledged, for example, that trade in services entails investment and establishment issues, since in many cases such trade requires having a local establishment. Therefore, measures relating thereto, such as the reciprocity provisions in the financial services directives, also come within the scope of the CCP. Similarly, international trade in services may require that a company temporarily transfer parts of its personnel abroad. Measures relating to such movement of workers (by, for example, restricting it to the company's key personnel) are also commercial policy measures.

To the scope of the CCP as described above should be added the concept of external harmonization.[37] Without introducing this concept, there would be a lacuna in the Community's commercial policy powers. As measures aimed at protecting, for example, the environment or public security, and applying to trade with third countries, do not come within the scope of the CCP, as interpreted in line with the rule of reason, the Member States remain entitled

---

[37] See Ch. 7, pp. 252–60.

to adopt such measures. None the less, this poses the risk of having divergent external policies, thereby creating deflections of trade or distortions of competition within the Community. The example of strategic export controls has been analysed above.[38] In the context of intra-Community trade, Article 100*a* provides the necessary powers for harmonizing national legislation with a view to eliminating distortions of competition caused by divergent national policies relating to the protection of the environment, of public health, etc.[39] Similarly, Article 113 must be interpreted as providing the necessary powers to perform such harmonization when external trade is at stake. That clearly follows from the *Chernobyl* judgment.[40] Consequently, one could say that Article 113 is to some extent the external counterpart of Article 100*a*.

The concept of external harmonization partly removes the tension which exists between the exclusive character of the Community's competence to conduct a commercial policy and the gradually expanding scope of this competence.[41] For measures coming within this concept, there is no such tension since the Member States remain competent to adopt them as long as the Community has not acted. That is justified because the respective competences are different in character. Those of the Member States are concerned with safeguarding public health, external security, or protecting the environment, whereas those of the Community are limited to bringing about a uniform external regime in order to prevent deflections of trade or distortions of competition.

The above-mentioned tension is of course not completely eliminated by the concept of external harmonization. It still exists for a number of important areas, one of which is trade in services. However, the difficulties associated with this tension should not be exaggerated. The Court of Justice has never outlawed national commercial policy measures adopted in those fields in which it had not yet been possible to lay down uniform common rules.[42] Instead, it allows for transitional periods. Similarly, the Commission is obviously prepared, as its proposals concerning civil aviation demonstrate, gradually to take over external competences.[43] In addition, the concept of exclusivity does not necessarily mean that the Member States have no longer any role to play with respect to the implementation of the common policy. In the services sector, there may be more room for Member State involvement than in the area of trade in goods, where uniformity depends much more upon the details of common rules.

---

[38] Ibid.

[39] Again see the *Titanium Dioxide* case, *supra* n. 35.

[40] Case C-62/88, *Greece* v. *Council*, [1990] ECR I-1527, see Ch. 7, p. 254.

[41] On this tension, see Paul Demaret, 'La politique commerciale: perspectives d'évolution et faiblesses présentes', in J. Schwarze and H. G. Schermers (eds.), *Structure and Dimensions of European Community Policy* (Baden-Baden: Nomos, 1987), 83–5.

[42] See Ch. 5, pp. 150–2.   [43] See Ch. 3.

Conclusions

It is submitted that this approach towards the scope of the CCP could substantially contribute to a better definition of the external dimension of the internal market, especially in the services sector. Not only should newly developed policies, such as a possible General Agreement on Trade in Services, be the sole responsibility of the Community, there are also serious efforts to be undertaken to ensure that existing bilateral or multilateral agreements, to which the Member States are parties, are brought into conformity with Community law.[44] Similarly, the Community should fully participate in the work of international organizations dealing with international services transactions, in accordance with its competences.[45]

One last word on implied powers. The fact that in these paragraphs nothing has yet been said on the role which they can play in defining the external dimension of the internal market is already an indication that I am not convinced that they are important in that respect. As was mentioned, implied powers are difficult to delineate, leaving a lot to the discretion of the institutions which apply them.[46] That is one thing, but admittedly the same goes to some extent for the CCP. However, implied powers merely grant an external competence to the Community, they have nothing to do with developing a comprehensive external policy. Under the provisions on the CCP, the Community is required to draw up uniform rules covering the entire field of trade relations with third countries. Implied powers require nothing of the kind. Moreover, as analysed above, there are two sorts of implied powers.[47] The *AETR* type is almost self-evident: when the Community has drawn up internal rules governing one or other kind of subject-matter, the Member States are of course no longer entitled to conclude agreements with third countries which would affect the operation of these rules. It is, as has been observed, more a rule of conflict than of competence.[48] The *Opinion 1/76* type is clearly wider: whenever the realization of a specific objective of the Community necessitates the conclusion of an international agreement, the Community is competent. Those who argue in favour of a wide interpretation of these two types of implied powers should list their arguments. It then would become apparent that these are the same arguments militating in favour of a wide interpretation of the CCP. It could be said, for example, that with the completion of the internal market in civil aviation, the continued existence of bilateral agreements binding the individual Member States and third countries, and relating

---

[44] The expression used is not intended to mean that such bringing into conformity is a one-sided affair, in which the relevant international agreement simply has to be adapted to Community law. It may also be necessary that the Community enters into negotiations and subsequently modifies its own rules.

[45] See e.g. Ch. 2, p. 74, on the OECD.

[46] See Chs. 1 and 3.   [47] Ch. 1, p. 39.

[48] John Temple Lang, 'The *ERTA* Judgment and the Court's Case-Law on Competence and Conflict', F. G. Jacobs (ed.), 6 *Yearbook of European Law* (1986) (Oxford: Clarendon Press, 1987), 216.

to the exchange of traffic rights, is liable to affect the operation of the internal rules, at least in an economic sense. But that is no more than the argument that in the absence of a common external regime competition within the internal civil aviation market is liable to be distorted. As a result, implied powers should only be allowed to play a role in those cases in which it is established that the CCP does not apply.

Finally, it is submitted that the Maastricht Treaty on European Union, if it enters into force, can only serve to strengthen the CCP. Unfortunately, the CCP did not figure highly on the agenda of the negotiations leading to this Treaty, which did not lead to a clarification of the Community's powers.[49] None the less, the Treaty expands if not the Community's then at least the Union's external competences, by adding a Common Foreign and Security Policy.[50] Moreover, in Article B the Union sets as one of its objectives 'to maintain in full the "acquis communautaire" and build on it ... ' whereas in Article C it is said that '[t]he Union shall in particular ensure the consistency of its external activities as a whole in the context of its external relations, security, economic and development policies'. These objectives cannot be attained if the CCP, which is the core of the Community/Union's external policies, is not strengthened.

The principle of subsidiarity is not of a nature to change this, on the contrary. First, according to the new Article 3*b* subsidiarity does not apply to areas falling within the Community's exclusive competence, such as the CCP. Secondly, even if this principle were to be applied to the CCP, it is hoped that this study demonstrates clearly enough that it would lead to expanding the scope of the CCP, instead of reducing it, because indeed the objectives which are pursued cannot be sufficiently achieved by the Member States acting independently.

---

[49] See Youri Devuyst, 'The EC's Common Commercial Policy and the Treaty on European Union', 16 *World Competition* (1992), 2: 80; Marc Maresceau, 'The Concept "Commercial Policy" and the Difficult Road to Maastricht', in M. Maresceau (ed.), *The European Community's Commercial Policy after 1992: The Legal Dimension* (Dordrecht: Martinus Nijhoff, 1993), 3–19. It is also unfortunate that the Maastricht Treaty did not strengthen the role of the European Parliament in the formulation of commercial policy. As is well known, Art. 113 does not even provide for the Parliament to be consulted, and this has not changed. Given the increasing importance of commercial policy (one need only think of the hefty debate accompanying the Community's external policy in the agricultural sector) that is, from a democratic point of view, unacceptable. There is only one improvement, and it depends on giving a wide interpretation to the relevant provision. According to the new Art. 228 (3), last sentence, the assent of the Parliament is required for certain categories of important agreements. It remains to be seen whether this also applies to the field of trade policy.

[50] The European Union Treaty also amends the EEC Treaty in the field of external relations by, for example, adding a title on development co-operation (Arts. 130*u*–130*y*). The relevant provisions are, however, more a clarification and confirmation of the existing practice than a genuine extension of the Community's powers, cf. Anon., 'Redactionele signalen', 40 *SEW* (1992), 7: 609.

On the instruments of preference

It has been said that the question of preference is the basic policy question underlying the external dimension of the internal market. More attention will be paid to how this question has been answered by the Community in the next section since this answer cannot be dissociated from its context, which is the world trading system. More from an internal perspective, however, an additional question must be put, which at first sight may seem rather technical: does the Community have the necessary instruments to implement preference, i.e. to draw a line between those goods, services, and companies which are considered domestic and thus entitled to the benefits of the internal market, and those which are foreign and not, or only to a lesser degree entitled hereto? It is one thing to decide that Europe's domestic car production should continue to be shielded from fierce Japanese competition, but it is another to determine what a Community and what a Japanese car is. Or, to give another example, the Community can well decide that banks from a third country not granting national treatment to Community banks are no longer allowed to establish themselves in the Community, but how does one determine which banks 'originate' from this country?

In the field of trade in goods, the instruments are clearly there. The Community has its well-established set of rules of origin, determining which products have Community origin and which not.[51] Whether, however, these rules are sophisticated enough to implement preference policies in a satisfactory manner is another matter. The much-publicized dispute on the status of Nissan car production in the United Kingdom has illustrated well that the general criterion of 'last substantial transformation' is totally unadapted for being applied to complex products such as cars.[52] Much more precise criteria are needed for these kinds of products.[53] Moreover, the ever increasing internationalization of manufacturing, especially in high-technology sectors, with R. & D., design, the production of parts and their final assembly taking place in various countries, makes trying to determine the 'nationality' of a product a more and more precarious exercise.[54] Because this is so difficult, it also risks becoming more dependent on the politics of international trade. Again cars offer the nicest example of this danger. Within the USA, Japanese transplant production of cars is seen as a big threat to 'US' manufacturers (mainly the Big Three, i.e. Ford, General Motors, and Chrysler). However, when the Community negotiated with the Japanese government the export-restraint arrangement discussed in Chapter 6, it was obvious that the restraints would not apply to this US-based transplant production because the US

[51] Regulation 2913/92, OJ L 302/1 of 19 Oct. 1992.
[52] See Ch. 6, p. 225.
[53] Cf. also the preference rule in public procurement, and the comments related thereto, Ch. 9, p. 311.
[54] See Ch. 6, p. 225, and Ch. 9, p. 312.

authorities would certainly not accept that exports of (this time) 'US cars' should be limited.[55]

In the field of services, there are no rules of origin. In all cases, therefore, in which the Community seeks to introduce some kind of internal preference, it has to devise something equivalent to rules of origin in order to determine the scope of the preference rules. In view of the complexity, variety, and especially individuality of service transactions, it almost goes without saying that this is an even more haphazard exercise than determining the origin of products. The definition of European programmes in the broadcasting directive makes this clear.[56]

However, in this respect not only are rules of origin applying to the services themselves relevant. For services trade, it was said, having a local establishment is in many cases as important as the provision of cross-border services. This means that, to implement a preference policy, one also needs rules determining the nationality of companies. Before the internal market programme, such rules only partly existed in European Community law. Article 58, EC Treaty, determines the scope of the freedom of establishment as applied to companies, and by so doing determines which are 'Community' companies and which not. But there were no rules determining the country of origin of non-European companies. In order to be able to implement the reciprocity policy in the financial services sector, the Community has had to lay down provisions determining the country of origin of non-European financial services companies. It was observed above that it might prove difficult to apply these provisions.[57] In addition, the rule of Article 58 is a liberal one, making it very easy to set up a 'Community' company, thereby benefiting from the internal market.[58] It will be recalled that it was for this reason that the Community considered it necessary, in the framework of the Utilities Directive, to introduce a preference rule concentrating on the origin of the products constituting a tender. Merely limiting the scope of this directive to tenders emanating from companies established in the Community was deemed to be insufficient for protecting 'genuine' domestic companies.[59]

[55] Cf. Written Question No. 1277/92 by Mr Christian de la Malène, MEP, OJ C 51/12 of 22 Feb. 1993.
[56] See Ch. 4, p. 131.
[57] See Ch. 2, p. 62.
[58] See e.g. Yvon Loussouarn, 'Le droit d'établissment des sociétés', 26 *RTDE* (1990), 2: 236–9; A. Renshaw, 'Le regime appliqué dans la Communauté aux sociétés contrôlées par des intérêts non-communautaires', in P. Demaret (ed.), *Relations extérieures de la Communauté européenne et marché intérieur: aspects juridiques et fonctionnels* (Bruges: Story-Scientia for the College of Europe, 1988), 144–6; Loukas Tsoukalis, *supra* n. 5, p. 275. In the 1962 General Programmes for the abolition of restrictions on the freedom of establishment and the freedom to provide services, adopted on the basis of Arts. 54 and 63 of the Treaty (OJ 1962, pp. 32–46) an attempt has been made to narrow the scope of Art. 58 by laying down that companies seeking to benefit from these two freedoms need to have an effective and continuous link with the economy of one of the Member States. However, the legal status of this requirement is uncertain (see Renshaw, p. 146).
[59] See Ch. 9, p. 308.

None the less, the Community has until now not attempted to tighten, in a general way, the rule of Article 58 in order to implement preferential policies.[60] Only in the field of civil aviation have stricter rules been laid down, linking the Community status of air carriers to the nationality of their shareholders or of the people who control them.[61] This absence of a more rigid general policy relating to the nationality of companies is not to be deplored, for reasons similar to those which are valid for rules of origin for products. As has been observed, there is nowadays 'a colossal criss-crossing of foreign direct investment flows which are constantly reducing the freedom of manœuvre of governments in their own economic and trade policies'.[62] There are more and more companies operating on a global basis, with establishments and investment ties in many countries. Trying to determine the nationality of these companies on any firmer basis than the criteria offered by Article 58 of the Treaty risks becoming an even more precarious and haphazard operation than implementing rules of origin for sophisticated high-technology products.

There is a clear lesson to be drawn from these observations on the instruments of preference. When one looks at the combined effects of the internationalization of production as well as investments, trying to limit the benefits of economic integration to domestic products and companies is getting more and more difficult, even from a purely technical point of view. That puts the preference question itself in perspective. One should not only ask: is it useful to reserve the benefits of the internal market to Community products and companies? The question whether this is feasible without distorting normal trade and investment flows by drawing up detailed nationality rules should immediately be added.

The external dimension as hiatus in the establishment of the internal market

In this last subsection, attention is drawn to those policies relating to the external dimension of the internal market which, from the perspective of Community integration, are most deplorable, because they work to the detriment of the completion and the proper functioning of the internal market. Indeed, in some cases external policies have not strengthened, but, conversely,

[60] According to François Lamoureux, member of the Cabinet of Commission President Delors, it is not excluded that after 1992 the Community would decide 'to harmonize the conditions of constitution of a company in the Community', see 'Reciprocity and 1992', in B. Hawk (ed.), *1992 and EEC/U.S. Competition and Trade Law: Annual Proceedings of the Fordham Corporate Law Institute 1989* (New York: Transnational Juris Publications, 1990), 11.
[61] See Ch. 3, p. 115.
[62] Paul Luyten, 'A View from a Fortress that never was', in T. Oppermann and J. Molsberger (eds.), *A New GATT for the Nineties and Europe '92* (Baden-Baden: Nomos, 1991), 278. See also, in the same sense, Gary Clyde Hufbauer, 'An Overview', in G. C. Hufbauer (ed.), *Europe 1992: An American Perspective* (Washington, DC: The Brookings Institution, 1990), 48; Jagdish Bhagwati, *The World Trading System at Risk* (New York: Harvester Wheatsheaf, 1991), 16–17.

weakened the integration of the various national markets into a genuinely single one. Hence the title of this subsection: the external dimension as hiatus in the establishment of the internal market. In this respect, not much more can be done here but to list these hiatuses again.

In the field of trade in goods, the most significant one is probably the EC–Japan arrangement relating to cars.[63] If it were only for the subquotas, protecting five national markets, which this arrangement provides for, the damage would still be limited. But there are also the possible effects on competition policy.[64] The EC–Japan arrangement is an inhibiting factor for a pro-competitive review of the group exemption for motor vehicle distribution agreements, because the only way the subquota system can be maintained is through restraints on competition at the level of the distribution of cars. One can of course defend the view that the group exemption regulation currently operates in a satisfactory manner, but that view will not be shared by everyone. There still is no single market for cars, due to a number of circumstances, one of which is the distribution policies of the manufacturers.

Related to the case of cars is the fact that the Community appears determined to continue to be able to take regional safeguard measures against imports from third countries, i.e. to be able to protect national markets instead of the overall Community market.[65] A lot depends here on the conditions under which the Community's institutions would be willing to take such action, whether it would really be exceptional or not, and whether the measures would be accompanied by restrictions on intra-Community trade based on Article 115 of the EC Treaty. Those conditions are not defined in Community legislation, which in itself is already unfortunate. It should also be recalled that in this study the point of view is defended that regional safeguard measures are inconsistent with the Treaty provisions on the CCP if they apply to products which are (in the absence of such measures) subject to a common import regime. Such measures disregard the uniformity requirement of Article 113, and are therefore not allowed.[66]

Also concerning trade in goods, there are the rejection and preference rules of the Utilities Directive, governing public procurement in the sectors of water, energy, transport, and telecommunications.[67] As these rules concentrate on the origin of the products constituting a tender, and do not differentiate between products which are in free circulation and those which are not, they make inroads into the principle that once goods are imported into the Community, they are definitively and wholly assimilated to goods originating in the Community. That principle, it should be remembered, is a result of the fact that the Community is a customs union, which, in the words of the EC Treaty, is its very basis.

[63] See Ch. 6, part 2.
[64] See Ch. 6, pp. 216 *et seq.*
[65] See Ch. 5, pp. 166 *et seq.*
[66] See Ch. 5, p. 168.
[67] See Ch. 9, p. 305 *et seq.*

In the services sector, the external dimension of the internal market is to a large extent not yet defined. That in itself is of course a hiatus in the establishment of the internal market, but its seriousness depends on the economic context of the various sectors which are involved. For example, there are no common rules governing the transmission of television programmes in the Community, broadcast by television stations located in third countries. However, the absence of such rules does not appear to affect, at this stage, the establishment and functioning of the internal market for broadcasting.

There is one sector, though, in which the persistent absence of a common external policy (in spite of the efforts of the Commission) does seriously affect the functioning of the internal market, and that is civil aviation.[68] There may now be an internal market for the provision of air transport services within the Community, but there is as yet no completed internal market at the level of competition between Community air carriers. The lack of a common regime governing the provision of air transport services to and from the Community is, because of the economic importance of these services, liable dramatically to distort the conditions under which such competition takes place. The Council of Ministers should therefore, regardless of the discussion on the Community's competences, try to develop a common external policy as soon as possible, if it takes the completion of the internal civil aviation market seriously.

The External Dimension and the World Trading System

Fortress Europe?

A concluding discussion of the relationship between the completion of the internal market and the world trading system should of course start off with the question: has the Community been constructing a Fortress Europe or not?[69] And the answer is of course: quite clearly not. For one thing, the Community's institutions have not even paid enough attention to the external dimension of the internal market for a malicious master plan, which the concept of a Fortress Europe presupposes, to be possible. Admittedly, in a number of cases restrictive external policies have been devised. But the general thrust of the programme is towards liberalization, internally as well as externally. As Pelkmans has said, one should compare the results of the internal market programme with what the situation would have been in the absence of

[68] See Ch. 3.

[69] For an account of the Fortress Europe debate as it was held from 1988 to 1990 across the Atlantic, see Stephen Woolcock, *Market Access Issues in EC-US Relations: Trading Partners or Trading Blows* (London: Pinter Publishers for the RIIA, 1991), 13–16.

this programme.[70] It can be assumed that without the programme it would have been much more difficult to eliminate the various national quotas on imports, especially in sensitive sectors such as cars and textiles. Similarly, without the renewed efforts to remove the trade-distorting effects of technical regulations and standards, third-country exporters would not have the benefit of being able to produce according to one harmonized regulation or standard. There might also have been much less respect for international standardization. In the field of public procurement, liberalization would in the absence of the internal market programme almost certainly have remained at the previous zero level. And as regards financial services, the focusing on reciprocity should not lead one to overlook that no measures have yet been taken under the reciprocity heading, which signifies that third-country financial companies remain completely free to establish themselves in the Community, and thus reap the benefits of the integrated financial services market—which would not exist in the absence of the programme. In the field of telecommunications services, national monopolies would probably have remained much more powerful, allowing much less for the liberalization of certain services which is of benefit to Community and foreign companies alike.

Looking at the subject from a more formal, legal angle, it must be emphasized that few clear infringements of international rules have been recorded in this study. There is the question of the compatibility with GATT of the EC–Japan car arrangement, of the common market organization for bananas and of the television quota, but in the event of a successful conclusion of the Uruguay Round these questions will probably be resolved.[71] There are also problems with the Chicago Convention, in the field of civil aviation, and with the OECD Codes, in the field of financial services. But here the problems stem from the fact that the Community does not yet sufficiently participate in the activities of the organizations responsible for these agreements.[72] It is therefore certainly not so that the Community would have defined the external dimension of the internal market by disregarding its international obligations.

In 1986 the late Jan Tumlir, referring to past experience with European economic integration, put before the Community the choice between a *common* market and a common *market*:

What matters in the first case is that an economic area comprising several national territories is administered by unified policy: that the common policy measures may interfere with competition, inside as well as from abroad, and aim at resource allocation patterns different from those that market forces would establish, is of secondary importance. The second case, in contrast, envisages a free field for economic

[70] Jacques Pelkmans, 'EC92 as a Challenge to Economic Analysis', *supra* n. 6, p. 20; see also, by the same author, '1992: Economic Effects on Third Countries', in *EG und Drittstaatsbeziehungen nach 1992, supra* n. 6, pp. 166–79.
[71] See Chs. 4 and 6.   [72] Ch. 2, p. 72, and Ch. 3, p. 100.

competition; here the common element consists of the absence of dirigistic distortions, whether introduced by individual Member States or from the centre. It would be an evasion to say both words are equally important. Emphasizing one or the other amounts to mutually exclusive conceptions, or at least conceptions most difficult to compromise in practice.[73]

At that time, the described choice may have been correct. However, the internal market programme has proven it wrong. This programme entails the construction of a much more *common* market and at the same time it leads to liberalization. In the framework of the programme, common policies have been used, not to protect certain sectors of economic life, but to expose them to more competition, also from the outside. There is therefore no Fortress Europe.

Regional integration and the GATT system

The Community's internal market programme is one case of what in trade policy parlance is called regional integration. This term indicates the trend towards greater economic integration within specific groups of countries, which are in most cases situated in the same region of the world. Such regional integration goes further than the degree of trade and economic liberalization agreed upon at the multilateral level, mainly within the GATT. Moreover, because non-discrimination is the most fundamental principle governing the GATT system, regional integration appears essentially antithetic to this system. As the internal market programme is undoubtedly the most prominent case of economic integration, given its all-encompassing and supranational character and the element of nation-building which it displays, one could conclude that it stands a model in the debate on regionalism versus multilateralism.[74] This debate deals with such questions as: is regional integration compatible with the current world trading system? Does it stimulate the disintegration of this system, leaving only a world characterized by opposing regional trade blocs, or is it simply a complementary route towards greater world-wide economic integration? This subsection aims at looking at the external dimension of the internal market from the angle of the debate on regionalism versus multilateralism, taking into account its legal dimension. It goes without saying, however, that the few pages which are devoted here to this fundamental issue are only a small contribution to the discussion on this subject, which is likely to stay with us for quite some time.

Above it was said that the preference question underlies the external dimension of the internal market. To the extent that internal liberalization is not

---

[73] *Supra* n. 24, pp. 16–17.

[74] There is a lot of literature on this debate. See, for a recent and fundamental discussion, Jagdish Bhagwati, 'Regionalism versus Multilateralism', 15 *World Economy* (1992), 5: 535–55.

extended to trade with third countries, it is obvious that the rule of non-discrimination, which underlies the GATT, is not observed. However, as is well known that is not necessarily inconsistent with the General Agreement, because the latter allows for departures from this rule of non-discrimination within the framework of customs unions and free trade areas, under the conditions laid down in Article XXIV. As the Community is a customs union, it is useful to look somewhat closer at this provision, to see which disciplines it imposes on a case of regional integration such as the internal market programme.

One can say that two main concerns lay at the basis of Article XXIV.[75] The first was that the setting-up of customs unions and free trade areas should not be detrimental to non-member countries. Indeed, classic customs union theory has revealed that such forms of regional integration have a positive and a negative effect: trade creation (more trade between member countries) and trade diversion (external trade is replaced by internal trade). Which of the two is predominant depends on the specific circumstances of each case. In line with this finding, Article XXIV aims at ensuring that any negative effects on trade with non-member countries are reduced to a minimum. Hence the requirement with respect to customs unions which was mentioned above, namely that external protection must not be enhanced with the creation of a customs union.[76] The second concern was that these forms of regional integration should remain exceptional, and not become standard practice. To achieve this, Article XXIV provides that the integration (i.e. the elimination of all duties and other restrictive regulations of commerce) has to cover 'substantially all the trade' between the constituent territories and that this has to be achieved within a reasonable length of time.[77]

In spite of these requirements (which have been subject to divergent interpretations and which have not always been observed) customs unions and free trade areas have flourished, a fact which is now perceived by many as undermining the foundation of non-discrimination on which the GATT is built. Particularly the Community has been the subject of much criticism, basically for two reasons.[78] One is that the acceptance in GATT of the customs union on which the Community is based was mainly induced by political motivations, and that this is regarded as having set in motion a lax attitude towards the creation of other customs unions and free trade areas. Secondly, it

---

[75] Cf. Jackson, *supra* n. 1, p. 141.

[76] See *supra*, p. 343.

[77] Paras. 8 and 6. See Bhagwati, *supra* n. 74, pp. 537–8.

[78] For such criticism see especially Gardner Patterson, 'The European Community as a Threat to the System', in W. R. Cline (ed.), *Trade Policy in the 1980s* (Washington, DC: Institute for International Economics, 1983), 234–7 and 'Implications for the GATT and the World Trading System', in J. J. Schott (ed.), *Free Trade Areas and U.S. Trade Policy* (Washington, DC: Institute for International Economics, 1989), 361. See also Ernst-Ulrich Petersmann, 'The EEC as a GATT Member: Legal Conflicts between GATT Law and European Community Law', in *The European Community and GATT, supra* n. 24, pp. 40–3.

is felt that the Community has further contributed to the said undermining by setting up an entire network of preferential trade agreements with a number of its trading partners.[79] In the light of this criticism, the question whether the internal market programme is in keeping with the requirements of Article XXIV becomes particularly relevant.

However, the requirements of Article XXIV are clearly not sufficient for imposing an effective discipline on an exercise of economic integration as complex as the internal market programme. On the one hand, it can be said that the programme is nothing more than the fulfilment of the condition, laid down in paragraph 8, that duties *and other regulations of commerce* are eliminated in internal trade.[80] On the other hand, however, the requirements imposed by paragraph 5 as regards the level of external protection are only very partially relevant for the completion of the internal market. The text provides, with regard to customs unions, that

the duties and other regulations of commerce imposed at the institution of any such union ... in respect of trade with contracting parties not parties to such union ... shall not on the whole be higher or more restrictive than the general incidence of the duties and regulations of commerce applicable in the constituent territories prior to the formation of such union ....

One can without difficulty apply this to a classical non-tariff barrier such as quantitative restrictions.[81] But it is much harder to do so with respect to non-tariff barriers resulting from domestic regulation, and these are precisely the prime target of the internal market programme. For example, when the Community harmonizes national technical regulations, is that more restrictive for trade with third countries or not? The fact that twelve different regulations are replaced by one single is of course beneficial, but it could also be that this harmonized regulation is more restrictive in the sense that it aims at, for example, a higher level of environmental protection. How can this be measured? Moreover, is it not positive to pursue a better protection of the environment (or of the consumer), even if this may restrict trade? To these and other questions Article XXIV provides no answer, because it was devised for a world in which border measures were perceived to be the main trade barriers.

Moreover, the Tokyo Round, which for the first time addressed the problem of non-tariff barriers resulting from domestic policies, has apparently not devoted much attention to the questions related to regional integration. The

[79] Such as the free trade agreements with the EFTA countries, the Lomé Convention, association and co-operation agreements with the Mediterranean countries; and, most recently, association agreements with Central European countries.

[80] Pieter Jan Kuyper, 'The Influence of the Elimination of Physical Frontiers in the Community on Trade in Goods with Third States', in *EG und Drittstaatsbeziehungen nach 1992, supra* n. 6, p. 53.

[81] Thus, one can apply it to the completion of the Common Commercial Policy in the field of imports of goods (Ch. 5). There is little doubt, in view of the envisaged general abolition of quantitative restrictions by the Community, that this completion is consistent with Art. XXIV (5).

Standards Code, for example, does not contain clear guide-lines in this respect, as was shown in Chapter 8.[82] In addition, the GATT does not extend to services and is therefore not able to impose any discipline on regional integration in the field of services trade.

It remains to be seen whether the Uruguay Round will result in a more comprehensive approach towards regional integration. The Draft Final Act of December 1991 is not entirely promising in this respect. Article XXIV does figure on the agenda of the negotiations, but the Understanding on its interpretation taken up in the Draft Final Act only addresses the more procedural and technical questions to which the application of the Article has given rise in the past. Thus, the reviewed Article XXIV continues to look at regional integration basically in terms of border protection, mainly addressing the tariff question. For example, with respect to the requirements of paragraph 5 concerning 'other regulations of commerce', it is only said that

[i]t is recognised that for the purpose of the overall assessment of the incidence of other regulations of commerce for which quantification and aggregation are difficult, the examination of individual measures, regulations, products covered and trade flows affected may be required.[83]

This states the problem, but gives no answer. Similarly, the revised Standards Code does not innovate with respect to regional integration.[84] On the other hand, in the draft General Agreement on Trade in Services a provision was inserted on 'Economic Integration' which is comparable to Article XXIV.[85] Leaving aside the merits of this provision, it would at least broaden the scope of multilateral supervision of regional integration, by extending it to the services sector.

The conclusion is that present GATT law offers little guidance for such a complex policy question as defining the external dimension of the internal market programme. Moreover, it is uncertain whether in the future it will be able to offer more in this respect, which is after all not surprising. The tension between regional integration and multilateral liberalization is a systemic one, which can probably not be fundamentally resolved by multilateral rules because these are by definition at one end of the spectrum. As Bhagwati has argued, the most vital question is whether regional integration strengthens or weakens the progression of multilateral trade liberalization.[86] That question

---

[82] See pp. 275–7.
[83] Draft Final Act embodying the results of the Uruguay Round negotiations, MTN.TNC/W/FA, p. U.2.
[84] See Ch. 8, n. 73.
[85] Art. V of the draft GATS, see MTN.TNC/W/FA, Annex II, p. 9. According to this provision agreements liberalizing trade in services are allowed provided that they have substantial sectoral coverage and provide for the absence or elimination of substantially all discrimination between or among the parties. Such agreements should not raise the overall level of barriers to trade in the sectors concerned.
[86] *Supra* n. 74, pp. 548–54.

surely applies to the case of the completion of the internal market. It does so in one very specific way: has the programme served as an incentive for the simultaneous multilateral negotiations of the Uruguay Round, or has it acted as a brake? Would the Community have been more or less inclined to contribute to these negotiations than if the programme had not existed? Have the Community's trading partners reacted to the programme by aiming for a strengthened multilateral trading system, or have they sought to protect their interests by other means? Beyond these specific questions lies a more structural one: to what extent can the Community's internal liberalization policies serve as a model or, more modestly, as a test case for multilateral liberalization? Are the Community's experiences transposable to the multilateral context? Both these sets of questions are examined below.

There is one last element to be highlighted in the regionalism versus multilateralism debate. As was mentioned, the Community has in the past been criticized for having set up an entire system of preferential trade agreements.[87] The question arises whether the same will happen as regards access to the internal market, as integrated by the 1992 programme. Until now, the Community has defined the external dimension in a non-discriminatory manner, with the exception of the European Economic Area which is, however, a special case in that it aims at completely extending the internal market to the EFTA countries. However, in a number of areas Community legislation provides that reciprocal agreements can be concluded, allowing for improved access to the internal market.[88] Therefore, there is scope for a comparable tendency to the one referred to above. If the Community also developed a network of bilateral agreements entailing preferential access to the internal market, that could again undermine the principle of non-discrimination. Suppose, for example, that the Community and the United States conclude an agreement regarding mutual recognition of certification and testing, will both sides display as much interest in multilateral policies in this field as they would in the absence of such an agreement?[89]

All this again brings the concept of reciprocity into focus. The following section deals with the Community's reciprocity policy (the formal answer to the basic question of preference).

Reciprocity

Reciprocity is the one concept characterizing the external dimension of the internal market, especially in those sectors or policies which are not yet

[87] See Ch. 10, p. 325 and this Ch., p. 360.
[88] That is the case as regards public procurement (Ch. 9, p. 310), certification and testing (Ch. 8, pp. 291 *et seq.*), television programmes (confined to Europe, Ch. 4, p. 128), and financial services (Ch. 2, pp. 55 *et seq.*).
[89] Again a lot depends on the outcome of the Uruguay Round: if it is concluded there will be much less need for bilateral agreements.

covered by multilateral rules.[90] At the same time it has been in the front line of the diplomatic attack on the allegations of a Fortress Europe, mounted in the course of 1988 and 1989. It is clearly worthwhile, therefore, to take a closer look at this notion and at what it signifies for the effect of the internal market programme on the world trading system.

The concept of reciprocity is a very treacherous one. There is an entire scale of meanings and functions that are attributed to it, even (or perhaps especially) if one limits oneself to the field of trade policy. For example, it has on the one hand been said that reciprocity is a fundamental GATT principle,[91] but on the other it is sometimes characterized as sheer protectionism.[92] Though it is not possible to list all these meanings and functions here, some kind of schematic overview may be useful.[93]

When reciprocity is seen as a fundamental GATT principle, it is to be considered the global balance of advantages and concessions without which multilateral trade liberalization would not be possible. Concessions are extended to all trading partners through the operation of the most-favoured-nation clause, which allows for the principle of comparative advantage maximally to perform its function. This kind of reciprocity is often contrasted with what is termed sectoral reciprocity. The latter means, evidently, that the scope of reciprocity is limited to one sector of trade. This is much less likely to be economically efficient, depending of course upon the size of the sector, because the role of comparative advantage is much reduced. At its extreme, this kind of reciprocity seeks a balance in actual trade flows or market shares.

Related is the phenomenon of a country seeking reciprocity, not at the multilateral, but at a bilateral level. Especially larger trading entities, such as the United States and the Community, are often accused of using their economic weight in order to extract unrequited concessions from smaller countries. It is obvious that such actions also seriously undermine the multilateral trading system.

Less negatively, the term reciprocity is sometimes used to indicate the

[90] See the Commission's 'Europe 1992: Europe World Partner' statement, *supra* Ch. 2, n. 32.

[91] Olivier Long, *Law and its Limitations in the GATT Multilateral Trade System* (Dordrecht: Martinus Nijhoff, 1985), 10.

[92] Thomas J. Berger, 'Preparing for 1992: A Yankee View on Europe's Internal Market Program', *USA Text*, 15 Sept. 1988, p. 3.

[93] Compare with William R. Cline, ' "Reciprocity": A New Approach to World Trade Policy', in *Trade Policy in the 1980s*, *supra* n. 78, pp. 121–52; Dell, *supra* n. 21, pp. 125–39; Jagdish Bhagwati and Douglas Irwin, 'The Return of the Reciprocitarians: U.S. Trade Policy', 10 *World Economy* (1987), 2: 109–30; L. Alan Winters, 'Reciprocity', in J. M. Finger and A. Olechowski (eds.), *The Uruguay Round: A Handbook on the Multilateral Trade Negotiations* (Washington, DC: World Bank, 1987), 45–51; Lamoureux, *supra* n. 60, pp. 1–11; Rudolf Dolzer, 'Reziprozität als Standard der EG-Drittlandsbeziehungen', in *EG und Drittstaatsbeziehungen nach 1992*, *supra* n. 6, pp. 114–17; Victoria Curzon-Price and Gerald Curzon, 'Non-Discrimination and Reciprocity in the GATT: Two Principles on a Collision Course?', in *Trade Laws of the European Community and the United States in a Comparative Perspective*, *supra* n. 20, pp. 311–14.

conditional most-favoured-nation (MFN) character of the Tokyo Round Codes. It then implies that the advantages of these Codes are only extended to the countries which have signed them, and not to other GATT members, the aim being to avoid free-rider behaviour. Although sometimes criticized by purists, this kind of reciprocity is generally tolerated as a useful device for getting around this free-rider problem and for countering the difficulties associated with trying to achieve meaningful liberalization with an ever expanding GATT membership.[94]

Reciprocity, lastly, has also been used to denote the fact that countries may require that other countries adopt regulatory policies similar to their own. It is then contrasted with the concept of national treatment, which leaves each country's policies intact, merely requiring that foreign products or companies are not discriminated against.[95]

As was mentioned, there are various areas, covered by the internal market programme, in which the Community insists on reciprocity. That has not been done, however, in trade sectors covered by the rules of the GATT. Even the EC–Japan arrangement concerning imports of Japanese cars, although it is probably one of the most protectionist pieces in the puzzle of the external dimension, does not provide for (sectoral) reciprocity. Admittedly, the Community has often voiced its concern with respect to the level of imports of European cars in Japan, but it has not linked this in the arrangement to the limits imposed on imports of Japanese cars in the Community.[96] It is well known that the United States, by contrast, does take such a course of action in its car trade with Japan.

Reciprocity is part of the Community's approach towards the external dimension of the internal market in the fields of public procurement and technical regulations and standards. As regards the first, the Utilities Directive provides that the benefits of non-discriminatory procurement practices will only be extended to trade with third countries in the framework of agreements ensuring reciprocity. As was mentioned, this provision is aimed at safeguarding the Community's negotiating position in the GATT negotiations on extending the disciplines established by the Government Procurement Code to the so-called excluded sectors.[97] It is not contested that the Community is prepared to accept such an extension. Therefore, this kind of reciprocity is surely defensible. It is in line with the above-mentioned conditional MFN treatment which this Tokyo Round Code entails. As regards technical regulations and standards, non-discrimination is the essential principle governing the external dimension, and reciprocity merely plays a small part. Indeed, in addition to non-discriminatory treatment of third-country products the Community has indicated that it is prepared to conclude agreements on mutual

[94] See the literature in n. 61 of Ch. 8.   [95] See Berger, *supra* n. 92.
[96] See Ch. 6, part 2.   [97] See Ch. 9, p. 307.

recognition of certification and testing.[98] Reciprocity seems to be inherent in the very concept of such agreements, as these require that at both ends testing bodies are designated whose activities will be mutually recognized. And although it can be said that bilateral agreements in this area may take away the incentive to conclude a multilateral agreement covering mutual recognition of certification and testing, it also has to be acknowledged that this is a field which lends itself more to bilateral negotiations than to multilateral ones. Moreover, it is not to be ruled out that at some stage a multilateral system could result from a comprehensive set of bilateral agreements.

But reciprocity is especially the key element of the external dimension of the internal market in the field of services trade. It was here that the impression was first created, when the Commission issued its proposal for a Second Banking Directive, that the Community was trying to impose on third countries its own views concerning how to regulate service transactions, and that if these countries would not go along with these views their companies would be barred from establishing themselves in the Community. Moreover, the kind of reciprocity the Community was seeking was clearly of a sectoral nature.[99]

However, this form of reciprocity has appeared much more threatening than it actually is. In the end, the Community opted for reciprocal national treatment: third-country companies will only have a right to national treatment in the Community (and thereby obtain full access to the internal market), if Community companies are also granted such treatment abroad. Surely, to the concept of national treatment was added that of effective market access so as to ensure that *de facto* national treatment would be assured. But in the meantime it has become clear that these twin concepts of national treatment and effective market access are essential components of a General Agreement on Trade in Services.[100] Here too, then, the Community's policy has to be understood as aiming at safeguarding the Community's negotiating position in the Uruguay Round negotiations. And again it must be emphasized that the Community (at this stage perhaps more than any of its trading partners) has been genuinely seeking to conclude a GATS.[101]

As to the sectoral character of this kind of reciprocity, the Uruguay Round negotiations have also shown that in the field of trade in services a sectoral approach is virtually inescapable. This has led one (impartial) commentator to conclude that

[i]n the services context determining [overall reciprocity] may be difficult. The basic issue here is how countries evaluate offers/tradeoffs, which in turn depends on the focal

[98] See Ch. 8, pp. 291 *et seq.*   [99] See Ch. 2.
[100] According to the draft GATS (*supra* n. 85), Parties must enter into 'specific commitments' (Part III), precisely concerning market access (Art. XVI) and national treatment (Art. XVII). See also Bernard Hoekman, 'Market Access through Multilateral Agreement: From Goods to Services', 15 *World Economy* (1992), 6: 719–21.
[101] Cf. 'End GATT talks, says Dunkel', *Financial Times*, 20 Jan. 1993, p. 3.

point used in discussions. In practice the simplest focal point or yardstick—perhaps the only one that is feasible in the services context—is sectoral coverage.[102]

Again, it is apparent that a lot depends upon the outcome of the Uruguay Round negotiations. If these negotiations are successful, the substance of the Community's demands for reciprocity will to a large extent be covered by their results. If they are not concluded, however, the Community will have to fill out its reciprocity form all by itself. It will have to determine more precisely what it seeks to achieve in return for granting access to the internal market. It will have to choose, basically, between an aggressive stance, insisting on trade liberalization in non-member countries to the benefit of European exporters and imposing its own views on regulatory policies, and a more moderate one in which reciprocity merely aims at safeguarding the Community's interests in cases of patent discrimination.

In this regard, the position of developing countries must be looked at. In the event that reciprocity, as a result of a failure of the Uruguay Round, is pursued on a bilateral basis, these countries could be the first to suffer. Although the Commission has stated that reciprocity is not aimed at them, the relevant Community legislation does not contain a limitation in that sense, and policy statements can be changed. Furthermore, it is obvious that in the services sector, the major terrain of reciprocity, developing countries often operate less liberal policies than the industrialized countries because they are at a comparative disadvantage.[103] They may also be more vulnerable to claims for reciprocity because they have less diplomatic weight and less scope for retaliation than the Community's major industrial partners.[104]

The internal market programme and the Uruguay Round

The relationship between the completion of the internal market and the Uruguay Round has already been mentioned a couple of times in this chapter, and in many of the preceding ones also. Indeed, the bonds between the internal market programme and the Uruguay Round are obvious. They range, to mention only the most important issues, from the question of safeguards and VERs, over technical regulations and standards and public procurement, to financial, audiovisual, and telecommunications services. As observed above, the Uruguay Round therefore offers an ideal opportunity to further define the external dimension of the internal market.[105] However, the Round has not yet

---

[102] Hoekman (who works in the GATT Secretariat), *supra* n. 100, p. 712.

[103] Hence the resistance put up by the developing countries against including services in the Uruguay Round.

[104] Moreover, in the financial services sector they can probably benefit less from grandfather rights than industrial countries (see Ch. 2, p. 56).

[105] Cf. Ernst-Ulrich Petersmann, 'The Uruguay Round of Multilateral Trade Negotiations and the Single European Market 1992', in *EG und Drittstaatsbeziehungen nach 1992, supra* n. 6, p. 208.

been concluded and the negotiations have experienced serious difficulties ever since the break-up of the December 1990 Ministerial Meeting in Brussels, which should have finalized the Round. One of the questions which this raises is whether the internal market programme has served as an incentive for or as a brake on the negotiating process. Or to use Pelkmans' expression, is Europe 1992 a handmaiden to GATT,[106] or has it been an uninvited and unwelcome guest, disturbing the party?

At face value, one could argue that the internal market programme has concentrated the Community's efforts on the internal integration processes, sapping part of the political and administrative energy necessary for a negotiating exercise as complicated as the Uruguay Round. Moreover, as the programme entails very substantial liberalization in a large geographical area which is, one should not forget, being extended to the EFTA countries, perhaps the Community is less inclined to commit itself to multilateral liberalization, since this only entails some additional benefits.

It is submitted, however, that this is not the correct view. Of course, it is true that the combination of such large agendas as the internal market programme and the Uruguay Round has put quite some strain on the Community's decision-making machinery. None the less, the programme has mainly contributed to forging meaningful and defensible negotiating positions in Geneva, rather than weakening them.[107] Again, one must consider what the situation would have been in the absence of the internal market endeavour. In the services sector, for example, the Community's market would have remained fragmented, with the various Member States each having their divergent views on how to regulate services. Actually, that was the situation when the Uruguay Round negotiations started, and the Community was reluctant at that stage to negotiate a General Agreement on Trade in Services. By contrast, as the internal market programme made progress, the Community became a more active participant in these negotiations, with the result that it can now be said that it is eager to conclude such a General Agreement.[108] Although the services sector is outstanding in this respect, comparable observations can be made as regards other policies.

The logic of this positive effect of the internal market programme is as follows. First, the programme has put the emphasis inside the Community on liberalizing trade by removing all kinds of barriers. This positive attitude towards trade liberalization is not confined to the internal market, but extends to external economic relations.[109] Moreover, from an institutional point of view it becomes much easier for the Community to agree on multilateral obligations once internal liberalization is already achieved. For example, once

[106] Pelkmans, *supra* n. 4.
[107] Cf. Tsoukalis, *supra* n. 5, pp. 271–2.
[108] Cf. n. 101.
[109] Pelkmans, 'Europe 1992: A Handmaiden to GATT', *supra* n. 4, p. 147.

the Community has decided to open up public procurement in the so-called excluded sectors, a common position on external liberalization is simply an additional step facilitated by the already existing common policy. By contrast, suppose such a common policy does not yet exist. The negotiations in Geneva would then deal with both internal and external liberalization at the same time. The Community's negotiators would at the same time be defining the external and the internal policy, and internal liberalization would be perceived as 'imposed' by the external context. It is beyond doubt that this would make it much more difficult for the Community to commit itself to multilateral liberalization.

Actually, this is confirmed by the history of the Uruguay Round negotiations in the field of agricultural policies. As is well known, this has for a long time been the most intractable problem, the Community being perceived as unwilling to reform the Common Agricultural Policy in the direction of a substantial reduction of support. It was mainly on this issue that the December 1990 Ministerial Meeting in Brussels broke up. In the meantime, a basic agreement was reached between the Community and the United States in November 1992, but this only proved possible after the Community had managed to decide, internally, that the Common Agricultural Policy had to be reformed, a decision taken in the course of 1991. Before that, it was nearly impossible to forge a common negotiating position in Geneva.

In addition, the completion of the internal market may have induced non-member countries to devote more attention to the Uruguay Round, precisely because this is a unique opportunity to consolidate the conditions governing access to this large market. With this completion, the Community has more clearly become a large trading power, alongside the United States and Japan. For smaller countries, the best guarantees against abuse of this power lie in an effective, rule-based multilateral trading system, the building of which is the purpose of the Round.

The internal market programme as a test-bed for multilateral liberalization

Not only has the internal market programme acted as an incentive for the Uruguay Round multilateral negotiations, it can also be looked at as a test-bed for the principles and instruments needed to achieve multilateral liberalization, especially in new areas, be they sectoral (such as trade in services) or horizontal (protection of the environment, public security, etc.).

That does not mean that the internal market can act as a genuine model for policies developed in the GATT framework.[110] The differences between the

---

[110] See, specifically as regards services, Claus-Dieter Ehlermann and Gianluigi Campogrande, 'Rules on Services in the EEC: A Model for Negotiating World-Wide Rules', in E.-U. Petersmann and M. Hilf (eds.), *The New GATT Round of Multilateral Trade Negotiations: Legal and Economic Problems* (Deventer: Kluwer, 1988), 482–9.

Community and the GATT system are much too fundamental for that.[111] The aims of the Community, to put it shortly, transcend the field of economic relations, and include an important element of nation-building. From a legal point of view, this has immense implications. The Community's legal order is a supranational one, integrating the legal orders of the Member States, with strong institutions and directly effective 'legislation'. GATT law is nothing of the kind; it is 'ordinary' international law, dealing with relations between States.

None the less, these differences should also not be exaggerated. For all practical purposes, both the Community and the GATT are engaged in trade liberalization between various countries. There is, in this complex world, no infinite range of methods for achieving such liberalization. Therefore, there may be quite some lessons to be drawn from the Community's experience, not only for the Uruguay Round (it is probably too late for that), but also, and perhaps mainly, for further multilateral efforts. Without of course claiming to be comprehensive, five subjects are touched upon below, namely the importance of case-law, the mixture between mutual recognition and harmonization, the principle of national treatment, the phased approach towards liberalization, and the tension between trade policy and other, non-economic policies.

It is well known and it has often been mentioned in this study that the concept of mutual recognition lies at the basis of the Community's approach in many segments of the internal market programme, particularly in the fields of goods and services. It is equally well known that this concept stems from the Community's experience in the field of free movement of goods, and, more particularly, from the case-law of the Court of Justice on Articles 30–36 of the EC Treaty. Without this case-law, arguably, the internal market programme would probably not have been possible or, at least, it would have had an entirely different outlook. This illustrates the dialectic between laying down general rules and applying them in specific cases. Such a dialectic often indicates the path which has to be followed when developing additional, more detailed policies. Especially for liberalization of trade in services, which depends even more than liberalization of trade in goods on the application of general rules, it is necessary to emphasize the importance of case-law. If a General Agreement on Trade in Services is concluded, it is to be hoped that sufficient attention will be devoted to developing a mature body of case-law on the interpretation of this Agreement, because such case-law will undoubtedly play a guiding role in exposing the possible directions of subsequent policies. The same may be true for an issue such as reconciling trade policies with non-economic policies.[112]

---

[111] See e.g. Tumlir, *supra* n. 24, p. 10; Anna Murphy, *The European Community and the International Trading System*, ii: *The European Community and the Uruguay Round*, CEPS Paper No. 48 (Brussels: CEPS, 1990), 131–2.

[112] See *infra*, p. 371.

A second subject concerns the concepts of mutual recognition and harmonization of domestic regulations affecting trade and investment flows, and the question concerning the most active mixture of these two ingredients.[113] The Community's experience shows the importance and, at the same time, the limits of applying the concept of mutual recognition. Especially when mutual recognition is merely employed as a general principle, which has to be applied by national legislators, administrations, and judges, its effectiveness is limited, even in a regulatory area as integrated as the Community. Otherwise, the internal market programme would not have been necessary. By contrast, mutual recognition becomes a much more useful device when its application is more specific. One can look at the Second Banking Directive, for example, as an instrument determining, specifically as regards banking, the scope of mutual recognition: it is indicated which national rules governing banking activities are subject to harmonization, and to what extent, implying that all other national rules may no longer be enforced against non-domestic banks.[114] The GATT context probably requires an even more detailed approach, because of the much lesser degree of integration and the much larger differences in regulatory policies and levels of economic development between the participants in multilateral liberalization. In the GATT, mutual recognition would probably have to be the subject of (perhaps bilaterally) negotiated concessions. Such an approach could be applied in areas such as services and technical regulations and standards.

Of course, it goes without saying that mutual recognition and harmonization go hand in hand. The former will only be possible when national regulatory policies, though technically divergent, arrive at comparable results. To achieve this, some degree of harmonization will often be necessary.[115] It is questionable whether the GATT is the appropriate forum for such harmonization, because the latter is more concerned with the substance of national policies than with their effects on trade. For example, one cannot imagine that the GATT would occupy itself with harmonizing national policies concerning the protection of the environment. However, such harmonization does take place in the framework of international agreements concluded outside the realm of GATT. At the moment, there is little co-ordination between such efforts (which are of course not limited to environmental protection) and multilateral trade liberalization.[116] That would need to be changed

[113] Cf. John H. Jackson, *supra* n. 1, p. 305. See also Ch. 8, pp. 284–6. For an analysis from a more theoretical perspective, see Phedon Nicolaides, 'Competition among Rules', 16 *World Competition* (1992), 2: 113–21.

[114] See Ch. 2, p. 47.

[115] Jacques Pelkmans and Niall Bohan, 'Towards an Ideal GATT TBT Code?', paper presented at the CEPS Conference on 'Reconciling Regulation and Free Trade', Brussels, Dec. 1992, pp. 7–8.

[116] Paul Demaret, 'Environmental Policy and Commercial Policy: The Emergence of Trade-Related Environmental Measures (TREMs) in the External Relations of the European

before a more systematic application of the mutual recognition technique was possible.

Specifically as regards the services sector, both the Uruguay Round negotiations and the external dimension of the internal market programme have shown the central position occupied by the concept of national treatment, to which a lot of attention was paid in Chapter 2.[117] It should be recalled here that the case-law of the Court of Justice offers a rich field as regards the various forms which a prohibition of discrimination may and should take. Among other things, this case-law demonstrates, first, that it is not sufficient only to address cases of formal discrimination, and, secondly, that the reach of a prohibition of discrimination in substance is potentially very wide, requiring, at its extreme, a review of the regulatory aims which are being pursued. Applying the concept of national treatment will therefore undoubtedly require some kind of judicial interpretation.

The Community's experience in the field of services, in particular transport, also demonstrates that in heavily regulated sectors liberalization can only be achieved in stages (or packages, to use the civil aviation terminology).[118] That puts a question mark against the hitherto used approach of all-encompassing rounds of multilateral negotiations, which are possible only once every decade. Such an approach leaves little room for a gradual process of liberalization, which may be the only one which is workable in the services sector.[119]

As regards the tension between trade policy and other, non-economic policies, the Community's experience also has a lot to offer. This tension has mostly been discussed in this study with respect to broadcasting services (cultural policies) and strategic export controls (public security). But it is certainly not limited to these fields. It also appears with respect to environmental policies (perhaps this will be the most prominent issue in the coming decade), and with respect to the protection of human rights. How to cope with this tension, how, in other words, to reconcile trade liberalization with non-economic policies acting as barriers to trade, is a difficult problem. It often cannot be resolved by applying one or other economic theory. These are genuinely political issues, requiring that a choice be made between conflicting objectives, a choice the costs and benefits of which are often diverse and not comparable.

The Community's experience, and again mostly the case-law of the Court of Justice, certainly teaches that the erection of trade barriers with a view to

---

Community', in M. Maresceau (ed.), *The European Community's Commercial Policy after 1992: The Legal Dimension* (Dordrecht: Martinus Nijhoff, 1993), 384–5.

[117] pp. 76–83.

[118] See Ch. 3, p. 86.

[119] Art. XIX of the draft GATS (*supra* n. 85) provides for 'successive rounds of negotiations', without specifying the frequency of such rounds.

(allegedly) achieving non-economic objectives must be looked at with some degree of suspicion.[120]

The Community and rule-oriented versus power-oriented diplomacy

Many authors have argued in favour of a world trading system based on fixed rules rather than on power politics. The difference between these two approaches has perhaps been most eloquently expressed by Jackson, who distinguishes between rule-oriented and power-oriented diplomacy. In the first case, disputes are resolved by referring to a set of mutually agreed rules, whereas, in the second case, only power elements are relevant.[121]

When one applies this distinction to how the Community has defined the external dimension of the internal market programme, it is obvious that both kinds of approaches are present—which is not surprising, of course. An example of power-oriented diplomacy is the EC–Japan arrangement regarding imports of Japanese cars. This arrangement was concluded without referring to the mutually agreed rules of the GATT; it was based on negotiations in which the balance of power between the two sides determined the contents of the arrangement.[122] An example of a rule-based approach, by contrast, is offered by the Community's external policy in the field of technical regulations and standards, where the rules of the General Agreement and the Standards Code are clearly the point of reference.[123]

However, in this context the most decisive developments are yet to come. As was said, the direction of the Community's reciprocity policy will be determined by the outcome of the Uruguay Round negotiations. If these negotiations are successful, they will at the same time to some extent determine the external dimension of the internal market. If, however, the Round fails, the Community could be tempted to use its economic power in order to impose its views on the kind of 'reciprocity' it would like to obtain from its trading partners. Such an aggressive stance, it is true, is not traditional for the Community, but in times of economic recession it could well emerge.

It is submitted that it is very much in the Community's interest to avert such a course of events—more, perhaps, than in that of its major trading partners. The impression that because of its economic power the Community would not run many risks if the application of multilateral rules is gradually replaced by power politics, is superficial and deceptive. Not only would the world-wide instability resulting from such a tendency surely also affect the Community, which is very dependent on international trade and investment flows. More importantly, it could also put the Community itself in jeopardy. One should

---

[120] See e.g. the case-law, dealt with in Ch. 4, pp. 120–3, on television broadcasting.

[121] See e.g. John H. Jackson, *Restructuring the GATT System* (London: Pinter Publishers for the RIIA, 1990), 51–4.

[122] See Ch. 6, part 2.   [123] See Ch. 8.

not forget that the very existence of the Community is dependent on the respect for important, fundamental rules agreed upon between the Member States. If at the world-wide level the respect for multilateral rules governing trade and economic relations is further eroded, there is every reason to believe that at one stage this erosion will also start to affect the rules governing the relations between the Member States, shaking the foundations on which the Community is built.

The conclusion is that the Community should, more than any other trading power, continue to labour for an effective, rule-based multilateral trade system, and further define the external dimension of its internal market accordingly.

Bibliography

ANON., *Trade Policies for a Better Future: The 'Leutwiler Report'*, the *GATT and the Uruguay Round* (Dordrecht: Martinus Nijhoff, 1987).

—— 'Redactionele signalen', 40 *SEW* (1992), 7: 609–10.

ANWAR, SYED TARIQ, 'The Impact of the Structural Impediments Initiative (SII) on U.S.–Japan trade', 16 *World Competition* (1992), 2: 53–65.

BALFOUR, JOHN M., 'Freedom to Provide Air Transport Services in the EEC', 14 *ELR* (1989), 1: 30–46.

BARAV, AMI, 'The Division of External Relations Power between the European Economic Community and the Member States in the Case-Law of the Court of Justice', in E. L. M. Völker and C. W. A. Timmermans (eds), *Division of Powers between the European Communities and their Member States in the Field of External Relations* (Deventer: Kluwer, 1981), 29–64.

BARENTS, RENÉ, 'Milieu en interne markt', 41 *SEW* (1993), 1: 5–29.

BEISE, MARC, 'Out of the Grey? Grey Area Measures and the Future of Multilateralism', in T. Oppermann and J. Molsberger (eds.), *A New GATT for the Nineties and Europe '92* (Baden-Baden: Nomos, 1991), 89–96.

BELLIS, JEAN-FRANÇOIS, 'The EEC Antidumping System', in J. H. Jackson and E. A. Vermulst (eds.), *Antidumping Law and Practice: A Comparative Study* (New York: Harvester Wheatsheaf, 1990), 41–97.

BESELER, ARIANE, 'Intra-Community Protection with Regard to Goods Imported into the EC: Article 115 EC', *International Business Law Journal* (1991), 8: 1119–44.

BHAGWATI, JAGDISH, 'Services', in J. M. Finger and A. Olechowski (eds.), *The Uruguay Round: A Handbook on the Multilateral Trade Negotiations* (Washington, DC: World Bank, 1987), 207–16.

—— 'Economic Costs of Trade Restrictions', in J. M. Finger and A. Olechowski (eds.), *The Uruguay Round: A Handbook on the Multilateral Trade Negotiations* (Washington, DC: World Bank, 1987), 29–33.

—— *The World Trading System at Risk* (New York: Harvester Wheatsheaf, 1991).

—— 'Regionalism versus Multilateralism', 15 *World Economy* (1992), 5: 535–56.

—— and IRWIN, DOUGLAS, 'The Return of the Reciprocitarians: US Trade Policy', 10 *World Economy* (1987), 2: 109–30.

—— and PATRICK, H. T. (eds.), *Aggressive Unilateralism: America's 301 Trade Policy and the World Trading System* (New York: Harvester Wheatsheaf, 1990).

BLECKMANN, ALBERT, *Europarecht* (Cologne: Carl Heymanns, 1985).

BLOKKER, NIELS M., *International Regulation of World Trade in Textiles* (Dordrecht: Martinus Nijhoff, 1989).

—— 'GATT en vrijwillige exportbeperkingen: Het panelrapport over Japanse halfgeleiders', 37 *SEW* (1989), 2: 90–104.

BORRELL, BRENT, and YANG, MAW-CHENG, *EC Bananarama 1992: The Sequel*, World Bank Working Paper (Washington, DC: 1992).

BOURGEOIS, JACQUES H. J., 'Some Comments on the Practice', in C. W. A. Timmermans and E. L. M. Völker (eds.), *Division of Powers between the European Communities and their Member States in the Field of External Relations* (Deventer: Kluwer, 1981), 97–110.

—— 'The Tokyo Round Agreements on Technical Barriers and on Government Procurement in International and EEC Perspective', 19 *CML Rev.* (1982), 1: 5–33.

—— 'The Common Commercial Policy: Scope and Nature of the Powers', in E. L. M. Völker (ed.), *Protectionism and the European Community*, 2nd edn. (Deventer: Kluwer, 1986), 1–16.

—— 'L'Espace économique européen', *RMUE* (1992), 2: 11–24.

BRONCKERS, MARCO C. E. J., *Safeguard Measures in Multilateral Trade Relations* (Deventer: Kluwer, 1985).

—— 'A Legal Analysis of Protectionist Measures Affecting Japanese Imports into the European Community: Revisited', in E. L. M. Völker (ed.), *Protectionism and the European Community*, 2nd edn. (Deventer: Kluwer, 1986), 57–120.

BRUHA, THOMAS, 'Normen und Standards im Wahrenverkehr mit Drittstaaten', in M. Hilf and C. Tomuschat (eds.), *EG und Drittstaatsbeziehungen nach 1992* (Baden-Baden: Nomos, 1991), 83–109.

CALINGAERT, MICHAEL, *The 1992 Challenge from Europe*, 5th edn. (Washington, DC: National Planning Association, 1990).

CHAPMAN, N. F. SPENCER, and GRANDJEAN, C., *The Construction Industry and the European Community* (Oxford: BSP Professional Books, 1991).

CHARLES-LE BIHAN, DANIELLE, and LEBULLENGER, JOEL, 'Common Maritime Transport Policy: Bilateral Agreements and the Freedom to Provide Services', in A. Barav and D. A. Wyatt (eds.), 9 *Yearbook of European Law* (1989) (Oxford: Clarendon Press, 1990), 209–23.

CLAROTTI, PAOLO, 'Harmonization for Banking and Securities Regulations in the European Communities: Its Implications for the Third Countries', in G. Sacerdoti (ed.), *Liberalization of Services and Intellectual Property in the Uruguay Round of GATT* (Fribourg: University Press, 1990), 177–89.

CLINE, WILLIAM R., ' "Reciprocity": A New Approach to World Trade Policy?' in W. R. Cline (ed.), *Trade Policy in the 1980's* (Washington, DC: Institute for International Economics, 1983), 121–58.

CLOSE, GEORGE, 'External Relations in the Air Transport Sector: Air Transport Policy or the Common Commercial Policy?', 27 *CML Rev.* (1990), 1: 108–27.

—— 'External Competence for Air Policy in the Third Phase: Trade Policy or Transport Policy?', 15 *Air Law* (1990), 5–6: 295–305, and in P. D. Dagtoglou, J. M. Balfour, and J. Stuyck (eds.), *European Air Law Association*, iii: *Second Annual Conference* (Deventer: Kluwer, 1991), 31–44.

CONSTANTINESCO, VLAD, 'Les compétences internationales de la Communauté et des États membres à travers l'Acte Unique européen', in P. Demaret (ed.), *Relations extérieures de la Communauté européenne et marché intérieur: Aspects juridiques et fonctionnels* (Bruges: Story for the College of Europe, 1988), 63–78.

COWHEY, PETER F., 'Telecommunications', in G. C. Hufbauer (ed.), *Europe 1992: An American Perspective* (Washington, DC: Brookings Institution, 1990), 159–224.

CUPITT, RICHARD T., 'The Future of CoCom', in G. K. Bertsch and S. Elliott-Gower (eds.), *Export Controls in Transition* (Durham, NC: Duke University Press, 1992), 232–48.

CURZON-PRICE, VICTORIA, and CURZON, GERALD, 'Non-discrimination and Reciprocity in the GATT: Two Principles on a Collision Course?', in P. Demaret, J. Bourgeois, and I. van Bael (eds.), *Trade Laws of the European Community and the United States in a Comparative Perspective* (Brussels: Story-Scientia for the College of Europe, 1992), 303–21.

DAKOLIAS, MARIA, 'The Second Banking Directive: The Issue of Reciprocity', *LIEI* (1992), 1: 69–100.

DANIS, FRANÇOIS, 'Le point de vue de la Commission des Communautés européennes', in G. Vandersanden (ed.), *L'espace audiovisuel européen* (Brussels: Éditions de l'ULB, 1991), 115–17.

DAVENPORT, MICHAEL, with PAGE, SHEILA, *Europe: 1992 and the Developing World* (London: Overseas Development Institute, 1991).

DE GROOT, JAN ERNST C., 'Cabotage Liberalization in the European Economic Community and Article 7 of the Chicago Convention', 14 *Annals of Air and Space Law* (1989), 139–88.

DELL, EDMUND, 'Of Free Trade and Reciprocity', 9 *World Economy* (1986), 2: 125–39.

DELWIT, PASCAL, and GOBIN, CORINNE, 'Étude du cheminement de la directive "télévision sans frontières": synthèse des prises de position des institions communautaires', in G. Vandersanden (ed.), *L'espace audiovisuel européen* (Brussels: Éditions de l'ULB, 1991), 55–74.

DEMARET, PAUL, 'La politique commerciale: perspectives d'évolution et faiblesses présentes', in J. Schwarze and H. G. Schermers (eds.), *Structure and Dimensions of European Community Policy* (Baden-Baden: Nomos, 1988), 69–110.

—— 'Environmental Policy and Commercial Policy: The Emergence of Trade-Related Environmental Measures', in M. Maresceau (ed.), *The European Community's Commercial Policy after 1992: The Legal Dimension* (Dordrecht: Martinus Nijhoff, 1993), 305–86.

DENYS, CHRISTINE, *Impliciete bevoegdheden in de Europese Economische Gemeenschap* (Antwerp: MAKLU, 1990).

DEVUYST, YOURI, 'The United States and Europe 1992', 13 *World Competition* (1989), 1: 29–42.

—— 'GATT Customs Union Provisions and the Uruguay Round: The European Community Experience', 26 *JWT* (1992), 1: 15–34.

—— 'The EC's Common Commercial Policy and the Treaty on European Union', 16 *World Competition* (1992), 2: 67–80.

DICKE, DETLEV C., 'Switzerland as an EFTA-Country and the "Fortress Europe"', in T. Oppermann and J. Molsberger (eds.), *A New GATT for the Nineties and Europe '92* (Baden-Baden: Nomos, 1991), 339–44.

DOLZER, RUDOLF, 'Reziprozität als Standard der EG-Drittlandsbeziehungen', in M. Hilf and C. Tomuschat (eds.), *EG und Drittstaatsbeziehungen nach 1992* (Baden-Baden: Nomos, 1991), 111–35.

DONY-BARTHOLME, MARIANNE, 'L'audiovisuel et les règles relatives à la libre prestation des services', in G. Vandersanden (ed.), *L'espace audiovisuel européen* (Brussels: Éditions de l'ULB, 1991), 33–54.

D'ORVILLE, MICHAEL, *Die rechtlichen Grundlagen für die gemeinsame Zoll- und Handelspolitik der EWG* (Cologne: Carl Heymanns, 1973).

ECCLES, RICHARD, 'When is a British Car not a British Car? Issues Raised by Nissan', 10 *ECLR* (1989), 1: 1–3.

EECKHOUT, PIET, 'The External Dimension of the Internal Market and the Scope and Content of a Modern Commercial Policy', in M. Maresceau (ed.), *The European Community's Commercial Policy after 1992: The Legal Dimension* (Dordrecht: Martinus Nijhoff, 1993), 79–104.

EGGER, ANTON, 'Ursprungsregeln aus schweizerischer Sicht (Art. 9 EWR-A)' in O. Jacot-Guillarmod (ed.), *EEA Agreement: Comments and Reflexions* (Zurich: Schulthess Polygraphischer Verlag, 1992), 133–48.

EHLERMANN, CLAUS-DIETER, 'The Scope of Article 113 of the EEC Treaty', in *Mélanges offerts à Pierre-Henri Teitgen* (Paris: Pedone, 1984), 148–69.

——'Application of GATT Rules in the European Community', in M. Hilf, F. G. Jacobs, and E.-U. Petersmann (eds.), *The European Community and GATT*, 2nd edn. (Deventer: Kluwer, 1989), 127–40.

—— and CAMPOGRANDE, GIANLUIGI, 'Rules on Services in the EEC: A Model for Negotiating World-Wide Rules?', in E.-U. Petersmann and M. Hilf (eds.), *The New GATT Round of Multilateral Trade Negotiations: Legal and Economic Problems* (Deventer: Kluwer, 1988), 481–98.

EMMERT, FRANK, 'Die Entwicklung der Ursprungsregeln bis zum EWR-Abkommen', in O. Jacot-Guillarmod (ed.), *EEA Agreement: Comments and Reflexions* (Zurich: Schulthess Polygraphischer Verlag, 1992), 115–32.

ERGEC, RUSEN, 'Le Conseil de l'Europe et l'espace audiovisuel européen', in G. Vandersanden (ed.), *L'espace audiovisuel européen* (Brussels: Éditions de l'ULB, 1991), 107–14.

ERHART, MICHAEL, 'Öffentliches Auftragswesen', in M. Röttinger and C. Weyringer (eds.), *Handbuch der europäischen Integration* (Vienna: Manzsche Verlags- und Universitätsbuchhandlung, 1991), 735–57.

ESTIENNE-HENROTTE, ELISABETH, *L'application des règles générales du Traité de Rome au transport aérien* (Brussels: Éditions de l'ULB, 1988).

EVERLING, ULRICH, 'The Law of the External Economic Relations of the European Community', in M. Hilf, F. G. Jacobs, and E.-U. Petersmann (eds.), *The European Community and GATT*, 2nd edn. (Deventer: Kluwer, 1989), 85–106.

FARR, SEBASTIAN, *Harmonisation of Technical Standards in the EC* (London: Chancery Law Publishing, 1992).

FEKETEKUTY, GEZA, *International Trade in Services: An Overview and Blueprint for Negotiations* (Cambridge, Mass.: Ballinger for The American Enterprise Institute, 1988).

FIELDING, LESLIE, *Europe as a Global Partner*, UACES Occasional Papers 7 (London, 1991).

FLAMME, MAURICE-ANDRÉ, and FLAMME, PHILIPPE, 'Vers l'Europe des marchés publics?', *RMC* (1988), 320: 455–79.

FLORY, THIÉBAUT, 'Les marchés de fournitures et les accords GATT', *RMC* (1989), 332: 654–7.

FREEDENBERG, PAUL, 'The Commercial Perspective', in G. K. Bertsch and S. Elliott-Gower (eds.), *Export Controls in Transition: Perspectives, Problems, and Prospects* (Durham, NC: Duke University Press, 1992), 37–58.

FROMENT-MEURICE, HENRI, *L'Europe de 1992: espace et puissance* (Paris: La Documentation française, 1988).

GAUDISSART, MARC-ANDRÉ, 'La portée des avis 1/91 et 1/92 de la Cour de justice des Communautés européennes relatifs à la création de l'espace économique européen: entre autonomie et homogénéité: L'ordre juridique communautaire en péril...', *RMUE* (1992), 2: 121–36.

GERTLER, JOSEPH Z., 'Towards a New, Rational and Fair Exchange of Opportunities for Airlines', in P. P. C. Haanappel *et al.* (eds.), *EEC Air Transport Policy and Regulation, and their Implications for North America* (Deventer: Kluwer, 1990), 199–210.

GILSDORF, PETER, 'Portée et délimitation des compétences communautaires en matière de politique commerciale', *RMC* (1989), 326: 195–207.

GOHON, Jean-Pierre, *Les marchés publics européens*, Que sais-je No. 2625 (Paris: Presses universitaires de France, 1991).

GOLEMBE, CARTER H., and HOLLAND, DAVID S., 'Banking and Securities', in G. C. Hufbauer (ed.), *Europe 1992: An American Perspective* (Washington, DC: The Brookings Institution, 1990), 65–118.

GORMLEY, LAURENCE W., *Prohibiting Restrictions on Trade within the EEC* (Amsterdam: North-Holland, 1985).

GOVAERE, INGE, 'Intellectual Property Protection and Commercial Policy', in M. Maresceau (ed.), *The European Community's Commercial Policy after 1992: The Legal Dimension* (Dordrecht: Martinus Nijhoff, 1993), 197–222.

——and EECKHOUT, PIET, 'On Dual Use Goods and Dualist Case Law: The *Aimé Richardt* Judgment on Export Controls', 29 *CML Rev.* (1992), 5: 941–66.

GREENWALD, JOSEPH, 'Negotiating Strategy', in G. C. Hufbauer (ed.), *Europe 1992: An American Perspective* (Washington, DC: The Brookings Institution, 1990), 345–88.

GROEBEN, H. VON DER, THIESING, J., and EHLERMANN, C.-D. (eds.), *Kommentar zum EWG-Vertrag*, 4th edn. (Baden-Baden: Nomos, 1991).

HAANAPPEL, PETER P. C., 'The External Aviation Relations of the European Economic Community and of EEC Member States into the Twenty-first Century', 14 *Air Law* (1989), 3: 122–46.

HILF, MEINHARD, 'The Application of GATT within the Member States of the European Community, with Special Reference to the Federal Republic of Germany', in M. Hilf, F.-G. Jacobs, and E.-U. Petersmann (eds.), *The European Community and GATT*, 2nd edn. (Deventer: Kluwer, 1989), 153–86.

——'The Single European Act and 1992: Legal Implications for Third Countries', 1 *EJIL* (1990), 1–2: 89–117.

——'Europa '92: Festung oder Partner?', in M. Hilf and C. Tomuschat (eds.), *EG und Drittstaatsbeziehungen nach 1992* (Baden-Baden: Nomos, 1991), 9–16.

HINDLEY, BRIAN, 'Voluntary Export Restraints and the GATT's Main Escape Clause', 3 *World Economy* (1980), 3: 313–41.

HOEKMAN, BERNARD, 'Market Access through Multilateral Agreement: From Goods to Services', 15 *World Economy* (1992), 6: 707–28.

HORDIES, JEAN-PAUL, and JONGEN, FRANÇOIS, 'La directive "télévision sans frontières": Analyse juridique', in G. Vandersanden (ed.), *L'espace audiovisuel européen* (Brussels: Éditions de l'ULB, 1991), 75–88.

HUFBAUER, GARY C., 'An Overview', in Gary Clyde Hufbauer (ed.), *Europe 1992: An American Perspective* (Washington, DC: The Brookings Institution, 1990): 1–64.

—— ERB, SHELTON J., and STARR, H. P., 'The GATT Codes and the Unconditional Most-Favored-Nation Principle', 12 *Law Pol. Int. Bus.* (1980), 1: 59–93.

—— and SCHMITZ, CLAUDIA, 'The North American Argument about a "Fortress Europe" ', in T. Oppermann and J. Molsberger (eds.), *A New GATT for the Nineties and Europe '92* (Baden-Baden: Nomos, 1991), 307–34.

ISHIKAWA, KENJIRO, *Japan and the Challenge of Europe 1992* (London: Pinter Publishers for the RIIA, 1990).

JACKSON, JOHN H., *World Trade and the Law of GATT* (Indianapolis: Bobbs-Merrill, 1969).

—— 'Consistency of Export-Restraint Arrangements with the GATT', 11 *World Economy* (1988), 4: 485–500.

—— *The World Trading System: Law and Policy of International Economic Relations* (Cambridge, Mass.: MIT Press, 1989).

—— *Restructuring the GATT System* (London: Pinter Publishers for the RIIA, 1990).

—— LOUIS, JEAN-VICTOR, and MATSUSHITA, MITSUO, *Implementing the Tokyo Round* (Ann Arbor, Mich.: University of Michigan Press, 1984).

JACOBS, FRANCIS G., 'Review by the Court of Justice of Commercial Policy Measures: Recent Trends and Future Prospects', in M. Maresceau (ed.), *The European Community's Commercial Policy after 1992: The Legal Dimension* (Dordrecht: Martinus Nijhoff, 1993), 63–77.

JAUME, A., 'La libéralisation du secteur des télécommunications: Aspects techniques et juridiques', *RMUE* (1992), 1: 117–42.

KAPTEYN, P. J. G., and VERLOREN VAN THEMAAT, P., *Introduction to the Law of the European Communities*, 2nd edn., ed. Lawrence W. Gormley (Deventer: Kluwer, 1990).

KLODT, HENNING, 'International Trade, Direct Investment, and Regulations in Services', 12 *World Competition* (1987), 2: 50–67.

KOHNSTAMM, MANUEL, 'Conflicts between International and European Network Regulation: An Analysis of Third Parties' Rights in European Community Law', *LIEI* (1990), 2: 45–99.

KORTLEVEN, JOZEF, 'Enkele externe aspecten van de Europese interne markt', *Documentatieblad Studie- en Documentatiedienst Ministerie van Financiën* (June 1991), 141–209.

KOSTECKI, MICHEL, 'Export-Restraint Arrangements and Trade Liberalization', 10 *World Economy* (1989), 4: 425–53.

KOVAR, ROBERT, 'Les compétences implicites: Jurisprudence de la Cour et pratique communautaire', in P. Demaret (ed.), *Relations extérieures de la Communauté européenne et marché intérieur: aspects juridiques et fonctionnels* (Bruges: Story for the College of Europe, 1988), 15–36.

KRENZLER, HORST G., 'Exportselbstbeschränkungen: ein aktuelles Problem der Handelspolitik der Europäischen Gemeinschaft', 12 *EuR* (1977), 2: 177–81.

KROMMENACKER, RAYMOND J., *World-Traded Services: The Challenge for the Eighties* (Dedham: Artech House, 1984).

—— 'Multilateral Services Negotiations: From Interest-Lateralism to Reasoned Multilateralism in the Context of the Servicization of the Economy', in Ernst-Ulrich Petersmann and Meinhard Hilf (eds.), *The New GATT Round of Multilateral Trade Negotiations: Legal and Economic Problems* (Deventer; Kluwer, 1988), 455–73.

KUTSCHER, H., 'Methods of Interpretation as Seen by a Judge at the Court of Justice', in *Reports of the 1976 Judicial and Academic Conference* (Luxembourg: Court of Justice, 1976), I-21/2.

KUYPER, PIETER JAN, 'The Influence of the Elimination of Physical Frontiers in the Community on Trade in Goods with Third States', in M. Hilf and C. Tomuschat (eds.), *EG und Drittstaatsbeziehungen nach 1992* (Baden-Baden: Nomos, 1991), 51–68.

—— 'European Economic Community', in K. M. Meessen (ed.), *International Law of Export Control* (London: Graham & Trotman, 1992), 57–78.

—— 'De invloed van het verdwijnen van de fysieke grenzen in de Gemeenschap op de handel in goederen met derde staten', 40 *SEW* (1992), 1: 18–32.

—— 'Trade Sanctions, Security and Human Rights and Commercial Policy', in M. Maresceau (ed.), *The European Community's Commercial Policy after 1992: The Legal Dimension* (Dordrecht: Martinus Nijhoff, 1993), 387–422.

LAMOUREUX, FRANÇOIS, 'Reciprocity and 1992', in B. Hawk (ed.), *1992 and EEC/U.S. Competition and Trade Law: Annual Proceedings of the Fordham Corporate Law Institute 1989* (New York: Transnational Juris Publications, 1990), 1–11.

LAUWAARS, RICHARD H., 'The "Model Directive" on Technical Harmonization', in R. Bieber, R. Dehousse, J. Pinder, and J. H. H. Weiler (eds.), *1992: One European Market?* (Baden-Baden: Nomos, 1988), 151–74.

—— 'Scope and Exclusiveness of the Common Commercial Policy: Limits of the Powers of the Member States', in J. Schwarze (ed.), *Discretionary Powers of the Member States in the Field of Economic Policies and their Limits under the EEC Treaty* (Baden-Baden: Nomos, 1988), 73–90.

—— and TIMMERMANS, CHRISTIAAN W. A., *Europees Gemeenschapsrecht in kort bestek* (Groningen: Wolters Noordhoff, 1989).

LEENEN, A. T. S., *Gemeenschapsrecht en volkenrecht* (Deventer; Kluwer, 1984).

LENAERTS, KOEN, 'Les répercussions des compétences de la Communauté européenne sur les compétences externes des États membres et la question de la "préemption"', in Paul Demaret (ed.), *Relations extérieures de la Communauté européenne et marché intérieur: aspects juridiques et fonctionnels* (Bruges: Story, 1988), 37–62.

—— 'L'égalité de traitement en droit communautaire', 27 *CDE* (1991), 1–2: 3–41.

LÉONARD, J., 'L'ouverture des marchés publics japonais', *RMC* (1989), 332: 658–60.

LEVITIN, MICHAEL J., 'The Treatment of United States Financial Services Firms in Post-1992 Europe', 31 *Harvard International Law Journal* (1990), 2: 507–64.

LOCHMANN, MICHAEL WILLIAM, 'The Japanese Voluntary Restraint on Automobile Exports: An Abandonment of the Free Trade Principles of the GATT and the Free Market Principles of United States Antitrust Laws', 27 *Harvard International Law Journal* (1986), 1: 99–157.

LONG, OLIVIER, *Law and its Limitations in the GATT Multilateral Trade System* (Dordrecht: Martinus Nijoff, 1985).

LOUIS, JEAN-VICTOR, in J. Mégret *et al.* (eds.), *Le droit de la Communauté économique européenne,* xii: *relations extérieures* (Brussels: Éditions de l'ULB, 1980).

LOUSSOUARN, YVON, 'Le droit d'établissement des sociétés', 26 *RTDE* (1990), 2: 229–39.

LUKOFF, F. L., 'European Competition Law and Distribution in the Motor Vehicle Sector: Commission Regulation 123/85 of 12 December 1984', 23 *CML Rev.* (1986), 4: 841–66.

LUPINACCI, TIMOTHY M., 'The Pursuit of Television Broadcasting Activities in the European Community: Cultural Preservation or Economic Protectionism?', 24 *Vanderbilt Journal of Transnational Law* (1991), 1: 113–67.

LUYTEN, PAUL, 'A View from a Fortress that never was', in T. Oppermann and J. Molsberger (eds.), *A New GATT for the Nineties and Europe '92* (Baden-Baden: Nomos, 1991), 275–90.

MACDONALD, STUART, *Technology and the Tyranny of Export Controls: Whisper Who Dares* (Basingstoke: Macmillan, 1990).

McLACHLAN, D. L., 'Discriminatory Public Procurement, Economic Integration and the Role of Bureaucracy', 23 *JCMS* (1985), 4: 357–72.

McMILLAN, J., 'La "certification", la reconnaissance mutuelle et le marché unique', *RMUE* (1991), 2: 181–211.

MARENCO, GIULIANO, 'The Notion of Restriction on the Freedom of Establishment and Provision of Services in the Case-Law of the Court', in A. Barav and D. A. Wyatt (eds.), 11 *Yearbook of European Law* (1991) (Oxford: Clarendon Press, 1992), 111–50.

MARESCEAU, MARC, *De directe werking van het Europese Gemeenschapsrecht* (Antwerp: Kluwer, 1978).

—— 'The Internal Market and its Impact on the Legal Framework of Trade Relations Between the EEC and CMEA', in *Matters of Promoting CMEA-EC Economic Cooperation* (Moscow: CMEA, 1989), 175–84.

—— 'The Concept "Common Commercial Policy" and the Difficult Road to Maastricht', in M. Maresceau (ed.), *The European Community's Commercial Policy after 1992: The Legal Dimension* (Dordrecht: Martinus Nijhoff, 1993), 3–19.

MARGUE, T. L., 'L'ouverture des marchés publics dans la Communauté', *RMUE* (1991), 2: 177–221; 3: 177–221; 4: 111–73.

MASLEN, JOHN, 'European Community-CMEA: Institutional Relations', in Marc Maresceau (ed.), *The Political and Legal Framework of Trade Relations between the European Community and Eastern Europe* (Dordrecht: Martinus Nijhoff, 1989).

MATSUSHITA, MITSUO, 'Coordinating International Trade with Competition Policies', in E.-U. Petersmann and M. Hilf (eds.), *The New GATT Round of Multilateral Trade Negotiations* (Deventer: Kluwer, 1988), 395–435.

MATTERA, ALFONSO, 'L'achèvement du marché intérieur et ses implications sur les relations extérieures', in Paul Demaret (ed.), *Relations extérieures de la Communauté européenne et marché intérieur: aspects juridiques et fonctionnels*, (Bruges: Story, 1988), 201–24.

MATTERA, ALFONSO, *Le marché unique européen: Ses règles, son fonctionnement*, 2nd edn. (Paris: Jupiter, 1990).

—— 'Les principes de "proportionnalité" et de la "reconnaissance mutuelle" dans la jurisprudence de la Cour en matière de libre circulation des personnes et des services: de l'arrêt "Thieffry" aux arrêts "Vlassopoulou", "Mediawet" et "Dennemeyer"', *RMUE* (1991), 4: 191–203.

MAZZOLA, BRUNO, 'Some Thoughts on the Liberalization Process of European Banking and Financial Activity', in G. Sacerdoti (ed.), *Liberalization of services and intellectual property in the Uruguay Round of GATT* (Fribourg: University Press, 1990), 202–12.

MEESSEN, KARL M. (ed.), *International Law of Export Control* (London: Graham & Trotman, 1992).

MÉGRET, J., *et al.*, *Le droit de la Communauté économique européenne*, xii: *Relations extérieures* (Brussels: Éditions de l'ULB, 1980).

MENDES DE LEON, PABLO, *Cabotage in Air Transport Regulation* (Dordrecht: Martinus Nijhoff, 1992).

MENGOZZI, PAOLO, 'Trade in Services and Commercial Policy', in M. Maresceau (ed.), *The European Community's Commercial Policy after 1992: The Legal Dimension* (Dordrecht: Martinus Nijhoff, 1993), 223–47.

MIDDLETON, R. W., 'The GATT Standards Code', 14 *JWTL* (1980), 3: 201–19.

MIFSUD, PAUL V., 'New Proposals for New Directions: 1992 and the GATT Approach to Trade in Air Transport Services', 13 *Air Law* (1988), 4–5: 154–71.

MILNER, CHRISTOPHER, and ALLEN, DAVID, 'The External Implications of 1992', in D. Swann (ed.), *The Single European Market and Beyond: A Study of the Wider Implications of the Single European Act* (London: Routledge, 1992), 162–90.

MOLSBERGER, JOZEF, and KOTIOS, ANGELOS, 'The Single European Market of 1992 within the GATT of the Nineties', in T. Oppermann and J. Molsberger (eds.), *A New GATT for the Nineties and Europe '92* (Baden-Baden: Nomos, 1991), 359–72.

MÖSCHEL, WERNHARD, 'La distribution sélective d'automobiles en droit européen de la concurrence', 44 *RTDC* (1991), 1: 1–26.

MURPHY, ANNA, *The European Community and the International Trading system*, i: *Completing the Uruguay Round of the GATT*, CEPS Paper No. 43 (Brussels: CEPS, 1990).

—— *The European Community and the International Trading System*, ii: *The European Community and the Uruguay Round*, CEPS Paper No. 48 (Brussels: CEPS, 1990).

NAYYAR, DEEPAK, 'Some Reflections on the Uruguay Round and Trade in Services', 22 *JWT* (1988), 5: 35–47.

NELL, PHILIPPE, *Les pays de l'AELE face au marché intérieur de la CE: Défi, enjeu et stratégie*, EFTA Occasional Paper No. 24 (Geneva, 1988).

NEMÉ, COLETTE, '1992 et la clause de l'article 115: à quand une politique commerciale commune?', *RMC* (1988), 322: 578–82.

NICOLAIDES, PHEDON, *Liberalizing Service Trade: Strategies for Success* (London: Routledge for the RIIA, 1989).

—— 'Economic Aspects of Services: Implications for a GATT Agreement', 23 *JWT* (1989), 1: 125–36.

—— *The Hydra of Safeguards: An Intractable Problem for the Uruguay Round?*, RIIA Discussion Paper No. 21 (London: RIIA, 1989).

—— 'Competition among Rules', 16 *World Competition* (1992), 2: 113–21.

NICOLAS, FLORENCE, and REPUSSARD, JACQUES, *Common Standards for Enterprises* (Luxembourg: Commission, 1988).

NUSBAUMER, JACQUES, 'The GATT Standards Code in Operation', 18 *JWTL* (1984), 6: 542–52.

OLIVER, PETER, *Free Movement of Goods in the E.E.C.*, 2nd end. (London: European Law Centre, 1988).

OLMI, GIANCARLO, *Commentaire Mégret*, ii: *Politique agricole commune*, 2nd edn. (Brussels: Études européennes, 1991).

OVERBURY, COLIN, and RAVAIOLI, PIERO, 'The Application of EEC Law to Telecommunications', in B. Hawk (ed.), *1992 and EEC/U.S. Competition and Trade Law: Annual Proceedings of the Fordham Corporate Law Institute 1989* (New York: Transnational Juris Publications, 1990), 271–312.

PATTERSON, GARDNER, 'The European Community as a Threat to the System', in W. R. Cline (ed.), *Trade Policy in the 1980's* (Washington, DC: Institute for International Economics, 1983), 223–42.

—— 'Implications for the GATT and the World Trading System', in J. J. Schott (ed.), *Free Trade Areas and U.S. Trade Policy* (Washington, DC: Institute for International Economics, 1989), 353–65.

PELKMANS, JACQUES, 'The New Approach to Technical Harmonization and Standardization', 25 *JCMS* (1987), 3: 249–69.

—— 'Europe 1992: A Handmaiden to GATT', in F. Laursen (ed.), *Europe 1992: World Partner? The Internal Market and the World Political Economy* (Maastricht: European Institute of Public Administration, 1991), 125–54.

—— '1992: Economic Effects on Third Countries', in M. Hilf and C. Tomuschat (eds.), *EG und Drittstaatsbeziehungen nach 1992* (Baden-Baden: Nomos, 1991), 163–94.

—— 'EC92 as a Challenge to Economic Analysis', in S. Borner and H. Grubel (eds.), *The European community after 1992: Perspectives from the Outside* (Basingstoke: Macmillan, 1992), 3–28.

—— *Applying 1992 to Textiles and Clothing*, CEPS Working Document No. 67 (Brussels: CEPS, 1992).

—— and EGAN, MICHELLE, *Fixing European Standards: Moving beyond the Green Paper*, CEPS Working Document No. 65 (Brussels: CEPS, 1992).

PERREAU DE PINNINCK, FERNANDO, 'Les compétences communautaires dans les négociations sur le commerce des services', 27 *CDE* (1991), 3–4: 390–421.

PESCATORE, PIERRE, 'La politique commerciale', in *Les Novelles: Droit des Communautés européennes* (Brussels: Larcier, 1969), 917–42.

PETERSMANN, ERNST-ULRICH, 'Grey Area Trade Policy and the Rule of Law', 22 *JWT* (1988), 2: 23–44.

—— 'The EEC as a GATT Member: Legal Conflicts between GATT Law and European Community Law', in M. Hilf, F. G. Jacobs, and E.-U. Petersmann (eds.), *The European Community and GATT*, 2nd edn. (Deventer: Kluwer, 1989), 23–72.

—— 'The Uruguay Round of Multilateral Trade Negotiations and the Single

European Market 1992', in M. Hilf and C. Tomuschat (eds.), *EG und Drittstaats-beziehungen nach 1992* (Baden-Baden: Nomos, 1991), 195–212.

PETERSMANN, ERNST-ULRICH, *Constitutional Functions and Constitutional Problems of International Economic Law* (Fribourg: University Press, 1991).

PISUISSE, C. S., 'De bevoegdheid van de Europese Gemeenschap met betrekking tot de liberalisatie van de internationale dienstverlening', 35 *SEW* (1987), 3: 179–93.

PORTER, VINCENT, 'The Janus Character of Television Broadcasting', in G. Locksley (ed.), *The Single European Market and the Information and Communication Technologies* (London: Belhaven Press, 1990), 59–72.

RENSHAW, A., 'Le regime appliqué dans la Communauté aux sociétés contrôlées par des intérêts non-communautaires', in P. Demaret (ed.), *Relations extérieures de la Communauté européenne et marché intérieur: aspects juridiques et fonctionnels* (Bruges: Story Scientia for the College of Europe, 1988), 137–60.

ROBERTS, DAVID, *GATT Rules for Emergency Protection*, Thames Essay No. 57 (London: Harvester Wheatsheaf for the Trade Policy Research Centre, 1992).

ROBSON, PETER, *The Economics of International Integration* (London: Allen & Unwin, 1980).

SALVATORE, VINCENZO, 'Quotas on TV Programmes and EEC Law', 29 *CML Rev.* (1992), 5: 967–90.

SAPIR, ANDRÉ, 'Comments', in J. J. Schott (ed.), *Free Trade Areas and U.S. Trade Policy* (Washington, DC: Institute for International Economics, 1989), 313–16.

—— 'Does 1992 Come before or after 1990? On Regional versus Multilateral Integration', in R. W. Jones and A. O. Krueger (eds.), *The Political Economy of International Trade* (Cambridge, Mass.: Basil Blackwell, 1990), 197–222.

—— 'Le commerce international des services audiovisuels: une source de conflits entre la Communauté européenne et les États-Unis', in G. Vandersanden (ed.), *L'espace audiovisuel européen* (Brussels: Éditions de l'ULB, 1991), 163–70.

SARRE, FRANCIS, 'Article 115 EEC Treaty and Trade with Eastern Europe', 23 *Intereconomics* (1988), 5: 233–40.

SCHEELE, JONATHAN, in G. Sacerdoti (ed.), *Liberalization of Services and Intellectual Property in the Uruguay Round of GATT* (Fribourg: University Press, 1990), 213–38.

SCHERMERS, HENRY G., 'The Effect of the Date 31 December 1992', 28 *CML Rev.* (1991), 2: 275–89.

—— Opinion 1/91 of 14 Dec. 1991; Opinion 1/92 of 10 Apr. 1992, with annotation, 29 *CML Rev.* (1992), 5: 991–1010.

—— and WAELBROECK, DENIS, *Judicial Protection in the European Communities*, 5th edn. (Deventer: Kluwer, 1992).

SCHRICKE, CHRISTIAN, 'La CEE et l'OCDE à l'heure de l'Acte unique', 93 *Revue générale de droit international public* (1989), 4: 797–829.

SCHULTE-BRAUCKS, REINHARD, 'L'ouverture des marchés publics des télécommunications', *RMC* (1989), 332: 649–53.

SCHWARTZ, IVO E., 'Broadcasting and the EEC Treaty', 11 *ELR* (1986), 1: 7–59.

SCHWARZE, J., BECKER, U., and POLLAK, C. (eds.), *The 1992 Challenge at National Level: Reports and Conference Proceedings 1991/1992* (Baden-Baden: Nomos, 1993).

SCHWOK, RENÉ, *U.S.–EC Relations in the Post-Cold War Era* (Boulder, Colo.: Westview Press, 1991).

Scott, Hall S., 'La notion de réciprocité dans la proposition de deuxième directive de coordination bancaire', *RMC* (1989), 323: 45–56.

Secchi, Carlo, 'Recent Trends in International Trade in Services', in G. Sacerdoti (ed.), *Liberalization of Services and Intellectual Property in the Uruguay Round of GATT* (Fribourg: University Press, 1990), 7–25.

Shawcross and Beaumont, *Air Law*, 4th edn, vol. ii (London: Butterworths, 1990).

Smith, Alasdair, and Venables, Anthony J., 'Automobiles', in G. C. Hufbauer (ed.), *Europe 1992: An American Perspective* (Washington, DC: The Brookings Institution, 1990), 119–58.

—— 'Counting the Cost of Voluntary Export Restraints in the European Car Market', in E. Helpman and A. Razin (eds.), *International Trade and Trade Policy* (Cambridge, Mass.: MIT Press, 1991), 187–213.

Snyder, Francis G., *Law of the Common Agricultural Policy* (London: Sweet & Maxwell, 1985).

Steenbergen, Jacques, 'Trade Regulation since the Tokyo Round', in E. L. M. Völker (ed.), *Protectionism and the European Community*, 2nd edn. (Deventer: Kluwer, 1986), 185–225.

—— 'Europe 1992 and the Uruguay Round', 8 *International Financial Law Review* (1989), 4: 37–9.

—— 'EG/EFTA en de Europese economische ruimte', 39 *SEW* (1991), 1: 15–29.

—— Annotation on Opinion 1/91, 40 *SEW* (1992), 5: 402–31.

Sweeney, Robert E., 'Technical Analysis of the Technical Barriers to Trade Agreement', 12 *Law Pol. Int. Bus* (1980), 1: 179–217.

Temple Lang, John, 'The *ERTA* Judgment and the Court's Case-Law on Competence and Conflict', in F. G. Jacobs (ed.), 6 *Yearbook of European Law* (1986) (Oxford: Clarendon Press, 1987), 183–218.

Timmermans, Christiaan W. A., 'Division of External Powers between Community and Member States in the Field of Harmonization of National Law: A Case Study', in C. W. A. Timmermans and E. L. M. Völker (eds.), *Division of Powers between the European Communities and their Member States in the Field of External Relations* (Deventer: Kluwer, 1981), 15–28.

—— 'Verboden discriminatie of (geboden) differentiatie', 30 *SEW* (1982), 6: 426–60.

—— 'Community Commercial Policy in Textiles: A Legal Imbroglio', in E. L. M. Völker (ed.), *Protectionism and the European Community*, 2nd edn. (Deventer: Kluwer, 1986), 159–83.

—— 'Noot onder *Tezi*', 36 *SEW* (1986), 11: 762–7.

—— 'Common Commercial Policy (Article 113 EEC) and International Trade in Services', in *Du droit international au droit de l'intégration: liber amicorum Pierre Pescatore* (Baden-Baden: Nomos, 1987), 675–89.

—— 'La libre circulation des marchandises et la politique commerciale commune', in P. Demaret (ed.), *Relations extérieures de la Communauté européenne et marché intérieur: aspects juridiques et fonctionnels* (Bruges: Story for the College of Europe, 1988), 91–108.

Toll, Christopher T., 'The European Community's Second Banking Directive: Can Antiquated United States Legislation Keep Pace?', 23 *Vanderbilt Journal of Transnational Law* (1990), 3: 615–51.

Тотн, A. G., 'The Legal Status of the Declarations Annexed to the Single European Act', 23 *CML Rev.* (1986), 4: 803–12.

Tsoukalis, Loukas, *The New European Economy: The Politics and Economics of Integration* (Oxford: Oxford University Press, 1991).

Tumlir, Jan, 'GATT Rules and Community Law: A Comparison of Economic and Legal functions', in M. Hilf, F. G. Jacobs, and E.-U. Petersmann (eds.), *The European Community and GATT*, 2nd edn. (Deventer: Kluwer, 1989), 1–22.

Ungerer, Herbert, with Costello, Nicolas P., *Telecommunications in Europe*, 2nd edn. (Luxembourg: Office for Official Publications of the EC, 1990).

Usher, John A., *Legal Aspects of Agriculture in the European Community* (Oxford: Clarendon Press, 1988).

van Dartel, R. J. P. M., 'The EEC's Commercial Policy Concerning Textiles', in E. L. M. Völker (ed.), *Protectionism and the European Community*, 2nd edn., (Deventer: Kluwer, 1986), 121–58.

van de Gevel, Ad (rapporteur), *The European Community without Technical Barriers*, CEPS Working Party Report No. 5 (Brussels: CEPS, 1992).

Van den Bossche, Anne-Marie, 'GATT: The Indispensable Link between the EEC and Hungary?', 23 *JWT* (1989), 3: 141–55.

van der Pas, Nikolaus G., 'The European Economic Area Aspects Concerning Free Movement of Goods', in O. Jacot-Guillarmod (ed.), *EEA Agreement: Comments and Reflexions* (Zurich: Schulthess Polygraphischer Verlag, 1992), 101–14.

van Empel, Martijn, 'The Visible Hand in Invisible Trade', *LIEI* (1990), 2: 23–43.

van Rijn, Thomas, 'Transport Policy and Commercial Policy', in M. Maresceau (ed.), *The European Community's Commercial Policy after 1992: The Legal Dimension* (Dordrecht: Martinus Nijhoff, 1993), 249–66.

Vermulst, Edwin, and Waer, Paul, 'European Community Rules of Origin as Commercial Policy Instruments?', 24 *JWT* (1990), 3: 55–99.

Vigneron, Philippe, and Smith, Aubry, 'Le concept de réciprocité dans la législation communautaire: l'exemple de la deuxième directive bancaire', *RMC* (1990), 337: 351–60.

—— 'Le fondement de la compétence communautaire en matière de commerce international de services', 28 *CDE* (1992), 5–6: 515–64.

Vogelenzang, Pierre, 'Two Aspects of Article 115 E.E.C. Treaty: Its Use to Buttress Community-Set Sub-quotas, and the Commission's Monitoring System', 18 *CML Rev.* (1981), 2: 169–96.

Völker, E. L. M., 'The Major Instruments of the Common Commercial Policy of the EEC', in E. L. M. Völker (ed.), *Protectionism and the European Community*, 2nd edn. (Deventer: Kluwer, 1986), 17–56.

—— Annotation of *Bulk Oil*, 24 *CML Rev.* (1987), 1: 105–9.

—— 'Technical Regulations and Standards and Commercial Policy', in M. Maresceau (ed.), *The European Community's Commercial Policy after 1992: The Legal Dimension* (Dordrecht: Martinus Nijhoff, 1993), 285–303.

—— *Barriers to External and Internal Community Trade* (Deventer: Kluwer, 1993).

Waelbroeck, Denis, 'L'harmonisation des règles et normes techniques de la CEE', 24 *CDE* (1988), 3: 244–75.

—— 'La libre transmission des messages audiovisuels et la protection des intérêts culturels', in G. Vandersanden (ed.), *L'espace audiovisuel européen* (Brussels: Éditions de l'ULB, 1991), 137–54.

WAINWRIGHT, RICHARD, and JESSEN, ANDERS, C., 'Recent Developments in Community Law on Telecommunications', in A. Barav and D. A. Wyatt (eds.), 11 *Yearbook of European Law* (1991) (Oxford: Clarendon Press, 1992), 79–110.

WALLACE, REBECCA, and GOLDBERG, DAVID, 'The EEC Directive on Television Broadcasting', in A. Barav and D. A. Wyatt (eds.), 9 *Yearbook of European Law* (1989) (Oxford: Clarendon Press, 1990), 175–96.

WASSENBERGH, H. A., 'EEC-Cabotage after 1992', 13 *Air Law* (1988), 6: 282–5.

—— (ed.), *External Aviation Relations of the European Community* (Deventer: Kluwer, 1992).

WEBER, LUDWIG, *Die Zivilluftfahrt im Europäischen Gemeinschaftsrecht* (Berlin: Springer-Verlag, 1981).

—— 'External Aspects of EEC Air Transport Liberalization', 15 *Air Law* (1990), 5–6: 277–87.

WEISS, FRIEDL, 'The Law of Public Procurement in EFTA and the EEC: The Legal Framework and its Implementation', in F. G. Jacobs (ed.), 7 *Yearbook of European Law* (1987) (Oxford: Clarendon Press, 1988), 59–111.

—— 'Public Procurement in the EEC: Public Supply Contracts', 13 *ELR* (1988), 4: 318–34.

WHITE, ERIC L., 'In Search of the Limits to Article 30 of the EEC Treaty', 26 *CML Rev* (1989), 2: 235–80.

WIJKMAN, PER MAGNUS, 'Economic Interdependence', in H. Wallace (ed.), *The Wider Western Europe: Reshaping the EC/EFTA Relationship* (London: Pinter for the RIIA, 1991), 60–8.

WILS, GEERT, 'The Concept of Reciprocity in EEC Law: An Exploration into these Realms', 28 *CML Rev.* (1991), 1: 110–274.

WINKEL, KLAUS, 'Die Grundsätze des freien Warenverkehrs im Verhältnis zu Drittländern', 44 *NJW* (1977), 1992–7.

WINTERS, L. ALAN, 'Reciprocity', in J. M. Finger and A. Olechowski (eds.), *The Uruguay Round: A Handbook on the Multilateral Trade Negotiations* (Washington, DC: World Bank, 1987), 45–51.

—— 'Partner Interests in Customs Union Formation: An Economic View', in P. Demaret, J. Bourgeois, and I. van Bael (eds.), *Trade Laws of the European Community and the United States in a Comparative Perspective* (Brussels: Story-Scientia for the College of Europe, 1992), 285–90.

—— 'Integration, Trade Policy and European Footwear Trade', in L. A. Winters (ed.), *Trade Flows and Trade Policy after '1992'* (Cambridge: University Press, 1992), 175–213.

WOOLCOCK, STEPHEN, *Market Access Issues in EC–U.S. Relations* (London: Pinter Publishers for the RIIA, 1991).

ZAVVOS, GEORGE S., 'Banking Integration and 1992: Legal Issues and Policy Implications', 31 *Harvard International Law Journal* (1990), 2: 463–506.